PENGUIN CLASSICS

THE NICOMACHEAN ETHICS

ARISTOTLE was born in 384 BC in Stagira in the northern Aegean. His father, Nicomachus, was personal physician to King Amyntas of Macedon. Aged about seventeen, he moved to Athens and became a student in Plato's Academy, where he remained for the next twenty years. Around the time of Plato's death in 347 he moved to Assos, in modern-day Turkey, where he attached himself to the household of his friend Hermias, the local ruler. He married Hermias' niece, Pythias. In Assos, and then in Mytilene on the island of Lesbos, he pursued intensive research in marine biology. In 343 he returned to his native Macedonia to serve as tutor to King Philip's young son, the future Alexander the Great, a post he held for two or three years. After Alexander succeeded to the throne in 336, Aristotle returned to Athens and established his own school, the Lyceum. He attracted a large number of young scholars, and he taught there on a wide range of philosophical and scientific questions for the next twelve years. The 'Peripatetic' (i.e. Aristotelian) school of philosophy takes its name from the *peripatos*, the Lyceum's covered walkway where he gave his lectures. Following Alexander's death in 323, there was a surge of anti-Macedonian feeling in Athens, and Aristotle was formally charged with impiety. He went into voluntary exile in Chalcis in Euboea, where he died the following year at the age of sixty-two. The philosophical dialogues he published during his lifetime have all been lost. But his students preserved other extensive writings, apparently derived from research notes and lecture materials, on a huge variety of topics – metaphysics, theology, physics, astronomy, biology, zoology, psychology, epistemology, logic, rhetoric, aesthetics, politics and ethics – that profoundly shaped the course of ancient, medieval and Renaissance thought, and continue to be widely read and appreciated by philosophers today. Besides the *Nicomachean Ethics*, the Penguin Classics series offers editions of the *Politics*, the *Metaphysics*, the *De Anima, The Art of Rhetoric*, the *Poetics* and *The Athenian Constitution*.

ADAM BERESFORD is Associate Professor of Philosophy at the University of Massachusetts, Boston. He has previously translated Plato's *Protagoras* and *Meno* for Penguin Classics.

ARISTOTLE

The Nicomachean Ethics

Translated by ADAM BERESFORD

PENGUIN BOOKS

PENGUIN CLASSICS

UK | USA | Canada | Ireland | Australia
India | New Zealand | South Africa

Penguin Books is part of the Penguin Random House group of companies
whose addresses can be found at global.penguinrandomhouse.com.

Penguin
Random House
UK

First published in Penguin Classics 2020

009

Translation and editorial material copyright © Adam Beresford

The moral rights of the translator have been asserted

Set in 10.25/12.25pt Sabon LT Std
Typeset by Jouve (UK), Milton Keynes
Printed and bound in Great Britain by Clays Ltd, Elcograf S.p.A.

A CIP catalogue record for this book is available from the British Library

ISBN: 978-0-140-45547-2

Contents

(8) Our moral virtues are human; they have no connection with God. (Contemplating the cosmos, by contrast, is a quasi-divine activity.) The gods do not need or possess any of our moral virtues or interests.

(9) How do we become good people? We need the right upbringing; carefully planned public education. We need good laws. It's time to turn to political questions.

Introduction

My aim here is not to walk the reader through everything Aristotle says in each book of this famous treatise. It makes more sense for you to read its arguments for yourself. Nor do I plan to spend much time explaining Aristotle's key terms and concepts or warning you about his strange vocabulary. The translation is in standard English, and does not contain too many terms that need much explanation, or, I hope, anything that you won't be able to understand well enough when you come across it on your own (with a little help from the relevant notes from time to time).[1]

Instead, I will briefly discuss the unusual form and the physical origin of this peculiar work, then pick out two of its more important philosophical features, which I hope will bring out some of what is distinctive and innovative and rich in Aristotle's approach and maybe shed a little light on his character.

I warn the reader that nothing that follows is entirely uncontroversial. But if I had to confine myself to claims that no scholar would disagree with, I would have to say nothing at all.

*

What *is* the *Nicomachean Ethics*? What kind of text is this? How was it first produced? How did it take its current form?

You don't always have to ask questions of that sort of a major philosophical work, but they're appropriate in this case, because we don't know. At least, not with any certainty.

For that matter, what does the odd title, *Ēthika Nikomacheia*, even mean? It probably originated as a librarian's tag, for use within the Lyceum (the school that Aristotle founded in

Athens), rather than as the informative title of a published work. It is opaque enough to have confused readers for millennia. Ever since late antiquity, people have wrongly thought that it meant 'A Treatise on Ethical Questions, Dedicated to [my son] Nicomachus'. Aristotle did have a son called Nicomachus, and Nicomachus probably has something to do with the title. But this treatise was certainly not dedicated to him.

Put that bit of the title to one side for now. The other bit seems straightforward enough. The Greek term *ēthika* means 'relating to character' (Greek for 'character' is *ēthos*). And various ancient sources suggest that this was shorthand for *ēthika hupomnēmata*: not just 'things relating to character', but more precisely 'notes on character', or '*records* on character'. And that, in turn, probably means 'records [of Aristotle's lectures] on character'. In origin, and especially in the context of philosophy, *hupomnēmata* meant 'records of a lecture'.

That's to say, these are not the notes from which Aristotle delivered his lectures (as is widely believed) or notes that he wrote himself and gave to his students. These are records of the lectures as delivered, taken down by someone who attended them, written up and edited later.[2]

There are two parallel sets of *Ēthika* in the surviving Aristotelian corpus. We have the *Nicomachean Ethics* and the *Eudemian Ethics*. Curiously, their three central books are identical (the 'common books'). Outside of those, they shadow one another, and make most of the same claims, often to the point of having very similar arguments (complete with the same examples), but never to the point of being the same text. Here and there they diverge on important details of philosophical doctrine. It seems that Aristotle gave essentially the same course of lectures over and over again (every year, say, like a modern university professor) and that they were taken down at least twice, perhaps a few years apart, perhaps many years apart, by two different listeners. The extensive and systematic similarities between these two sets of 'records', but also the fact that (outside the common books) they are two fully independent and separately formed texts, can be quite neatly explained that way.[3]

Most surviving Aristotelian treatises started as his lecture courses. That's why they are so unlike the great works of Greek literary prose. We think they derive from lectures he gave in the Lyceum in the 330s and 320s BC, the final phase of his career. They were probably then written up in the decades following his death, and may not have been more widely published till much later than that. He did also produce works for publication that were widely read and admired – including for a fine prose style that is sadly absent here – and he occasionally mentions their existence, rather sheepishly. For some reason none of those has come down to us.

So you'll find him referring, in this treatise and others, not to 'readers' but to 'listeners': the people actually there, listening. There are also countless details that suggest live speech. Aristotle repeats himself, he backtracks, he changes his mind, he starts a line of thought then immediately decides it's irrelevant, he is colloquial and clipped, or infuriatingly unclear; he wonders out loud about answers to tough questions, he constantly declares that 'we've said enough' about this or that, and he sometimes seems to take questions from the audience. He makes frequent obscure references and occasional inside jokes that only his live and very familiar audience could have followed. He constantly quotes from poetry, especially Homer, but often gets the quotations wrong, or gives ungrammatical snippets, because he is quoting from memory, on the spot. At one point, for example, he quotes a line that he says is what 'Calypso advises Odysseus to do', when in fact it's Odysseus passing on the advice to his helmsman, and it wasn't Calypso who gave him the advice, it was Circe. He mangles a line of Agamemnon's and wrongly assigns it to Hector. What's remarkable about this is that neither Aristotle himself (who probably had no hand in editing these records anyway) nor his students (who did) bothered to correct even these very fixable errors. The approach seems to be: 'That's what he said, so there it stays.'

We should be thankful that his editors had that sort of reverent attitude. It means that the recorded lectures are vivid, and probably pretty accurate in most respects. (If they were reluctant to fix even trivial inaccuracies, we can be fairly sure they didn't mess around with the main arguments.) Some scholars worry that if these records were taken down and edited by students, then what we have here is not really written by Aristotle. True. But it is arguably even better to have such detailed records of actual talks he gave in the seclusion and relative safety of his school. Even once edited, they were probably only ever intended for internal use. So they are sure to be less guarded than whatever he wrote, and edited, for the general public. This is raw Aristotle.

The downside to his editors' reverence is that they didn't want to leave any of their precious records out of the final text – and should have. A few parts of it read like collections of miscellaneous points that they didn't know where to put; some parts seem to combine more than one version of the same bit of the lecture, like a movie where two different takes of the same shot have weirdly both found their way into the final cut. Books V to VII in particular (the 'common books') are full of strange repetitions and duplicated arguments and other general glitches, probably because they are a rather flawed blending of the two sets of records otherwise kept separate as the *Nicomachean* and *Eudemian* versions. (That is why they are the 'common' books, in my view. They belonged to both edited versions of *Ethics* for as long as either version has existed at all.)

So who did this editing? The title of the *Eudemian Ethics* points us helpfully to one of Aristotle's well-known students: Eudemus of Rhodes. We know that Eudemus was involved in preserving and editing Aristotle's work, and it seems almost certain that the title means '*Lectures on Character, Eudemus version*', so named because he edited that version or because it derived from his own records, or most probably both. Aristotle's even more famous protégé, and his successor as head of the Lyceum, was Theophrastus. It is a good bet that the other set of records were originally his. Nicomachus, Aristotle's son, is said to have been Theophrastus' student, and it's reported that Nicomachus did scholarly work on Aristotelian material too. So we can explain the title of the *Nicomachean Ethics* as follows: Theophrastus took his own treasured records of Aristotle's lectures on ethical topics and asked one of his more

talented and promising students, Nicomachus, to take on the
job of editing them, or at least to assist him. The result was
'*Lectures on Character, Nicomachus version*'.[4]

Nicomachus died a young man, in war, not long after performing this editorial task, if our story is correct. He probably
thought of it as no more than a rather tedious favour to his
mentor; a graduate student's task of gathering, organizing and
copying out several boxes of wax tablets with their messy jot-
tings. He did not do a particularly good job. The result was a
plain, dry, unadorned and rather choppy presentation of the
lectures that Theophrastus had attended some twenty years
earlier.[5] And, as it turned out, one of the most influential works
of Western philosophy.

*

So, what does 'On Character' mean?

The lectures have that title not because they discuss human
character in general (they don't), but because they discuss one
important aspect of human character: what it is to be a good
person.

For Aristotle, that's implicit in the term *ēthos*, 'character'.
To say something about your character, he tells us, is to say
something about 'what kind of person you are', and by that he
means whether you are a good person or a bad one: 'a decent
man or a scoundrel'. It's to say something about your virtues
or your vices. That's why it's not at all misleading (as some
scholars worry) to claim that these are indeed discussions of
ethical or moral questions, in roughly, or even exactly, the current (plain-English) sense of those terms.

People sometimes point out here, cautiously, that by 'moral
questions', in English, we tend to mean, rather precisely, questions of right and wrong. Surely 'things relating to character' is
broader, more spacious. Well, yes and no. Aristotle does discuss several topics that range beyond narrow questions of right
and wrong: friendship and love, for example, the nature of
pleasure and pain, and what it is to live a good life, to flourish
as a human being. But the treatise was not called 'the *Ēthika*'
because it discusses pleasure and human flourishing. It is called

'the *Ēthika*' because it is mostly about good and bad people
and what defines them, and the place of moral goodness in our
lives. Other topics are covered because they have some clear
bearing on those central questions. And good people, as Aristotle tells us over and over again, are people who consistently
choose to do the right thing and to behave honourably, while
bad people do things that are wrong and shameful. So, apart
from a difference of focus – the good person rather than the
right thing to do is the central topic of these lectures – the treatise is, much of the time, about right and wrong, and honourable
and shameful actions.

It was only later that the Greeks regularly started to refer to
ēthika, 'ethics', as a philosophical subject matter. They did so
because of Aristotle. It's his term, in a sense. But he hardly ever
seems to have used it that way himself.[6] In this treatise, he
never calls his subject *ēthika*. He calls it *politikē*:[7] 'statesmanship' or 'political philosophy'. That doesn't match normal
English and can sound odd. But it's based on the fairly simple
idea – one that Aristotle inherited from Plato – that it is the job
of statesmanship, and political thought, and political deliberation, to think about what is good and bad and right and
wrong for human beings (because it is statesmen who make
laws) and also to understand human flourishing (because
statesmen must aim, ultimately, to make their citizens flourish).[8] So ethics is really politics; politics subsumes ethics.

Aristotle also offers us an alternative title right at the end of
the course of lectures: he calls everything that he has discussed
so far (combined with the political questions that he will turn
to next) 'the philosophy of human things'.

Both these labels – 'Ethics', given to the treatise by its editors, and 'On Human Things', the title Aristotle might have
given it himself – are grounded in some of his most fundamental ideas, and in his disagreements with his mentor, Plato. Let's
consider each of them in turn.

Virtues begin as habits

The first, 'Ethics', derives from Aristotle's habit of calling virtues 'virtues of character' (*ēthikai aretai*) and moral goodness 'goodness of character' (*ēthikē aretē*).

The virtues of character are the moral virtues. Our term 'moral' derives from the Latin translation of Aristotle's word. And though its sense is a little thinned out by the passage of time, it remains fundamentally accurate. At any rate, it points us efficiently at the qualities that Aristotle has in mind: the ones that make you a good person; the ones that make you behave honourably and do the right thing. But there's an extra implication in Aristotle's term that has dropped out of our word 'moral'. He calls the moral virtues 'virtues of character' because he believes they are grounded in the non-rational elements of human psychology: in our feelings and emotions, our likes and dislikes, our loves and hates, our pleasures and pains, our pre-rational intuitions. 'Character' is his way of referring to all of those things collectively. So it's almost as if he is calling the moral virtues 'the virtues of emotion, desire and feeling'.

Aristotle rejected the famous Socratic view that virtues are mostly forms of knowledge (a disagreement he discusses explicitly in II.4 and VI.13). For Aristotle, since goodness depends on stable patterns of emotion and desire, it's not about what you know or how you reason, or only to a much lesser extent. 'Our virtues involve reason, rather than just *being* forms of reason.' (See VI.13.) And it's this disagreement that is embedded even in his terminology. Goodness is now 'goodness of character', *ēthikē aretē*. The phrase itself is staking his claim. To use it at all, in his time, was to approve of this newfangled view. Plato never once uses it in all of his voluminous surviving works, not because he predated it, but because he pointedly ignores it.[9]

It's easy to misrepresent Plato's views (at Plato's expense) when discussing Aristotle. It's also easy to exaggerate the differences between them. Both speak of the need for reason to 'be in charge of' emotion and desire. Both often say that good people are also wise, and always do what reason tells them to do; and there are places in these lectures where Aristotle still sounds very Platonic in his view of the emotions' role (notably, in his discussion of selfishness in IX.8). But here are several clear ways in which Aristotle does at least usually depart from his mentor – and for that matter, from almost all other Greek philosophers – in his view of the emotions.

First, he gives emotions a much more central role. Plato typically speaks of our emotions and desires as if they were corrupting and dangerous forces that only need to be restrained, tamed and checked. In the *Phaedo* he exhorts us to get away from them as much as we possibly can. In the *Republic* he defines a righteous person, simply, as someone in whom reason fully rules emotion and desire, with the implication that reason and knowledge alone provide the direction in which a righteous person needs to go. When emotion and desire direct our actions, they are usurping reason's role. He suggests that we grasp the very highest truths – including truths about right and wrong – only by escaping from the dark cave of our worldly attachments (the influences of our desires and emotions and pleasures and pains).[10] Aristotle, by contrast, tells us (in VI.1) that truths about right and wrong, and indeed all 'practical truths', i.e. all truths about what we should do, wouldn't even exist without desire. It is desire (broadly construed), not reason, that gives us our goals and pushes us in any direction at all. 'Thought on its own doesn't move {or motivate} anything.' And correct desires, the right desires, push us in the right direction. It's reason's job to grasp and reflect on those goals and guide us wisely in our pursuit of them.

In Aristotle's view, reason, when it works well, is like a smart GPS that's full of useful facts, knows where you're going and shows you the best way to get there. And Plato's mistake is to think that your GPS can also tell you where you should be going in the first place.

It isn't the job of human wisdom or reason to justify its own 'starting points', he says several times. Reasoning has to start somewhere. And our starting points come from human character; from the things that we (adult) human beings already care about, that we love or we loathe, that we praise or we blame, that we fear or long for. We shouldn't look to reason for an argument to prove that it's good to fall in love, or good to have friends and that your friends and family matter to you, or that being brave and fair is better than being a coward and a cheat. And though we often need to think long and hard about how to treat other people fairly, say, or how to be kind, we don't need reason to tell us that we should be treating people fairly in the first place, or to explain the value of kindness. If you're an adult and still mystified about those basics, you're not in need of an argument. You need a psychiatrist.[11] We may well have to reason very carefully about how to balance our various goals. But we can't reason ourselves into those goals from outside all of our existing desires.

Another way of thinking about Aristotle's view is that it accepts what our emotions are telling us, while Plato and most other Greek philosophers warn us, over and over again, that our emotions lie to us: they mislead and confuse and delude us. I'll illustrate this with two of the simplest examples.

Socrates, in the *Apology*, famously argued that our fear of death – a fear felt by virtually all human beings – is a kind of ignorance. Our fear is telling us something false, namely that death is a bad thing. In reality, says Socrates, we have no reason at all to think of death as a bad thing. Plato develops the argument further in the *Phaedo*. Fear of death, he says – a delusion caused by lack of philosophy – makes cowards of ordinary people. To be brave on the battlefield, in the face of death, you have to come to see, against those fears and through philosophical enlightenment, that death is actually a good thing.[12]

Aristotle's view (III.7–9) is that if you are not afraid of death then there's something wrong with you. You're misinformed or mad. Death is a very bad thing, and your fear of it is not a delusion. It's useful. It's doing the important job of steering you in the right direction in the presence of danger – away from death. And it does not make you a coward. On the contrary, if you aren't afraid of death you can't be brave. A brave person isn't someone who faces death because they're convinced it isn't a bad thing. (Someone like that is unafraid, but not brave, just as I am unafraid, but not brave, when I confront a piece of buttered toast.) A really brave person is someone who loves life deeply, fears death powerfully, but faces it boldly when they have some strong and honourable reason to do so – for example, to save their family or defend their country (see III.9). It's only because death *is* so frightening that risking your life is such a brave thing to do.

Or consider anger. A few generations after Aristotle, Stoic philosophers (influenced by Socrates and Plato) argued that, ideally, we should never get angry with anyone at all. Anger, in their view, like our fear of death, is fundamentally deceptive: it asserts, in effect, that someone has done us real and meaningful harm. But deeper reflection reveals that nothing that someone else can do to you should ever count as real harm. ('Nothing bad can ever happen to a good man', said Socrates.)[13] So the Stoics were also against retaliation, like Plato before them. The same view then also turns up in Christianity. 'If someone strikes you on the cheek,' says Jesus, 'just offer them your other cheek as well.'[14] But Aristotle's view is that anger is not misleading. Again, he sees it as functional and perfectly normal in good people. Of course, you can easily get too angry (and that's the failing that tends to attract our attention disproportionately). But you can also not get angry enough. And you can be just the right amount of angry. There are things you should get angry at, he says. To fail to feel any anger at the things you should – the things that merit anger – doesn't make you more saintly. It's a serious moral failing. It gives bullies a free pass and is often a danger to the people who depend on you. It also makes you a bad friend (we need our friends to get angry with us, to just the right degree, when we do shameful things or make terrible mistakes). And payback, into which anger drives us, is important and valuable too. It's crucial to the existence of human society. 'It's the ability to pay people back', says Aristotle, 'that holds society together. People want to pay back harm, or benefits. And if they can't repay harm, they feel like slaves.' He is not saying he approves of violent revenge. He is saying something we all know: that one of the key functions of law in any well-ordered and fair society is to enable people to obtain redress, reliably, against wrongdoers.

But the most famous consequence of his view that the virtues have a major non-rational component is his idea that we also acquire them by a non-rational process. He thinks that you become a good person by habituation – which is to say, by training your emotions, your likes and dislikes, without knowing too much about why you're acting that way. He thinks virtues of character come to all of us naturally, to some degree (see II.1 and VI.13) and are then triggered, and developed, by the right kind of upbringing. That is, by good habits. Neither element involves very much thinking.

This idea has aged well, and seems very nicely in line with what we think we know about human evolution and human nature. It was ahead of its time.

It seems a better idea, to me, than supposing (as Plato did) that you can only become a truly good person by seeking out, or being exposed to, the best philosophical ideas; or even (as he sometimes seems to claim) that true goodness demands very complex, difficult and rare insights into the nature of the universe.

Aristotle thinks that becoming a good person is far simpler than that, but also much harder. To become brave, for example, you don't need to do any philosophy. You don't need to gaze upon the Form of the Good. Nor do you need the right theology. But you do need to put yourself in danger. Over and over again. You need to get out there and do the things brave people do. So, in that different sense, it's much harder than talking to Socrates, or having the right view of the cosmos.

He is not saying that being a good person doesn't have a cognitive component at all (it seems likely that his critics accused him of implying something of that sort).[15] To be a fully and properly good person, he says, you'll certainly also need wisdom (VI.12–13, X.8), which includes consciously held and articulate moral beliefs, and common sense, and an overview of life's goals, and the ability to reason well about how to achieve those goals and balance them against one another in the best possible way. But his view still reverses the core Socratic and Platonic idea that some form of wisdom, or knowledge, or higher philosophy, will make us good people by providing us with special and powerful reasons for being one kind of person rather than another.

'First, let's attain knowledge', says Socrates, 'of what bravery is, say, or what generosity is, and of exactly why it's a good thing to be brave, or generous, or righteous, and then surely that kind of knowledge will make us act the right way without fail. And conversely, without that knowledge, won't we just flounder around aimlessly?'

No, says Aristotle. You'll never find that kind of foundational moral knowledge. If you aren't already a generous person no mere argument, no philosophical discovery of whatever kind, will crowbar you into becoming one. We have to reverse that approach. First make yourself a generous person. (How?) Do lots of generous things. (But why am I doing them?) Don't ask that. Just do them. Then, once you now *are* a generous person, by long habit, once it's part of your character – well, you'll easily see why we should be generous. You probably won't even think to ask.

The key point is that wisdom, and knowledge, and argument, and precepts and principles, whatever else they do, cannot create character. Reading the Sermon on the Mount or Buddhist Sutras won't make you a better person, any more than reading a biography of Muhammad Ali will make you a champion boxer. Your wisdom, says Aristotle, can't even exist before basic goodness of character (see VI.12–13). Rather, the motivational muscle memory we call good character must develop first, long before we are any good at reasoning about anything at all, and then it will feed into and inform and provide the crucial 'starting points' for our wisdom (as well as being guided, moderated and tweaked by it). Good character must develop blind, and only then open its eyes.

Humanism; right and wrong without God

Aristotle also calls his subject 'human philosophy'.

That is because he thinks that all the questions he is discussing here – questions of right and wrong, good and bad – are tied specifically to the human condition and to human nature, and hence are a purely human concern.

That is to say, he wants us to do ethics without God.

More generally, he believes that facts about right and wrong do not depend on facts about the nature of the whole cosmos. I shall call this his 'humanism'. (That term means rather different things in different contexts and historical periods, and it especially tends to mean something different for people who feel they are against it. Here, I use it only to refer to this very basic idea that morality does not depend on God, or on our beliefs about God, or the gods.[16] I suspect that our term ultimately derives from Aristotle himself and from Aristotelian idiom: 'All the ways we exercise moral goodness are human', he says. 'Right and wrong is a human thing'. 'It's human questions we're investigating here' (see 1178a9, 1137a30, 1155b9). But it doesn't matter whether I am right about that.)

Let's consider three or four different ways in which these ideas show themselves through the treatise.

For one thing, Aristotle never discusses the virtue of piety. For most Greeks this must have seemed a strange omission. Piety was regarded as a central and important virtue. Plato discusses it several times,[17] and tells us in the *Laws* (I assume he is also reporting a standard view) that piety is an absolutely crucial motivator of morality. By 'piety' he means having the right views about the gods, namely that they exist and take a keen interest in human action and expect us to do what is right. Traditional Greek piety means believing both that the gods are foundational to right and wrong, and that they will make sure, somehow, that good people always prosper.

But Aristotle does not believe that the gods are foundational to right and wrong or that they take any interest in human actions. (Strictly, he is a deist. He does not think that God has any needs, emotions or desires at all.) So he also does not think that having the correct views about the gods, or God, or the wider universe, can make us better people. Hence he cannot accept that piety is a moral virtue. And his way of dealing with this potentially awkward fact is ingenious. He just never mentions it at all. In these lectures, we enter a world which is otherwise thoroughly Greek, but where the virtue of piety seems never to have existed, and all the terms associated with it and so closely intertwined with morality in other Greek texts have mysteriously vanished.

This is all the more striking when you consider the virtues, or other qualities, he does discuss. According to this treatise, having a sense of humour, being appropriately lavish in your spending, being honest about your accomplishments and talking in a deep voice are all more important than being religious. (At least they get a mention.) Most Greeks would have found this deeply weird.[18]

Actually, there is one place where Aristotle invokes piety. He says (at 1096a16) that it is a matter of piety – his religious duty – to disagree with Plato about the Form of the Good. I assume that this is a joke. That famous part of the *Republic* (the parable of the cave) makes the claim that we need to study the whole cosmos and grasp its principles, see that it is beautifully governed – organized at the highest level according to what is good – and then use that sublime knowledge in our ethics and our politics.[19] This looks like a philosophically sophisticated version, a brilliant reimagining, of traditional Greek piety. (Facts about the governance of the universe, Plato is saying, must still serve as the foundation of human right and wrong.) And Aristotle says that his only duty of piety is to reject Plato's view.

There is another partial exception. Aristotle does talk about piety, in a sense, in book VI. But he does so cautiously and indirectly. What he says is that we have to separate wisdom – i.e. *phronēsis*, which includes our ideas about right and wrong – from *sophia*.

But what does that mean? What is *sophia*? As it turns out, Aristotle uses that term to refer to the highest branches of philosophy and science: our knowledge of the 'constituents of the cosmos', and 'the best things in the universe', and 'things that are the most divine in their nature'.[20] And that, by very clear implication, includes our knowledge of the nature of God. So when the subtexts are properly brought out, we see that Aristotle is arguing directly for his humanistic idea itself. He is arguing that we have to separate theology from our ideas about right and wrong.

Sophia is what you eventually obtain when you do lots of *philo-sophia*. It is what Plato's philosopher-kings are supposed to obtain by their years of punishingly complex higher studies. Aristotle himself sees metaphysics and theology as an important science, related to cosmology, astronomy, physics and biology. All of those, if successful, will count as forms of *sophia*. And his point is that however wonderful and uplifting that kind of knowledge is, it will not make us any wiser; it will not make us morally better people, or help us make better laws. Because it isn't about us. People with that kind of knowledge, he says, 'know things that are extraordinary and amazing and difficult and marvellous – but useless, because they aren't investigating what's good for human beings'.[21]

Aristotle thinks it is not the job of science to provide us with our moral wisdom. That view is widely held today. But he also thinks, on what seem quite reasonable grounds, that theology is a science. So, just like the other hard sciences, it can't tell us anything about right and wrong. Human wisdom, and correct theories and beliefs about God, in his view, have non-overlapping magisteria.

*

These expressions of his humanism are quite discreet. Readers sometimes barely notice them. It seems clear that Aristotle doesn't wish to be too blatant, or to offend sensibilities, in his rejection of both traditional and newer Platonic ideas about piety.

But there is at least one part of the treatise, a very important section of book X, where he speaks more openly on this issue.

For most of the treatise Aristotle has argued (or assumed) that we human beings flourish, mostly, by exercising our moral virtues. But in X.7–8 he offers what seems like a different view. He now says – unexpectedly[22] – that the very best activity available to us is one of exercising our higher intellect on purely scientific and philosophical objects. More precisely, he argues that the best thing you can do in life is contemplate the most sublime, eternal truths.

In the course of making this case, he carefully compares a life of exercising your virtues with a life of contemplating the cosmos.

Scholars have spilt a lot of ink arguing over whether we can comfortably reconcile the book I account of human flourishing with these rather different claims in book X. I have my own views on the problem (some of which I offer in the relevant notes). But let's set that controversy to the side. It's something else Aristotle claims in the book X passage, just in the course of the argument, that is more relevant to the aspect of the *Ethics* that we're discussing here. As part of his case for the wonderfulness of contemplation, he says that contemplative activity is superior to moral activity because contemplation is divine, whereas 'all the ways we exercise our moral virtues are human'. That's to say, our moral virtues are specifically uniquely human; they have no connection with God. He makes humanism itself serve as one premise of the argument for the value of contemplating the universe.

As far as I can tell, Greeks had vanishingly little interest in whether it's better to be a contemplator or a statesman. (The question only ever seems to have troubled philosophers themselves, as if from a nagging suspicion that their choice of career had been a huge mistake.) But lots of people at the time cared very deeply about the sub-question that gets slipped without fanfare into this part of the discussion: whether the gods share and applaud our virtues and take an interest in human affairs. And Aristotle's argument, which casually separates God from human virtues and human conduct, is one of the starkest, boldest rejections of traditional piety that comes down to us from ancient times:[23]

We take it for granted that the gods are especially 'blessed'; they're an ideal of 'flourishing'.

But what kinds of actions are we supposed to attribute to them?

Can they do things that are fair {and honest}? Or isn't there something absurd in imagining the gods trading, returning money that's been lent to them, all that kind of thing?

Can we assign them brave actions? – [shall we have the gods] standing up to frightening situations and facing down danger because it's the honourable thing to do?

Or generous actions? Who are they going to be giving stuff to? And it's absurd to think of them using cash or anything like that.

And how could they do things that are moderate? It's a pretty paltry sort of praise, to say that the gods don't have any sordid cravings.

In fact, if we go through them all like that, it seems quite clear that all things related to actions are trivial to the gods, and beneath them. (1178b8–18.)

Most Greeks would have found this argument scandalous.

Consider the claim that the gods could have no need for fairness. Why not? Why couldn't the gods be fair, not in their treatment of each other – obviously – but in their treatment of humanity? For example, why couldn't their fairness show itself in the fact that they reward the good and punish the wicked? It seems a little disingenuous of Aristotle to ignore that possibility. As if it had never even occurred to him. Or consider his rhetorical question: 'Who are they going to be giving stuff to?' Us! – replies just about every Greek who ever lived.

But Aristotle does have his deeper reasons for these views.

Let's take just one example. Fairness, in his view, is something especially tailored to our distinctive human problems. We human beings must struggle for food, shelter, health, money and power – and all the rest – because we are mortal, short-lived, fragile beings, living down here on the earth. We are a social animal, and there is by no means a limitless supply of those goods. They are contested. So we have to share them, and divide them, and apportion them, and earn them, and pay for them. And that is why we need our instinctive love of fairness. It's obviously a tool provided by *our* nature, nurtured and captured and expressed by *our* laws and institutions and traditions, for our particular form of life. The gods do not live anything like our life. They are not mortal or fragile. They do not struggle for food or shelter or safety. They do not need to share or apportion anything whatsoever. So why would they ever have developed the virtue of fairness, or any interest in it, or the ability to treat us, or anyone else, fairly? Why would they know the first thing about it? You might as well expect human beings (just because they're so smart) to have acquired and honed the hunting techniques of a giant squid, or a koala's knack for knowing which eucalyptus leaves are wholesome. God cannot have our wisdom, or make our laws, because He does not live our life. He does not feel the emotions or cares or strivings that, as Aristotle says, provide our human form of wisdom with all its 'starting points'.

So for Aristotle our moral virtues are ours. We human beings must develop them, understand them and exercise them as well as we possibly can, for ourselves and on our own, without any help or backing from God (even if studying the nature of God, and of this awe-inspiring cosmos, is also one of the best things that we can do if we are lucky enough to get a moment's respite from our mundane struggles).

Aristotle's humanism also shows itself in his far greater acceptance of ordinary human interests, desires, sorrows and loves; his respect and affection for his fellow human beings, whose opinions and feelings, at least when they all point in the same direction, he is happy to trust. ('Every animal homes in on its own good.' 'What seems to be the case to everyone, we assume *is* the case.')[24] His defence of common human fears, and anger, and physical pleasures, and his deep interest in friendship and love and family attachments can all be seen in that light.

There is a connection between this acceptance of common human attitudes and the respect for the role of the emotions that we discussed earlier. If you think (as Plato does) that most people are wrong most of the time about what really matters in life, you are bound to be suspicious of the emotions and feelings that so obviously push people in those silly directions. Conversely, if you think that human emotions are functional, normal and a key part of human goodness, as Aristotle does, then you are much more likely to value the things that they so vividly attach us to.

This is why Aristotle is the only Greek philosopher (at least, that we know of)[25] who makes any defence of the 'material', 'external' or 'worldly' goods that the rest of Greek philosophy seems to run so scared of: money, health, power, beauty, respect, reputation, children, physical pleasures, luck and so on. Ordinary people can't be completely wrong about those things, says Aristotle. We might often overvalue them; but there is a wisdom, of a sort, to the common view. They have their place in a flourishing life too:

> [Human flourishing] does seem to require external goods as well ... Because it's impossible, or certainly pretty hard, to do honourable things if you don't have any resources. There are lots of things that we do by using friends and family or wealth or political power as tools, so to speak. And there are other things you need in the sense that missing out on them mars your blessedness, like, say, noble birth, having fine children, being physically attractive. You're a long way from the typical idea of 'blessed' if you're hideously ugly, or low-born, or solitary and childless; and perhaps even further from it if you have really awful children or friends; or if they were good ... but they've died.
>
> So as we said, a flourishing life does also seem to depend on certain things like that falling in your favour. (1099a31–1099b7)

These reasonable claims appalled other philosophers. Aristotle was violently attacked for them; for his unacceptable embrace of the worldly. Here, for example, is an angry denunciation by Atticus, a second-century Platonist (the same attack was enthusiastically retweeted by the Christian philosopher Eusebius, which is why it survives):

> Aristotle's treatments on these questions – the *Eudemian* and *Nicomachean Ethics* – offer us thoughts on human goodness that are piffling, degraded and vulgar; the sort of thing any layman or uneducated fool or teenager or woman might think up.
>
> He has the temerity to rob moral goodness of its crown and kingly sceptre, inalienably bestowed upon it by Zeus. He denies that being a good man, on its own, is enough to make you blessed.

He sets goodness on an equal footing with mere wealth, reputation, noble birth, health and beauty, and all the other things
that might just as easily be possessed by evil men. According to
Aristotle, while none of those things on its own will make you
flourish if you aren't also a good man, by the same token, merely
being a good man apparently isn't enough either, if you don't
have those worldly goods! On such a view, is not the value, the
dignity, of virtue cast down and destroyed?[26]

This is one of the more revealing ancient discussions of Aristotle's *Ethics*. It's a little overwrought. But it is also at least partly
correct, and an unintended, powerful compliment to Aristotle.

Aristotle thinks that what mostly makes your life go well is
being a good person; exercising your moral virtues as fully as
you can. And he has the optimistic view that the quality of
your life is therefore very substantially in your own hands. But
he concedes that other, purely external goods have their role
to play too. Why does Atticus find that thought so horrifying?
To answer this, you need to see that a commitment to a certain
kind of piety is deeply woven into this reaction. (The flowery
reference to Zeus is a pretty good clue.)[27] It is Aristotle's
humanism – his impiety, Atticus would call it – that he is sniff-
ing out, like some Platonic Grand Inquisitor, and denouncing
as heretical.

Consider beauty, money, power, health and children: the
things Aristotle sweeps over in the passage we just read. We
can all agree that those things are not distributed very fairly,
in the bigger picture. Evil people can easily have more power
and money than good people (in fact, it's a common view that
evil people usually have more power and money than good
people);[28] anyone, whether good or evil, can be beautiful; anyone can be struck down by illness in their prime, however kind
and decent, while some blowhard dictator enjoys ninety infuri-
ating years of perfect health. Anyone's child can be taken from
them by tragedy. Innocent people die, or suffer horribly, every
day. Most of us are lucky enough to be born with body and
mind well set for the activities of life, others with cruel obs-
tacles set in their way from the start. So if we concede that all

those kinds of things have real importance, we must conclude that life is not very fair.

Now, Aristotle says here that these kinds of things, by coming or going, by being given to us or taken away, can make a serious difference to our lives. He accepts that life is at least somewhat exposed to tragedy, in the sense that really extreme misfortunes – in any sane view – mar and blight a human life. But that view is impious, says Atticus. It is blatant impiety to assert that life, and the cosmos, and its ruler, distribute important goods unfairly; that it could be so callous and indifferent to what we deserve.

Conversely, if you firmly believe that life is fair, that the world is perfectly governed by higher powers, then you really have no option other than to conclude that those material, worldly goods cannot have nearly as much value as most people think they do. And that is exactly the view that most Greek philosophers settled on.

Not Aristotle. Impiety of that sort doesn't trouble him. He does not think the gods share any of our concerns or any interest in fairness, or that they watch over us or provide any guarantee that good people will prosper. On the Aristotelian view, if we want a fair world we'll have to roll up our sleeves and make it ourselves. If we want good people to prosper we'll have to find ways, by the laws and institutions and societies that we create, to thwart our worst impulses and unleash our own better angels.[29]

He does, as it happens, think that life is very much better for good people than for bad people. But only as a general rule. He remains free to accept that terrible things sometimes happen even to very good people. So he is also free, philosophically, to retain a more normal, more humane, more sympathetic attitude to the 'external' goods that are vulnerable to fortune. And that's just what he does.

This makes him a bit of an outlier. Within wider Greek philosophy, Aristotle's positive view of worldly goods gained hardly any more traction than Aristarchus' heliocentric theory among Greek astronomers. And yet it is one of the greatest strengths of his ethical system. For Aristotle, the importance of those 'external' goods can play a major role in our moral virtues as well – as it should. Or rather, as it does.

The view that he is rebelling against goes something like this. We do wrong because of our desires, and because of all our worldly attachments. That's why we'll be righteous if and only if our reason fully takes charge of those desires. For example, people commit adultery because of sexual desire (so if they could purify themselves of that kind of desire, they wouldn't ever do that kind of wrong). They steal because of their greed; their grubby love of material gain (so if they could rid themselves of their love of money, they won't steal). They do cowardly things in battle because of their ignorant attachment to staying physically alive (so if they could just see that death is not such a bad thing, they would be perfectly brave).

But none of this makes sense.

If you want to understand why stealing is wrong, you need a healthy sense of the value of a dollar. Otherwise you won't understand why other people's money has value *to them*. (If you thought that the cash in your friend's wallet was literally worthless, you'd be more likely to take it, not less – for example, to blow your nose on it, or make an origami pelican.) And to know why you shouldn't interfere in other people's sexual relationships, you have to understand why those relationships have the importance they do to those people; and if you have no sexual desire and no interest in sex yourself, that importance will be opaque to you. (That's why eight-year-olds don't know why adultery is wrong.) Or how can you possibly understand why it is wrong to injure someone if you don't set any value on the body? How would you grasp how shockingly cruel it is for a young person to be deliberately disfigured if you don't know the value of beauty and its role in young people's lives? How could you be a good father, or mother, if you don't see your children's death as a life-changing disaster? And if you're going to fight for your friends on the battlefield, obviously you want *them* to remain physically alive – and with a passion. And you'll be a hopeless political leader if you think your fellow citizens only need moral virtues. They don't. They also need food and safety, money, health and families. And fun, from time to time. And power – especially the power to remove you from office for having such a crummy grasp of their needs.

I find this point nicely made, in defence of Aristotle's view of external goods, by one of the Greek commentators. He teases it out more explicitly than Aristotle ever does himself:

> Stoics and Platonists like to say that only our virtues – like the virtue of being a fair person – have intrinsic value. But fairness is a virtue we use for sharing things out. And not just anything. It's for sharing out external goods, like money, health, survival, respect and so on. (Obviously we don't use fairness for sharing out virtues.) But if those external goods themselves have no intrinsic value, what does it matter whether we distribute them fairly or unfairly? What difference does it make? So, on their view, being a fair person is pointless. Virtue doesn't have any value either.[30]

Exactly.

Think of our character virtues as the plants growing in a farmer's field. One famous view is that all the 'cares of the world' are like weeds. They swamp and smother the crop and prevent it bearing fruit. Aristotle would say that's very confused. Our attachments to the good things of this life, and to this wonderful world, are not the weeds in that image at all: they're the soil. Our virtues are deeply rooted in all our other values and inseparable from them. Earthly cares and struggles nurture and inform every single exercise of our goodness. They're the only setting in which our virtues could have any point to them; the only matrix in which they could possibly have formed.

In his view, the key to moral virtues is not (as Plato argued in the *Phaedo*) ever greater detachment from bodily and worldly desires. The defining feature of our virtues is that they direct our gaze and energies towards the interests *of others* – and typically, and most often, to their bodily and worldly needs. And to understand and serve those needs, we most certainly need to share in them and sympathize with them.

Most obviously of all, if life itself – another of those 'external' goods – is not something to be treasured, then why is it wrong to take other people's lives? If death is not a bad thing, why is it wrong to bring it upon someone else? Aristotle is the only Greek philosopher who doesn't need to answer that profoundly silly question, because he is the only one to hold on to the common-sense view that death is a very bad thing indeed. He dismisses, without argument, Socrates' famous claim (enthusiastically taken up by Platonists, Stoics, Epicureans and Christians alike) that we should not fear it. He has the opposite view: 'And the most frightening thing of all? Death. Because death is the end, and surely once we're dead that's it, there's nothing more for us, good or bad.' A refreshingly humane attitude, but a rebellious one for any Greek philosopher, and especially Plato's star student. And yet it does have its antecedent somewhere in Greek thought. There is a familiar, deeply wise voice behind it. But not a philosopher's. We need to search more widely to see who has shaped Aristotle's thinking here.

When Odysseus journeys to the underworld to consult Tiresias, he runs into Achilles, and rather tactlessly suggests that he must be having a wonderful time:

> Achilles, no man was ever more blessed than you, or ever will be again. When you were alive, we Greeks revered you like a god; and now that you're here, you're the ruler of the dead! So, you shouldn't be too upset about your death.

Achilles sets him straight:

> Just don't, Odysseus. Don't try to console me about death. I'd rather be a field hand, toiling for some lowly man with a few measly acres to his name, up above the ground, than be lord of all the dead whose lives are spent.[31]

Consciously or unconsciously, Aristotle closely echoes the Homeric attitude in his claim that death is the most terrible thing of all, because it ends everything for us. He expresses the same Homeric view, in distinctly Homeric language, in his discussion of the afterlife (the main point of which is to dismiss it entirely from the discussion of human flourishing and human goals): 'if anything from [later events] gets through to [the dead], good or bad, it must be faint and slight'. And again in his discussion of bravery: 'dying will be all the more distressing for [a good man], because a man like that has so much to live for, and he'll be conscious of the fact that he's being robbed of the greatest blessings'.

For that matter, several of the more unorthodox moral virtues that Aristotle discusses (including some never so much as mentioned by other philosophers) – the importance of 'lavish spending', for example; the value of standing tall and knowing your worth; of having healthy ambitions and a desire for esteem; of getting angry at people when they deserve it – quite clearly have a very Homeric flavour to them too, once you see it. This is a useful way of thinking about Aristotle, I think. By his embrace of human character as he finds it, and of the whole great, messy variety of human cares and pleasures and pains, by his evident love of life here on the surface of the earth, and not least by his Iliadic view that the gods do not protect or reward good people or help us solve any of our problems – in all those things, he is the most Homeric of the Greek philosophers.

*

Aristotle's humanism also gives rise to some interesting puzzles and problems – and, of course, some modern readers, like Atticus before them, will see this aspect of his thought as very unattractive in itself.

For one thing, he has to stay clear of areas of morality that are too deeply mixed up with piety and traditional Greek ideas about the gods.

That's why he gives no explicit account of the practice of making and keeping promises and vows. For Greeks, promises were intimately bound up with oaths. And oaths were always sworn by the gods – as, indeed, they still are.[32] But presumably Aristotle does not think it is good theology to invoke the power and wrath of Zeus, or any god, to make sure that the parties to a contract keep their word. But instead of giving some alternative, humanistic account of why we should keep our promises, he just gives no account at all. He barely mentions them. By extension, he offers no account of the related virtue of honesty. That seems a very serious omission for any moral philosopher, especially for one whose stated aim is to list and discuss all our most important virtues.

Other areas of morality that Greeks would normally beef up with notions of sanctity and sacredness likewise have to be revised, passed over with careful evasions, or significantly toned down. Aristotle agrees that it is 'more terrible' to strike your own father than anyone else; and that 'there are some things' – he means things like matricide, or mistreating the body of a loved one – 'that nothing could ever force you to do'.[33] For most Greeks that kind of language is tame. Orestes and Oedipus weren't hounded by the Furies because what they did was 'terrible': they were guilty of monstrous sins, vile pollutions, loathsome to all the gods. And while most Greeks would readily agree with Aristotle that 'nothing could force them' to kill their parents, almost all of them would also say that there is a further obvious reason for that: the fact that it is an act of unspeakable impiety.

Aristotle never mentions incest in the *Ethics*. At least, not directly. He perhaps touches on it rather vaguely in his discussion of moderation (for example, at 1118b25, where he says there are certain 'despicable' pleasures 'that nobody should [ever] enjoy'). In which case, by his account of that virtue and its corresponding vice, he is saying that incest results from an excess of physical desire. So he places it on a moral par with drinking too much wine. That seems inadequate, and it is surely not what he actually believes.[34] Incest arouses a very distinctive moral sentiment: disgust. It activates that particular taste-receptor in the human moral palate, one that shows up in many areas of human conduct and many of our moral judgements. Feelings of moral disgust are subject to a strikingly large amount of cultural malleability. But the examples we've just noted, incest, violence to one's parents and the mistreatment of the dead, evoke that same response in almost all of us, along with sexual abuse of children, cannibalism, murder, treason and acts of monstrous cruelty. Disgust often lies behind our strongest, most absolute moral commitments – 'I'd rather die than do that' – and is closely related to notions of moral purity and integrity.

It surely doesn't depend on any particular metaphysical view. It is a human universal. But Aristotle does not discuss it, and I suspect he feels he cannot discuss it, because in Greek culture it is too tightly bound up with notions of sanctity, and those traditional ideas about the gods that he rejects. My guess is that he cannot see a way to tease apart the moral sentiment from the troublesome metaphysics. (He's grappling with an interesting problem, and one we still face.)[35] He does say, a few times, that a good upbringing, among other things, trains you to 'hate the things you ought to hate'. (See, e.g., 1172a23, 1179b25.) Perhaps he thinks that just about covers it. But it simply doesn't. He fails to give an account of the relevant virtue here. And the relevant virtue, at least for most Greeks, is piety.

There is also a problem of inconsistency. Aristotle does not embrace the *whole* range of human values after all. He leaves one out. He has no room for Antigone. Arguably, that actually undermines his humanism. When it comes to piety, he assumes that most people's instincts and emotions have deluded them. (Isn't that a Platonic move?) Or, at the very least, he refuses to tell us what he thinks. He shies away from the topic. (There are only the briefest hints, in these lectures, of his attitude to traditional religious beliefs and practices.) That runs against his Homeric policy of celebrating and analysing the whole of human life.

The paradox here is that even if we grant that right and wrong belongs to the human domain, it seems very plausible that piety is a 'human thing' too. It should be part of the conversation.

*

These seem like rather minor problems. Let's confront the deeper worries that many readers may have about the whole humanistic project.

If right and wrong has no connection with God, or with the kind of higher truths that Plato thought were so important to human values, what does Aristotle think is their real foundation? Does he have a satisfactory replacement? Or any?

I suggest that one useful way to approach the treatise is to see that he is thinking about and addressing this question all the time.

In book II he proposes that our moral virtues have a grounding in our biology. We are 'primed' by our nature to develop a rich set of character virtues that serve as the basis of our moral intuitions. (That is also why he often calls human beings a 'social animal'; a moral animal.) Then, in book V, he claims (like other Greek humanists before and after him) that right and wrong depend on laws and social norms. He implies that right and wrong formally comes into being only once a community of equals articulates and codifies a set of common rules. Morality exists 'between fellow citizens'.

Laws, he adds, are supposed to create and sustain human flourishing. So that offers a third foundation for morality, of a sort. Laws and moral norms can be considered sound, and wise, if and only if they promote general human flourishing, which itself (he implies) can be given a reasonably clear outline in the shared and objective demands of human life.

So the removal of God does not make Aristotle a subjectivist or a relativist. Rather, his ethics is anthropocentric. Facts that are relative to the needs and interests of human beings, and human communities, are its new foundation.

Later, in book VIII, he offers what looks like another, slightly different answer to the same question. He suggests that our relationships with the people we care about, all our friendships and family ties and various wider partnerships, generate and are sustained by corresponding obligations; corresponding facts about right and wrong (i.e. right and wrong ways of treating those people). And he catalogues a very wide array of such relationships that between them cover just about every form of right and wrong that most of us could think of.

'When people are friends, that's all the righteousness they need' (1155a26). By that Aristotle means, I assume, that if people are friends, that fact alone – with no outside force, no higher authority – will make them see and do what's right by another. Friendship serves as the alternative, entirely human origin of our strongest obligations.

And by extension, right and wrong apply more widely if and when we succeed in expanding our attachments and partnerships more widely: for Aristotle that means, as we just noted, to the all-embracing 'partnership of fellow citizens', where right and wrong find their broadest and most characteristic domain (but also, it seems, their usual outer limit). And if we want to extend morality wider than that, we have to ground it in the sorts of partnerships that cross borders, or the natural fellowship of all human beings (an idea that Aristotle touches on but never discusses in much depth).

Of course, for many readers this simply won't do. It's a respectable and perfectly intelligible view that right and wrong demand, or inevitably imply, a higher and non-human authority.

Some people say, in our age of rising secularism, that if right and wrong have the strong hold over you that they do for most people, then whatever you say about your beliefs, you are acting as if there is a righteous God. You are treating others as if there are moral facts with the sort of absoluteness only God could sustain. And it is only because of the many centuries during which people did believe that morality came from God that it retains the same hold over you now. So it is a little ungrateful of you to disparage those beliefs while benefiting so much from their cultural legacy.

How might Aristotle respond to this line of argument?

Well, for one thing, he doesn't think there is a God who shares our moral interests or could possibly play that role. So, in his view, this allegedly crucial belief in a righteous God would be a false belief, or at best a very implausible one. And it seems highly unsatisfactory for morality to be grounded in an illusion, or a hunch.

He might at least have half agreed about the role of religion. He believes, as we saw, that well-crafted cultural practices must instil good habits and, from those, the right ethical principles. And he is aware that religious traditions and narratives are the most common way that Greeks present those principles to one another and build those habits. He shows no interest in altering that fact. On the contrary, he is a great lover of Greek literature and mythology. He knows the tales of gods and heroes are full of wisdom.

But stories are not scientific theories. Nor are they history. And on the Aristotelian view, it's ultimately the habit itself that matters, not the story it comes with, and certainly not the detailed metaphysics. Train your children to be fair, kind and brave in any manner you like. Tell them (almost) any tales you like. Just get them to do it. Wax on, wax off. The idea that their virtues need very precise beliefs about the cosmos to be their foundation rests, in his view, on confusion about that process.

What does such a foundation look like? 'I should respect my parents because that is one of God's commandments.' 'I should treat people fairly because that is what was revealed to the prophet.' 'I should care about others because I have discovered that the self is an illusion.' Aristotle thinks there shouldn't be a 'because' here at all. We don't explain the obvious on the basis of the very unobvious.

This is just another application of the larger idea we already discussed above: that ethical 'starting points' come from human character, not from reason. We don't need theological beliefs or cosmic insights to explain why we should treat people fairly, or respect our parents, because we don't need *any* prior beliefs, or *any* prior argument, to explain why we should do those things, or to explain anything else so ethically basic.

Is this a strange view? On the contrary, I think we all accept it quite happily when it's applied to other characteristically human cares and passions. People who don't believe in Aphrodite will fall in love just the same. And when they do, nobody thinks that their actions show they really believe in Aphrodite after all. Bad leaders and angry young men don't need to worship Ares or Mars to be eager to blight the world with violent conflicts. We blunder on regardless, with or without any help from the gods of war. And if you've ever admired a painting, or a beautifully made film, nobody insists that you're piggybacking on centuries of faith in Athena, goddess of the arts. Why should our moral interests be the exception? Why do only they need metaphysical support, instead of arising unstoppably from human character like the rest?

This Aristotelian view is optimistic and philanthropic. Perhaps a little naïve. It offers grounds for faith in your fellow human beings, across theological and ideological divides. It proposes – a deeply civilized idea – that each of us should instead be measured only by the content of our character. And it's good news (if true) that we don't need theology and metaphysics to sustain morality. It means we can expect decency to be relatively common, a normal human thing, instead of being parcelled out to a few enlightened sections of humanity. It means we can stop hating and killing our fellow human beings for being raised under a different set of stories. We can stop worrying that the *wrong* metaphysical views will corrupt us, or depress us, or sink us into nihilism.[36] On Aristotle's view, we might just as well worry that the wrong beliefs about the laws of gravity will cause those laws to lose their hold on us and send us floating into space. Relax. Our virtues are made of sterner stuff. They aren't going to melt away like snowflakes in the face of a few heated arguments about the nature of the cosmos.

I think we all harbour a natural sympathy for this view of things. Here's a way of testing your intuitions, if you aren't sure. When you travel to some new country, knowing nothing whatsoever about its theology (or lack of it), do you expect people to exhibit the central human virtues? (Do you expect to be treated fairly? To encounter friendship, generosity, humour and kindness? To see parents looking after their children?) You probably do. Aristotle invites us to reverse the claim I cited above. You may say that you're convinced that morality depends on having the right beliefs about the right kind of God. But every day you will *act* as if it doesn't. In the way you treat others and in what you demand of them, you will often act as if you know that we are a moral animal, and that right and wrong is a human thing.

*

These ideas, and the rest that are covered by this extraordinarily rich and varied set of discussions, enjoyed rather limited success in Aristotle's day.

For two or three centuries hardly anyone seems to have noticed the *Nicomachean Ethics* at all, possibly because it barely circulated outside of the Lyceum, or possibly because (according to one ancient report) the surviving records of Aristotle's lectures spent two hundred years hidden in a dank and mouldy basement.[37] By late antiquity a few adherents of Aristotle and other specialist philosophers were studying it closely. Some, as we saw, were angrily denouncing it. (Christians, at least in antiquity, firmly decided that Aristotle was on the wrong team.)

It bided its time, hiding out in the nooks and crannies of Constantinople and a few Greek monasteries for another seven centuries or so while not many people were reading much philosophy at all. Byzantine scholars occasionally worked on it. Wider interest in Aristotle (mostly his logic and metaphysics) eventually resurged, first in the great centres of Arab learning, and from there, starting around the twelfth century, in Arab and Christian Spain and the rest of Western Europe. But the *Ethics* itself still kept a very low profile. Finally, in the Renaissance, amidst a hunger for ancient wisdom and a growing fashion for humanism in particular – and in a much emptier field, now that so many once-dominant works of ancient ethics had vanished – it found its moment. It emerged, an authoritative work and a philosophical must-read for the first time, a mere 1,700 years after Aristotle gave his last talk.

NOTES

1. But it goes without saying that my aim was to translate the text as accurately as possible. For that reason, I decided not to use the special scholars' dialect traditionally used for translating Aristotle. For more on this, see below, in the Note on the Text.

2. Plutarch, who is usually well informed, refers to this treatise not as the *Nicomachean Ethics* but as Aristotle's *Ēthika Hupomnēmata* (see *Adversus Colotem* 1115b). I assume the term is traditional. There is also the fact that the school treatises

like the *Ethics* (as distinct from Aristotle's published works) were called 'acroamatic' works by later scholars. That term, in origin, meant 'lecture-based'. Chrysippus, speaking just after the time of Aristotle's editors, says: 'I don't see you as ready for philosophy just because you keenly attend lectures and take down your *hupomnēmata* of what philosophers say; you also have to be prepared to apply the instructions of philosophy to your actions; to live by them.' (Stobaeus 2.7.11.) 'Records' of this sort were taken down on wax tablets, not papyrus (which was far too expensive for that purpose). That fact is important. Delivering lectures of this length from wax tablets is impossible. (So we know these cannot be records from which Aristotle spoke.) Also, when notes were then copied and written up onto papyrus, the result was one single (very costly) library text, not something that could feasibly be distributed to students.

It seems likely that scribes or secretaries (probably educated slaves) were given the task of doing more thorough 'recordings' (rather like minute-takers at meetings).

3. There is also a third ethical treatise in the Aristotelian corpus, the *Magna Moralia*, or '*Big Ethics*', so called because its individual books are much longer than in the other two. It is clearly a later recasting, in generally simpler and more fluent Greek (and often by way of different arguments) of the main material and doctrines of the other two treatises (mostly the *Eudemian*).

4. Suda's lexicon records, under the entry for Nicomachus, that 'He was a philosopher; son of the philosopher Aristotle; student of Theophrastus, and (according to some) his lover; he left six books of *Ethics*, and also wrote on his father's *Lectures on Nature* [i.e. *Physics*].' The 'six books of *Ethics*' seems likely to be a reference to the seven (unique) books of these *Nicomachean Ethics* (i.e. its ten books less the three common books) that he edited. Because of the unclear title, the idea that he wrote this work himself circulated in antiquity. (It is taken seriously by Cicero, for example.) The incorrect number of books is hardly significant, given the fluctuations in how the books were divided up and the widespread inaccuracies in the transmission of details of that kind. (It is surprising that it is only off by one.) Regarding the terms 'Eudemian' and 'Nicomachean': these unusual forms never meant '*by* Eudemus' or '*by* Nicomachus', and would certainly not have been taken at the time to mean 'dedicated to so and so'. But in just the right period this

form of nominal adjective was used to designate editions. Thus the scholar Aristophanes' edition of Homer was known as *The Aristophanean Homer*; and Aratus' edition of the *Odyssey* was known as *The Aratean Odyssey*; and so on (see *Vitae Arati* 7.18). This offers a good parallel and a satisfying explanation of our title (at least in the light of the other evidence).

5. I mentioned above that it was probably secretaries who did higher-quality, more accurate record-taking. Theophrastus had an educated slave named Pompylus (see Diogenes Laertius 5.36), whom he later freed, and who, in his will, was left in charge of several tasks in the Lyceum, including 'supervision' of the *peripatos* (the covered walk) where these lectures were given. Aulus Gellius records (2.18) that he was a philosopher 'of some renown'. Pompylus, I suspect, is the man who actually took down the records that became this text.

6. It does occasionally appear elsewhere in Aristotle's works (five times in all) in references to these discussions. But it is clear that Aristotle hardly ever used it. There is one place in this treatise where *ēthika* comes quite close to meaning 'ethics' in our sense: 1178a19.

7. E.g. in the second chapter of book I; also in I.3, I.4, I.9, I.13, VI.7, VI.8, and (in a sense) X.8.

8. So *politikē* was, more or less, philosophical Greek for the *topic*, 'ethics', for Plato, and hence also for Aristotle. It means 'statesmanship', 'statecraft', but with a tendency to slide towards 'moral and political [know-how]'. It is an adjective. Strictly, the noun that went with it, and explains its feminine ending, is *technē*. *Politikē technē* means 'statesman's expertise'; 'moral and political expertise'; 'civic and ethical know-how'. This is awkward for Aristotle, because his own view is that moral qualities, and moral wisdom, are not a form of technical expertise (see VI.4–5). So he always leaves the noun out. 'Moral and political . . . *something*'; 'statesman's . . . *something*'.

9. Plutarch's essay 'On Goodness of Character', *Peri Ēthikēs Aretēs*, illustrates my point. It is a close and intelligent discussion of parts of books II, III, VI and VII of the *Nicomachean Ethics*. But it is not just an essay on 'moral goodness'. Rather, it defends the idea that the virtues involve emotion and desire, and that those have a positive role to play. And it's clear that for Plutarch, even writing 500 years after Aristotle, that debate is still implied just by the title.

10. I am referring to the cave parable: *Republic* 514a–520e.

11. See, for example, *Nicomachean Ethics* VII.8, 1151a15–19, VI.12, 1144a31–36, also the *Eudemian Ethics* 1214b28–1215a3.

12. Socrates speaks on death in the *Apology* repeatedly, but see especially 40c–42a. The *Phaedo* argument I am referring to unfolds from 63d to 69e.

13. *Apology* 40d1.

14. For Plato's arguments against retaliation, see *Crito* 49a–e and *Republic* 335a6–d13. The Jesus saying is found at Matthew 5:39.

15. In VI.12 he raises the question, 'What's the use of wisdom, and what's the use of higher philosophy?' Why do we even need them? He then points out that you might argue that his own view of the virtues leaves no role for those things in human goodness. He disagrees (at least about wisdom). But it seems that the problem was raised by others in response to the arguments of book II.

16. Some people take 'humanism' to be functionally equivalent to moral relativism, or to the idea that 'anything goes', or to the idea that right and wrong depend on human whim or do not exist at all; or, most bizarrely of all, to the idea that individual human beings have infinite value and should replace God as an object of worship. I absolutely do not mean any of those things by 'humanism'. Nor does Aristotle hold any of those positions. He thinks that right and wrong belong fully to the human world (the details can be filled in, reasonably and charitably, as we proceed).

17. E.g. explicitly in *Euthyphro*; *Protagoras* 330b6–332a1; *Laws* X; *Republic* 337b11–391e, 612–13. Several famous discussions have humanism and piety as their subtext, in my view: Thrasymachus in the *Republic* (335–344) and then Glaucon (357–367), and Callicles in *Gorgias* (482–492) present humanistic and deeply impious views that Plato encourages us to regard with horror. The remark in the *Laws* about the powerful motivating force of piety comes at 885b.

18. Even Aristotle's own students apparently thought it was weird. In the later Peripatetic work *On Virtues and Vices* we find a catalogue of the virtues that Aristotle discusses in this treatise; and piety is there too, restored to its conventional role and importance (1251a31).

19. The idea that philosophers have to 'go back down' from the one domain of knowledge to the other (to sort out human morality and politics) is discussed at 520a6–521b10.

20. See 1141a18–b7. Strictly, he says that it makes no sense to think that *phronēsis* (human and moral wisdom) is the highest form of knowledge, since human beings are not 'the best thing in the cosmos', the latter being, by implication, the object of the highest form of knowledge, *sophia*. And he notes that the objects of *sophia* are 'far more divine in their nature' than mere human beings.

21. The word for 'marvellous' here is *daimonia*. In some older contexts that means 'divine'. That also hints at the motivating thought here: knowledge *of the divine* is of no practical use to us.

22. But not entirely unexpectedly. There are several minimal allusions, in book I, to the later argument; and another brief anticipation of it in book VI, at 1144a5.

23. This argument turns up again in Cicero's *De Natura Deorum*, where it is used as a Middle Academy (i.e. Sceptic) argument against Stoic theism. See III.15. Cicero seems unaware that it comes from Aristotle. Sceptics may have taken it directly from Aristotle, or perhaps by way of Epicurus. There are other hints that Epicurus was influenced by it. *Principal Doctrines* I (a terse statement of Epicurean humanism) retains its structure and conclusion.

24. Both these claims are in X.2, in the second discussion of pleasure. They are drawn from biology. Aristotle assumes that all animals are wonderfully well designed. Hence, we should assume that their characteristic desires and their feelings of pleasure and pain (for human beings that includes all the normal human emotions) typically push them in the right direction. For another statement of his respect for common and traditional views (in ethical matters) see 1198b27.

25. Huge swathes of ancient philosophy have vanished, of course. And Aristotle's own students, and later followers, no doubt had similar views. We know that Theophrastus did. But it is true, I think, to say that Aristotle's are the only surviving texts of ancient philosophy that express this attitude.

26. Fragment 2; quoted by Eusebius, *Praeparatio Evangelica* XV.4.9.

27. Atticus does not literally mean that Zeus, as traditionally conceived by Greek polytheism, makes moral goodness the supreme value in life. This is a philosophical usage. The Stoics, for example, were monotheists, but still referred to God using the old idioms – i.e. sometimes as 'Zeus'. Atticus is following that convention. Plato likewise talks about Zeus in this semi-metaphorical way, e.g. in the chariot allegory in the *Phaedrus*.

28. Aristotle mentions this common view at 1120b17. He also notes that since good people often don't care about making a lot of money, it's hardly very surprising when they don't make a lot of money.

29. US President John F. Kennedy knew this treatise fairly well. (He alluded to it in his sixty-third press conference, when asked if he liked being president.) And it seems he also wove an Aristotelian view into the final words of his inaugural address: 'Let us go forth ... asking His blessing and His help, but knowing that, here on earth, God's work must truly be our own.'

30. This is the gist of it. I am rather freely paraphrasing a section of Michael's commentary on V.9. I strongly suspect, from the wording, that Michael is recycling an argument from a much earlier source. The reference to Platonists implies that this may be a contemporary response to Atticus, or to arguments very like his.

31. *Odyssey* 10.482–91. Plato quotes these beautiful lines in the *Republic*, to single them out as philosophically unacceptable and to insist that they should be deleted from the poem.

32. That's to say, we still make some of our deepest promises either in a church (marriage vows) or touching the Bible (in court, or being sworn into the military, or citizenship, or high public office), thereby invoking God's oversight and inviting His displeasure if we defect. For the Greeks, a far larger range of promises, agreements and contracts took this form.

33. See III.1, 1110a26. Aristotle tells us that he has matricide in mind (at 1110a29). And I am struck by the echo of a famous passage in Herodotus (3.38): 'King Darius asked some Greeks what sum of money would induce them to eat the bodies of their parents. They replied that they would never do that; not for *any* amount.'

34. In the *Politics*, Aristotle criticizes Plato's proposal that wives should be held in common in an ideal community, making everyone's paternity invisible. He notes (1262a37–40) that such an arrangement might well lead to incest. But he evidently means accidental incest: i.e. *unknowingly* sleeping with your own parent. Clearly, that has nothing to do with excess sexual desire.

35. Plato thought hard about the same problem. But his impulse was to reform Greek ideas about the gods, in such a way as to be able to retain the core elements and advantages of piety. Socrates, in the *Apology*, does not exactly have orthodox Greek

religious views; but he constantly links his deeply held principles to his ideas about the gods.

36. In almost the last thing Plato ever wrote, the tenth book of the *Laws*, he proposed that works of atheists and also humanists (like Aristotle) should be banned, and that people who held such views should be imprisoned and re-educated, and executed if they did not change their views. His reason for those astonishing proposals was that the materialist/physicalist world view and humanistic ethics of those various thinkers were a threat to the whole moral fabric of society. The parable of the cave also seems to claim that the wrong metaphysical views leave us morally blighted and wretched.

37. See Strabo 13.1.54; Plutarch, *Sulla* 26.1–2.

Note on the Text

[square brackets]

These indicate something not explicitly in the Greek text, but which may or must be understood as part of the thought. Aristotle's text is terse and elliptical because of its spoken-lecture style and its minimalist editing. But there is usually no doubt about how the sense fills out, and some excellent translators do not bother indicating such supplements at all (even when they provide them in exactly the same way).

The supplements include (a) things that could not possibly be doubted by any scholar; (b) things that most scholars would confidently supply, but some might query; (c) things offered as a plausible example, among other possibilities, of how to fill out a gap in the sense.

I also use square brackets when Aristotle is directly discussing Greek words or Greek etymology, and occasionally for slightly filling in a line of thought that is mysterious for modern readers only for cultural or historical reasons.

In certain rare cases I supply a sentence to bridge what seems like a hole in the argument. Such gaps may have been easier for Aristotle's listeners to skip over, from context or because of their familiarity with the material. But in a few places there does seem to be an actual gap in the transmitted text or a defect in the editing. (Readers are invited to assume that longer additions of this particular kind are a little more speculative.)

In some places I considered it likely that part of the text is a response to a question or objection from a student. Those moments are signposted by suggestions set outside the main text, again in square brackets. (I offer guesses as to what the questions were.) Obviously, as with the longer supplements just mentioned, the reader should feel free to regard these cues as merely probable.

There are also a few places where the text seems to me to preserve actual questions, or actual objections presented to Aristotle by someone in the audience. It is hard to be sure about this, because Aristotle often rehearses opposing views himself; but subtle details seem to make it a fair possibility that we are hearing someone else's voice at those points. Those brief sections of the argument are italicized.

{squiggly brackets}

These indicate double translation. I sometimes find it helpful to translate a given Greek word twice (or occasionally three times), offering different senses or shades of meaning, or the same sense with different historical flavours. So any word or phrase squiggly brackets has already been translated in the immediate vicinity. Readers should have no trouble spotting the partner.

English has a much larger vocabulary than Greek. So we often use two or three words that cover, in fine-grained ways, the various uses of a single Greek term that acquires its different senses from context. For example, the Greek verb *lupeisthai* means 'to be in pain', 'to experience pain', but also 'to be upset', 'to be distressed'. The adverb *kalōs* means 'well' (with an all-purpose sense), but also 'honourably' (with a strongly ethical sense). The noun *nomos* means 'law', 'social norm', 'custom', 'convention'; *koinōnia* means 'partnership', 'cooperation', 'sharing', 'community', 'society'; and so on.

An argument might toggle between a word's different senses, or subtly employ more than one of them. In such cases it can be useful both to register the different senses and the continuity of the term, if the latter is playing a role within a single argument. The importance of purely lexical connections is, in my view, exaggerated by translators. But in some places Aristotle does lean on them a little, and I use double translation to help the reader see what he is up to.

In many cases the best translation I could devise was an

English doublet. 'Friends and family', or 'friends and loved ones', is frequently the correct translation of the single Greek word *philoi*. 'Complete and perfect' often feels like the best way to translate *teleia*. 'Lecherous and gluttonous', though clumsy, is sometimes the most accurate translation of *akolastos* as it is used by Aristotle. 'Right and wrong' (i.e. treated abstractly, as a single philosophical topic) is the normal English for the Greek abstract noun *to dikaion*. 'Laws and social norms', for *nomoi*, is the best way of capturing Aristotle's more theoretical claims about the origins of right and wrong. I do not mark any of those as double translations in the same way as the other cases, since my view is that the whole doublet accurately translates the single Greek term, as distinct from those cases where I am offering stand-alone alternatives.

Book and chapter divisions

I have used the standard, traditional division of the treatise into ten 'books' and the traditional chapter divisions within those books. A 'book' in this ancient sense was originally a separate papyrus role. Each is now about twenty-five printed pages of Greek text. The book divisions go back at least to late antiquity (though it is very difficult to figure out when, exactly, the ten books acquired their current boundaries) and the chapter divisions have probably been used for at least 1,000 years. But these do not reflect Aristotle's (or his first editors') own choices, and they do not always correspond to natural divisions of subject matter. Some of the books (II, IV, VIII, IX) have single subjects. Most have at least two. Some chapters are self-contained sections; many continue an argument seamlessly or change topic abruptly. Even so, it seems to make little sense to disturb these old divisions. In my experience the only effect of reforming them is to make it much harder for people to find their way around the treatise.

Bekker numbers, derived from the pages and columns of Immanuel Bekker's 1831 edition of the complete works of Aristotle, are supplied in the usual way in the margins to enable more exact reference to sections of text, and for line-by-line checking against the Greek. Chapter divisions are marked by the large Arabic numerals in the text.

I have decided, most of the time, not to supply headings or summaries for each section of argument, preferring to present the text as cleanly as possible. The English version aims to be as close as possible to the experience of reading the Greek text (i.e. if you speak late-classical Greek natively). Subject headings were obviously not part of these lectures as they were actually delivered, and no such headings appear to have been any part of the original version of the text. Also, like all lecturers, Aristotle typically declares when one subject has come to an end and a new one is beginning. He is also good at indicating each new subdivision of a topic. (He often begins a section with the exact question that is now to be addressed, for example.) So usually the reader needs no extra help tracking the argument. The lectures are, for the most part, about as easy to follow as any modern professor's lecture delivered freely from a rough outline, shaped by elements of improvisation, low-level repetition and accidental digression.

On the other hand, in the common books (V, VI and VII) it is often distinctly harder to see where the argument is going without extra help. There the text seems to jump around abruptly, or to repeat itself in a way that seems too confusing to be natural. There are sections that read like collections of short, miscellaneous points connected only by their wider topic (one in book V, from chapter 6 on, and one in the later part of the discussion of self-control in book VII). It is as if the editors had various little pieces left over after editing the longer discussions and decided, naturally enough, to form them into scrapbooks of related material rather than dispensing with them altogether. There it seemed useful to label the miscellaneous sections, or at least to divide them clearly, rather than expect the reader to try to join them all together as a continuous discourse.

Diagrams and other illustrations

The translation includes several diagrams and one chart. We know from clear indications in several of the surviving treatises that Aristotle, like modern classroom lecturers, used diagrams, and sometimes wrote out syllogisms in some sort of abbreviated form. My assumption is that he used a vertical board for his illustrations. In this text he is obviously using and labelling a diagram at least six times in his discussion of fairness in book V alone. (In two cases, the surviving Greek text effectively *is* the diagram.) I have reconstructed those diagrams as best I can. My reconstructions largely match those of other commentators.

In book II Aristotle says that he is going to illustrate his theory that all virtues are 'middle states' by applying it to a set of particular cases 'from our chart' or 'from our list'. The parallel ethical treatise, the *Eudemian Ethics*, preserves just such a chart (i.e. a table of virtues and their corresponding vices) in the manuscripts, and I supply a Nicomachean version closely based on the Eudemian one (except that I put the virtues in the middle).

Near the start of book V, I present a small portion of the text in the form of four diagrams of my own. I found the diagrams useful for dealing with the special difficulty of presenting Aristotle's complex claims about the Greek terms themselves – not the underlying concepts – in English.

The Greek text

I follow Bywater's Oxford text, with a number of minor departures from it. All alterations to the text, however small, are marked with this larger asterisk* and listed separately in an appendix. (A longer version of that list, with a full discussion of all the problems, is available on my page at academia.edu.)

The most serious difficulties are in the common books (V, VI and VII), which are also by some way the worst-edited. But even there, in almost all cases, the changes to the text make no substantial difference to the local sense or the wider argument.

Most are simply aimed at getting the text to say what most scholars agree it is supposed to be saying, with minimal departure from the manuscripts.

However severe the editorial problems, at no point have I removed or repositioned substantial chunks of text, as some editors have proposed doing. I present it as received. The translation typically looks rather different from the Greek text in its layout, but that is only because I have introduced paragraph divisions and clearer punctuation. Bywater's text (like Bekker's, and like the medieval manuscripts from which our texts derive) is almost completely uncontaminated by paragraphs.

In the few places where I feel that a longer passage is not just mildly out of place – a common occurrence – but confusingly so, or if a passage obviously interrupts and conceals a continuous train of thought, I obelize it or otherwise mark it as a separate portion of text, with a brief explanation in the Notes.

In two places I direct the reader's attention to what I take to be lengthy duplicate passages (where each part of the duplicate takes up more than an entire page of Bywater's text). By 'duplicate' I mean a passage where Aristotle repeats himself, in detail, in a way that by any reasonable standard goes beyond the allowances of normal lecturer's discourse. The simplest explanation for duplicates is that they derive from two versions of the same lecture, given and recorded at different times (e.g. two different occasions on which Aristotle gave his lecture on self-control, or fairness, or wisdom). The wider Aristotelian corpus contains a large number of such duplicated discussions. Within this treatise, all the duplicates are in the common books (except for the largest, on pleasure, which is parcelled out between book VII and book X). So it seems plausible that they are a result of some sort of blending of the two sets of records that were elsewhere separated into Nicomachean and Eudemian material.

There are a dozen or so duplicated passages in all by my count. Most are too small to matter very much. I mark the two largest. One takes up almost all of book V, chapter 5, the other most of book VII, chapter 4. Before deciding to flag them, I noticed that the author of the *Magna Moralia*, in paraphrasing these parts of books V and VII, collapses the duplicates into single passages. Clearly, that author was quite happy to assume that these were indeed editorial duplicates. (Later commentators from Aspasius onwards, for whom such imperfections in Aristotle's text were unthinkable, preferred fanciful explanations for why Aristotle was saying the same thing twice.) So my presentation of the duplicated text records a view of those passages that goes back almost to Aristotle's own time and is of historical importance in itself.

The translation

This translation is conservative in interpretation and traditional in aim. It aims to translate the text as accurately as possible.

I translated every page from scratch, from a clean Greek text, rather than revising an existing translation. In part I wished to avoid unconscious duplication of errors. (Ross's version, in particular, is so influential that his minor mistakes are often accidentally copied into later versions.) But mostly I wanted to avoid the scholars' dialect that is traditionally used for translating Aristotle and work from a first draft that was in standard English even in its smallest details.

Typically, with about a chapter in hand I consulted several of the best recent translations, and the parallel passages in the *Eudemian Ethics* and *Magna Moralia* (where they exist) and the surviving ancient or Byzantine commentaries of Aspasius, Eustratius, Heliodorus and Michael. I checked all debatable decisions about the construal of the Greek against the best editors and philological commentators (especially Stewart and Susemihl). I also discussed a large number of particular passages and problems with colleagues over seven annual meetings of the Aristotle Workshop, dedicated to close reading and study of books III, IV, V, VIII and IX.

In places where some word or idiom still remained opaque or open to significantly different readings, I checked other instances of the same item in other passages, first in Aristotle and then in other contemporary or later but still pertinent

Greek writers – typically dozens of other passages in all – until I found something that I felt settled the question one way or another. Modern technology has made that process much quicker and easier than in the past. I often refer to those findings in the Notes.

I almost always went with the majority of voices (modern and ancient) as to what Aristotle was saying and at other times follow a credible minority. Places where I have introduced interpretations that are purely my own are extremely rare (usually a result of minor emendations to the text). So, all in all, I offer for the modern reader of the *Ethics* a cautious and consensus reading, based on the accumulated research of dozens of other scholars stretching back over two millennia.

No doubt plenty of errors remain. I think that is inevitable with this text. I have never discussed a single paragraph with two other scholars without finding that we had six different views as to the meaning of at least one puzzling detail.

I accept the modern scientific consensus as regards the translation of ethical vocabulary and related discussions of 'human things'. In the light of forty years of advances in evolutionary psychology, I believe that there are a number of universal, familiar features of human character that Aristotle can talk to us about, whatever our disagreements about details, whatever the many cultural differences between us and the ancient Greeks. Because of that (and for several other reasons) I am fairly optimistic about translation. I reject the approach of Arthur Adkins, Elizabeth Anscombe and others who followed Nietzsche in supposing that the main elements of modern thinking about right and wrong were unknown to the Greeks, or known to them only in some radically different form. My view of humanity and of our shared moral instincts is shaped by a newer paradigm. This is a post-Darwinian translation. (It is also more in line with the older, both Aristotelian and Christian view of human character.)

Having said that, I have no interest at all in modernizing Aristotle's ideas. All the attitudes of this treatise remain fully Greek, very patriarchal, somewhat aristocratic and firmly embedded in the fourth century BC. My choice of dialect (standard

English) has no bearing on that whatsoever. (It is perfectly possible to express distinctively Greek and ancient attitudes in standard English.) Of course, some ideas expressed in these lectures will sound familiar to modern readers. That's because plenty of things in human life do not change. I have also not simplified the text in any way. I have translated every iota, particle, preposition, noun, verb, adjective, phrase, clause and sentence of the original. Every premise and every argument therefore remains – unfortunately – exactly as complex and annoyingly difficult as in any other version in whatever dialect.

Set against wider norms of translation there is nothing special about this version at all. My approach is boringly conventional. Taking care to avoid any bold theorizing (whether about Aristotle, 'the Greeks', or translation itself), I translated the text into standard English as accurately as I could. The only difference of any note between this version and (some) others is that I fully set aside the scholars' dialect. In my view that requires no explanation. (You wouldn't say, for example, that a notable feature of this version is that it isn't in Swedish.) Some scholars and students unwarily assume that the traditional dialect has a special connection with Greek and that using it brings readers closer to the original text; and that it makes the translation more accurate. In reality, it has no special tie to the Greek language, either in its main philosophical glossary or in its dozens of minor (and pointless) deviations from normal English. And in my view it certainly makes any translation much less accurate.

But this is not the place for a detailed defence or explanation of that view. I will occasionally refer to the scholars' dialect ('Gringlish') and its traditional glossary in the Notes. For a full discussion of that dialect and its origins, and all other aspects of my methods and philosophy of translation, please see my longer essay ('Translating the Ethics').*

---

* As of publication of this translation, that essay is available on my page at *academia.edu*.

BOOK I

Every {art and} technical skill, every systematic method [asso- 1094a
ciated with those], and in the same way every action and choice
seems to aim at something good.

That's why they were right to propose that 'good' is what all
things strive for.[1]

But it seems there are two different kinds of goal. Some
of our goals are activities, and some are various products
beyond them. (And where there are goals beyond our actions, 5
in those cases the products are by nature greater goods than
the activities.)[2]

But there are lots of things we do, lots of different skills and
forms of knowledge, so that makes for lots of different goals.
The goal of medicine, for example, is health. The goal of ship-
building, a ship. The goal of generalship, victory. The goal of
running a household, wealth.

And whenever those kinds of skills fall under some single 10
ability – like, say, the way bridle-making and other skills
for making cavalry equipment fall under horsemanship, and
then horsemanship (and every other war-related action) falls
under generalship ... and others fall under this or that other
one in the same sort of way – so my point is, in all those cases,
the goals of all the higher, master skills are more valuable
than the sub-goals. Because they're the reason for pursu- 15
ing those in the first place. (And that's true whether it's our
activities themselves that are the goals of our actions, or some
other thing beyond them, as with the forms of knowledge just
listed.)

2 So if there's a goal of [all] the things we do, something
   that we want for its own sake, something that's our reason for wanting everything else – assuming we aren't always
20 choosing everything just to get some other thing, because then
it would go on for ever, and our strivings would be empty and
pointless – then obviously that must be the key good [in life];
the highest good.

So in that case, won't knowing about it also have a major
bearing on our lives? Like archers, if we have a target to aim
at, won't we be more likely to hit upon what we've got to do?
25 And if that's so, then we'd better try to get at least a rough
idea of what it is, and what branch of knowledge, or what ability, it falls under.

Surely the most authoritative. The most all-encompassing.
And clearly that's statesmanship. After all, that's the one that
determines which forms of knowledge should even exist in city
1094b states, and which ones each set of people should learn, and up
to what point. And we can see that even the most high-status
abilities – being a general, a head of family, an orator – are
subordinated to it. It employs all other branches of knowledge
and, of course, it makes the laws, tells us what we have to do
and what we may not do; so its goal must encompass the goals
of the others.

Its goal must be the [key] good for human beings.

Because even if that's the same thing for an individual as for a
city, it certainly seems a greater thing, more perfect, to attain it
and preserve it for a whole city state. True, we should be pleased
10 enough [to bring it about] even for just one person. But a finer
thing, more divine, [would be to achieve it] for a nation, or a state.

So those are the aims of our enquiry. So this is statesmanship –
of a sort.[3]

3 Now, we'll only need our claims to be as explicit and
   detailed as the underlying material allows. We mustn't
demand precision in the same way in all areas of discourse –
just as we don't [expect it] in things made by craftsmen.[4] There's
a lot of variation and fluidity in what's honourable and what's
15 right, the sort of thing that statesmanship is concerned with.

So much so that some people think they only exist by social convention, not by nature. And what's good for people shows that kind of fluidity, too, in a sense, because people quite often find themselves being harmed by good things. (There are cases of people being destroyed by wealth, for example, or by their bravery.)[5] So the best we can hope for, in making claims about things of this sort, and on the basis of facts of this sort, is to 20 indicate the truth in thick strokes; rough outline. We're making claims about things that hold for the most part, and on the basis of for-the-most-part facts, so we'll have to be content with conclusions of the same sort.

And that means you'll need that same approach in taking on the various claims we'll be making. An educated person only demands precision in each field to the degree that the nature of 25 the thing permits. Asking for scientific proofs from a political orator surely makes about as much sense as accepting a mathematical proof because it 'sounds pretty plausible'.

Each of us is good at judging the things we know. That's 1095a what you're a good judge of. So that might be some particular thing, if you're educated [in that field], and things in general, if you've had an all-round education. That's why lectures on moral and political questions aren't suitable for the young. Young people have no experience of the actions of life. And that's what the arguments will be based on. That's what they'll be about. Plus, young people tend to act purely on their emotions. So for them, taking the course will be a waste of time. 5 They won't get anything out of it.

Because our goal here isn't just about knowing. It's about doing.

And it makes no difference whether you're actually young in age, or just immature in character. What's lacking isn't just a matter of time. It's about whether you live your life, and pursue the things you pursue, by your emotions. For people like that, knowing doesn't help, just as it doesn't help people with no self-control.

But if you can form your desires, and act, according to 10 reason, then knowing about these things might well do you a lot of good.

All right, so that's all we need to say, by way of introduction, about who should be at these lectures, the right way to be receptive to the material and what we're aiming to do here.

4   Now let's pick it up from where we were.
        Given that every kind of knowledge, and every choice
15 we make, strives for some kind of good, what is this thing that we're saying statesmanship aims to achieve? What is this 'highest of all goods' achievable by action?

So, pretty much everyone at least agrees on what it's called.
    Eudaimonía – {'flourishing', 'prospering', 'being blessed'}: that's what everyone calls it, across all social classes. And we all take 'having a good life' or 'doing well' to be the same thing
20 as 'flourishing'.
        But as for what 'flourishing' {or 'being blessed'} actually is – people disagree about that, and most people don't offer the same view of it as philosophers. Most people say it should be some plain, obvious thing like [a life of] pleasure, or wealth, or prestige. Different people have different ideas about it. Or often even the same person. (When you were sick, it was healthy people who were 'blessed'; now that you're poor, it's the rich.)
25 Others, aware that they lack ideas of their own, are dazzled by other people's grand and pretentious[6] theories about it. And some [of you] used to think there was something extra, beyond all the particular good things [that we're familiar with]; something 'Good in itself'; the cause of all those things being good as well.[7]
        All right, so, let's not examine every single view that's out there. That would surely be a bit of a waste of time. Let's just
30 look at the most prevalent, or the ones that seem the most plausible.
        And let's not forget that there's a difference between arguments that work *from* our first principles[8] and arguments that get us *to* first principles. Plato was quite right to puzzle over that, and try to figure out whether we move from first prin-
1095b ciples or towards them; from the judges to the far end of the stadium, so to speak, or back towards them?

Well, clearly we have to start from knowables. But that means two different things. 'Knowables' are either the things we easily know [i.e. familiar, particular facts] or 'knowables' in the absolute sense [i.e. universal scientific truths].

So surely we have to start from the things we easily know.

That's why you already have to have been pointed in the right direction by good habits, if you hope to get very much out of a course of lectures on what's honourable and right, or any other moral or political question. Because our starting point is the fact that X, and if X seems pretty obvious, that's all we need. We won't need [to talk about] *why* X is the case.[9]

People like that [with the right upbringing] either already have, or can easily grasp, [the right] principles. If neither of those applies to you . . . well, Hesiod says it best:

> Best of them all is a man
> who relies on his own understanding.
> Next best, someone who knows
> how to take good advice when he hears it.
> So, if you're clueless yourself,
> and unwilling to listen to others,
> taking to heart what they say –
> then, sorry, you're pretty much hopeless.[10]

5 We went off on a bit of a tangent there . . . Let's start from where we were.[11]

When it comes to the key good, and what it is to flourish, people seem to base their ideas – understandably enough – on their own lives.

So ordinary people, the most vulgar and uncouth, think the key good is pleasure. That's why they're satisfied with a life of indulging themselves.

. . . You see, there are three forms of life; or three that stand out. That one, and the life of a statesman, and third, the contemplative life . . .

So ordinary people seem utterly slavish, opting for a life of [well-fed] cows![12] But their view gets some plausibility from the fact that powerful rulers so often behave just like [King] Shardanapal.[13]

The higher classes, at least those who choose an active life, assume that the key good is respect. Respect, roughly speaking, is the goal of the life of statesmanship.[14] But it seems a bit too superficial to be what we're looking for here. It seems to depend on the people who respect you, rather than on you, the person being respected; and we have the strong intuition that the [key] good [in life] should be something that's your own, and hard to prise away from you.

Also, people seem to pursue respect to reassure themselves that they're good men. At any rate, they seek to be respected by people who are wise, and well informed about them; and to be respected for being good men.

So it seems clear that, on their view, being a good man itself matters more [than being respected]; and maybe it makes more sense to regard that as the goal of a life of statesmanship.

But then even that – [goodness] – seems somehow incomplete. After all, it seems perfectly possible to have it and be in a coma, or do nothing at all, for your entire life. What's more, [a good man] can still experience the worst kinds of suffering and really awful misfortunes; and nobody – unless stubbornly defending some [crazy] theory[15] – would say that someone living a life like that was flourishing {or blessed}.

And that's all we'll say about that. I've already talked about it enough in my public writings.

The third form of life is the contemplative life, which we'll be taking a close look at later on.

And a life of earning money? That's one of drudgery, pretty much.[16] And wealth clearly can't be the 'key good' that we're looking for. Because it's just something we use. It's just for getting something else with.

That's why [the key good] is more likely to be one of the other goals we just talked about. At least they're valued for their own sake. And yet it doesn't seem to be any of those either, in spite of the many arguments already expended on them.

So, let's drop these questions [for now].

6 I suppose we'd better investigate the 'Universal Good' – see if we can figure out what on earth that's supposed to be about – though it's a question I'm a little uncomfortable with, seeing as the people who introduced the 'Forms' were like family to me. But I think it would probably be better to dispense with personal ties – I think we really have to when the truth is at stake – especially as we're philosophers.   15

We love them both – [our mentors, and the truth] – but it would be a sin[17] not to respect the truth more.

All right, so the people who brought in this view didn't propose Forms for sets of things where some things in the set were (in their terms) 'prior' to others, and some 'secondary'. (That's why they didn't even try to construct a common Form for the [set of all] numbers.)[18] But we use the term 'good' of (1) existing things and (2) qualities of things and (3) relations between 20 things. And something that exists on its own – an entity – is naturally prior to a relation. A relation is surely a sort of offshoot of, a feature of, an existing thing. So there can't be a common Form for all those.

Also, we use the term 'good' in as many senses as we use the word 'is'. We use it, for example, of good things (e.g. God, and mind) but also of good qualities (virtues)[19] and quantities ('the 25 right amount') and relations ('this is useful for that'); we apply it to time ('the right moment') and place ('habitable')[20] and so on and so forth. So it's obvious that there can't be some single Universal Good common to all. If there were, we wouldn't use the term 'good' in all the different [predicating] categories. Just in one of them.[21]

Also, for sets of things that come under some single Form there's also a single branch of knowledge. So [on this theory] 30 there also ought to be a single science of all good things. But there isn't. In fact there are multiple sciences even for things that are just in one category of good. Take [knowing] 'the right moment'. In war that's a matter of generalship; but in treating an illness it's medical knowledge. Or 'the right amount' – of what? Food? That's medical knowledge. Of exercise? That's physical training.

And you might well wonder what on earth they even mean 35

by an 'X in itself'? I mean, whether it's this 'human being in
1096b itself' or just a human being, the account of [what it is] – a
human being – is one and the same. There'll be no difference
in what makes them human. And if that's right, then [the same
goes for 'the Good in itself' versus particular good things].
There'd be no difference in what makes them good.[22]

And no, being 'everlasting' does not make it somehow more
of a good thing. If A is white for a really long time, and B just
for one day, does that make A whiter than B?

5   The Pythagoreans surely have a more plausible claim here,
when they place 'Unity' in their column of good things.[23] And
in fact even Speusippus[24] seems to have adopted their view. But
we should talk about these things another time.

Back to what I just argued – I can just, faintly, see an objection you might raise, on these grounds:

These claims weren't supposed to apply to every kind
10   *of good. Things we pursue and value for their own sake,*
those are called 'good' according to a single Form; and then
there are things that bring those about or preserve them or
prevent their opposites. The second kind are 'good' {deriva-
tively}, because of the first kind – it's a different sense of the
term.

So clearly things can be 'good' in two different senses: some
good in themselves, the rest 'good' because of the first kind. So
15   [let's call the second sort 'instrumental']; and let's set instrumental goods to one side, and single out things that are good
in themselves, and consider whether those are good according
to a single Form.

But what kinds of things are you supposed to classify as
good in themselves? All the things we pursue even taken on
their own? Like, say, being wise, being able to see, certain
kinds of pleasure, certain forms of respect? You'd classify all of
those as good in themselves, even if we also pursue them for
the sake of something else.

Or is the idea that nothing else, at all, is good in itself. Just
20   the Form? If so, the Form turns out to be pointless.[25]

And if those other things are good in themselves, then the
account of what makes them good ought to be, conspicuously,

the same across all the different cases, like the way an account of whiteness is the same for snow as for face-paint.

But actually there are distinct and different accounts of what it is that makes respect, {status}, wisdom and pleasure good things. So what's good isn't a universal, determined by a single 25 Form.

So why exactly do we call all those things 'good'? I mean, they're surely not just random homonyms.[26]

Is it that they all derive from some single thing? Or contribute to some single goal?

Or – more plausible, maybe – is it a matter of analogy? What sight is in the body, intellect is in the soul, and likewise A is in B, and C is in D, and so on.

We should probably just drop this question for now. Work- 30 ing it all out in detail really belongs to a different area of philosophy.[27] And let's not talk about the Form [of the Good] any more either. Because even if there is some single, universally predicated Good, or something separable, existing 'alone and by itself', it obviously couldn't be a good that any human being can do, or possess. But that's the kind of good we're looking for here.

Here one of you might have the idea[28] that it's better to know 35 about [the Form] with a view to the good things that we can 1097a do, or possess.

Maybe if we have it as a kind of paradigm, we'll be more likely to know what things are good for us as well. And if we know that, then we'll be able to attain them.

All right, sure, that argument has a certain plausibility to it. But it seems to be at odds with actual forms of knowledge {and expertise}. I mean, all of those are aiming at some kind of 5 good, and all of them are on the lookout for ways to improve themselves, but none of them show any interest in knowing about [the Form of the Good]. So here's this huge resource, and yet craftsmen are all unaware of it, and never even think to look into it! Doesn't sound very plausible.

And I can't for the life of me see how a tailor or carpenter is going to get any help exercising his craft if he does know about this 'Good in itself', or how anyone is going to be a better 10 doctor[29] or general because they've 'beheld the Form itself'. I mean, doctors don't even seem to investigate health that way.[30] They investigate human health, or really just the health of this person in front of me. Right? Because you practise medicine on particular people.

All right. That's as far as we need to go with that.

15 7 Let's go back again to the kind of good we were looking for [the key good in life].

What could it be?

Because there's evidently a different good for each [sphere of] action and each skill: one for medical skill, one for generalship, and so on for the rest.

So for each of those, what [do we mean by] 'the good' of it? Surely it's the thing that is your reason for doing all the other things you're doing [in that sphere]. In medicine, that would be
20 health. In generalship, victory. In building, a house. It's one thing here, another thing there, but every action and every choice has its goal, and it's for the sake of that goal that we're doing all the other things we're doing.

So if there's a goal of all the things that we ever do [in life], then that would be the key good achievable by action.

(Or if there's more than one, those.)[31]

We're making great progress. We're right back where we started![32]
25 But we have to try to explain this even more clearly this time.

So, we're faced with this variety of goals. But some of those goals, [we said], are things we only want to have as a means to something else – wealth, bridles,* any sort of tool.[33] So they obviously aren't all ultimate goals. But the highest good seems like something ultimate.

So, if there's one, single, ultimate goal [in life], then that would be what we're trying to find here.
30 (And if more than one, then it would be whichever of them is the most ultimate.)[34]

Something we pursue for its own sake is a 'more ultimate' goal than one we pursue [only] as a means to something else;

and if there's something, X, that we *never* value as a means to something else, then that's a 'more ultimate' goal than the things we value both for what they are themselves and as a means to X.

So, an *absolutely* 'ultimate' goal is one we always value just for itself, and never as a means to anything else.

And that applies, exactly, to 'flourishing'. That's something 1097b we always value for itself, and never as a means to something else, whereas respect, pleasure, intellect and every kind of virtue – we value those, yes, partly for their own sake (even if nothing else came out of them, we'd still choose to have them); but we also value them for what they contribute to a flourishing life, that is, with the idea that through those things we will 5 be flourishing. But [it doesn't work the other way]: nobody wants to flourish so as to have those things (or as a means to anything else at all).

We seem to get the same result from [the idea of it] meeting all your needs. Because the 'ultimate good', surely, ought to be something that meets all your needs. And when I say 'your needs' I don't mean just yours (the way someone living the life of a hermit can 'meet his own needs'). I mean it to include your parents and your wife and children and all your family and 10 friends . . . and your fellow citizens,[35] too, because people are by nature social beings. (Of course, we have to set some kind of limit to it. I mean, if you stretch it out to include your ancestors, your grandchildren, your friends' friends and so on, it'll go on for ever. But we can address that question later.)

We're saying here that [the highest good] 'meets all your needs' if, on its own, it makes your life [not just] a desirable 15 one, but a life from which nothing is missing.

And that's exactly what we think 'flourishing' implies.

More than that, we think of 'flourishing' as the most desirable good [there can be], but not one that you count alongside other good things.[36] (If you counted it with the others, then obviously it would become more desirable if you added even the smallest good thing to it. The addition means you have a larger total of goods than before; and a larger set of good things is always more desirable.)[37]

20   So:
        To flourish {and prosper} is our ultimate goal.
        It [means living a life that] meets all our needs.
        It's the goal of everything we do.

        But to say the highest good is 'to flourish' isn't exactly ground-
        breaking. What we're missing here is a detailed account of
        what flourishing actually is.
        We might well be able to give that account if we first get an
        idea of the task {or function} of a human being.
25   For a flute-player or a sculptor or any artist {or craftsman}
        or anyone that has some sort of task, something that they're
        supposed to do, the '[key] good' for them, and their 'doing
        well', lies in that task, surely. So that's probably how it is for
        human beings too, assuming that there's such a thing as the
        human task.
        So [isn't there?] Could it be that a carpenter and a shoe-
        maker each has his task, his thing that he's supposed to do, but
30   not a human being as such? Is a human being born into the
        world jobless and idle?
        Or if our eyes and hands and feet and all our other parts so
        clearly have their tasks, {their functions}, surely we can safely
        assume that, in the same way, the [whole] human being has
        some sort of task, beyond all of those?
        So what on earth could that be?
        Well, there's just being alive. But that's clearly something we
        have in common even with plants, and we're trying to find the
1098a   task that's specifically ours. So we should rule out a life of just
        feeding, reproducing, growing.
        Next might be some kind of life based on our capacity to
        perceive {and feel}. But that form of living, too, is clearly one
        we have in common even with horses and cows and any other
        animal.
        So that leaves a life of doing,[38] [based on] the rational part
        of us. (And that means the part that's responsive to reason[39] as
        well as the part that possesses reason, i.e. actually thinks.)
5   And ['life'] is ambiguous here too, so we'd better specify that
        we mean the exercising [of that part of us, as opposed to just

having it]. Because that's surely the more natural sense of 'living'.[40]

So, given that:

(1) our task as human beings is the exercising of the soul's rational and partly rational [elements],[41] and

(2) we say that the task of any X is the same in general as the task of a good X.[42] The task of a guitar-player, for example, is the same in general as the task of a good guitar-player, and that holds as a rule across all cases; that superiority, [10] implied in its being a good X, just gets added to [the description of] the task. As in, the task of a guitar-player is 'to play the guitar', and the task of a good guitar-player 'to play the guitar well'.

And if that's so, and

(3) we're saying that the task of a human being is a certain form of living, namely, a life of exercising the soul and of rational agency; and

(4) the task of a good man is to [exercise] those [capacities] well, in every sense;[43] and

(5) performing anything well means performing it with the [15] appropriate goodness, {or the appropriate virtues}[44] . . .

. . . If all that's the case, then the [key] good for human beings turns out to be: activity of the soul that expresses our goodness {or our virtues}.

(And if there is more than one sort of goodness[45] {or if we have different virtues}, then such as expresses the best, and the most complete.)

Also, over a complete life. Because 'one swallow doesn't make a summer',[46] nor does just one day; and in the same way, one day, or a small amount of time, isn't enough to make someone flourish or qualify as 'blessed'.

So that will do as an outline of the key good. We should prob- [20] ably just do a rough sketch first, then fill in the picture later. And as long as things are sound in outline, surely anyone can take them forward and work out the details. Time is good at discovering those kinds of things too, or at least good at help-ing. That's also how there's been progress in the arts and [25] technology. It's easy to add something; improve what's already there. Anyone can do that.[47]

We also have to remember what we said earlier, and not require the same degree of precision all the time. Let's just be as precise as the underlying material allows, and to a degree that makes sense for our particular enquiry. Look at the way a carpenter and a mathematician have different ways of thinking

30 about a right angle. One only [needs to think about it] to the extent that it's useful to his task; the other investigates exactly what it is, and its [mathematical] properties; he's studying truth. So that's exactly the approach you need in other areas as well: never let the side issues become more important than the main tasks.

1098b   We also shouldn't demand explanations in the same way in all areas. In some it's enough just for the facts to have been stated clearly and correctly. That's how it is with starting points, for example. And facts come first. They're our starting points.

(Some of our starting points are discerned by induction, some by perception, some by a sort of habituation.[48] Different ways for

5 different kinds. And we have to try to investigate each sort only in the way that fits with their nature. And take great care to set them out correctly. Because they have a big impact on what follows. As they say, 'the start is more than half[49] the job' – that's to say, a lot of the things you're trying to figure out immediately become clear once you have [the right] starting point.)

8   We need to think about this – [flourishing] – not just on
10   the basis of our conclusion, and the premises we used to get to it, but also by looking at what people tend to say about it.

After all, if something's true, all the available evidence harmonizes with it. But if it's false, it quickly clashes with the truth.

So, first of all, good things are divided up three ways: there are 'external goods', 'goods of the soul' and 'goods of the body'. And we say that goods of the soul are goods in the strictest and

15 fullest sense. And 'actions, and exercisings of the soul' count as goods of the soul. So our definition is looking pretty good, at least according to that long-standing view, widely agreed on by philosophers.

[*Can you repeat that, please?*]

[Sure.] Something we've got right[50] is our claim that certain
'actions and exercisings' are the goal [of life], because that puts
it among goods of the soul, not external goods.   20

Also, the [common] idea that flourishing means 'living well'
and 'doing well' chimes nicely with our view, because that's
pretty much exactly how we've defined it: as a sort of well-
living and well-doing.

And the way we've defined it, it seems to have all the expected
features that people associate with flourishing.

Some people think [you're flourishing just by] being a good
person.

Some think, by being wise.

Some think, by [attaining] some sort of [higher] philosophical knowledge.[51]

Some think it's those things, or one them, plus pleasure (or   25
at least not without pleasure).

Some think you also need an abundance of external goods.

Some of these are popular and traditional views, some are
held by just a few highly regarded [thinkers]. And neither of
those sources is likely to be completely wrong. They've probably got at least something right. Or even most of it.

So, first, my definition agrees with people who identify   30
it either with being a good person or with [having] some particular virtue. Because 'exercising your goodness' is *dependent
on* being a good person. Mind you, I'd say it makes a pretty
big difference, whether we take the highest good to lie in
just possessing [virtues], or using them; a mere disposition,
or its exercise. After all, a disposition can be there without
producing any good effect, e.g. if you're asleep, or otherwise   1099a
totally inactive. But when you're exercising [your virtues]
that's not possible, because you'll inevitably be doing things,
and doing them well {and hence, doing well}. It's not the strongest athletes on the practice ground* who win the Olympic
crowns.[52] It's the ones who take part in the contests. You have   5
to be in the contest to win. And it's the same in life: you have
to actually do things, and do them right, to win life's greatest
blessings.

And life for such people is also pleasurable in itself.

Feeling pleasure is [not an external thing]; it's in the soul. And everyone gets their pleasure from whatever they're really devoted to. If you're a devoted horse-lover, say, you get pleasure from riding horses; if you love sightseeing, you get pleasure from seeing the sights. And in the same way, if you love doing what's right, then doing what's right is something you take pleasure in; and every other aspect of being a good person gives you pleasure, if you love being a good person.

Now, most people, it's true, find themselves fighting[53] the things they take pleasure in. That's because those things aren't naturally pleasurable. But people who love what's honourable take pleasure in things that *are* naturally pleasurable. All the actions that go with being a good person are like that. So that means they're pleasurable for those people, but also in themselves.[54]

So life for those people doesn't need any extra pleasure, tied onto it like some sort of magic trinket. It already has its pleasure in itself.

Besides, here's another thing: a person who doesn't enjoy acting honourably isn't even a good person [in the first place]. You wouldn't call someone fair and honest, for example, if they didn't enjoy treating people fairly and honestly, or generous if they didn't enjoy acting generously, and the same for the rest. But in that case, it follows that the actions that go with being a good person are intrinsically enjoyable. And of course, they're also good for you, and they're also honourable. In fact they're every one of those things more than anything else in life, at least if good people are correct in their judgement about them. (That's certainly what good people judge them to be.)

So it turns out that flourishing is the best thing there is, and the most honourable, and the most enjoyable, and those three things are not incompatible, as the [famous] inscription on the temple at Delos[55] implies they are:

> The most honourable thing? To be righteous as can be.
> But the best thing in life? To be healthy and hale.
> But the sweetest thing is to get your heart's desire.

Because you get all three of those features in the best activities {the best ways of exercising your soul}. And it's those
activities – (or one of them, the best one) – that we're saying   30
constitute a flourishing life.

But even so, it does seem to require external goods as well,
as we said. Because it's impossible, or certainly pretty hard, to
do honourable things if you don't have any resources. There
are lots of things that we do by using friends and family or
wealth or political power as tools, so to speak. And there are   1099b
other things you need in the sense that missing out on them
mars your blessedness, like, say, noble birth, having fine children, being physically attractive. You're a long way from the
typical idea of 'blessed' if you're hideously ugly, or low-born,
or solitary and childless; and perhaps even further from it   5
if you have really awful children or friends; or if they were
good . . . but they've died.[56]

So as we said, a flourishing life does also seem to depend on
certain things like that falling in your favour.

That's why some people think[57] that flourishing {or being
blessed} is basically the same as being fortunate; rather different from the view[58] that it's a matter of being a good person.

9 And that gives rise to another puzzle. Is it something you
   can learn? Or do you [achieve it] by forming good habits,
or by some other kind of training? Or does it come to us by   10
some sort of divine dispensation? Or just by luck?

So if anything else is a gift of the gods to humankind, it
would make sense for a flourishing life to be something God-
given, more than all other human things, seeing as it's the
greatest human good. This is surely a question that more naturally belongs in a different investigation.[59] But even if it's not
bestowed upon us by the gods, even if you attain it through   15
being a good person, and through some kind of learning or
training [as we've claimed], it still feels[60] like the most divine of
things. Because the prize for goodness, the thing you're aiming
for {in being a good person}, feels like . . . [not just] the best
thing there is . . . but also something divine and blessed.

It also turns out to be widely available. Anyone can achieve

it, unless congenitally incapable of being a good person,[61]
through some form of learning and by their own efforts.

20   And if it's better that we flourish that way, rather than just by
mere luck, it also makes sense for it to be that way. After all,
it's nature, [not chance], that structures things in the finest
{and most beautiful} ways, as well as human design and every
cause of that sort* (especially the very best one).[62] [So] to
entrust the most important and finest thing [in human life] to
luck – something seems very wrong with that.

25   We can also see the answer to our question right in the definition. We defined [flourishing] as a certain kind of activity of
the soul, expressing our virtues. As for the rest of life's good
things, they're either just the background conditions for that,
or they're of a nature to contribute to it or be useful for it –
they're just tools.

And that also seems to fit well with what we claimed at the
start. We said there, remember, that the highest good was also
30 the goal of statesmanship. And statesmanship concerns itself,
above all, with turning citizens into certain kinds of people,
namely good people, who consistently behave honourably.[63]

So it makes sense that we don't call a cow or a horse or any
other animals 'blessed'.[64] It's because none of them is able to
1100a share in that kind of activity. For the same reason a child can't
[fully] 'flourish' either, because a child is too young to be able
to do those kinds of things. If we do call children 'blessed' it's
because we think they have a bright future. Because, as we said,
you need to exercise complete goodness, over a complete life.

5   [And that's not so easy.] Life is full of sudden reversals and
strokes of fortune of every kind, and someone can be thriving
to the full but then suffer terrible disasters in old age, like King
Priam in the tales of the Trojan War. And when someone experiences that level of misfortune and meets a miserable end,
nobody calls them 'blessed'.

10   **10** So does that mean that we should never call anyone
blessed – anyone human – while they're still alive?
Do we have to agree with Solon[65] and 'wait and see how it
ends'?

But then, supposing that's right, does that mean – what? – you flourish once you're dead? Or is that totally absurd? Especially for us, since we're saying that you flourish by activity of some sort.

And suppose we're not saying the dead are flourishing; suppose that's not what Solon means either; suppose he just means that it's only then that you can safely declare a human being blessed, because now they're beyond the reach of further evils and misfortunes – well, even that's somewhat debatable. Because we do tend to think that bad things and good things (of a sort) can happen to you after you're dead (just as they can happen to someone who's alive but unaware of them) like, for example, your being revered or reviled [by later generations], or the successes and failures of your children and your descendants in general.⁶⁶

But that raises another puzzle. Suppose you've lived a {wonderful}, blessed life right to old age, and then you've passed away in a manner in keeping with such a life. Your descendants might experience multiple changes of fortune; and some of them might be good people who achieve the life they deserve, others the opposite. (And of course, how distantly related they are, too, makes for all sorts of different degrees of relevance to you.) So it would be pretty strange if – though dead – you were to share in all those changes too: if you became blessed one day and went back to being a miserable wretch the next!⁶⁷

But then it's also strange to think that the lives of our descendants have no impact on us at all – not even for just a little while.

We should go back to our last question. That one might well help us discern the answer to the one we're asking now.

So, suppose we do have to 'wait and see how it ends', and it's only then that we should call a man blessed; and we don't mean he *is now* blessed, we mean he *was*, before [he died]. So how is it not absurd that when he actually is living that blessed life it's not true to say that he is?⁶⁸ To state that fact about him? And all because we refuse to declare any living person blessed 'because fortunes can change' – that's to say, because a flourishing life is supposed to be something stable and not at

all easy to alter, and fortunes have a way of turning full circle
on people, again and again.

Clearly, if we were basing it on a person's fortunes, we'd have
5 to say that the same person is flourishing one day, then pitiful
again the next, over and over again; our man who 'flourishes',
on that view, turns out to be a sort of chameleon; [or] set on
very shaky foundations.

Maybe focusing on people's fortunes is fundamentally a mistake. Because those don't determine whether [your life] goes
well or badly. Yes, a human life needs those things as an extra,*
as we said, but what really determine whether we flourish are
10 the ways we exercise our goodness. And the opposite sort of
activities give us the opposite kind of life.

Even the question we just worked through supports our
claim. [A flourishing life, we just noted, is supposed to be
stable, and] no task in human life involves as much stability as the
various ways we exercise our goodness. [Our virtues] are more
durable even than bits of knowledge.[69] And the most precious[70]
15 of them are also the most durable of all, because people spend
the largest portion of their lives [exercising] them, and the
most uninterruptedly – at least, if they're blessed. That's likely
to be the reason we don't forget them.

So it follows that anyone who's flourishing will have the
characteristic we're looking for here: they'll be that way their
whole life. Because they'll always, or more than any other thing,
be doing, and contemplating [in others],[71] things that express
20 goodness. As for fortunes [good or bad], they'll handle those
in the [best and] most honourable way, and fittingly in absolutely every respect, at least, if they're 'truly good; straight as a
die, without a single flaw'.[72]

Lots of things in life happen to us by luck. And they vary in
scale. Some are important, some trivial. Of those, the minor
bits of good luck, or minor bits of bad luck, clearly don't have
25 much of an impact on your life. But if you experience major
strokes of fortune, and a lot of them, well, if those go in your
favour they'll make your life more blessed (for one thing they're
a natural embellishment of life, considered in themselves, and
for another you can take advantage of them in honourable,

morally good ways); but if they go the other way they weigh down on, and damage, your blessedness. Because they cause you pain and suffering, and also hinder lots of your activities.

Then again, even in those situations honourable [behaviour] 30 can shine through – when, say, you handle a series of terrible disasters with poise; not because you're insensitive to the pain, but because of your nobility and your sense of pride.

And if exercising [our virtues] is what really matters in life, as we said, then nobody who's blessed can ever become a miserable wretch. Because they're never going to do things that are morally despicable or vile. If someone's 'truly good' (and sane), 1101a we fully expect them to handle every misfortune with grace and dignity, and always conduct themselves as {well and as} honourably as circumstances allow (just as we expect a good general to make the best possible military use of whatever troops are to hand, and a good shoemaker to make the finest possible shoes with whatever hides he's supplied with; and the 5 same goes for all other experts). And if that's the case, then a man who flourishes can at least never become wretched – not that he'll be blessed, either – if he suffers misfortunes on the scale of King Priam's.

So he's not chequered and changeable, either. He won't easily be prised from his state of flourishing, and not by just your 10 run-of-the-mill misfortunes. It will have to be a long series of major calamities. And [conversely], after misfortunes of that kind, he isn't going to be able to go back to flourishing in any short amount of time. If he manages it at all, it will take a long time: a whole lifetime in which he'll have to accomplish great and glorious things.

So why shouldn't we say that someone is flourishing {or is blessed}, if they've been exercising complete goodness, and 15 they're adequately supplied with external goods, and they've been that way not just for some trivial amount of time but for their entire life? Or do we have to add that they're going to carry on living that way, and then also die in a manner in keeping with that life? After all, the future is invisible to us, and we assume that a flourishing, {blessed} life is not just our goal, but also something perfect and complete in every possible way.

In that case, fine – yes, we *will* call people blessed, even
20 while they're still alive (if they have all the characteristics I've
just listed, and look set to keep them into the future), but we'll
say 'as blessed as is humanly possible'.

All right, I think we've sorted out those questions. Let's
move on.

11 The idea that the fortunes of our descendants, and of
our friends and loved ones in general, have no effect on
us whatsoever[73] is surely far too unloving. And it goes against
common sense.

But lots of different things happen to them, of every conceiv-
25 able category and kind, some of them touching our lives more,
some less, and to sort through all of them, case by case, seems
a long – in fact, endless – task.

Let's just say something general, and in broad outline.
That'll probably be enough [for our purposes].

So, [think about] the misfortunes you experience yourself.
Some have a heaviness to them and an impact on your life,
30 others seem more bearable. The same is true of misfortunes
suffered by all our family and friends. [They vary greatly in
how much they affect us.] And it makes a big difference, for
each such thing suffered by them, whether it happens while we're
alive or after we're dead – far more difference than whether the
grisly crimes in a tragedy have already taken place [off-stage]
or are being acted out [before our eyes].[74] So we have to factor
in that difference. More to the point, [let's not forget] that we
35 have major doubts as to whether the deceased can experience
any kind of good thing at all, or anything of the opposite kind.
1101b Because it seems likely that if anything from [later events] gets
through to [the dead], good or bad, it must be faint and slight,
either absolutely, or at least for them,[75] or at any rate not important enough, and not the sort of thing to make people blessed if
5 they're not already blessed, or rob them of their blessedness[76]
if they are.

So while it seems that, yes, there may be some effect on the
departed when the people they love do well in life, and some
effect when those people do poorly, the nature and scale of

those effects surely isn't such as to make the blessed unblessed, or do anything else like that.

12 So now that we've sorted that out, let's consider the 10 question of whether flourishing in life is something we praise in other people, or rather something that's . . . precious.

(Because obviously it shouldn't be classed as a mere capacity.)

So it seems clear that with anything we praise, we praise it because it has a certain quality, or stands in a certain relation to something.

We praise someone who's fair, for example, or brave, and in general a good person, both for [having that quality] – for 15 being a good person* – and also because of their actions[77] and what they accomplish; and we praise someone who's strong, or a fast runner, and so on, both for having a certain physical quality, and also for standing in a certain relation to some kind of good;[78] something we value.

We can also see this clearly when people praise the gods. It makes the gods look ridiculous,[79] to think of them as bearing any relation to us {and our needs}. And that's just what 20 happens [when we praise them], because praise always involves some such relation, in the sense we just explained.

So, if those are the kinds of things we praise, it seems clear that things that are the best of all aren't praised. They get something greater, something better, than praise.

And that's just how it seems to work. Take the gods. We [don't praise them, we] declare them blessed; we aspire to the wonderful life they have; and likewise the men who are the most godlike among us.

And the same is true of [the greatest] of all good things. No 25 one praises people for flourishing {or being blessed}, the way we praise people for doing what's right. Instead we feel it's something more divine, something above [mere praise]: we aspire to it.

Eudoxus [used the same point] to make what I thought was a pretty good case for 'the primacy' of pleasure. The fact that it's a good thing, but one that we don't praise, he thought, was a clear indication that it's superior to things we praise. That's

30 true of God, he thought, and it's also true of the key good in
life. [We don't praise those things] because they're the things
we judge everything else in relation to.

[Think about it like this, too.] You're praised for being a
good person. Because goodness makes you reliably do honourable things. And eulogies celebrate accomplishments – of any
sort at all, of body, mind {or character}.[80] We don't need to go
35 into all the details. This isn't my advanced class on eulogy-
writing ... But even from what we've said, it's clear enough
1102a that flourishing should be classed [apart], as something precious, perfect, complete.

It also seems to have that status by virtue of being a principle, in the sense that it's the reason all of us do all the other
things we do. And something that's the principle, {the source}
of all good things, the thing that makes them good – we treat
that as something precious and divine.

5 13 Since flourishing is a kind of activity of soul, expressing
complete goodness, next we'd better investigate goodness. Because that way we'll surely gain more of an insight into
the nature of [human] flourishing as well.

But surely a statesman – at least, a statesman in the true sense
of the word – is also someone who, above all, makes a close
study of human goodness? Because the aim of a statesman is
to make his citizens good people; law-abiding people. As our
10 model for that we have the lawmakers of Crete and Sparta;
and various others that were like them.

(If our current question does fall under the scope of statesmanship, that just shows that our investigation is proceeding
nicely in line with our original purpose.)

And in saying that we need to investigate 'goodness', obviously we mean human goodness {and human virtues}. After all,
15 it's the key good for human beings that we've been investigating: human flourishing.

Also, 'human goodness' doesn't mean good qualities of the
body; we mean goodness of the soul, {virtues of the soul}.
Remember, we define flourishing as activity of the soul.

And if all of that's the case, then obviously a statesman [or

anyone studying moral and political questions as we are] has
to have some degree of knowledge about the soul, like the way
[a doctor], if he's going to treat someone's eyes, has to know
something about the whole body, and all the more so, to the 20
extent that moral and political [wisdom] is better than medical
knowledge and more valuable.

Certainly, the better class of doctors put a lot of effort into
knowing about the body. In the same way, a statesman needs
to study the soul.

But we also only have to study it for our particular reasons,
i.e. only to the extent that's enough for the questions we're asking. To go into it in more detail is probably too time-consuming 25
for our purposes.

I've made claims about it in my public writing, too. They're
not too bad. Some of them. We can use those claims here.

For example, I've said that there's an irrational part of the
soul and a rational part. Whether those are separate in the way
parts of the body are separate (or anything made up of actual
bits), or only distinct in the way we describe them, but physic- 30
ally inseparable (like the concave and the convex side of the
circumference of a circle) – that doesn't make any difference
for now.

One aspect of that irrational part seems common [to all
living things]. Even plants. I mean the part responsible for
nourishment and growth. That sort of capacity in the soul is
something that you can see exists in all things that feed and
grow. Even in embryos. And we should assume it's the very 1102b
same capacity in the fully grown. (That makes more sense than
thinking that it's a different one.)

Now, that part of the soul can be good [at what it does]. But
that's clearly something all living things are good at. That's
obviously not human goodness.[81] In fact that part of the soul,
that capacity, seems to operate most of all when we're asleep,
whereas good and evil people are pretty much indistinguish- 5
able when they're asleep. (That's why they say that 'for half
their lives there's no difference at all between the wretched and
the blessed'.) It makes sense that it works that way. Sleep is
the inactivity of precisely those aspects of the soul by which it's

termed a good or bad soul. (Unless, to some small extent, certain [mental] processes get through to us while we're asleep, so
10 that the dreams of decent people are better[82] than the average
person's.)

But enough about that. Let's just forget about the nutritive
part of the soul, since it has no natural connection with human
goodness.

The soul seems to have another part that's irrational in its
basic nature, but has some degree of {or a sort of overlap with}
reason:

Consider that in someone who's exercising self-control (or
experiencing a failure of self-control) we praise [one part of
15 them, namely] their reasoning, and the rational part of their
soul. Because that bit is doing its job right and urging them to
do what's best. But it seems there's another element in them,
besides reason, that's fighting with reason. Straining against it.

It's like when parts of the body are paralysed, and people
20 mean to move them to the right but they pull the opposite way,
to the left. That's how it can be with the soul. When people
lack self-control their impulses pull them in opposite directions. It's just that, with the body, we can actually see the part
pulling the wrong way. With the soul it's invisible. But all the
same, surely even in the case of the soul we have to assume that
there's something else there, something other than reason,
opposing itself to reason and working against it. (Exactly how
25 it's a 'separate' thing doesn't matter here.)

And this other bit of us seems to have some overlap with
reason too, as we said. At any rate, it obeys reason's command
in someone who has self-control. And surely it's even more
responsive and obedient in someone who's moderate or brave.
Because there it's in total harmony with reason all the time.

So it seems that the irrational bit of the soul itself has two
parts. There's the plant-like bit, which doesn't share in reason
30 at all. And then there's the part that feels physical desires, and
desires in general, which is partly rational, in the sense that it
can listen to reason and obey reason's command.

So it 'has reason' [in Greek, 'has *logos*'] in the sense in which
we speak of someone paying attention to their father or their

friends. [Greek for 'pay attention to' is 'have *logos* of', i.e. 'take account of'.] But not in the sense that you 'have a *logos*' [a reasoned proof] of a mathematical proposition.

And a further indication that this irrational part can be persuaded by reason, in some sense, is the fact that we chastise one another; and every time we ever criticize or encourage anyone.

And if we must say that that bit of us actually 'is rational', then [fine], the 'rational' bit of us will turn out to have two parts. There'll be the bit that's properly speaking rational, in itself. And there'll be the bit that's rational in the sense of *listening to* [reason], like the way you listen to your father.   1103a

Goodness {and virtues} can be divided according to the same distinction. That's to say, we speak of virtues of thought and intellect, and also virtues of character. Philosophical knowledge, insight and wisdom – those are virtues of the intellect. Being generous or moderate – those are virtues of character. If we're saying something about someone's character we don't say 'he's a great philosopher' or 'he's insightful', we say 'he's a good-natured person', or 'he's a moderate man'.   5

But we do praise the philosopher, too, for that state [of his intellect]. And all praiseworthy states [whether of character or intellect] are 'virtues'.[83]   10

BOOK II

So, there are two kinds of virtues: intellectual virtues, and
virtues of character. Intellectual virtues, for the most part, are
created and are developed through teaching.[1] But character
virtues[2] come about through *habit*, and hence need time and
experience.* That's why our word for character – *ēthos* – is
only a slight variation on the word for habit – *ĕthos*.

From that, we can also be sure that none of our moral virtues
develops in us just naturally. Because nothing that's naturally
what it is can be habituated {or trained} into being otherwise.
A stone, for example, which by its nature moves downwards,
can't be trained to fall upwards, even if you 'trained' it by hurl-
ing it up in the air 10,000 times, and you can't train fire to
move downwards, or anything else that's by its nature one way
to be some other way.

So [the role of habituation] shows that our virtues don't arise
either [purely] by our nature, or against our nature. Rather,
our nature primes us to receive them, and then we're perfected
by our habits.

Also, with things that do just develop in us naturally, we
always acquire the capacities first and then manifest the exercising of those capacities. That's obvious in the case of the
senses: it wasn't by seeing, over and over again, or hearing,
over and over again, that we first got those senses. It's the other
way round. We already had [our sight and our hearing] before
we used them. We didn't get them by using them.

But with virtues, we exercise them first, and that's how we
acquire them – just like the way it is with technical skills.[3] In
general, when we have to learn how to do something, that's

how we learn it: by doing it. People become builders by building things, for example, and they become guitar-players by
playing the guitar. So it's the same [with virtues]: we become
fair and honest[4] people by doing things that are fair and hon-   1103b
est, moderate people by doing things that are moderate, and
brave people by doing brave things.

Another piece of evidence for this is what goes on in cities {at
the political level}. Lawmakers try to make citizens good people
by habituating them [with laws]. That's the intention, at least,
of every lawmaker. When they don't do it well, it's only because   5
they get something wrong [in their laws]. That's the difference
between a good system of government[5] and a bad one.

Also, with every virtue, the things that give rise to it and
develop it are the same things that can mess it up.

The same thing applies to technical skills. It's by playing the
guitar, for example, that people become good guitar-players or
bad guitar-players. The same goes for builders (and the rest):   10
people will become good builders by building things well, or
bad ones by building things badly. (If that weren't the case,
then why would they even need anyone to teach them? They'd
all just be born already good or bad at it.)[6]

So that's how it is with our virtues too. By the way we act in
our dealings with other people, some of us become fair and   15
honest, some of us unfair and dishonest; and by the things we
do in frightening situations, habituating ourselves to be afraid
or unafraid, some of us become brave men, some of us cowards.
Likewise for situations that involve physical desires or that make
us angry: some become moderate and good-natured people,
others lecherous and gluttonous, and bad-tempered, depending   20
on whether they behave one way or the other in those situations.

So our overall claim: our dispositions, {our character traits},[7]
are created by the activities that correspond to them.

That's why we've got to manifest activities, {behaviours} of
the right sort – because differences in those will lead to different character traits.

So it's no small matter, whether we get into these habits or
those habits right from childhood. It makes a very, very big
difference. Really, all the difference.   25

2 Now, this investigation isn't just theoretical, like other [areas of philosophy]. We're not just asking these questions so that we'll know what 'being a good a person' is {or what 'virtues' are}. We want to actually become good people. Otherwise what would be the point of it?

30 So that means we have to carefully think about the nature of actions: how, exactly, should we do the things we do? Because it's our actions that will determine what our dispositions end up being like – as we've just said.

All right, so first we [have to] act according to correct reason.[8] That applies across the board,[9] and we can just take it as given for now. We'll be talking about it later, and we'll say what 'correct reason' means and how it relates to the other virtues.

1104a Let's also agree from the start that any claim about what people should and shouldn't do ought to be stated in rough outline only, not precisely, as we said back at the start. Remember, we said that we should expect our claims to suit their subject matter.[10] Nothing connected with human action is hard and fast, and {there's nothing fixed} about what's in people's interests, any more than what makes us healthy. And if

5 that's how it is even for universal claims, it'll be all the more true of claims about particular situations that they can't be precise.[11] These things don't fall under any technical expertise or set of rules.[12] It's the people actually doing things, in each case, who have to think for themselves about what that situation calls for, like a doctor treating a patient or a helmsman steering a ship.

10 Still, even though that's the kind of subject[13] we're dealing with, we've got to do the best we can with it.

So the first thing for us to observe is that it's in the nature of these kinds of things to be messed up if we *fall short*, or *go too far*.

We can see that in the case of strength and health – and we should use the obvious cases as evidence for the ones that

15 aren't so clear. Doing too much exercise, or not enough, messes up your strength, and likewise having too much food and drink, or too little, messes up your health, but just the right amount creates and increases it, and preserves it.

So, it's just the same with moderation and bravery and our other virtues. Someone who runs away from everything is 20 afraid of everything, never stands and faces anything, becomes a coward; someone who isn't afraid of anything at all and saunters into anything becomes a reckless person. And likewise, someone who indulges in every kind of pleasure and never refrains from any sort of pleasure becomes a lecherous, gluttonous man; while someone who avoids every pleasure, like dour yokels,[14] becomes some kind of ... 'feel-nothing' person.[15]

So, moderation and bravery are messed up by our going too 25 far, or by our falling short, and are preserved by the middle state.

And [virtues] aren't just created and developed and also [sometimes] messed up as a result of, and by way of, the very same [sorts of behaviours].[16] We'll then exercise them in those same areas, too. That's also how it is with the other very obvi- 30 ous cases, like strength. People become strong by consuming lots of food and enduring lots of hard toil, and it's a strong person who can then do those things more than anyone. And it's the same with our virtues: we become moderate people by refraining from pleasures, and once we've become moderate people we're then more able to do that than anyone else. Same 35 with bravery: by habituating ourselves to be untroubled by 1104b frightening things and face them we become brave people; and once we've become brave, we'll be better than anyone else at facing frightening situations.

3 We should take as evidence for someone's dispositions – {their character traits} – the pleasure or pain that arises with their actions.   5

For example: if you hold back from physical pleasures, and enjoy doing exactly that, you're moderate. If it pains you to have to do so, you're a lecherous man or a glutton. If you face frightening things and enjoy it, or at least aren't distressed by it, you're brave. If it distresses you, you're a coward.

The fact is, being a morally good person is all about pleasures and pains.

10   After all, we do bad things because they give us pleasure,
and [typically] fail to do honourable things because they're
painful. That's why it's important for us to have been brought
up a certain way right from childhood – as Plato says[17] – so
that we enjoy the things we should and feel pain at the things
we should. That's what a good upbringing is.

Also, if virtues are all about our actions and our emotions,
and if every emotion and every action has a feeling of pleasure
15 or pain that goes with it, that's another reason for thinking
that being a good person is all about pleasures and pains.

It's also indicated in the fact that punishments work through
[pleasures and pains]. That's because punishments are remedies; and remedies naturally work through opposites.[18]

Also, as we said earlier, for every disposition of your soul,
20 the kinds of things that make it better or worse are also the
things that determine what it naturally relates to; its scope.
And it's through pleasures and pains that people become bad,
i.e. by pursuing and avoiding them, or at any rate the wrong
ones, or at the wrong time, or in the wrong way, or all the
other ways of getting it wrong that reason may determine.[19]

That's why some people even define the virtues as 'tranquillity states'[20] or 'states of inner calm' or whatever – {i.e. as the
25 *absence of* feelings of pleasure and pain}. But that's not right,
just to say [we shouldn't feel them] at all, rather than saying
how we should feel them, or *how* we shouldn't, or *when* – and
all the other extra qualifications.

So here's our basic claim: being a good person[21] is a matter of
[feeling] pleasures and pains in such a way that you do what's
best; and being a bad person, the opposite.

And here's another way for us to see that it's all about [pleas-
ures and pains].

30   There are three classes of things – things that are honourable,
things that are in our interest, things that are pleasurable – that
are the targets of our choices, and [three] opposites of those –
things that are shameful, things that are harmful, things that
are painful – that we try to avoid. And it's in all three areas, of
course, that a good person regularly gets it right while a bad

person regularly makes mistakes; but it's mostly with respect to pleasure. Because pleasure, something we share with all animals, accompanies all possible objects of choice. Because even 35 what's honourable, and what's in our interest, *presents itself* as 1105a pleasurable.

Also, it's been nurtured into all of us right from infancy. That's why it's hard to scrub these feelings out of us, when our whole life is deep-dyed with them.

We also regulate our actions (some of us more than others) using the pleasure and pain [they produce] as our standard.[22] So that means our whole task[23] here is bound to be all about 5 pleasure and pain; because it's going to make a really big difference to our actions, whether we feel pleasure and pain at the right things or the wrong things.

Also, it's 'a harder thing to fight pleasure than anger', as Heraclitus says, and the harder tasks are the ones that call for technical skills, and virtues. The [tougher the job], the greater 10 the good in doing it well.

† So that's another reason why the whole business of being good people (and the whole business of statesmanship)[24] is to do with pleasures and pains. Depending on whether you feel them the right way or the wrong way, you'll be a good person or a bad one. †[25]

So here's what we've claimed so far: that virtues are all to do with pleasures and pains; that the [activities] that produce them can either augment them or diminish them (depending 15 on whether they're done one way or the other); and that they're exercised in the very same activities that produced them. Let's move on.

4 You might well wonder how we can claim that to become a fair person you've got to do things that are fair, and to become a moderate person you've got to do things that are moderate.

After all, if you're doing things that are fair and moderate, doesn't that mean you already are a fair and moderate person? – 20 just like, if you're doing things that are literate or musical, then you must already be literate or already a musician.

Or is that not right, even with technical skills? Because it's perfectly possible to produce a bit of writing just by luck, or by following someone's guidelines. So you're only really literate not just when you do some writing, but also when you do it the
25 way someone who can write does it, and that means by way of your own knowledge of how to write.

Also, it's not the same for virtues as it is for skills. With the products of technical skills, yes, how good or bad they are is in the things themselves. So it's enough for those to turn out a certain way. But with things we do by way of our virtues, it doesn't follow just from those being a certain way, themselves,
30 that we're doing them (say) fairly, or moderately. You, the person doing them, also have to be a certain way when you do them. First, you've got to know [what you're doing].[26] Second, you've got to be choosing to do those things, and be choosing them for what they are. Third, you've got to be acting from a constant and unvarying state [of character].

1105b   Those things aren't factored in when it comes to having technical skills – just the knowing. But when it comes to having virtues, knowledge doesn't really matter much at all. Or maybe just a little. But the other two certainly don't matter just a little. They make all the difference. And they're the ones that can [only] be brought about by your doing fair and moderate things over and over again.

5   So we call *things* fair and moderate when they're the kinds of things a fair or moderate person would do. But a fair or moderate *person* isn't just anyone who does those things; it's someone who also does them exactly the way that fair and moderate people do them.

So there's no problem with our claim that you become a fair
10 person by doing things that are fair, and a moderate person by doing things that are moderate.

You certainly have no hope whatsoever of becoming a good person by not doing any of those things. But the fact is, most [young men like you][27] don't do them; they shelter themselves in mere theory, fancy themselves 'philosophers' and think that's going to turn them into good men. That's like patients
15 who listen carefully to their doctors, but don't actually do

anything the doctors tell them to do. Patients aren't going to
make their bodies well by that kind of treatment, and those
people aren't going to improve their souls by that sort of [pure]
philosophizing, either.

5 Next we should consider exactly what a virtue is.
Here are three kinds of things that can be present in
your soul: emotions, capacities, dispositions. A virtue has to be 20
one of those.

By emotions, {or feelings}, I mean things like desire, anger,
fear, boldness, envy, joy,[28] love, hate, longing, jealousy, pity –
in general, things that are accompanied by pleasure or pain.

By capacities I mean the things that make us capable of those
feelings – capable of feeling angry, capable of feeling annoyed, 25
capable of feeling sorry for someone.

By dispositions, {or states}, I mean the things that set us in a
good or bad way as regards our emotions, e.g. with respect to
feeling angry, we're set in a bad way if our feelings of anger are
either [typically] intense or typically feeble, and in a good way
if they're somewhere in the middle; and similarly for our other
emotions.

So, first, virtues (and vices) aren't just emotions.

We aren't called good or bad people just on the basis of our 30
emotions, but we are called good or bad on the basis of our
virtues and vices.

Also, we aren't praised or blamed just for having emotions
(you don't praise someone for being afraid or for being angry;
you don't criticize someone simply for being angry either; it
depends on the way they get angry). But we are praised and 1106a
blamed for our virtues and vices.

Also, when we get angry or feel afraid, it's not a matter of
choosing to feel that way, but virtues are choices, of a sort – or
at any rate they involve making choices.[29]

As well as that, we say that our emotions move us. But we 5
don't say our virtues and vices move us. We say they set us –
into a certain condition.

For the same reasons, [virtues] aren't capacities either: we
aren't called good or bad people, we aren't praised or blamed,

just for being capable of feeling certain emotions. Also, it's our
nature that gives us capacities, but we don't become good or
10 bad people just by our nature – we talked about that earlier.

So if virtues aren't emotions or capacities, then they must be
dispositions; {states of character}. That's what's left.

So that tells us, in general,[30] what a virtue is.

6   But we can't leave it at that – 'it's a disposition'. We also
       have to say what sort of disposition.
15   So here we need to explain that virtues,[31] whatever they're the
virtues of, always put the thing itself into a good state, and also
make it good at performing its task. E.g. the [physical] virtues of
an eye make the eye a good eye, and make it [perform its] task
well – which is to say, the eye's virtues make us see well.

Likewise, a horse's virtues make it a good horse, and [specif-
20 ically] good at running, carrying its rider, facing the enemy.

So, if that's how it is for all cases, then human virtues, similarly, are presumably dispositions that make someone a good
human being, {a good person}, and good at performing the
task of a human being.[32]

As for how they do that, we've said something about it
25 already,[33] but another way for us to get a clear idea of what I
mean is by examining the exact nature of a virtue.[34]

So whenever something comes in different amounts, on a
sliding scale, you can have a more-than-X amount of it, a less-
than-X amount of it, or an equal-to-X amount of it, and those
can be set either {objectively}, by the thing itself, or relative to
us.[35] The equal-to-X amount is then a sort of mid-point between
overshooting X and falling short of it.

Now, by an 'objective' mid-point I mean the amount that's
30 equidistant from each of the two extremes. That doesn't vary.
It's the same for everyone. But the mid-point relative to us [is
an amount that] isn't too much and isn't too little. And that
can vary. It isn't the same for everyone.

Example: suppose ten [of something] is a lot, and two is a
little; then six is the mid-point, if we take it {objectively}, going
by the thing itself. Because it's four more than two and also
35 four less than ten. That's the mathematical mid-point. But that's

not the way to take [the middle] relative to us. Suppose ten
pounds of food is a lot[36] for someone to eat and two is a little. 1106b
It doesn't follow that the trainer's [always] going to tell someone to eat six pounds of food. Because even six pounds might
be a lot for the person who's going to consume it, or it might
be a little. It might be a small amount for a Milo,[37] for example,
but a lot for someone who's just starting out on their training.
And the same goes for running, or wrestling.

So in the same way, every expert avoids going too far and 5
avoids falling short, and tries to figure out the mid-point and
chooses that – not the objective mid-point: the mid-point relative to us.

So that's how every sort of knowledge {and technical skill}
does its task well and perfects {its product}: with its eye on the
mid-point, and by drawing its works towards that mid-point.
(That's why people typically say of well-formed works [of art] 10
that 'you couldn't possibly add or take away a single thing',
implying that going beyond that sweet spot, or falling short of
it, would mess it up, while the middle state preserves it. And
good artists {and craftsmen} do their work with their eye on
that mid-point – as I said.)

But of course virtues are more precise than any {art or} technical skill, and better, as nature is.[38] So virtues must aim at a 15
mid-point too.

[*Do you mean both kinds of virtues? Even intellectual
virtues?*]

I'm only talking about character virtues. Those are to do
with actions and feelings, and it's in those that you can have
too much, too little and a mid-point.

You can be afraid, for example, or feel bold, or feel physical
desire, or get angry, or feel sorry for someone (and in general 20
feel any pleasure or pain) more or less; too much or too little.
And [to have those feelings] when you should, and at the things
you should, and towards the right people, and for the right reason and in the right way – that's the mid-point; and optimal,
and [to be optimal] is characteristic[39] of good people. Likewise
with actions: you can do something too much or too little
or a middle amount. Virtues apply to feelings or actions where 25

going too far, or falling short, means getting something wrong, while the mid-point means getting it right and is something people praise – both of which [getting things right, being praised] are characteristic of good people.[40]

So a virtue is a 'middle state', at least in the sense that it aims at the mid-point.

Also, there are lots of ways of getting it wrong, but only one way of getting it right. (That's what the Pythagoreans had a vague sense of when they classified bad as 'infinite' and good as 'finite'.) That's also why one is so easy and the other so hard. It's easy to miss your target, hard to hit the bull's eye. So for that reason too, going too far or falling short is characteristic of bad people, and the middle state characteristic of good people:

There's only one way for the good to be good,
But so many ways to be bad!

So a virtue is a disposition to choose certain things; it lies in a middle state (middle relative to us) as determined by reason, or as a wise person would define it. It's a 'middle' state both because it's between two ways of being bad – {two vices} – one caused by going too far and one caused by falling short, and also in the other sense that vices either make us fall short of or go beyond what's required in our feelings and our actions, while the [relevant] virtue finds and chooses the mid-point.

That means that [we can think of virtues in two different ways]: in essence, and by the definition stating what it fundamentally is, a virtue is a middle state. But in terms of being optimal, and as well [set as it can be], it's also a high point.

[*Does everything have a middle state? Is there, say, even a right amount of being unfair, or a right amount of being a coward?*]

Not every kind of action or emotion allows a middle state. In some cases you just name the thing and you've automatically implied its badness – things like 'gloating',[41] 'shamelessness', 'envy'; or in the case of actions, 'adultery', 'stealing', 'murder'. With all of those, and other things like that, it's implicit in the mere mention of them that they're bad per se. Never mind too much or too little of them. So there's never any way of getting it right where they're concerned. You're always getting it wrong. 15 With things like that there's no good or bad way of doing it, like, say, depending on whether you commit adultery with the right woman ... or at just the right moment ... or in just the right way. To do any of those things at all is to do the wrong thing.

So it's the same with being unfair, {being dishonest}, being a coward, being lecherous – you shouldn't expect there to be a middle state, or ways of going too far, and falling short with those. If there were, we'd end up having a middle amount of 20 going too far and a middle amount of falling short, and you'd be able to go too far in going too far, and fall short of falling short. Just as there's no such thing as too much or too little of being moderate or being brave (because the mid-point is also, in a sense, the high point), there's also no middle state, no going too far, and no falling short with any of those. No matter how you do them, you're getting something wrong.

The general rule: there's no middle point of going too far or 25 middle point of falling short, and there's no such thing as too much, or too little, of being in the middle.

7 We can't just make this very broad kind of claim. We also have to make it fit particular cases. When we're making claims about actions, general claims may have a wider scope, 30 but particular claims are more dependable. Actions are all about the particular situations, and that's where [our theory] has to ring true.

So let's take these examples from our chart:[42]

FALLS SHORT	IN THE MIDDLE	GOES TOO FAR
coward	brave	reckless
'feel-nothing'	moderate	lecherous, gluttonous
ungenerous	generous	extravagant
cheapskate	lavish	tacky, vulgar

FALLS SHORT	IN THE MIDDLE	GOES TOO FAR
lacks pride	has a sense of pride	full of himself
unambitious	ambitious [in a good way]	[too] ambitious
'angerless'	good-natured	bad-tempered
self-deprecating	truthful [about yourself]	phoney, charlatan
humourless yokel	witty, funny	crass, buffoonish
cantankerous, grumpy	like a friend	people-pleaser, flunky
shameless	has a sense of modesty	extremely shy

With feelings of fear and boldness, the middle state is being
brave. If you go too far in feeling no fear, there's no name for
1107b what you are (there's often no name for these things), but
someone who goes too far in feeling bold is 'reckless'. Someone
who feels too much fear or not enough boldness is a coward.

In the sphere of pleasures and pains, the middle state is being
5 moderate (but not with all kinds of pleasure, and this has less
to do with pains than pleasures). Someone who goes too far
[i.e. indulges too much in physical pleasures] is lecherous and
gluttonous. As for people who enjoy [physical] pleasures too
little – there pretty much aren't any people like that, so there's
no word for those kinds of people either. But let's call them
'feel-nothings'.[43]

In the sphere of giving and making money, the middle state
is being generous {and gentlemanly}. If you do too much or too
10 little, you're either extravagant or ungenerous. [Ungenerous
and extravagant people] do too much and too little in opposite
ways: an extravagant person goes too far in giving stuff away,
and not far enough in making money; while an ungenerous {or
ungentlemanly} person goes too far in [the ways] they make
money,[44] and not far enough in giving. (For now this is just a
15 rough outline, which is all we need. We'll give a more detailed
description of them later on.)

There's also another set of dispositions to do with money:
a middle state we call being lavish. Being lavish isn't just the
same as being generous. A lavish spender spends on a grand
scale; generosity applies to small-scale [spending]. Going too
far, in this case, is being 'tacky' or 'vulgar', while spending
too little is 'being a cheapskate'. Those are different from the 20
[vices] that [are the opposites of] being generous. We'll explain
later exactly how they're different.

When it comes to [how you feel about] being respected or
disrespected, the middle state is having a sense of pride, going
too far is what we call being 'full of yourself', and falling
short is 'having no pride'.

And then there's another disposition, related to having a
sense of pride in the same way that we said being generous relates to being lavish – namely, by being on a smaller 25
scale. It applies to the more minor forms of respect {and pres-
tige}, while a sense of pride applies to the major ones. Because
you can desire respect {and prestige} to the right degree, or
more than you should, or less than you should. And someone who goes too far in those strivings is 'ambitious', while
someone who falls short is 'unambitious'. But there's no word
for the person in the middle, and there are no words for 30
the dispositions either (except for the ambitious person's, i.e.
'ambition'). That's why the people at the two extremes both
lay claim to the middle spot, and we [go along with that, in
that we] sometimes call the person in the middle 'ambitious'
and then other times 'not ambitious' [in a good sense]; i.e.
sometimes we praise people for being ambitious, and sometimes we praise them for not being ambitious. We'll explain 1108a
why we do that in a later [lecture]. But for now let's say something about the rest of the list, following the method we've
sketched out.

You can also go too far, or fall short, or be in the middle
with feelings of anger, and there are pretty much no names 5
for those dispositions; but since we call the person in the middle 'good-natured' {or 'gentle'}, let's call the middle state 'being
good-natured'. As for the extremes, a person who gets too
[angry] is bad-tempered, so the vice is 'having a bad temper',

while someone who falls short is a 'never-gets-angry' sort of
a person, and so the fall-short state is, [let's say], 'anger
deficiency'.

Then there are three other middle states, somewhat similar
10 to one another but distinct. All three are about how we are in
the company of others, either in conversation or doing things
together. They differ in that one is to do with telling the truth
in those contexts, while the other two are about being pleasant
(in one case, pleasant in the context of jokes and amusement,
in the other case, pleasant in all areas of life). So we should say
15 something about those as well, to help us to see[45] more clearly
that the middle state is, in all contexts, something we praise,
while the extremes are always things that aren't praised and
aren't correct; people are criticized for them.

All right, so, here again, there aren't any words for most
of these things, and we'll have to try to come up with names
for them as we did in the other cases, for clarity and to make
everything a bit easier to follow.

So, as regards telling the truth [about yourself], the person
20 in the middle is just 'truthful', let's say, and we can call the
middle state 'being truthful'. Giving a false impression of yourself, if you talk yourself up, is 'phoniness', and someone who
has that disposition is a 'phoney' {or a 'charlatan'}, and if
you're always talking yourself down that's 'self-deprecation',
and someone with that disposition is 'self-deprecating'.

As for being pleasant: in the context of {playing around,
and} telling jokes, the person in the middle state is witty, and
the disposition a good sense of humour. Going too far is buf-
25 foonery, and the person with that disposition is a buffoon; and
someone who falls short is a sort of . . . humourless yokel.[46]
And the disposition: being humourless.

As for being pleasant in other areas of life, the person who's
pleasant in just the right way is '[like] a friend' {or 'friendly'}
(and the middle state is 'friendliness'); someone who goes too
far (with no ulterior motive) is a 'people-pleaser' or (if it's to
further their own interests) a 'flunky' {or 'hanger-on'}; and
someone who falls short, i.e. is unpleasant in all situations, is
30 a 'grumpy' and 'cantankerous' sort of person.

There are also middle states for certain emotional responses and feelings.

Shame, for example, although it isn't a virtue, is still something we praise, as is someone who has a sense of shame; {a sense of modesty}. Because even here we say that someone can be in the middle, or go too far (someone extremely shy, say, who feels embarrassed at everything); and someone who falls short, or feels no shame at all, is 'shameless'; and someone 35 'with a sense of modesty' is in the middle.

Then there's the feeling of indignation; it's the middle state between being envious and gloating over other people's mis- 1108b fortunes. [All of them] have to do with the pleasure and pain we feel at things that happen to the people around us. An 'indignant' sort of person is someone who gets upset when people enjoy successes that they don't deserve, whereas an 'envious' person goes too far, beyond indignation, to the point of being annoyed at *everyone's* successes; and [while an indignant person feels upset when people experience suffering that they don't deserve,] a 'gloater' falls so far short of being upset by it, he 5 actually delights in it.[47]

But we'll have a chance to talk about these things elsewhere.[48] (And after that, we'll distinguish the two different senses of being *díkaios*, {'being righteous' and 'being fair'}, and talk about each of those, [and say] in what sense they're middle states.[49] We'll also talk about the virtues of thought and 10 reason.

8 So when you have three possible dispositions, two of them vices (one caused by going too far, one caused by falling short) and one of them a virtue (the one in the middle), all of them are opposites of all the others in some way or other. The two extremes are the opposite of the middle, and also of each other, and the middle is the opposite of the extremes. Because just as an X amount is 'bigger' compared to less-than-X, but 15 'smaller' compared to more-than-X, likewise, in feelings and actions, the middle states [seem to] overshoot if you compare them to the ones that fall short, but [seem to] fall short if you compare them to the ones that overshoot. A brave man, for

example, seems reckless compared to a coward, but looks like
20 a coward compared to someone reckless. And in the same way,
a moderate person seems lecherous compared to a 'feel-nothing'
but looks like a 'feel-nothing' compared to someone lecherous;
a generous person seems extravagant compared to someone
ungenerous, but ungenerous next to someone extravagant.
That's also why the two people at the extremes both try to push
the person in the middle towards the other end: that is, a coward
25 calls a brave man reckless, and a reckless man calls the brave
man a coward – and the equivalent with the other virtues.[50]

So in that sense all these dispositions are opposites of each
other. But the strongest contrast is between the two extremes,
less so between the extremes and the middle. That's because
they're further away from one another than they are from the
middle, just as 'big' is further from 'small' and 'small' is fur-
30 ther from 'big' than either of them is from 'medium-size'.* Plus,
in some cases one of the extremes is somewhat similar to the
middle – e.g. being reckless looks a little bit like being brave;
being extravagant looks a little bit like being generous – whereas
the two extremes are always totally different from one another.
And people define 'opposites' as things that are as far apart from
one another as possible, so things that are further apart are the
35 more natural opposites.[51]

In some cases it's falling short that seems more like the
1109a opposite of being in the middle, and, in other cases, going too
far. The more natural opposite of being brave, for example,
isn't being reckless (i.e. going too far) but being a coward (i.e.
falling short). And the more natural opposite of being moderate
isn't being a 'feel-nothing' (i.e. the shortfall) but being lecherous and gluttonous (i.e. going too far).
5   There are two reasons that happens. One is based on the
thing itself. Namely, if one of the extremes is closer to and more
like the middle than the other, then we're more inclined to treat
the other extreme, not that one, as the opposite. Being reckless, for instance, seems more similar to being brave, and closer
10 to it; being a coward seems less like it, so that's the one we're
more inclined to treat as its opposite. The one further from the
middle seems the more natural opposite.

So that's the first reason, based on the thing itself. The second reason comes from us. If there's one extreme that we're somehow naturally more drawn towards, that one feels more like the opposite of the mid-point. We're naturally more drawn to [physical] pleasures, for instance, and because of that we're more likely to gravitate towards being lecherous and gluttonous than towards behaving ourselves. So we're more likely to call that the 'opposite' of the middle: the thing we more often give ourselves over to. And that's why being lecherous and gluttonous (in this case, going too far) is the more natural opposite of being moderate.

9 So we've said that a virtue (of character) is a middle state, and we've said how – namely, that it's in the middle between two vices, one caused by going too far and one caused by falling short, and also that it's a middle because it aims for the mid-point in our feelings and actions. That just about covers it.

That's also why being a good person is a tough task. It's a task to find the mid-point all the time. It's like finding the mid-point of a circle – not just anyone can do it; it takes knowledge – and in the same way, sure, anyone can just get angry or give money to someone or spend money. That bit's easy. But as for doing it to the right person, and to the right degree, and at the right time, and for the right reason, and in the right way – that's not so easy any more. Not just anyone can do it. That's why getting it right is rare, and something we praise, and something honourable.

So, if you're aiming for the mid-point, first of all you've got to move away from the more natural opposite, just like Calypso advises [Odysseus]:[52]

'Pilot the ship well clear
            of the spray and the roar of the whirlpool!'

Because, of the two extremes, one of them implies getting it wrong more, the other less. So, since it's so hard to hit the mid-point dead on, the next best thing is to take 'the lesser of two

evils', as they say.⁵³ And the best way to do that is the way I'm
saying.

1109b   We also need to think about what we're individually more
inclined towards. After all, we're all naturally drawn towards
different things. We can figure it out from our own feelings of
pleasure and pain, {our individual likes and dislikes} – and then
5   the trick is to drag ourselves in the opposite direction. That's to
say, by drawing ourselves a long way away from getting it
wrong, we'll end up at the mid-point, just like the way they
straighten out warped planks of wood [by over-bending them].

And in every situation, above all, we have to keep a close
watch on what we find pleasurable. {Watch out} for Lady
Pleasure!⁵⁴ Because whenever we're judging her she bribes us.
10   We need to have the same feelings towards pleasure as the
Trojan elders had towards Helen, and in every situation make
their words our mantra.⁵⁵ That way we can send her on her
way, and we'll be less likely to go astray.

So, in short, if we do all that we'll give ourselves the best
chance of hitting the mid-point. But no doubt that's a pretty
hard thing to do – especially in the particulars. It's not easy, for
15   example, to determine how you should get angry, and who with,
and over what kinds of things, and for how long. After all, [even
as observers] we sometimes praise people who fall short and say
they're 'good-natured', and then at other times we praise people
who are being [too] harsh and call them 'tough and manly'.

But in any case, we don't criticize someone who's only a
little bit off getting it right, whether to one side or the other.
20   They have to be further off. Because that's when we notice. But
as for how much someone [has to be off], or what point they
have to reach, before they should be criticized – there's no easy
way to define that by theory alone, just like with everything
else that depends on perception. These kinds of things are in
the particulars, and judging them depends on perception.

So what all of this goes to show is that although the middle
state, in all cases, is what people praise, we should sometimes
25   lean towards going too far, and sometimes lean towards falling
short, because that'll actually be the easiest way of hitting the
mid-point and getting it right.

BOOK III

Now, since being a good person is all about feelings and
actions, and since it's only things we do willingly {and wil-
fully} that we're praised or blamed for, whereas things we do
unwillingly are forgivable, and in some cases even make people
feel sorry for us, surely a definition of 'willing' and 'unwilling'
actions is crucial for anyone investigating moral goodness, as
well as useful for people drafting laws that deal with rewards
and punishments.

So we regard as unwilling: (a) things we're forced to do, and
(b) things we do by mistake {or unknowingly}.

(a) You're 'forced to do something' when it has an external
cause, such that you, the person doing it (or rather, the person
it's happening to), don't contribute anything at all – like, say,
when you're simply carried somewhere by the wind[1] [at sea], or
by people who've captured you.

Then there are all those cases where you do something
through fear of something even worse, or for some honourable
reason. Suppose some tyrant orders you to do something
shameful {or degrading} and he's holding your parents and
children hostage, and if you do it they'll live but if you refuse[2]
they'll be killed. In situations like that are you acting willingly
or unwillingly? You could argue it either way.

Something similar happens in those cases where people
throw their cargo overboard in a storm. Normally, nobody
willingly dumps their cargo, but if it's to save their own life
and the lives of the rest of the crew, anyone would. They'd be
crazy not to.

So actions like that are mixed. But they seem a bit more like

things we do willingly. After all, they're your best option at the
moment when you're doing them, and the goal of your action
is set by the particular situation. So 'willingly' and 'unwillingly' have to apply to the moment you're actually doing it.
15 And [at that moment]³ you're doing it willingly. After all, in
those kinds of actions the source of all your bodily movements
is within you, and if an action has its cause within you that
means it's up to you to do it or not do it.

So it follows that we do those kinds of things willingly. But
I suppose broadly speaking⁴ they're done unwillingly – in the
sense that nobody would ever choose to do anything like that
for its own sake.

20 In some cases people are even praised for what they do in
those situations, when they submit to something shaming {or
degrading} or painful for some very important and honourable
reason. And they're criticized if it's the other way round. Submitting to extreme humiliation⁵ for no honourable reason, or
not much of one, seems pretty shabby.

In other cases, even if you aren't praised you're at least for-
given: cases where you do the wrong thing under the kinds of
25 pressures that strain human nature to breaking point and that
nobody could possibly endure.

Then again, there are surely some things that nothing could
ever force you to do – 'I'm not doing *that*. I'd rather die a horribly painful death.' I mean, the things that 'compelled' Alcmaeon
to kill his own mother, in the Euripides play, for example, seem
pretty ridiculous.⁶

And in some of these cases it's very hard to determine
30 whether option A is better than option B, or whether it's worth
submitting to X to avoid [outcome] Y,⁷ and even harder to
stick to your decision⁸ once you've made it. Because in most
of these cases, on one side there's the prospect of something
painful [if you refuse], but on the other you're being pressured
into something shameful {or humiliating}. Hence the praise or
blame people receive for giving in, or for not giving in, to the
pressure.

1110b So when exactly should we say we're 'forced' to do something, then?

How about this: you're forced to do it, plain and simple, when the cause is external; so you're doing it, but not contributing to its cause in any way. But as for things we do unwillingly considered in themselves, but which we choose to do at that moment and to avoid X (and where the cause is within the person doing it) – why not just say those are done unwillingly considered in themselves, but willingly-at-that-moment, and willingly-to-avoid-X. 5

But they're more like things we do willingly. Because all actions take place in particular contexts, and those [particular things, in that situation] are being done willingly.[9]

And as for when your option A is better than your option B, there just aren't any easy answers. The particular situations throw up so many variables.

And if someone's tempted to think that we're even 'forced' to do things that are pleasurable or honourable – 'because those [features] are external, and they compel us' – well, that would mean that we're forced to do every single thing we do. Because those are the two reasons anyone does anything. Also, when people are forced to do something, and do it unwillingly, it's painful; but when they do something because it's pleasurable or honourable they enjoy doing it. And it's ridiculous to blame external causes, rather than yourself, for being so easily hooked[10] by things like that; or to give yourself the credit for doing things that are honourable, but then blame 'pleasures' the moment you do something shameful. 15

So [overall] it seems you're 'forced to do X' when X has an external cause, to which you, the person forced, contribute nothing at all.

(b) Something you do by mistake {or unknowingly} is always non-wilful. But it's only unwilling if it upsets you and you're sorry about it. That's to say, if someone does something by mistake but then isn't remotely bothered by what they've done, then, sure, they haven't acted wilfully (since they didn't even know they were doing it), but they haven't [exactly] acted unwillingly either – not if it doesn't upset them. So in cases of doing something by mistake, it seems you did it unwillingly if you're then sorry about it, but if you aren't, since that's different, let's 20 say you did it 'non-wilfully'. Since it's a different thing, it's better to give it its own label.

25   There's also a difference between (a) 'doing something by mistake' {or 'unknowingly'} and (b) 'not knowing what you're doing'. We wouldn't say that someone who's drunk or angry is doing things unknowingly {or by mistake}. We'd say they're acting that way because they're in that state. But [we do tend to say] they 'don't know what they're doing'; they're 'not aware of their actions'.

And of course every wicked person is 'mistaken' – mistaken, that is, about what sorts of things people should and should not do. Being mistaken in that sense is what makes us unethical;

30   makes us evil. We don't call it 'acting unwillingly' when someone just doesn't know what's best.[11] Being mistaken in your [basic] choices doesn't make your actions unwilling, it makes you a bad person. Neither does ignorance of a general principle. For that kind of ignorance you'll certainly be criticized. It has to be ignorance of the particulars; the context of the action,

1111a   the particular things it involved. Whether or not people are going to forgive you or sympathize [with your mistake] depends on those. Because it's [only] when you're mistaken about one of those that you're acting unwillingly.

So it's probably not such a bad idea if we set them out in full – say what they are and how many there are.

So, there's (a) who's doing the thing, and (b) what they're doing, and (c) what it affects, or who they're doing it to, and in some cases (d) what they're doing it with (as in with what {tool

5   or} implement) and (e) the intended result[12] (e.g. to save someone's life) and (f) how they're doing it (e.g. gently, or violently).

Now there's no way, short of being crazy, that you could be mistaken about all of those at once. And obviously you can't be mistaken about who's doing it, either. (How could you not realize that you're the one doing it?) But you might not realize (b) what you're doing, like when people are talking* and say 'it just slipped out',[13] or that 'they didn't know it was a secret',

10   like with Aeschylus and the Eleusinian mysteries; or the catapult case, where he just meant to show it to someone and fired it. Or (c) you might mistake your own son for one of the enemy,

the way Meropē did;[14] or (d) you might think that the spear
is ball-tipped when it's actually bladed, or that the rock you're
throwing is just pumice. Or (e) you might give someone a potion
to save their life and kill them with it; or (f) you might mean
to just scuff someone, like when you're sparring, and actually
punch them.

So those are all the ['details'] of the action you could be 15
mistaken about. And when you're mistaken about one of those,
people feel you've done the thing unwillingly. Especially if it's
one of the really important ones. The really important ones are
who you're doing it to, and its [intended] purpose.

So you're acting unwillingly when you do things by mistake
{or unknowingly} in that sense – provided that the action also
upsets you and you're sorry about it.   20

So, if you're acting unwillingly when you're either (a) forced
to do something or (b) do it by mistake, then presumably you're
acting willingly whenever (a) the cause of your action is internal
and (b) you're fully aware of all the particulars of what you're
doing.

It's surely not right to say (as some people do) that fighting
spirit, {anger}[15] and physical desire also cause us to do things
unwillingly.

First, because that will mean that no animal besides us ever 25
does anything willingly {or wilfully}. Or children.

And second, what's the claim here, that we do none of those
things willingly? Nothing that we do out of fighting spirit {or
anger} or physical desire? Or is it that we do all the honourable
ones willingly, but all the shameful ones unwillingly? Surely
that's ridiculous, when it's one and the same thing causing both.
But then it's surely also absurd to say we're doing X unwillingly 30
in cases where we *should* be motivated in that way.[16] There are,
after all, things we ought to get angry about, things we should
desire,[17] † like health and learning †.

And surely unwilling actions are painful. But don't we [by
definition] enjoy doing things that fulfil our physical desires?

Also, why aren't mistakes caused by [poor] reasoning[18] just as
'unwilling' as mistakes done in anger? What difference does it

make? The fact is we should avoid both kinds of error, and
1111b our non-rational emotions seem just as much a part of human
nature; and that means the actions that flow from physical
desire {and anger} and fighting spirit are very much actions of
the person.

So it's absurd to class them as things we do unwillingly.

2 Now that we've sorted out what it means to do something
willingly {and wilfully} or unwillingly, the next thing to
5 do is explain the concept of choice.

Making choices is absolutely central to being a good person,
and [our choices] are a more reliable indicator of our character
than our actions.

All right, so choosing [to do something] implies doing it
wilfully, but not vice versa. 'Willing' {and 'wilful'} is broader.
Children and non-human animals can certainly do things willingly {and wilfully}, but they aren't capable of making choices.
10 Also, we regard snap reactions as wilful, but we don't say people
choose them.

Some people say (a) that choice is desire, or (b) that it's *thumos*, an [impulse] of spirit,[19] or (c) that choosing is wanting, or
(d) that a choice is a sort of belief.

[Here's why] none of those ideas seems to be right.

(a) [It can't just be desire.] Non-reasoning animals aren't
capable of making choices, but they are capable of desire and
fighting spirit.

Plus, if you lack self-control you do things out of [physical]
desire but without choosing to, and, conversely, in exercising
15 self-control you're choosing to act against your desire.

Plus, you can desire the opposite of what you choose, but
you can't desire the opposite of what you desire.[20]

Plus, desire targets what's pleasurable or painful, but choice
doesn't target pain or pleasure.[21]

(b) [As for it being] *thumos*, a spirited [impulse] – that's
even less plausible. Spirited actions seem the very least based
on choice.[22]

(c) But then choosing certainly isn't just wanting, either –
although they certainly feel very similar.

For one thing, you don't choose things that are impossible (if 20
you claimed to be 'choosing' impossible things, people would
think you were a halfwit), but you can certainly want things
that are impossible. You can want eternal life, for instance.

Plus, you can want things that you couldn't possibly bring
about through your own actions – e.g. you can want some
actor or athlete to win.[23] But nobody chooses things like that. 25
You only choose things you think it's in your power to make
happen.

Plus, we're more likely to want the thing that's our goal, and
then choose the things that will get us to our goal. E.g. we
want to be healthy, and we choose the things that make us
healthy; and we want to flourish and be blessed, and we *say*
[we're blessed],[24] but it sounds a bit weird to say 'I choose to be
blessed' – because there's a general sense that choice is about
things that are in our power.[25]   30

(d) It doesn't seem to be [just] a belief, either. A belief can be
about anything at all. We can just as easily have beliefs about
eternal, unchanging facts, or things that are impossible, as
about things that are up to us.

Plus, we classify beliefs as true or false, not good or bad, the
more usual way[26] of classifying a choice.

No doubt nobody claims that choice is just the same thing as
belief in general. But it isn't even the same as a certain sort of 1112a
belief, [namely, as some people say, the belief that X is good].

Choosing good or bad things makes us the kind of people
we are;[27] merely having beliefs about them doesn't.

Plus, we choose to get or to avoid good and bad things, whereas
we have beliefs about what they are, who they're good for,
or how. Our beliefs certainly aren't 'to get them' or 'to avoid 5
them'.

Plus, we normally praise a choice if someone chooses what
they should, or for being the right choice, but we praise a belief
for being true.

Plus, it's very typical to choose things we know are good;*
but if we *believe* that X is good, we certainly don't *know* that
X is good.

Plus, people who make the best choices don't seem to be the

10 same as the ones who have the best beliefs [about what's good and bad]. Some people seem to have the better beliefs but then choose the wrong thing, because they're bad people.[28]

And even if a belief always precedes any choice, or is implied by it, so what? That's not the claim we're considering here. We're asking if a choice is the same thing as some kind of belief.

So what is it then? What does it involve, if it's none of the above?

Well, [what we choose to do] we certainly do willingly. But not all the things we do willingly are things we also choose. 15 So, could it be that it's just the ones we've deliberated over beforehand? Yes, because choosing implies reasoning and thinking. And even the word [in Greek] seems to hint at deliberation: [*pro-haireisthai*, to choose,] implies taking A *over* B.[29]

3 Do people deliberate about everything? Can you deliberate about anything at all, or are there some things where deliberating doesn't apply? (And we should probably say that 20 what you 'can' deliberate about doesn't mean whatever some halfwit or madman might deliberate about. Let's say it means something you could sanely deliberate about.)

So – nobody deliberates over eternal, unchanging facts, like the nature of the cosmos or the fact that the square root of two is an irrational number. Or things that are in motion but occur with perfect regularity (by necessity, or maybe by their nature, 25 or for some other reason), like the turning of the seasons or the rising of the stars. Or things that happen unpredictably, like droughts or rainfall. Or things that are just a matter of luck, like finding buried treasure. And we don't deliberate about all human matters either, e.g. no Spartan ever deliberates over what would be the best form of government in Scythia. The 30 point is, none of these can be brought about through our own agency. We deliberate about things that are up to us and that are doable. Those are still left. Because the causes of things are (a) nature, (b) necessity and (c) chance; but also (d) mind and every kind of human agency. (And each group of human beings deliberates about the things that *they* can do.)

With precise, self-contained forms of knowledge – like know- 1112b
ing how to write – there's no place for deliberation. We're never
in two minds about how to write an A. We only deliberate about
things that happen through our agency but that don't always
turn out the same way – like things we do in medicine, or business. And piloting a ship, say, involves more deliberating than 5
athletic training does, to the extent that its rules are less precisely honed, and the same applies generally; and skills involve
more deliberation than sciences, because with skills we're more
likely to be in two minds about what to do.

Deliberating takes place with things that usually happen a
certain way, but where it's unclear how they'll turn out this
time; where there's a bit of indeterminacy.

We get other people to help us deliberate – {advise us} – on 10
big things, because we don't trust ourselves to make the right
decision on our own.

We don't deliberate about our goals. We only deliberate about
the things that will get us to our goals.

A doctor doesn't ask, 'Should I cure the patient?' or an orator, 'Should I try to persuade [my audience]?' or a statesman,
'Should I bring about law and order?' In general, nobody deliberates about their goal.[30] No, they take their goal as set, and 15
think about how to bring it about, i.e. by what steps. And if it
seems like there are several possible ways of making it happen,
the question then becomes which would be the best way, or the
easiest. And if their goal, A, can only be achieved through one
thing, B, they then consider *how* to make A happen through B,
i.e. what's the C that will make B happen – and so on, until
they come to a starting point in the chain of causation, which
is the end point in finding the answer. Because when you're
deliberating it's like you're working something out: you're work- 20
ing backwards through a problem, the way I've just described,
rather like {working back through} a proof in geometry. (Working something out doesn't always imply deliberating – it doesn't
in mathematics, for instance – but deliberating always implies
working something out.) And the end point in working back
through the problem is then the first step in making the thing
happen. So if we come up against an impossible first step, we

25 give up on the whole idea (if we need money, say, and there's
simply no way of getting any). But if it seems possible, we set
about doing it. And by 'possible' here we mean things that
can be brought about through us – [or through our friends],
because that *is* through us, in a sense, because we initiate [our
friends' actions].

Sometimes we're trying to figure out what tools we need; sometimes, how to use them. Likewise, in general sometimes the
30 question is 'What X will make this happen?' and sometimes
it's 'How [do we make X happen]?' or 'Who's going to do X?'

So, to recap: (a) human beings, we've said, are a cause – they
cause their own actions; and (b) we deliberate about the things
that we can do, and (c) our actions are always for the sake of
some other thing, because it isn't our goal that we deliberate
about, just the things that get us to our goals.

You don't deliberate about particulars, either – like 'Is this
1113a bread?' or 'Is it cooked?' That's the job of perception.

If you deliberate at every level you'll go on for ever.

You deliberate about, and choose, the very same set of things,
except that something you choose has got as far as being decided
on. That's to say, what you choose is what you've approved after
5 deliberating over it. There's a point where figuring out how
you're going to do something stops, namely when you've traced
the initiating of it back to yourself, and [in particular] to the part
of you that's in charge. That's the part that does the choosing.
(That's illustrated by those older forms of government, the ones
that Homer described, where the chieftains would announce
their choices to the rank and file.)

10 Something we choose is (a) a thing we deliberate about, and
(b) a thing we desire to do, and (c) in the class of things that are
up to us. So it seems that overall a choice is a deliberation-based
desire to X, where X is something that's up to us. As a result of
deliberating we've approved X, and now desire to X, in line with
our deliberation.

So that will do as our outline of what a choice is, and what
kinds of things we choose, namely the things that get us to our
goals. Let's move on.

4 What we want, as we said, is our goal.

But [beyond that], some people think that you can only 15
want what's good, others think that you [just] want whatever
seems good to you.

Now, if we say that you can only want what's good, the
upshot is that if someone picks the wrong thing to want, then,
[weirdly], the thing they want is unwantable.[31] Because to be
wantable it has to be good, and (as it turned out in this case) it
was bad.

But if we say you [just] want whatever seems good, the upshot 20
now is that there's no such thing as naturally wantable; 'wantable' is [on this view] just whatever seems so to each of us. And
that's one thing to me and something else to you, and in some
cases the very opposite things.

So if we're unsatisfied with both those ideas, maybe we should
say that wantable in the normal sense – and truly wantable –
is what's good; but wantable-by-you is whatever seems good
to you.

On that view, a good person [can only want] what's really 25
wantable[32] [i.e. good], while a bad person can want whatever.

(That's how it is with our bodies, too: what's 'healthy' for
people in good physical condition are things that really are
healthy; but when you're sick a different set of things are
'healthy' for you; and the same goes for 'bitter' or 'sweet' or
'hot' or 'heavy' and the rest.)

A good person, we're saying, judges everything correctly, and
in all situations the way things seem to a good person is the way 30
they really are. Each character-state brings its own particular
[view of] what's honourable, and pleasurable. And if you're
a good person, what makes you special (maybe more than
anything else) is the fact that in every situation you see [those
things] as they really are. A good person is the standard, the
measure of them, so to speak.[33]

Most people {get it wrong}. It seems they're fooled by pleasure, which seems to be a good thing but isn't. So they choose 1113b
what's pleasurable, as if it were [the only] good thing; and
avoid pain, as if it were [the only] bad thing.

5   So, if what we want is our goal, whereas what we deliber-
    ate about and choose are the things that get us to our goal,
it follows that all the actions that get us to our goal are things
we do by choice, and therefore willingly.

5   But that's also exactly where we exercise our virtues. So that
    means that being good people, in general, or bad people is up
    to us as well.

        Because if doing something is up to us, so is not doing it, and
    if not doing it is up to us, so is doing it.[34] So if doing something
    is up to us and it's the honourable thing to do, then failing to
10 do it will also be up to us, and shameful. Or if not doing some-
    thing is up to us and that's the honourable thing, then doing it
    is also up to us, and shameful. And if doing or not doing hon-
    ourable and shameful things – which is just to say, being good
    or bad people – is up to us, then it follows that whether we're
    decent people or scoundrels is up to us.

15   To say that 'no man is willingly nasty,[35] or unwillingly blessed'
    seems partly right, partly wrong. True, nobody's unwillingly
    blessed. But being a terrible person is certainly wilful. Or should
    we dispute the claims we've just made? Should we claim that
    people aren't the source of their actions, the parents of their
    actions, as surely as of their children? No, that seems right.
20 There are no other causes we can trace our actions back to
    besides the ones inside us. And when things have their causes
    inside us, those things themselves are up to us, and wilful.

        That's surely the view endorsed by all of us, individually,
    and by all lawmakers.* Lawmakers punish and penalize people
    who do wicked things (unless they were forced to do them, or
    did them without realizing and weren't to blame for not real-
25 izing) and reward people for behaving honourably, with the idea
    of encouraging the latter and thwarting the former. But we
    can't possibly be encouraged to do something that isn't up to us
    and that we don't do willingly. There's no point being persuaded
    not to feel hot, say; not to have a headache; not to feel hungry,
    or anything like that. What difference will it make? We'll just
    feel it anyway.

30   For that matter, lawmakers even punish people for not real-
    izing what they were doing, if they seem responsible for not

realizing. They [sometimes] set double penalties for people who [commit crimes] while drunk, for example, since that counts as an internal cause. They had the power not to get drunk, and being drunk was what made them unaware [of what they were doing]. And they punish people for being ignorant of some detail of the law if it's something that they ought to know and that isn't very hard to know, and likewise in other cases if it 1114a seems careless of them not to realize [what they were doing] – on the assumption that it was up to them to avoid the oversight, because it's in their power to be more careful.

But what if he couldn't help being careless? What if he's just that kind of person?

Well, but people have only themselves to blame for becom- ing 'that kind of person' through slack living; and for becoming 5 unfair, {dishonest} men by cheating people,[36] or for becoming gluttons by constant boozing and suchlike. Remember: our activities, in any area, give us dispositions that match them. It's obvious: just look at people who are in training for any kind of competition, or for doing whatever. [They train] by spending all their time in that activity. So you'd have to be incredibly obtuse not to see that our various activities create our char- 10 acter traits. And it makes no sense to say that someone who keeps treating people unfairly nevertheless 'doesn't want to be an unfair person', or that a man who keeps behaving lecher- ously 'doesn't want to be a lecherous man'. If you knowingly do things that are going to make you an unfair person, well, that means you are then wilfully an unfair person – mind you, that's not to say that you can stop being an unfair person whenever you like and go back to being someone who's fair. Just like, if you're sick [you can't just go back to being] healthy again either. And let's suppose you're wilfully sick, as the case 15 may well be, because you've been living your life without any self-control and you've never listened to your doctors. In that case, yes, early on you may have had the option of not being sick, but once you let yourself go you lost that option, just like the way, when you throw a stone, once you let go it's impos- sible to take it back – and yet throwing it was certainly up to you; the cause was internal. Likewise, with someone who's

now an unfair person, or someone who's now a lecherous man:
20 they certainly had the option, back at the start, of not becoming those kinds of people. (That's why they're wilfully what
they are.) But once they've become those kinds of people they
no longer have the option of not being that way.

And it isn't just defects of character[37] – {vices} – that are wilfully acquired. So are physical defects, in some cases, and we
criticize people in those cases. Nobody criticizes people for
being born ugly.[38] But we do criticize people who are unattractive because they don't exercise enough or don't take care of
25 themselves. The same goes for being weak or disabled. You
certainly wouldn't reproach someone for being blind from
birth, or through sickness or injury. You'd surely just feel sorry
for them. But you'd certainly reproach a man who was blind as
a result of constant boozing, or from some other sort of over-
indulgence. In other words, we criticize the physical defects
that are our responsibility, but not the ones that aren't. And
30 that suggests that in other areas, too, the defects {or vices} that
we criticize are up to us, {our own responsibility}.

But suppose someone said this:[39]
*All you can do is strive after whatever seems good to you.
But you don't have any control over how things seem to you.
It's just a matter of the kind of person you are: that determines*
1114b *what seems [good to you, and] what goal you have.*

Well, first, that means that if we *are* responsible, in some sense,
for being the people we are, then it turns out we *are* responsible,
in some sense, for how things seem to us as well . . .
*But if that's not the case, then nobody's ever to blame for
the evil things they do. They're just doing those things because*
5 *they have the wrong goal. They mistakenly think those things
will get them what's best [in life]. But being driven towards our
goal isn't something we choose for ourselves. You just have to
be born with a sort of vision which will make you judge things
well and choose what's actually good. {So it's a talent}: a 'talented' person is someone nobly natured in that respect. After
all, this is the most important and the finest [part of you], and*
10 *if it can't be acquired or learnt from anyone – if what it's like
is purely a matter of your nature – then to be well natured,*

*nobly natured, in that respect would be the most perfect and
complete natural talent; talent in the truest sense.*

Well, if all that's true, doesn't that mean that being a good
person is every bit as involuntary[40] as being a bad person?
Because it's the same for both. A good person and a bad one, [on
this view], both have this innate, fixed goal[41] that seems [good]
to them (whatever it might be)[42] and then they both do every- 15
thing else they do (whatever that is) with reference to that goal.*

So, maybe our goal (whatever it is that seems good to us) is
not innate, it's also partly down to us. Or maybe our *goal* is
innate, but because a good person then does everything else
wilfully, being a good person is [still] voluntary {and wilful}.
Either way, being a bad person turns out to be voluntary {and
wilful} as well, because a bad person, in the same way, at least 20
has responsibility for their actions, even if not for their goal.

So, if it's the case (as we've claimed)[43] that our ways of being
good – {our virtues} – *are* voluntary (because we *are* partly
responsible for our character traits, and the kind of goal we set
ourselves depends on the kind of people we are), then our ways
of being bad – {our vices} – must be voluntary too. Whatever
goes for one goes for the other. 25

All right, so we've completed our overview of virtues.

We've said what kind of thing they are, in outline: dispositions {or character-states}, and specifically middle states.

We've said the actions that create them are also the things
they make us do, and do *for what they are*.*

We've said that they're up to us, and wilful.

We've said they always [operate] subject to the orders of
correct reasoning.

But our character traits aren't 'wilful' in quite the same sense 30
as our actions. We're in full charge of our actions from start to
finish, and aware of all the details, but with character traits we
only have control over starting them off; we don't have a fine-
grained awareness of them growing – just like with illnesses. 1115a
But they're still wilful [overall], because it was up to us [at the
start] to behave that way, or not.

*

So now let's pick it up by discussing each virtue separately. Let's say what they are, what kinds of things they're concerned
5 with, and how. (That will also show us, in the process, how many there are.)

First, bravery.

6 So, we've already explained that being brave is a mid-point connected with feeling afraid and feeling bold.

What we're afraid of, obviously, are things that are frightening, and that basically means things that are bad. (That's why they define being afraid of X as 'thinking that X is going to be bad for you'.)
10 Now, we're afraid of all bad things – disgrace, poverty, sickness, having no friends, dying – but not all of them seem relevant to being brave. For a start, there are some things you ought to be afraid of and that it's honourable to fear, and actually shameful not to fear – like disgrace. To fear disgrace is to be a decent person, with a sense of shame. A man with no fear of disgrace is shameless. (He might sometimes be called 'brave' –
15 but that's a kind of metaphor. It's because he resembles a brave man in one respect: they're both 'fearless' in some sense.) Poverty, on the other hand, you probably shouldn't be afraid of. Or sickness. Or anything else that doesn't come from being a bad person and that you don't bring upon yourself. But having no fear of those kinds of things doesn't make you brave either. (Although, again, you might be called brave by resemblance.)
20 After all, some people who are cowards in the heat of battle are also generous, i.e. cool and calm about losing money.

You're also not a coward if you're 'afraid' of violence being done to your wife and children.[44]

Or [if you're afraid that X might make you feel] envy; or anything like that.[45]

And you're not brave just because you can keep your cool when you're about to get a whipping [from your master].[46]

All right, so what kinds of frightening things is a brave man
25 brave about? Presumably the most frightening of all. Because a brave man is by definition the very best at facing the things we dread.

And the most frightening thing of all? Death. Because death is the end, and surely once we're dead that's it, there's nothing more for us, good or bad. Yet it seems not even every kind of death gives a brave man scope for being brave. Not death at sea, or from sickness, for example. So death in what circumstances, then? Presumably the most honourable {and glorious}. And that means death in battle. That's where men die facing the greatest and most glorious peril – as indicated in the way those men are highly esteemed by city states and by monarchs. 30

So a brave man, in the strict sense, is a man who is fearless in the face of an honourable death, and in the face of all the things that threaten instant death – which means, above all, the dangers of battle. Of course, brave men will also be unafraid in the face of death at sea or from sickness – though not in the same way as professional sailors. Brave men resign themselves to the fact that their lives are lost; they're only bothered to be dying in that way. Sailors have the confidence that comes of long experience. Also, men show their bravery in situations where they can go down fighting, or where their death is glorious. Neither of those applies when they perish at sea or from sickness. 35 1115b 5

7 What's 'frightening' isn't the same thing for everyone. But we do speak of some things as being superhumanly frightening, and those are certainly frightening for anyone – at any rate anyone who isn't crazy. But things that are frightening within human limits vary in scale and might be more, or less, frightening. (Likewise, things might be more, or less, emboldening.) A brave man is unflinching, as far as any mere human being can be. So, yes, he will be afraid of those humanly frightening things too, but to the right degree, the reasonable degree, and he'll face them whenever it's the honourable thing to do. Because that's the goal of being a good man. 10

You can fear these things too much or too little, and you can also be afraid of things that aren't frightening as if they were. There are various ways of getting it wrong: you can be afraid of the wrong thing, or to the wrong degree, or at the wrong time – and so on. Similarly with things that embolden us. So 15

a brave man is someone who fears (or is emboldened by) and
faces the right things, for the right reason, to the right degree,
at the right time. Because a brave man always both feels and
acts as the situation merits, and just as reason [says he should].

20   The goal of every activity is set by your character-state. And
for a brave man [that character trait], being brave, is an honourable thing. So its goal must also be honourable. Because
every [aspect of character] is defined [as honourable or shame-
ful] by reference to its goal. So that means he faces the dangers,
and does all the things bravery calls for, because it's the honourable thing to do.

There are different ways of going too far.

(a) Someone might go too far in feeling no fear. There's no
25 name for that (as we said earlier, there's often no name for
these things), but you'd have to be a kind of lunatic, or imper-
vious to all pain, if you weren't afraid of anything at all, not
even earthquakes or tidal waves – as they say about the Celts.[47]

(b) Someone who's too bold in frightening situations is reckless. And a reckless man is surely a bit of a phoney, too – someone
30 who just pretends to be brave. In frightening situations he wants
to seem the way the brave man is. So at every opportunity he
mimics him. That's why most reckless men are actually cowards under the bravado. They put on a bold show while they
can, but once things get frightening they don't stick around.

(c) Someone who feels too much fear is a coward. He's afraid
of the wrong things, and to the wrong degree, and so on. Every
35 way of getting it wrong goes with being a coward. He falls
1116a short, too – in boldness, that is. (But it's his distress, in which
he goes too far, that more often gives him away.) So a coward
is prone to despair, because he's afraid of absolutely everything. A brave man is the opposite, because boldness implies
confidence, {optimism}.

So cowards, the reckless and the brave are all involved with
5   the same things, but relate to them in different ways. Two of
them go too far and fall short, and one is set nicely in the middle and gets it right.

Plus, reckless men are impetuous, and eager before the danger, but once they're in the thick of it they back off, whereas

brave men get fired up in the action but stay calm and steady beforehand.

So, to recap: bravery is a middle state concerned with things 10 that frighten or embolden us (in the situations we've specified) and a brave man chooses to do what he does, and face what he faces, because it's the honourable thing, or shameful not to.

(Committing suicide to escape poverty, or a broken heart, or some kind of pain or distress is not brave. It's more something a coward would do. Running away from your troubles is spineless. You're not facing [death] because it's honourable to do so; 15 you're just running away from something bad.)

8 So that's what true bravery is like. But there are also other things we *call* bravery – which we can divide into five types.

(a) First – because it's the most similar – there's citizens' bravery, {patriot bravery}. Fellow citizens face the dangers of battle, as it seems, to avoid the penalties set by their laws and because of the reproaches or the respect they'll receive. That's why you always seem to find the 'bravest' men in city states 20 where cowards are treated with scorn and brave men highly respected. There are characters who illustrate this sort of bravery in Homer – like when Hector says: 'Polydamas shall be first to pile his reproaches upon me!' Or Diomedes:

[But if I run], just imagine what Hector will say to the Trojans! 25
'[The famous Diomedes], Tydeus' son – I sent him packing!'

This is the closest to the kind of bravery we described earlier, because it still comes of being a good man – specifically, it's caused by shame and a desire for respect (hence, for something honourable) and a fear of reproach (i.e. a fear of something shameful).

You might also be tempted to put men who are coerced by their commanders in the same category. But theirs is actually 30 a rather lower grade of bravery, considering that they act out of fear rather than shame, and to avoid pain rather than what's shameful. They're coerced by men who hold the power of life and death over them – like when Hector says:

> Any man I spy a-skulking, far behind the line,
35 > You mark my words, he'll soon be meat for dogs!

And when [generals] put men in the front line and then whip
1116b them if they fall back, they're doing the same, or when they line up their men in front of ditches and suchlike. Those are all forms of coercion. But a man shouldn't be brave under duress. He should be brave because it's honourable.

(b) Technical expertise in a given field can also look like bravery, which is what Socrates had in mind when he thought
5 bravery was knowledge. Different sorts of people are 'brave' in that sense in different fields, and in warfare it's the professional soldiers. Because in war, as they say, 'many a scare is just hot air' and mercenaries have seen it all before, which makes them look brave, because the others don't yet know the ropes. On top of that, their expertise enables them to attack or defend themselves better than anyone else, since they know how to
10 use their weapons and generally possess superior weapons, the best for attack or defence. So they're almost like armed men fighting unarmed opponents, or professional athletes against novices. (In those combat sports, too, it isn't the bravest men who are the best fighters; it's the ones who are the strongest
15 and fittest.) But they turn into cowards once the danger becomes too much for them to handle: once they find themselves outnumbered, or up against superior equipment. They're the first to run away, while civilian units stand their ground and fight to the death. (That's just what happened in the Battle of Hermes' Precinct.) That's because, for citizens, running away is shame-
20 ful. So they'd rather die than survive that way. But mercenaries only face the danger in the first place on the assumption that they're the stronger side, so as soon as they realize they're not, they cut and run. They're more afraid of death than of acting shamefully. A brave man isn't like that.

(c) People also connect fighting spirit with bravery. Men driven
25 by fighting spirit – like the way wounded animals will rush at

their attackers – can seem brave, on account of the fact that genuinely brave men are certainly also spirited. It's fighting spirit, above all, that fires us up and propels us into danger, hence those phrases in Homer: 'it filled his spirit with strength' and 'it roused his valour and his spirit' and 'he sucked a fierce breath of valour up his nose' and 'his blood boiled'. All those stock phrases seem to refer to the arousal, and the impetus, of 30 fighting spirit. So the reason brave men do what they do is that it's honourable. But fighting spirit helps them do it.

With animals, it's really just pain that drives them. It's because they've been hit [and wounded] or they're afraid. Certainly, if [the hunt] is in a forest or a reed-marsh, they stay well away. Then, when they're flushed out, intense pain and fighting spirit can make them rush at the danger without any foresight {or any 35 awareness} of what's frightening and what isn't. That doesn't make them brave. Otherwise we'll have to say that donkeys are brave when they're hungry. (A hungry donkey, after all, will endure a beating to keep on eating its hay.) Plus, even adulter- 1117a ers, driven by sexual desire, do plenty of daring things.

But it does seem that the most natural sort of bravery is the kind caused by fighting spirit, and that once that's combined with [conscious] choice and a reason for action, the result is 5 [full] bravery.

People feel pain, too, when they're angry, and then pleasure when they take revenge, and men who fight from those motives are certainly belligerent, but not brave. They're not thinking about what's honourable or doing what reason tells them to. They're driven by an emotion. But the state they're in is fairly close to bravery.

(d) Men who simply feel confident aren't thereby brave, either. They're bold in the face of danger because, let's say, they've 10 won lots of battles in the past against lots of opponents. And they're similar to brave men in so far as both act boldly. But brave men are bold for the reasons we explained, confident men only because they feel unbeatable and think there's no way they can come to any harm. (Men who are drunk behave in pretty much the same way. Getting drunk makes you confident, too.) But as soon as events prove them wrong, they run away.   15

A brave man is different. He faces things that are, and seem, frightening to [any normal] human being because it's the honourable thing to do, and shameful not to.

That's also why it seems braver of a man to be fearless and to keep his cool in a sudden crisis than one that he anticipated.
20 Because then it's more a matter of character, less of preparation. When you can plan ahead, what you choose to do may be a result of calculation and reason. But a spur-of-the-moment choice has to be based on character.

(e) Men also seem brave when they're just unaware of the danger. They're in more or less the same state as men who feel confident, but worse, to the extent that they have no sense of self-worth, whereas confident men do. That's why confident men stand their ground at least for a while, but men who are
25 simply under some misapprehension run away the moment that they realize, or so much as suspect, that things are not as they thought. (That's what happened to the Argives when they attacked the Spartans thinking they were just Sicyonians.)[48]

All right, so we've said what brave men are like, and we've described the various kinds of men who merely seem brave.

9 So bravery, we're saying, applies to things that frighten us
30 and embolden us – but not to both equally. It's really more about the things that frighten us. A brave man is someone who keeps his cool in frightening situations, and is the way a man should be in the face of things that frighten us, more than things that embolden us.

So that means it's for {facing and} enduring painful things that people are called brave, as we've explained. [Because fear is a form of pain.] That's why being brave is painful {and stressful}, and that's why men are praised for it, and rightly so.
35 It's harder to endure things that are painful than to abstain from pleasures.

1117b   Having said that, it seems plausible that at least the goal of bravery is actually something pleasurable, but that it gets overshadowed by all the things around it. Something like that happens in combat sports. Boxers, for example, certainly have a goal that's pleasurable: the thing they're doing it all for. The prize. The glory. But being punched hurts (assuming they're made of flesh and blood). It's painful. So is all the training. And because there's a lot of that stuff, and the point of it all is such a small, distant thing, overall it doesn't seem to involve any pleasure. So if that's how it is with bravery as well, then certainly dying, or being wounded, will be painful for a brave man and he won't want them to happen, but he'll endure them because it's the honourable thing to do, or shameful not to. In fact, if he's a good man in every way – so, he's flourishing – dying will be all the more distressing for him, because a man like that has so much to live for, and he'll be conscious of the fact that he's being robbed of the greatest blessings – and that's painful.

But it won't make him any less brave, and perhaps he's actually more brave[49] for choosing an honourable [death] in battle over living out such a life.

So it's not true[50] of all the virtues that exercising them is enjoyable – [being brave is painful] except in so far as it attains its goal.

And perhaps it isn't men of that sort who make the best soldiers. It may very well be men who are less brave but have nothing else to lose. Men like that are happy to run risks, and they trade their lives away cheaply.

All right, that's all we need to say about bravery. From what we've said it should be easy enough to get at least a broad sense of what it is.

10 After bravery we should talk about moderation. Because those seem to be the two virtues connected with the non-rational parts [of the soul].

So, we said earlier that being moderate is a middle state with regard to pleasures. (It's less connected with pains, and not in the same way, we said.) And having unruly appetites[51] {that is, being lecherous and gluttonous} clearly applies in the same contexts. So now let's set out exactly what kinds of pleasures they're concerned with.

So first we need to distinguish mental and physical pleasures.

Consider people who crave respect, or have a passion for learning. In both cases they derive enjoyment from the thing

they feel that way about. But it isn't a physical experience; it's
really their mind that's affected. Being moderate, or lecherous
and gluttonous, doesn't apply to those kinds of pleasures, or to
any other pleasures that aren't physical. People who love tell-
35 ing tales, gossiping, spending the whole day talking about any
old thing – they're 'garrulous', not 'gluttonous'. And we'd never
1118a say that people who get very upset about losing money or family are being 'gluttons' for those things either.

So being moderate seems to be about physical pleasures. But
not even all of those. When people enjoy the objects of vision,
for instance – colours, shapes, pictures – we don't speak of
5 them being 'moderate' or 'gluttonous'. (And yet arguably you
can enjoy even those things to the right degree, or go too far,
or fall short.) Similarly with pleasures connected with hearing.
If you're excessively fond of songs or plays, nobody calls you a
glutton (or moderate, if you enjoy them the right amount). You
can't be moderate or gluttonous or lecherous through smell,
10 either – except by association. If you love the smell of apples,[52]
roses or incense, for example, nobody's going to call you gluttonous or lecherous. But they might if you love the smell of a
woman's perfume, or a curry. That's because lecherous and
gluttonous men typically enjoy those smells since they remind
them of the objects of their cravings. (And notice that the rest
15 of us like the smell of food as well, when we're hungry.)[53]

Other animals get no pleasure through those three senses
either, except by association. Dogs, for example, don't enjoy the
smell of rabbits. They just enjoy devouring them. But the smell
alerts them to the presence of the rabbit. A lion doesn't enjoy
20 the sound of a cow mooing. It just enjoys eating the cow. But
the mooing makes it aware there's a cow nearby, and for that
reason it appears to enjoy the sound. Similarly, a lion doesn't
enjoy '*seeing* a deer or a wild goat' – it's just happy that it's
going to get a meal.

The kinds of pleasures involved in being moderate, or gluttonous and lecherous, are the ones that we share with the other
25 animals (which is why we think of people like that as being like
slaves or beasts). And that means the pleasures of touch[54] and
taste. And even then they seem to make very little use of taste,

or none. Taste is for discriminating between flavours – the sort of thing we do when we're checking the quality of a wine or seasoning a curry, say – and they don't really enjoy that kind of thing, at least not if they're true gluttons. They just enjoy the 30 consuming, which is an entirely tactile[55] experience, whether it's in drinking, eating or sexual activity, so-called. That's why that famous foodie[56] wished his throat could be longer than a crane's – because it was the contact with the food that he took pleasure in.

So being lecherous and gluttonous depends on the most uni- 1118b versal of the five senses – touch. And it seems quite right to regard it as especially reprehensible, seeing as it comes from our animal nature, not our human nature. That means that to enjoy those kinds of things, and to value them above all else, is to live like a mere beast.

(It goes without saying that the gentlemanly forms of tactile pleasure, like the pleasures of a massage or a hot bath at the 5 gymnasium, are a different matter. It isn't the pleasure of contact with any part of your body that marks you out as a lecherous man, just . . . certain parts.)

11 Of the various kinds of physical desire, some are common to everyone, some are individual and acquired. Desire for food, for example, is natural. Everyone desires nour- 10 ishment (liquid or solid, or both) when their body needs it, and every young man in his prime desires to 'bed' someone,[57] as Homer puts it. But not everyone desires this or that kind of food, or this or that kind of the other, and we don't all have the same desires. That makes it seem a [purely] individual thing.[58] But actually it's still at least partly natural: different sorts of people get pleasure from [predictably] different things, and there are some things that give everyone a more than average amount of pleasure. 15

So, in the case of our natural desires, not many people go wrong, and when they do it's always in one direction: too much. Eating or drinking beyond the point of being full means overshooting the naturally appropriate quantity. Because natural desire, here, is all about refilling – satisfying a need. That's why

you call a man like that a 'greedy-guts': he's always filling
20 up his gut beyond what it needs. Only the very worst kind of
riff-raff are like that. But when it comes to our more individual
tastes for pleasure, plenty of people go wrong, and in lots of
different ways. We say of people [in Greek] that they're *philo-*
somethings', {'X-addicts'}[59] when they enjoy things that you
shouldn't enjoy, or more than most of us do, or in the wrong
way. And in all respects lecherous and gluttonous men go too
25 far. They enjoy some things – vile, disgusting things – that
nobody should [ever] enjoy. And with any of the kinds of pleasures you should enjoy, they enjoy them more than you should,
or more than most people do.

So, going too far with respect to physical pleasures means
being lecherous and gluttonous. And it's blameworthy. That's
clear.

What about pains? Well, you aren't considered a moderate
man for enduring them (as in the case of bravery) or gluttonous
30 and lecherous for not enduring them. Rather, you're gluttonous and lecherous if you feel more pain than you should at not
getting physical pleasures (such that the pain is actually caused
by the pleasure) and a moderate man if you don't feel pain at
the absence of pleasure or when you abstain from it.

1119a   So a gluttonous, lecherous man desires all physically pleasurable things, or the most pleasurable, and is constantly driven
by his cravings to choose those things over anything else. That's
why he feels pain when he doesn't get them, and pain in craving
them. His desire itself causes him pain. And that seems pretty
silly – to be in pain on account of pleasure.

5   As for people who fall short with respect to pleasures, i.e.
who enjoy them less than one should – there aren't any such
people. That kind of lack of feeling simply isn't human. All other
animals, after all, show preferences for certain foods: there are
things that they enjoy eating and things they don't. If there's
anyone for whom nothing is pleasurable, for whom nothing
feels any different from anything else, well, they're a long way
10 from human. There's no special word for a person like that
because they basically don't exist.

A moderate man, on the other hand, is set nicely in the middle with respect to pleasures. He doesn't take any pleasure in the things that gluttonous, lecherous men enjoy the most – if anything, he finds them distasteful – or in general anything you shouldn't enjoy. And he doesn't ever feel intense pleasure at any of those kinds of things. He also doesn't feel pain at the absence of pleasures or crave them, or he desires them within measure and never more than one should or at the wrong time or the wrong anything else. All the pleasures that keep you healthy or in good shape he'll desire within measure, and in the way that you should, and other pleasures too as long as they don't undermine his health or his fitness and as long as they don't go against what's honourable and aren't beyond his means. That would be to place more value on those kinds of pleasures than they're worth. A moderate man wouldn't do that. He always goes by what's reasonable.

12 Being gluttonous and lecherous seems a more wilful [character trait] than being a coward. It's caused by pleasure, something we choose, whereas cowardice is caused by pain, something we try to avoid. Plus, pain disrupts and damages the nature of whatever's experiencing it, but pleasure doesn't do anything like that. So that makes it more wilful, and therefore more reprehensible. And after all, it's easy to get yourself into good habits with respect to pleasures. Life offers plenty of instances of that kind of pleasure and there's no danger involved in training yourself. The opposite is true of situations that are frightening.

And it seems that being a coward – [the character-state] – and the particular actions of a coward aren't wilful to the same degree. The disposition itself may well be painless, but the particular situations drive a man out of his mind with pain {and stress} to the point where he throws down his arms and does those other disgraceful things. That's why it can seem that he's forced to act that way. But for a lecherous, gluttonous man it's the reverse. His particular actions are wilful (after all, he's motivated by his own cravings) but his general disposition less so. Nobody yearns to be a lecherous man.

We use the same term[60] *akolastos* for naughty little children

1119b as well, because that's a somewhat similar thing. It doesn't
matter for our purposes which sense of the term derived from
which, although it's pretty clear that the later, adult sense
['lecherous', 'gluttonous'] derives from the one applied earlier
in life ['unruly', 'undisciplined']. And the transfer of the term
seems appropriate. Because anything that craves shameful things
and has a great potential for growth needs to be disciplined.
5 And that exactly describes both physical desire and children.
(Children live by their cravings, and their desire for pleasure is
especially pronounced.)

So unless a thing like that becomes obedient and falls under
the [appropriate] controlling force, it will get more and more
out of hand, because desire for pleasure in a thing without any
sense is insatiable and can be triggered by anything. Also, the
exercising of desire will cause its kindred [desires] to grow, and
10 when a man's desires are large and powerful they can knock
out his deliberation. So a man should have only a few moderate physical desires, and they mustn't go against reason in any
way (which is just what it is for something to be obedient and
disciplined), and, just as a little boy has to live by the instructions of his minder, desire has to follow reason. That's why [we
15 often say that] in a moderate man desire has to be 'in harmony'
with reason. His desire and reason both aim at what's honourable, and a moderate man desires what he should, the way he
should, when he should – just as reason also instructs him to do.

All right, so that's all we need to say about being moderate.

BOOK IV

Next, let's say something about being generous {and gentle-manly}.

So, it seems it's the middle state relevant to money. When a man is praised for being generous it's not in warfare,[1] or in situations where he's praised for being moderate, and it's not about the judgements he passes. It's about the way he gives money to others and makes money – but more about giving.

(By 'money'[2] here I'll mean everything that has a measurable cash value.)

Then there's being extravagant and being ungenerous {and ungentlemanly} – the ways of going too far, or falling short, when it comes to money.

Of those, 'ungenerous' {or 'ungentlemanly'} always applies to people who care too much about money. The other – *asōtos* – we sometimes apply to a blend of different things: we use it of people who have no self-control and spend a lot[3] of money on debauchery. That's why those people seem especially awful: because they have more than one vice at once. So that's not the proper way to use the term. *Asōtos* ['extravagant'] should mean someone with just one bad thing about them, that they waste their resources. An extravagant person [as the word *asōtos* implies] is self-destructive,[4] and wasting your resources seems like self-destruction because they're your means of staying alive.

So that's the sense of *asōtos* that we're assuming here: ['extravagant'].

There are things that we use. And you can use them well or badly. Wealth is one of those. It's useful.

5   And the man who makes the best use of any given thing is
the one with the virtue relevant to that thing.

So the person who makes the best use of money is the one
with the virtue relevant to money. And that's someone generous {and gentlemanly}.

Using your money means spending and giving. Making money,
and keeping it – that's more possession [than use]. That's why
10 being generous {and gentlemanly} is more about giving to
the right people, and less about making money[5] from the right
sources and not making it from the wrong sources. After all,
being a good person is more about benefiting others than being
benefited; it's more about doing honourable things than merely
not doing shameful things; and it's easy to see that by giving
you're benefiting others and doing something honourable,
whereas in making money you're being benefited and, [at best],
15 avoiding shameful behaviour.

Also, we thank someone for giving. We don't thank someone
just for not making money.[6] And we're more likely to praise
someone for giving.

Also, not taking {or making} money is easier than giving.
People are less inclined to freely give away what's theirs than
merely not take what belongs to others.

Also, it's people who give that we *call* 'generous'. When people
are praised for not making money [in indecent ways], they
aren't [typically] praised for generosity {or for being gentle-
20 manly}. They're just as likely to be praised for their 'moral
standards'. And we aren't praised at all for the ways we do
make money.

Also, of all the different types of good man, generous men
are arguably the ones we like the most. Because they help us.
And they do that by giving.

Actions that express any moral virtue are honourable. We
do them 'because it's the honourable thing to do'. So a generous man will give because it's the honourable thing to do, and
25 in the right way – that is, to the right people, the right amounts,
at the right time, and all the other things that go with correct
giving.

And he'll do so gladly, or at least it won't be painful.

Remember, whatever expresses a moral virtue gives us pleasure, or is painless – certainly not actually painful.

If someone gives to the wrong people, or not because it's the honourable thing to do but for some other reason, he won't count as generous. That's something else.

It also doesn't count if giving is painful. That shows he'd rather keep his money than do something honourable, which 30 means he's not a generous man.

Also, he won't make money from the wrong sources. Making money that way doesn't fit with being someone who doesn't really care about money.

He also won't be one to beg and scrounge. Someone who [likes to] help out others doesn't feel comfortable receiving help.

But he will make money from the right sources. For example, by raising it from his own property, not because that's an hon- 1120b
ourable thing to do [in itself], but as a necessity, so that he has money to give. And he certainly won't neglect his own wealth. (Of course not. He wants to support people with it.) He also won't give indiscriminately, to ensure he has enough to give to the right people, on the right occasions, and where it's the honourable thing to do.

Also, a defining feature of being generous is outdoing others 5
in your giving, so that you leave too little for yourself. Not being all that bothered about their own interests – that's typical of generous people.

And part of what's implied by 'being generous' is giving relative to your means. A generous action doesn't depend on the amount given. It depends on the disposition of the giver, a disposition that gives relative to means. So there's no reason why you can't be more generous even in giving a smaller amount, if 10
you're giving from smaller resources.

People who've inherited their wealth, rather than acquiring it for themselves, are typically more generous {and gentlemanly}. That's because they've had no experience of poverty; and because people are always fonder of their own creations – just think of parents, and poets.

Also, it's hard for a generous man to be rich, because he's 15 not interested in making or keeping hold of money, but is inclined to freely give it away. And he doesn't value it for itself; only so he can give to others. That's why people complain about Lady Luck: 'the most deserving people are the least likely to be rich'. But it makes sense that things turn out that way. You can't expect to have money if you make no effort to get it – like with anything else [in life].

20   But that's not to say that a generous man will give to the wrong people, or at the wrong time, or the wrong anything else. That wouldn't even count as a properly generous action any more; and if he spent money on the wrong things he wouldn't have it to spend on the right things. Because, as we said, a generous man spends in proportion to his means and on the right things. Someone who spends beyond his means is extravagant.

25   (That's why we tend not to call tyrants 'extravagant'. They have such a vast amount of wealth that it seems hard for them to give, or spend, beyond it.)

So, being generous {and gentlemanly} is a middle state that covers both giving and making money. A generous man will give, and spend, on the right things, and in the right amounts, whether it's on large things or small, and will enjoy doing so; he'll also make money from the right sources, and in the right amounts. The virtue here is a middle state that covers both, so a generous man, {a gentleman}, will do both in the right way. Decent giving goes with decent ways of making money too, and is inconsistent with [making it] other than decently. So the matching forms of each are found together in the same person, while those that don't match aren't. Clearly.

1121a   If a generous man finds himself spending beyond what he should, and beyond what's acceptable, he'll be displeased – but not especially annoyed, and in the right way. (A key part of being a good person is being pleased and displeased by the right things in the right way.)

        Also, a {gentlemanly}, generous man is very easy-going[7] in
5   financial dealings. He can be given an unfair deal, because he doesn't really care about the money. In fact he's more likely to be annoyed to find he didn't spend what he was supposed to

than to get upset about having spent money he didn't have to. (He's kind of an anti-Simonides.)[8]

An extravagant man, here too, gets it all wrong. He isn't pleased when he should be and doesn't get upset when he should be. That will get clearer as we go on.

So we've already said that (a) being extravagant and (b) being ungenerous {and ungentlemanly} are the ways of going too far and falling short here; and that they have two domains: giving and making money. (We're treating spending as a category of giving.)

Of those, being extravagant means (1) going too far in giving and in not making money, and (2) falling short in making money. Conversely, being ungenerous {and ungentlemanly} means (1) falling short in giving, and (2) going too far[9] in the ways you make money (albeit on a small scale).

Now, it's rare for both aspects of extravagance to be combined in one person. It's not easy for someone to give to everyone while also not making any money[10] from anywhere. When people do that, their resources quickly run out (if they're private citizens, that is – and only private citizens are ever seen as extravagant). And anyway, someone like that seems a far better sort of person than an {ungentlemanly and} ungenerous man. He's easily cured, when he grows up a bit or runs out of money. And then he's well placed to arrive at the middle spot. After all, he's already got the [main] characteristics of someone generous {and gentlemanly}: he gives, and avoids making money. It's just that he doesn't do either in the right way. He doesn't do them well. So if he could just fix that, either by better habits or some other way, he'd be a generous man. He'll now give to the right people and only avoid making money from the wrong sources.

That's why we don't see someone like that as being such a bad character. Going too far in giving to others and in not making money doesn't make you a low or nasty person – just rather foolish. And that type of extravagant man seems far better than an ungenerous one, for the reasons given, and also because he helps a lot of people, whereas an ungenerous man is no help to anyone. Not even himself.

30   But most extravagant men, as we said,[11] also make money from the wrong sources, which makes them ungentlemanly.[12] They become money-grubbers because their desire to spend meets an inability to do so with ease (because they so quickly run through their resources). So they're forced to turn to new sources 1121b of income. Then add in the fact that since they don't care about what's honourable, they make their money unscrupulously and from any source. All they desire is to give. As for how they do it, or where the money comes from, they really couldn't care less.

That's why when they give it's not even generous {or gentle-manly}. Because it's not honourable, and they don't give for 5 the right reasons, or in the right way.[13] Sometimes they make men rich who ought to be poor. And while they never seem to give anything to decent folk, they give huge amounts to their flunkies {and hangers-on} and people who provide them with some other amusement. That's why most of them are also into debauchery. They throw money around, squandering it on their wild living. They live their life with no thought for what's hon-10 ourable, and so gravitate towards physical pleasures instead.

So an extravagant [young] man, with no one to tutor him, transitions into that kind of life. But with the right kind of care and attention he can arrive at the middle, where a man ought to be.

Being ungenerous, by contrast, is incurable. Old age, for example, and any sort of disability seem to make people un-generous.

We're also naturally more prone to it than we are to being 15 extravagant. When it comes to money, most people are more inclined to greed than to giving.

Also, it has a broad range and is multifaceted. That is, there seem to be lots of different ways of being ungenerous {and ungentlemanly}. That's because it has two domains – (a) fall-ing short in giving, and (b) going too far in the way you make money – but not all cases involve the complete pair. They can 20 come separately, with some people [only] going too far in mak-ing money, others [only] falling short in giving.

Take the people we label as 'misers', 'penny-pinchers', 'stingy' – all of those people fall short in giving, but they don't covet what isn't theirs and have no special interest in making {or taking} money.

Some of them are like that because of a kind of decency: their anxiety about being put into shameful situations. It seems that's why some people hoard their money (or so they say): 25 so that they won't be forced into doing anything {shameful or} degrading. And that includes 'cumin-splitters'[14] and all those kinds of people, so named because of the extremes they go to so as to not give anything away. Then there are others who keep their hands off other people's goods through fear [of having to reciprocate]. They worry that if you take from others, it's hard to stop them taking from you. So they're content to 30 not give or take.

Then there are the people who go too far in the way they make money. They make a living from any source, whatever they can get; like people who do ungentlemanly kinds of work (pimps and so on, and loan sharks, charging high interest on small loans). All of those make money from the wrong sources, 1122a and in the wrong amounts. And what they're seen as having in common is that they degrade themselves for their gains. They tolerate infamy for profits.

And small profits, too. Because when people make large amounts of money from the wrong sources, or take what they shouldn't {on a large scale} – like tyrants who sack entire cities 5 and loot religious sanctuaries – we don't call them 'ungentlemanly'. We're more likely to call them 'evil', 'heinous', 'criminals'. But gamblers, petty thieves, muggers[15] – they're 'ungentlemanly'. They degrade themselves for gain.

Both types, [thieves and gamblers], are in their line of work, and tolerate their ill repute, for profit. The former take enormous 10 risks for their loot, the latter profit from their own friends – the very people they should be giving money to. But both types are willing to profit from the wrong sources, and degrade themselves in doing so.

So all those ways of making money are ungentlemanly.

So it makes sense that we treat being ungenerous {and ungentlemanly} as the [standard] opposite of being generous. For one thing, it's a greater evil than being extravagant, and

15   for another, people are more inclined to go wrong in that direction than by being extravagant in the way that we described earlier.

All right, that's about all we need to say about being generous {and gentlemanly}, and the several vices that are its opposites.

2   Here we can segue nicely into an account of being lavish. Because that's another virtue that seems connected with money.

20   But it doesn't apply to all money-related actions, the way being generous does. Only to spending. And in that area it outdoes generosity in scale. [Greek for 'lavish' is *megaloprepēs*, and] as the word itself implies, it means spending on a grand scale [*megalo-*] in a way that's fitting[16] [*prep-*].

'On a grand scale' is relative. Commissioning a trireme, for example, won't involve the same expenditure as leading a reli-
25   gious embassy. So what's 'fitting' is also relative, to the spender, the thing he's spending the money on, and the context.

Someone who spends as required on something small or middling isn't being 'lavish'. (As in, 'many a time I gave [food] to a drifter'.)[17] You're only 'lavish' when you spend fittingly on a grand scale.

In other words, being lavish always implies being generous, but you can be generous without thereby being lavish.

30   Falling short, in this particular case, is being a 'cheapskate'. Going too far means being 'tacky' and 'tasteless' and things like that. And that doesn't mean spending too much money on the right things. It means spending [too much] on the wrong things, and in the wrong style – garishly. We'll say something about that later.

35   A lavish spender is like a connoisseur. He's good at discerning what's fitting and spending large amounts in a classy way.
1122b   As we said earlier, a given character-state can be defined by the ways you exercise it and by the things that it applies to. So a lavish man's spending will be on a grand scale, and fitting. And his works {and projects} will also be lavish. That way his expenditure can be on a grand scale and appropriate to the project.

So that means he needs a project worthy of his [grand] spending, and conversely he has to spend on a scale worthy of 5 the project – or even overdo it a bit.

And he'll be motivated to spend in these ways because it's an honourable thing to do. (That's common to all the virtues.)

And he'll do so gladly.

And he'll spend freely. Only cheapskates count pennies. He's more likely to be thinking, 'How can I make this as beautiful as possible, as fitting as possible?', not 'What's it going to cost?' or 'What's the cheapest way to do it?'

So a lavish man is necessarily generous. A generous man, 10 after all, is also someone who'll spend what he should, and spend in the right way. But it's the grandeur of that spending that marks someone as lavish. The same things, without grandeur, just fall under generosity.*

Even if he spends an equal amount, he'll create something more lavish. Because the qualities[18] we look for in a mere possession aren't the same as the ones we look for in a [public] work. 15 With possessions, the most valuable is just the most costly (gold, for example). But with a [public] work, what we value most is the grand, the beautiful – the kind of thing that is a wonder to behold. And it's the lavishness that supplies wonder. Lavishness is the special quality we look for in a public work on a grand scale.

It characterizes what we call 'prestige' spending: like spending on the gods (votive monuments, {statues}, temple-building, 20 sacrifices and so on; anything connected with religion); plus the ways ambitious men like to spend on the public, like when they choose to produce a stylish play, say, or commission a trireme, or lay on a banquet for the whole city.

And in all these things, as we said, we match [the spending] to the man doing it: 'Who is this person? What resources is he using? {What's his background?}' Because it has to be worthy 25 of those factors, too. That is, it has to be suitable not just to the work, but also to the man.

That's why someone poor can't be lavish. A poor man doesn't have the resources {or background} from which to spend large amounts in a fitting way. If he tries, he makes a fool of himself by spending above his station, and more than [someone like that] ought to. And exercising any virtue requires [doing everything] correctly.

30   It suits people who already have this kind of thing in their background,[19] either personally or through their ancestors or family connections; that is, it suits people of noble birth, people of distinction and so on. Because people like that are grand and important.

So that's the paradigm case of a lavish man, and lavishness is mostly a feature of those forms of [public] spending, as we've
35 said. Because those are the grandest and most prestigious.

As for private spending, [it makes sense to spend lavishly] on
1123a once-in-a-lifetime events like a wedding (or whatever else is in that category); or on something the whole city is enthused[20] about (or at least the important people); or on hosting and sending off foreign guests; and on gifts and counter-gifts. (A lavish man doesn't typically spend on himself. He likes to
5 spend on the public, and his 'gifts' tend to be rather like public {offerings and} monuments.)

A lavish man also furnishes and decorates his house in a manner appropriate to his wealth. Because that's another form of beautification.

Also, he prefers to spend money on works that are long-lasting. (Those are the most beautiful.)

And in all these various things he does what's fitting. (The
10 same things aren't suitable for the gods as for human beings, for instance; and what suits a temple may not suit a tomb.)

Also, everything he spends money on is [at least] grand for the kind of thing it is. So while the most lavish thing [he can possibly do] will be some grand version of something grand-scale, 'lavish' in a given context might just be a grand example of one of those, [whatever it might be].* There's a difference between the grand scale of the work itself and grandeur in the expenditure. A very beautiful ball or oil flask can be a {'grand' and} 'lavish' birthday
15 present for a child, though its cost is small and modest.[21] So being lavish means always making a lavish version – something of near-unsurpassable quality – of whatever it is you're making; but also in a style proportionate to the expense.

All right, so that's what we mean by someone lavish.

Now, someone who goes too far here is tacky. He goes too far by spending beyond what he should, as we said. That's to 20 say, he spends large amounts even on what [ought to be] minor expenses, with a garishness that's in bad taste. Like when someone provides a dinner for his dining-club friends on the scale of a wedding banquet, or produces a chorus for a comedy and they come on stage dressed in purple, like in Megara.[22]

And he'll do all these kinds of things not because it's the honourable thing to do but to show off his wealth, and because 25 he sees it as a way to impress people.

Also, when he should spend a lot he spends a little, but when he only needs to spend a little he spends a lot.

A 'cheapskate' is someone who'll fall short in his spending on all these things. Even after spending a huge amount on something, he'll spoil the beauty of it over some trifling sum. Whatever it is he's paying for, he drags his feet, thinks about how to spend as little as possible, complains even about that, and always 30 thinks that what he's producing is grander than it needs to be.

Now, these dispositions are obviously bad qualities. But they don't bring a man into too much ill repute because they don't harm other people, and they're not especially disgraceful.

3 A sense of pride[23] – as the [Greek] word itself implies – involves great things. But in what sense exactly? Let's get 35 an idea of that first. (And it doesn't make any difference whether we investigate the disposition or a person who has it.)   1123b

So someone with a sense of pride sees himself as worthy of great things – and *is*. (Because if he were wrong to see himself that way he'd just be a twit, and no exemplar of a virtue can be foolish or silly.)

So that's a man with a sense of pride. Note the wording. It's not someone of little worth who sees himself as being of little 5 worth.[24] Someone like that is 'sensible',[25] but doesn't qualify as having a sense of pride. Size matters here: {you need great worth} for a sense of pride, just as you need physical size to be attractive. (Short men can be dapper and well proportioned, but not attractive.)

A man who sees himself as worthy of great things, and isn't, is 'full of himself' {and vain}. (But not everyone who overestimates himself at all is thereby 'full of himself'.)

10   Someone who underestimates himself 'has no pride', whether his actual worth is great or middling . . . or he may even be a man of small worth who rates himself even lower. Probably of those it applies best to someone of great worth [who underestimates himself]. Because just think what someone like that would do if his actual worth were any less.

So a man with a sense of pride, in terms of his worth, is at the top, but in terms of attitude he's right in the middle: his 15   self-estimation is just right, whereas the others go too far or fall short.

So if he feels worthy of great things – and is – and especially the greatest, then perhaps [this virtue] concerns one particular thing most of all. And 'worth' here means in terms of external goods. [We're talking about people deserving, or not deserving, external goods.] And we can assume that the greatest of those is the one that we award even to the gods; the thing that important people strive for most of all; the prize for the most 20   glorious exploits. And that exactly describes respect. Respect is the greatest of all external goods.[26]

So a man with a sense of pride is someone with the right attitude to respect and disrespect (in all forms). (In fact, even without argument it seems pretty clear that men with a sense of pride are all about respect. Respect is what they think they deserve, more than any other thing – and they do.)

Someone who lacks pride falls short, both by underestimat-25   ing himself and by having less self-worth than someone with a sense of pride.

Someone who's full of himself {and vain} goes too far, {in that he overestimates} himself. But that's not to say he has more [self-worth] than someone with a sense of pride.

Someone with a sense of pride, if he's worthy of the greatest things, has to be an exceptionally good man. The better the man, as a rule, the more he deserves; and it's the very best people who deserve the greatest things. So to truly have a sense of pride you have to be a good man.

You might say that a sense of pride adds a kind of greatness 30
{or grandeur} to every virtue.

It would be completely out of character for a man with a
sense of pride to run pell-mell from battle; or to cheat somebody. What reason would he have for doing shameful things like
that? This is a man for whom nothing is all that important.[27]
Think it through case by case,[28] and the very idea of someone
having a sense of pride without being a good man seems utterly
absurd.

Also, he wouldn't deserve respect if he were a bad person.
That's what respect is: the prize for being a good man. We 35
award it to good men.

So a sense of pride seems like a kind of embellishment of the 1124a
virtues. It amplifies them. And it can't exist without them. That's
why it's difficult to genuinely have a sense of pride. Because it
is not possible without being a fully decent man.

So, as I said, a man with a sense of pride is defined, mainly,
by his attitude to respect and disrespect.   5

When he's offered great respect, and by good people, he'll be
somewhat happy about it. He'll feel he's getting his due – or less
than his due, because no amount of respect can really match up
to his total goodness. Mind you, he'll take it, since they don't
have anything greater to offer him. But as for respect he gets 10
from mediocre people, and for trivial things – well, he'll just
completely ignore it. That stuff's beneath him. And likewise
any disrespect he receives. Because it won't be justified.

So someone with a sense of pride, we've said, mostly has a
certain attitude to respect. But he'll also have a cool, reserved
attitude to wealth, power and every success or setback[29] in life –
however things turn out. He's not one to be either overjoyed 15
when things go well or especially upset when things go badly.

The thing is, he doesn't even feel that way about respect. (It's
not like it's hugely important to him.) And power and wealth
are only desirable in the first place on account of respect. (At
least, for the people who have them, the point is to be respected
for them.)[30] So when even respect is a minor thing to someone,
so is the other stuff. That's why a sense of pride makes people 20
come across as haughty.

It's also a common view that the advantages of fortune contribute to a sense of pride.

People of noble birth, for instance, are seen as worthy of respect, as well as wealthy or powerful men. That's because they have a kind of superiority, and superiority in any kind of good always wins you more respect. Hence those kinds of things enhance a man's sense of pride. Because [those things] are respected – at least, by some people.

25 Strictly, only a good man truly deserves to be respected. But if someone has both – [e.g. he's a good man and wealthy] – he's seen as even more deserving of respect.

What if people have those advantages without being good men? In that case they're wrong to see themselves as having any great merit, and it's incorrect to speak of them as 'having a sense of pride'. That cannot be so if they aren't completely good people.

But those advantages, too, [rather like a sense of pride], can 30 make people haughty and scornful. If you aren't a good man it's hard to handle the advantages of fortune gracefully. So some men just don't know how to handle them, and because they 1124b think they're above everyone else they end up {being snobs,} and looking down on others even though their own achievements are distinctly mediocre. They play the role of a man with a sense of pride (even though they're not like him) and they do that the only way they can. So even though they don't do any of the things that go with being good men [because that's beyond them], they still 5 look down on everyone. (Because a man with a sense of pride looks down on people too; but he's right to do so – his opinions are correct. Most people do it for no good reason at all.)[31]

He doesn't often take risks, and doesn't seek out danger*[32] because there aren't many things he sets that high a price on. But he'll face great dangers [if need be], and when he does he's willing to give up his life. For him, not every form of life is worth living.[33]

He likes to do good for others, but he's embarrassed to receive 10 help himself. That's because helping implies a superior position, being helped implies an inferior one.

And he likes to return a favour by one-upping it. That way the first person will be in his debt by the difference, and will be the one who's been benefited [overall].

Also, he remembers the good he's done for others but not the help he's received. That's because a man who has been helped has a lower status than the man who helped him; and he wants to be top dog. He also likes hearing about the one, but not the other. (That's why Thetis doesn't tell Zeus about the ways 15 she'd helped him in the past; neither did the Spartans before the Athenian assembly – they just talked about the help they'd received from Athens.)

Also typical of a man with a sense of pride is not needing anybody, or hardly anybody, while being eager to be of assistance to others.

Also, it's only in the company of important people, or the wealthy or powerful, that he stands tall. In more modest company he tones it down. That's because being superior, in the first 20 case, is difficult and impressive, but in the second case easy. A bit of swagger in the presence of [the rich and powerful] has a certain nobility to it, but among humbler folk it's rather boorish. Like a strongman beating up weaklings.

And he won't enter into the high-prestige [spheres of life], or at least not the ones where other people are at the top.

He doesn't like work,[34] and he always takes his time, except where there's great respect {and glory} [to be won] or a great 25 exploit [to perform]. He doesn't do much, but the things he does are big and memorable.

He invariably lets people know who his enemies are and who his friends are. Hiding it would imply he was scared; and he cares more about being truthful than about what people think of him.* So he speaks, and acts, openly. He says whatever he wants – because he basically doesn't give a damn [what people will think] – and tells it like it is (unless he's understating him- 30 self, which he will in the company of ordinary people).

He's incapable of living his life deferring to someone else (apart from family). Because that's the life of a slave. That's 1125a why flunkies are all from the lowest classes, and [only] meek-spirited men are other men's flunkies.

He's not easily impressed. Because nothing's a big deal to him.

He doesn't hold grudges. It doesn't suit a sense of pride to dwell on the past, especially not on the harms [he's been done]. He's more likely to see past that stuff.

5   He doesn't talk about people. He won't say anything about himself, or anyone else. Because he's not interested in being praised, or in stirring up criticism of others. And he's not one to praise other people either. Hence he also doesn't speak ill of others, not even his enemies – unless [stirred] by some outrageous wrong.

When it comes to necessities – the little things – he's the last person to start whining or begging, because to behave in that 10   way would suggest someone who actually cared about that stuff.

Also, he prefers to own things that are beautiful and profitless, rather than productive and useful. That's more in keeping with a man who has all he needs.

We expect a man with a sense of pride to be slow in his movements. To have a deep voice. Steady speech. A man who's 15   not really bothered about all that much isn't going to be in a hurry. And if nothing's a big deal, why be stressed? A high-pitched voice, and haste, go with those things.

All right, so that's a man with a sense of pride.

Someone who falls short here 'has no pride'. And someone who goes too far is 'full of himself' {and 'vain'}.

Now, here too, we don't see these people as morally bad. They don't do any harm. But we do think there's something not quite right about them.

A person who lacks pride is someone who does deserve good 20   things but denies himself what he deserves. So he gives the impression of having some kind of defect, from the fact that he doesn't see himself as deserving those things. It's as if he doesn't know himself. If he did, he'd strive for the things he deserved – they're good, after all.

Having said that, people like that certainly don't come across as silly. More like, hesitant.

Then again, I think having that kind of opinion of yourself does actually make you a worse person. People will always

aspire to what they think they're worthy of. So they hold back 25
from doing honourable things, and from honourable ways of
life, if they don't feel worthy of them. People also hold back
from external goods in much the same way.

When people are full of themselves, they certainly do come
across as silly – as well as not knowing themselves – and glaringly so. They try their hand at high-prestige [areas of life]
when they aren't worthy, and then they get found out.

And they embellish themselves – by their dress, their demean- 30
our and so on. And they want everyone* to see just how
fortunate, {how wealthy, how powerful}, they are and talk
about it, as if they'll be respected for those things.[35]

Having no pride is the [natural] opposite of having a sense of
pride, rather than being full of yourself. Because we're more
inclined to it, and it's worse.

So, a sense of pride concerns respect on the grand scale,
we've said . . .   35

4   But there seems to be [another, nameless] virtue here con- 1125b
     nected with respect – we talked about this right back at
the start[36] – which you might say relates to having a sense of
pride in something like the way that being generous relates to
being lavish. Because both are outside the grand scale. It's in
medium-size and small-scale matters that they set us in the right 5
state. And just as there's a middle state when it comes to giving and making money, and a way of going too far, and a way
of falling short, likewise when it comes to desire for [ordinary
levels of] respect there's such a thing as desiring it more than
you should, and less than you should, and for the right things,
and in the right way.

Consider: we criticize someone for being 'philotimos' –
{'status-loving', 'ambitious'} – meaning that they strive for
respect {or status} more than a person should, and for the wrong
things. We also criticize someone for being 'unambitious' if 10
they aren't interested in winning respect – even for honourable
achievements.

Conversely, there are times when we praise an 'ambitious'
man, meaning he's energetic, {forceful}, eager to do honourable

things. But we also praise someone for 'not being ambitious', meaning he's reserved, sensible. (We said all this back at the start.)

15 Clearly, 'he's someone-who-loves-X' can have various implications; and we don't always use *philotimos*, {'ambitious'} to pick out the same thing. As a compliment, it means you [want respect] more than most people do. As a criticism, it means you [want it] more than anyone should.

Since there's no word here for the middle state, in its absence it's as if the two extremes are both laying claim to it.

But in anything, where there's a way of going too far and a way of falling short, there's got to be an in-between. And people do desire respect both more than they should and less 20 than they should. So you can also desire it just the right amount.

At any rate, there's a character trait here that we praise: a middle state to do with respect. We just don't have a word for it. Compared to ambition [in the bad sense], it seems a bit like lack of ambition, and compared to lack of ambition [in the bad sense], it seems a bit like ambition; and compared to both, it can sort of seem like both. (That seems to happen with all the other virtues too.)

And in this case it's the people at the extremes who seem to 25 be opposites, because we don't have a word for the person in the middle.

5 Being good-natured {or gentle} is a middle state to do with feelings of anger.

Actually there's no name for the middle here (and pretty much no names for the extremes, either), but we use 'good-natured' {or 'gentle'} for the middle, even though it leans a bit towards the shortfall[37] – that there's also no word for.

What about going too far? We might call it something like 30 being 'anger-prone'. Because the emotion here is anger, though any number of different things might be causing it.

So if someone gets angry at the right things, and at the right people, and as angry as they should, and when they should, and for as long as they should – we praise them. So I suppose

that's a 'good-natured' person – since being good-natured is
something we praise.

Being good-natured means keeping your cool, not being carried away by emotion. It means only getting as angry as reason 35
tells you to; at the things it tells you to; for as long as it tells you
to. And maybe a good-natured person errs on the side of not 1126a
getting angry enough. Because they don't like having to retaliate. They're more inclined to be forgiving.

As for falling short, which is ... I don't know ... being
'angerless', or whatever we want to call it ... that's something
we criticize. People who don't get angry at the things they should
get angry at come across as saps; or if they don't get angry in 5
the right way, or at the right time, or at the right people. It's as
if they're not sentient; as if they don't feel the pain. And if you
don't get angry, people assume you won't stick up for yourself.
And to let yourself be abused and insulted – or to allow your
family to be insulted – seems pathetic and servile.

As for going too far, that can happen in all respects. You can
get angry at the wrong people and over the wrong things, and
you can get more angry than you should, or too quickly, or 10
stay angry for too long. (That's not to say all of those occur
in the same person. That wouldn't be possible. Any defect [as
well as being harmful to others] is also self-destroying, and if
it's total it becomes unsustainable.)

So bad-tempered people get angry quickly, and at the wrong
people, and over the wrong things, and more than they should.
But they're quick to stop being angry. That's the best thing 15
about them. And that happens because they don't hold their
anger in. They retaliate, which means they express how they
feel by their fiery reaction. And then their anger eases off.

And 'touchy'[38] people take that fieriness to an extreme; they
lose their temper at anything, over anything; {at the slightest
touch}. Hence the name.

Then there are 'bitter' people who refuse to reconcile and
stay angry for a long time. They bottle up their rage. But you 20
get relief by [letting it out, and] paying people back. Retaliat-
ing puts a stop to your anger because it produces a pleasure that
replaces the pain. And when that doesn't happen, people are

weighed down. And since they don't express their feelings,
nobody even tries to talk them round. Time passes, and that
25 makes their anger fester away inside them. People like that cause
huge problems for themselves and the people nearest to them.

Then there are harsh people. By 'harsh' we mean people who
react harshly to the wrong things, and more harshly than they
should, and for longer than they should, and refuse to reconcile without payback or punishment.

We're more likely to see going too far, {getting too angry}, as
the [natural] opposite of being good-natured. Because it's more
30 common. (It's more human to retaliate.) Also, harsh people are
harder to live with.

And the [general] point I made before is very clear in what
we're talking about here too.

It isn't easy to determine exactly how angry you should get, or
who you should be angry with, and over what kinds of things,
and for how long – and up to what point someone is getting
35 it right or getting it wrong. If someone only goes a little bit
off-target (in either direction) we don't blame them. In fact,
1126b sometimes we even praise people who fall short; call them 'good-
natured'. And sometimes we praise people when they're being
harsh; we call them 'tough' and say they 'know how to lead'.[39]

So exactly how far someone has to be off-target, and in what
way, before it's right to criticize them – it's not easy to lay that
out in a general theory. Because when it comes to particulars,
judgement also depends on perception.

5 But at least this is clear: that the middle state here is
praiseworthy – the one that makes us [reliably] get angry at
the right people, and over the right things, and as angry as we
should (and so on and so forth), and that when people go too
far, or fall short, they deserve to be criticized – a little when
they're slightly off, more when they're further off, severely
10 when they're way off. So it's clear that we've got to get hold of
that middle state.

All right, that's all we need to say about the character-states
relating to anger.

6 In social interactions, and in spending time with others and sharing in conversation or action, some of us are 'people-pleasers'. 'People-pleasers' applaud everything in order to please people. They never say no to anything. They think they should *never* offend the people they're interacting with.

Others are the exact opposite. They say no to everything and couldn't care less about offending people. We call them 'grumpy' and 'cantankerous'.

So we criticize those dispositions. That's pretty clear. And the character trait in between them is obviously something we praise: the one that will make you accept the things you should, and in the way you should, and likewise object to [the right things, in the right way]. But there's no special name for that.

It most closely resembles being a friend.

That's to say, someone who's in the middle state here is just the same as what we mean by a morally decent friend, except that a friend has the extra element of affection. This differs from being a friend by the fact that it involves no emotion; no affection for the people you're interacting with. You respond to everything in just the right way, not because you love {or are friends with} the person or are their enemy, but just because that's the way you are. You'll do the same whether you know them or not; whether they're close to you or mere acquaintances – except of course that you'll also do whatever suits each case. (It's not appropriate to be as concerned about strangers as family and friends, or to hurt their feelings in the same ways either.)

So that's the general description: you interact with others in just the right way.

[Specifically], you'll always think about what's honourable and what's in their best interests, and on that basis aim not to offend, or to humour people.

This seems all about feelings of pleasure and pain that arise in social interactions; {it's all about making people feel good, or hurting their feelings}. And whenever it's not honourable, or it's harmful, to humour someone, you'll voice your objections. You'll prefer to hurt their feelings. And if doing X is going to bring them disgrace – let's say really major disgrace – or harm,

35 and confronting them about it will only hurt them a little, then
you won't tolerate it. You'll object.

But how you treat people will also vary depending on whether
1127a they're important or ordinary people, famous or more obscure,
and so on with all the other ways we categorize people – you'll
give everyone their due.

You'll prefer, ideally, to be pleasant and to avoid offending
anyone, but you'll be guided by the consequences if those carry
more weight; that's to say, {you'll go with} what's honourable
5 and in people's best interests. (You'll also cause them a little
hurt now, if it helps them to greater pleasure in the future.)

So that describes the person in the middle. And there's no
word for someone like that.

As for humouring people,[40] well, if someone is just aiming to
be pleasant, with no ulterior motive, that's a 'people-pleaser'.
But if they're doing it for the benefits they get out of it – for
money, or the things that money buys – that's someone's
'flunky' {or 'hanger-on'}.

10 And someone who objects to everything, as I said, is 'grumpy'
and 'cantankerous'.

In this case, the extremes appear to be opposites of one
another because there is no name for the middle.

7 Applying to more or less the same domain is the character
trait that's in between being a charlatan {or phoney} and
being self-deprecating.

Again, there's no word for this quality.

(It's not such a bad idea, by the way, to address even these
15 kinds of qualities.[41] For one thing, we'll get a better knowledge of human character in general if we go through it all
in detail; and we can also be more confident that virtues are
middle states if a full survey shows that that's how it works for
everything.)[42]

So in the context of spending time with others, we've just
talked about people interacting in ways that please or offend;
next let's talk about the ways people can be truthful and
20 untruthful – in what they say, or what they do, or the way they
present themselves.

So a charlatan is someone who pretends to have impressive [abilities or qualities] that they don't really have, or exaggerates the ones they do have.

Someone self-deprecating is the opposite. They deny outright or downplay their [attributes].

And the person in the middle, a kind of straight-talker,[43] likes to be truthful, in the way they live and in what they say; admitting what's the case about themselves without either exaggerating 25 or downplaying it.

(You can do each of those things either with or without an ulterior motive. And what someone is really like is reflected in what they say and do and in the way they live when they aren't acting with any ulterior motive.)

In itself, telling lies is bad and blameworthy; telling the truth is honourable and praiseworthy. And in line with that, 30 we praise a truthful person (the one in the middle here) and we criticize untruthful people – both kinds, but more so the charlatan.

So let's talk about the one then the other.

First, someone truthful. And we're not talking about someone who tells the truth in their contracts {promises, agreements}, or all those cases of truth-telling that have a direct bearing on wrongdoing, or doing what's morally right.[44] (That would come under a different virtue.) No. We're talking about someone 1127b who, even if nothing like that is at stake, is truthful anyway, in what they say and in the way they live, because that's just the sort of person they are by disposition.

But arguably, being like that is morally significant. Because if you like telling the truth even when nothing major is at stake, you'll be all the more likely to be truthful when it is. Because 5 now you'll be avoiding falsehood as something shameful – and you were already avoiding it just for its own sake. A commendable[45] way to be.

But maybe [a 'truthful' person] leans a little towards understatement, rather than telling just the truth [about themselves]. That comes across as more gracious, on account of overstatements being kind of annoying.[46]

Someone who exaggerates their [abilities] with no ulterior

10 motive at all certainly still seems like a bad person – why else
would they enjoy telling lies? – but comes across as silly more
than nasty.

If they do have an ulterior motive – well, if it's for reputation
or respect, they're not really all that blameworthy (at least, not
by the standards of charlatans).* But if it's for money or anything money-related, that's rather more disreputable.

(And note that being a charlatan doesn't just depend on an
ability. It depends on choice. Someone's a charlatan by charac-
15 ter; by being that kind of person. It's like being a liar. A liar is
someone who likes telling lies, per se, or tells lies from a desire,
e.g. from a desire for reputation or material gain.)[47]

So people who make phoney claims just to enhance their
reputation pretend to have things that people will praise them
for; or congratulate them for.

But charlatans who are out for material gain pick the kinds
of abilities that other people benefit from and that are easily
20 faked; like being a prophet, an intellectual,[48] a healer. (That's
the reason most of them pretend to have those kinds of abilities
and are phonies {in those fields}: because those fields have the
said features.)

As for self-deprecating people, they understate themselves
and come across as more charming characters. Nobody thinks
they're talking that way for material gain; just to avoid being
pompous.

25 In most cases, again,[49] they play down noteworthy [abil-
ities]. (That's what Socrates used to do, for example.) But some
disclaim even rather trivial things [like wealth], that everyone
can plainly see [they have]: so-called 'upper-class tramps'.[50] It's
rather easier to look down on people like that.

Sometimes [understating yourself] even comes across as a
form of being phoney – like when people wear Spartan clothes.[51]
Going too far [in how you present yourself] or falling way too
short – they're both phoney.

30 But people who only employ their self-deprecation moderately (and don't deny things about themselves that are in front
of our eyes and perfectly obvious) – they come across as
charming.

It's the charlatan {and phoney} who's the [natural] opposite of someone truthful. Because that's worse [than being self-deprecating].

8 There are also times in life when we relax. And in relaxing we sometimes pass our time {playing around, and} telling jokes. And there too we feel there's an appropriate way of conversing; a way of saying, and listening to, the sorts of 1128a things you should, and in the right way. (And it will also make a difference what kind of company you're speaking in, or what kind of people you're listening to.)

And obviously here too there'll be a way of going too far or falling short, and an in-between.

So people who go too far in their humour we see as buffoonish and crass – people who strain to be funny by any means at 5 all, and are more concerned about raising a laugh than about speaking in a dignified way and not offending the target of their joke.

Then there are people who would never tell a joke themselves and who get annoyed with people who do. We see them as humourless yokels[52] and stiffs.

And people who tell jokes tastefully are 'witty'. Our word for them is *eutrapeloi* – as it were, *eutropoi*, 'good at turning', 10 {deft, nimble}. That's because this sort of thing is like character in motion.[53] And just as people's physiques can be judged from the way they move, so can their characters.

In places where comedy is very prevalent, and almost everyone likes joking and mockery more than one should, even vulgar buffoons are called 'witty'; seen as 'charming'. But buf- 15 foonery is different [from wit, and a good sense of humour]; and it's no small difference. That's clear from what we've said.

Closely connected with the middle disposition here is the quality of being tactful. Being tactful is about saying, and [being willing to] hear from others, the kinds of things that are appropriate to someone decent and gentlemanly. The fact is, only certain things are suitable for someone like that to say and hear when the time comes for jokes. Gentlemanly humour 20 is different from servile, {riff-raffish} humour. Cultivated jokes differ from those of uncultivated people. You can see this in the difference between old and new comedies. In older comedies,[54] the jokes were bawdy and foul-mouthed. In more recent comedies, it's more a matter of innuendo. That makes them considerably more dignified.

25 So, is that how we should define someone who tells jokes well? Is it a matter of telling jokes not inappropriate to a gentleman? . . . Or is it just a matter of not offending your audience (or that, plus entertaining them)? Isn't that far too vague? Because different audiences find such different things offensive, or amusing . . .

And [we need to add] that he'll also only listen to those kinds of jokes. (Because the jokes you can put up with, as a listener, seem to be the same as the jokes you tell.)

So he won't tell just any joke.

30 To make fun of someone is, after all, a sort of abuse. Some forms of verbal abuse are actually illegal. Maybe certain forms of mockery should be illegal too. So someone courteous and gentlemanly will be that way anyway, just by his character – he'll be his own law, so to speak.

So that's what our person in the middle is like, whether we're calling him 'tactful' or {'witty' or} someone with 'a good sense of humour'.

As for a buffoon, that's someone who can't resist a joke and 35 won't treat anyone – himself or other people – as off-limits, as long he can make people laugh; and who tells the kind of jokes 1128b that no courteous person would ever tell, and some that they wouldn't even ever want to hear.

As for humourless people – well, they're useless in these kinds of social settings. They contribute nothing and take offence at everyone else's [jokes]. But surely relaxation and humour are something life cannot do without.

So we've now discussed three different middle states that 5 apply to the way we live our lives. All three relate to sharing in certain kinds of conversations and actions. They differ from one another in that one of them is about being truthful and the other two are about [certain forms of] pleasure. And of the two that are about pleasure, one of them applies specifically to contexts of telling jokes, the other applies to our interactions with others in every other sphere of life.

9 What about shame?   10
    It seems odd to speak of shame as a virtue at all. It seems more like a feeling than a character trait. At any rate we define it as the fear that people will think badly of you. And its effect on us is rather similar to the effect of [standard] fear – fear of frightening things. People who feel shame turn red. People in fear of their lives turn white. Both seem in some sense physiological, which is more what you expect of a feeling, or a [temporary] state of mind, than a disposition {or   15 character-state}.

    And even as a feeling, it isn't appropriate to every stage of life; just to young people. Young people, we think, should be {bashful and} prone to shame because they live by their feelings and constantly make mistakes, and shame keeps them in line. And though we praise the young for being prone to shame, no one would praise an adult for constantly feeling ashamed {or   20 embarrassed}, because we don't think an adult should ever be doing any of those shameful things [in the first place]. Shame is what we feel when we do morally bad things. So obviously it isn't something that a decent person ever feels. Because you just shouldn't be doing things like that. (And it doesn't make any difference here if we're talking about things that are actually shameful or things that you regard as shameful. You shouldn't do either. So you shouldn't ever feel shame.) If you're someone   25 who occasionally does something shameful, well, you're a bad person.

    But what about being the sort of person who, if they did do something like that, would be ashamed of it?

    It makes no sense to think that that makes you a decent person. We feel shame about things that we do wilfully. And no decent person will ever wilfully do morally bad things.

    All right, yes, perhaps we could say that shame is hypothetically a decent thing, in the sense that 'if they were to do that,   30 they would feel shame'. But [hypotheticals] are irrelevant to our moral virtues.[55]

Even if it's a bad thing to be 'shameless' about doing shameful things, that certainly doesn't mean that doing those things, and then feeling ashamed about them, is a morally good thing!

It's a bit like self-control. That's not a virtue either. Or, it kind of is and kind of isn't. We'll explain that later.

35   But now let's say something about fairness.

BOOK V

Now let's talk[1] about being *díkaios* {being righteous, being fair} 1129a
and being *ádikos* {being unrighteous, being unfair.}

We need to think about what sort of actions they're concerned with, and in what sense being fair is a middle state, and
how what's fair is in the middle – middle of what and what?   5

Let's use the same method as we did with the virtues we've
already talked about.

All right, so, it's clear that everyone thinks of being *díkaios*
{being righteous, being fair} as a disposition of character,
namely, the one that makes us do what's right {or fair} and
treat people rightly {or fairly}, and also want what's right {or
fair}.

And in the same way, everyone assumes that being *ádikos*
{being unrighteous, being unfair} is what makes us do wrong   10
{or act unfairly} and also want things that are wrong {or
unfair}. So we can take that as our initial, rough outline of
what these things are.

Remember, a disposition is not like a piece of knowledge or
an ability. We think an ability to X also implies an ability to do
the opposite of X; and knowing how to Y implies also knowing how to do the opposite of Y. But a disposition to X [is
different]; it can't make you do the opposite of X.[2] Health, for
example, can't make [the body] do things that are the opposite   15
of healthy. It only makes it do things that are healthy (e.g. have
a sound, healthy walk – as we say of someone who walks the
way a healthy person walks).

Now, often, the way to figure out what a given disposition
involves is (a) from its opposite, and often both dispositions can

be figured out (b) from the things they operate over. Example:
(a) if it's obvious what being in good physical shape is, that
20 automatically makes it obvious what being in bad shape is.
And (b) you can figure out what being in good shape is from
things that are in good shape; and you also know what gets
you into shape once you know what being in good shape is.
(Suppose, for example, that being in good shape means having
a hard, toned body. In that case being in bad shape obviously
means having a soft, flabby body, and what gets you into shape
is obviously whatever produces a hard, toned body.)

It goes along with this that, usually, if one of two opposites
25 has more than one sense, then so will the other, e.g. if *díkaion*
{right, fair} has more than one sense, then so will it's opposite,
ádikon {wrong, unfair}.

And as a matter of fact, these words do seem to have more
than one sense. It's just that the two senses are rather close,
so we tend not to notice that they each refer to two different
things – unlike when the two senses of a word are so far apart
that it's obvious it has two senses, since it refers to two quite
different types of thing ... like with the word *kleis*, for
30 instance, which means the bone below your neck {'collarbone'}
but also the thing you lock a door with {'key'}.

So let's start from the different senses of our term *ádikos*:
{'unrighteous person' or 'unfair person'}.

So, we think of someone *ádikos* as being

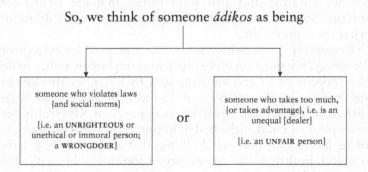

someone who violates laws
{and social norms}

[i.e. an UNRIGHTEOUS or
unethical or immoral person;
a WRONGDOER]

or

someone who takes too much,
{or takes advantage}, i.e. is an
unequal [dealer]

[i.e. an UNFAIR person]

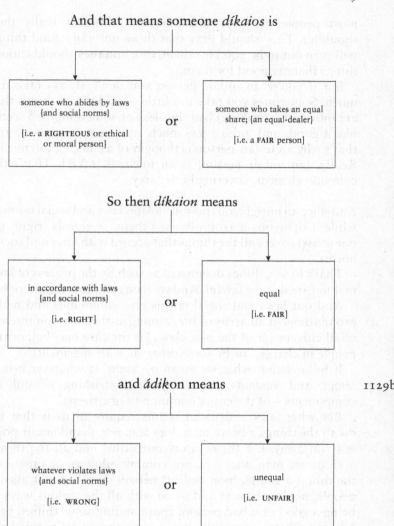

And that means someone *díkaios* is

someone who abides by laws
{and social norms}

[i.e. a RIGHTEOUS or ethical
or moral person]

or

someone who takes an equal
share; {an equal-dealer}

[i.e. a FAIR person]

So then *díkaion* means

in accordance with laws
{and social norms}

[i.e. RIGHT]

or

equal

[i.e. FAIR]

and *ádikon* means   1129b

whatever violates laws
{and social norms}

[i.e. WRONG]

or

unequal

[i.e. UNFAIR]

Now, since an unfair person[3] takes too much, being unfair will
have to apply to goods – not all good things, just all the ones that
good or bad luck can affect. (Those are normally good things,*[4]
but not always good for a given person. They're also the things

most people pray for and pursue – although really they
5 shouldn't. They should pray that those normally good things
will turn out to be good for them, too, and they should choose
things that are good for them.)

But if you're an unfair person you don't always take too
much. Sometimes you take too little – too little of things that
are (normally speaking) bad. But less-of-something-bad seems
like a good, and 'taking too much' applies to any good, and
that's why an unfair person is thought of as 'taking too much'.
10 Really, [an unfair person] is an unequal [taker]. That's the
common element, covering both cases.

And since an unrighteous person violates laws and social norms,[5]
while a righteous person observes them, obviously 'right' (in
one sense) covers all the things that accord with laws and social
norms.

That's to say, things designated as such by the process of lawmaking are thereby lawful. And we then call those things 'right'.

And our laws and social norms give commands and make
15 prohibitions in all areas of life, aiming at the common interest
of all citizens (or of the best class, [as the case may be], or the
people in charge,[6] or by some other such arrangement).

It follows that what we mean by 'right' is whatever brings
about and sustains the complete flourishing – and its
components – of the entire community of citizens.

But what laws and social norms require of us is that we
20 do all the things a brave man does (e.g. not abandon our post,
not run away, not throw away our arms) and all the things
a moderate man does (e.g. not commit adultery or rape) and
the things a gentle, {non-violent} person does (e.g. not assault
people, not be abusive) and so on with all the various ways of
being a good or a bad person, commanding some things, pro-
hibiting others – correctly, if our laws and social norms have
25 been correctly laid down, not so well, if carelessly.

So this first way of being *díkaios* – {being righteous} – is
really the same thing as complete goodness (with one qualification, that it refers to complete goodness in relation to other
people).

That's why being righteous so often seems like the most important virtue of all, and 'not even the morning star, or the evening star, is quite so wondrous'; and hence the proverb: 'In being a righteous man is every virtue, all in one.'   30

Also, being a righteous person is the most complete virtue because it's the using of your complete goodness.

It's also complete because someone who has it knows how to exercise their goodness in dealing with other people, not just on themselves. (There are plenty of people who know how to exercise their goodness on their own family, but don't know how to exercise it in dealing with other men.) That's why that saying of Bias' seems right: 'Power will show you the man.'   1130a Because a man who has power is now automatically dealing with other men, [beyond his own family], and doing things in partnership with others.

For the same reason being a righteous man is the only one of the virtues that's thought of as 'a good thing for someone else'[7] – because it's used on other people, in the sense that it makes us do things that serve the interests of some other person: a ruler, say, or a partner {or cooperator} of some sort.   5

Now while it's true that the very worst sort of man is one who inflicts his badness even on himself and his own family, the best sort is one who uses his goodness not just on himself [and his family] but in his dealings with others [beyond that group]. Because that's a greater challenge.

So this very general virtue, being a righteous {or ethical person} isn't just one part of being a good person. It's really the whole of being a good person. And it's opposite, being unrighteous, isn't part of being a bad person. It's the whole of it.   10

So in that case, what's the difference between being a good person and a righteous one? Well, that should be clear from what we've just said – namely, that they're really the same thing, but two different aspects of it. We call it 'being righteous' {or 'being ethical'} in so far as it affects others, and we call the very same character-state, unqualified, 'being a good person'.

2   But we think there's another sense of 'being *díkaios*'
    [namely, 'being a fair person'] that's just one part of being
a good person, and that's what we're interested in here. And
15 likewise, we're interested in the particular sense of 'being
ádikos' [namely, 'being an unfair person'].

And here's how you can tell there is such a thing [even if you
speak Greek and are using the same words for both].

With all the other moral failings, the corresponding behaviour is certainly *ádikon*, {'wrong'}, but in no sense implies
taking too much of something – like, say, if a man throws
away his shield (because he's a coward) or says something abusive (because he's bad-tempered) or refuses to give money to
help someone out (because he's ungenerous).

20 Conversely, when someone does take too much, often they
aren't acting from any of those kinds of vices (and they're not
acting from all of them at once, either); but they're certainly
exhibiting a moral failing (we criticize them for it) – and {we
still call it} *adikía*, [now in the sense 'being unfair'].

So there must be another kind of *adikía*, {'being unfair'},
which is part of general *adikía*, {'wrongdoing'}, and there must
be a particular kind of *ádikon*, {'unfair'}, that's just part of the
universal *ádikon*, {'wrong'}, that covers everything that violates
laws and social norms.

Also, suppose one man sleeps with someone else's wife
25 for profit, i.e. makes money out of it, while another does it out of
lust, and has to spend money and makes a loss. We'd say the
second man was lecherous rather than greedy {or taking too
much}. The first one, by contrast, seems *ádikos* {unfair} but not
lecherous. That's got to be because he's making a profit out of it.[8]

Also, with all the other forms of *adikía*, {wrongdoing}, we
can always relate them to some particular moral failing: he
30 committed adultery? Because he's lecherous. He abandoned
the man beside him? Because he's a coward. He punched someone? Because he lost his temper. But if what he did was profit
at someone's expense, then [in Greek] there's no other moral
failing we relate that to, besides *adikía*.[9] So obviously there
must be another, particular kind of *adikía*, {being unfair},
besides the general kind: a related use of the term, with broadly

the same definition, in that both kinds apply to our dealings 1130b
with other people, it's just that one of them – {being unfair} –
specifically concerns respect, {status}, money and survival (or
whatever term we might come up with to cover all of those)
and is caused by the pleasure we get from personal gain, while
the other – {wrongdoing} – covers everything in any way relevant to being a good person.   5

All right, so it's clear we've got two different senses of 'being
díkaios' – {being a righteous person, and being a fair person} –
and that one of them is not the same as the whole of being a
good person.

We need to figure out what it is and what it involves.

So, we've already said that ádikon-wrong means against law
and social norms and ádikon-unfair means unequal, and that
díkaion-right means in line with law and social norms and
díkaion-fair means equal.

So, corresponding to the first of these is the general adikía 10
{wrongdoing} that we've already talked about.

But 'unequal' is not the same thing as 'against laws and
social norms'. It's a different concept, related to it as part to
whole. That's to say, every case of unequal [dealing] is contrary to law, but not everything against laws or social norms is
an unequal [dealing].[10]

So there are also two different senses of ádikon, and two
different ways of being ádikos, related to one another as parts
to wholes. That's to say, being an unfair person is part of being
unrighteous. And likewise, being a fair person is part of being a 15
righteous {or ethical} person.

So it's time to discuss the particular virtue of being a fair
person, and the particular vice of being an unfair person, and
likewise what's fair and unfair.

So for now let's put the wider notions of being a righteous or unrighteous person, which correspond to the whole of
being a good person (one being the exercise of your all-round
goodness on others, and the other the exercise of all-round
badness) – let's put them to one side.   20

And anyway, it's obvious how to define the general kind of right and wrong that correspond to those. Roughly speaking, most of the things required by law and custom [and hence right] derive from [our conception of] all-round goodness. That's to say, what the law does is require us to live our lives according to every virtue and forbid us to exercise any of the vices. And to
25 promote this all-round goodness are all the laws {and customs} that determine the way young people are educated for civic life.

(As for your individual upbringing, which aims to make you simply a good man [as opposed to a good citizen], we can determine later whether that should be a matter for state control or belongs to some other sphere. Maybe being a good man and being a good citizen aren't the same thing in every society.)

30 The particular virtue, being a fair person, and the corresponding particular *díkaion* – what's fair – come in two forms.

One form applies to distributions, i.e. sharing out respect, {status}, wealth and whatever else can be divided up between a community of citizens. Because with those things one person's share can be equal or unequal to another's.

1131a   The other form, compensatory fairness, applies to making amends in our dealings with one another, and it divides into two parts, corresponding to the two kinds of dealings: willing and unwilling. Dealings that are willing are things like buying, selling, lending, insuring, renting, investing, hiring. We call these kinds of dealings willing in the sense that they're
5 entered into willingly. And unwilling dealings are unwilling either because they're done without the other's knowledge (e.g. stealing, adultery, poisoning, aiding an adulterer, slave-enticement, premeditated murder, giving false evidence) or because they're forced on someone (e.g. assault, imprisonment, manslaughter, kidnapping, maiming, verbal abuse, insult).[11]

10 3 An unfair person, we said, takes an unequal share, and unfair means unequal; so there's obviously also a mid-point here, i.e. a mid-point of the range 'unequal to X', and that mid-point is equal to X. (Because in any sort of action where you can get more than someone, or less, you can also get an equal amount.)

So if an unfair share is an unequal share, then a fair share is an equal share – exactly as everyone feels is the case without even having to think about it.

And since equality is a mid-point, it follows that what's fair is also a mid-point. And equality implies equality of at least 15 two variables. So, if what's fair has to be both a mid-point and a kind of equality, then:

(a) as a mid-point, it has to lie between something and something (i.e. between getting too much and getting too little) and

(b) as a kind of equality, it has to be the equality of two shares, C and D, and

(c) considered as fair, it has to be fair for two people, A and B.

So for something to be fair you need at least four variables: two people for whom it's fair, and two shares over which it's fair. 20

Of course, the equality of the shares will have to be the same as the equality of the people. That's to say, the shares have to stand in the same relation to each other as the people do. That means, if the people involved aren't equals, it won't be fair for them to get equal shares. That's exactly what causes all the bickering and the recriminations: it's either when equals don't get equal shares, or when people who aren't equals are awarded equal shares.

That's also clear from [all the talk about] what we deserve. Everyone agrees that fairness in distributions has to be based 25 in some sense or other on what people deserve; but they disagree about what makes one person deserve the same as the next. Democrats say[12] it's merely not being a slave. Oligarchs say wealth, or sometimes pedigree. And people who support aristocracy {or 'rule by the better class'} say moral worth.

In other words, a fair share is, in some sense, proportional. (Proportion isn't just a property of numbers in the abstract: it 30 applies to anything that can be quantified at all.) Proportionality means equality of two ratios, and so needs at least four variables. (In a case where there's no overlapping term [i.e. A is to B as C is to D], it's easy to see the four variables. But even with an overlap[13] there are still four variables, because one of them serves as two – you say it twice; e.g. 'A is to B as B is to 1131b C'. There. We said 'B' twice. So as long as you put down the 'B'

twice, you get four proportional variables.) And that's like fairness. Fairness also needs a minimum of four variables, and it
too has ratios that are the same, in the sense that the shares are
5 divided in a ratio that matches the gap between the persons.

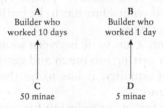

[Translator's example: fair pay, when 10:1 = 50:5 and
10:50 = 1:5 ; A-getting-50 matches B-getting-5]

So that means, for example, that A will be to B as C is to D,
and conversely A will be to C as B is to D. And consequently
the whole [A-getting-C] matches the whole [B-getting-D], the
'whole' being the coupling brought about by the distribution,
and when they're put together that way the couplings are fair.
In other words, the joining of A with C, and B with D, makes
10 a fair distribution. And what's fair here is also a mid-point,
because the proportional share is a mid-point, and the fair share
the proportional one. And an unfair distribution is one that
breaks that proportionality. (Mathematicians call this kind of
proportionality 'geometrical', because it's something you find
in geometry, where one whole figure stands in relation to another whole figure as each part of it to each part of the other.
15 But in the case of fairness the proportionality can't have overlapping terms [i.e. can't be of the form 'A is to B as B is to C']
because a person and a share can't be one and the same term.)
   So that's what fair means in this context: proportional. And
unfair means out of proportion, meaning that one of the shares
is too big and one of them too small. And that's just what happens in actual cases of unfairness: the person who's being unfair
gets too much of some sort of good, and the person who's
20 being treated unfairly gets too little of it. Or the reverse, if
it's something bad, because a smaller share of something bad,

relative to a larger one, counts as a good. (The smaller share of
something bad is more desirable than the larger one. Desirable
implies good, and if X is more desirable, X is a greater good.)
    So that's one kind of fairness.

4 The other kind is compensatory {or corrective} fairness, 25
which applies in our individual dealings with one another
(willing or unwilling).
    This sort of fairness takes a different form. Here's why. Fair-
ness in distributions of public goods is always based on the
kind of proportion we just talked about. When you're sharing
out public funds, for instance, the fair thing is to do it in the 30
same ratio as existed between the amounts that people put into
the funds. And unfair – the opposite of fair in that first sense –
means out of proportion.
    But when it comes to our individual dealings with one another,
what's fair is certainly still a form of equality, and unfair still
means unequal, but this time the equality isn't 'geometrical' [i.e. 1132a
same-ratio] equality. It's 'numerical' [i.e. same-amount] equality.
    It's completely irrelevant, for example, who stole whose money,
whether a decent man {of higher rank} stole from some {lowly}
scoundrel, or the other way round, or whether the decent man
or the scoundrel slept with the other's wife. Now the law only
looks to the difference brought about by the harm. It treats A 5
and B as equals if A has committed a crime and B is the victim;
if A has done harm and B has been harmed. The wrongdoing
results in a sort of inequality between A and B; one that the
judge must now try to equalize. (Even when A throws a punch
and B gets punched; even when A kills B and B dies, A's action
and its effect on B, set one against the other, amount to an
inequality.) So the judge tries to even out B's loss [and A's profit]
by taking something away from the profit. (That's the term, 10
broadly speaking, that we use in these sorts of cases: we speak
of the one person's 'profit', e.g. the 'profit' to the man who
threw the punch, even if it sometimes might not seem like quite
the right word to use, and we speak of the 'loss' to the victim.
At any rate, [in court] we call them the 'loss' and the 'profit'
once the harm done to the victim[14] has been quantified.)

All right, so equality, we said, is a mid-point between getting
15 more and getting less, and profit and loss mean getting more or
less (in opposite ways: profit is getting more of the good, less of
the bad, and loss is the other way round). And in the middle of
those is the point of equality – and that's what we call 'fair'. So
it follows that what's fair, in the context of compensation, is the
mid-point between making a profit and making a loss.

That's why when people have a dispute they go and appeal
20 to the judge. Going to the judge means appealing to fairness
itself. Because that's what a judge is supposed to be: fairness
in the flesh, so to speak. And they want a judge who's in the
middle – some people even call judges 'mediators', i.e. middle-
ators – because they feel that if they get a judge who's in the
middle, they'll get what's fair. (So what's fair must be a mid-
point, if even judges are 'in the middle'.)

25 So a judge is an equalizer. Think of it as like a line that's been
cut into two unequal sections. What a judge does is take away
the bit of the larger section that extends beyond halfway and add
it to the smaller section. When the whole line is divided exactly
in two,[15] then people say they've got what's theirs – when they get
what's equal (which is also the middle, in the sense of the mathematical average, of the larger and the smaller sections).

30 That's why the word for 'fair' in Greek is *díkaion*. Because
of the dividing *in two* [Greek for 'in two' is *díkha*]. So it's as if
we were calling what's fair the 'divided-in-two' thing (*díkhaion*),
and a judge (*dikastēs*) a 'cutter-in-two' (*dikhastēs*).

Suppose X and Y are equal, and some amount, *a*, is taken from
X and added to Y. Y is now larger than X by exactly 2*a*. (Obviously if *a* was taken from X but *not* added to Y, Y would just
1132b be larger by *a*. As it is, Y is now larger than the average [of X
and Y] by *a*, and the average is also larger than X by *a*.) So it's
by using that average that we can figure out what we need to
take away from Y, the one that now has more, and add to X,
the one that now has less – like this: how much is X short of
5 the average? That's the amount we need to add to it. How
much is Y larger than the average? That's what we need to take
away from it.

Let's say we have three equal lines,[16] AA', BB', CC'. Now let's take away a section, AE, from AA' and add it to CC' (mark that as C'D), so that now the whole length CD is longer than EA' by both the length of C'D and the length of CF. That means CD is longer than BB' [the average] by the length of C'D.

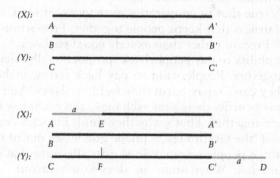

The terms 'loss' and 'profit' originally come from the context 11 of willing exchange. To make a profit means to get more than is yours, and to make a loss is to have less than you did before, e.g. in buying and selling stuff, and any other dealings where the law 15 sets no restrictions on us.[17] And when people don't get either more or less through their dealings, but just the same, then they say that they haven't made a loss or a profit, and just have 'what's theirs'. From that, fairness in the context of unwilling interactions is likewise a mid-point between a 'profit' (of a sort) and a 'loss'. It's when what you end up with is equal to what you had before. 20

5 Some people think that fairness is simply a matter of reciprocity. That's what the Pythagoreans said. They defined fairness simply as 'doing unto others as they've done unto you'. But reciprocity doesn't work either for distributive or compensatory fairness – even though they'd have us believe that Rhadamanthus[18] himself defined it that way: 25

> Let him suffer each one of the things that he did.
> That will serve a man perfectly right.

It doesn't work, because in lots of cases it gives an obviously
odd result. If a man with authority over you strikes you, for
example, it doesn't follow that you should hit him back. And if
a subordinate strikes his superior, he shouldn't *just* get a return
30 slap. He also needs to be punished.[19] Also, it makes a big difference whether or not something was done wilfully.

But it's true that in cooperative exchanges, at least, it's this
form of fairness that keeps people together. Proportional reciprocity,[20] I mean, rather than exactly equal payback.

It's the ability to pay people back (proportionally) that holds
society together. People want to pay back harm, or benefits.
1133a And if they can't repay harm they feel like slaves. And if they
can't repay benefits there's no exchange, and exchange is what
holds them together. That's why they think Eteocles even built
a temple of 'the Gratitudes',[21] [made goddesses out of them]:*
to encourage people to repay [his] gifts. Because that's gratitude's function. When someone does you a favour – {earns
your gratitude} – you're then obliged to do them a favour in
5 return, and to take the initiative the next time round.

[Translator's note: *In what follows there are two versions of
the same section of the discussion, including two similar diagrams. In the first version, I offer different stages of the diagram;
in the second, only its final stage.*]

[Version A]
And what makes for a proportional exchange of goods is coupling the terms along the diagonals of our square, like this:

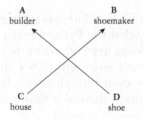

So the builder has to get the shoemaker's product from the
10 shoemaker and give him his own product in exchange. So as

long as proportional equality is in place first, and then they reciprocate, you'll have what we're talking about. Otherwise the [trade] is unequal and the partnership unworkable. Because, of course, one of the products [e.g. a house] may well be more valuable than the other [e.g. a pair of shoes].

[*We may assume that Aristotle indicates the relative values of house and shoes.*]

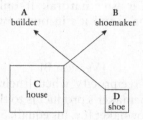

So their goods have to be equalized.[22] † . . . † Because of course 15 cooperative partnerships like this aren't between a doctor and another doctor. They're between, say, a doctor and a farmer, and in general between people who are different and [in that sense] unequal. OK, so they've got to be equalized. So we have to have some way of comparing all the things they exchange. And that's what money was invented for. It serves as a sort of middle {or 20 medium of exchange}. Money can measure anything. So it can measure the higher and lower values of two products – hence, how many shoes are equal to a house, say, or a supply of food.

So what builder is to shoemaker,[23] *x* number of shoes has to be to a house, or supply of food. If that isn't the case, there'll be no exchange, no partnership, {no cooperation}. And it won't be the case unless their goods can somehow be made equal.

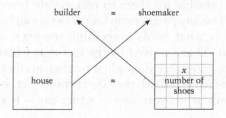

25 That's why everything has to be measured by a common unit, as we said. And that common unit is money. Well, strictly speaking, it's need. Need is what binds the whole community together. If people didn't have any needs (or didn't have the same needs as they do), then either there wouldn't be any exchange at all, or there wouldn't be the same kind of exchange. But by convention we've created a sort of token of need, and 30 that's what money is. (That's why [in Greek] we call money *nomisma*. Because it isn't natural. It only exists by social convention – *nomos* – and it's in our power to change it or make it worthless.)

[Version B]

There can only be reciprocity when [their goods] are equalized, so that the shoemaker's product is to the farmer's product 1133b what farmer is to shoemaker [i.e. his equal]. So they have to bring their goods* into a proportional relation when they trade.[24] Otherwise, one or other of them [farmer or shoemaker] – here at the top – will get an advantage over the other, both ways.[25] But when their goods are (in some sense) equalized, that way they can be equals; and hence also partners because that equality can be brought about between them:*

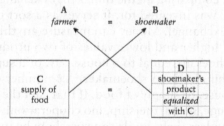

5

If it weren't possible for them to reciprocate [proportionally], there couldn't be any partnership {or cooperation} between them.

And need is what holds everything together, as a kind of common unit. That's proved by the fact that when two people don't need one another (i.e. when neither needs the other, or one doesn't need the other), they don't trade. E.g. it's only when someone needs what you have – wine, say – that they trade

with you, e.g. by giving you their exports of grain † . . . † And for 10
the purpose of future exchange, in the case of someone who
doesn't need your goods right now, we use money, as a sort of
promise[26] that he'll be able to get them when he does need
them. The idea is, when he brings that money [and pays], he's
got to be able to take them.

Of course, the very same thing happens to money, too. It
doesn't always have the same value.[27] But it does tend to be a
bit more stable.

That's why everything has to be given a price. Because that 15
ensures that exchange will always be possible, and, with
exchange, partnership {and cooperation}.

So money is a sort of unit of measure that equalizes goods by
making them commensurable. There could be no cooperation
without exchange; no exchange without goods being equal; and
that can't happen without their being commensurable.

Of course it's impossible for goods that are so different to be
truly commensurable. But it can be done well enough to serve 20
our needs.

So we need a common unit: money. (An arbitrary one – that's
why we call it *nomisma*.) Money makes everything commensurable, because everything can be measured in money:

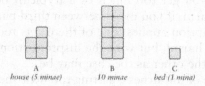

A   B   C
house (5 minae)   *10 minae*   *bed (1 mina)*

A is half of B, if five *minae* is the value of, or equal to, one
house. And the bed, C, is a tenth of B. So that makes it obvious 25
how many beds are equal to one house. Five. (And it's obvious
that that's how all trading was done [i.e. by use of a common
unit of some kind] even before the existence of money. Because
it doesn't make any difference whether we swap five beds, or
whatever five beds are worth, for a house.)

*

All right, so we've now said what it is for [outcomes] to be fair, and unfair.

30   And now that we've defined those, it's clear that fair dealing is a middle. Namely, it's the mid-point between giving someone else an unfair deal and getting an unfair deal. Because one of those means getting more than you should, and the other means getting less.

And being a fair *person* is a middle state, of a sort. But not quite in the same way as the other virtues. It's a middle only in the sense that it produces a middle.[28] (And unfairness produces 1134a both extremes.) That's to say, fairness is the disposition that makes you reliably do what's fair, by choice, i.e. share out goods (whether between yourself and someone else, or between third parties) in such a way that you don't get more of the desir-5 able good and the other person less of it (or vice versa if it's something harmful); you get a proportionately equal amount. Likewise between third parties.

Unfairness is the opposite: [it makes you choose] unfair outcomes. And what's unfair is someone getting too much, or too little, of something beneficial or harmful; a disproportionate amount.

That's why unfairness is both an overshoot *and* a shortfall: because it produces an overshoot and a shortfall. If you use it 10 on yourself, you get too much of a (typical) benefit and too little of the harm; if you use it between third parties, the same general description applies [one of them gets too much benefit and too little harm], but with the disproportion going against one party or the other as the case may be.

For any act of unfairness, getting too little means getting an unfair deal; and getting [or awarding] too much means dealing unfairly, {treating someone unfairly}.

So that's all we need to say for now about fairness and 15 unfairness [as character traits] and the nature of each, and about what's a fair and what's an unfair outcome in general terms.

[*When does doing wrong make you an
unrighteous person?*][29]

6 Since you can do wrong without yet being an unrighteous person, {'wrongdoer'}, what sort of wrongs do you need to commit to qualify as a wrongdoer {or 'criminal'} for each class of wrongdoing? To be, for example, a thief, an adulterer, a bandit?

Or do your actions per se not make the difference? After all, a man could sleep with someone's wife, knowingly, but in a moment of passion rather than by deliberate choice. So that means he does wrong without yet being an unrighteous person {or a criminal}. 'He's not a thief but, yes, he did steal something', or 'He's not an adulterer but, yes, he did sleep with that guy's wife.'

† . . . So we have discussed (earlier) the relationship between reciprocal exchanges and fairness. But let's not forget that . . . †

[Right and wrong derive from the laws of a community of equals]

What we're now investigating is right and wrong in their standard sense, and that means right and wrong between citizens.

That means between people living together in a self-sustaining community of free and equal partners (either fully equal[30] or equals by proportion).

It follows that whenever people don't stand in that relationship to one another, no right or wrong exists between them such as exists between citizens; just, [at best], some sort of right and wrong, by resemblance to it. Right and wrong [only] exist for people subject to law; and [conversely] laws only arise among people who can do one another wrong.[31] (Courts of law pass judgment on questions of right and wrong.) . . .

[Three miscellaneous points]

Being an unrighteous, {unethical} person[32] always implies doing wrong. But just doing wrong [e.g. once] doesn't always make you an unrighteous person.

[Being unfair] means assigning too much of the (normally) good things to yourself, and too little of the (normally) bad ones.

35   ... That's why [in a well-governed state] we don't allow any individual man to be sovereign; we give sovereignty to reason [in the form of law]. Because [when individuals rule] they do so
1134b   for themselves. They become tyrants. Instead a ruler [should be] a sort of guardian of what's right {and fair}; and that means a guardian of equality. And since he doesn't make a profit out of being such a guardian – at least not if he's a righteous, {honest} ruler – since he doesn't award himself a larger share of the typical goods (except in proportion to his merits), it follows
5   that he's working [not for himself but] for others. (That's why they say being a righteous man is 'a good thing for other people' – as we said earlier.) So he has to be given some sort of reward, then. And the reward is respect and prestige. And if those kinds of things aren't enough for someone ... that's when people become tyrants.[33]

[Right and wrong derive from the laws of a community of equals, continued]

... Right and wrong between master and slave,[34] by contrast, or between father and child, is not the same [as between citizens]. It's just somewhat similar. Because there's no way of
10   doing wrong to what's simply yours. And your chattel, or your child until it reaches a certain age and becomes independent, is effectively a part of you. And you can't intentionally harm yourself. So you can't wrong yourself. So no right or wrong exists between you and them – {you have no obligations[35] to them} – such as exists between citizens. Because that depends on law, and hence (we said) only exists for people who are natural partners under law, which means people who are equals
15   with respect to ruling and being ruled.

That's why you have obligations to your wife more than to your children and slaves. [She's more like an equal]. You have obligations to her as a husband[36] {and head of the household}. But that still isn't the same as right and wrong between citizens.

7 Right and wrong † between citizens † comes in two kinds:
natural, or based [purely] on law {and custom}.

What's naturally right has the same force everywhere, whether
or not people regard it as such. But with the kind based on law 20
{and custom}, well, at the start it doesn't really matter whether
things are done this way or that way; but it matters once people
establish the custom, e.g. that the price for releasing a pris-
oner is one *mina*, or that you have to sacrifice one goat rather
than, say, two sheep [to this or that god]; plus all the particular
little customs that cities establish (like offering sacrifices to
Brasidas); plus the [temporary] obligations created by special
decrees.

Some people think that's the only kind of right and wrong
that exists, since what's natural is invariable and has the same 25
force everywhere (fire, after all, burns just the same in Persia as
in Greece); and then they see all the variation in [what people
regard as] right and wrong.

That's not correct. But at the same time it's ... kind of
correct.

The fact is, in our world – maybe not in the divine realm,
where there's surely no change whatsoever – but here in our
human world some things are certainly natural, but everything
is subject to change {and variation}. Even so, some things are
natural and some aren't.   30

And while all of them could be some other way,[37] it's still
obvious which sort are naturally [right] and which sort are
based only on custom and convention, *not* nature – even if it's
true that both can vary, in much the same way.

The same kind of distinction will work in other areas as
well. The right hand, for example, is naturally the stronger;
and yet it's perfectly possible for everyone to be [trained to be]
ambidextrous.

Moral norms based on convention and expedience are like 35
units of measurement. The measures we use for wine and for 1135a
grain aren't the same size everywhere. (Buyers use larger ones,[38]
retailers use smaller ones.) Likewise with moral norms that are
man-made rather than natural: they're not the same everywhere, just as forms of government aren't all the same (although

5 there's only one form of government, everywhere, that's naturally the best.)

Each case of what's right or lawful works the way a universal
relates to particulars. There's just one of each – one universal –
and it covers lots of particular actions.

To say 'X is a wrongdoing' is different from saying 'X is wrong'.
And 'X is a right action' (*dikaiōma*) is not the same as 'X is
right' (*díkaion*). A thing is wrong, naturally or by some stipu-
10 lation, and then when somebody does it, that's a wrongdoing.
But until somebody does it it's not a wrongdoing yet. It's just
wrong. Likewise with a right action (*dikaiōma*).

(We usually call a right action, in the broad sense, a
dikaiopragēma. *Dikaiōma* means *righting* a wrong: making
amends for a wrongdoing.)[39]

† Let's think some more about each of these later, and figure
out what kinds of them there are, and how many, and what
they apply to. †

[*Different degrees of wilfulness in our right and wrong
actions imply different character-states*]

15 8 So, if the forms of right and wrong are as we've said,
somebody 'does wrong' or 'does the right thing' whenever
they do those things willingly {or wilfully}.
But when they do them unwillingly they aren't 'doing wrong'
or 'doing the right thing' – except incidentally. That is, they're
doing X, and X also happens to be right or wrong. Wrong-
20 doing, or doing the right thing, is determined by whether or not
it is wilful. When a wrong action is wilful people will blame
you for it, and that's also when it's 'a wrongdoing'. That means
that an action can be wrong, but not a wrongdoing – if it doesn't
have the extra element of being wilful.
By wilful I mean – as we explained earlier – anything you do
that's in your power and that you do knowingly and without

being mistaken about who you're doing it to, or what you're 25
doing it with, or about the result, etc. E.g. you know *who* you're
hitting, what you're hitting him *with* and *why*, and (in each
respect) it's not by accident or forced on you (like, say, if somebody took hold of your arm and hit somebody else [with *your*
arm], then that's not wilful because it's not in your power) ...
or, I don't know, maybe the person you hit is your own father,
and you know you're hitting someone, or 'one of the people
who was there', but you don't realize it's your father ... and 30
similar distinctions can be made about the intended result and
indeed the action as a whole.

So you're acting unwillingly:

(a) when you do something unknowingly {or by mistake}, or

(b) you're not doing it unknowingly, but it's not something
in your power, or

(c) when you're forced to do it.

(There are plenty of naturally occurring things that we do and
undergo knowingly, and none of those is wilful {or volun- 1135b
tary}* – like getting old or dying.)[40]

Also, doing something 'incidentally' applies, in the same
way, to doing right and doing wrong. Suppose a man pays back
some money he owes, but unwillingly, out of fear. We wouldn't
say that he's 'doing the right thing' or 'acting ethically' – except 5
incidentally. Conversely, if someone fails to pay back the money
because of circumstances beyond his control and thus *fails*
unwillingly, we'd now have to say that he's only 'wronging'
anyone {or 'cheating' anyone} or 'doing wrong' incidentally.

Of things we do willingly, some are also by choice, some
aren't. We act by choice whenever we act *after deliberating*; 10
and *not* by choice when it's *not* deliberate.

So there are three forms of doing harm in our dealings with
others.

(a) Harmful things that we do unknowingly are mistakes.
I.e. when you're confused about who you're doing something
to, or what you're doing, or what with, or the intended result.

E.g. you didn't think you were firing at someone; or firing at
him with one of those; or firing at *him*; or you didn't mean that
to happen (it just turned out that way, not the way you intended, 15

e.g. you didn't mean to wound him, just to prick him, or that wasn't who you meant to do it to, or what you meant to do it with).

When the resulting harm was very unlikely, that's a mishap {or unlucky accident}. If it wasn't unlikely but there was no malice involved, that's a mistake. A mistake is when the cause originates inside you; when the cause is external it's a mishap.[41]

20 (b) When you do something knowingly but without deliberating over it beforehand, that now does count as a wrongdoing, e.g. the wrongs we do out of anger or any other emotion {or state of mind} that's simply inevitable or natural for any normal human being. When people harm others in that way – when they err in those ways – yes, they're certainly doing wrong, and yes, those do count as wrongdoings {and crimes}, but they don't yet make you an unrighteous, {unethical} or evil person. Because the harm you do isn't a result of wickedness.

25 (c) When someone does the same things by deliberate choice, that does now mean that they're an unrighteous, {unethical} and wicked person.

That's why we're quite right not to judge things done from anger as premeditated. If a man acts in anger, he isn't the one who initiated his action. The guy who made him angry initiated his action. Also, [in a case like that], there's no argument afterwards over whether or not he did it, just about whether it was justified. Because his anger was a reaction to a perceived wrongdoing. It's not like in disputes over business dealings,

30 where people argue over what happened (and where one man or the other must be a crook, unless it's just because they can't remember)[42] – no, they agree on what happened and just argue over whether or not it was justified. So one of them feels he's been wronged and the other feels otherwise[43] (whereas a man who has deliberately done wrong [always] knows it).

1136a [So, as I was saying,] if you do harm by deliberate choice, then (a) you are doing wrong, and (b) that kind of wrongdoing also makes you an unrighteous person.[44] † . . . † And conversely, you're an {ethical or} righteous person if you do the right thing by deliberate choice. (And you're only 'doing the right thing' if you're acting willingly.)

Of things people do unwillingly, some we're inclined to forgive, 5
some not. We're inclined to forgive people for mistakes they make
unknowingly. [And I don't mean] when 'they aren't aware of their
actions'. When people make mistakes [in that way], *not* unknowingly, but because they 'aren't aware of their actions' as a result of
some emotion {or state of mind} that isn't natural or normal for a
human being – then we're *not* inclined to forgive them.

[*Can you be willingly wronged? Can you
wrong yourself?*]

9 So, if we've given a reasonably good account of what it is 10
to be wronged and to do wrong, one puzzle to consider
is whether what Euripides describes is possible, when he says,
absurdly,

A: I slew my mother! – the long and short of it.
B: Slew her? Wilfully? And she was willingly slain?
Or was the act against your will, and hers?

Can you really be willingly wronged, as that suggests? Or is 15
that impossible? Is being wronged always unwilling, just as
every case of doing wrong must be wilful?

And we might also ask if it has to be all one thing or all the
other? Maybe some cases are willing and some are unwilling.

The same question applies to being treated rightly, or {rightly
dealt with}. Because doing right by someone is always voluntary, too. But as for being dealt with rightly, it's surely absurd
to say that it's always willing. Some people are clearly unwilling to have what's right dealt out to them.

So it seems somewhat plausible that each pair of opposites
would work the same way, i.e. that both of them, being 20
wronged and being treated rightly, are sometimes willing and
sometimes unwilling.

And here's another puzzle. If it's true that what happened
to me was wrong, does that always mean that I've been
wronged?

Or can you be wronged incidentally,[45] just as you can inciden-
25 tally do wrong? After all, an action can be incidentally right,
both ways [i.e. whether you do it, or it happens to you]. Clearly
the same is true for wrongs: 'he's doing X, and X is wrong' is
not the same as 'he's doing wrong', and 'X happened to him,
and X was wrong' is not the same as 'he was wronged'. The
same goes for doing the right thing versus being the object of a
30 right action. It's impossible to be wronged unless somebody is
wronging you, or to have X rightly done to you, unless somebody is rightly doing X.

Doing wrong, in the ordinary sense, means willingly harming
someone, where willingly means knowingly (i.e. knowing who
you're harming, what with, how).
    But if you lack self-control you can willingly harm *yourself*.
So that would mean you can be willingly wronged; and it
makes it possible for you to wrong yourself. (That's another
1136b one of our questions here: Can you wrong yourself?)
    Plus, through a lack of self-control you might willingly allow
yourself to be harmed by someone else who willingly [inflicts
the harm]. So there again it seems possible to be willingly
wronged.
    Or was our definition of doing wrong incorrect? Maybe
it isn't just 'doing harm to someone, knowingly' (i.e. knowing
whom, what with, how); maybe we need to add that it has
5 to be contrary to what that person wants. In which case, yes,
someone can be willingly harmed and willingly submit to X
(where X is wrong), but nobody can ever be willingly wronged.
Because nobody wants to be wronged. Not even a man who
lacks self-control. A man like that acts contrary to what he
wants. Nobody wants what they don't think is good for them
[and think they shouldn't be doing], but a man who lacks self-
control[46] does things that he thinks he shouldn't be doing.
    When someone gives away his own things – like the way, in
10 Homer, Glaucon gives Diomedes 'gold armour for bronze, a
hundred-cow'orth for nine!' – he isn't being wronged; {he isn't
being cheated}. Because the giving of it is up to him. But being

wronged can't be up to you. There has to be someone wronging you.

So that's clear: you can't be willingly wronged.

Also, of the things we planned to talk about, here's two we can 15
do [at the same time]: (a) whether it's the person who awards
someone more than they deserve who's the wrongdoer, or the
person who then has it, and (b) whether it's possible to wrong
yourself.

Because if the first is possible, i.e. if the distributer is the
wrongdoer, and not the person who gets more than they should,
then if you knowingly and willingly assign more to someone
else than to yourself you're thereby wronging yourself; {being
unfair to yourself}.

But surely that's just what reasonable people do [all the 20
time]. Any kind and decent person typically takes less than
they're entitled to.

Or is it not quite as simple as that? Maybe (as the case may
be) they're really taking more, but more of a different kind of
good, like reputation, or more of what's simply honourable.

Also, the problem is solved anyway by our earlier definition of wrongdoing. [In that situation] nothing is happening
to you contrary to what you yourself want, which means that
you certainly aren't being wronged. At most, perhaps you're
being harmed; not wronged.   25

It's also obvious that the distributer is the wrongdoer, not the
person who thereby gets too much. The beneficiary of a wrongful [e.g. unfair] decision isn't thereby the wrongdoer. The
wrongdoer is whoever wilfully brings about that unfair situation. And that means whoever is the source of the action. And
the source of the action is the person who distributes the goods
unfairly, not the receiver – or not always.

Also:

(a) To 'bring about' can mean different things, and there's a
sense in which even inanimate objects can 'kill' someone, or 30
your hand can 'kill' someone, or a slave acting on his master's

instructions; [so the recipient], although he isn't *wronging* anyone, is still 'bringing about' things that *are* wrong.

(b) Also, if he judged the case without knowing all the facts,
then he hasn't [technically] done wrong and it isn't a wrongful
judgment according to the law. But it is still wrong in a sense.
(What's right according to the law is not the same as what's
absolutely right.)

(c) If, on the other hand, he knowingly makes a wrong-
1137a ful judgment, then he must be getting something out of it
himself: someone's gratitude; or perhaps revenge.[47] So just as
if he were to take a cut of [the profits of] the wrongdoing,
the man whose wrongful judgment has those motives behind
it gets more than he should. E.g. when A makes a corrupt
judgment (on condition of getting a cut) awarding the piece
of land to B, then, no, A doesn't get the land; but he does get
the money.

[*Doing right or wrong is not simply a matter of
physically doing certain things*]

5 People think that it's in their own power to do wrong [when-
ever they like], and for that reason they think doing what's
right is easy too.

Not so. I mean, yes, sleeping with your neighbour's wife,
punching someone, handing over that bribe – that's easily done
[physically speaking], and in our power. But doing those things
from a particular character-state is not easy, and not in our
power.[48]

10   In the same way, people also think there's nothing particularly clever about knowing right from wrong, since it's not so
hard to understand everything the law says. But that's not the
same as knowing what's right – except incidentally. You need
to know exactly *how* those things should be done, so as to
be right, or *how* things should be shared out, so as to be fair –
and that's a tough task. Harder than knowing what's healthy.
There, too, it's easy enough to know that honey and red wine
15 and hellebore and cauterizing and surgery keep people healthy;
but knowing how to dispense them so as to make someone

healthy, and to whom and when, that's a major task – if you can do that, you're a doctor.

For the same reason people think that a righteous person should be just as good at doing wrong as right, because, after all, a righteous person is just as capable (and maybe even more capable) of doing any of those things. He could sleep with someone else's wife. He could punch someone. And a brave 20 man could throw away his shield, turn and run in whatever direction he likes. But being a coward and doing wrong isn't the same as just [physically] doing those things – except incidentally. It's a matter of doing them from a particular state of character, just like the way being a doctor[49] and making people healthy isn't simply a matter of cutting someone open or not cutting them open, giving them a drug or not giving them 25 the drug – it's a matter of doing those things in a very particular way.

[Right and wrong is tied to the human condition]

Right and wrong only applies at all to those who
  (a) can have some share of (normally) good things, and
  (b) can also have too much of them or too little.

For some, (the gods, surely), it's impossible to have too much of them. For some (e.g. people who are incurably evil), it's impossible to have any amount of any kind of benefit (because everything harms them). But some – [normal human beings] – can have them up to a point.

That's why right and wrong is a human thing.   30

10 Next we should talk about being kind and decent;[50] and [what we mean by] the kind and decent thing [to do], and how being a kind and decent person relates to being simply righteous, and how what's kind or decent relates to what's right.

Because if you think about it, they don't seem to be simply the same thing, or truly distinct from one another either.

Sometimes we praise a 'kind' or 'decent' action and a 'kind 35 and decent' man. (We even apply the term 'decent' to other

1137b things as well, as a term of general approval – i.e. meaning simply 'good' – clearly implying, the more decent, the better.)[51]

On the other hand, if you think it through logically, it seems absurd if the kind and decent thing to do deviates from what's right and yet is still praiseworthy. Because that either means that doing the right thing isn't good; or that doing the kind and decent thing isn't right – if it's different from what's right.

5   Or if they're both good, surely they must just be the same thing?

So those are the points – I think that's about all of them – that make the idea of what's 'kind' or 'decent' a little puzzling.

In fact these ideas are all correct in a sense. They don't contradict one another. At all. Because the kind and decent thing to do *is* the right thing to do. But it's right by being better than one particular form of what's right.

And it's better than what's right without being distinct from it.

10   So the 'kind and decent' thing, and the right thing, are the same. And they're both good. But kind and decent is better.

What causes the puzzle is the fact that doing the kind, decent thing is also certainly right, but it's not [always] the right thing strictly according to the law. Rather, it's an amelioration of what's strictly right according to the law.

The reason for that is that every law has to be stated in general terms, but with some things it isn't possible for it to be perfect in that general form. So in cases where we're forced to

15   state general rules and it's impossible for [a general rule] to be perfect, the law assumes what will usually be the case, fully aware that by doing so it introduces a flaw. And it might well still be a perfectly well-drafted law. The shortcoming isn't in the law or the lawmaker. It's in the nature of the thing itself. It's just a question of the basic stuff that all practical questions are made of. So when the law states a general rule, and then

20   something happens that goes against [the intent of] that general rule in that particular case, it's entirely proper, where the original lawmaker fell short and got it wrong, by stating it in general terms, to correct the shortcoming: 'This is what the lawmaker himself would have said if he were here in person';

or 'That's how he would have drafted the law if he knew [that it would lead to this problem].'

That's why doing the 'kind and decent' thing is certainly right, but at the same time actually better than (one form of) what's right. It's not better than the unqualified, [general] rule 25 itself. It's just better than the imperfection caused by its very lack of qualification.

And that's the fundamental nature of being kind and decent: it's a corrective to law, in so far as law is always imperfect for being stated in general terms.

That's also why not everything [rulers and lawmakers do] can be done through law in the first place. With some things it's impossible to draft a law that covers them. So then you need a special, one-off decree. Because for indeterminate matters you need an indeterminate standard, like those lead 30 rulers used by builders in Lesbos:[52] the ruler isn't rigid; it flexes to the shape of the stone – and a one-off decree can be fitted to events.

So it's now clear what we mean by what's 'kind and decent'; and it's clear that it's both right and at the same time better than (one form of) what's right.

And that should make it obvious what it is to be a kind, decent person. A kind and decent person is simply someone 35 who reliably chooses and does those sorts of things and who, instead of being rigid about what's right (in a way that makes 1138a things worse), tends to demand a little less than they're entitled to, even when they have the law on their side.

That character trait is kindness; decency. It's just a [better] way of being righteous, not a separate trait.

[*Can you wrong yourself? Second discussion.*]

11 As for whether or not it's possible to wrong yourself, that should be clear from what we've already said. [But here are some more arguments.]

Some things that are *díkaia* [in the broader sense, 'right'] are 5 the sort ordained by law in accordance with every way of being a good person.

And the law orders us not to take our own lives (and what it orders us not to do, it forbids).*

And when someone wilfully inflicts harm (not in retaliation) he's doing wrong. And he's doing it wilfully if he knows who he's harming, and what with, etc.

And a man who kills himself, out of anger, does so wil-
10 fully and contrary to the law* – he does something the law doesn't permit. So that means he's doing wrong. But who is he wronging?

Is the answer that he wrongs his city, but not himself? After all, he's a willing victim, and nobody can be wronged willingly. And that's why it's the city that punishes him: when a man has taken his own life he suffers a kind of public disgrace for his wrong against the city.

And with the [other] kind of *ádikon* – the kind that only
15 makes someone an unfair person, but not an all-round bad person – it's impossible to wrong yourself [i.e. it's impossible to deal unfairly with yourself].

(Note that this kind of *adikía* is indeed distinct from the other,[53] [general] kind. There's a way of being *ádikos* that implies one particular moral failing, [namely, being an unfair person], on a par with, say, being a coward, and doesn't imply all-round badness.)

So, with that kind of *adikía* [unfairness], no, you can't wrong yourself. Because that would mean you getting X and having X taken from you at the very same time.[54] And that's impos-sible. Fair and unfair actions always have to play out between
20 at least two people.

Also, [wrongdoing] has to be wilful, deliberate and un-provoked – the last, because someone who acts because a wrong was done to him, and does the same thing in return, isn't seen as doing wrong.

But if you wrong *yourself*, you're [literally] doing the very same thing that's being done to you.[55] [So it's retaliation. So it's not wrong.]

Also, that would make it possible to be willingly wronged.

And on top of all those, here's another reason. You can't 'do
25 wrong' except by one of the particular forms of wrongdoing.

But you can't commit adultery with your own wife; or break
and enter into your own house; or steal your own stuff.

And in general the idea of doing wrong to yourself is also
ruled out by our earlier definition anyway – when we talked
about whether you can be wronged willingly.

[Doing wrong is worse for you than being wronged – usually]

Obviously being wronged, and doing wrong, are both bad things.
† ... †* Even so, doing wrong is worse [for you]. Because doing 30
wrong involves you being a bad person and is reprehensible – it
implies you're either completely, absolutely bad, or getting there
(maybe not every wilful wrongdoing makes you a [fully] unrighteous person).

But being wronged doesn't involve you being a bad person,
or an unrighteous, {unethical} person. So in itself being 35
wronged is the lesser of the two evils.

Having said that ... there's nothing to say being wronged 1138b
can't sometimes be worse for you, through some turn of events.

[Here's a parallel. Medicine tells us that] a lung infection is
a much worse illness than stubbing your toe. And yet ...
though of course this has nothing to do with the medical
facts ... stubbing your toe could turn out worse, through some
turn of events – like, say, if you stub your toe, [stumble] and,
because you stumbled, end up being captured or killed by the 5
enemy.[56]

[You can wrong yourself in a metaphorical sense]

In a metaphorical sense, or by analogy, you have obligations to
yourself; or not to yourself exactly, but maybe to some of the
parts of yourself. The analogy isn't even with every kind of
obligation. Just those of a master and a husband. Because it's
in those relations[57] that the rational part of the soul is set over
the irrational part.

So some people reflect on that, and think you can [in a sense] 10
wrong yourself – because one part of you can do things to

another part that go against its {wishes or} desires. So just as ruler and ruled have obligations to one another, so do the different parts of the self.

All right, there, so that completes our account of being *díkaios* {being righteous, being fair} and of all the other virtues – of character, that is.

BOOK VI

We claimed earlier that you've always got to choose 'the middle' and avoid going too far or falling short, and that the middle is set by correct reason. Let's explain what we mean by 20 that.

So, for all the dispositions of character we've talked about (and for that matter all others, too) there's a sort of target that someone who possesses reason aims for as they increase or decrease their efforts; a sort of . . . [sense of the] boundary of those middle states that we say lie between going too far and falling short, determined by 'correct reason'.

So, when we put it that way, what we're saying is certainly 25 true. But very vague.

I mean, in other pursuits too – all those that involve any kind of knowledge – it's a truism that you have to exert yourself or ease off, {just the right amounts}, 'the middle amount' – not too much and not too little – and 'as correct reason says'. But if that was all you had to go on, you'd be none the wiser . . . say, about what substances exactly to apply to your body, if 30 someone said 'the ones medical expertise says you should' or 'the ones determined by the expert doctor'. That's why it's important here as well, in talking about dispositions of soul, not to just make this [vague] claim – true as it is – and leave it at that. We've also got to make sure we've determined exactly what 'correct reason' is, and how we define it.

All right, so earlier we divided up virtues of the soul into two classes. We said that some are character virtues, {moral virtues}, and some are intellectual virtues.

So now that we've completed our account of character

virtues, it's time for us to say something about the remainder, after first saying something about the soul. So let's do that.

So, earlier we said that there are two parts of the soul: the
5 part with reason and the irrational part. Now we need to divide up the rational part itself in the same way.

Let's start from the idea that there are really two parts that 'possess reason': one that we use to contemplate all those kinds of facts whose {causes and} principles cannot possibly be other than they are, and one that we use to contemplate things that can be otherwise. (Because for each of those two different kinds of things there's a corresponding part of the soul, itself differ-
10 ent in kind, naturally suited to the one or the other – if it's by a sort of sameness or relatedness that each part is able to be conscious of its object.)

Let's call one of these the 'scientific' part and one the 'calculating' part (deliberating is the same as calculating, and nobody deliberates about things that can't possibly be otherwise).

That means the calculating part[1] is just one aspect of the rational part of the soul.

15 So we need to get a sense of what's the best possible state for each of these parts to be in. Because that's also the distinctive virtue of each, or what it is for it to be good at its designated task.

2 So, there are three things in the soul that are in control of action and truth: perception, cognition, desire.

Of those, perception isn't ever a source of action. That's
20 clear from the fact that the lower animals have perception but don't share the capacity for action.

Affirmation and denial in [practical] thought have to have their desire equivalents: pursuing X and avoiding X.[2]

So if a virtue of character is a disposition to reliably make certain choices, and a choice is a desire shaped through deliberation, it follows that for a choice to be a good choice,

(a) reason has to be [saying something] true, and

(b) desire has to be correct,

25 and what reason is asserting has to match what desire is pursuing.

That's how it works with practical thought and practical

truth, {truth about what you should do}. Purely contemplative thought, by contrast, unconnected with doing anything or making anything, succeeds or fails just by being true or false. That's the goal of every part that thinks: [truth]. But for the part that not only thinks but is also involved with doing, it's truth in agreement with correct desire. 30

The starting point of an action (in the sense of its efficient cause, not its purpose) is choice. And the starting point of choice itself is desire combined with goal-directed reason. That's why you can't have choice unless you have both (a) cognition and thought *and* (b) disposition of character. Doing well or badly in our actions is impossible without a combination of thought 35 and character. Thought on its own doesn't move {or motivate} anything. Only goal-directed thought, practical thought, can [move us]. (Practical thought also governs thoughts about making. Anyone who makes something does so with a goal. But the 1139b thing they're making isn't their overall goal. It's always relative to, or part of, something else. The thing they're *doing* is their overall goal.)[3]

Doing well – that's [always] your goal. And that's the object of desire.[4]

That's why choice is either cognition-tied-to-desire, or desire-tied-to-thought.[5] That's the distinctive human way[6] of being a 5 cause of things.

† Nothing that's past can be an object of choice. You can't choose to have sacked Troy. Because you can't deliberate about the past, either. You can only deliberate about things that are still going to happen and that might come to be. But what's happened can't *not* have happened. That's why Agathon's couplet is right:

> The only power that even heaven lacks: 10
> To change the past, to make what's done undone.†

So the task of both of the thinking parts of the soul is truth. So whatever states enable each to grasp truth the most are the specific virtues corresponding to each part.

3 All right, let's go back a bit and begin our account of them again.

15   Let's say that there are five faculties in all where the soul hits the truth {or gets it right} in its affirmations and denials: (a) technical skill, (b) scientific knowledge, (c) wisdom, (d) [higher] philosophical knowledge and (e) [direct] cognition.

But not belief and opinion, because those can sometimes be entirely false.

So what do we mean by scientific knowledge? Well, if we're going to be precise about it (ignoring merely related uses [of the term 'knowledge']) we might make it clear like this: we
20 all assume that if we scientifically know X, then X cannot possibly be otherwise (whereas with things that can be otherwise, once they're outside our observation we lose track of whether they are or aren't the case). Hence an object of science must be a necessary truth. Hence it must be an eternal truth, because strictly necessary truths are also always eternal. And by eternal truth we mean things that don't ever come to be or cease being the case.

25   Also, we assume all science is teachable, and that whatever can be scientifically known can also be learned. And all teaching has to be based on things you already know (as we explain in the *Analytics*) because it arises either by induction or deduction. And of those, induction is the source of our universal scientific principles, and then deduction works from those uni-
30 versals. That means there are principles that are the basis of our deductions that aren't themselves arrived at by deduction. By induction, then.

So scientific knowledge is the condition [of mind] arrived at through proof, plus all the other qualifications we set out in the *Analytics* (e.g. that it's only when you trust your starting points in a particular way, and they're known to you in that particular way, that you have scientific knowledge. If they weren't any more known to you than the conclusion, scientific
35 knowledge would be accidental.)[7]

All right, so that'll do as our definition of scientific knowledge.

4 Of the set of things that can be otherwise, some are also 1140a
   things we can make; and some are things we can do.

But making and doing are two different things. On that point we can follow common sense. So that means that the disposition to do things in a reason-guided way must be different from an ability to make something in a reason-guided way. So it isn't even the case that one includes the other. Doing isn't 5 even a form of making. Making isn't even a form of doing.

Now, a builder's technical skill, say, is a clear case of 'an ability to make something in a reason-guided way'.

In fact, every technical skill {or expertise} is an ability to make something in a reason-guided way. And conversely, every such ability is a skill. So it looks like a technical skill precisely *is* an ability to make something in a reason-guided way.   10

Every technical skill is concerned with creating, i.e. with considering and contriving how something or other – something that can either be or not be – can be brought into being, assuming that the source [of its existence] depends on the maker, not on the thing being made. (No skill creates things that are as they are or come into being by physical necessity or naturally. 15 Those things have the source of their existence in themselves.)

And since making is different from doing, it follows, unavoidably, that technical skill {and expertise} is concerned with making, not with doing[8] {or action}. Plus, in a sense skill and luck cover the same domain, as Agathon says: 'Skill's the friend of luck, and luck of skill.'

So technical skill {or expertise}, as we've said, is an ability 20 to make something, using reason, getting it right; and lack of skill the opposite:[9] a disposition to make something, using reason and get it wrong. Both are concerned only with things that can be other than they are.

5 What about wisdom?
   Perhaps we can get a sense of what wisdom is by considering the kinds of people we call wise.   25

All right, so we think of a wise person as someone who's able to deliberate well, {make good decisions}, about what's good for them and what's in their interests; and not just particulars,

like what's going to make them healthy or strong, but what kinds of things make for a good life in general. In support of that, notice that we call people 'wise' even in a particular field[10] when they succeed at figuring out how to achieve an important
30 goal that isn't a matter of their expertise. That suggests that, in the general sense as well, to be wise is to be good at deliberating {or a good decision-maker}.

But nobody deliberates about things that can't possibly be otherwise, or that it's impossible for them to do anything about.

So, given that (1) scientific knowledge involves proof, and (2) you can't prove X if the principles from which we derive X
35 could have been otherwise (because then X itself could always
1140b have been otherwise) and (3) you can't deliberate about things that are necessarily the way they are, it follows that wisdom is not a form of scientific knowledge or technical expertise. It isn't a science, because things we do, by definition, can be otherwise; and it isn't technical, because [as we just explained] doing and making are two separate categories. Because any case of making something has to have some further, separate goal. But that's not the case with doing, where doing well is itself the goal.[11]

So that leaves us with this: wisdom is a truth-hitting, rational,
5 action-guiding disposition concerned with what's good and bad for human beings.

That's why we think of Pericles, and men like that, as wise: wise people have a talent for discerning what's good, for themselves and for human beings in general, and we regard
10 good family men, and good statesmen, as exactly fitting that description.

That also explains why [in Greek] we call moderation sōphrosunē: because it preserves [sōzei] our wisdom[12] [phronēsis]. But what it 'preserves' is those kinds of notions. Pleasure and pain don't mess up or distort just any notion at all, like, say, the notion that the internal angles of a triangle
15 add up to two right angles. They only disrupt your ideas about what you should or shouldn't be doing. Because the starting point for action is the purpose of the things you're doing, and

when someone is corrupted by pleasure or pain, then from the outset they fail to see that starting point, so then they also don't see that they should be choosing and doing all the other things for that purpose and for that reason.

That's what being a bad person does to you. It warps your [ethical] starting points.

So it follows that wisdom must be[13] a rational, truth-sensitive 20 disposition that guides our actions with respect to what's good for human beings.

[Resuming the claim that wisdom is not a technical expertise]

What's more, you can be good at a technical skill, but you'd never say 'he's good at being wise'.[14]

Plus, in the case of technical skill, it's actually better to be someone who makes a mistake on purpose.[15] But with wisdom, as with [character] virtues, that's not the case. So it's clear that wisdom is a kind of [character] virtue, not a technical skill.

There are two parts of the soul that possess reason, and wis- 25 dom seems to be the virtue specific to one of them, namely the part that forms beliefs. Because belief is concerned with what could be otherwise, and so is wisdom. But it isn't a purely rational quality. That's clear from the fact that you can forget those kinds of [purely intellectual] abilities,[16] but you don't forget your wisdom.   30

6 Scientific knowledge is all about what's universal and necessarily the case; and there are starting points, {first principles}, for whatever we prove, and hence for all scientific knowledge, because all such knowledge is supported by reasons. So that means the principles from which we derive what we know scientifically can't themselves be objects of our scientific knowledge;[17] or for that matter of technical expertise or wisdom, because what can be known scientifically can be 35 proved [and hence is necessarily the case] and both those concern things that could be otherwise. And we can't have [higher] 1141a

philosophical knowledge of them either, since that always involves proving at least some things.

So if the four faculties which hit the truth, and which [by definition] cannot be wrong (whether it's about things that can or cannot be otherwise), are scientific knowledge, wisdom, 5 philosophical knowledge and direct cognition, and if it can't be any of those three ('those three' being wisdom, scientific knowledge or philosophical knowledge) that just leaves direct cognition.

We must directly intuit[18] the first principles [of science].

7 As for *sophia*, well, [by one use of the term] we attribute it to the most exact, {consummate} craftsmen {and artists}. 10 So, we might say that Phidias is *sophos*, '{a master} mason', or that Polycleitus is *sophos*, '{a master} sculptor'. In that context what we mean by *sophia* is technical virtuosity.

But we also think of some people as having a general sort of *sophia* [higher philosophical knowledge], as opposed to *sophia* at some particular thing . . . like when Homer says Margites isn't *sophos*, {a master}, 'at anything else':

15   He couldn't handle a spade –
               'cos that wasn't the way the gods made him –
         Nor could he master a plough –
               or anything else for that matter.

So this [older sense, 'precise technical mastery'], implies that *sophia* – [in its new sense, 'philosophical knowledge'] – should be the most exact of all the sciences.[19] So it requires us not just to know the things that we derive from our first principles, but to grasp [by induction] the truth of the first principles themselves. So that makes [higher] philosophical knowledge a combination of direct cognition[20] and scientific knowledge.

It is scientific knowledge crowned, so to speak, by having the most exalted things that exist as its subject matter.

20   It's absurd to imagine that statesmanship, or wisdom, is the best kind of knowledge there is, when human beings are far from the best thing in the cosmos.

Also, if 'healthy' or 'good' means one thing for fish and something quite different for human beings, while what's white or straight is always the same, then having philosophical knowledge [i.e. of metaphysics, theology, physics] will always mean the same thing, but 'being wise' will mean something different [for different species]. Anything that's good at per- 25 ceiving all its own interests would qualify as 'wise', and that [species] will be the authority on its interests. That's why people even call[21] some wild animals 'wise': the ones that evidently have the capacity to anticipate their needs {and make provisions} for their survival.

Another reason it's obvious that philosophical knowledge [e.g. metaphysics, theology, physics] is not the same thing as statesmanship {or moral and political wisdom}: if knowing what's beneficial to one's own [species] is going to count as 30 'philosophical knowledge',[22] then there'll be multiple forms of philosophical knowledge – [which is absurd].[23] There won't be just one, encompassing what's good for all animals. There'll be a different version for each [species] of animal, just as there isn't a unified medical knowledge for all living things.*

And even if human beings are the best of all animals – so what? There are still other things in the universe far more divine in their nature. To give only the most obvious examples, 1141b the constituents of the cosmos.

So it's clear from all we've said that *sophia* – [i.e. knowledge of metaphysics, theology, physics] – is a combination of scientific knowledge and [direct] cognition, applied to things that are by their nature the most exalted things in the cosmos.

That's why people say that Anaxagoras, Thales and men like that are 'great philosophers', {'geniuses'}, but don't think of them as wise, because they see that they're clueless about their 5 own best interests. 'Yes, the things they know are extraordinary and amazing and difficult and marvellous – but useless, because they aren't investigating what's good for human beings.'

Wisdom is all about human concerns. Stuff you can deliberate about. That's the defining talent of a wise person: to be good at deliberating; {good at decision-making}. And nobody 10 deliberates about things that cannot possibly be otherwise, or

about things that don't involve a goal: specifically, some good
thing that can be achieved by doing something. A good decision-
maker in the general sense is someone good at homing in on
the highest of human goods achievable by doing things.

15   Wisdom isn't just about general principles either. You also
have to know the particular facts. Because it determines what
we do. And doing is all in the particulars. That's why sometimes people can be ignorant of some general principle but still
more likely to do the right thing than people who know it –
notably, people with experience. If someone knows, say, that
'lean meat is easy on the stomach, and healthy' but doesn't
know which particular kinds of meat are lean, they're not
20   going to eat healthily. The person who only knows that chicken
is healthy is more likely to do the healthy thing.

But wisdom determines what you actually do. So that means
you need both kinds of knowledge, or the particular kind more
so. Though of course even here there can be general, master-
plan wisdom, too.

8   Being a good statesman, {or a good leader}, and being wise,
are the same character trait, but different aspects of it. And
even in the political sphere wisdom takes two forms: the
25   general, master-plan kind is legislative wisdom, the day-to-day
kind gets the name that really applies to both: statesmanship,
{politics}. And that involves action as well as deliberation. Passing a decree, for example, is an action in the first-step sense.
That's why only those people are called 'statesmen'. It's because
they're the only ones doing things. They're the hands-on craftsmen [of public life].

30   'Wisdom' is most naturally thought of as applying to yourself, to the individual, and so that's what we usually mean by
the general term 'wisdom.' But there are those other kinds too:
wisdom in managing your family, in lawmaking, in politics;
and the last includes both deliberative and judicial wisdom.

So, really, knowing what's good for you is just one particular form of wisdom. But it's a very distinct form of it, so there's
1142a this idea that a man who knows his own interests and 'minds
his own business' is thereby wise, whereas statesmen [who are,

by definition, concerned about other people's lives] are seen as
'busybodies'. Hence those lines in Euripides:

> How unwise I've been! I must be mad!
> I could have stayed out of trouble,
> been a grunt, one of the troops, content with my equal share.   5
> [People hate] a man who sticks out from the crowd,
> and does something special . . .

He means people look to their own interests, and assume that's
what we ought to do. From that attitude you get the idea that
that's what it is to be wise.

But does that make sense? Surely your own interests can't
be well served if you [only think about yourself]; if you aren't
also a family man, and a citizen. Also, exactly how you should   10
manage your own affairs[24] is not obvious; you have to think
about it.

[Resuming the claim that wisdom is not an abstract science; it requires experience of life]

Another bit of evidence for this claim is the fact that young
people can certainly learn geometry and mathematics and become
brilliant at that kind of thing, but we don't think the young
can be wise. The reason for that is that wisdom requires knowing the details of life, and we only become acquainted with
those through experience, and experience is exactly what young   15
people don't have. It's sheer quantity of time that gives you
experience. The same thing explains that other curious fact:
why is it that children can be good at mathematics but not at
[metaphysics, theology] or the natural sciences? Is it because
mathematics studies things in abstraction [from the physical
world] whereas the principles of those other subjects have to
come from experience? Children can recite that stuff, but they
don't believe it. But in mathematics all the basic concepts are   20
easy enough to grasp.

Also, you can be wrong about either the universal or the
particular in deliberating. For example, you might not know

that 'high-density water isn't drinkable' or not realize that 'this water here is high-density'.

It's also clear that wisdom isn't a science from the fact that it has to grasp the ultimate facts, the particulars. Because those
25 are the stuff of action. So that means wisdom is at the opposite end of the process from direct cognition. Direct cognition, at one end, gives us our [general] concepts, which are not deduced from anything, and wisdom, at the other, grasps particular facts.[25] And they're not deduced scientifically either. They're something we just perceive. I don't mean the way we perceive qualities specific to each sense [e.g. colours, sounds, tastes]. I mean the way we perceive, say, in a mathematical proof, that this particular shape here is a triangle. Because at that end of the process too there's a point where [explanation] just has to stop. Of course, that's more perception than wisdom; but a
30 different form of perception.

9   Problem-solving and decision-making aren't the same thing. Decision-making is a particular form of problem-solving. We need a sense here of what good decision-making is.

Is it a matter of having some sort of scientific knowledge, or belief? Is it the same as being sharp and quick-witted? Or some other kind of thing?

So, to begin with, it isn't knowledge. With things we know,
1142b there's nothing for us to work out. But good decision-making is deliberation, and when you're deliberating you are working things out, {problem-solving}, figuring something out.

Then again, it isn't just a matter of being quick-witted, either. That doesn't involve reasoning and is on the spot, whereas people spend a long time deliberating, and they say 'Decide slowly, then act quickly.'
5   Being a quick, shrewd observer is also not the same as good decision-making. It's just a form of being quick-witted.

Good decision-making is also not equivalent to having any particular belief.

Here's a better idea. Since someone who deliberates badly {or makes bad decisions} is thereby making mistakes in their deliberation, whereas good decision-making means deliberating

correctly, it's clear that good decision-making is a kind of correctness. But not correctness of knowledge or belief. There's no
such thing as 'correct knowledge' (because there's no such thing 10
as incorrect knowledge). And a correct belief is just a true belief.
Plus, the content of a belief is already fully determined.

Of course, good decision-making also involves reason. So
there's still the option of it being the correctness of the thought
process itself. Because a thought process is not yet an assertion. (That's what rules out belief: a belief is not a form of
working anything out. It's already an assertion. But when
you're making a decision, whether you're doing it well or badly, 15
you're still working something out; you're calculating.)

So good decision-making is correctness in deliberation.[26]
† . . . †

But we can mean various different things by correct deliberation, and clearly not every kind counts.

Take a case where someone who lacks self-control, or an evil
person, figures out a way to achieve the goal he sets himself. So
that means he'll have 'deliberated correctly' even though he's 20
done himself a lot of harm.[27] But deliberating correctly should
be a good thing. That's the kind of correctness in deliberating
that we have to mean here: the kind that helps you attain something good.

Then again, you can also achieve a goal by a false chain of
reasoning: you can achieve what you're supposed to, but by the
wrong means. You might have a false middle premise.[28] So that
isn't yet good decision-making either, if you attain the right 25
result by the wrong means.

Also, you can succeed after taking a really long time deciding what to do, when you might have got there quickly. That
doesn't yet count as good decision-making either. 'Correctness' here is determined by what benefits you: right goal, right
means, right time.

Also, we can say someone 'has made good decisions' either in
an absolute sense [that is, in life] or relative to some particular
goal. So good decision-making in the absolute sense is the kind 30
that's successful relative to the overall, absolute goal [of life].
The particular forms of it are relative to our particular goals.

So, if it's a defining feature of wise people that they've made good decisions [in life], then it seems good decision-making is correctness in our deliberations, as determined by whatever advances us towards that [overall] goal that our wisdom gives us a true conception of.

1143a **10** We also call some people 'insightful' and 'good at understanding [people]', and those qualities, insight and being good at understanding others, aren't just a matter of knowledge or belief in general (if they were, we'd all be 'insightful'),[29] and they aren't the same as having a particular kind of knowledge either. Medical knowledge doesn't make you 'insightful' about health, geometry doesn't make you 'insightful' about triangles. In fact you can't really be insightful about any [objects

5 of scientific knowledge], things that are eternal and unchanging; or even about just anything in the domain of things that come to be, either. You can only be insightful about the kinds of things a person can be facing some problem over and trying to make a decision about.

So it has the same domain as wisdom. But that doesn't mean being insightful is the same as being wise.

The difference is that your wisdom gives you orders (its goal is to figure out what you should or shouldn't do) while

10 being insightful is only for offering judgement[30] {and advice}. Being insightful is the same as being good at understanding people; insightful people have a knack for understanding [people's situations].

So being insightful isn't a matter of possessing or acquiring wisdom. Rather, just as learning something [in general], when you use your existing knowledge to do it, implies *seeing your way into it*,[31] likewise insight is about using your existing views to make a judgement on something – something within

15 the scope of wisdom – when someone else tells you about it, and making the morally right call, or judging it well (which is the same thing).

That's why [in Greek] we call insight *sunesis*. It makes us good at understanding people [*eusunetoi*]; the word comes from the context of learning. [You can see this in the fact that, in

Greek,] the word for 'to learn', *manthanein*, often also means 'to understand', *sunienai*.[32]

11 'Understanding', used in that other way, to refer to the quality that makes people sympathetic and forgiving,* is a matter of correctly judging the kind and decent thing to 20 do. We think of kind and decent people as especially likely to be sympathetic, and being able to forgive (at least, certain things) *is* kind and decent.

A sympathetic outlook[33] is the sort of understanding that makes us correctly judge the kind and decent thing to do. 'Correctly', as in you get it right.

And all these various traits tend in the same direction, as 25 you might expect, because [typically] we attribute [all of them together], understanding and insight and wisdom and {'sense'} and awareness, to the same people. If we say they have understanding, we'll [typically] also say they have sense, they're wise, they're insightful. That's because all these abilities are directed at the immediate facts, and the particulars . . .

† And it's in offering [other people] your advice (on matters 30 that fall within the scope of wisdom) that you can be insightful, and considerate – or sympathetic, because of course kindness[34] is common to all good people in their dealings with others. †

. . . and all the things that we do belong to that set of immediate facts and particulars. A wise person has to know them; and insight and understanding also only apply to the things people are doing, i.e. to particulars. And awareness, too, is of 35 'ultimates' – at both ends. We have [that kind of direct] awareness of first principles, and of particular facts. We don't reason our way [to either]. In our scientific proofs, that means direct 1143b cognition of the unalterable first principles. And in our practical reasoning it means direct awareness of the last term, the thing that could have been otherwise, the 'minor premise'. Those [– the particular facts –] are the source material of all our goals: we get our universals from the particulars [of life]. So we have to have perceived those particulars, {have a sense of them}, and 5 that kind of perception is 'awareness', {'common sense'}.

That's why these things seem to develop in us naturally. [Metaphysics and theology] don't come naturally to anyone, but understanding, insight, {sense}, awareness – those do seem to come naturally. We can see that from the fact that we think of them as arising at certain stages of life: 'that's the age when you acquire some sense, and understanding', we say – implying that nature causes these things.

11   Hence we should pay attention to experienced people, to our elders and people who are wise. We should listen even to their unproven assertions and opinions, no less than to the proven claims of science. Those people have the keen eye of experience, so they see things right.

15   All right, so we've explained what wisdom is, and what philosophical knowledge is, and what each of them is about; and said that each is the special virtue of a different part of the soul.

12   But you might well wonder about these things: what's the use of them?

Philosophical knowledge, [like knowledge of metaphysics and theology], won't help you contemplate any of the things that make a person flourish. It's not about making things happen. And while wisdom does have that feature, what do you really need it for? Wisdom is all about what's right and wrong, honourable and shameful, good and bad for human beings: it's about the things a good person is supposed to *do*. But what if we're no more likely to do them by knowing about them, since virtues are traits of character – just as we're no more able to do things that are healthy and fit, just from knowing about them (I mean things that depend on our already being in that state, not things that *make us* healthy and fit). Obviously, we're no more able to do those things just by being experts in medicine or physical training.

But maybe we shouldn't call someone wise for that reason. Maybe wisdom is what makes you become a good person.

But then it would be of no use to people who already are good.

30   Or even to people who don't have it, [and aren't]. Because what difference will it make whether we possess it ourselves or just follow the advice of the people who do? That would work

well enough for us, just as with health. (We [all] want to be healthy, but we don't all study medicine.)

What's more, it seems absurd that [mere moral and political] wisdom, although clearly inferior to philosophical knowledge [like theology and metaphysics], should nevertheless exercise authority over it (because it's the one that makes things happen, is in charge and gives the orders in every area of life).   35

So those are things we need to say something about. So far all we've done is set out the problems.

So first let's make the point that they're bound to be worth 1144a having in themselves just because they're virtues (each of its respective part of the soul), even if neither of them has any other effect whatsoever.

Second, they do have an effect:

(a) Philosophical knowledge [like metaphysics, theology, cosmology] does make us flourish. Only, not the way that medical expertise makes you healthy. It does it the way *health* makes you healthy. It's part of the whole set of virtues;[35] {part of 5 being good at everything you should be good at}. So by having it and exercising it, you *are* flourishing.

(b) Also, our human task is only achievable through goodness of character working in combination with wisdom. Goodness gives us the right target but wisdom shows us how to attain it.

(There's no equivalent 'virtue'[36] {or 'goodness'} of the fourth part of the soul, by the way, the nutritive-reproductive part, 10 because it isn't responsible for our doing or not doing anything.)

As for the idea that wisdom doesn't make us any more likely to do what's honourable and right, well, we'd better go back to what we said a little while ago.

Let's start with this.

We said that some people do the right thing without yet being righteous, {ethical} people. They might do all the things required of them by the law, for example, but unwillingly, or just by 15 mistake, or for some other reason; not for what those things are. But they're certainly doing the things they should be doing: all the things a good person ought to do.

So, conversely, we think there's such a thing as doing all

those things from a certain state of character, such that you are thereby a good person. That means doing them by choice, and for what they are in themselves.

20   So, in that case, being a good person is what makes your [basic] choice, {your aim},[37] the correct one. But as for [figuring out] all the things that need to be done to carry out that aim – that's not just part of goodness [of character]. It requires a further ability.

We need to really concentrate here and explain this more clearly.

All right, so there's the ability we call being clever. That's the ability to do the things that help you move towards whatever
25   goal you happen to have set yourself, and accomplish it. So now, if that goal is an honourable one, being clever is a praiseworthy ability. But used on a bad goal, [we call it] being cunning.

(That explains why clever, cunning people* are also [sometimes] called 'wise'.)[38]

Wisdom is not that ability. But it does include it. The [full]
30   disposition cannot develop, here in this 'eye of the soul', without goodness [of character] – as we said, and as should be obvious by now. Because practical reasoning always has to have its starting point: 'Given that X is my goal; given that X is the best thing for me to do . . .' whatever it might be, any [decent] goal you like . . . The point is, that goal is only visible at all to a
35   good person. Being an evil person distorts your practical starting points; it makes you consistently wrong about them.

Hence, clearly, you can't be wise if you aren't also a good person.

1144b **13** So we need to take another close look at what's involved with being a good person.

The situation with goodness is rather like what we just said about wisdom and cleverness (namely, that they're not the same thing, but closely related): there's a similar relationship between natural goodness and goodness in the full sense.

Everyone agrees that all character traits come to us natur-
5   ally to some extent. Right from birth we're [predisposed to] fairness, moderation, bravery – and so on. But we look for

something more in the fully good person; we expect those traits to be there in a different way. After all, even children, and animals, can have those natural dispositions. But if they're not combined with {sense and} awareness, they're manifestly harmful. A powerful animal that rushes around without vision is bound to crash into things just as powerfully – and we can easily imagine that something like that applies here (to say the least). But once they gain awareness – well, that makes a big difference in how they act. And their disposition of character (while still fundamentally the same one) will then be full moral goodness.

So with the part of us that forms beliefs [about what to do] there are these two related abilities: cleverness and wisdom. And similarly, when it comes to character, there's natural moral goodness and full moral goodness, and the latter can't exist without wisdom.

That's why some people say that all the moral virtues just are forms of wisdom. Socrates was partly right in the way he tried to explain the virtues, but also partly mistaken. He was wrong to think that all moral virtues are forms of wisdom; but quite right when he said that they require wisdom.

Here's evidence for that. All [philosophers] these days, when they're defining a moral virtue, first outline the disposition, then say what its domain is, and then add the qualification: 'consistent with correct reason' – which means consistent with wisdom. So it's as if everyone has this vague sense that the disposition needs that feature to count as a full moral virtue: it has to be consistent with wisdom.

But we need to adjust that slightly. Strictly, it's not just that it has to be consistent with correct reason to be a virtue; it also has to actually involve your own correct reason. And correct reasoning about these kinds of things is wisdom.

So Socrates thought all the virtues were just reasoning (he thought they were all forms of knowledge) – but we say they involve reason.

So the upshot of everything we've said is that it's not possible to be a fully good person without also being wise, or wise without goodness of character.

*

This also gives us a way to dismiss that dialectical argument that tries to show that the virtues can exist separately from one another. 'The same person isn't going to be naturally inclined
35 to a high degree to all the virtues; so he might well acquire virtue A before virtue B.' Yes, maybe that's true of the natural virtues. But with the virtues that make you a good person in
1145a the full sense, it's not possible. Because once you have wisdom, when you have any one virtue, you'll have them all.

It's clear (a) that even if wisdom didn't make us more likely to do [the right thing] we'd still need to have it, just because it's the special virtue of its part of the soul, and (b) that in fact our choices won't be the right ones without a combination of wis-
5 dom and moral goodness. (Goodness makes us have the right goal, wisdom makes us do the things that lead to that goal.)
     What's more, it isn't really 'in charge of' philosophical knowledge, or of the better part of the soul, just as medicine is not 'in charge of' health. Wisdom doesn't employ the knowledge that comes from higher philosophy [like theology and metaphysics]. It just makes sure that it can exist. So it gives orders in the interest of philosophical knowledge, but not to it.
10 [That misconception] is rather like saying that statesmanship rules the gods, because it gives orders for everything that goes on in the city [including religious matters].

BOOK VII

Next, let's make a fresh start, and say that when it comes to 15
undesirable states of character there are three distinct types:
(a) being a bad person; (b) having no self-control; and (c) being
like a beast.

The opposites of those are obvious for the first two: 'being a
good person' and 'having self-control'. As for the third – being
bestial – well, it might make most sense to say the opposite of
it is being superhumanly good, like a god or demi-god, like the
way, in Homer, Priam says that Hector (because he was such 20
an exceedingly good man), 'seemed more like he was born of a
god than a child of a mortal'. So, if (as they say) human beings
become gods through exceptional goodness, clearly something
like that is the natural opposite of being like a beast.

That makes sense in another way too: a beast isn't good or 25
evil, and neither is God. [God has] something more exalted
than goodness, and [being a beast] is a wholly different category from being evil.

Also, it's rare for a man to be 'godly' – as they say in Sparta
when they really admire someone: *seios anēr!* {godly man!}[1] –
and equally rare for a human being to be bestial. It's mostly a 30
barbarian thing. But it's also sometimes caused by illness or
[mental] impairment.

(We also use ['beast!' and 'animal!'] as terms of abuse, of
people who are extremely evil.)

But we'll say something about that condition later. And we've
already talked about what it is to be a bad person. So here we 35
should talk about (a) lacking self-control (and being 'soft' and
'pampered') and (b) having self-control (and being 'resilient').

We shouldn't treat the one as the same as being a bad per-
1145b son, or the other as the same as being a good person;[2] nor
should we treat them as entirely distinct from those things.

Let's go with our usual method. We should lay out the things
that appear to be the case, first run through all the puzzles and
problems, and then explain ... well, ideally, all the standard
5 views about these experiences, but if not all then at any rate most
of them, and the most important. Because if the difficulties can
be cleared up, and the standard views are left standing, we can
feel we've done a decent enough job of explaining things.

All right, so people think that:

(a) Self-control (and resilience) are good qualities and praise-
10 worthy, while lacking self-control and being soft are bad qualities
and blameworthy.

(b) People with self-control stick to what they've decided;
people who lack self-control deviate from what they've decided.

(c) When people lack self-control, feeling and emotion[3] makes
them do things they know are bad; when people have self-
control reason makes them not follow desires they know are bad.

(d) People say a moderate person always has self-control
15 (and resilience). But only some people think that everyone with
self-control is also moderate. Others say that's not right. Some
treat 'having no self-control' as equivalent to being lecherous
and gluttonous, and vice versa – they just lump them all together.
Others say they're different.

(e) Sometimes you hear people say a wise person must also
have self-control. Other times, that some people are wise –
clever – but have no self-control.

(f) Also, we use the same word [in Greek] – *akrateis* – of people
who can't control their temper, or have no self-control when it
comes to prestige {and fame}, or where money is concerned.
20   So those are the things people say.

2   And our first puzzle.
        (a) In what sense exactly does someone correctly grasp
[that they shouldn't be doing what they're doing] when their
self-control fails?
Do they know?

Because some people say that's impossible. 'Shocking!' –
Socrates thought – 'that there's knowledge inside them, and yet
something else is able to control it, push it around like a mere
slave!'. In fact, Socrates was firmly against the whole idea of 25
'failures of self-control'. He thought there was no such thing.
'Nobody ever goes against what they think is best. They must
just not realize [that what they're doing is bad].'

Well, there's a theory glaringly at odds with the apparent
facts. You've got to ask about what's happening to people here:
if they 'don't realize',[4] what sense of 'don't realize' does that turn
out to be? Because they certainly think they shouldn't do it, 30
before they experience their loss of self-control. That's a given.

(b) Others partly go along with Socrates, partly disagree.
They agree that knowledge can't be overpowered. But they
don't agree that you can't even act against what you merely
believe is better. So on those grounds they claim that when you 35
lose control and are 'overpowered by pleasures' you don't have
knowledge; you just have a belief [that you shouldn't be acting
that way].

But if it's just a belief rather than knowledge, which is to say,
if it's not a strong conviction telling you not to do it, just a 1146a
rather half-hearted one – like when people can't quite make up
their minds about something – surely you can be excused for
deviating from those beliefs in the face of really powerful
desires? But we don't excuse a moral failing [like lack of self-
control], or anything else we blame people for.

(c) So is it your wisdom telling you not to do it? That's very
strong.

No. That's absurd. That would mean the same person could 5
be wise and also have no self-control. And literally nobody
would say that wilfully doing really awful things[5] is compatible
with being wise. On top of that, we showed earlier that a wise
person is [by definition] good at actually doing the right thing –
a particulars guy[6] – and has all the other moral virtues.

(d) Also, if self-control comes into play when you have desires 10
that are strong and bad, a moderate person will not be someone who needs to use self-control, and a person who needs to
use self-control[7] will not be someone moderate. Extreme [desire

of that sort] is incompatible with being moderate, and so is having bad desires.

And they do have to be [strong and bad]. Because if the desires in question were good, the disposition that stopped you acting on them would be bad, so then, [weirdly], self-control wouldn't always be a good quality. And there's nothing very
15 impressive about controlling desires that are weak and not so bad. Even if they're bad, but also weak, what's the big deal?

(e) Also, if self-control is what makes you stick to any and every belief [about what you ought to do] then it can be a bad quality (if it even makes you stick to a false one). Conversely, if deviating from any such belief is a 'lapse of self-control' then lack of self-control will sometimes be a good thing. Remember
20 Neoptolemus in Sophocles' *Philoctetes*. We applaud him precisely for not following through on what he was persuaded to do by Odysseus, because he feels bad about telling a lie.

(f) There's also that sophists' argument. That creates another puzzle.

(Sophists try to force you to accept weird conclusions [based on your own views]. It makes them look clever when they pull it off. So you get a chain of reasoning that amounts to a paradox. Your mind gets all tied up in knots. It doesn't want to stay
25 where it is, with a conclusion it can't possibly accept, but it can't move beyond it either because it can't see how to unknot the argument.)

So there's this [sophists'] argument to the effect that being an idiot, combined with having no self-control, amounts to being a good person.

The idea is, since you have no self-control you always do the opposite of whatever you think [you should be doing]; but [since you're an idiot], you think good things are bad and that
30 you shouldn't be doing them. So you end up always doing good things[8] and never bad ones!

(g) And another:

Person A does [something he shouldn't do], pursuing pleasures, convinced it's a good idea. He does it by choice.

Person B does it not because he reasoned that he should, but just through a lapse of self-control.

So, you could argue that A is morally better than B,[9] on the grounds that he's more easily cured. Because he can be persuaded otherwise. But B, the one with no self-control, fits the old saying: 'When even water makes you choke,[10] what can you 35 wash it down with?' If he'd been doing it because he was 1146b convinced it was a good idea, he might have stopped by being persuaded otherwise. As it is he's already convinced he shouldn't be doing it, and it doesn't make any difference. He's doing it anyway.

(h) Also, if self-control and lack of self-control can apply to anything at all, what's the standard sense of 'having no self-control'? Nobody lacks self-control in all the ways [we mentioned]. But we do speak of some people as simply 'having no self-control'.   5

All right, so those are the various problems and puzzles that come up here. We need to clear away some of these ideas and hold on to some of them. Remember: clear up the puzzles and you find the answer.

3 So first we need to consider whether or not these people know [they shouldn't be doing what they're doing], and if so, in what sense.

Second, what kinds of things should we take self-control and lack of self-control to apply to? Can they apply to any kind 10 of pleasure and pain, or only certain kinds?

Also, is self-control the same as resilience, or different?

And so on, through all the other questions connected to this enquiry.

† The starting point[11] for our investigation is this: are people who have or who lack self-control distinguished[12] by the sorts 15 of things they do,[13] or by the way they are when they do them? What I mean is, does someone who lacks self-control lack self-control just by virtue of doing A-, B-, C-type things. Or is it not the A, B, C but the way they are when they do them? Or both?

Second, can lack of self-control, and self-control, apply to anything? Because someone who 'lacks self-control' in the

standard sense doesn't lack self-control about just anything.
20 He lacks self-control in a particular area: he does the same
things[14] that gluttonous and lecherous men do. Plus, it's not
just about [doing] those things at all (otherwise lacking self-
control would be the *same* as being lecherous and gluttonous).
It's about being in a particular state [when you do them]. A
gluttonous, lecherous man is driven to them by choice: he
believes he should, whenever possible, pursue immediate grat-
ification. Someone who lacks self-control thinks they *shouldn't*,
but do it anyway. †

So, as for that idea that it's only true belief, not knowledge,
25 that people go against when their self-control fails – that just
doesn't make any difference to the explanation. Because sometimes people might only have a belief, but that doesn't mean
they're unsure about it. On the contrary, they can feel 100 per
cent certain. So if the idea is that people with 'mere' beliefs
only have a kind of half-hearted confidence in them, and so are
more likely to act against what they take to be the case than
people with knowledge – wrong. Knowledge or belief, it won't
make the slightest difference. Some people have just as much
30 confidence in what they believe as other people do in the things
they know. I mean, just look at Heraclitus.

No, [here's a better idea]. 'Knowing' means two different
things. It can mean having the knowledge but not using it, or
it can mean actually using it. And it will make a difference,
whether you (a) have the knowledge [that you shouldn't do X]
but aren't actually thinking about it, or (b) are actually thinking about [the fact that you shouldn't be doing X] when you do
35 X. Maybe that seems 'shocking'. It's not so shocking if you
aren't thinking about it.

1147a   Also, since there are two kinds of premises [universal and
particular], there's no reason why you can't have both of them
when you act against your knowledge, but only be using the
universal one, not the particular.[15] Because it's particular things
we actually do.

It also makes a difference what kind of universal it is. It can
5 be about you, or it can be about the thing. So, for example:

[Case A]: You know that 'dry foods are good for every human being' and [automatically] also know [the particular]: 'I'm a human being.'

[Case B]: You know that 'food of type X is dry', but you don't know [the particular],[16] that this food here is of type X; or maybe you have the knowledge, but it's not active.

So these various senses [of 'knowing'] will make a massive difference here, such that your 'knowing' in one sense [that you shouldn't be doing what you're doing] seems perfectly normal, while your 'knowing' it in the other sense seems astonishing.

Also, there's yet another way that people can 'have knowledge', different from the ones we've mentioned so far. Within the class of having the knowledge but not using it we know there's a different sense of 'having it', such that you kind of have it but also kind of don't have it – like someone who's asleep, or mad, or drunk. And isn't that exactly the condition people are in when they're in the grip of those feelings? Anger, sexual desire and various other things like that actually alter your physical state[17] in obvious ways, and sometimes they drive people insane. So it makes clear sense to say that people who lose their self-control are in the same sort of condition as those people. The fact that they can still mouth all the arguments that come from their knowledge means nothing. After all, even people who are [drunk or mad] can recite scientific proofs and verses of Empedocles, and when children first learn [about right and wrong] they can string together the arguments, but they don't yet know what they mean. (They have to mature and grow[18] into those ideas, and that takes time.)

When people say [all the right] things in the middle of a loss of self-control we can think of them as being like actors, reciting lines.

We might also try looking into the cause of it by a scientific approach. Like this.

There's one kind of belief that's universal, and another kind that's about particulars (the latter determined by perception, of course). And when they come together to form a single belief, then, in other cases,[19] your soul is bound to assert that conclusion, and in special cases where the conclusion is 'I should do X' you're bound to do X, right away.

For example, suppose your premises are:

[Universal]   if it's sweet, I must have a taste of it, and
[Particular]   this is sweet – (i.e. this particular bit[20] of food).

30 As soon as [you put them together] you're also bound to do that thing [i.e. eat it] – if you can, and nothing prevents you.

So now consider a case where you have one universal belief telling you *not* to have a taste, but another one saying that

[U2]   every sweet thing is delicious, and
[P2]   this thing is sweet,

and that's the one that's active,[21] and physical desire happens to be in the mix as well, then there's one universal telling you not to, but desire is driving you on. (Desire can set all your 35 bodily parts in motion.)[22]

1147b   So it turns out that, in a sense, it's actually reason, and a belief [P2], that cause your loss of self-control. But the belief doesn't in itself contradict correct reason. It only contradicts it because it happens to meet with desire. It's desire that really opposes correct reason, not the belief.[23]

(So that's why animals can't 'lack self-control'; because they 5 don't have universal notions. All they have is an impression of particular facts, and memory of particular facts.)

As for how your fit of 'not realizing' [what you're doing] dissipates, and you get your knowledge back after a loss of self-control – well, the explanation is the same as for someone who's been drunk or asleep. It isn't specific to this experience. We should ask the physiologists.

And since that final premise is a belief about something per-10 ceived, and the one that determines our actions, that's the one you either don't have at all while you're in the grip of emotion, or you only have it in such a way that 'having it' doesn't really mean actually knowing it, it just means mouthing it,[24] like the drunk guy reciting Empedocles. And since that final term isn't a universal, and isn't really part of knowledge in the same way as the universal is, it seems we do even get the result 15 Socrates was after. Because it isn't what we take to be knowledge in the strict sense that gets disrupted[25] or 'dragged around' by the effects of feeling and emotion – just your perceptual knowledge.*[26]

All right, that's all we need to say about whether or not it's possible to know [that you shouldn't be doing what you're doing] when your self-control fails, (and if so, in what sense). Let's move on.

4 Is there a standard sense of 'lacking self-control' – {without qualification}? And if so, what kinds of things does it apply to? Or are there just the various particular forms of it? That's what we should talk about next.

So, first, it's quite clear that having self-control, being resilient, lacking self-control and being soft – it's clear they're all to do with pleasures and pains.

[Translator's note: *In what follows there are two versions, A and B, of the same section of the discussion.*]

[Version A]
Some things that give us pleasure are necessary [to life]; others [though non-essential] are worth having considered in themselves, but you can have too much of them. The necessary sources of pleasure are the bodily ones: I mean things like the pleasures of eating and drinking, sex and all the kinds of physical pleasures that we earlier said were involved in being lecherous and gluttonous, or moderate. As for sources of pleasure that are non-essential but desirable in themselves, I mean things like winning, being respected, being rich, and those kinds of good and enjoyable things.

(a) So when people overshoot correct reason (i.e. their own) with regard to the second kind, we don't simply say they 'lack self-control', we qualify it. We say: 'he has no self-control when it comes to money', or 'he has no self-control when it comes to fame', or 'he can't control his temper',[27] not simply he 'has no self-control', because these cases are different, and only described that way by resemblance. It's like with 'Man, the

1148a Olympic champion':*[28] for him, the general expression ['man']
was only a little bit different from the one that specifically
referred to him. But it makes quite a difference.

Here's a way to see the difference here. We *blame* people for
failures of self-control. And it's not just seen as a mistake. We
think that it (sort of) makes you a bad person, or is (sort of)
a vice.[29] But nobody gets blamed for any of those [qualified
forms of lacking self-control].

5   (b) When it comes to physical enjoyments, the sort you can
be moderate or lecherous and gluttonous about, when someone pursues excessive pleasures † ... †[30] not because they're
choosing to but against their choice and intent – that person

10 'lacks self-control'. We don't qualify it. There's no 'with
respect to this or that', as with someone who 'can't control *his*
temper'. They simply 'lack self-control'. {That's the standard
sense.}

You can see this in the fact that people are only called 'soft'
with respect to those kinds of [pleasures], not any of the other
kinds.

That also explains why we tend to lump together lack of
self-control with being lecherous and gluttonous – and, conversely, self-control with moderation – but wouldn't think to

15 do that with any of the qualified forms. It's because they
involve the same kinds of pleasures and pains. Strictly speaking,
though, while [all those types of people] do the same things,[31]
they aren't the same way when they do them. In one case they're
choosing to do them, in the other case they aren't. That's why
we're more likely to call someone lecherous or a glutton if they
aren't acting on any desire at all, or only a mild desire, when
they pursue excessive pleasures or avoid minor discomforts –
as opposed to someone who does the same thing because of

20 extremely powerful desires. Because just imagine what the first
type of person would do if they also felt a vigorous desire
for pleasure, or really serious pain, caused by a lack of basic
necessities.

[Version B]

Some desires and pleasures are in the class of honourable and good things. Because, as we distinguished them earlier, some things that give us pleasure are intrinsically desirable, others are the opposite, some in between. Examples of the first class 25 are money, material gain, victory, respect.

So with all those kinds of things, and the in-between kind, people aren't criticized just for having feelings about them – just for desiring them or liking them. They're criticized for the way they feel about them – for going too far. We criticize people for pursuing one of those intrinsically honourable and good things obsessively,[32] and beyond reason. Think of people 30 who care more than they should about respect {and prestige}, or more than they should about their children or parents. Because [children and family] are good things too, and people are praised for caring about them. But you can go too far even with those, like, say, if you insist you have better children than the gods, the way Niobe did, or if you love your father as much as 'father-loving' Satyros.[33] I mean, [to go and throw himself 1148b off a cliff just because his father died] – that was a really stupid thing to do, surely.

Not that there's any moral failing in liking these things too much, for the reason already given: each of them is an intrinsically desirable thing, just in itself. But going too far with them is a bad thing and to be avoided. For the same reason, there's no way of lacking self-control about them either. Because lack 5 of self-control isn't just something 'to be avoided'. It's also something we actually blame people for.

But by resemblance to the standard phenomenon, we do speak of 'lacking self-control' about those things, with a qualification: 'no self-control when it comes to X'.

It's like calling someone a 'bad doctor' or 'bad actor' when you wouldn't call them simply bad – [i.e. a bad person]. Neither of those amounts to being simply bad. They just resemble 10 it by analogy. And that's clearly how it works in the self-control case too.

We should assume that [standard] self-control and lack of self-control only apply to the things that people can be moderate or lecherous and gluttonous about. But as for 'not controlling your temper' – that's something we only say by analogy. That's exactly why we qualify it with the reference to temper; likewise with 'he can't control himself when it comes to fame', or 'he's got no control when it comes to money'.

15   5   Some things are naturally pleasurable (and some of those universally so, some only for certain classes of animals or people).

And some things aren't naturally pleasurable, they just come to be pleasurable through physical impairments {and abnormalities} or by habituation; and in some cases because people have depraved natures.

And you can see dispositions closely corresponding to each of those phenomena.

By 'bestial' {or 'animalistic'} dispositions I mean . . . people 20 like that slave-woman who they say used to cut open pregnant women and devour the foetuses; or the kinds of things they say some of the savage tribes around the coast of Black Sea take pleasure in – they say some of them like to eat raw meat, or human flesh; and that some of them supply their children to one another for banquets. Or the thing about Phalaris.[34]

Those are bestial, {animalistic} dispositions.

25   But others are {pathological}: caused by illnesses – including insanity in some cases; like the man who sacrificed and ate his mother, or the one who ate his fellow slave's liver.

The pathological kind may result either from people's nature* or from habituation. I mean things like . . . pulling your hair out . . . biting your nails . . . eating charcoal, or clay[35] . . . and, we might add, female sexuality in males.*[36] Because in some people those things arise from their nature, in others from 30 habituation, i.e. when they're trained into them* from childhood. So in all cases where the cause is their nature, nobody would speak of them 'not being able to control' [those urges] (just as you wouldn't say women 'lack self-control' for having the non-penetrative role sexually), and the same goes for any pathological states that result from habituation.

So having any of those conditions is outside the bounds of being a bad person; as is [the other kind], being like an 1149a animal.

And having [such a condition], and controlling it or not controlling it – that's not standard 'lack of self-control'. We just call it that by resemblance – just like with someone who's the same way with fits of anger: we say 'he can't control his emotion', but we shouldn't simply say 'he lacks self-control'.*

In fact, all extremes – extreme mental deficiency, cowardliness, 5 lecherousness, aggressiveness – they're all either animalistic or pathological. A man whose nature makes him afraid of everything, even the squeak of a mouse, has an animalistic cowardliness. And the guy who was scared [every time he saw] a weasel – that was an illness.

As for the mentally deficient, some lack the power of reason innately, and live by perception alone. That's animalistic. 10 (Some tribes of distant barbarians are like that.) Others are that way through illness (seizures, for example) or madness. That's pathological.

And with some of these things, it's possible to have the condition but not be controlled by it. (Imagine a Phalaris who was able to *restrain* his desire to eat a child, say, or abuse it for some perverse sexual pleasure.) Or you can be controlled by 15 them, as well as having them.

It's the same with being 'depraved': being a 'depraved person' in the standard sense implies within the normal human range. Then there's the kind we qualify – X is a bestial depravity, Y is a pathological depravity, not the standard kind. In the same way, it's clear that, yes, there's such a thing as 'failing to control' bestial urges or 'failing to control' a pathology; but standard-sense 'lack of self-control' is strictly just the kind that corresponds to [normal] human levels of lechery and gluttony.[37] 20

So [basically], lacking self-control, or having self-control, properly apply to the things people can be lecherous and gluttonous or moderate about. Applied to other areas it's a different sense of 'self-control',[38] and we only use the same expression by crossover from the normal sense. That's settled.

6   It's also the case that not controlling your temper is less
25   shameful than not controlling [physical] desires. Let's look
at that.

Anger seems to listen to your reason – a bit. Only, it mis-
hears it. It's like those hasty servants who dash out of the room
before they've heard the whole of what you're telling them and
then get your instructions wrong; or dogs who start barking
when they hear the slightest noise before checking to see if
30 it's a friend. That's how anger is. Because of its hot and hasty
nature it listens, yes, but it doesn't wait long enough to hear a
command before lunging towards retaliation. Reason, or your
impression of the situation, sends the signal: 'You're being
insulted. You are being belittled.' Then anger, so to speak,
makes the inference – 'When someone does that sort of thing . . .
you MUST ATTACK!' – and immediately gets all fired up.

35 But with desire – reason or perception just has to tell it, 'X
will give you pleasure', and [that's enough], it lunges towards
consuming X.

1149b So that means that anger, in a sense, follows reason,[39] but
desire doesn't. That makes desire more shameful. Someone
who can't control their temper is, in a way, actually overwhelmed by their reason. Whereas in the other case, it's desire
that overwhelms them, not reason.

5   Also, we're more inclined to excuse people for acting on natural impulses. After all, even with physical desires we're more
[tolerant when people act on] the kinds that are universal, and
to a degree that's universal. And anger, and bad temper, is a
more natural thing than extreme and non-necessary[40] physical
desires. (Remember the one about the man whose defence
for beating up his father was: 'Well, he hit *his* father too. And
10 Grandpa hit *his* father.' Then he points to his little boy, 'And
when he grows up, he'll hit *me*! It runs in the family.' Or the
guy being dragged across the floor by his son: 'You have to stop
at the doorway!' 'Why?' 'Because that's as far as I dragged Dad!')

Also, the more that people scheme against others, the more
immoral they are. And a hot-tempered person isn't a schemer.
Anger doesn't scheme. It's right out there in the open. But
15 lust certainly schemes.[41] That's why they call Aphrodite 'the

Cyprus-born weaver of many wiles'; and 'on her broidered gir-
dle', says Homer, she's got those 'sweet little lies, to beguile a
man's mind, be he ever so wary'. So that kind of lack of self-
control is more immoral, and more shameful, than failing to
control your temper.

That's why it's the standard case.

And that's why it (kind of) makes you a bad person.

Also, if you [lash out] because you're pained and upset, that's   20
not an act of abuse[42] {or cruelty}. But anyone acting from anger
precisely *is* acting that way from [a kind of] pain, whereas treating someone abusively involves pleasure. So if the things we're
most right to be angered by – [i.e. acts of abuse, especially sexual
abuse] – are the greater wrongs, then lack of self-control caused
by physical desire, {by lust}, must also be the more immoral kind.

There's nothing abusive[43] about reacting angrily [to mistreat-
ment].

All right, so failing to control your desires is more shameful
than not controlling your temper; and [standard] self-control,   25
or lack of it, applies to physical desires and pleasures. That's
settled.

But we need to grasp the distinctions among those. As we
said back at the start, some are normal and natural for human
beings, both in kind and in extent; others are bestial {and ani-
malistic}, caused either by [physical or mental] impairments or
by pathologies.

Being moderate, or lecherous and gluttonous, only applies to   30
the first kind.

That's why we don't call animals 'moderate' or 'lecherous' or
'gluttonous', by the way – except metaphorically, if one whole
species of animals, compared to another, is violently randy,[44]
or scoffs everything in sight. Because animals don't have a
faculty of choice or reasoning. They're crazy and impulsive[45]   35
by nature, the way human beings are when they're insane.*

Also, when someone's bestial that's actually less harmful   1150a
than their being a bad person – though a more frightening
thing. Because it's not that their better part is corrupted, as in
someone who's a [normal] human being. They just don't have
that better part.

(a) So it's like comparing an inanimate evil with an animate one, and asking which is worse. The badness of something that
5 doesn't have the power to initiate {and devise} [harm] is always less destructive. And intellect is just such a power.

(b) So it's rather like comparing, say, a lion[46] to an unrighteous human being.* There's a sense in which each is worse. Because an evil human being can do many times more harm than any beast.

7 When it comes to pleasures, pains, desires and aversions
10 that depend on touch and taste – which, we determined earlier, are the domain for being lecherous or gluttonous, or moderate – the various ways you can be[47] are [as follows].

(a) If you can't resist the pleasures most people can, you lack self-control.

(b) If you can resist the pleasures most people can't, you have self-control.

(c) If you can't handle the pains that most people can, you're soft.

(d) If you can handle the pains that most people can't, you're resilient.

15   The majority of people are set somewhere in between (even if they lean a little more to the inferior states).[48]

Some pleasures are necessary, and some aren't. And some are necessary up to a point, but too much of them, or too little, isn't necessary. And the same goes for desires and pains. That being so:

(a) Someone who pursues excessive pleasures, or [necessary
20 ones] excessively, by choice,* and for the pleasures themselves, not some other consequence of them – that's your lecherous, gluttonous man. He's [called] *akolastos* – [literally, 'uncontrollable', 'unstoppable'] – because, by definition, he never feels any regret; so he's incurable. Because if you don't feel regret, you're incurable.[49]

And someone who pursues pleasure too little is . . . the opposite of that, [whatever that's called].

And the person in the middle is someone moderate.

(b) Similarly [with pains]: one type of person shirks* physical pains, not because they can't handle them, but by choice.

Others [shirk pain] against their choice {and intent}. Of those, 25 some are driven by pleasure and some by [the need to] escape the pain of their desire. (So those are different from one another.)

And anyone would agree that:

(a) if you do something shameful [e.g. commit adultery] without even feeling any desire, or from only mild desire, that's worse than if you [only] do it because of a really intense desire. And

(b) if you hit someone when you aren't even angry, that's worse than doing it because you're angry.

Because [if you're the first type], just imagine what you'd be 30 doing if you did feel those emotions!

That's why a lecherous man is, in fact, a worse person[50] than someone who lacks self-control.

Of the two types just described – [people who shirk pain by choice and people who pursue excessive pleasure by choice] – the first is, more strictly, a form of being soft; the second is the lecherous, gluttonous man.

The opposite of someone who has self-control is someone who lacks self-control; and the opposite of someone soft is someone resilient.

Being resilient is about holding out. But self-control is about controlling, {mastering}. And holding out against X is different 35 from mastering X; rather in the way that not being defeated by the enemy is different from defeating them. That's why self-control is a more valuable quality than resilience.

Someone who falls short here – who [can't handle] the kinds 1150b of pains that most people make an effort against, and succeed – that's someone 'soft' or 'delicate'. Being delicate is another way of being soft, by the way. Think of someone who trails his cloak along the ground to avoid the terrible pain and suffering of having to lift it up. Or [the hypochondriac] who impersonates an invalid and thinks he isn't pitiful, even though he [behaves] 5 like someone who is.

The same applies to having, or lacking, self-control.

The point is, if someone's overwhelmed by powerful and extreme pleasures or pains, that's understandable. We're forgiving towards that kind of thing if they put up a struggle – like Philoctetes (in the Theodectes' version) when he's been bitten
10 by the snake, or Cercyon in *Alopē* (by Carcinus); or people who try to hold back their laughter then crack up explosively (remember when that happened to Xenophantus?).[51] It's only [significant] when someone is overwhelmed by or can't withstand the kind of pleasures or pains that most people can hold out against – assuming it's not because of some natural family trait, {or gender trait}, or illness (like the softness that runs in
15 the family of the kings of Scythia,[52] or the gap between men and women).

We also tend to think of people who 'love to party' {and 'playboys'} as lecherous. Actually, they're just soft. Partying is a form of relaxing. It's a way of taking a break. And some people go too far with their relaxing. Party-lovers are in that group.

There are two forms of lacking self-control: being impulsive and being weak.
20   In some cases people deliberate beforehand but then feeling {and emotion} makes them fail to stick to what they decided. [That's weakness.]

In other cases it's because people haven't deliberated that they're carried away by emotion. Because, like the way you can stop yourself from being ticklish by tickling yourself first, some people, if they're aware ahead of time, see what's coming and pump themselves up and rouse their reasoning in advance. Then they aren't overwhelmed when the emotion {or feeling}
25 hits them, whether it's pleasure [they're up against] or pain.

It's mostly quick-tempered or hot, passionate people who lose control the impulsive way. Because of the speed of their temper or the intensity of their feelings, they don't wait around for reason [to do its work]. They just go with their first impressions.

8 So a lecherous, gluttonous man, as we said, isn't going to regret his actions. He's chosen [to behave that way] and is sticking to his choice. 30

But anyone who lacks self-control is bound to feel regret.

That's why that paradox that we mentioned earlier is, in fact, not correct. It's actually the first type who's incurable. Lack of self-control is curable.

If it were an illness, then being a wicked person is like dropsy, say, or tuberculosis; but a loss of self-control is more like a seizure. One is a constant defect, the other only strikes now and then.

And in general, lacking self-control is a different kind of thing from being a bad person. For one thing, you can be a bad person without realizing it; but you can't lack self-control without realizing it. 35

And of people who do lack self-control, the ones who lose their heads are better people than the ones who retain their reason but don't stick to it. The second sort can be overwhelmed by less powerful emotion. And you can't say they act without any forethought, like the other sort. 1151a

Someone who lacks self-control is like those people who get drunk quickly, without drinking a lot of wine – and less wine than it takes for most people to get drunk. 5

All right, so it's clear that lacking self-control doesn't make you a bad person. (It makes you sort of a bad person, arguably.) Because it's contrary to your choices {and aims}. But being a bad person *is all about* your choices {and aims}.

Having said that, they certainly amount to the same thing when it comes to your actions. Remember what Demodocus said about the Milesians: 'The Milesians aren't stupid. But they sure act like it.' It's the same with people who lack self-control: they aren't immoral people, but they'll still do wrong.[53] 10

So [here are two different types of people]:

Person A: the kind of person who – not because they're

convinced they should do so – pursues excessive physical pleasures against their own correct reasoning.

Person B: who, because they're the kind of person who pursues them, is actually convinced they *should* pursue them.

So it's the first type who can be fairly easily talked into behaving differently; but the second type can't.

15   Here's why. Being a good person, or being a nasty person, preserves or destroys your [ethical] starting point. In the context of actions, your 'starting point' means your purpose, {your goal}. It plays just the same role as starting assumptions in mathematical problems. So, as in mathematics, here too, it isn't reason's job[54] to explain {or justify} our starting points. No. It's our goodness – coming either from our nature or from habituation – that makes us have[55] the right belief about that starting point.

So [in this context] someone like that, [with the right starting point], is moderate. And a lecherous, gluttonous man is the opposite: [he has the wrong starting point].

20   But then there's another kind of person: someone who's prone to being unhinged by emotion and going against their own correct reasoning; someone over whom emotion and feeling exert just enough power to stop them actually doing what correct reason is telling them to do, but not enough to turn them into the sort of person who's convinced they actually should be pursuing those kinds of pleasures with abandon.

That's the person who lacks self-control: a better person than the lecherous man and not a bad person in the normal sense. Because the best part of him, that [ethical] starting point, is still there, intact.

25   And then [finally], there's the person who's the opposite of that, someone who's able to stick to [what reason tells them to do] and *doesn't* get unhinged by emotion.

So it should be obvious, from all this, that self-control is a good quality and lack of self-control a bad one.

9   So is it self-control if you stick to reason, whatever it says, or to a choice of whatever sort – or only if it's correct?

30   And is it a lapse of self-control if you fail to stick to any choice, of whatever sort, or to reason whatever it says? Or not

if what it says is false? Not if the choice isn't correct? (We raised this puzzle earlier.)

Maybe the answer is that, incidentally, yes,[56] you could be sticking to, or not sticking to, any choice at all; but if we mean per se, then your reason has to be saying something true and your choice has to be correct.   35

Let me explain. Suppose someone chooses, or pursues, X in order to get Y.[57] That means that per se they're pursuing and 1151b choosing Y, and only incidentally choosing and pursuing X. And the standard sense [of 'choosing' or 'pursuing'] is the per se one.

So yes, in a sense you can be sticking to or deviating from any 'opinion' whatsoever, but by the normal sense [of 'opinion'] it has to be a true one.

And there's another class of people who 'stick to their opinion':   5 we call them 'pig-headed', i.e. people who are hard to persuade and can't be easily made to change their minds. They're certainly a little bit like people with self-control, rather in the same way that an extravagant man is a little bit like a generous one, and a reckless man is a little bit like someone bold. But they're also different, and in multiple ways. When someone has self-control it's emotion and desire that can't shift them. They're certainly open to persuasion, under the right circumstances. But   10 with pig-headed people it's reason that can't shift them. They're certainly susceptible to desires. As a matter of fact, a lot of them are [precisely] driven by pleasures.

Pig-headed people can be (a) fanatics, (b) ignorant or (c) yokels. Of those, fanatics are certainly motivated by both pleasure and pain. They relish the 'victory' when you can't get them to change their mind, and they're distraught when their ideas . . .   15 their decrees {and dogmas} aren't enacted, so to speak. So they're actually more like people who lack self-control[58] than people who have it.

There are also people who fail to stick to what they've decided, but not because they lack self-control, like the Neoptolemus case in Sophocles' *Philoctetes*. It's true he failed to stick to his decision because of pleasure. But it was an honourable

pleasure. Telling the truth was the honourable thing for him to
20 do,[59] and he'd been persuaded to lie by Odysseus. The general
point being: just because someone is doing something for pleasure, that doesn't always mean they're lecherous or a bad person
or that they lack self-control. It has to be a shameful pleasure.

There's also the kind of person who enjoys physical pleasures less
than one should, and who fails to stick to their reasoning by way
of that feature of their character.* Someone with self-control is
25 between[60] that person and someone who lacks self-control.
I'll explain. Someone who lacks self-control fails to stick to
their reasoning because something in them, [their desire], is
too strong. And this other kind of person, because it's too
weak. And someone with self-control, [in the middle], does
stick to what reason says, without either of those things shift-
ing him off course.
And if having self-control is a good thing, then it must be
that both of these opposing character traits are bad – just as
30 people assume they are. It's just that, because one of them is
observed in so few people and so rarely, we tend to think of
lacking self-control as the only opposite of having self-control;
like the way we think the only opposite of being moderate is
being lecherous.[61]
And since we often use words just on the basis of a resemblance, here too we've come to speak of the 'self-control' of
someone moderate, because of the resemblance. After all, some-
35 one with self-control 'never does anything contrary to reason
on account of physical pleasures'; and exactly the same goes
1152a for someone moderate. The difference is that the former has bad
desires, the latter doesn't. Also, a moderate person is someone
who doesn't enjoy things that go against reason; whereas a
person with self-control is someone who does {and would} enjoy
them; they just aren't carried away by them.
Then there's the resemblance between someone who lacks self-
control and someone lecherous or gluttonous. They're different
5 kinds of people, of course. But they both pursue physical pleasures. The difference is that one of them is thinking, 'This is
what I should do' and the other, 'I should not be doing this.'

10 Also, it's not possible for the same person to be wise and lack self-control. We showed earlier that being wise implies being a morally good person as well. Also, you're not wise just by knowing [what you should do]; you also have to be good at actually doing it. And someone who lacks self-control isn't good at actually doing it.

But there's no reason why you can't be clever and lack self-control. That's why some people, sometimes, seem like they're wise, but also lacking in self-control. It's because [they're clever; and] being clever differs from being wise [only] in that [subtle] way that we explained in our earlier discussion: i.e. in terms of their [means-end] reasoning they're very close; they differ in terms of choice {and intent}.[62]

Also, [someone who lacks self-control] isn't like someone who knows [what they should do] and is actually thinking about it. They're more like someone who's asleep or drunk.

Also, though they're certainly acting wilfully (because, in a sense, they know what they're doing and why they're doing it), they're not wicked people, because their [underlying] choice remains decent. They're sort of *semi*-wicked.

And they're not unethical people, because they don't plan the harm they do. Because, [by definition], they either (a) fail to stick to what they planned or (b) are the hot, impulsive types who act without any planning at all.

Someone who lacks self-control is like a city that passes all the resolutions that it should and has perfectly good laws, but fails to observe any of them. Like that joke in Anaxandrides:

A: The city has decreed . . .
B: Yeah, the city where no one gives a hoot about the law!

A wicked {or evil} person, by contrast, is like a city that does observe its laws, but actually has wicked laws.

Having or lacking self-control is about going beyond the average character-state. It's about being able to stick to what you've decided, more, or less, than most people are capable of doing.

Of the different kinds of lack of self-control, the one that's

easier to cure is the kind of lapse of self-control experienced by
impulsive people, as opposed to people who do deliberate but
then fail to stick to their decision; plus, people who lack self-
control through bad habits [are easier to cure] than people who
30 have it in their nature. A habit is easier to shift than your
nature. After all, that's exactly what makes a habit hard to
shift, too – the fact that it's quasi-nature. Like Evenus says,

> Training yourself, dear friend,
> > takes a very long time to accomplish.
> But when it comes to an end,
> > it will form a new part of your nature.

All right, so we've said what self-control is; and lack of self-
35 control; and being resilient and being soft; and how those
dispositions relate to one another. We're done.

1152b **11** Pleasure and pain – moral and political philosophy is
the right place for thinking about those, because it's
the part of philosophy that makes the master plan, {lays out
life's} goal, which we can use as our criteria for calling anything good or bad (without qualification).[63]

Plus, investigating them is something we really have to do.
First, because we made the claim[64] earlier that 'being a (morally)
5 good or bad person is all about pleasures and pains'; and also
because most people say that a blessed, {flourishing} life must
include pleasure. That's why even the word [in Greek] for
someone blessed, {makarios}, comes from the word for feeling
joy, {pleasure, happiness}: khairein.[65]

All right, so:

(a) Some people think that no pleasure is a good thing, either
in itself or derivatively. They take the view that what's good
and pleasure are [simply] not the same.

10 (b) Others think that some pleasures are good, but most
are bad.

(c) And there's a third position: that even if all pleasures are
a good thing, pleasure still can't possibly be the highest good.

*

(a) All right, so [people say] pleasure is not a good thing at all, on the grounds that:

(1) Every pleasure is a process of change towards some natural state, and no process of change can be the same kind of thing as its endpoint[66] {or goal}. For example, no instance of building is the same kind of thing as a house.

(2) A moderate person avoids pleasures.   15

(3) A wise person pursues freedom from pain, not pleasure.

(4) Pleasures get in the way of thinking, and the more intense the pleasure, the more it gets in the way. Take sexual pleasure. It's impossible to have any thought at all when you're experiencing it.

(5) There's no technical expertise that governs pleasure. Yet surely every good thing is the product of some form of expertise.

(6) Children and animals pursue pleasures.   20

(b) And people claim that not all pleasures are good, on the grounds that:

(1) Some pleasures are shameful, and people are reproached for them; and

(2) Some are harmful, in the sense that certain pleasurable things make you ill.

(c) As for the claim that pleasure couldn't be the best thing in life, they say that on the grounds that it's not an endpoint {or goal}; it's an A-to-B process, {it brings something about}.

So those are pretty much the things people say about it.

12 In fact, it doesn't follow from any of these [arguments] 25
that pleasure is not a good thing, or that it can't be the very best thing [in life]. We'll make that clear from the following.

So first of all, 'good' means two things: it can mean simply {or normally speaking}[67] good, or it can mean good for a given person; and a corresponding distinction[68] will apply to natures and dispositions {and physical states}, and hence also to motions and A-to-B processes {that bring about those states}.

And of [pleasures] considered bad, some are, normally speaking, bad, but not bad for a given person. Maybe for person X
they're desirable. And some maybe aren't even {unequivocally}
30 desirable for person X, they're just sometimes desirable or for
a while, but not all the time.*

And some of them aren't even [really] pleasures at all;[69] they're
just experienced as pleasures: the ones that involve pain as well,
and that are part of medical treatment; i.e. the sort experienced
by people who are ill.

Also, one kind of good is activity, and another kind is disposition {or state}. And it's merely incidental that [processes]
that restore us to our natural {physiological} state give us pleas-
35 ure. In fact [pleasure] is activity – in the case of physical desires,
activity of the remaining, [intact] physiological disposition.[70]
There are, after all, also pleasures that involve no pain and no
1153a physical desire, like the pleasures of contemplation, where our
nature is not lacking anything [at any stage].

You can see this[71] in the fact that people don't find the same
thing pleasurable when their nature is being refilled as they do
once it is restored. Once it's restored {and settled} they enjoy
things that are, in the normal sense, pleasurable. But when it's
being refilled they [may] even enjoy the very opposite things.
5 They [may] even enjoy things that are sharp or bitter, for
example,[72] and none of those is naturally or normally pleasurable. Hence those aren't [natural] pleasures either. Because that
distinction, between different kinds of pleasurable things – [some
are naturally pleasurable, some aren't] – implies an equivalent
distinction between the pleasures arising from them.

Also, there doesn't always have to be some other thing that's
better than the pleasure, the way some people say[73] the endpoint, B, must be better than the A-to-B process. Because
pleasures are not A-to-B processes (not all of them even involve
10 any such process). They are {activities}, exercisings [of our
capacities], and hence are endpoints {and goals}.

They don't arise when we're changing from A to B.[74] They
arise when we're using [some part of our nature].

Not all pleasures have some other thing as their endpoint.
That's only true when people are being brought to a completion

of their nature. That's why it's simply not right to say that pleasure is a 'perceptible A-to-B process'. It would be better to say that it's the exercising of our natural dispositions.[75] And instead of 'perceptible' we should say 'unimpeded'.   15

[Ultimately], the reason some people think that pleasure is a process is the [very] fact that it's a paradigm good[76] – [namely, a form of activity]. They think activity is an A-to-B process.[77] But it's not. It's something quite different.

As for the idea that pleasures are bad because some pleasurable things make you ill, you might just as well argue that some healthy things are bad because they make you lose money. Yes, maybe they're bad in that respect (in both cases). But that certainly doesn't make them bad things [in general]. I mean, for that matter, even philosophy is sometimes bad for your health.   20

Also, pleasure does not 'get in the way of' thinking, or any disposition, if it's the very pleasure that arises from that disposition. Only pleasures that arise from something else do that. Obviously, the pleasures that arise from philosophical thinking and from learning are only going to make you better at that style of thinking, and better at learning.

As for the claim that no pleasure is the product of a technical expertise, well, that's just what we'd expect to be the case. No other kind of activity is the product of an expertise   25 either. Expertise only produces capacities.

(Having said that, expertise at making perfume and culinary expertise do have pleasure as their object, don't they?)

As for the claim that a moderate person avoids pleasure and a wise person pursues a life free from pain, and the claim that children and animals pursue pleasure – all of those arguments can be dismissed by the same single point.

We've explained in what sense [some] pleasures are simply good, and in what sense pleasures are not good (not all of them).   30 And the fact is it's only *certain kinds* of pleasures that even animals and children pursue and that a wise person aims 'not to be disturbed' by: the ones that involve physical craving and pain, i.e. the bodily pleasures – they're the ones that are like that – and specifically the excessive amounts of those pleasures that define someone as lecherous and gluttonous. That's why a

moderate person only avoids those. (Moderate people have
35 their pleasures too, after all.)

1153b 13 And of course it's also uncontroversial that pain is
a bad thing and to be avoided. In some cases pain is
straightforwardly a bad thing, in other cases because it hinders
us in some respect. But the opposite of something that is to be
avoided, considered as something to be avoided and bad, is
good. So it follows that pleasure must be a good thing.

5 The way Speusippus tried to get around that argument, by
saying that it's like the way bigger is the opposite of smaller[78]
and also the opposite of equal – that doesn't work. [Nobody's]
going to agree that pleasure is, by definition, a bad thing.[79]

And there's no particular reason why some sort of pleasure
can't be the best thing in life, even if some pleasures are bad,
just as it might be some kind of knowledge, even though some
forms of knowledge are bad.

10 And if each of our dispositions [or mind or character] has
its corresponding unimpeded activities, and if flourishing is
either the exercising of all our dispositions or one of them,
surely {that activity}, that exercising, must take its most desirable possible form if it is unimpeded. But that's [how we just
defined] pleasure – [unimpeded activity]. So that would mean
that the best thing in life is some form of pleasure, even if it
turned out that most pleasures are (normally speaking) bad.

That's why people all assume that a flourishing, {blessed} life
15 must also be a pleasant life; we all weave pleasure into our
conception of human flourishing. With good reason. Because
no activity can be perfect if it's impeded; and flourishing is
something complete and perfect.[80]

That's why, to flourish, you also need goods of the body and
external goods and goods of fortune: so that you aren't thwarted
in those respects. People who claim that even someone who's
being tortured on the rack or suffering through the most awful
20 disasters is still flourishing as long as he's a good man are talking pure nonsense, and probably know they are. And it's because
we need luck, as an extra, that some people think that being
{lucky or} fortunate is the same thing as flourishing in life. But it

isn't. In fact, even good fortune, if you have too much of it, can be an impediment. (Maybe we shouldn't even call that good fortune any more. It's only good fortune if it helps you flourish.)

The fact that 'all things' – all animals and human beings – 25 pursue pleasure is good evidence that it is, in some sense, the highest good. [As Hesiod says:]

> A truth set forth will never fade away,
> when it's a thing that many nations say.

But people don't all have the same nature or the same best-possible state (and nobody thinks they do),[81] so they also don't 30 all pursue the same pleasure.

But they do all pursue pleasure. And maybe they're not pursuing the pleasure they think they are, or the pleasure they'd say they're pursuing. Maybe they are all pursuing the same pleasure. Because all [living] things have something divine in their nature.

But physical pleasures have come to monopolize the term 'pleasure', since they're the kind that people most often direct themselves towards and that everyone experiences. So since 35 they're the only kind [most people] are familiar with, [most] people think they're the only kind there are.

It's also clear that if pleasure isn't a good thing, along with 1154a activity, then – [bizarrely] – it won't be the case that a man who's flourishing is living a pleasant life! Why would he need any pleasure if it's not a good thing and he could just as well live a painful life [and still be flourishing]? Because [on that view], pain isn't good or bad (since pleasure isn't either). So why would you bother avoiding it?   5

So that means that the life of a good man won't be a more enjoyable one either, if his activities are also no more enjoyable [than anyone else's].

14 On the subject of physical pleasures ... Some people claim that 'some pleasures are extremely desirable, namely the honourable kind, but not physical pleasures, not the pleasures that lecherous and gluttonous people pursue'. And here's something for those people to think about.   10

Why, in that case, are the pains that are the opposite of those pleasures bad? After all, the opposite of what's bad is good.

Is it that necessary [physical] pleasures are 'good' just in the sense that even something that's not bad is good?

Or are they good up to a certain point?

Let me explain. With some dispositions and processes of change, you can't go too far – more is always better – so there's also no such thing as too much of the pleasure. But with others you can, so there is.

15 And there is such a thing as going too far with respect to bodily goods, and we only fault someone for pursuing excessive amounts of them, not for pursuing necessary pleasures. After all, everybody enjoys, in some manner or other, food, wine and sex. But not everyone enjoys them the right way.

It's the reverse with pain. [There's nothing wrong with you if][82] you avoid excessive pain; just if you avoid it entirely. Pain isn't [something to be avoided at all costs; it isn't] the opposite

20 of excessive pleasure except to someone who's pursuing excessive pleasure.

It isn't enough just to state what's true. You also need to give an explanation for why people get it wrong. Because that strengthens our conviction. (When you have a clear, plausible explanation for why something seems true even though it isn't,

25 that makes you all the more confident in the truth.)

So we have to say why it's physical pleasures that seem more desirable.

So first of all it's because they drive away pain. When they're experiencing extremes of pain, as a kind of remedy people pursue extreme pleasure, and in general [that means] physical pleasure. These remedial [pleasures] end up being very intense –

30 which is why people pursue them – because they're highlighted by the opposite extreme.

† And pleasure seems not to be a good thing, as we said earlier, for these two reasons: (a) because some pleasures are the actions of a bad nature (whether bad from birth, as in the case of a beast, or from habituation, like those of bad people). And

(b) because some are remedies for something lacking (and it's better to be in [the required] state than to be getting into it); and some arise when people are being brought to completion. So 1154b those pleasures are only indirectly good. †

Also, people pursue physical pleasures, because of their intensity, when they aren't capable of enjoying other kinds of pleasures. Some people* [are so desperate for pleasure] that they even find ways to make themselves thirsty.

So when the [physical pleasures they pursue] are harmless, there's really nothing wrong with that. When they're harmful, 5 that's bad.

The problem is that [most people] don't have anything else they enjoy, and also, for most people, even the neutral state [of neither pleasure nor pain] is painful. That's our nature. 'An animal is always in pain', [as Anaxagoras said], and the physiologists say the same: they claim even seeing and hearing are painful. It's just that after a while we get used to them. So they say.

Along the same lines, young people, because they're grow- 10 ing, are in a condition that's a bit like being drunk, and youth is a pleasure; but impulsive, {black-biled} types, by contrast, are in constant need of [pleasure as a form of] medication. Their body is continually over-stimulated because of the mixture [of their bile], so they're always in a state of intense desire. And pleasure drives out their pain – whether it's the opposite kind of pleasure, or any pleasure as long as it's strong. For those reasons they tend to become lecherous men and bad people.   15

With pleasures where there are no corresponding pains, there's also no way of going too far. Those are the pleasures that arise from things that are naturally pleasurable and not indirectly pleasurable. Pleasures that act as a remedy I call 'indirectly pleasurable'. (The remaining, healthy part of you is active in some way that happens to result in your being cured, and that in turn gives the [false] impression that [being cured itself] is pleasurable.)

What's 'naturally pleasurable' [for X] are those things that 20 bring about the action {and activity} characteristic of X's particular nature.

But there's no one thing that can give us pleasure all the time, because our nature isn't simple {or uniform}. There's another element in it [besides intellect], in so far as we are material, perishable beings. So that means that if you're doing the one kind of thing, it's actually unnatural for your other nature. (And if you try to bring them into balance, then what you're doing doesn't feel either painful or pleasurable.)

25   Certainly, if there were something [here on earth] that had a simple, {uniform} nature, then for that thing one and the same activity would always be the most pleasurable possible.

That's why God for ever enjoys the same, single, uniform pleasure. (Activity doesn't always require motion and change; there's also the exercising of changelessness. Indeed, there is more pleasure in rest {and tranquillity} than in motion.)

30   But 'variety is the spice of life', the poet says. That's because of a kind of defect in us. Just as it's a bad person who's fickle and shifty, similarly it's a defective nature that's constantly in need of change. It needs change because it isn't simple or decent.

All right, so we've talked about having and lacking self-control. We've talked about pleasure and pain. We've explained what each of those things is and in what sense some of them are good and some bad.

We still need to talk about friendship and love.

BOOK VIII

Next it would make sense to give an account of *philia*:[1] friend- 1155a
ship and love. Because that's a virtue – of a sort;[2] or tied to
being a good person.

It's also absolutely necessary to life. Who would choose to
live their life without any friends or family, even if it had all 5
other good things in it? In fact, isn't it people with lots of
money, and men of great authority and power, who need family and friends more than anyone? Because what's the point of
all those resources if you subtract doing any good with them?
And 'doing good' means, most often, doing good for friends
and family; and that's the most praiseworthy kind.

Or how could they protect or maintain their power and
wealth without friends and family? The greater it is, the more 10
easily it slips away.

And if you're broke, or up against one of life's other misfortunes, they say your family and friends are the only people you
can turn to.

Also, young people need help from family and friends to
avoid mistakes, and the old to have someone to care for them,
and for the things they can't cope with any more because of
their frailty. And men in their prime need friends for carrying
out honourable actions – 'better when two men go together'[3] – 15
because with friends they're better at 'thinking' and at getting
things done.

Also, in parents there's surely a natural love for their offspring, and in offspring for their parents, not just in human
beings but also in birds and indeed most animals. And in members of the same species there's a natural love for one another

20 too, and that's especially true of human beings, which is why
you're praised simply for 'loving your fellow human beings'.

And when you're travelling,[4] you soon see that any human
being is family, and friend, to any other.

Also, friendship seems to hold cities together, and lawmakers seem more concerned about it than about their citizens
being righteous. At any rate, what they mostly aim for in their
25 citizens is harmony (which is basically the same thing as friendship), and they try above all to eliminate civil strife {and
partisanship} (by which citizens are, in effect, enemies).

Also, when people are friends,[5] that's all the righteousness
they need; {they don't need anything else to make them treat
each other rightly}; but people who are [merely] doing right [by
one another] still also need friendship.

Also, of the various kinds of right and wrong the clearest
case is the kind that holds[6] between friends and family.*

And it's not just necessary. It's also honourable. We praise
30 people who care about their friends and family; and having
lots of friends is considered an honourable thing.

Plus, we tend to regard as friends the same people we think
of as being good.

But then there are various things to do with love and friendship that people disagree about.[7] Some people say friendship is
a kind of sameness, i.e. that friends always have things in common, hence the sayings 'like with like' and 'birds of a feather
35 flock together' and so on; but some people take the opposite
view and say that people who have a lot in common – like the
1155b proverbial[8] potters – dislike one another. And some people look
for its more abstract principles in the workings of nature. Euripides, for instance, says:

> Love is in the parched Earth, yearning for the downpour.
> Love's is in the proud, rain-swollen Sky, yearning to plunge to
> Earth.

5 And Heraclitus says: 'opposites benefit opposites' and 'different
notes make the sweetest harmony', and that the whole universe
came into being 'through strife'. But then other philosophers

take the opposite view, notably Empedocles, who says that 'like strives towards like'.

But let's not bother with questions of natural science. They're irrelevant to what we're investigating here. It's human questions, anything that has a bearing on our characters and on {feelings 10 and} emotions – that's what we should be looking into.

Questions like this: is friendship and love something everyone experiences, or is it impossible for bad people to have friends? Is there just one kind of friendship and love, or are there several? (Some people think that there's only one kind, because it comes in degrees; but that's not a valid reason. A thing can exist in different forms and come in degrees. We've talked 15 about that before.)⁹

2 We'll get a clearer idea of things if we first figure out what's lovable. Because you can't love just anything. You can only love what's lovable. And that means something good, or something that gives you pleasure, or something useful. (And surely a useful thing is useful by being a means to something good or 20 pleasurable. So that would mean the only lovable things, considered as goals, are what's good and what's pleasurable.)

(So do people love what's good, or just what's good for them? Because sometimes those aren't the same. The same goes for what's pleasurable. Well, it seems everyone loves what's good for them, and that although, normally speaking, lovable means good, for each individual what's lovable is what's good for them. Plus, each person loves what seems good to them, not 25 [always] what is good for them. But that won't make any difference. Because what seems good for them will then also just be what *seems* lovable.)

So there are three ways something can be 'lovable'. But loving inanimate objects doesn't count as friendship. Because they can't love you back. Plus, there's no wanting what's good *for them*. (It would be pretty bizarre to want what's best for your wine, for instance. I suppose you might want it to be safe – but 30 only so that you can have it for yourself.) But they say you should want what's best for a friend for the friend's own sake.

Even when people do want the best for someone else, we still

only call it 'goodwill', not friendship, if the feeling isn't mutual. Because friendship, they say, has to be a mutual feeling of goodwill. And we'd better add that they also have to be aware of it. Because often someone can feel goodwill towards people he's never even set eyes on, because he thinks they sound mor-
1156a ally decent (or useful to him). And what if one of those people felt the same way towards him? In that case they'd apparently feel 'mutual goodwill'. But how could you possibly call them friends if they aren't aware of how they feel about each other?

So friends have to feel goodwill towards one another and be aware of it, and want what's good for one another – because of
5 one of the three things listed above.

3 And note that these are three different types of thing. So there'll also be different forms of liking {or loving} someone, and hence different kinds of friendship.

So there are three kinds of friendship, corresponding to the three things you can love. Each kind involves a mutual feeling of attachment (that both people are fully aware of), and in each kind the people who have that attachment want what's good for one another – but in different ways, depending on exactly what it is they like about each other.
10 People whose attachment is based on what's useful don't like each other for what they are in themselves. Each likes the other in so far as they're getting something good out of them. And the same goes for attachments based on pleasure. (We like people who make us laugh, for example, not for the kind of people they are overall but because they're fun to be around.) So if your attachment is based on what's useful, you like the
15 other person because of what's good *for you*, and a pleasure attachment is based on what's pleasurable *for you*. You don't like the person for who they are. What you like about them is just the fact that they're useful to you or give you pleasure. So these kinds of friendships are incidental, in the sense that you don't like the friend for being the person they are, but because they happen to be providing you with something good or pleasurable.

That means those friendships can easily break down if the

people don't stay the same. If they're no pleasure to each other 20
any more, or no longer useful, they stop being friends. And of
course what's useful to a man doesn't stay the same. First it's
one thing, then it's something else. So when the thing that
brought them into the friendship in the first place breaks down,
the friendship dissolves as well, because that's what it was
based on.

Useful friendship is especially common in old people, because 25
people at that age aren't after pleasure or having fun. They just
need help. (And among men in their prime and the young you
find it in people whose priority is material gain.)

Friends like that don't really spend much time together, either.
After all, they may not even enjoy each other's company. So they
don't need their friends to spend time with them, except when
they're actually being helpful. That's to say, they enjoy their
company only to the extent that they expect some direct benefit 30
out of it.

(People usually class *xenia*,[10] {guest-friendship}, with this kind
of friendship as well.)

Friendship in the young, on the other hand, seems pleasure-
based. The young live by their feelings {and emotions}, and they
mostly chase after what's pleasurable and fun, and the here and
now. But as they get older what gives them pleasure changes.
That's why they're quick to become friends and quick to stop
being friends. Their friendships shift along with their pleas- 35
ures, and that kind of pleasure changes quickly. Falling in love 1156b
is typical of young people too. That's almost entirely emotional
and pleasure-driven. That's why young people make and break
those relationships so quickly. They seem to fall in love with
five different people a day.

Pleasure-friends, of course, do like to pass their days together
and live their lives together because that's exactly how they do 5
all the things that their friendship involves.

But complete and perfect friendship is friendship between
good people, where being good people is precisely the thing
they have in common. They want what's good for one another
because, and in so far as, they're good people. And that's a
fact about their own, true selves. And wanting what's good for

10 their friends for their friends' own sake makes them friends
in the fullest sense. Their relationship is based on something
about *them*,[11] not something incidental. So their friendship lasts
as long as they remain good people. And goodness is something durable.

Also, [in this kind of friendship], each friend isn't just good
in general but also good to his friend. Because good people are
good in general, plus helpful to one another. And they're like-
15 wise a pleasure to each other. Because good people are pleasant
in general, and also enjoy one another's company. (Everyone
enjoys their own actions, and others that are like their own,
and two good people's actions are bound to be the same, or
similar.)

And it makes sense that this kind of friendship should be
long-lasting, because it combines all the things that there ought
to be in a friendship. Every kind of friendship is based on
20 what's good or pleasurable (either absolutely, or for the friend)
and depends on [the friends] being alike in some sense. And in
this kind of friendship, [the friends] have all [three] of those
features, in themselves. The other two kinds resemble this one
† . . . †[12] and what's absolutely good is also pleasurable absolutely. And those things are lovable in the truest sense. So these
kinds of friends also love each other in the truest and best
sense, and their friendship [is the truest and best kind].

25   But these kinds of friendships are understandably rare because
there aren't many people like that. Plus it takes time and closeness. As the saying goes, people can't get to know one another
until they've 'gone through a pile of salt together'. So they can't
fully accept one another either and be friends until each has
gained the other's trust and shown themselves to be lovable,
{love-worthy}.

30   When people are quick to start acting in a friend-like way
towards one another they may well want to be friends, but
they aren't; not unless both of them deserve to be loved and are
convinced of that fact. Wanting to be friends with someone
can certainly happen quickly. Actually being friends is a different matter.

4 So that kind of friendship is complete and perfect, both in
   its durability and in all other respects. And in every respect
both friends get the same things, or the same kind of things,
from the friendship – exactly as friendship ought to be.   35

Pleasure-based friendship resembles it (because good people 1157a
take pleasure in one another's company too), as does friendship based on what's useful (because good people are useful to
one another too).

Even for those other kinds of friends, the friendship lasts
longer if they're getting the same thing out of it. If they're both
getting pleasure, for example, and, more precisely, pleasure 5
from the very same thing, like people who enjoy each other's
sense of humour; but not like an older suitor and his young
boyfriend. That's a case of two people not getting pleasure
from the same things. What the suitor enjoys is the teenager's
looks; what the teenager likes is being pampered. But when his
prettiness begins to fade sometimes their relationship wanes
too, because now the suitor isn't getting the same pleasure from
his looks and the pampering stops. Then again, they quite often 10
do stay together if as a result of their closeness they become
fond of each other's characters, assuming they have similar
characters to begin with. But when people aren't exchanging
pleasure for pleasure in those romantic relationships – when
they're just in it for something useful[13] – they're 'friends' in a
weaker sense and less likely to remain so.

In general, a friendship based on what's useful dissolves
as soon as it stops benefiting the friends. Because they didn't 15
really like each other to begin with. What they really liked was
advancing their own interests.

Now, even bad people can have friendships with one another
that are based on pleasure or what's useful to them, and decent
people can have those friendships with bad people, and people
who aren't exactly good or bad can have them with anyone.
But only good people, obviously, can have a friendship based
on what they are themselves. Because bad people don't enjoy
being around other people like themselves, unless they're getting some sort of benefit out of it.

Friendship between good people is also the only kind that's 20

proof against lies and slander. Because you're hardly going to believe someone [when they lie to you] about a friend who's thoroughly proven himself to you over a long period of time. Plus, something these friends have is that they trust one another, and would never do one another wrong; and all the other things you expect to find in a real friendship. But in the other kinds
25 there's no reason why those sorts of things can't happen.

Now, seeing as people use the term 'friends' even in cases where the friendship is based on what's useful, like so-called friendships between city states (i.e. alliances, which city states seem to enter into purely on a basis of self-interest), and for attachments that are pleasure-based, like children's, I suppose we'd better use the term 'friends' in those cases too. But let's
30 say that really there are various kinds of friendship, and that friendship in the primary and strict sense is between good people who are friends because and in so far as they're good people, and that the other kinds are called friendship by resemblance: they're friends in so far as they're a good thing to one another of some sort and have something in common.[14] Pleasure, for instance, is a good thing for people who like pleasure.

Also, these other kinds almost never tie together. That's to say, you don't get people who are friends because they're useful
35 and pleasurable to each other. Incidental features hardly ever match up that way.

1157b   So with friendship divided into these [three] kinds, bad people will only have friendships based on pleasure or what's useful to them, and that's all they'll have in common. Good people, on the other hand, will have friendships based on themselves, i.e. because they're good people. So those are friends in the standard sense. The others are friends incidentally, and they're called 'friends' because they bear some sort
5 of resemblance to standard-sense friends.

5   Now, with moral virtues, 'being good people' means either just having a certain character trait or actually exercising it. It's the same with being friends. Friends can either be actually spending time together, enjoying each other's company and providing one another with good things, or they can be

asleep or miles apart, in which case they aren't exercising their
friendship, although they retain the disposition to do so. Being
apart in itself doesn't dissolve a friendship. It just stops it being   10
active. But if friends are apart for a long time, that does seem
to make them forget their friendship. Hence the lines:

> For want of a handshake, a simple 'G'day!'
> Many a friendship fades away.

Old people and grouches aren't good friend material. They have
a limited capacity for pleasure, and nobody can spend their   15
day with a person who's a pain to be with or gives them no
pleasure. Our strongest natural impulse, after all, is to avoid
pain and aim for pleasure.

If people approve of one another but don't actually spend
time together, that's more like mutual goodwill than friendship. Nothing's as crucial to friendship as spending time
together. Not even helping one another out. Only needy friends   20
want help, but even blessed, {prosperous}[15] people want someone to spend their time with. In fact they're the last people
you'd expect to be solitary. And people simply can't spend time
together and do things together unless they're a pleasure to
one another and enjoy the same things – as in a 'best friends'
relationship.

So friendship in the fullest sense is friendship between good   25
people, as we've now said several times. Because, as we said,
what's lovable and desirable is what's (absolutely) good, or
pleasurable. And what's lovable for a given person is whatever's
good, or pleasurable, to them. And to a good person, another
good person is lovable on both counts.

It seems that, while the feeling of love is an emotion, love [in
the other sense, the relationship between friends and family] is
a disposition, {a state of character}. You can feel love in the
first sense even for inanimate objects. But reciprocated love   30
involves choice.[16] And that comes from a disposition of character. Plus, wanting the best for the people you love, for their
sake, depends on a disposition, not just an emotion.

Also, by loving a friend people are actually loving what's

good for themselves, because a good person, by becoming someone's friend, thereby becomes part of the well-being of the person whose friend they now are. So each friend [in loving
35 the other] is also thereby loving their own well-being, and each gives the equal of what they get in return, both in wanting the best for them and in pleasure. Because 'friendship is equality', they say, and it's especially the friendship of good people that
1158a has those [kinds of equality].

6   Grouches and old fogies form friendships less easily. They're grumpier and get less pleasure from people's company – surely the key to friendship, and in particular to forming a
5 friendship. That's why young people form friendships quickly, but not old people. They struggle to make friends because they don't enjoy people's company. The same goes for grouches. People like that can certainly feel mutual goodwill: they can want the best for one another and they meet each other's material needs. But they're hardly 'friends', because they don't spend time together and don't enjoy being around one another –
10 surely the key features of any friendship.

You can't have the complete, perfect kind of friendship with lots of people, just as you can't be in love with lots of people (that seems a sort of maximum, and as such something you naturally only feel towards one person). It's hard to feel a really strong liking for lots of people at the same time; and they surely couldn't all be good people either. Plus you'd have to
15 get to know them all and become close to all of them, which would be extremely difficult to do.

But it's certainly possible to like a lot of people* on the basis of their usefulness or for pleasure. There are plenty of people like that, and the [mutual] benefits can [be up and running] quickly.

And of the two, the pleasure-based kind is more like real friendship, provided both friends are getting the same things out of it and enjoy each other's company (or enjoy the same
20 things) – like friendships in young people. Pleasure-friendships are more gentlemanly, whereas a friendship based on what's useful to you is transactional, {and vulgar}. Indeed, the well-to-do

have strictly no need for useful friends, but they do need friends
who are a pleasure to be around because they certainly want to
pass their time in someone's company, and although we can all
tolerate pain for a short while, you can't possibly endure something continuously – not even the Form of the Good itself[17] – if 25
you find it painful. So they look for friends who'll be a pleasure
to be around. And they'll probably have to be good people as
well, plus good to them. That way they'll be all three things
that friends ought to be.

Powerful rulers, on the other hand, seem to compartmental-
ize their friends. They have their useful friends, and their
pleasure-friends; but no friends at all who are both at the same
time. That's because they don't look for friends who are fun to 30
be around and also good people, or useful friends [who'll be
useful] for doing honourable things with. When they're after
pleasure they just look for people who'll amuse them, and then
they want other people who are efficient at carrying out their
orders. And those two things are not at all likely to be found in
the same person.

But we just said that a good man is both a pleasure to be
with and useful at the same time.

Yes, but a good man doesn't become friends with some
[powerful ruler] far above his station unless he's also inferior
to him in goodness; otherwise he can't balance things out, by 35
being proportionately outclassed [in both areas].

But it's extremely unusual for [rulers] to be like that.[18]

Now, all the friendships we've described are between equals. 1158b
Both friends get the same things out of them and want the
same things for one another. (Or they exchange one type of
thing for another, e.g. pleasure for aid.)

And we've said there are these two lesser forms of friendship, which tend not to last very long. [Are they friendships?]
In a sense they are and in a sense they aren't, in so far as they're 5
both like and unlike the same thing. In so far as they resemble
the sort that depends on goodness, they do seem to be friendships. One involves pleasure, one is mutually useful, and that
[complete] kind of friendship has both those features too. But

on the other hand, that kind is immune to lies and gossip, and
it has staying power, whereas the other kinds are rapidly shift-
ing, and differ in several other ways as well. In that respect
10 they *don't* seem to be friendships – because of the ways in
which they're unlike [complete] friendship.

7 But there's another distinct class of love and friendship:
the kind you get between a superior and a subordinate.
Examples are a father's love for his son (and in general, any relationship between an elder and a junior) or a husband's love for
his wife (or any relationship where one person has authority
over the other). And there are further distinctions within that
15 group. Parents' love for their children, for example, isn't the
same as a ruler's love for the people he rules. For that matter, a
father's love for his son isn't even the same as the son's for his
father, and a husband's love for his wife isn't the same as the
wife's for her husband. Because each of these roles implies a
different way of being good [i.e. being a good father is different
from being a good son, a good husband, a good wife, a good
ruler, etc.] and different tasks, and so brings a different basis for
loving that person. Hence these are [all] different forms of love
[in both senses: different feelings, and different dispositions].
20 So in these cases, each party certainly doesn't get the same
things out of the relationship. Nor should they look to. But
when (for example) children pay their dues to their parents
(the things they owe them for bringing them into existence)
and parents do what they owe to their children, then the love
between them, as long as they stay like that, is enduring and
morally decent.
And in all relationships like this (between a superior and a
subordinate), the amount of love people feel needs to be pro-
25 portional [to the gap between them]. Someone who is your
better, for example, or someone with greater resources needs
to be loved by you more than they love you back, and likewise
for every other kind of superiority. When the love offered
corresponds to what each party deserves, you get a sort of
equality – which we think is essential to love and friendship.
But equality in love and friendship doesn't seem to work the

same way as in cases of fairness. In cases of fairness, equality 30
primarily means equality relative to what each party deserves,
and in secondary cases it might mean same-amount equality.
But in friendship, equality primarily means same-amount equality. It's the secondary cases where it's relative to what people
deserve.

That becomes clear when a really big gap opens up between
two friends, e.g. in how good or bad they are, {or their social
rank}, or how wealthy they are, or anything else. In that case
they can't be friends any more, and don't expect to be. That's 35
especially obvious with the gods. [We can't possibly be friends
with them] because the gods are so vastly superior to us in
every kind of good. It's also clear with kings. The people far 1159a
below them don't expect to be their friends. And ne'er-do-wells
don't expect to be friends either with people who are very good
men {or of very high rank} or with famous philosophers.

Of course, there's no formula in these cases for determining
precisely how large a gap will stop two people from being
friends. You can take away lots of things from one of them and
still find that the friendship carries on. But if the gap is really
big – like between man and god – then it certainly can't.   5

And that has a curious implication. Perhaps people don't
strictly want their friends to have the very greatest goods. They
don't want them to be gods, for example. Because then they
couldn't be their friends any more and so they wouldn't be part
of their own well-being. (Friends, we said, add to our own well-
being.) So if we were right to say that you always want what's
good for your friend, for your friend's sake, we meant as long 10
as they continue to be the same kind of thing as you are. In
other words, you'll want them to have the greatest goods on
condition they're still human. (And probably not all[19] of those
goods. Because you mostly want the best things for yourself.)

8 Ordinary people, because they crave respect, want other
people to love them more than they want to love other
people. (That's why ordinary people love flunkies. A flunky {or
hanger-on} is a friend who's a social inferior, or he pretends to 15
be [a friend] and to love you more than you love him back.)

Being loved feels similar to being respected, and that's what
ordinary people are really after.

And yet people don't even seem to value respect for itself.
They value it because of what it implies. Ordinary people, for
example, enjoy being respected by powerful rulers because
20 it excites their hopes. They think they'll be able to get anything
they need out of them. So they enjoy the respect, as a prelude
to the perks. Then there are those who want to be respected by
decent people, who know them well. They're trying to confirm
their good opinion of themselves. They enjoy the respect
because they trust the judgement of the people telling them
25 that they're good men. But being loved – that's something
they enjoy in itself, which implies it's more important than
being respected, and that love and friendship are intrinsically
desirable.

Also, friendship and love depend more on loving others than
on being loved. Good evidence for that are those mothers who
are content just to love [their children]. I'm thinking of mothers who give away their children to be raised by others, and
still love them (assuming they know who they are) without
30 expecting to be loved back, if that's their only option. It seems
it's enough for them if they can observe their children doing
well. They keep up their one-sided love, even though the
children – not knowing who they are – never perform any of
the duties a child owes a mother.

If friendship depends more on loving, and we praise people
for loving their friends, it seems it's loving [rather than being
35 loved] that's the key to being a good friend. So when friends
[love one another], as much as each deserves, they stay friends
1159b and their friendship is durable. And that's also the best way
for people who are unequal to be friends[20] – [the best they can
manage]. Because that way they can equalize the gap between
them.

'Friendship means being equals' – and being similar. And
the best case is between friends who are similar in their goodness. Because they're stable in themselves, and they remain
the same in the way they treat one another. Plus they make no
5 demands that are morally shabby, and don't do any morally

shabby favours for their friends either. If anything, they actually prevent that kind of thing. That's to be expected of good
people: that they do no wrong themselves and stop their friends
from doing wrong. Horrible people, on the other hand, certainly aren't stable (they aren't even consistent in the way they
treat themselves); but they can be friends for a little while, if   10
they get a kick out of each other's horribleness.

Friends who are useful or a pleasure to one another can stay
friends for longer – namely, for as long as they keep providing
one another with pleasures or material benefits.

Friendship based on what's useful most often seems to arise
between people who are opposites – e.g. rich and poor, ignorant and expert. Because often when a man lacks something he
tries to obtain it by giving something different in exchange for
it. You might push suitors and their teenage boyfriends into   15
that category, especially if one's cute and one's ugly. That's
why suitors sometimes make fools of themselves by expecting
to get the same kind of love as they give. I mean, if they were
desirable in just the same way, sure, that might be a reasonable
expectation. But when they're not even remotely attractive it's
just silly.

(Come to think of it, maybe opposites aren't really attracted
to one another per se. Maybe it's indirect, and desire's real   20
target is the mid-point, because that's what's good for each
opposite. What's good for something dry, say, isn't becoming
wet but moving towards the mid-point of wet and dry. Likewise for something hot, and so on . . . But let's not talk about
that now. It's a bit off-topic.)

9 As we said back at the start, it seems that right and wrong   25
{and obligation}[21] exist in the same contexts and in the
same people as friendship and love. Because any kind of partnership[22] {or cooperation} brings along its obligations – and
some sort of love or friendship.

At any rate, people call their shipmates or their fellow soldiers
'friends', and likewise the other people in any kind of partnership. And the extent of the partnership determines the extent of   30
the friendship – because it also [sets] their obligations. So the

old saying that 'friends are partners'[23] is right. Love and friendship always exist in a partnership. Brothers and best friends,
for example, {share everything, and} are partners in everything,
others within certain defined limits and to varying degrees, just
35 as there are degrees of love and friendship; and, of course,
different forms of right and wrong, {different obligations}.

1160a   The obligations parents have to their children, for example,
aren't the same as the obligations brothers have to one another,
and our obligations to our close friends aren't the same as to
our fellow citizens – and so on with the various forms of love
and friendship. And that means that wrongs also vary for each
category of person, i.e. a wrong becomes more serious if done
to a closer friend or loved one. Stealing from your best friend,
5 for example, is far worse than stealing from a fellow citizen.
Failing to help your own brother is far worse than failing to help
a stranger. Punching your father is far worse than punching . . .
anyone else at all.

So right and wrong {and obligation} naturally expand in
step with love and friendship, because they exist in the same
people and have an equal range.

And all forms of partnership {and cooperation} are parts, so
to speak, of the grand partnership of fellow citizens.

10 People go on trading voyages together, for example, in
pursuit of some particular interest, and to get some particular
thing they need in life. And that's also why people originally
came together as a community of citizens, and that's why they
stay together – because it's in their interest to do so. That's
what lawmakers aim for, and they call anything that serves the
common interest[24] 'right'. So, [as I was saying], all other forms
of partnership {or cooperation} only aim at some particular
15 interest – e.g. fellow sailors pursue their interests within the
context of their voyage (which is for making money, or something like that) and fellow soldiers pursue theirs in the context
of war (they're after loot, or victory, or a city), and likewise
members of the same clan or district. And some associations
seem to come into being for pleasure – like religious guilds
20 and dining clubs. Those are for organizing a religious festival,
or a banquet.

All of these associations seem subordinate to the one that exists between citizens. The community as a whole doesn't just aim at our interests of the present moment. It concerns itself with our whole life.

[*What was that you just said about religious guilds? They're just for pleasure?*]

[Well, those people] organize {festivals and} sacrifices and the public gatherings for those. They're paying their respects to the gods. They're also providing themselves with occasions for pleasure and relaxation. The earliest religious festivals and 25 gatherings seem to have taken place right after people harvested their crops, as a sort of 'first fruits' offering. Because that's when people had the most free time.

So [as I was saying], all forms of partnership {and cooperation} seem to be subdivisions of the one that exists between citizens. And each form of cooperation will have its corresponding type of friendship. 30

10 There are three types of government, with three deviations – corrupt versions of them, so to speak. The three types of government are rule by a king, rule by the best class of people, {'aristocracy'}, and the third is based on property qualifications, so it would make sense to call it government 'by property-holders',[25] but in fact most people usually call it 'republican'[26] government. Of the three, the best is rule by a 35 king and the worst is rule by property-holders.

The deviation from rule by a king is tyranny. Both are one- 1160b man rule. But they're worlds apart. A tyrant only thinks about his own interests, while a king thinks about the interests of the people he rules. Because if he doesn't already have everything he needs, if he isn't far above everyone in all goods, then by definition he isn't a king. And a man like that has no further needs. 5 (The only 'kings' not like that would be the ceremonial kind, appointed by lot.) So a king won't think about ways of benefiting himself. Just the people he rules. Tyranny is the opposite of that. A tyrant pursues what's good for himself. And it's perfectly obvious, in the case of tyranny, that it's the worst form of government. And the worst is the opposite of the best.

10　　Kingship can slide into tyranny. Tyranny is one-man rule gone bad. A wicked king turns into a tyrant. And rule by the better class {'aristocracy'} slips into oligarchy through bad rulers, i.e. rulers who distribute public resources without regard for merit, keep all or most goods for themselves and always give

15　out all the political offices to the same set of people; and pretty much the only thing they care about is being rich. So then you get a clique of nasty people in charge instead of the most decent class of people.

Government open to property-holders slides into democracy. Those are next to one another. Because even rule open to all property-holders [or 'republican' government] tends to empower the majority anyway, and creates [political] equals out of all the people who meet the qualification.

20　　Democracy is the least bad[27] of the bad ones. It's only a slight deviation from republican government.

So those are the most common ways in which governments change, with the smallest and easiest shifts from one type to another.

And you can find analogies for them – models, so to speak – in the family.

A father's relationship with his sons, for example, has the

25　same basic form as kingship. Because a father takes care of his children. That's also why Homer calls Zeus 'our father'. A king's rule is supposed to be fatherly. But in Persia a father's authority is more like tyranny, because [Persian fathers] treat their sons as slaves. (A master's relationship with his slaves is

30　also a kind of tyranny. It exists only to carry out the interests of the master. And, of course, there's nothing wrong with that kind. But there is something wrong with the Persian kind. Different classes of people [slaves and children] should be under different forms of control.)

The partnership between man and wife is like aristocracy: rule by the better class. The husband has the authority that he's entitled to, in the areas where a man should be in charge. All matters that a woman is suited to, he delegates to her. But if he

35　puts himself in charge of absolutely everything, he shifts their relationship into oligarchy. He's now [exercising authority]

beyond his entitlement, and not just in the areas where he's her better. And in some cases it's the wives who are in charge – 1161a wealthy heiresses. So in those two cases authority isn't based on who's better. It's just derived from force or wealth respectively, rather like in an oligarchy.

The relationship between brothers resembles rule open to all property-holders. Because brothers are equals, except in so far as there are differences in their ages. (Which is why if there's a 5 really big age gap they can't really love one another *as brothers* any more.)

And there's domestic democracy too: most obviously, in households that have no master at all (because there everyone is equal); also in households in which authority is weak, and it's a free-for-all.

11 Under each form of government, love and friendship 10 exist to the same degree as right and wrong, {and civic obligations}.

A king's [love for] his subjects, for example, depends on his being their supreme benefactor. That's to say, he benefits his subjects (since he's good, by definition, and only cares about their interests) and ensures that they flourish. He's like a shepherd looking after his flock. That's why Homer calls Agamemnon 'shepherd of the people'. A father's love is like that too, but 15 differs in the far greater extent of the benefits. Fathers, after all, are the cause of our existence, which we think of as the greatest good of all, as well as being responsible for our upbringing and education. We credit our forefathers with those blessings as well. And a father has a natural authority over his sons, forefathers over their descendants, kings over their subjects. These forms of love are between superior and subordinate – 20 that's why we also *respect* our parents. So obligations in these cases aren't the same on both sides. They're based on what each party deserves. As is the love.

A husband's relationship with his wife is like the one that exists [between the classes] in government by the better class (aristocracy): [in both cases] it's based on moral worth, and the greater good goes to the better party, and everyone gets

25 what they're suited to. Obligations are [proportioned] the same way.

Love between brothers is like the love between best friends. They're equals, and of the same generation, which means that they have the same attitudes and the same character (more or less). And that kind of relationship resembles the [civic] friendship under a government open to all property-holders. Because there, citizens are supposed to be equals, and all [members of the] 'decent' [class].*28 So they take turns at holding power and 30 govern on a basis of equality. Hence their friendship is also the kind you get between equals.

In the deviant forms of government [rulers have] very limited obligations, and there's correspondingly little love or friendship [between ruler and ruled]. Least of all in the worst: in a tyranny there's none at all or very little. Because when ruler and ruled are not in any sense partners there's no love or friendship between them. Because there are no obligations either. A craftsman, for instance, has no obligations to his tools; the 35 soul has no obligations to the body; masters have no obliga-1161b tions to their slaves. All of those things are certainly benefited by their users. But we don't love inanimate objects and we have no obligations to them, and likewise we have no obligations to horses, or cows, or slaves, in so far as they're slaves. Because they aren't in any sense our partners. A slave is just a tool – an animate tool – just as a tool is an inanimate slave. So there can 5 be no love[29] for a slave, considered as a slave. Considered as a human being – [maybe]. There's always some degree of right and wrong between any human being and any other who's [even] capable of being a partner[30] to an agreement or system of law. So there can also be love for a slave, in so far as he's a human being.

So even under tyrannical governments, friendship and love, and obligations, can exist [between rulers and ruled] to a limited degree. But in democracies they're more extensive, because citizens of democracies are partners in lots of things, 10 because they're equals.[31]

12 So every kind of love or friendship exists in some form of partnership {or cooperation}, we've said. But you might well treat love between family and close friends as a special case. (Friendships between fellow citizens, or between shipmates and suchlike, resemble partnerships rather more obviously. They're quite clearly based on an agreement. And you might put guest-friendship in the same category.)

Plus, family love itself seems to come in various forms, but it all depends on the love of parent for child. Parents love their children as something created from them, and the children love their parents because they're something that came from them. And the parents' love is the stronger because they more easily know [that their offspring] came from them than the offspring know they're from the parents.

(Also, the thing created belongs to its creator more than the creator belongs to the thing created; e.g. we say that hair and teeth belong to an animal; we're much less likely to say that an animal belongs to its hair. Plus it's a matter of time: parents love their offspring from the moment they're born, but offspring can only love their parents later, once they acquire awareness or perception.)

That's also why mothers love their children more.[32]

So parents love their children as versions of themselves. Offspring are like other selves, created by the physical division. And children love their parents because they're born from them. And siblings love each other because they're born from the same parents. Their sameness relative to their parents creates a sameness with one another – hence the talk about 'the same flesh and blood' and 'branches on the same tree' and so on. So it's as if they're the same thing, even in separate persons. (And a big factor in their love is growing up together and being the same age. 'Old loves old and young loves young', as they say, and people who do everything together tend to be close friends. That's why love between siblings often resembles a close friendship.) And cousins and other relatives derive their attachment to one another from the siblings – i.e. by being from the same family. And the strength of their attachment depends on how closely or distantly related they are.

Children's love for their parents, like humankind's love for
5 the gods, is a love for something both good and superior. Our
parents have benefited us in the greatest ways possible. They're
responsible for our existing at all and for our growth, and,
having given us existence, for raising and educating us.

Love between family members also has more pleasure and is
more useful than friendships with non-family, because a family
lives a life that's more closely shared.

10 Love between brothers (as long as they're both decent, and in
general similar to one another) is like love between best mates,
only more so, to the extent that siblings are closer, have an
instinctive fondness for one another from infancy and are more
likely to share the same likes and dislikes, because they're born
of the same parents and reared together and given the same
upbringing. Plus, a sibling gets to sound out your character –
which takes time – more fully and accurately than anyone.

15 The same factors explain the love between other relatives
too, in proportion [to how closely related they are].

Love between man and woman – {husband and wife} – seems
to be instinctive. Human beings are naturally a pair-bonding
animal even more than a social animal, to the extent that family comes before, and is more fundamental than, the state, and
because producing offspring is something more basic; something we share with all other animals.

20 Of course, for other animals that's the only purpose of
this kind of partnership. But human beings don't live together
in couples just to have children. They do so for all the things
they need in life. Their tasks are naturally divided, a man's
being different from a woman's. So they meet each other's needs,
each contributing their own particular tasks to their shared
well-being.

So that explains why that kind of relationship is useful to
25 us and gives us pleasure. But it can also be based on moral
goodness – if the husband and wife are also decent people.
Each has their way of being good, and they can be happy in the
other's being that kind of person.

Plus, having children seems to tie them together. (That's why
childless couples break up more easily.) Their children are a

blessing they share, and it's their shared interests that hold them together.

And to ask how a man should treat his wife, and in general 30 how we should treat our family and friends, seems no different from asking how to do what's *right* by them {or what our obligations are to them} – the point being that we evidently don't have the same obligations to family as to a stranger, say, or a best friend, or a classmate.

13   So we've got three kinds of friendship and love, as we said back at the start, and within each kind people 35 can be friends either on a basis of equality, or in the relation of superior and subordinate. Two equally good people can become friends, for example, but also a better man and a worse one. 1162b Likewise, pleasure-friends and friends who're after what's useful can be evenly or unevenly matched in the benefits they provide. So equal friends, in line with their equality, have to offer each other an equal amount of love and equal everything else, whereas unequals have to offer whatever's in proportion to the friends' superiority.

Complaints and criticisms only arise, or mostly arise, in 5 friendship based on what's mutually useful – as you'd expect. After all, in friendship based on being morally good, friends are strongly motivated to help one another, because that's part and parcel of being good people and being friends. And if friends are competing to help one another, you won't get any complaints or quarrels. You'd never get annoyed with someone for loving you and doing good things for you. If you're well 10 mannered, you just take revenge by doing them good right back. And if he manages to outdo you (which is exactly what he's aiming to do), what would he have to complain about? In that case you both desire the [same] good.[33]

You don't get any complaints between pleasure-friends, either. They're both getting what they desire as long as they still enjoy passing their time together. Plus, you'd look pretty silly com- 15 plaining that someone isn't any fun any more when you can just stop spending time with them.

But mutually useful friendship does generate complaints.

When people are using each other for material benefit they constantly ask for too much and always think that they're getting less than is due to them, while grumbling that their friends don't actually deserve as much as they're asking for. And when
20 they're helping one another they never seem to be able to satisfy each other's demands.

It seems that just as there are two different kinds of obligation – unwritten, {purely moral} obligations, and formal, legal obligations – there are two corresponding forms of mutually useful friendship: one is {informal, and} just a matter of character,[34] one relies on law. So complaints are especially likely to arise when people enter into an exchange on the one basis
25 but then try to settle accounts[35] on the other.

The law-based kind operates on clearly stated terms. It can be the entirely vulgar kind of exchange where you pay over the counter, or the more gentlemanly kind where the payment is postponed, but there's a contract stipulating that X is to be paid for Y. In the second kind what you owe is still fully spelt out, but the delayed payment makes it somewhat friend-like. (That's why in some countries you can't sue people for break-
30 ing those kinds of contracts. The attitude is that when you make deals on trust, you just have to take your chances.)[36]

But the informal kind lacks clearly stated terms. Instead it's like this: someone offers you a 'gift' (or whatever it might be) 'as one friend to another'. But really he expects to get as much or more in return. So to his mind it wasn't a gift. It was a loan. And the complaining starts when he doesn't settle the exchange on the same [friendly] terms[37] on which he entered into it.
35   That kind of thing happens because while almost everyone would quite like to behave honourably, [in the end] they opt for whatever serves their interests. (The honourable thing is to
1163a help others without wanting anything in return. But it's in our interests to benefit from it.)

So, if you can, you just should pay back the full cost of what he gave you. If he doesn't want to be your friend, you shouldn't force him.[38] Really, it was a mistake to have accepted the gift from him in the first place – because he wasn't a friend and
5 wasn't doing it just to help you – so now you should act exactly

as if you'd received the benefit for an agreed price, and settle
the debt. Or you can agree to pay him back when able to do so.
(Even your gift-giver wouldn't expect you to pay him back if
you can't. So you only have to pay him back if you can.)

And be sure to consider carefully, at the outset, who is offering you help and what they expect in return, so that you can
decide whether or not to accept their help on those terms.

People also argue over whether it's just the benefit to the 10
recipient that should be the measure here – I mean, for determining the size of a repayment – or the effort someone made to
give that aid. When we've been helped out, we tend to say that
what we got from our benefactors was 'just some little thing'
for them and we 'could have got it from someone else'. We
minimize it. And they do the opposite: they say it was 'the
most valuable thing they had', and that we 'couldn't have got 15
it from anyone else', and they 'risked their lives' [helping us] or
they were 'very hard up at the time'.

Maybe it depends on the type of friendship. For mutually
useful friendships, yes, the measure should just be the objective
benefit to the recipient. Because he's the one in need, and the
other meets that need with the idea that he'll get an equal
amount in return. So the amount of aid there's been is exactly
the benefit to him, and he should pay back the amount that he 20
gained (or more – that would be more honourable). But with
friendships based on moral goodness – not that there'll ever be
any complaints, of course – the measure for repayments should
be the choice {or intent}[39] of the giver. Because with moral
goodness, and character in general, choice is key.

14 You get quarrels in friendships between superiors and
subordinates, too. Each thinks he deserves more than 25
the other, and when that happens the friendship ends. The
better man, {of higher social rank}, thinks he should get more
'because after all, a good man deserves the larger share'. Likewise the [wealthy friend] with the greater resources: 'A friend
who's no use to me shouldn't get an equal share. If what I get
out of this friendship doesn't match the cost of all I've done
[for him], that's not friendship, that's charity!' They think a 30

friendship should be like a financial partnership, where the
people who contribute more get more of the profits. But the
[poor and] needy friend, or the friend of inferior rank, sees it
the other way round. A high-ranking friend is supposed to provide for his friends' needs! What's the point of being friends
with 'a good man',[40] or a powerful man, they say, if I'm not
35 going to get any benefit out of it?

1163b They're actually both correct in their expectations. Each one
should indeed get a greater share than the other – but not of
the same thing. The superior friend should get more respect,
the needy friend should profit more {materially}. Because the
proper reward for being a good man, and for helping others, is
respect; material gain is what helps a friend in need.

5   This seems to apply in political life as well. A [statesman]
earns no respect if he doesn't contribute to the common good.
Public goods are only granted to people who benefit the public,
and respect is a public good. It's impossible, for example, to
make money from public office and earn respect at the same
time. Nobody tolerates a situation that makes them worse off
10 in every sense, so if [public office] makes you worse off financially, people will compensate you with respect. If you're
corrupt, on the other hand, you just get the money.[41]

Giving people what they deserve is a way of equalizing, and
preserves love and friendship, as we said earlier. So that's also
how unequal friends should interact with one another: when
one friend is benefited financially, or by being made a better
person,[42] he should pay the other back with his respect – which
is paying him back the only way he can. Because friendship
15 and love only demand of us what's possible, not the full amount
we owe. After all, sometimes that's just impossible – like with
the forms of respect we offer the gods, or our parents. Nobody
could possibly ever pay them back in full. All any decent man
can be expected to do is care for his parents as best he can.

That's probably also why we feel that a son has no right to disown his father, although a father may disown his son. Because
20 as long as you owe a debt, you have to keep paying it back; and
no son has ever done enough for his father to match the value
of what he's already received from him. So he'll always be in

his debt. But the person to whom a debt is owed has the right
to cancel it – including fathers. But even so, chances are that
no father would ever renounce his son, unless the son was
an extremely nasty person. Because apart from a father's
instinctive love for his son, it's human nature not to drive away 25
a [future] means of support. A son, on the other hand, might
well try to avoid providing for his father, or have no interest in
doing so, if he's a terrible son. After all, that's typical: people
are happy to receive help but shy away from doing good for
others, because they don't see what they have to gain from it.

I think that's all we need to say about that.

BOOK IX

In all asymmetrical friendships,[1] proportion equalizes and preserves the friendship – as we said. In civic friendship, for example, a shoemaker trades shoes for things of equivalent value, and likewise a tailor, and so on.

35

1164a Now, in that context, people have devised a common unit – money – and all goods can be matched to that and measured in it.

But between lovers, [it's not so simple]. Sometimes the older suitor complains: 'I'm devoted to you, but you don't love me back' – even though (as sometimes happens) there's really nothing lovable {or attractive} about him. Often the younger boyfriend complains: 'You promised me all those things. And now you're not doing anything[2] you said you would!' That kind of thing happens when [the older man] loves his young boyfriend for pleasure, but he only likes the older guy because he's useful; [so it only works as long as they] both still have those attributes. Since their love is based on those things, they break up once they're not getting them. Those things were their reason for being in the relationship. They didn't like one another for who they are. What they liked were those [extrinsic] features. And since those don't last, neither do those kinds of relationships.[3] (But love of people's characters[4] is intrinsic. So that does last, as we said.)

5

10

Disputes also arise when friends find themselves getting the wrong thing – something that isn't what they want. If you don't get what you're aiming for, you may as well be getting nothing at all. Like when [the king] promised to pay the guitar-singer:[5] 'and the better you sing,' he said, 'the more I'll pay'. So

15

next morning, when he asked him to pay up, he claimed he'd
already paid – pleasure for pleasure. [He'd given him the pleasure of anticipating all that money.] So that might have been
OK if that's what both of them wanted; but since only one of
them wanted enjoyment, and the other wanted profit, and one
has what he wanted and the other doesn't – that doesn't quite 20
count as respecting the terms of the deal.

The point is, what you need [from a friendship] – whatever
that happens to be – is also what you focus on.[6] You'll give X
so as to get Y.[7]

But who decides how much X is worth? The person who
offers it, up front, or the taker, after getting it? If you offer
something up front, it looks as if you're leaving [the question
of payment] to the other person. (That's what they say Protagoras used to do. Whenever he taught whatever it might 25
be, he'd ask the student to set the price – 'whatever you think
knowing these things is worth' – and he'd accept that amount.)

But some people in these situations prefer the motto: 'state
your fee up front – [even with friends]'.[8]

But, then, if people do take a cash payment up front, and
then don't do anything they said they would (because they
made such extravagant promises), they can expect to face complaints for not carrying out what they agreed. (Sophists are 30
surely forced to do that, because nobody would pay money for
what they know.)

So those people, by failing to do what they've been paid to
do, understandably face complaints. But in cases where there
isn't any fixed agreement about the value of the benefit:

(a) If people give freely [to their friends] just because of who 35
they are,[9] they won't get any complaints – as we said earlier.
That's the nature of friendship based on goodness. And repay- 1164b
ment should be sensitive to the friend's choice {and intent}.[10]
Because choice is key to being a friend, and to being a good
person.

(b) And that's surely how [we should repay] our philosophical mentors[11] too. You can't measure the value of that kind
of thing in money. No amount of respect could ever balance
out [what they've given us]. It's enough, I'd say, if we offer 5

them whatever we can, like the way we respect the gods[12] or our parents.

But when giving isn't like that – when there's a quid pro quo – then, ideally, repayment should be made according to what both parties think is the right amount. But failing that, surely it's both unavoidable and fair that the person who received the benefit gets to set its value. However much that person was benefited (or however much they would have given in exchange for that pleasure), that's the right amount for the giver to get in return.

After all, that's clearly the way things work with buying and selling. (And in some places it's against the law[13] to sue people for breaking voluntary contracts. The idea is that if you trusted someone, you just have to settle with them on the same [informal] terms as you entered into the deal.)

[Also], people think* that if person A [in effect] left it to person B to set the payment, it's fairer for B to do so rather than A.

[Also], typically the possessors of X, and the people who want to get hold of X, don't value it equally. We always think that things that are ours, and that we're offering to others, are worth a lot. But even so, when the exchange takes place it's based on the amount that the people who are getting X say it's worth. (Though perhaps its value should be based on what they thought it was worth before getting it, not once they've got it.)

2   And here's another set of difficult questions.

Do you owe your father everything? Do you have to obey him in everything? Or is it that when you're sick you should trust your doctor, and when you're voting for a general you should pick the man with actual military skill?

Similarly, is it better to do favours for friends and family, or good people? Should you repay a favour to someone who helped you out or spend [that money] on a close friend, assuming you can't do both?

Perhaps it isn't easy to determine all of those sorts of things exactly. There are so many variables; all manner of differences in how important it is [to do it], or unimportant, or how

honourable, or how urgent. But it's at least fairly clear that you 30
don't owe everything to the same person. Also, that you should
repay people who've helped you out – for the most part – rather
than [using those resources to] do favours for your close friends
(just as you should repay a debt to a creditor rather than gift
the money to a friend).

But maybe even that isn't always the case.

Suppose you were kidnapped by pirates, and someone paid
your ransom. [Then the man who paid your ransom, and your
father, are both kidnapped.] Should you ransom the person
who ransomed you, whoever he is? Or what if he hasn't even 35
been kidnapped, what if he's just asking for the money back?
Should you pay him back, or ransom your father? [Your father, 1165a
surely.] After all, you'd probably even ransom your father instead
of yourself.

So as we said, as a general rule you should pay your debts.
But if giving that money to someone else is overwhelmingly the
more honourable thing to do, or more urgent, then you should
lean towards that.

In any case, sometimes repaying a favour isn't even equiva- 5
lent; like, say, when someone helps you out, knowing you're a
good man, and then you find yourself having to return a favour
to someone you think is a horrible person.

And if someone has lent you money, that doesn't always mean
you have to do the same for them. Suppose someone made you
a loan, assuming he'd be repaid, because you're a decent guy,
but you don't expect him to pay you back what you lend him
because [you think] he's a crook. So in that situation, if he
really is a crook, then his expectation [of a return loan] isn't 10
equivalent. And even if he's not, but people think he is,[14] it
surely wouldn't be so wrong of you [to refuse].*[15]

So, as we've said many times before,[16] all claims {and the-
ories} that involve human feelings and actions can only be as
definite as their subject matter. But it's at least pretty clear that
you don't owe the same things to everyone, and that you don't
owe everything to your father – just as people don't only offer 15
sacrifices to Zeus.[17] We owe different things to our parents,
our siblings, our closest friends, people who've helped us out;

and we have to grant and give what's appropriate and fitting to each.

And that's just what people seem to do. They invite their relatives to weddings, for example, because they share family
20 with those people, so they also share family-related events. They also mostly expect relatives to attend funerals, for the same reason.

And surely we have a duty to provide support {and sustenance} for our parents, before all others, because of our debt to them. They're the reason we exist at all, and [if we had to choose] it's better[18] to provide for them than for ourselves. We also owe our parents respect – as to the gods. But not every
25 kind. After all, you don't even owe the same respect to your father as to your mother. And you don't owe your father the respect you owe a philosopher, or a general. You just owe him the kind a father deserves; and your mother, the kind a mother deserves.

We also owe respect to any elderly person just on account of their age – by standing up [when they enter the room], offering them a seat,[19] that kind of thing.

As for our close friends and our siblings, what we owe to
30 them is to speak frankly;[20] and to share everything.

As for relatives, fellow tribesmen, fellow citizens and so on – in each case we have to try to give them their due, and to weigh up their competing claims on us in terms of kinship, {social rank}, how good they are, or how useful. If people are in the same category, comparing them is easier; when they're in different categories it's a bit harder. But that's no reason to give
35 up. We've just got to sort it all out as best we can.

3 Another difficult question is whether or not you should end friendships with people who don't stay the same.

1165b   So maybe when people are friends on the basis of what's useful, or for pleasure, there's nothing wrong with them ending the friendship when they're no longer getting those things out of it. After all, it's those things that they were friends with. So when the supply of them runs out, it makes sense for them to not be friends.

But you might well complain if someone liked you for your usefulness, or for pleasure, but pretended it was because of your character. Because, as we said at the start,[21] all sorts of disputes arise between friends when there's a difference between what they think is the nature of their relationship and what it actually is.

So when you mistakenly think that someone likes you for your character, without them doing anything to give you that idea, you only have yourself to blame. But if you're deceived by pretence on their part, you have every right to call them out for their deceit – more so than people who make counterfeit coins, since the harm they're doing concerns something much more valuable.

And what if you accept someone as a friend, thinking that they're good, but then they turn into – and you now think they are – a horrible person? Should you still love them, {keep them as a friend}? Or is that impossible, given that not everything is lovable? Only what's good. Evil is not lovable {or love-worthy}, and should not be loved. You shouldn't be an evil-lover. And you shouldn't let yourself become like your awful friend either. (We said before, like tends to be friends with like.)

So does that mean that you should end the friendship straight away? Or not in every case? Maybe just if they're incurable in their wickedness? If there's a possibility of reform, then you should help them. It's much more important to help a friend fix their character than, [say], to help them increase their wealth, to the extent that character is something better and more crucial to friendship.

But it surely wouldn't be so wrong of you[22] to end the friendship either. After all, you weren't friends with someone like that. So if they've become a different person and there's nothing you can do to bring them back, you just give up on them.

Or what if your friend stayed the same and you became a better person, so you significantly diverge from them in how good you are? Should you still treat them as a friend? Or is that impossible?

The problem becomes especially clear when the gap is really large – as [sometimes happens] with childhood friendships.

That's to say, if one friend remained mentally a child and the
other became as good a man as any, how could they be friends?
If they don't have the same likes and dislikes, aren't pleased
or pained by the same things? (In fact, that won't even be true
of how they relate to each other.)[23] But without those features
30 there's no way that they could be friends, because it's impossible for them to share their lives. We talked about that already.

So should the one now treat the other exactly as if they'd
never been friends at all? Or take account of the closeness that
they once had? We say we ought to favour friends and loved
ones over strangers. Perhaps, in the same way, you owe at least
35 something to the people who were once your friends, on account
of the friendship that existed between you in the past – as long
as the break-up of your friendship wasn't caused by any really
extreme nastiness on their part.

1166a   4   The things that characterize friendship and love towards
others – the features by which we define them – seem to
derive from the way we relate to ourselves.

Consider: people define 'a friend' {or 'someone who loves
you'} as:

(a) someone who wants and does things that are good for
5 you, or that they think are good for you, for your sake, or

(b) someone who, because they love you, wants you to exist –
to be alive – for your own sake. (That's how mothers feel about
their children, for example; or friends and family who've had
a falling-out.)[24] Or

(c) someone who spends their time with you and makes the
same choices as you, or

(d) someone who, because they love you, shares your pains
and your joys. Again, that's especially true of mothers with
respect to their children.

And it's by one or other of those that people always define
philia, friendship and love, as well.

10   But [now notice that], if you're a good person, every single
one of those is true of your relationship with yourself, and
they hold for anyone else to the extent that they can think of
themselves as good. And as we've said before, we assume that

goodness, and the good person, are always the measure[25] of the facts.

Consider: if you're a good person, then:

(a) you're always in agreement with yourself; you desire the same things in every part of your soul; and

(b) you want good things (or what you think is good) for yourself, and you do what's good for you (a good person works to achieve what's good) and for your own sake (that's to say, for the sake of the part of you that reasons {and thinks}; and that's the part we think of as being *you*). Also,

(c) you want yourself to be alive, and to survive (especially the part of you that thinks). Existing, for a good person, is a good thing, and you always want good things for yourself.

[But that means, as what you are;][26] you'd never choose to have all possible good things if it meant first becoming something else – a god, for example – [i.e. choose] for that other thing that's now come into existence [to have them].* (God already has the highest good,[27] anyway.) You only want them if you can still be what you are. (And the part of you that thinks – surely that's what you are, or mostly.)

(d) Also, if you're a good person you want to spend time with yourself. That's something you like doing because you have pleasant recollections of things that you've done, and optimism about your future, which is also enjoyable, and you're supplied with plenty of [higher] contemplations by your intellect.

(e) Also, you sympathize with your own pains and pleasures more than with anyone else's, in the sense that a given thing causes you pain or pleasure consistently; not one thing one moment, something else the next. You pretty much never regret anything.

So all of those things are true of your relationship with yourself if you're a decent person. And you relate to a friend in the same way. Because a friend is another self. That explains why we think of love and friendship as one or other of those things [listed above], and 'friends' and 'loved ones' as the people you relate to in those ways.

As for whether you can or can't actually experience love for

Margin line numbers: 15 (at "yourself"), 20 (at "for yourself."), 25 (at "have pleasant"), 30 (at "with your-")

yourself {or be your own friend} – for now we can put that to
one side.

35   . . . But you might think you can, in so far as you are [made
up of] two or more elements (going by what we've said before);
1166b and also because the most extreme form of love [of others] is
so like your relationship with yourself.

All the things we've just mentioned seem to apply to ordinary people too – bad as they are.

So is it only in so far as they're happy with who they are,
and consider themselves decent people, that they can share
5   in them? After all, when people are utterly bad – the sort who
commit heinous crimes – they certainly don't have any of those
features and nobody even imagines that they do.

And, roughly speaking, neither do [any] bad people. Consider:

(a) Bad people are conflicted.[28] The have desires {and cravings}
that are at odds with what they want [to do] – just like people
who lack self-control. Instead of the things they think are good
for them, they choose things that give them pleasure but cause
10   them harm. For others, it's their cowardice or their laziness that
makes them give up on doing what they think is best for them.

(b) And [sometimes] people who've done lots of really terrible things, on account of being such horrible people, hate
being alive,[29] and escape from it by killing themselves.*

(c) Also, horrible people seek out others to pass their days
15   with, but shun their own company. They remember all sorts of
disturbing things when they're on their own and have equally
disturbing thoughts about their future. But when they're
around other people they can forget.

And there's nothing to love[30] about them, so they don't feel
any sort of love for themselves.

(d) People like that don't even sympathize with their own
joys or their own pains. Their soul is in a state of civil war.
20   Part of it, because of their wickedness, feels pained when they
abstain {or refrain} from something. Part of it is pleased. One
part pulls them in one direction, another in some other
direction – tearing them apart, as it were. Even if it's not strictly
possible to feel pain and pleasure at the very same instant, at
any rate, right after enjoying something they're upset that they

enjoyed it: 'Why did I enjoy that? I wish I hadn't!' Bad people
are stuffed full of regrets.

So a bad person doesn't seem to feel any sort of friendship or 25
love even towards himself – because there's nothing lovable {or
attractive} about him.

So if being that way is utterly wretched and pathetic, that's
a very good reason to make every effort to avoid being a horrible person, and to try as hard as you can to be a kind and
decent one. Only then can you have friend-like feelings towards
yourself or be anyone else's friend {or earn anyone's love}.

5 What about goodwill? That certainly seems related to 30
friendship. But it isn't friendship. It's something that you
can feel even towards people you don't know, and without
them being aware of it. That's impossible with friendship. (We
talked about that before.)

Nor is goodwill just a matter of liking {or loving} someone.
It doesn't involve any effort or motivation – standard features
of loving someone. Also, loving someone implies knowing
them well, but a feeling of goodwill can be instantaneous – like 35
when we feel it towards athletes in sporting contests. We feel 1167a
goodwill towards them – want them to succeed – but wouldn't
actually do anything to help them because, as I said, our goodwill arises just in that instant and our affection is fleeting.

But goodwill does at least seem a sort of starting point for
being friends. It's a bit like the way the pleasure of seeing someone can be a starting point for falling in love. Nobody falls in
love if they don't first like the look of someone, but just liking 5
someone's looks doesn't amount to being in love. (You're in
love once you also miss someone whenever they're gone, and
long for them to be around.) In the same way, it's impossible
for people to be friends if they haven't come to feel goodwill
towards one another; but they can have mutual goodwill without yet being friends. People want the best for the objects of
their goodwill, that's all. That doesn't mean they'd do anything to help them or go to any trouble over them. You could 10
call goodwill lazy friendship, metaphorically speaking.

But if it continues for a while and gets to the point where you

know each other well, it can grow into friendship. And [when it does, it won't be a friendship] based on what's useful or based on pleasure. Because those aren't the things that trigger our goodwill. It's when someone has been good to you, that's
15 when you offer them your goodwill, in return for how they've treated you. You feel you owe it. By contrast, if your reason for wanting to do someone a good turn is that you're hoping for some advantage from them, you're not really acting out of goodwill, at least not towards them – towards yourself, more like – just as you aren't someone's friend if you're tending to their needs because it's useful to you to do so.

In general, goodwill is a response to someone's moral goodness, or some kind of decency or kindness on their part. You
20 feel it when someone comes across as attractive,[31] brave, something like that – as happens with athletes, as we said.

6   Harmony seems closely tied to friendship too. That's why it's not just a matter of people having the same views about things. That could be the case with people who don't even know each other.

We also don't speak of 'harmony' when people have the same views on just anything, like when they agree about the sun,
25 moon and stars.[32] Being in harmony on those kinds of things has nothing to do with being friends. Rather, we speak of harmony in city states when [citizens] have the same views about what's in their interests; when they make the same choices, {have the same values}[33] and do the things that they've all decided on as a community.

So harmony means harmony on practical and moral questions and, more precisely, the important ones, where options
30 are open and things are at stake for both sides or for everyone. There's harmony in city states when everyone agrees, say, that 'there should be elections for public offices'; or that 'we should have an alliance with Sparta'; or that 'Pittacus[34] should rule' (when that was also what *he* wanted to do). But not when two people are both saying '*I* want to rule' – like [Eteocles and Polynices] in Euripides' *Phoenician Women*. That's civil strife. Harmony isn't just a matter of both parties having the same

idea, whatever it might be. It's a matter of people having the 35
same view applied to the same person, like when the common
people and the decent classes all agree that the best people 1167b
should rule. That way everyone's getting what they want.

So it seems clear that harmony is {civic friendship}, friendship between citizens (exactly what the word usually means).
Because it's about things that are in people's interests and that
affect the way we live.

Harmony in that sense is a feature of decent people. Decent
people are in harmony, within themselves and with one another, 5
since they have pretty much the same attitudes. With people
like that {you know where you stand}; what they want stays
fixed. It doesn't flow back and forth like the [shifting currents
of the] Euripus. And they want what's right {and fair}, and
in people's best interests, and strive for those things for their
community as well.

Bad people, on the other hand, can't experience harmony,
except to a limited degree (just as they can only be friends to 10
a limited degree). [When they live together,] they all strive
to get more than their share of the benefits, but fall short
when it comes to the burdens and their public duties. Every
man is only out for himself, so everyone investigates and
thwarts his neighbour. And the fact is, if people don't look
after the common good, it's destroyed. So they end up falling
into faction and civil strife – coercing one another {to do
what's right}, never wanting to do the right thing of their own 15
accord.

7 When people have helped others, they seem to love {and
care about} the people they helped more than the people
who received that help love their benefactors.

It's surprising it works that way, and people have tried to
figure it out.

So most of them think it's because helpers are owed a debt
by the people they helped. 'What happens with debts is that, 20
while the people who owe the debt would like their creditors to
cease to exist, the lenders take great care to make sure that
their debtors stay alive; and in much the same way, when people

have been helpful to others they want the people they helped to
stay alive long enough to return the favour, whereas the people
25 they helped aren't so concerned about paying them back.'

'A scoundrel's view[35] of things!' Epicharmus might say about
that claim. But true to human character. Most people *are*
inclined to forget and *are* more interested in being helped than
in doing good for others.

And yet, maybe the reason is deeper in nature. Maybe it's
30 not like the lender case. After all, lenders don't actually love
{or care about} their debtors. They only want them to survive
so they can collect the debt. But people who've helped others
actually care about, and love, the people they've helped, even
if they're not useful to them in any way and are unlikely ever
to be so in the future.

The same thing happens with craftsmen: every craftsman
loves his own work, {his own creation}, more than the work
35 would love him back if it came to life. And it probably happens
1168a most of all with poets. They just adore their own poems and
plays; love them like their own children.

So it seems that something similar is also going on with people
who've helped out others. The person that they've helped is
their creation, {their handiwork}. So they love that work more
than their work loves its creator.

5   And the reason for that is that existence is something desirable for everyone; something we all love. But we exist by being
actualized. By being alive and by doing. And a creator is actualized, so to speak, in his work. So he loves his work because
he loves existence. That's natural. What he is in his capacities,
his creation reveals and makes actual.

10   Also, if you've helped someone your action is honourable, so
you cherish the person who embodies that fact about you. If
you've been helped, the person who helped you doesn't embody
anything honourable of yours. At most they represent a benefit
to you, and that gives you less pleasure and is less lovable.

We get pleasure from our activities in the present, from our
expectations about the future and our memories of our past.
15 But we get most pleasure from our activities, and it's those
that we love the most. So for someone who's done something

[helpful], their work lasts, because [it was honourable; and] what's honourable endures. For the person who received that help, the usefulness of it is soon gone.

Also, the memory of our honourable actions gives us pleasure; the memory of things that were useful to us gives us no pleasure at all, or less. (With our expectations, it seems to work the other way round.)

Also, loving someone seems like the active role, being loved the passive role. So outdoing others in your actions [naturally] 20 goes with loving them and being a friend.

Also, people always feel greater fondness for things they've toiled hard to bring about. People who've made their money themselves, for example, are more fond of it than people who've inherited their wealth. And being helped seems effortless, while helping others is hard work. (That's also why mothers love their children more [than fathers]. For mothers, producing a child 25 involves a lot more toil. It's also easier for them to know the child is theirs – which, come to think of it, is another thing that might apply[36] to benefactors.)

8 Another puzzle: should you love {and care about} yourself most of all, or someone else?

We criticize people who mostly care about themselves; call them 'selfish' as a rebuke. The common view is that a bad per- 30 son does everything for himself, and the nastier he is the more that's the case; and people hold that against someone, as in 'everything he does, it's always about him'. A decent person, by contrast, does things 'because it's the honourable thing to do', and the better they are the more they act for that reason; they also do things for their friends and loved ones. As for their own interests, they put them to one side. 35

But the facts are at odds with these claims, and with good reason.

People say you should love your 'dearest friend' the most; and your 'dearest friend' is the person who wants what's good for you just for your sake (even if nobody's ever going to know about it). But that applies above all to your relationship with yourself – as do all the other things by which we define a friend.

5 We said earlier, remember, that all [the main] features of friendship and love start from your relationship with yourself and
extend from there to others. And all the sayings[37] support the
same idea: as in 'friends are a single soul', 'friends share everything', 'friendship is equality', 'knee's closer than shin': all of
those would apply most of all to your relationship with yourself. Because you are your own dearest friend.

10   It follows that you should also love yourself the most.

So, reasonably enough, there's a puzzle here as to which of
these sets of claims we should go along with. They both seem
pretty plausible.

Maybe what we should do is analyse the two lines of argument and try to determine to what extent, and in what way,
each is correct.

All right, so we can probably clear things up if we get a sense
of what each set of claims means by 'selfish'.

15   So, the people treating it as a term of reproach are calling
someone 'selfish' if they assign themselves the larger share when
it comes to money, prestige, {status}, physical pleasures. Those
are the things that most people desire and care about, as if they
were the best things [in life] – that's why they're the 'fought-
over' goods.[38]

So when people are greedy over those things, they're indul-
20 ging their desires {and cravings}, and in general their feelings
and the non-rational part of their soul. And that's what most
people are like. So that's also how the term 'selfish' arose –
from that crummy, {flawed} majority. So it's right to reproach
people for being selfish in that sense.

And it really is clear that for most people, by common usage,
'selfish' only applies to people who assign themselves those kinds
25 of things. Because think about it: suppose you were always keen
to do the right thing – i.e. keen for you to be the one doing it
rather than anyone else – or the moderate thing, or anything
else based on any of the virtues, and in general always laying
claim to [every chance to do] what's honourable, for yourself.
Nobody's going to call you 'selfish' or criticize you for *that*.

But you might think that's actually a way of being more selfish. At any rate, you're now awarding yourself the finest, {most

honourable} things – 'goods' in the fullest sense – and you're 30
indulging the most authoritative element of yourself and fully
obeying that part of you. And just as we think a city state (or
any other union of parts) is, above all, its most authoritative
part – so too a human being. So if you love and indulge that
part of yourself you're 'selfish', {you 'care about your *self*'}, in
the truest sense.

Also, we say someone 'has *self*-control' or 'lacks *self*-control',
depending on whether or not their mind is controlling them, 35
implying that your mind is you.[39]

Also, we think people have performed an action themselves, and willingly, above all when they've done it using their 1169a
reason.

So it's quite clear that the individual is that part of them,
or mostly. And it's also clear that a decent person loves that
part of themselves most of all. That's why you could say that
they're the most fully selfish – though by a different kind of
selfishness from the kind that gets reprimanded. They're as
different [from that other kind of selfish person] as living by
reason is from living by your emotions; as different as desiring 5
what's honourable is from desiring whatever you take to be in
your interests.

So when people are extremely eager to perform honourable
actions everybody welcomes it, everyone applauds them. And
if everyone competed [only in that way], over doing the honourable thing, and put all their effort [only] into behaving
as honourably as they could, society as a whole would have
everything it needs and individually everyone would have the 10
greatest of all goods (since the greatest of all goods is to be a
good person).

It follows that a good man actually should be selfish. Because
that way he himself will benefit from doing honourable things
and he'll also be helping others. But a wicked man should not
be selfish. Because he'll harm both himself and his neighbours
by acting on his bad impulses.

For a wicked man, what he should be doing is different from 15
what he does. But with a decent man, whatever he should be
doing – that's always what he does. That's because intellect

always chooses what is best for itself, and a decent person always obeys his intellect.

20 It's true that a good man does lots of things for the sake of his friends and loved ones, or for his country – even giving up his life for them if he has to. He'll freely give up money, prestige and in general all the 'fought-over' goods if it means securing for himself [a chance to do] the honourable thing.

He'd rather experience a brief moment of extreme bliss than live a long life of being weakly satisfied. He'd rather live honourably for a year than for many in moral mediocrity. He'd rather perform a single great and glorious action than a long series of minor ones.

25 That's surely what's happening with people who give up their lives for others. So that means they're choosing a great good – what's honourable – for themselves.

And they'll happily give up money if it means their friends and loved ones having more of it. That way, the friend gets money but they get [to do] the honourable thing. So really they're awarding themselves the greater good.

The same goes for prestige and positions of power: [a good 30 man] will give it all away for his friend or someone he loves. Because that's the honourable thing for him, and praiseworthy.

(It's no wonder he's thought of as a good man if he chooses what's honourable over everything.)

It's even possible to give up *actions*[40] to a friend. It can be more honourable to be responsible for your friend's doing something than to do it yourself.

So in all these kinds of praiseworthy actions, a good man is 35 clearly awarding himself the larger share – of what's honourable.

1169b So you should be selfish in that sense, as we said. But not in the way most people are.

9 Another thing people disagree about is whether, to flourish in life, you will or won't need friends and loved ones.

People say that the most blessed, {well-off} people, who can meet all their needs, have no need for friends because they 5 already have the good things [in life]. So since they can meet their needs they don't need anything further; and a friend, who's a kind of other self, is only there to supply the things that you can't get on your own. Hence the line: 'When the gifts of god[41] are good, what need of friends?'

But it seems a bit absurd, if we're assigning all the good things in life to our {'blessed'}, 'flourishing' man, not to grant him any friends – supposedly the greatest of external goods!   10

Also, if being a friend is more about doing good than receiving it, and if a key feature of being a good person is helping others, and if it's a finer, {more honourable} thing to do good for friends and loved ones than for strangers, then a good man will need the people he's going to do good things for.

That's why people puzzle over whether you need friends more when you're enjoying good fortune or when you're down on your luck. Both, it seems. If you're down on your luck you need   15 the friends who are going to help you. And when you're enjoying good fortune you need friends to have someone to help.

And surely it's absurd to make our flourishing, {blessed} man a loner. Nobody would choose to have every good thing in life on their own. People are social beings. It's our nature to share our lives with others. So that must apply to {flourishing}, prosperous people too. Because they have [all] the naturally good things. And it's obvious that it's better to pass your time   20 with friends and loved ones, and with good people, than with strangers or just anyone.

So to flourish, you do need friends and loved ones.

In that case, what are those first people saying? And is there any truth in it?

Maybe it's that most people think that 'friends' just means friends of the useful kind? It's true that a flourishing [i.e. prosperous] man won't have any need for those kinds of friends, since he already has all the good things [in life]. He also won't   25 need pleasure-friends, or only to a limited degree. (His life is pleasant, and has no need for extra, imported pleasure.) So since he doesn't need those kinds of friends, people think he just doesn't need friends.

But that's surely not the case.

We said, back at the start, that flourishing is a kind of activity.

And activity is obviously something ongoing, not something
30 you just have, like a possession. And if
(1) flourishing depends on living, and activity, and
(2) a good person's activity is morally good and pleasant in
itself (as we said right at the start) and
(3) what's our own is one of the things that gives us pleasure,
and
(4) we're more able to observe others than ourselves, and the
actions of others more than our own actions, and
35   (5) the actions of good people, who are also our friends, give
1170a us pleasure (if we're good people) because they have both
naturally pleasurable features . . .

. . . it follows that to flourish you'll have to have morally
good friends, given that one of your aims is to observe actions
that are (a) morally good and (b) your own, and the actions of
a good person who's your friend nicely fit that description.

Also, people think that if you're flourishing, you should be
5 enjoying life; {you should be happy}. But a loner's life is hard.
It's not easy to exercise [your virtues] continually on your own.
But with others, and on others – that's easier. So that way your
activity (enjoyable in itself) will be more continuous – which
has to be a feature of any flourishing life.

† A good person, as a good person, takes pleasure in [others']
actions that express goodness, and is bothered by actions
10 caused by badness, just as a musician enjoys beautiful songs
but finds bad ones painful. †[42]

Also, by sharing your life with good people you get a sort of
training in how to be a good person – as Theognis says.

Thinking about it more scientifically, it does seem that a morally good friend is a naturally desirable thing* for any good
person.
(1) We said earlier that what's naturally good is always good,
15 and pleasant, to a good person.
(2) And people define being alive, for all animals, by their
capacity for perceiving, and for human beings by their capacity
for perceiving or thinking. But a capacity only exists for the
exercising of it; the key thing is in the exercising of it. So that

implies that being alive, in the key sense, means actually perceiving, or thinking.

(3) Being alive is something good and pleasant in itself. It's a   20
determinate state, and what's determinate is part of the nature
of what's good.

† And whatever's naturally good is also good [and pleasant]
for a good person. That's why [being alive] seems pleasant to
everyone. [Because everyone sees themselves as good.] But [for
our purposes] we shouldn't assume a depraved or corrupted
form of life – not even for [talking about] pains. That kind of
life is indeterminate, and so are all its features. (This will be
explained more fully in the next section, on pain.) †   25
So being alive, in itself, is good, and something we enjoy.

(That also seems to be the case from the fact that everybody
desires it, and especially people who are morally good, and
flourishing. Theirs is the most desirable kind of life; for them,
living is flourishing in the fullest sense.)

(4) When you see something, you also perceive that you are
seeing; and when you hear something, you perceive that you
are hearing; and when you walk, you're aware that you're   30
walking; and with all the rest, there's always a part of us that's
aware that we're exercising that capacity. So if we're perceiving, we're also aware that we're perceiving, and if we're
thinking, we're aware that we're thinking.

(5) To be aware that we're perceiving, or thinking, is to be
aware that we exist. Because to exist, {or to be alive}, we just
said, is to be perceiving or thinking.

(6) To be aware that you're alive is something that gives you 1170b
pleasure in itself, since being alive is a natural good, and to be
aware that you hold that natural good gives you pleasure.

(7) Being alive is especially desirable for good people. For
them [above all], existing is good and pleasant (they experience
pleasure from perceiving the intrinsic good that they have).   5

(8) As a good person, you relate to a friend the same way as
to yourself (because a friend is a second self). So just as your
own existence is desirable for you, so is your friend's – or in
very nearly the same way.

(9) And existing, we said, is desirable through your perceiving

yourself, and that you are good. That kind of awareness is
10 pleasurable in itself. Hence you need to share the awareness
of your friend's existence; and that's what happens when you
share your life with a friend, converse with them, share your
thoughts. (Surely for human beings that's what 'sharing a life'
or {'spending your time with someone'} means. We don't just
mean grazing the same patch of grass, like cattle.)

So if you're really flourishing in life, existing is intrinsically
15 desirable (because naturally good and pleasant) and your friend's
existence is desirable, for you, in very nearly the same way. So
it follows that the friend, too, is something desirable.

And what's 'desirable' for you is [by definition] something
you've got to have, or you'll be missing out in that area of life.

So, yes, to flourish you will need some friends, [and you'll
need them to be] good people.

20 **10** So does that mean that you should make as many
friends as possible?

In the case of *xenoi*, {guest-friends}, people tend to agree
with [Hesiod's] motto, 'bad idea to have too many; just as bad
to not have any'. Will that apply to having friends as well? Is it
not just a bad idea to have no friends, but also to have a huge
number of them?

Well, if we mean the useful kind, the saying seems exactly
right. Returning favours {and services} to a large number of
25 people is hard work. I mean, life's too short. You just don't
have time for that. So any such friends that you have beyond
the number that you need for your own livelihood are superflu-
ous. They actually get in the way of living well {and honourably}.
So you simply don't need them.

A small number of pleasure-friends is also enough, just as
you only need a little bit of spice with your food.

What about morally good friends? Should you make as many
30 as you can? Or is there some sort of measure of the quantity of
friends you can have – like with a city? You can't make a city
out of ten people, and if you have 100,000 people that's not a
city any more, either. As for the right amount, well, it's surely

not some single number. It's a whole range between an upper
and a lower limit. Likewise with friends, there's an [upper]
limit to the number of friends that you can have. Surely it's the 1171a
largest number of people that you can share your life with.
(Because that's what we thought was the key thing in friendship.) And it's pretty clear that it's not possible to share your
life with a large number of people; to spread yourself so thin.
Also, they'd all have to be friends with one another (if you're
all planning to hang out together). And for that to be true of a 5
very large number of people is pretty tricky. It's also hard to
sympathize with all the joys and pains of a lot of other people
and make them your own. Chances are you'll find yourself
[having to] feel happy for one friend and upset for another at
the same time.

So maybe it's a good idea not to try to have as many friends
as you possibly can; just as many as are enough for sharing a
life with.

In any case, it doesn't even seem possible to be a very close 10
friend to lots of people, for the same reason that you can't be
in love with more than one person. That tends to be a sort
of maximum of love; something you can only feel towards
one person. And very strong friendship, too, can only be with
a small number of people.

And that's just the way it seems to work in practice. You
don't find large groups of people all becoming very close
friends;[43] and in the famous cases in the stories, it's always two 15
people.

People who do have lots of 'friends' and interact with everyone on familiar terms surely aren't actually friends with anyone
(except in the way fellow citizens are). We call those types
'people-pleasers'. Well, no, you can be friends with lots of people
in that fellow-citizen way without being a people-pleaser; just
as a genuinely nice person. But to be friends with lots of people
on the basis of their goodness and their intrinsic qualities – you
can't do that.

You should be happy to find even a small number of friends 20
like that.

11 Question: when do you need friends more? In times of good fortune or in adversity? Because they're required in both. When people are down on their luck they need support; when their fortunes are up they need people to share their life with and people they can help, because they want to do some good.

So in adversity, [friendship] is more of a necessity. That's
25 why in that situation you need the useful kind of friends. When you're enjoying good fortune, it's more something honourable. So then you look for morally decent friends, since those are the people it's more desirable to do good things for and pass your time with.

In fact, just the mere presence of our friends, both in times of good fortune and in adversity, gives us pleasure.

We get relief from our distress when friends share our pain . . .
30 Which raises another question: are they, as it were, helping us carry a burden? Or is that not it? Maybe it's that their presence is a pleasure, and the realization that they're feeling our pain with us lessens our own distress . . . Anyway, whether it's for that reason or for some other reason that people are uplifted in that way by their friends – let's not worry about that for now. The point is, it does seem to work that way.

35 But the presence of friends seems kind of a mixed [experience].

On the one hand, just seeing your friends is a pleasure, espe-
1171b cially when you're having a hard time, and acts as a support; stops you feeling too distressed. A friend is a thing with the power to make you feel better, by the mere sight of them and by what they say, if they're good at saying the right thing. Because a friend knows your character, and knows what pleases you and what pains you, {what cheers you up and what upsets you}.

On the other hand, the awareness that your friend is upset at
5 your misfortunes is painful. Nobody wants to be a cause of pain to their friends. That's why people who are tough by nature take care not to spread their own pain and distress to their friends. [A man like that] may even outdo his friends[44] in not being upset, and, if not, he certainly doesn't tolerate his friends getting upset as well, and in general he doesn't let his

friends moan [about his misfortunes] because he doesn't even like to moan about them himself.

But females, and womanish men, enjoy it when people whine 10 and wail along with them. They love those people: 'They care about me; they feel my pain.'

And in all things, obviously you should imitate the better type of person.

When you're enjoying good fortune, the presence of your friends offers both a pleasant way of passing your time and the awareness that they're taking pleasure in your blessings. So I'd say what you should do is this: be eager to invite your friends 15 to share in your good fortune – doing good for others is an honourable thing – but be reluctant to invite them into your misfortunes. You should share the bad stuff in your life as little as possible. (Hence the line: 'One of us being miserable is plenty.') Ideally, you should call on them [only] when they're going to be a very big help to you with very little trouble to themselves.

But when it comes to going [to people's aid], I'd say the 20 reverse applies. If your friends are in trouble you should go to their aid without being called, and eagerly. Because being a friend means helping out, and especially helping out friends in need – and without them even having to ask (because that's more honourable, and a greater pleasure, for both of you). But as for when friends are enjoying good fortune {and success} . . . well, by all means be eager to help make it happen (we need our friends for that), but when it comes to taking favours from them, you should hang back. There's nothing honourable in 25 hankering after perks from your friends. On the other hand, you should probably avoid a reputation for being a killjoy by constantly refusing [such things], too. That sometimes happens.

So [all in all] the presence of our friends seems desirable in all contexts.

12 So is it like this? When people are in love with someone, what they cherish most of all is seeing them. They'd choose that way of perceiving them over all the others, since 30 their love arises and exists mostly through that sense. So is it

that, in a similar way, what friends want more than anything else is to share life? Because friendship is a kind of sharing, {a kind of partnership}, and your relationship with your friend matches your relationship with your own self. And in your own case, your awareness that you exist is desirable. So your awareness that your friend exists must be too.

35   Also, we exercise friendship by sharing a life. So it's no sur-
1172a prise that that's what friends aim to do.

And whatever existing means to each group [of friends] – i.e. whatever their reason is for wanting to be alive at all – that's what they want to spend their time doing with their friends. So some friends drink together, some play dice together, some train
5 together, some hunt together, some do philosophy together – in each case they spend their time doing whatever it is that they most cherish in life. Because what they want is to share life with their friends; so they do the things, share in the things, that they think amount to really living.

Now, for bad people friendship is corrupting. They share in their morally bad [actions]; and they're fickle {and impression-
10 able}, [so] they become wicked by assimilating to one another. But the friendship of decent people is itself decent, and grows more and more [so] as they spend their time together. It's as if they become better people by exercising their friendship; by correcting one another's mistakes. They're shaped by one another, by their likes and dislikes. Hence the line in Theognis: 'From noble men [you'll learn] noble things.'

All right, I think that's all we need to say about friendship and love.

15   Next we should give an account of pleasure.

BOOK X

Next I think it would make sense to give an account of pleasure.[1]

Pleasure, after all, seems something deeply ingrained in 20 human nature. That's why people educate the young by steering them with pleasure and pain. Also, enjoying the things you should, and hating the things you should, seems hugely important to your goodness of character. Those things extend through the whole of your life and have a major bearing, a powerful influence, on how good a person you are and on whether you flourish in life. Because {pleasure shapes our choices:} people 25 choose {and value} the things that give them pleasure and they avoid the things that cause them pain.

So we certainly don't want to skim over such an important topic, not least since it involves a major controversy.

Some people say pleasure is the key good [in life].

Others say the exact opposite, that it's an utterly bad thing.

Maybe some of the people who make that second claim are actually convinced that it's the case. But some of them just think it's better, for the effect it'll have on people's lives, to 30 declare that pleasure is bad even though it isn't. 'Ordinary people tilt strongly towards it; they're slaves to pleasures; so we have to lead them in the opposite direction; that way they might end up in the middle.'

I'm not so sure that's a good argument. The thing is, [theoretical] claims about any matters that involve our emotions and feelings, and actions, are always less credible than how life really 35 works.[2] So when they clash with what we plainly perceive is the case people dismiss them as nonsense, and the truth gets

1172b thrown out along with them. Some [philosopher] might *say* that pleasure is bad, but when he's then seen at some point striving after it, his inclination implies that it's something desirable – i.e. desirable in any form,[3] because most people can't make the distinctions here.

So it seems to me that the most useful philosophical claims
5 are always the ones that are true; not just for knowing what is the case, but also for their effect on how we live. Since they're in harmony with how life really works, people find them believable. And that's how they come to motivate people (who understand them) to live their lives by them.

But enough about that. Let's have a look at the things that people have said in the past about pleasure.

2 All right, so Eudoxus[4] thought that pleasure was the key
10 good [in life] because he saw that all things strive after it, [i.e. all animals], rational and non-rational. And in all cases (he said), desirable for X implies good for X, and what's most desirable for X must be X's highest good. So the fact that all [animals] gravitate towards the same thing indicates that it's the highest good for all (we can assume that each of them homes in on its own good, exactly as each homes in on its own food). And if it's good for all, and what all things strive for, it must be the key good [in life].

15 His arguments seemed plausible more on account of his goodness of character than on their merit. He was known as a man of extraordinary moderation. So people assumed he wasn't making those claims as a partisan for pleasure; hence things must actually be the way he claimed.

He thought it was equally obvious from pleasure's opposite. Pain, he said, is intrinsically undesirable for all animals. So its
20 opposite, pleasure, must be intrinsically desirable for all.

Also, what's most desirable [by definition] is whatever we choose, not because of something else or for the sake of some other thing. And pleasure undeniably fits that description. We never ask someone [who's doing something for pleasure], 'Yes, but why experience pleasure?' We treat pleasure as desirable in itself.

Also, when pleasure is added to any other good thing it makes it more desirable (for example, if you add pleasure to acting fairly or moderately), and what's good only increases by 25 more of itself.

(That particular argument, by the way, only seems to show that pleasure is one sort of good, i.e. no more than any other. After all, any good combined with any other becomes more desirable than it is on its own. In fact, Plato even uses much the same argument *against* the idea that pleasure is the key good. He argues that a pleasant, {enjoyable} life is more desirable combined with wisdom than without it; and if that combin- 30 ation is better, pleasure can't be the key good. Because nothing can be added to the key good such that it becomes more desir- able.[5] And obviously that applies to anything else: X can't be the chief good if X becomes more desirable by being combined with any other intrinsic good.)

(So what does fit that description, while also being some- thing we can actually share in? That's the outline of what we're 35 looking for here.)[6]

Now, some people object by denying that 'what all things strive after [must be] good'. But that's got to be nonsense. What seems to be the case to everyone {and everything}, we assume 1173a *is* the case. If you dismiss that sort of evidence, you're certainly not going to put something more plausible in its place. I mean, if it was just the non-thinking animals desiring* [pleasure], those people might have had a point. But since it's the smart ones too, how could there possibly be anything in their claim? (And surely, even in the lower animals there's a kind of natural [force],[7] something greater than they are, that strives for their 5 proper good.)

They don't seem to be right in what they say about its oppos- ite, either. Even if pain is a bad thing, they say, it doesn't follow that pleasure is a good thing. 'Because one bad thing, A, can be the opposite of another bad thing, B, and both can be op- posites of something that isn't A *or* B.'[8] And they're not wrong about that. But that's not to say it applies in this case, [to pleas- ure and pain]. If both of them were bad things* then they should 10 both be undesirable, and neither should be in the [desirable] 'neutral' class (or both equally).⁹ But that's not how it is. People obviously shun pain as something bad and choose pleasure as something good. So that's the way that they're opposites: [one's bad, one's good].

3   Also, the fact that pleasure isn't a quality doesn't mean that it's not a good thing. After all, the activities {and 15 behaviours} that express our [moral] goodness¹⁰ aren't qualities either. Neither is flourishing.

They also say that what's good is determinate {and definite}, while pleasure is indeterminate because it comes in degrees.

So if they're basing that judgement on the way we feel pleasure, then the same thing is going to be true even of, say, being fair and the other moral virtues. They'd agree that we evidently possess those qualities to greater or lesser degrees and act on 20 our virtues to varying degrees. That's to say, we can be brave people, or fair people, by degrees; and we can act fairly or moderately in varying degrees.

And if it's just a judgement about pleasures [as such],¹¹ then I suspect that's not the real explanation, given that some pleasures are pure and some are mixed.

And anyway, why shouldn't pleasure be like health? Health 25 is determinate *and* comes in degrees. It isn't the same balance of elements in everyone, or even the same one in a given person all the time. It can be relaxed (up to a point) and persist; it exists in different degrees. So something like that could also be the case with pleasure.

Also, they assume that the key good is something perfect and complete, and that processes, and [in particular] processes 30 that bring about something, are incomplete, and then they try to show that pleasure is a process and brings about something.

But I don't think that's right. Not even that it's a process. Every process seems to have its way of being fast or slow, if not in itself (as in the case of the motion of the cosmos)¹² at least relative to something else. But neither of those applies to pleasure. You can certainly be quick to take pleasure in something 1173b (just as you can be quick to get angry), but you can't feel pleasure at high speed – not even relative to something else. It's not like walking or growing, or anything like that. In other words, you can transition into pleasure quickly or slowly, but you can't then exercise it (I mean feel pleasure) quickly.

And does pleasure bring about something? How so? [They can't just be vague about that.] You don't get just anything coming into being from anything. When X comes into being, what it comes out of is what it also dissolves back into.

[They] also [say]: 'What pleasure brings about, that's what pain destroys'; and that pain is the lacking of your natural state and pleasure the refilling {and the restoring} of that natural state. But those are things that happen to the body. So if pleasure is the refilling of your natural state, it should be the thing where the refilling is going on that feels the pleasure. So, the body. But it doesn't seem to be. So pleasure is not the refilling. Rather, we should say that, when the refilling is going on, you feel pleasure (just as when you're being cut* you feel pain).[13]

Their view seems to be based only on the pleasures and pains to do with eating and drinking. The idea is that people get into a state of need and first experience that pain, then feel pleasure at filling up again.

But that doesn't happen with all pleasures. The pleasures of learning, for example, are painless [throughout], and of the sensory pleasures so are the pleasures of smell; as are hearing and seeing (in plenty of cases); remembering and anticipating. So what shall we say all those pleasures 'bring about'? There's no prior need {or lack} of anything here. So there's nothing that can be 'refilled'.

And to those people who go on about the 'disgraceful' kinds of pleasures, you could reply, [first], that those things aren't actually pleasurable. When things are pleasurable to people whose [character] is in poor condition, we don't have to think those things actually are pleasurable, except to those people – just like with things that are only healthy, sweet or bitter to people who are sick; or that only look white to people with an eye infection.

Or you could say this: that those pleasures *are* desirable, they're just not desirable when they arise from those things, just as we might say that being rich is desirable, but not if it comes from an act of betrayal, or that health is desirable, but not if you have to eat just anything[14] for it.

Or maybe there are different kinds of pleasure. The pleasures that arise from honourable things are just of a different kind from those that arise from shameful things; it's not even possible to experience the pleasure that an ethical person ex-
30 periences without being an ethical person, or the pleasure a musician experiences without being a musician, and so on with the rest.

And the fact that a friend is a different thing from a flunky shows, arguably, that pleasure is not the highest good,*[15] or [at least] that there are different kinds of pleasure. A friend spends his time with you with a view to what's good, a flunky with a view to pleasure. And flunkies are vilified, friends
1174a praised; so we must see a friend's companionship as having different aims.

Also, nobody would choose to live their whole life with the mind of a child, even if it meant enjoying to the absolute full the things that children enjoy.

And nobody would choose to get pleasure from doing something utterly shameful, even if they were never going to experience any pain [as a result of it].[16]

Also, there are plenty of things that we'd still value highly
5 even if they didn't bring us any pleasure at all, like seeing, remembering, knowing things, having our moral virtues. Even if pleasures inevitably do accompany those things, that doesn't affect my point. The point is, we'd choose to have them even if no pleasure came from them.

So it seems pretty clear that pleasure is not the key good [in life], and that not every pleasure is desirable; but also that
10 there are some pleasures that are desirable, i.e. in themselves, and those are different in kind [from the undesirable ones], or in what they arise from.

All right, that's enough on the things other people say about pleasure and pain.

4 So what is it, or what kind of thing? Maybe we'll get a clearer
sense of that if we take it up again from the beginning.

{Consider seeing.} Seeing is complete at any moment that it's
occurring. That's to say, it's not lacking anything that has to   15
come about at some later stage to bring its form to completion.

And pleasure seems to be something like that.

That is, it's something whole; there's no instant you could
freeze[17] a pleasure, such that it has to go on for more time
before its form is completed.

That's why it's not a process; {or a movement towards some-
thing}. Every process {or movement} takes a certain amount
of time and is towards a goal – the process of building, for   20
example – and is only complete once it produces the thing it's
aiming at. So it's only complete [viewed] over the whole time[18]
it takes, or at that endpoint. But all processes, in their parts,
and during the time [they take], are incomplete, and differ in
kind both from the whole process and from each other.

Fitting the stones [of a column] together, for example, is a
different process from fluting the column; and both are different from the [whole process of] making the temple. And [as for
'making'], though making the temple is 'complete' (it doesn't   25
lack anything relative to the overall project), making the foundation or the triglyph is 'incomplete', in that each is just the
making of a part of the whole.

So processes differ in kind, and it isn't possible to freeze a process at any particular moment and {catch} it complete in its form.
It's only complete, if at all, over the whole of the time it takes.

The same is true even of walking and suchlike. If moving is a
kinēsis, {a process of change} from one place to another place,   30
then there are different forms of that, too – flying, walking,
jumping, and so on. And they don't just differ in that way; there
are also different [processes going on] even, say, within walking itself. Moving 'from one place to another' isn't the same
over the whole length of the stadium as over a part of it, and it
isn't the same in one part as in another. Even crossing the fin-
ishing line here isn't the same as crossing it there. Because you
don't just cross a line: you cross a line in a specific location;   1174b
and this [bit of the] line is in a different location from that one.

So, though our detailed treatment of *kinēsis* – {processes of change and movement} – is set out elsewhere, it's safe to say[19] that a process is not complete at each moment; rather, most processes are incomplete[20] and differ in kind [at each moment] –
5 if, [for example], moving from this spot to that one makes for a different kind [of moving].

Pleasure, by contrast, is complete in its form at every moment. So it's clear that these two things must be different from one another, and pleasure belongs to the class of things that are whole and complete.

The same thing also seems to follow from the fact that it's not possible for a process {of change} to take place other than over a certain time. But it is possible to feel pleasure [without it being over any period of time]. It's complete in every instant, [however small].

From these facts it's also clear that they're not right to say
10 that pleasure can be the object of a process[21] {of change}; or that any process brings about pleasure.* You can't attribute those things to everything; just to things that are divisible into parts and that aren't whole. There's no process, for example, that brings about seeing,[22] or that brings about a point or a unit (and conversely, none of those *is* a process or brings any X into being). So there's no process that brings about pleasure either. Because it's something whole.

Every sense operates on an object of perception and is com-
15 pletely and perfectly active when it's in good working order and operating on the finest of the objects that fall under it. That's what we see as the paradigm case of complete, perfect activity. (And let's say it doesn't matter whether we say it's the sense itself that's 'active', or the thing that has it.) So, for each of the senses, the best kind of activity is of a sense organ in the best possible working order operating on the best object that falls under it.

20   That's the most complete and perfect – and also the most pleasurable. Because for every kind of perception, and also every kind of thought and higher contemplation, there's a corresponding pleasure; and it's most pleasurable when at its most complete and perfect; and that means the activity of a [faculty] in good condition operating on the best thing that falls under it.

The pleasure perfects and completes the activity.

But the pleasure doesn't 'perfect' or 'complete' the activity in the same sense as the object of perception (when it's good) and the faculty (when working well)[23] 'perfect' the activity, just as 25 health and a doctor[24] don't cause you to be healthy in the same sense.

It's clear that for each kind of perception there's a corresponding pleasure. (For example, we speak of sights and sounds that give us pleasure.) And it becomes especially obvious when the perception in question is the best kind and operating on the best possible object. If they both fit that description – the object perceived, A, and the thing doing the perceiving, B – there'll be 30 a continuous pleasure, as long as A is there to act upon B and B is there to be acted upon by A.

And the pleasure perfects and completes the activity, not in the same way as the disposition does (by already being in place),[25] but as a kind of emergent, perfecting feature – like the 'bloom' of youth. So as long as the object of thought or perception is as it should be, and likewise the thing doing the discriminating or the contemplating, then there will be pleasure in the resultant activity. As long as they stay the same and 1175a stand in the same relation to one another – i.e. both the thing acted upon and the thing that acts upon it – you naturally get the same outcome.

In that case, why is it that you can't ever be in a continuous state of pleasure?

Is it that you get tired? That's true of all human things: they're incapable of continuous activity. So you don't get con- 5 tinuous pleasure, either. Because pleasure tracks activity.

Some things delight us when they're new and fresh, but don't give us the same pleasure later, for the same reason. At first our mind is drawn into them and engages with them very intensely (in visual terms, like staring at them); later its engagement isn't the same. It's more casual. So the pleasure fades. 10

You might think the reason everyone desires pleasure is that everyone also strives to be alive.

Being alive is a kind of activity, and each of us [lives by] exercising whatever [faculties] we value most, on whatever things

we value most. If you're a musician, for example, you exercise
your hearing, on music. If you love learning you exercise your
15 intellect, on objects of contemplation – and so on for everyone
else. And pleasure perfects and completes our activities. So
that means it perfects being alive, too; and that's what people
desire.

So it makes sense that people also strive for pleasure. Because
for each person, pleasure perfects and completes being alive,
which is something desirable.

As for whether we choose being alive for the sake of pleasure, or pleasure for the sake of being alive – for now let's not
worry about that. The two things seem to be tightly bound
20 together. There's no way of separating them. Without [life's]
activity there can be no pleasure; but pleasure perfects {and
completes} every activity.

5   That's also why [pleasures] surely differ in kind.
    We assume that things that are different in kind are
completed and perfected by things that are different in kind.
That seems to be true, for example, both of products of nature
(e.g. animals as opposed to trees) and products of human craft
(a painting as opposed to a statue; a house as opposed to a
25 tool). And in the same way, we assume that activities that differ in kind are perfected by things that are different in kind.
And intellectual activities are different in kind from the activities of our senses, and they both differ (in kind) from one
another. So the pleasures that perfect those activities must also
differ in kind.

It's also clear from the fact that each pleasure is intimately
30 tied to the activity it perfects. Because the corresponding pleasure enhances the activity. People are better at judging all the
details, more able to master [an activity], when they get pleasure from engaging in it. For example, people become expert at
geometry, better at figuring out all the answers, if they enjoy
geometry. And the same goes for people who love music, or
35 people who love building, and so on – they all improve at their
particular task if they enjoy doing it. So* the corresponding
pleasures enhance [the activities]. But the things that enhance

X, Y and Z have to be specific to X, Y and Z; and if X, Y and
Z are different in kind, so are the things specific to them.[26]   1175b
    We can see the same thing even more clearly from the fact
that our activities are actually impeded by pleasures that arise
from another source. For example, people who love flute music
can't pay attention to a conversation if they hear someone playing a flute in the background, because they enjoy the flute music
more than the activity they're engaged in. So the pleasure they   5
get from flute music disrupts their other activity, engaging in
conversation. And the same thing happens in other cases: whenever someone engages in two activities at the same time, the one
that gives them more pleasure knocks out the other; and if it
gives them a lot more pleasure, all the more so, to the point
where they can't even engage in the other activity at all. That's
why when we're enjoying something intensely we can't do any-   10
thing else; and, conversely, if we aren't particularly entertained
by something, we do other stuff – like people eating snacks at
the theatre. They're most likely to do it when the acting is lousy.
    So, given that the pleasure specific to our activities refines
them, prolongs them and improves them, while outside pleasures mess them up, it's clear that the two are very different.   15
    In fact, outside pleasures have pretty much the same effect
as the pains specific to an activity. Pains specific to our activities disrupt them. Like, say, if you find writing or doing
arithmetic boring and tiresome. You just don't do it – {you
simply don't write}, you don't do the arithmetic – if the activity
is painful like that. So the pains specific to an activity have   20
exactly the opposite effect on it as its pleasures. (By 'specific to
it' I mean the ones that arise in the activity itself.) And outside
pleasures, as I just said, have pretty much the same effect as
pain. They disrupt the activity; only not in the same way.
    Now, activities differ from one another in their decency or
badness; and some are desirable, some undesirable, some nei-   25
ther. So the same goes for the corresponding pleasures. Because
there's a pleasure specific to each activity. So a pleasure specific to morally good activity is a decent pleasure, and one
specific to a bad activity is a nasty pleasure. It's just like with
desires. Desires for honourable things are praiseworthy, desires

for shameful things are blameworthy. But the pleasures of
30 our activities are actually more specific to them, {more tied to
them}, than our desires. Desires are distinct from the activities,
both in the times they occur and in their nature. But the pleasures are right in on the activities, and so hard to distinguish
from them that people even argue over whether the activity is
the same thing as the pleasure. Not that anyone thinks that
pleasure just *is* (e.g.) thinking, or just *is* perceiving. (Of course
35 not. That would be silly.) I just mean that because they can't be
separated, to some people they feel as if they're the same thing.

So pleasures differ from one another in all the same ways
as activities do. Seeing differs from touch by being purer, and
1176a hearing and smell are purer than taste. So their corresponding
pleasures differ from one another in the same respect. And
intellectual pleasures [are purer] than all sensual pleasures;
and in both groups, some are purer than others.

Also, each kind of animal seems to have its specific kind of
pleasure, just as it has its specific task {or function} – i.e. the
pleasure that corresponds to its [characteristic] activity. If we
5 just look at it case by case we can make that clear. Horses,
dogs and human beings, for example, all have different pleasures. As Heraclitus says: 'Donkeys would rather have the
sweepings off your kitchen floor than gold.' Food is a more
pleasurable thing than gold if you're a donkey.

So the pleasures of the different kinds of animals themselves
differ in kind, and it seems likely that the pleasures of a given
species of animal don't vary.[27]

10 But there's certainly plenty of diversity in the pleasures of
human beings. The very same things give some people pleasure
but cause other people pain; are painful {and distressing} and
loathsome to some people, enjoyable {and pleasing} and attractive to others. That also happens with the way things are sweet:
the same things don't seem sweet to someone in a fever as to
someone healthy. And the same thing won't seem hot to someone who's unfit as to someone in good shape. And it works the
15 same way with other things too.

But surely, in all those kinds of cases, how things are is how
they seem to a good person, {or someone in good condition}.

And if we're right about that – as we surely are – and the measure of each thing is goodness and the good person as such, then it follows that [actual] pleasures are what seem to be pleasures to a good person; and actually pleasurable things are the ones a good person enjoys.

And if the things a good person finds distasteful seem pleasurable to someone else, what's so surprising about that? There 20 are so many ways that human beings can be depraved and damaged. Those things aren't [really] pleasurable. They're just pleasurable to those people; to people in that condition.

So the undeniably shameful ones – clearly, we just shouldn't say they're pleasures at all, other than for people who are depraved.

And as for pleasures we think of as morally decent, which sort, or which of them,[28] should we say is the characteristically human form of pleasure?   25

Or is that clear from our activities? Because our pleasures match those. So whether there's just one kind of activity, or several, that go with being a man [whose life is] complete, perfect and blessed, the pleasures that perfect those activities can properly be termed the pleasures of a human being.[29] The rest can be treated as human pleasures of the second rank,[30] or the third or fourth rank, like their corresponding activities.

6 So now that we've talked about virtues, and forms of 30 friendship and love, and pleasures, what remains is for us to give an outline account of what it is to flourish {and prosper}, since we're assuming that's our overall goal as human beings.

Maybe we can shorten the discussion by recapitulating some of what we've already said.

So, we said that flourishing isn't just a [matter of having] a certain state of character. If it were, you could be 'flourishing' even if you were in a coma your whole life, living the life of a vegetable; or even while suffering the most appalling misfortunes. 35

So if we're not happy with that, and it seems more plausible to assume that it's some kind of activity (as we said in our earlier 1176b discussion), and if, of our various activities, some are necessities, only desirable because they get us other things, and some are

desirable in themselves, obviously we have to assume that flourishing is one of the latter: an activity desirable in itself, and not
5 because it gets us something else. Because a flourishing, {blessed}
life has nothing missing from it. It meets all its own needs.

Activities are 'desirable in themselves' when there's nothing
you're trying to get out of them besides the activity itself.

And surely something that fits that description is [a life of]
being an actively good person. Doing things that are honourable and good – that's something desirable in itself.

[You might say:] So are parties, and having fun. People don't
10 choose to party to get other things out of it. If anything, they're
harmed more than benefited, through neglect of their health
and their finances. And most of the people typically hailed as
'flourishing', {'prosperous'} men throw themselves into those
kinds of pursuits. That's why tyrants have especially high
regard for men who are good at making people laugh in those
settings. {Funny guys} are a pleasure to have around in exactly
15 the pastimes [tyrants] are attracted to. So those are the kind of
men they need.

The reason these things are thought to imply a flourishing,
{blessed} life is that powerful rulers tend to spend all their time
[partying].

But surely those kinds of people don't prove anything.

Moral goodness and intellect – the things that give rise to
good activities – don't depend on being powerful.

And just because those people have never tasted the purer
20 kind of pleasure, the more gentlemanly kind, and instead
throw themselves into physical pleasures – that's no reason to
think those pleasures really are more desirable. After all, don't
little boys assume the things they like the most are the best,
too? So it's only to be expected that bad people and decent
people will see different things as valuable, just like little boys
and grown men.

25 So, as I've said several times, what's actually valuable or
actually pleasurable is whatever's [valuable or pleasurable] for
a good person. And for each person, the exercising of their
particular disposition is the most desirable kind of activity. So
for a good person, that means exercising goodness.

So, no, flourishing is not about partying, {or fun and games}.

In any case, it seems absurd to say that the goal of life is just our amusement, and that we go to all the trouble that we go to, and suffer hardships our whole lives, just so we can play around and party.   30

All the things that we choose, pretty much, we choose for the sake of some further thing, except flourishing itself. Because that's the goal of life. And the idea that we do the serious things in life and toil away just so that we can play around seems silly. What an extremely childish suggestion!

[The opposite idea,] that you play so that you can get on with serious things, as Anacharsis says – that seems right. Play is surely a form of relaxation, and it's because people can't toil continuously that they need to relax. So relaxation isn't a goal.   35
It's there for the sake of activity.   1177a

And we think a flourishing life is one of [exercising] goodness. But that kind of life is a serious business. You can't do that while playing around.

And we speak of *spoudaia*,[31] 'serious' things, as also better than things that are jokey and playful. And we say that the activity of anything better – the better part of us, or the better   5
person – is itself more *spoudaia* [i.e. 'better', but by etymology 'more serious']. And the activity of something better must itself be a superior activity, which means more important to our flourishing.

Also, anyone at all can indulge in physical pleasures – a slave just as much as the best. But nobody would say that a slave is flourishing! To any degree. (Would we say a slave is even living?)[32]

No, flourishing doesn't depend on those kinds of diversions. It depends on the ways we exercise our goodness, as we said before.   10

7   If flourishing is about exercising our goodness, {exercising our virtues}, it makes sense for it to be the exercising of our very best kind of virtue. And that would have to be the virtue specific to the best part of us.

Now, whether that's our intellect or something else – whatever it is that by its nature seems to rule us and to lead us,

15 and to have a conception of all that is beautiful and divine [in
the cosmos], whether it's actually divine itself or as divine as
anything in us can be – surely the exercising of that part of us,
according to its specific virtue . . . surely that ought to be the
most perfect form of flourishing.

And that means contemplating [the higher truths of the
cosmos] – as we've said before.

That seems consistent both with what we said before and
with the truth. That kind of activity really is the best, just
20 as intellect is the best element within us, and the best possible objects of knowledge are the ones we use our intellect to
grasp.

Also, it's the most continuous kind of activity. It's easier for
us to contemplate [the cosmos] continuously than to perform
any kind of action [continuously].

Also, we assume pleasure is an ingredient of flourishing.
And of the various forms of exercising our virtues, the exercising of higher knowledge [of the cosmos] is undeniably the most
25 pleasurable. Certainly philosophy, {the pursuit of that know-
ledge}, involves the most extraordinary pleasures: extraordinary
in their purity and dependability. And it stands to reason that
people who possess that knowledge must pass their time even
more enjoyably than people who are still seeking it.

Also, we've talked about [a flourishing life] meeting its
own needs. And that will surely apply, above all, to contemplation.

Someone with higher knowledge and someone who's fair
(and the rest)[33] both need the bare necessities of life. But assum-
30 ing they're adequately supplied with those, a fair person still
needs the people he's going to treat fairly, and people to help
him do it. The same goes for someone moderate or brave, and
all the rest.[34] But a man with higher knowledge can contemplate it all by himself. And the more such knowledge he has,
the more he can contemplate alone. Sure, it's probably better to
have collaborators. But even so he can 'meet his own needs'
more than anyone.

1177b   Also, this is surely the only activity we value purely for itself.
After all, we get nothing out of it beyond the contemplating

itself. But with our practical activities we gain something (sometimes more, sometimes less) besides the doing itself.

Also, surely a flourishing, {blessed} life should be one of leisure. When we're busy [in life] it's so that we can be at leisure. 5 We fight wars so that we can have peace. Now our practical virtues are exercised largely in political life or warfare. And our actions in those domains surely take away our leisure [and must be aiming at something beyond themselves] – completely so, in the case of warfare. Nobody chooses to go to war just so they can be at war, or works to achieve war. (You'd have to be 10 a sort of homicidal maniac to [want to] turn your allies into enemies, so as to bring about battles and bloodbaths.) But even the activity of a statesman allows no leisure and aims to achieve other things beyond the engaging in politics itself, like power and prestige – or, more to the point, a flourishing life for himself and for his fellow citizens, which is [therefore clearly] not the same thing as the political activity itself. It's what we're searching for. Obviously, we assume it's something other than 15 [the search itself].³⁵

Of all the ways of exercising virtues by action, it's actions in politics and war that stand out as by far the {finest}, most honourable, most important. But they're exactly the ones that rob us of leisure; and they aim at some [further] goal; and they aren't desirable just in themselves. Exercising your intellect, by contrast, is exceptionally leisurely*³⁶ because it's [purely] contemplative and doesn't aim at any goal beyond itself; and it has 20 its own particular pleasure, and that pleasure enhances the activity. So [it has all the required features]:³⁷ it meets its own needs; it's leisurely; you never get tired of it (within human limits);* and all the other things we attribute to a blessed, {flourishing} life are quite clearly what you get with this kind of activity.

So that must be how to flourish, completely, as a human being – provided it goes on for the length of a complete life (nothing 25 connected with a flourishing life should be incomplete).

A life like that is surely superhuman. That's to say, it isn't as a human being that you'll live a life like that. It's in so far as there exists something divine within you. And that bit of us is far superior to the compound being [that we are], so to the same degree its activity is superior to the exercising of our other sort of virtue, [our moral virtues].

30   So if intellect is something divine compared to the human being, then a life of the intellect is also a divine life in comparison with a human life. But that doesn't mean we have to follow the motto and think human,[38] since we're human, or 'think on mortal things since we're mortal'. No. We should transcend our mortality as much as possible and do everything we can to live our life by the very best element within us. Yes, it may be

1178a small in bulk, but in its power and exaltedness it far surpasses everything else [we have].

It's also, surely, what you are. Because it's the part of you that's in charge; the better part of you.

So it would be absurd not to choose the life {of what you are}; your own life; to choose some other thing's life!

5   And what we said before will apply here as well: what's proper to each thing's nature is best and most pleasurable for that thing. So that means that for a human being, a life of the intellect is the best and the most pleasurable, since that's what a human being is (most of all).

So that's the form of life by which you're flourishing the most, too.

8 The second-best way [to flourish] is to live a life of exercising the other type of virtue:[39] {your moral goodness}.

All the ways we exercise that are human.[40]

10   We do things that are fair, for example, or brave, and the other things that express our virtues, to one another, taking care in our exchanges and in [meeting each other's] needs[41] and in all manner of actions, and in our feelings, to observe what's fitting for each case. And all those things are clearly tied to our humanity.

Some of these things even seem to arise from the body;[42] and

15 goodness of character, {moral goodness}, has multiple ties to our feelings. And then wisdom in turn is closely bound up with moral goodness, and goodness with wisdom, seeing as the

principles wisdom uses are set down by the virtues of character; but then getting things exactly right, in all aspects of character, depends on wisdom.

So since they're dependent upon our feelings too, these virtues must be features of our composite being; and the virtues of our composite being are human. Hence, so is a life of exercising those virtues, and the kind of flourishing that goes with it.

But the [exercise] of the intellect has no such ties. (For now that's all we need to say about it. To explain what I mean in detail is beyond our purpose here.) And surely it only needs external resources to a small extent, or to a lesser extent than being a morally good person does. I mean, let's grant, for the sake of argument, that both need the bare necessities equally (even if, in fact, a statesman is more likely to exert himself physically, and so on). Because there won't be much difference there. But when it comes to their activities there's going to be a huge difference. To be generous, for example, you'll need money for doing generous things; and as a fair person you'll need it for paying people back. (Just wanting to isn't enough. That's invisible. And even people who aren't fair can pretend that they want to treat everyone fairly.) And to be brave you need power,[43] if you're actually going to accomplish anything that goes with that virtue; and to be moderate you need opportunity.[44] Otherwise how's anyone supposed to know you're moderate – or indeed have any other virtue?

Also, people argue over whether what matters with moral goodness is choice {and intention}, or actions. It seems to depend on both.

So the complete package obviously must require both. And for actions you need lots of resources; and the greater the actions and the more honourable they are, the more you need.

But someone engaged in contemplation doesn't need any of those kinds of things,[45] at least not for the activity itself. If anything, those things just get in the way (at any rate, of his contemplating).

But as a human being, and as someone who lives a life with other people, he still chooses to do all the things that go with being a good person. So he will need those kinds of things – for being human.

The fact that we flourish, perfectly and completely, by engaging in contemplation can also be made clear by the following.

We take it for granted that the gods are especially 'blessed'; they're an ideal of 'flourishing'.

10   But what kinds of actions are we supposed to attribute to them?

Can they do things that are fair {and honest}? Or isn't there something absurd in imagining the gods trading, returning money that's been lent to them, all that kind of thing?

Can we assign them brave actions? – [shall we have the gods] standing up to frightening situations and facing down danger because it's the honourable thing to do?

Or generous actions? Who are they going to be giving stuff to? And it's absurd to think of them using cash or anything like

15   that.

And how could they do things that are moderate? It's a pretty paltry sort of praise, to say that the gods don't have any sordid cravings.

In fact, if we go through them all like that, it seems quite clear that all things related to actions are trivial to the gods, and beneath them.

On the other hand, everyone takes it for granted that the gods are at least alive. So they must have [some sort of] activity. Right? They can't just be asleep [the whole time], like

20   Endymion. So, if something's alive, but doing things isn't an option – much less making things[46] – then what's left for it other than contemplation?

So it follows that God's activity – exceptional in blessedness – must be one of [pure] contemplating. So it also follows that, of all possible human activities, the one most closely akin to that will make us flourish more than any other.

Another indication of this is the fact that none of the other animals[47] can in any sense 'be blessed' {or 'flourish'} – and

25   [notice that] they're completely deprived of that kind of activity. The gods have a life that is wholly blessed, and human life

to the extent that it allows some sort of imitation of that kind
of activity, but none of the other animals gets to 'flourish' since
none of them can experience contemplation to any degree at
all. So flourishing is exactly coextensive [in the universe] with
contemplating. The more X has the ability to contemplate, the 30
more X flourishes, and not just by coincidence, but because of
its contemplating. (Contemplation's value is in itself.)

So that shows, [again], that flourishing, {being blessed}, is
some form of contemplating.

You'll also need external wealth {and good fortune}, as a
human being. Our nature can't meet its own needs (for contemplating).[48] Your body has to be healthy; it needs a supply of 35
food and the other forms of care and attention.

That being said, we certainly shouldn't think you'll need 1179a
huge quantities of stuff to flourish, just because it isn't possible
to flourish without external goods. 'Meeting your needs'
doesn't require excessive [wealth]. And neither does action. It's
quite possible to do honourable things without being lord of
land and sea. You can be an actively good person even from 5
moderate means. That's perfectly plain to see. After all, ordinary citizens are surely able to do morally decent things as much
as powerful rulers – in fact, more so. So it's enough to have
that amount of stuff. A life of exercising your goodness in that
way *will* be a life of 'flourishing' {and 'prospering'}.

Solon[49] was surely right about the people he declared 'blessed': 10
he named men only modestly provided with material wealth,
but who'd performed, as he saw it,[50] 'glorious deeds' and lived
out their lives moderately.

It's perfectly possible to do the things you ought to do [as a
good person] with only a modest amount of property.

Anaxagoras, likewise, evidently thought that a 'flourishing'
{'prosperous'} man wasn't someone wealthy or powerful: he said
he wouldn't be surprised if [his idea] seemed absurd to most 15
people. Because most people judge flourishing {and prospering}
only by external goods. It's the only thing they notice at all.

So the views of other philosophers seem to be in harmony
with our claims.

And that kind of thing does carry a certain amount of
weight. Some. But the truth in practical matters is ultimately
judged from the realities of life. Those must have the final
20 word. So we should always test the claims that people have
made in the past by holding them up against how things actually work. Against life. And if they're in harmony with those,
then we should accept them. But if they're at odds with life, we
should take them for [what they are] – mere theories.

Someone who exercises their intellect and cultivates their intellect is surely in the best possible condition [any person can be
in], and is the most beloved by the gods.
25   Because if the gods have any concern for human affairs, as
people assume, then it would make sense that they take pleasure in the best element [in human beings], the thing most
closely akin to themselves – our intellect, in other words – and
that they reward those people who value and cherish that part
of themselves most of all; reward them for caring about the
things *they* love. † And who act correctly and honourably. †[51]
    And it's quite clear that all of those things apply, above all,
30 to a man of higher philosophical knowledge. So that kind of
person is most beloved by the gods; and it stands to reason that
the same person must be flourishing the most.
    So by that argument, too, it's higher philosophy {and sci-
ence} that makes us flourish.

9   So, if we've said enough, in broad outlines, about those
    things, and the virtues, and friendship and love, and pleas-
35 ure, should we feel that we've achieved what we set out to do?
    Not really. Because, as we said,[52] our goal in practical mat-
1179b ters isn't just to theorize about all the things {we're supposed to
do}, and *know* about them. Our real goal is to *do* them. So the
same applies to goodness. Knowing about it isn't enough. We
also have to try to have it and use it. We have to strive, in every
way we can, to actually become good people.
    Now, if philosophical arguments were enough on their own
5 to make people decent, they'd rightly 'earn many a fine, fat

fee', as Theognis says; and all we'd need to do is provide people with plenty of those.

But as it is, they only seem to have the power to motivate and encourage young men of gentlemanly character; they can take an already noble nature, genuinely devoted to what's honourable, and make it ready for goodness to take hold. But with most people, {the common people}, arguments seem powerless 10 to motivate them to become decent men.

The trouble is that common people by their nature don't respond to shame. They only respond to fear. They don't refrain from bad behaviour because it's shameful; they need [the threat of] punishments. They live by emotion and feeling and pursue the pleasures that go along with that, and whatever will get them those pleasures, and avoid any pains that are the opposite of those pleasures. But as for what's honourable – and truly 15 pleasurable – they're not even aware of it. Because they never even get a taste of it.

So with people like that, how could philosophical argument transform them? It's simply not possible, or at least not easy, when things have long taken hold in people's characters, to pry them out with argument alone.

But we *may* be able to get hold of goodness if all the things that we need to become decent people are already in place.

That's probably the best we can hope for.

How do people become good? Some think it's a matter of your 20 nature. Some say by habit. Some say by being taught.

So the bit of it that's innate obviously isn't something you can do much about. It's something that some people have through some divine cause; lucky people, in the truest sense.

As for argument and teaching, I suspect that it may not be effective for everyone. The student's soul has to be well tilled beforehand – by good habits, so as to already enjoy the right 25 things, and already hate the right things – like a field that's going to nurture seed. Someone who lives by their emotions[53] {and feelings} wouldn't listen to any argument that tried to turn them from their course. Or even understand it. How can

you possibly persuade someone like that to see things differently? In general, emotion seems not to yield to argument.
Only to force. So the student's character has to be, in a sense,
30 already germane to goodness; it has to already have a liking for
what's honourable and a distaste for what's shameful.

But it's hard to get the right kind of pointers on being a good
person, from early childhood, if you haven't also been raised
under the right kinds of laws and social norms. To live with
moderation and resilience isn't something most people enjoy,
especially not young people. That's why the rearing of children, and their day-to-day activities, need to be regulated by
35 law. (They won't find those things so painful once they're
accustomed to them.)

1180a   And it surely isn't enough just for people to get the right kind
of upbringing and care only while they're young. As grown
men, too, they have to engage in the pursuits and acquire the
habits proper to their age.* So we need laws to cover that too,
and in general to govern every stage of life. Because most
people respond to compulsion more than to reason; to penal-
5 ties more that to what's honourable.

That's why some people think that while, of course, lawmakers should call upon [all citizens] to be good people, and
urge them to do what's honourable for its own sake (in the
knowledge that at least those who've been set on a decent path
by good habits will respond to that appeal), they also have to
impose punishments and penalties on people who disobey, and
whose natural tendencies aren't as good; and some people –
10 the incurables – they have to remove from society altogether.
Only a decent person, on this view, lives his life guided by
what's honourable, or will be responsive to reason; a scoundrel, striving only for pleasure, has to be kept in line with pain,
like a beast of burden. That's also why they say that the pain
needs to be, in each case, whatever kind is the precise opposite
of the pleasure they're attracted to.

So, as we've said, anyone who's going to be a good person
15 has to be brought up the right way and given good habits, and
from there live their life in decent pursuits and never do bad
things, 'wilfully or otherwise'.[54] And that can only happen if

people live their lives according to some sort of intelligence and under the right sort of order; and that order has to be strong.

Now, a father's orders just don't have that strength. They can't compel. Nor, in general, can the orders of any one man 20 (unless he's a king, or something like that).

But law does have the power to compel. And law is reason. It derives from some sort of wisdom and intelligence. And though people can't stand it when other human beings oppose their impulses (even if they're right to do so), law can order us to do what's decent without being oppressive [to anyone].

Yet it's only in Sparta (along with one or two other cities) 25 that their lawmaker seems to have taken any interest in [children's] upbringing, or in how people are to employ their time. In the vast majority of cities those kinds of things have been neglected and everyone lives just as they please, with each man, like the Cyclops, 'acting as lawman to his children and his wench'.

So the best thing would be for there to be public provisions for those things – {communal education} – of the correct kind. 30 But if such things are being neglected by the community, I suppose it falls to each individual to help his own children, and his family and friends, become good people. Or at least that should be his aim.

And from what we've been saying, it seems you'd be most able to do that if you became an expert on law and lawmaking. Because all public education[55] obviously works through laws (and decent public education is the product of good laws). And 35 whether that means written laws or unwritten [norms], that 1180b shouldn't make any difference, nor should it matter if they're for the education of just one person or many (just as it wouldn't make any difference in the case of music, athletics or other pursuits). And a father's ideas and habits hold sway within each household in much the same way as laws and national character hold sway in each city – or even more so, given family bonds, 5 and all the good things he's done for [his children]. That makes them instinctively affectionate and obedient from the outset.

In fact, individual education may even be better than communal education – as with medical treatment. It might be a

general rule that someone with a fever benefits from rest and
fasting, but that might not be the case for this or that individ-
10 ual. And a boxer surely doesn't use the same style of fighting
with all his opponents.[56] So when the care taken over someone
is personal, it's likely to be more precisely honed to the individual. Each person is more likely to get what's just right for them.

Of course, you're certainly best able to attend to someone, as a doctor, physical trainer or whatever, by having the
general, {scientific kind of} knowledge; by knowing what's the
15 case for everyone, or for anyone in that condition. (The 'sciences', after all, are supposed to be knowledge of universals – and
they are). But, that being said, there's no reason why you can't
do a perfectly good job of attending to one particular person,
even without any scientific knowledge, as long as you've
observed through experience {and experiment} exactly what
happens, every time, with each thing[57] [you try on them] – just
like the way some people seem to be really good at being their
own doctors, even though they wouldn't have a clue how to
cure someone else.

20 Still, the fact remains that if you want to master a technical
expertise or theoretical science, for that at least you surely
have to make your way to its universal [principles], and get as
much knowledge of those as you possibly can. Because that's
what sciences are about, as we said. So, case in point,* if you
want to make people better by attending [to their education] –
whether lots of people or just a few – you probably have to try
25 to become expert at laws and lawmaking, since it's through
laws that we become good people.* Because to take whoever it
is – whoever's put in front of you – and put them into the right
condition, that's no ordinary ability. If anyone can do it, it'll
be someone with knowledge – just like with medical treatment, and everything else that requires care and attention and
wisdom.

So does that mean that what we should think about next is
how you can become an expert lawmaker? Where [do you get
that knowledge] from? Will it be, as in other cases, [from the
30 people who have that knowledge; so,] from statesmen? Because
we said lawmaking was part of statesmanship.

Or does it seem different with statesmanship, compared to the other sciences and abilities? With the others, we see the same people practising the abilities and passing them on to others. Like doctors and painters. But when it comes to political matters, the people offering to teach it are 'sophists'. But 35 none of them does anything [in politics]. Only the politicians 1181a do, and they seem to do that by some kind of [intuitive] ability and by experience rather than thought. We never see them writing or speaking about those kinds of questions – (And why not? Wouldn't that be a finer thing to do than write speeches for the courts and the assembly?) – and we never find that 5 they've turned their own sons into good statesmen, or anyone else among their family or friends. But surely they would have, if they could. Because what better legacy could they have left their cities? And there's no other kind of ability they'd rather have themselves, so they ought to have wanted the same for the people they cared about the most.

On the other hand, experience surely counts for quite a lot. 10 Otherwise they wouldn't have become good statesmen [the way they did,] just by being familiar with political life. That's why anyone who aims to know all about statesmanship surely also needs to experience it.

As for those sophists who profess to teach these things, they're clearly a very, very long way from doing so.

I mean, in general terms, they don't even know what kind of thing [statesmanship] is, or what kind of things it's about. If they did, they'd never have assumed that it was the same as the art of public speaking (or inferior to it, some of them say),* or 15 thought that it was an easy thing to make laws, just by collecting together [existing] laws that are highly thought of. 'It's just a matter of picking out the best ones' – as if the selection itself weren't something that required insight! As if being able to evaluate laws correctly isn't extremely difficult, just like making judgements about music. It's only people who have experience in each area who can correctly judge its products 20 and understand the means and methods of achieving them, and what sorts of things are suited to one another. When people don't have the relevant experience, the best they can

hope for is to just about notice whether the finished product
is good or bad. Like with paintings, for instance. But laws are
the products of statesmanship, so to speak. So how, just from
1181b those, could someone possibly become expert at lawmaking,
or able to judge which laws are the best?

People don't even seem to be able to become good doctors
from medical casebooks. And yet [those] do at least attempt to
explain not just the treatments, but also how people can be
cured, and how to give the treatment in each case, distinguish-
5 ing the different states [the patients might be in]. But those
things only seem useful to people with medical experience. To
people with no knowledge [of medicine] they're useless. It's
probably the same with laws: catalogues of laws and forms
of government may well be useful things, yes, for people with
the ability to study them and to assess what works and what
doesn't, and what kinds of things suit what kinds of people.
But when people without that ability work their way through
10 those kinds of things, well, they certainly won't be making any
sound judgements – unless it's by fluke. (But perhaps it'll make
them a bit more insightful about political questions.)

So, since our predecessors left the whole question of lawmaking unexplored, maybe it's a good idea for us to look into
it more thoroughly ourselves, and the whole question of forms
of government in general – so as to bring to completion, as
15 fully as we can, our philosophy of human things.

So first of all, let's try to go over the (one or two) particular
claims made by our predecessors that were right.

Then, using our collection of different forms of government,
let's try to ascertain what kinds of things preserve or destroy
cities; what kinds of things preserve and destroy each of the
different forms of government; what things cause some cities
20 to be well governed and some not. If we can ascertain all of
that, we're likely to get a better overview of what form of government is the best, and the best way for each to be ordered,
the best laws and customs for it to employ.

All right, so let's begin by saying . . .

Note on *eudaimonia, aretē*
and *dikaiosunē*

Eudaimonia

It is of some importance that the term *eudaimonia* does not mean 'happiness', though there is, of course, a very long tradition of translating it that way.

This isn't just something we say because, although it really does mean 'happiness', the Greek conception of happiness is different enough from ours that it feels safer not to use our word. Actually happiness, exactly as we understand it, is something that the Greeks talk about all the time. It just isn't the same thing as *eudaimonia*.

Eudaimonia refers to a *state* of well-being, not to a *sense* of well-being. If you are *eudaimon*, then you are doing well in life; your life is going really well; you are living a wonderful life; you are prospering; flourishing; you are blessed. To be *eudaimon* is to be living a life that has every good thing in it; a life that meets all our needs as human beings.

Now, it is perfectly possible to say in English: 'My life is going extremely well. As well as it possibly could. There is nothing whatsoever I would want to add to it. And yet I am very unhappy.' Or, conversely: 'Every single thing has gone disastrously wrong in my life. But, for some strange reason, I am very happy.' There is nothing illogical or self-contradictory about this (though it may sound psychologically unusual) because 'happiness' refers to a state of mind, not to the state of living described in the other portions of the sentences. But if you made the same claims in Greek using *eudaimon* in place of 'happy' you would produce an actual self-contradiction. It would be like saying, 'My life is going extremely badly in every way but going extremely well in every way.'

The fact that *eudaimonia* does not mean 'happiness' is not a cultural matter. The Greeks, as I said, fully possess our concept of happiness too. They speak of feeling happy, being happy about something, being happy with something, being happy for someone, making someone happy, being happy to do something. They think very hard about how to stay happy in the face of hardship and misfortune. It's just that they never use the word *eudaimon*, or any related term, to say or ask any of those things.

If you want to check your own existing conception of *eudaimonia*, here are two easy ways to do it. (a) Make a list of the ten or so things that you most want your life to have in it. A life with all those things in it constitutes your vision of *eudaimonia*. (b) Make a list of the ten or so things that you're most likely to congratulate someone for, and then imagine a life with all of those things in it.

We do not have a single, neat noun that maps perfectly onto all the uses of *eudaimonia*. But the verb *eudaimonizo* (literally, 'to declare someone *eudaimon*') also means, very precisely, 'to congratulate someone'; so the correspondence with the Greek concept, by the second test, is exact. (Also, we certainly never congratulate people just for being happy. That in itself neatly proves that *eudaimon* does not mean 'happy'.)

The term 'flourishing', and the expression 'human flourishing', started out as a way of referring specifically to Aristotle's and the Greek idea of *eudaimonia*. It has now also started to be widely used in normal English, in a variety of other, non-scholarly and non-Aristotelian contexts. That wider usage itself has helped make it easy to understand, in the right sense. So I have used it as the central translation of the term. (It does not quite work perfectly, because it has connotations of growth and flowering that are absent from the Greek word. Aristotle does use a word that literally means 'flourishing' – i.e. has the very same metaphor of growth – as a synonym for *eudaimonia*, but only once, at 1100a7.)

In wider Greek usage both *eudaimon* and its synonym *makarios* have a very strong tendency to mean simply 'wealthy'; rather like English 'prosperous', 'well off', 'well to do'. The word *eudaimon* is used of 'prosperous cities', 'prosperous households' and 'the wealthy classes'. There are several places in the text where Aristotle leans heavily on that common usage. A similar conceptual connection (going in the opposite direction, as it were) lies behind the English word 'wealth' (originally 'wellth', i.e. general wellness, well-being). And we see it again in the fact that 'good fortune' is quite close in sense to *eudaimonia*, but 'a fortune' means 'lots of money'. And in the fact that we use the very same metaphors: we speak of our lives being enriched by the activities that we most value, and impoverished by the lack of them. Those are claims about *eudaimonia*.

Eudaimonia also traditionally implies being well treated by the gods. In that respect it corresponds quite well to English 'blessed', which can have similar historical connotations and which otherwise also carries a similar broader meaning (a person whose life is full of good things is 'blessed'). The synonym *makarios* has those connotations too, in part because Homer often uses a related word, *makares*, of the gods themselves; 'the blessed gods', as most English versions say.

Closely related to this, *eudaimonia* in ordinary Greek usage sometimes directly implies good fortune. According to Aristotle, some Greeks speak as if being *eudaimon* is just the same as 'being lucky' or 'being fortunate'. By a similar connection, in English we sometimes use 'lucky' in almost exactly the sense of *eudaimon*. We say 'Lucky you!' or 'You're a lucky woman!' simply to mean 'Congratulations!' Or we might say: 'We're so lucky to have this job' when we simply mean 'This is a really good job.' 'Lucky' in that kind of statement is not a reference to luck in its normal sense; it means *eudaimon*.

This connection with luck and fortune is also why 'happiness' was used in this context in the first place. The English term 'happy' used to mean 'lucky'. In Shakespeare's English 'You are happy that ...' meant, and only meant, 'You are lucky that ... '. So the noun 'happiness' meant 'luckiness', 'good fortune'. That's why it was used to translate *eudaimonia*. (You can see the older sense of 'happy' in its cognates: 'happen', 'hapless', 'haphazard', 'mishap', 'happenstance', 'perhaps'.) But the term has now shifted in sense quite sharply. In modern English, 'You are happy that ...' cannot mean, in any context, 'You are lucky that ... '. It has drifted off in a different direction. That is why 'happy' is no longer able to serve as a translation of *eudaimon*.

The resulting difference between *eudaimonia* and happiness is not exactly vast, but it is important. If we attribute to Aristotle the idea that the ultimate goal of life is happiness (taken in its standard current English sense), then we give him a view that is indistinguishable from ancient hedonism. But hedonism was not his view. He does not think the goal of life is just to be happy (i.e. content, satisfied, pleased with life; tranquil; enjoying a steady and stable sense of well-being). He thinks the goal of life is to live a genuinely desirable, worthwhile life; one that really does have all the greatest blessings in it (whether you feel that way about it or not). Further, his own distinctive view of *eudaimonia* is that you will attain such a life if you exercise the best human virtues to the full; if you live a life of action, of achievement and accomplishment. He also argues, somewhat differently, that the most wonderful life available to us is one of higher philosophy and pure science; a life of contemplating the cosmos.

He thinks such a life will also, mostly and usually – but not infallibly, and not all the time – be a happy one. And that's an extra observation about *eudaimonia*.

Aretē

In Aristotle's Greek the term *aretē* has two distinct uses: general and particular. In its particular sense it means 'a virtue', typically 'a moral virtue', and most often occurs in the plural ('virtues'). I discuss the particular sense of the term at some length in the notes on books I, II and IV. (See notes I.19, I.83, II.2, IV.18, IV.42.) Here I will confine myself to discussing a key feature of general *aretē*.

Aretē does not mean 'excellence'. That's a common misconception. It means 'goodness' (and most often, moral goodness). When unqualified, it refers to the state of being a good person.

It is the noun that corresponds to the adjectives *agathos* or *spoudaios*; and it gets its sense very precisely and tightly from those adjectives.

Agathos, when unqualified, means 'a good man' or 'a good person'. (So does *spoudaios*.) That's to say, the unqualified adjective does not have a generic sense. Even though, when suitably qualified, it can mean 'a good X' (e.g. 'a good guitar-player', 'a good doctor', 'a good actor'), the unqualified adjective does not thereby mean 'a good something'. Rather, it reverts to meaning 'a good person', with a very specific, ethical sense.

The English dummy qualifier 'person' performs exactly the same role as the masculine ending of the Greek adjective (which shows that you are referring to a person). So we have the very same phenomenon in English that I am trying to explain in the Greek case. A 'good person' is not 'a person who is good at something'. Obviously. And just as obviously to a Greek speaker, *agathos* or *spoudaios* ('good person') does not mean 'good at something', or 'good at anything'.

The same is true of the opposite, *kakos*. Aristotle discusses this (at 1148b8). He tells us that if someone is 'a bad doctor' (*kakos iatros*), it certainly does not follow that you can call them just *kakos*. That is because *kakos* unqualified means 'a bad person'. Being a bad doctor does not make you an evil person. Obviously. (Note that if the unqualified sense of *kakos* were generic, i.e. if it meant 'bad at something', then you *could* call a bad doctor *kakos*, unqualified. Because a bad doctor *is* 'bad at something', namely, bad at being a doctor.)

Since *kakos*, unqualified, means 'a bad person', the noun that goes with it, *kakia*, when similarly unqualified, takes on the corresponding specifically moral sense: 'being a bad *person*'.

The same is true of its opposite. Just like the adjectives to which it is tied, the noun *aretē*, as long as it is unqualified, specifically means 'being a good *person*' – which further has a specifically character-related sense, to about the same degree as its English equivalent (even if modern ideas about what makes someone a good person are different, in some details, from Greek ones). Nor is this a coincidence. All human cultures have some easily identifiable way of talking about good people and bad people. We should not be surprised that *aretē* corresponds, pretty closely, to our concept of 'being a good person' and *kakia* to our concept of 'being a bad person', just as we should not be surprised that there are Greek words for 'father', 'mother', 'right', 'wrong', 'brave', 'anger', 'funny' and 'feet'.

The translation 'excellence' is thus, at least in part, based on a simple and precisely identifiable mistake: that of thinking that because the noun *aretē* can be used in other senses when suitably qualified, the unqualified noun must retain a neutral, generic sense: 'being good at X', hence 'excellence [i.e. of whatever sort]'. The English word 'excellence' was chosen here because it is generic by default. It has to be qualified (strangely) to have an ethical sense, and even then has trouble bearing a clearly ethical sense. But the word *aretē* (in the Greek of Plato and Aristotle's time and later) behaves in exactly the opposite way. It is ethical by default, naturally and easily carries its default ethical sense, and has to be qualified (strangely) not to have an ethical sense.

Dikaiosunē

There is a long-standing tradition of translating the term *dikaiosunē* as 'justice'. It is a feature of the special dialect that we use for translating Aristotle. But in standard English *dikaiosunē* does not mean 'justice'.

Dikaiosunē is a virtue. It is the virtue of being *díkaios*, that is, of being someone who reliably does what's right. In normal English we refer to this as the (broad) quality of being a moral or ethical person. We also call it righteousness, the virtue of being a righteous person.

That is the 'general', i.e. broadest, sense of the terms, closely dependent on the broader sense of the underlying, more basic concept of *díkaion* and *ádikon*: right and wrong.

Those more basic terms also have a 'particular' or narrower sense: fair and unfair. And corresponding to that narrower, particular sense of *díkaion*, the virtue term, *dikaiosunē* now picks out the narrower virtue of being a fair person, and *adikía* refers to the narrower vice of being an unfair person.

Now, in standard English we do not refer to either of these virtues (general or particular) as 'justice', and we never have. That is why you cannot, for example, 'admire someone's justice', or say that 'your friend's two best qualities are her kindness and her justice'. 'Justice' is *never* analysed by native English speakers as a character trait. *Dikaiosunē*, by contrast, is *only* analysed by Greek speakers as a character trait. You can, of course, call someone 'a just person', and thereby refer to a character trait. I am not denying that. My point is that the noun, 'justice', cannot serve as the relevant virtue term, and that fact makes it very inaccurate as a translation of *dikaiosunē*. (Of course, there may be other reasons for preferring the traditional term, unconnected with accuracy.) The error is on a par with translating 'sense of humour' into another language by way of a term that only ever means 'laughter'.

Latin (classical or medieval) for 'righteousness' (the quality of being a righteous person) is *iustitia*, or *justitia*. That Latin term is the origin of the Gringlish-dialect word 'justice', traditionally used to translate *dikaiosunē*. To be properly understood it has to be taken strictly in its Latin sense, not its English sense.

We could instead speak of the virtue of 'being just' or 'being a just person', rather than 'justice'. That would be an improvement. But 'being just' has little currency in normal English. It still implies some non-standard dialect and it prompts the reader to expect something unusual, quite wrongly.

As for the (action-describing) adjectives *díkaion* and *ádikon*, it is obvious that 'right' and 'wrong' are the most accurate English translations when they have their general sense, and equally obvious that their most common particular sense is 'fair' and 'unfair'. Hence there is no place where 'just' and 'unjust' are the best available terms. 'Just' and 'unjust' can be used (sometimes) to mean 'fair' and 'unfair', but are obsolescent in that sense. (To see this, imagine one child shouting at another: 'You got more than me! That's not just!' If you are a native English speaker, you know that the term cannot occur in that way in natural language, even if it is still intelligible in written texts.) The personal adjective 'just' is also moribund, in part because it never had much currency anyway, and in part because of its competition with the adverb. The sentence 'My friend is just' prompts most English speakers only to have the thought 'Your friend is just what?' All good writers of English carefully avoid the personal adjective.

Though 'justice' cannot translate the virtue term, it works more acceptably as a translation of *to díkaion* ('right and wrong', considered abstractly).

But then there is the problem of its very special domain. 'Justice' in English is strongly tied to the context of public institutions, governments and the judiciary. (When John Rawls says 'justice is fairness', he means that the rightness *of a political institution* depends on its fairness.) That makes 'justice' an important term in good English in those contexts. But the same fact also makes it too narrow to match the Greek terms *díkaion* and *ádikon* in their broader sense. Greeks use these terms to refer to *all* forms of right and wrong – including, indeed especially, between family and friends, and random individuals, even when there is no connection whatsoever with public institutions or the courts. Likewise, the narrower sense of *díkaion*, 'fair', applies to *all* domains of fairness (including, say, a backyard game of soccer, or sharing a birthday cake), not just to political institutions and legal systems.

So should we at least use 'justice' as the translation in those contexts? Not necessarily. Even in its special domain 'justice' belongs to optional registers of speech. It's quite normal to speak of government institutions, laws and legal rulings as being right and fair. Even in legal contexts it's more common to say 'he denies any wrongdoing' rather than 'he denies any injustice'; and it is more normal to speak of our 'civic obligations' than it is to say that voting and paying our taxes is 'political justice'. The latter expression, as an attempt to say the former, would baffle virtually all English speakers.

When Aristotle says in V.1 and V.6 that what is *díkaion* has a special connection with laws, social norms and the agreements formed between fellow citizens, he is offering a theory about the nature of right and wrong; a version of the social-contract theory that Greek humanists strongly favoured. He is not making a claim about the domain in which Greeks use those words. He is making a bolder claim, about where our ideas about right and wrong, as used across a wide range of contexts, come from in the first place. The rather trivial fact that, in English, 'just' and 'unjust' are by linguistic etiquette used for the political and legal domain is a different matter. It should not be confused with Aristotle's etiological theory.

Because of its long connection with the judiciary, 'justice' in English is also now increasingly used in the very narrow sense of 'punishment'. 'We demand justice' almost always means 'We demand that someone be punished', 'We demand redress against a wrongdoer'; 'to dispense justice' means 'to carry out punishments'; 'to evade justice' means 'to escape legal punishment'. To make similar claims in Greek, by contrast, you have to use words or idioms explicitly tied to punishment.

So here is a paradox. The pervasive use of 'justice', and 'just' and 'unjust', in translations of Greek philosophical texts (because of the use, there, of the Gringlish dialect and its medieval Latin vocabulary) has created the misconception that these are specially Greek concepts, and that without them the text is less authentically Greek. But that is the opposite of the truth. In reality, 'justice' is a word whose finicky boundaries and subtle connotations and idioms are intimately tied to the peculiar history of the English language (with its large vocabulary, and layers of Anglo-Saxon, French and Latin). The Greeks do not have any term at all that means (i.e. only means) 'justice'. They have no terms that mean (i.e. only mean) 'just' or 'unjust'. That is to say, they have no word, as we do, that refers (only) to what's right specifically within the domain of public institutions and the judiciary. They make do with their ordinary, common words for 'right' and 'wrong', 'fair' and 'unfair', whatever the context, public or private. That is why Aristotle can move seamlessly between those contexts in his discussions.

Suggestions for Further Reading

EDITIONS OF GREEK TEXTS

Bywater, I. (ed.), *Ethica Nicomachea*, by Aristotle (Oxford: Clarendon, 1894).

Ross, W. D. (ed.), *Fragmenta selecta*, by Aristotle (Oxford: Oxford University Press, 1955).

Susemihl, F. (ed.), *Aristotelis Eudemia Ethica, Eudemii Rhodii Ethica*, by Aristotle (1884).

Susemihl, F. and Apelt, O. (eds), *Ethica Nicomachea*, by Aristotle (3rd edn, Leipzig: Teubner, 1912).

ENGLISH TRANSLATIONS

Broadie, S. and Rowe, C. (eds), *Nicomachean Ethics*, by Aristotle (Oxford and New York: Oxford University Press, 2002).

Crisp, R. (ed. and trans.), *Nicomachean Ethics*, by Aristotle (Cambridge: Cambridge University Press, 2000).

Irwin, T. H. (trans.), *Nicomachean Ethics*, by Aristotle (2nd edn, Indianapolis: Hackett, 1999).

Kenny, A. (trans.), *The Eudemian Ethics*, by Aristotle (Oxford: Oxford University Press, 2011).

Pakaluk, M. (trans.), *Nicomachean Ethics: Books VIII and IX*, by Aristotle (Oxford: Clarendon Press, 1999).

Reeve, C. D. C., *Nicomachean Ethics*, by Aristotle (Indianapolis: Hackett, 2014).

Ross, W. D. (trans.), *The Nicomachean Ethics*, by Aristotle, revised with an introduction and notes by L. Brown; Oxford World's Classics (Oxford: Oxford University Press, 2009).

Taylor, C. C. W. (trans.), *Nicomachean Ethics, Books II–IV*, by Aristotle (Oxford: Clarendon Press, 2006).

PHILOLOGICAL COMMENTARIES
IN ENGLISH

Burnet, J., *The Ethics of Aristotle*, by Aristotle (London: Methuen, 1900).

Grant, A. (ed.), *The Ethics of Aristotle*, 2 vols (rev. 4th edn, London: Longmans, Green, 1885).

Stewart, J. A., *Notes on the Nicomachean Ethics of Aristotle*, 2 vols (Oxford: Clarendon Press, 1892).

ANCIENT AND BYZANTINE
COMMENTATORS

Aspasius, 'Aspasii in *Ethica Nicomachea* quae supersunt commentaria', in *Commentaria in Aristotelem Graeca*, vol. 19, ed. G. Heylbut (Berlin: Reimer, 1889).

Atticus, *Fragment*, ed. E. des Places (Paris: Les Belles Lettres, 1977).

'Eustratii et Michaelis et Anonyma in *Ethica Nicomachea*', in *Commentaria in Aristotelem Graeca*, vol. 20, ed. G. Heylbut (Berlin: Reimer, 1892).

Heliodorus (the Paraphrast), 'Heliodori in *Ethica Nicomachea* Paraphrasis', in *Commentaria in Aristotelem Graeca*, vol. 19, ed. G. Heylbut (Berlin: Reimer, 1889).

BOOKS ON THE *NICOMACHEAN ETHICS*

Annas, J., *The Morality of Happiness* (New York: Oxford University Press, 1993).

Aspasius, *On Aristotle: Nicomachean Ethics 1–4, 7*, trans. David Konstan (London: Bloomsbury, 2006).

Bostock, D., *Aristotle's Ethics* (Oxford: Oxford University Press, 2000).

Broadie, S., *Ethics with Aristotle* (Oxford: Oxford University Press, 1991).

Burger, R., *Aristotle's Dialogue with Socrates: On the Nicomachean Ethics* (Chicago: University of Chicago Press, 2008).

Garver, E., *Confronting Aristotle's Ethics: Ancient and Modern Morality* (Chicago: University of Chicago Press, 2006).

Hardie, W. F. R., *Aristotle's Ethical Theory* (2nd edn, Oxford: Clarendon Press, 1980).

Hughes, G. J., *The Routledge Guidebook to Aristotle's Nicomachean Ethics* (London: Routledge, 2013).

Irwin, T. H., *The Development of Ethics: A Historical and Critical Study*, vol. 1: *From Socrates to the Reformation* (Oxford: Oxford University Press, 2007).

Kraut, R., 'Aristotle's Ethics', in *The Stanford Encyclopedia of Philosophy*, ed. E. N. Zalta (Stanford: The Metaphysics Research Lab, Center for the Study of Language and Information, Stanford University, 2010).

Meyer, S. S., *Ancient Ethics: A Critical Introduction* (London and New York: Routledge, 2008).

Pakaluk, M., *Aristotle's Nicomachean Ethics: An Introduction* (Cambridge: Cambridge University Press, 2005).

Reeve, C. D. C., *Practices of Reason: Aristotle's Nicomachean Ethics* (Oxford: Clarendon Press, 1992).

Smith, T. W., *Revaluing Ethics: Aristotle's Dialectical Pedagogy* (Albany: State University of New York Press, 2001).

Sparshott, F., *Taking Life Seriously: A Study of the Argument of the Nicomachean Ethics* (Toronto: University of Toronto Press, 1994).

COLLECTIONS OF ARTICLES ON THE
NICOMACHEAN ETHICS

Anton, J. P. and Preus, A. (eds), *Essays in Ancient Greek Philosophy*, vol. 4: *Aristotle's Ethics* (Albany: State University of New York Press, 1991).

Barnes, J., Schofield, M. and Sorabji, R. (eds), *Articles on Aristotle*, vol. 2: *Ethics and Politics* (London: Duckworth, 1977).

Kraut, R. (ed.), *The Blackwell Guide to Aristotle's Nicomachean Ethics* (Cambridge, MA and Oxford: Blackwell, 2006).

Miller, J. (ed.), *Aristotle's Nicomachean Ethics: A Critical Guide* (Cambridge: Cambridge University Press, 2011).

Pakaluk, M. and Pearson, G. (eds), *Moral Psychology and Human Action in Aristotle* (Oxford: Oxford University Press, 2011).

Polansky, R. (ed.), *The Cambridge Companion to Aristotle's Nicomachean Ethics* (Cambridge: Cambridge University Press, 2014).

Rorty, A. O. (ed.), *Essays on Aristotle's Ethics* (Berkeley: University of California Press, 1980).

Sherman, N. (ed.), *Aristotle's Ethics: Critical Essays* (Lanham, MD: Rowman & Littlefield, 1999).

HISTORICAL SETTING,
LIFE OF ARISTOTLE

Dillon, J. M., *Morality and Custom in Ancient Greece* (Bloomington: Indiana University Press, 2004).

Dover, K. J., *Greek Popular Morality in the Time of Plato and Aristotle* (Indianapolis: Hackett, 1994).

Düring, I., 'Aristotle the scholar', *Arctos, Acta Philologica Fennica* 1 (1954), pp. 61–77.

Hansen, M. H., *The Athenian Democracy in the Age of Demosthenes* (Oxford: Blackwell, 1991).

Hansen, M. H., *Polis: An Introduction to the Ancient Greek City-state* (Oxford: Oxford University Press, 2006).

Natali, C., *Aristotle: His Life and School*, ed. S. Hutchinson (Princeton: Princeton University Press, 2013).

Whitehead, D., 'Aristotle the metic', *Proceedings of the Cambridge Philological Society* 21 (1975), pp. 94–9.

THE *PROTREPTICUS*

Barnes, J. and Lawrence, G., 'Fragments: Dialogues', in *The Complete Works of Aristotle: The Revised Oxford Translation*, by Aristotle, ed. J. Barnes (Princeton: Princeton University Press, 1984), pp. 2403–17.

Bywater, I., 'On a lost dialogue of Aristotle', *Journal of Philology* 2 (1869), pp. 55–69.

Chroust, A. H., *Protrepticus: A Reconstruction*, by Aristotle (South Bend, IN: University of Notre Dame Press, 1964).

Hutchinson, D. S. and Johnson, M. R., 'Authenticating Aristotle's *Protrepticus*', *Oxford Studies in Ancient Philosophy* 29 (2005), pp. 193–294.

Rabinowitz, W. G., *Aristotle's Protrepticus and the Sources of its Reconstruction* (Berkeley: University of California Press, 1957).

RELATIONSHIP BETWEEN *EUDEMIAN* AND *NICOMACHEAN ETHICS*

Kenny, A., *The Aristotelian Ethics*: *A Study of the Relationship between the Eudemian and Nicomachean Ethics of Aristotle* (Oxford: Oxford University Press, 1978).

Pakaluk, M., 'The egalitarianism of the *Eudemian Ethics*', *Classical Quarterly* 48.2 (1998), pp. 411–32.

Rowe, C. J., *The Eudemian and Nicomachean Ethics: A Study in the Development of Aristotle's Thought* (Cambridge: Cambridge Philological Society, 1971).

HISTORY AND COMPOSITION OF THE TEXT

Barnes, J., 'Roman Aristotle', in *Philosophia Togata II: Plato and Aristotle at Rome*, ed. J. Barnes and M. Griffin (Oxford: Oxford University Press, 1997), pp. 1–70.

Bobonich, C., 'Aristotle's ethical treatises', in *The Blackwell Guide to Aristotle's Nicomachean Ethics*, ed. R. Kraut (Malden, MA: Blackwell, 2006), pp. 12–36.

Chroust, A.-H., 'The miraculous disappearance and discovery of the *Corpus Aristotelicum*', *Classica et Mediaevelia* 28 (1962), pp. 50–67.

Düring, I., *Notes on the History of the Transmission of Aristotle's Writings*, *Göteborgs Högskolas Årsskrift* 56 (Gothenburg, Sweden: Elanders Boktryckeri Aktiebolag, 1950).

Lord, C., 'On the early history of the Aristotelian corpus', *American Journal of Philology* 107.2 (1986), pp. 137–61.

Pakaluk, M., 'On the Unity of the *Nicomachean Ethics*', in *Aristotle's Nicomachean Ethics: A Critical Guide*, ed. J. Miller (Cambridge: Cambridge University Press, 2011), pp. 23–44.

ON INDIVIDUAL BOOKS OF THE
NICOMACHEAN ETHICS

Book I

Baker, S. H., 'The concept of *ergon*: Towards an achievement interpretation of Aristotle's "Function Argument"', *Oxford Studies in
   Ancient Philosophy* 48 (2015), pp. 227–66.

Barnes, J., 'Aristotle and the Methods of Ethics', *Revue Internationale
   de Philosophie* 34.133/134 (1980), pp. 490–511.

Barney, R., 'Aristotle's argument for a human function', *Oxford
   Studies in Ancient Philosophy* 34 (2008), pp. 293–322.

Brown, E., 'Wishing for fortune, choosing activity: Aristotle on
   external goods and happiness', *Proceedings of the Boston Area
   Colloquium in Ancient Philosophy* 22 (2006), pp. 221–56.

Capuccino, C., 'Happiness and Aristotle's definition of *eudaimonia*',
   Philosophical Topics 41 (2013), pp. 1–26.

Cooper, J. M., 'Aristotle on the goods of fortune', in *Reason and
   Emotion: Essays on Ancient Moral Psychology and Ethical Theory*,
   ed. J. M. Cooper (Princeton: Princeton University Press, 1999),
   pp. 292–311.

Cooper, J. M., 'Plato and Aristotle on "finality" and "(self-)suffi-
   ciency"', in *Plato and Aristotle's Ethics*, ed. R. Heinaman
   (Burlington, VT and Aldershot: Ashgate, 2003), pp. 117–52.

Farwall, P., 'Aristotle, success, and moral luck', *Journal of Philosophical Research* 19 (1994), pp. 37–50.

Farwall, P., 'Aristotle and the complete life', *History of Philosophy
   Quarterly* 12.3 (1995), pp. 247–63.

Fine, G., *On Ideas: Aristotle's Criticism of Plato's Theory of Forms*
   (Oxford: Clarendon Press, 1993).

Heinaman, R., '*Eudaimonia* and self-sufficiency in the *Nicomachean Ethics*', *Phronesis* 33.1 (1988), pp. 35–41.

Irwin, T. H., 'Ethics as an inexact science: Aristotle's ambitions for
   moral theory', in *Moral Particularism*, ed. B. Hooker and M. Little
   (Oxford: Clarendon Press, 2000), pp. 130–56.

Irwin, T. H., 'Conceptions of happiness in the *Nicomachean Ethics*',
   in *The Oxford Handbook of Aristotle*, ed. C. Shields (Oxford:
   Oxford University Press, 2012), pp. 495–528.

Korsgaard, C. M., 'Aristotle on function and virtue', *History of Philosophy Quarterly* 3.3 (1986), pp. 259–79.

Kraut, R., 'The peculiar function of human beings', *Canadian Journal of Philosophy* 9.3 (1979), pp. 467–78.

Kraut, R., 'Two conceptions of happiness', *Philosophical Review* 88.2 (1979), pp. 167–97.

Lawrence, G., 'Aristotle and the ideal life', *Philosophical Review* 102.1 (1993), pp. 1–34.

Lawrence, G., 'The function of the function argument', *Ancient Philosophy* 21 (2001), pp. 445–75.

McDowell, J., 'The role of *eudaimonia* in Aristotle's *Ethics*', in *Essays on Aristotle's Ethics*, ed. A. O. Rorty (Berkeley: University of California Press, 1980), pp. 359–76.

Nussbaum, M. C., *The Fragility of Goodness: Luck and Ethics in Greek Tragedy and Philosophy* (Cambridge: Cambridge University Press, 1986).

Rowe, C., 'The good for man in Aristotle's *Ethics* and *Politics*', in *Studi sull' Etica di Aristotele*, ed. A. Alberti (Naples: Bibliopolis, 1990), pp. 193–225.

Vasiliou, I., 'The role of good upbringing in Aristotle's *Ethics*', *Philosophy and Phenomenological Research* 56.4 (1996), pp. 771–97.

White, S. A., 'Is Aristotelian happiness a good life or the best life?', *Oxford Studies in Ancient Philosophy* 8 (1990), pp. 103–43.

White, S. A., *Sovereign Virtue: Aristotle on the Relationship between Happiness and Prosperity* (Stanford: Stanford University Press, 1992).

Whiting, J., 'Aristotle's function argument: A defense', *Ancient Philosophy* 8.1 (1988), pp. 33–48.

Williams, B., *Ethics and the Limits of Philosophy* (Cambridge, MA: Harvard University Press, 1985).

Zingano, M., 'Aristotle and the problems of method in *Ethics*', *Oxford Studies in Ancient Philosophy* 32 (2007), pp. 297–330.

Book II

Audi, R., 'Acting from virtue', *Mind* 104.415 (1995), pp. 449–71.

Bosley, R., Shiner, R. A. and Sisson, J. D. (eds), *Aristotle, Virtue and the Mean* (Kelowna, BC: Academic Printing, 1995).

Bowditch, N., 'Aristotle on habituation: The key to unlocking the *Nicomachean Ethics*', *Ethical Perspectives* 15.3 (2008), pp. 309–42.

Brown, L., 'What is the "mean relative to us" in Aristotle's *Ethics*?', *Phronesis* 42.1 (1997), pp. 77–93.

Burnyeat, M., 'Aristotle on learning to be good', in *Essays on Aristotle's Ethics*, ed. A. O. Rorty (Berkeley: University of California Press, 1980), pp. 69–92.

Cooper, J. M., 'Reason, moral virtue, and moral value', in *Reason and Emotion: Essays on Ancient Moral Psychology and Ethical Theory*, ed. J. M. Cooper (Princeton: Princeton University Press, 1999), pp. 253–80.

Curzer, H. J., 'A defense of Aristotle's doctrine of the mean', *Ancient Philosophy* 16 (1996), pp. 129–39.

Curzer, H. J., 'How good people do bad things: Aristotle on the misdeeds of the virtuous', *Oxford Studies in Ancient Philosophy* 28 (2005), pp. 233–56.

Gottlieb, P., *The Virtue of Aristotle's Ethics* (Cambridge: Cambridge University Press, 2009).

Hursthouse, R., 'Moral habituation', *Oxford Studies in Ancient Philosophy* 6 (1988), pp. 201–19.

Hutchinson, D. S., *The Virtues of Aristotle* (London: Routledge and Kegan Paul, 1986).

Irwin, T. H., 'Aristotle's Conception of Morality', *Proceedings of the Boston Area Colloquium in Ancient Philosophy* 1 (1985), pp. 115–43.

Kraut, R., 'Aristotle on becoming good: Habituation, reflection, and perception', in *The Oxford Handbook of Aristotle*, ed. C. Shields (Oxford: Oxford University Press, 2012), pp. 529–57.

Lawrence, G., 'Acquiring character: Becoming grown-up', in *Moral Psychology and Human Action in Aristotle*, ed. M. Pakaluk and G. Pearson (Oxford: Oxford University Press, 2011), pp. 233–83.

Leighton, S. R., 'Aristotle and the Emotions', *Phronesis* 27.2 (1982), pp. 144–74.

Lorenz, H., 'Virtue of character in Aristotle's *Nicomachean Ethics*', *Oxford Studies in Ancient Philosophy* 37 (2009), pp. 177–212.

Pearson, G., 'Does the Fearless Phobic really fear the squeak of mice "too much"?', *Ancient Philosophy* 26.1 (2006), pp. 81–91.

Sherman, N., *The Fabric of Character: Aristotle's Theory of Virtue* (Oxford: Clarendon Press, 1989).

Taylor, C. C. W., *Aristotle: Nicomachean Ethics, Books II–IV* (Oxford: Clarendon Press, 2006).

Whiting, J., '*Eudaimonia*, external results, and choosing virtuous actions for themselves', *Philosophy and Phenomenological Research* 65.2 (2002), pp. 270–90.

Williams, B., 'Acting as the virtuous person acts', in *Aristotle and Moral Realism*, ed. R. Heinaman (Boulder, CO: Westview, 1995), pp. 13–23.

Young, C. M., 'Aristotle's doctrine of the mean', *Topoi* 15 (1996), pp. 89–99.

Book III

Bobzien, S., 'The inadvertent conception and late birth of the free-will problem', *Phronesis* 43.2 (1998), pp. 133–75.

Bobzien, S., 'Found in translation: Aristotle's *Nicomachean Ethics* 3.5, 1113b7–8, and its reception', *Oxford Studies in Ancient Philosophy* 45 (2013), pp. 103–48.

Bondeson, W., 'Aristotle on responsibility for one's character and the possibility of character change', *Phronesis* 19.1 (1979), pp. 59–65.

Brady, M. E., 'The fearlessness of courage', *Southern Journal of Philosophy* 43.2 (2005), pp. 189–211.

Brickhouse, T. C., 'Roberts on responsibility for action and character in the *Nicomachean Ethics*', *Ancient Philosophy* 11 (1991), pp. 137–48.

Curzer, H. J., 'Courage and continence', in *Aristotle and the Virtues* by H. J. Curzer (Oxford: Oxford University Press, 2012), pp. 19–64.

Destrée, P., 'Aristotle on responsibility for one's character', in *Moral Psychology and Human Action in Aristotle*, ed. M. Pakaluk and G. Pearson (Oxford: Oxford University Press, 2011), pp. 285–318.

Donini, P., *Aristotle and Determinism* (Louvain-la-Neuve: Peeters, 2009).

Everson, S., 'Aristotle's compatibilism in the *Nicomachean Ethics*', *Ancient Philosophy* 10.1 (1990), pp. 81–99.

Flannery, K., 'Force and compulsion in Aristotle's ethics', *Proceedings of the Boston Area Colloquium in Ancient Philosophy* 22 (2006), pp. 41–61.

Gottlieb, P., 'Aristotle and Protagoras: The good human being as the measure of goods', *Apeiron* 24.1 (1991), pp. 25–46.

MacIntyre, A. C., 'Sōphrosunē: How a virtue can become socially disruptive', *Midwest Studies in Philosophy* 13 (1998), pp. 1–11.

McDowell, J., 'Deliberation and moral deliberation in Aristotle's *Ethics*', in *Aristotle, Kant, and the Stoics: Rethinking Happiness and Duty*, ed. S. Engstrom and J. Whiting (Cambridge: Cambridge University Press, 1996), pp. 19–35.

Mele, A. R., 'Aristotle's wish', *Journal of the History of Philosophy* 22.2 (1984), pp. 139–56.

Meyer, S. S., *Aristotle on Moral Responsibility: Character and Cause* (Oxford: Oxford University Press, 2011).

Moline, J. N., 'Aristotle on praise and blame', *Archiv für Geschichte der Philosophie* 71.3 (1989), pp. 283–302.

North, H., *Sophrosyne: Self-knowledge and self-restraint in Greek Literature* (Ithaca, NY: Cornell University Press, 1966).

Pears, D., 'Courage as a mean', in *Essays on Aristotle's Ethics*, ed. A. O. Rorty (Berkeley: University of California Press, 1980), pp. 171–88.

Sisko, J. E., 'Taste, touch, and temperance in *Nicomachean Ethics* 3.10', *Classical Quarterly* 53.1 (2003), pp. 135–40.

Taylor, C. C. W., 'Wisdom and courage in the *Protagoras* and the *Nicomachean Ethics*', in *Pleasure, Mind, and Soul: Selected Papers in Ancient Philosophy* by C. C. W. Taylor (Oxford: Clarendon Press, 2008), pp. 281–94.

Tuozzo, T. M., 'Conceptualized and unconceptualized desire in Aristotle', *Journal of the History of Philosophy* 32.4 (1994), pp. 525–49.

Wiggins, D., 'Deliberation and practical reason', in *Essays on Aristotle's Ethics*, ed. A. O. Rorty (Berkeley: University of California Press, 1980), pp. 221–40.

Young, C. M., 'Aristotle on temperance', *Philosophical Review* 97.4 (1988), pp. 521–42.

Book IV

Athanassoulis, N., 'A defense of the Aristotelian virtue of magnificence', *Journal of Value Inquiry* 50 (2016), pp. 781–95.

Collins, S., 'Political wit and enlightenment', in *Aristotle and the Rediscovery of Citizenship* by S. Collins (Cambridge: Cambridge University Press, 2006), pp. 147–65.

Cooper, N., 'Aristotle's crowning virtue', *Apeiron* 22.3 (1989), pp. 191–205.

Crisp, R., 'Aristotle on greatness of soul', in *The Blackwell Guide to Aristotle's Nicomachean Ethics*, ed. R. Kraut (Malden, MA: Blackwell, 2006), pp. 158–78.

Crisp, R., 'Nobility in the *Nicomachean Ethics*', *Phronesis* 59 (2014), pp. 231–45.

Gooch, P. W., 'Socratic irony and Aristotle's *Eiron*: Some puzzles', *Phoenix* 41.2 (1987), pp. 95–104.

Gottlieb, P., 'Aristotle's "nameless" virtues', *Apeiron* 27.1 (1994), pp. 1–15.

Hadreas, P., 'Aristotle on the vices and virtue of wealth', *Journal of Business Ethics* 39 (2002), pp. 361–76.

Pakaluk, M., 'The meaning of Aristotelian magnanimity', *Oxford Studies in Ancient Philosophy* 26 (2004), pp. 241–75.

Reiner, P., 'Aristotle on personality and some implications for friendship', *Ancient Philosophy* 11.1 (1991), pp. 67–84.

Sarch, A., 'What's wrong with *Megalopsychia*?', *Philosophy* 83 (2008), pp. 231–53.

Ward, A., 'Generosity and inequality in Aristotle's *Ethics*', *Polis* 28.2 (2011), pp. 267–78.

Young, C. M., 'Aristotle on liberality', *Proceedings of the Boston Area Colloquium in Ancient Philosophy* 10 (1994), pp. 313–34.

Zembaty, J. S., 'Aristotle on lying', *Journal of the History of Philosophy* 31 (1993), pp. 7–30.

Book V

Aubenque, P., 'The twofold natural foundation of justice according to Aristotle', in *Aristotle and Moral Realism*, ed. R. Heinaman (Boulder, CO: Westview, 1995), pp. 35–47.

Brickhouse, T. C., 'Aristotle on corrective justice', *Journal of Ethics* 18.3 (2014), pp. 187–205.

Brunschwig, J., 'Rule and exception: On the Aristotelian theory of equity', in *Rationality in Greek Thought*, ed. M. Frede and G. Striker (Oxford: Oxford University Press, 1996), pp. 115–56.

Burns, T., 'Aristotle and natural law', *History of Political Thought* 19.2 (1998), pp. 142–66.

Curzer, H. J., 'Aristotle's account of the virtue of justice', *Apeiron* 28.3 (1995), pp. 207–38.

Drefcinski, S., 'Aristotle and the characteristic desire of justice', *Apeiron* 33.2 (2000), pp. 109–23.

Foster, S. E., 'Virtues and material goods: Aristotle on justice and liberality', *American Catholic Philosophical Quarterly* 71.4 (1998), pp. 607–19.

Frank, J., 'Democracy and distribution: Aristotle on just desert', *Political Theory* 26.6 (1998), pp. 784–802.

Harrison, A. R. W., 'Aristotle's Nicomachean Ethics, Book V, and the law of Athens', *Journal of Hellenic Studies* 77 (1957), pp. 42–7.

Harvey, F. D., 'Two kinds of equality', *Classica et Mediaevalia* 26 (1965), pp. 101–46.

Horn, C., '*Epieikeia*: The competence of the perfectly just person in Aristotle', in *The Virtuous Life in Greek Ethics*, ed. B. Reis and S. Haffmanns (Cambridge: Cambridge University Press, 2006), pp. 142–66.

Jackson, H. (ed.), *Peri Dikaiosunes: The Fifth Book of the Nico-machean Ethics of Aristotle* (Cambridge: Cambridge University Press, 1879).

Judson, L., 'Aristotle on fair exchange', *Oxford Studies in Ancient Philosophy* 15 (1997), pp. 147–75.

Keyt, D., 'Aristotle's theory of distributive justice', in *A Companion to Aristotle's Politics*, ed. D. Keyt and F. D. Miller Jr (Oxford and Cambridge, MA: Blackwell, 1991), pp. 238–78.

Kraut, R., 'Justice in the *Nicomachean Ethics*', in *Aristotle: Political Philosophy* by R. Kraut (Oxford: Oxford University Press, 2002), pp. 98–177.

Miller, F. D., Jr, 'Aristotle on natural law and justice', in *A Companion to Aristotle's Politics*, ed. D. Keyt and F. D. Miller Jr (Oxford and Cambridge, MA: Blackwell, 1991), pp. 279–306.

Neyers, J. W., 'The inconsistencies of Aristotle's theory of corrective justice', *Canadian Journal of Law and Jurisprudence* 11 (1998), pp. 311–28.

Nussbaum, M. C., 'Equity and mercy', *Philosophy & Public Affairs* 22.2 (1993), pp. 83–125.

Scaltsas, T., 'Reciprocal justice in Aristotle's *Nicomachean Ethics*', *Archiv für Geschichte der Philosophie* 77.3 (1995), pp. 248–62.

Shiner, R. A., 'Aristotle's theory of equity', *Loyola of Los Angeles Law Review* 27 (1994), pp. 1245–64.

Simpson, P. L. P., 'Aristotle on natural justice', *Studia Gilsoniana* 3 (2014), pp. 367–76.

Vega, J., 'Aristotle's concept of law: Beyond positivism and natural law', *Journal of Ancient Philosophy* 4.2 (2010), pp. 1–31.

Williams, B., 'Justice as a virtue', in *Essays on Aristotle's Ethics*, ed. A. O. Rorty (Berkeley: University of California Press, 1980), pp. 189–99.

Young, C., 'Aristotle on justice', *Southern Journal of Philosophy* 27 (1988), pp. 233–57.

Book VI

Broadie, S., 'Practical wisdom', in *Ethics with Aristotle* by S. Broadie (Oxford: Oxford University Press, 1991), pp. 179–265.

Broadie, S., 'Practical truth in Aristotle', *American Catholic Philosophical Quarterly* 90 (2016), pp. 281–98.

Cooper, J. M., 'The unity of virtue', *Social Philosophy and Policy* 15.1 (1998), pp. 233–74.

Devereux, D. T., 'Particular and universal in Aristotle's conception of practical knowledge', *Review of Metaphysics* 39.3 (1986), pp. 483–504.

Dominick, Y. H., 'Teaching nature: Natural virtue and practical wisdom in the *Nicomachean Ethics*', *Southwest Philosophy Review* 22.1 (2006), pp. 103–11.

Dryer, D. P., 'Aristotle's conception of *orthos logos*', *Monist* 66.1 (1983), pp. 106–19.

Fortenbaugh, W. W., 'Aristotle's distinction between moral virtue and practical wisdom', in *Essays in Ancient Greek Philosophy*, vol. 4: *Aristotle's Ethics*, ed. J. P. Anton and A. Preus (Albany: State University of New York Press, 1991), pp. 97–106.

Gómez-Lobo, A., 'Aristotle's right reason', *Apeiron* 28.4 (1995), pp. 15–34.

Gottlieb, P., 'Aristotle on dividing the soul and uniting the virtues', *Phronesis* 39.3 (1994), pp. 275–90.

Hursthouse, R., 'Practical wisdom: A mundane account', *Proceedings of the Aristotelian Society* 106 (2006), pp. 285–309.

Irwin, T. H., 'Disunity in the Aristotelian virtues', *Oxford Studies in Ancient Philosophy* (1988), supplementary volume, pp. 61–86.

Kirkland, S., 'The temporality of *phronesis* in the *Nicomachean Ethics*', *Ancient Philosophy* 27 (2007), pp. 127–40.

Lennox, J. G., 'Aristotle on the biological roots of human virtue: The natural history of natural virtue', in *Biology and the Foundation of Ethics*, ed. J. Maienschein and M. Ruse (Cambridge: Cambridge University Press, 1999), pp. 10–31.

Louden, R. B., 'What is moral authority? *Euboulia, sunesis*, and *gnome* vs. *phronesis*', *Ancient Philosophy* 17 (1997), pp. 103–18.

Mele, A. R., 'Aristotle on the roles of reason in motivation and action', *Archiv für Geschichte der Philosophie* 66 (1984), pp. 124–47.

Moss, J., 'Virtue makes the goal right: Virtue and *phronesis* in Aristotle's *Ethics*', *Phronesis* 56 (2011), pp. 204–61.

Moss, J., 'Right reason in Plato and Aristotle: On the meaning of *logos*', *Phronesis* 59 (2014), pp. 181–230.

Natali, C., *The Wisdom of Aristotle*, trans. G. Parks (Albany: State University of New York Press, 2001).

Olfert, C. M. M., 'Aristotle's conception of practical truth', *Journal of the History of Philosophy* 52 (2014), pp. 205–31.

Pakaluk, M., 'On an alleged contradiction in Aristotle's *Nicomachean Ethics*', *Oxford Studies in Ancient Philosophy* 22 (2002), pp. 201–19.

Reeve, C. D. C., *Practices of Reason: Aristotle's Nicomachean Ethics* (Oxford: Clarendon Press, 1992).

Reeve, C. D. C., 'Aristotle on the virtues of thought', in *The Blackwell Guide to Aristotle's Nicomachean Ethics*, ed. R. Kraut (Malden, MA: Blackwell, 2006), pp. 198–217.

Simon, A., '*Sunesis* as ethical discernment in Aristotle', *Rhizomata* 5.1 (2017), pp. 79–90.

Smith, A. D., 'Character and intellect in Aristotle's *Ethics*', *Phronesis* 41.1 (1996), pp. 56–74.

Taylor, C. C. W., 'Aristotle on the practical intellect', in *Pleasure, Mind, and Soul: Selected Papers in Ancient Philosophy* by C. C. W. Taylor (Oxford: Clarendon Press, 2008), pp. 204–22.

Walsh, M. M., 'Role of universal knowledge in Aristotelian moral virtue', *Ancient Philosophy* 19.1 (1999), pp. 73–88.

Wiggins, D., 'Deliberation and practical reason', in *Essays on Aristotle's Ethics*, ed. A. O. Rorty (Berkeley: University of California Press, 1980), pp. 221–40.

Woods, M., 'Intuition and perception in Aristotle's *Ethics*', *Oxford Studies in Ancient Philosophy* 4 (1986), pp. 145–66.

Books VII and X (Self-control, Pleasure)

Ackrill, J. L., 'Aristotle's distinction between *energeia* and *kinesis*', in *New Essays on Plato and Aristotle*, ed. R. Bambrough (London: Routledge & Kegan Paul, 1965), pp. 131–41.

Annas, J., 'Aristotle on pleasure and goodness', in *Essays on Aristotle's Ethics*, ed. A. O. Rorty (Berkeley: University of California Press, 1980), pp. 285–300.

Bostock, D., 'Pleasure and activity in Aristotle's *Ethics*', *Phronesis* 33.3 (1988), pp. 251–72.

Brickhouse, T. C., 'Does Aristotle have a consistent account of vice?', *Review of Metaphysics* 57.1 (2003), pp. 3–23.

Charles, D., *Aristotle's Philosophy of Action* (Ithaca, NY: Cornell University Press, 1984).

Charlton, W., *Weakness of Will* (Oxford: Blackwell, 1988).

Cook Wilson, J., *On the Structure of Book Seven of the Nicomachean Ethics* (Oxford: Oxford University Press, 1912).

Destrée, P., 'Aristotle on the causes of *akrasia*', in *Akrasia in Greek Philosophy: From Socrates to Plotinus*, ed. C. Bobonich and P. Destrée (Leiden: Brill, 2007), pp. 139–66.

Dillon, J. M., 'Speusippus on pleasure', in *Polyhistor: Studies in the History and Historiography of Ancient Philosophy*, ed. K. A. Algra (Leiden: Brill, 1996), pp. 99–114.

Frede, D., 'Pleasure and pain in Aristotle's *Ethics*', in *The Blackwell Guide to Aristotle's Nicomachean Ethics*, ed. R. Kraut (Malden, MA: Blackwell, 2006), pp. 255–75.

Gonzalez, F. J., 'Aristotle on pleasure and perfection', *Phronesis* 36.2 (1991), pp. 141–60.

Gosling, J. C. B. and Taylor, C. C. W., *The Greeks on Pleasure* (Oxford: Clarendon Press, 1982).

Gottlieb, P., 'The practical syllogism', in *The Blackwell Guide to Aristotle's Nicomachean Ethics*, ed. R. Kraut (Malden, MA: Blackwell, 2006), pp. 218–33.

Grgić, F., 'Aristotle on the akratic's knowledge', *Phronesis* 47.4 (2002), pp. 336–58.

Irwin, T. H., 'Some rational aspects of incontinence', *Southern Journal of Philosophy* 27 (1988), supplement 1, pp. 49–88.

Irwin, T. H., 'Aristotle reads the *Protagoras*', in *Weakness of Will from Plato to the Present*, ed. T. Hoffmann (Washington: Catholic University of America Press, 2008), pp. 22–41.

Kenny, A., 'The practical syllogism and incontinence', *Phronesis* 11.2 (1966), pp. 163–84.

McDowell, J., 'Comments on T. H. Irwin's "Some rational aspects of incontinence"', *Southern Journal of Philosophy* 27 (1988), supplement 1, pp. 89–102.

Natali, C. (ed.), *Aristotle's Nicomachean Ethics, Book VII: Symposium Aristotelicum* (Oxford: Oxford University Press, 2009).

Olfert, C. M. M., *Aristotle on Practical Truth* (Oxford: Oxford University Press, 2017).

Pickavé, M. and Whiting, J., '*Nicomachean Ethics* 7.3 on akratic ignorance', *Oxford Studies in Ancient Philosophy* 34 (2008), pp. 323–72.

Price, A. W., '*Acrasia* and self-control', in *The Blackwell Guide to Aristotle's Nicomachean Ethics*, ed. R. Kraut (Malden, MA: Blackwell, 2006), pp. 234–54.

Roochnik, D., 'Aristotle's account of the vicious: A forgivable inconsistency', *History of Philosophy Quarterly* 24.3 (2007), pp. 207–20.

Taylor, C. C. W., 'Pleasure: Aristotle's response to Plato', in *Plato and Aristotle's Ethics*, ed. R. Heinaman (Aldershot and Burlington, VT: Ashgate, 2003), pp. 1–27.

Warren, J., 'Aristotle on Speusippus on Eudoxus on pleasure', *Oxford Studies in Ancient Philosophy* 36 (2009), pp. 249–82.

Weinman, M., *Pleasure in Aristotle's Ethics* (New York: Continuum, 2007).

Weiss, R., 'Aristotle's criticism of Eudoxan hedonism', *Classical Philology* 74.3 (1979), pp. 214–21.

Welch, J. R., 'Reconstructing Aristotle: The practical syllogism', *Philosophia* 21.1–2 (1991), pp. 69–88.

Wiggins, D., 'Weakness of will, commensurability and the objects of deliberation and desire', in *Essays on Aristotle's Ethics*, ed. A. O. Rorty (Berkeley: University of California Press, 1980), pp. 241–66.

Books VIII and IX

Alpern, K. D., 'Aristotle on the friendship of utility and pleasure', *Journal of the History of Philosophy* 21.3 (1983), pp. 303–16.

Annas, J., 'Plato and Aristotle on friendship and altruism', *Mind* 86.344 (1977), pp. 532–54.

Annas, J., 'Self-love in Aristotle', in *Special issue: Spindel supplement: Aristotle's Ethics*, ed. T. D. Roche, *Southern Journal of Philosophy* 27 (1988), S1, pp. 1–18.

Belfiore, E., 'Family friendship in Aristotle's *Ethics*', *Ancient Philosophy* 21.1 (2001), pp. 113–32.

Biss, M., 'Aristotle on friendship and self-knowledge: The friend beyond the mirror', *History of Philosophy Quarterly* 28.2 (2011), pp. 125–40.

Cooper, J. M., 'Aristotle on the forms of friendship', in *Reason and Emotion: Essays on Ancient Moral Psychology and Ethical Theory* by J. M. Cooper (Princeton: Princeton University Press, 1999), pp. 312–35.

Cooper, J. M., 'Political animals and civic friendship', in ibid., pp. 356–77.

Curzer, H. J., 'Justice in friendship (*NE* VII–IX)', in *Aristotle and the Virtues* by H. J. Curzer (Oxford: Oxford University Press, 2012), pp. 275–92.

Flannery, K. L., 'Can an Aristotelian consider himself a friend of God?', in *Virtue's End: God in the Moral Philosophy of Aristotle and Aquinas*, ed. F. Di Blasi, J. P. Hochschild and J. Langan (South Bend, IN: St Augustine's Press, 2008), pp. 1–12.

Gottlieb, P., 'Aristotle's ethical egoism', *Pacific Philosophical Quarterly* 77.1 (1996), pp. 1–18.

Hardie, W. F. R., 'Friendship and self-love', in *Aristotle's Ethical Theory* by W. F. R. Hardie (2nd edn, Oxford: Clarendon Press, 1980), pp. 317–35.

Hitz, Z., 'Aristotle on self-knowledge and friendship', *Philosopher's Imprint* 11.12 (2011), pp. 1–28.

Hursthouse, R., 'Aristotle for women who love too much', *Ethics* 117.2 (2007), pp. 327–34.

Irrera, E., 'Between advantage and virtue: Aristotle's theory of political friendship', *History of Political Thought* 26.4 (2005), pp. 565–85.

Irwin, T., 'Aristotle's conception of morality', *Proceedings of the Boston Area Colloquium in Ancient Philosophy* 1 (1985), pp. 115–43.

Kahn, C., 'Aristotle and altruism', *Mind* 90.357 (1981), pp. 20–40.

Kenny, A., 'Friendship and self-love', in *Aristotle on the Perfect Life* by Anthony Kenny (Oxford: Oxford University Press, 1992), pp. 43–55.

Klonoski, R., '*Homonoia* in Aristotle's *Ethics* and *Politics*', *History of Political Thought* 17.3 (1996), pp. 313–25.

Kosman, A., 'Aristotle on the desirability of friends', *Ancient Philosophy* 24.1 (2004), pp. 135–54.

Kraut, R., 'Self and others', in *Aristotle on the Human Good* by R. Kraut (Princeton: Princeton University Press, 1989), pp. 78–154.

Lockwood, T. C., Jr, 'The best regime of Aristotle's *Nicomachean Ethics*', *Ancient Philosophy* 26.2 (2006), pp. 355–70.

Madigan, A., '*Eth. Nic.* 9.8: Beyond egoism and altruism?', *Modern Schoolman* 62 (1985), pp. 1–20.

Mansini, G., 'Aristotle on needing friends', *American Catholic Philosophical Quarterly* 72.3 (1998), pp. 405–17.

McKerlie, D., 'Aristotle and egoism', *Southern Journal of Philosophy* 36.4 (1998), pp. 531–55.

Nehamas, A., 'Aristotelian *philia*, modern friendship', *Oxford Studies in Ancient Philosophy* 39 (2010), pp. 213–47.

O'Connor, D. K., 'Two ideals of friendship', *History of Philosophy Quarterly* 7.2 (1990), pp. 109–22.

Payne, A., 'Character and the forms of friendship in Aristotle', *Apeiron* 33.1 (2000), pp. 53–74.

Perälä, M., 'A friend being good and one's own in *Nicomachean Ethics* 9.9', *Phronesis* 61 (2016), pp. 307–36.

Politis, V., 'The primacy of self-love in the *Nicomachean Ethics*', *Oxford Studies in Ancient Philosophy* 11 (1993), pp. 153–74.

Price, A. W., 'Aristotle on erotic love', in *Love and Friendship in Plato and Aristotle* by A. W. Price (Oxford: Clarendon Press, 1997), pp. 236–49.

Roberts, J., 'Political animals in the *Nicomachean Ethics*', *Phronesis* 34.2 (1989), pp. 185–202.

Rogers, K., 'Aristotle on loving another for his own sake', *Phronesis* 39.3 (1994), pp. 291–302.

Sherman, N., 'The shared life', in *The Fabric of Character: Aristotle's Theory of Virtue* by N. Sherman (Oxford: Oxford University Press, 1989), pp. 118–56.

Sihvola, J., 'Aristotle on sex and love', in *The Sleep of Reason: Erotic Experience and Sexual Ethics in Ancient Greece and Rome*, ed. M. C. Nussbaum and J. Sihvola (Chicago: University of Chicago Press, 2002), pp. 200–21.

Stern-Gillet, S., 'Self-love', in *Aristotle's Philosophy of Friendship* by S. Stern-Gillet (Albany: State University of New York Press, 1995), pp. 79–101.

Timmermann, J., 'Why we cannot want our friends to be gods: Some notes on *NE* 1159a5–12', *Phronesis* 40.2 (1995), pp. 209–15.

Whiting, J., 'The Nicomachean account of *philia*', in *The Blackwell Guide to Aristotle's Nicomachean Ethics*, ed. R. Kraut (Malden, MA: Blackwell, 2006), pp. 276–304.

Zingano, M., 'The conceptual unity of friendship in the *Eudemian* and the *Nicomachean Ethics*', *Apeiron* 48 (2015), pp. 195–219.

Book X (*Eudaimonia* and contemplation)

Ackrill, J. L., 'Aristotle on *eudaimonia*', in *Essays on Aristotle's Ethics*, ed. A. O. Rorty (Berkeley: University of California Press, 1980), pp. 15–34.

Baracchi, C., *Aristotle's Ethics as First Philosophy* (Cambridge: Cambridge University Press, 2008).

Burger, R., 'Aristotle's "exclusive" account of happiness: Contemplative wisdom as a guise of the political philosopher', in *The Crossroads of Norm and Nature: Essays on Aristotle's Ethics and Metaphysics*, ed. M. Sim (Lanham, MD: Rowman and Littlefield, 1995), pp. 79–98.

Bush, S., 'Divine and human happiness in the *Nicomachean Ethics*', *Philosophical Review* 117.1 (2008), pp. 49–75.

Charles, D., 'Aristotle on well-being and intellectual contemplation', *Proceedings of the Aristotelian Society* 73 (1999), supplementary volume, pp. 205–23.

Cooper, J. M., 'Contemplation and happiness: A reconsideration', in *Reason and Emotion: Essays on Ancient Moral Psychology and Ethical Theory* by J. M. Cooper (Princeton: Princeton University Press, 1999), pp. 212–36.

Crisp, R., 'Aristotle's inclusivism', *Ancient Philosophy* 12 (1994), pp. 111–36.

Curzer, H. J., 'The supremely happy life in Aristotle's *Nicomachean Ethics*', *Apeiron* 24.1 (1991), pp. 47–69.

Destrée, P. and Zingano, M. (eds), *Theoria: Studies on the Status and Meaning of Contemplation in Aristotle's Ethics* (Leuven: Peeters, 2014).

Hardie, W. F. R., 'Aristotle on the best life for a man', *Philosophy* 54.207 (1979), pp. 35–50.

Heinaman, R., 'Eudaimonia and self-sufficiency in the *Nicomachean Ethics*', *Phronesis* 33.1 (1988), pp. 31–53.

Heinaman, R., 'Eudaimonia as an activity in *Nicomachean Ethics* 1.8–12', *Oxford Studies in Ancient Philosophy* 33 (2007), pp. 221–53.

Irwin, T., 'The structure of Aristotelian happiness', review of *Aristotle on the Human Good* by R. Kraut, *Ethics* 101 (1991), pp. 382–91.

Kenny, A., 'The Nicomachean concept of happiness', *Oxford Studies in Ancient Philosophy* (1991), supplemental volume, pp. 67–80.

Lawrence, G., 'Human good and human function', in *The Blackwell Guide to Aristotle's Nicomachean Ethics*, ed. R. Kraut (Malden, MA: Blackwell, 2006), pp. 37–75.

Long, A. A., 'Aristotle on *eudaimonia, nous,* and divinity', in *Aristotle's Nicomachean Ethics: A Critical Guide*, ed. J. Miller (Cambridge: Cambridge University Press, 2011), pp. 92–114.

Mingay, J. M., 'How should a philosopher live? Two Aristotelian views', *History of Political Thought* 8 (1987), pp. 21–32.

Purinton, J., 'Aristotle's definition of happiness (*NE* I.7, 1098a16–18)', *Oxford Studies in Ancient Philosophy* 16 (1998), pp. 259–98.

Roochnik, D., 'What is *theoria*? Nicomachean Ethics book 10.7–8', *Classical Philology* 104.1 (2008), pp. 69–81.

Rorty, A. O., 'The place of contemplation in Aristotle's Nicomachean Ethics', in *Essays on Aristotle's Ethics*, ed. A. O. Rorty (Berkeley: University of California Press, 1980), pp. 377–94.

Scott, D., 'Aristotle on well-being and intellectual contemplation: Primary and secondary *eudaimonia*', *Proceedings of the Aristotelian Society* 73.1 (1999), supplementary volume, pp. 225–42.

Segev, M., *Aristotle on Religion* (Cambridge: Cambridge University Press, 2017).

Striker, G., 'Aristotle's ethics as political science', in *The Virtuous Life in Greek Ethics*, ed. B. Reis and S. Haffmanns (Cambridge: Cambridge University Press, 2006), pp. 127–41.

Thorsrud, H., 'Aristotle's dichotomous anthropology: What is most human in the *Nicomachean Ethics*?', *Apeiron* 48 (2015), pp. 346–67.

Vander Waerdt, P. A., 'The plan and the intention of Aristotle's ethical and political writings', *Illinois Classical Studies* 16.1–2 (1991),
pp. 231–51.

Whiting, J., 'Human nature and intellectualism in Aristotle', *Archiv
für Geschichte der Philosophie* 68.1 (1986), pp. 70–95.

Textual Appendix

The following are the places where this translation departs from Bywater's Oxford text. The majority of these changes are very minor. Most are adopted from other scholars, many with manuscript support. A longer version of this list of emendations, with a full discussion of all the more substantial problems, can be found on my page at academia.edu.

	THIS TRANSLATION	BYWATER
1097a27	χαλινούς	αὐλοὺς
1099a4	οὐχ οἱ ἐν παλαίστρᾳ ἰσχυρότατοι στεφανοῦνται	οὐχ οἱ κάλλιστοι καὶ ἰσχυρότατοι στεφανοῦνται
1099b23	πᾶσαν τοιαύτην αἰτίαν	πᾶσαν αἰτίαν
1100b15	μονιμώταται	μονιμώτεραι
1101b15	τὸν ἀγαθὸν διά τε τὴν ἀρετὴν ἐπαινοῦμεν καὶ διὰ τὰς πράξεις	τὸν ἀγαθόν τε καὶ τὴν ἀρετὴν ἐπαινοῦμεν διὰ τὰς πράξεις
1103a16	ἡ δ' ἠθικὴ ἐξ ἔθους περιγίνεται, διόπερ ἐμπειρίας δεῖται καὶ χρόνου	διόπερ ἐμπειρίας δεῖται καὶ χρόνου, ἡ δ' ἠθικὴ ἐξ ἔθους περιγίνεται
1108b30	τοῦ μέσου	τοῦ ἴσου
1111a9	λέγοντές φασιν ἐκπεσεῖν αὐτό	λέγοντές φασιν ἐκπεσεῖν αὐτούς
1112a7	μάλιστα ἃ ἴσμεν ἀγαθὰ ὄντα	ἃ μάλιστα ἴσμεν ἀγαθὰ ὄντα
1113b23	ὑπὸ πάντων τῶν νομοθετῶν	ὑπ' αὐτῶν τῶν νομοθετῶν

1114b14	τὸ τέλος φύσει ὁποιονδήποτε φαίνεται	τὸ τέλος φύσει ἢ ὁπωσδήποτε φαίνεται
1114b28	καὶ δι' αὐτά	<καὶ> καθ' αὐτάς
1122b12	ἄνευ μεγέθους περὶ ταὐτὰ τῆς ἐλευθεριότητος οὔσης	οἷον μέγεθος, περὶ ταῦτα τῆς ἐλευθεριότητος οὔσης
1123a11	καὶ μεγαλοπρεπέστατον μὲν τὸ ἐν μεγάλῳ μέγα	καὶ μεγαλοπρεπέστατον <ἁπλῶς> μὲν τὸ ἐν μεγάλῳ μέγα
1124b7	πυκνοκίνδυνος	μικροκίνδυνος
1124b28	καὶ μελεῖ αὐτῷ τῆς ἀληθείας μᾶλλον ἢ τῆς δόξης	καὶ ἀμελεῖν τῆς ἀληθείας μᾶλλον ἢ τῆς δόξης
1125a31	βούλονται τὰ εὐτυχήματα πᾶσι φανερὰ εἶναι	βούλονται τὰ εὐτυχήματα καὶ φανερὰ εἶναι
1127b12	ὥς γε ἀλαζών	ὡς ὁ ἀλαζών
1129b3	ἁπλῶς ἀγαθά	ἁπλῶς ἀεὶ ἀγαθά
1133a3	διὸ καὶ <ἱδρῦσαι> Χαρίτων ἱερὸν Ἐτεοκλῆν οἴονται, ἵν' ἀνταπόδοσις εἴη	διὸ καὶ Χαρίτων ἱερὸν ἐμποδὼν ποιοῦνται, ἵν' ἀνταπόδοσις ᾖ
1133b1	εἰς σχῆμα οὖν ἀναλογίας δεῖ ἄγειν	εἰς σχῆμα δ' ἀναλογίας οὐ δεῖ ἄγειν
1133b3	ὅταν ᾖ πως ἴσα τὰ αὑτῶν, οὕτως ἴσοι καὶ κοινωνοί...	ὅταν ἔχωσι τὰ αὑτῶν. οὕτως ἴσοι καὶ κοινωνοί...
1135b1	οὐθὲν ἑκούσιον ἐστιν	οὐθὲν οὔθ' ἑκούσιον οὔτ' ἀκούσιόν ἐστιν
1138a7	οἷον κελεύει μὴ ἀποκτιννύναι ἑαυτὸν ὁ νόμος, ἃ δὲ μὴ δρᾶν κελεύει, ἀπαγορεύει	οἷον οὐ κελεύει ἀποκτιννύναι ἑαυτὸν ὁ νόμος, ἃ δὲ μὴ κελεύει, ἀπαγορεύει
1138a10	παρὰ τὸν νόμον	παρὰ τὸν ὀρθὸν λόγον
1138a29	†...†	τὸ μὲν γὰρ ἔλαττον... ἐν γυμναστικῇ
1141a33	περὶ πάντων τῶν ζώντων	περὶ πάντων τῶν ὄντων
1143a20	ἔχειν φαμὲν συγγνώμην	ἔχειν φαμὲν γνώμην
1144a27	διὸ καὶ φρονίμους τοὺς δεινούς	διὸ καὶ τοὺς φρονίμους δεινούς

1147b15	οὐ γὰρ τῆς κυρίως ἐπιστήμης εἶναι δοκούσης ἔκκρουσις γίνεται – οὐδ' αὕτη περιέλκεται – διὰ τὸ πάθος, ἀλλὰ τῆς αἰσθητικῆς.	οὐ γὰρ τῆς κυρίως ἐπιστήμης εἶναι δοκούσης παρούσης γίνεται τὸ πάθος – οὐδ' αὕτη περιέλκεται διὰ τὸ πάθος – ἀλλὰ τῆς αἰσθητικῆς.
1147b35	νενικηκώς	νικῶν
1148b27	αἳ δὲ νοσηματώδεις ἢ φύσει ἢ ἐξ ἔθους	αἳ δὲ νοσηματώδεις ἢ ἐξ ἔθους
1148b29	ἡ τῶν ἀφροδισίων ἐν τοῖς ἄρρεσι θηλύτης	ἡ τῶν ἀφροδισίων τοῖς ἄρρεσιν
1148b30	ἐθιζομένοις	ὑβριζομένοις
1149a4	τοῦ πάθους ἀκρατῆ, ἀκρατῆ δ' οὐ λεκτέον	τοῦ πάθους, ἀκρατῆ δ' οὐ λεκτέον
1149b35	ἐξέστηκε τῇ φύσει	ἐξέστηκε τῆς φύσεως
1150a6	λέαιναν	ἀδικίαν
1150a19	ὁ μὲν τὰς ὑπερβολὰς διώκων τῶν ἡδέων, ἢ καθ' ὑπερβολὰς, διὰ προαίρεσιν	ὁ μὲν τὰς ὑπερβολὰς διώκων τῶν ἡδέων †ἢ καθ' ὑπερβολὰς† ἢ διὰ προαίρεσιν
1150a23	ὁμοίως δὲ καὶ ὁ μὲν φεύγει τὰς σωματικὰς λύπας	ὁμοίως δὲ καὶ ὁ φεύγων τὰς σωματικὰς λύπας
1151b24	οὐκ ἐμμένων τῷ λόγῳ ἢ τοιοῦτος	οὐκ ἐμμένων τῷ λόγῳ, ὁ [τοιοῦτος]
1152b31	ὀλίγον χρόνον αἱρεταί, <ἀεὶ> δ'οὔ	ὀλίγον χρόνον αἱρεταί, <ἁπλῶς> δ' οὔ
1154b4	τινὲς παρασκευάζουσι	τινὰς παρασκευάζουσιν
1155a28	τῶν δικαίων τὸ μάλιστα τὸ φιλικὸν εἶναι δοκεῖ.	τῶν δικαίων τὸ μάλιστα φιλικὸν εἶναι δοκεῖ.
1158a16	πολλοὺς	πολλοῖς
1161a29	καὶ πάντες ἐπιεικεῖς εἶναι	καὶ ἐπιεικεῖς εἶναι
1164b15	τοῦτον οἴονται	τοῦτον οἴεται
1165a12	οὐκ ἂν δόξειεν	οὐκ ἂν δόξαιεν
1166a20	γενόμενος δ' ἄλλος (οἷον θεός) αἱρεῖται οὐδεὶς πάντ' ἔχειν ἐκεῖνο τὸ γενόμενον	γενόμενος δ' ἄλλος αἱρεῖται οὐδεὶς πάντ' ἔχειν [ἐκεῖνο τὸ γενόμενον]

1166b12	μισοῦσί τε καὶ φεύγουσι τὸ ζῆν	μισοῦνται καὶ φεύγουσι τὸ ζῆν
1170a14	αἱρετὸν εἶναι	αἱρετὸς εἶναι
1173a2	ὠρέγετο	ὀρέγεται
1173a10	ἀμφοῖν γὰρ ὄντοιν κακῶν	ἀμφοῖν γὰρ ὄντοιν <τῶν> κακῶν
1173b13	ὥσπερ καὶ τεμνόμενος λυποῖτο	καὶ †τεμνόμενος† λυποῖτο
1173b32	οὐκ οὖσαν τἀγαθὸν τὴν ἡδονήν	οὐκ οὖσαν ἀγαθὸν τὴν ἡδονήν
1174b10	γένεσιν εἶναι τῆς ἡδονῆς	γένεσιν εἶναι τὴν ἡδονήν
1175a36	συναύξουσι δὴ αἱ ἡδοναί	συναύξουσι δὲ αἱ ἡδοναί
1177b19	σχολῇ τε διαφέρειν	σπουδῇ τε διαφέρειν
1177b22	ἐνέργειαν). καὶ τὸ αὔταρκες δὴ	ἐνέργειαν), καὶ τὸ αὔταρκες δὴ
1180a2	δεῖ ἐπιτηδεύειν αὖ τὰ οἰκεῖα καὶ ἐθίζεσθαι	δεῖ ἐπιτηδεύειν αὐτὰ καὶ ἐθίζεσθαι
1180b23	τάχα δὴ καὶ τῷ βουλομένῳ	τάχα δὲ καὶ τῷ βουλομένῳ
1181a15	οἱ δὲ χείρω	οὐδὲ χείρω

Notes

ABBREVIATIONS USED IN THE NOTES

In these notes I use abbreviations to refer to Aristotle himself and various frequently cited texts and commentaries.

Full details of the editions used for the texts listed here are provided in the Suggestions for Further Reading. I have not supplied page numbers for the parts of the Greek commentators that I refer to. The editions I have used display Bekker numbers, corresponding to the sections of the *Ethics* under discussion, at the top of every page. Those serve as well as page numbers for finding your way to the right part of the commentaries. Most often I paraphrase or summarize what a commentator says, rather than quoting word for word.

[A]	Aristotle
[NE]	The *Nicomachean Ethics*
[EE]	The *Eudemian Ethics*
[MM]	The *Magna Moralia*
[Asp.]	Aspasius
[E]	Eustratius
[H]	Heliodorus
[M]	Michael of Ephesus
[P]	Anonymous Paraphraser
[R]	Ross's Translation of the *Ethics*
[S]	Stewart's Commentary on the *Ethics*
[TA]	Textual Appendix
VI.3	Book VI, chapter 3 of [NE]
Note IV.12	Note 12 on book IV

BOOK I

1. The reference is to Eudoxus' hedonist definition of 'good', dis-
    cussed at some length later, at X.2. Eudoxus thinks that pleasure
    is 'the good', i.e. the key, or fundamental, or only good thing in
    life. The point cited by [A] here – that whatever all things strive
    for must be the key good – forms a part of one of his arguments.
    In Eudoxus' view, all things – i.e. all living things – strive for
    pleasure, so pleasure must be the key good. But [A] here appears
    to want to take 'all things' in a different sense, namely 'all
    aspects and forms of *human* striving' (some of which he has just
    listed). [A] is not a hedonist, but he agrees with Eudoxus that
    what is good for an X depends upon the (natural) strivings of an
    X. What is good for human beings depends upon human nature
    and human strivings.

2. *two different . . . the activities*: Some simple examples: if you go
    for a walk in a beautiful place, the walk itself, the activity, is
    your goal. (Clearly, if you walk in a circle, your goal isn't to end
    up in that place. If it were, you've already achieved your goal
    before you start.) But when you undergo surgery, that activity is
    not your goal. You don't have surgery for its own sake. Your
    goal is its result or product: health. And in such cases, though
    we may speak of heart surgery as being a very good thing, a
    healthy heart must be a greater good than heart surgery.

    This distinction is given prominence because [A] will claim
    that the most valuable things in life are activities, certain exer-
    cisings of our dispositions, not just the outcomes or results of
    those activities.

3. *statesmanship – of a sort*: I.e. *politikē*. The same term can refer
    to a topic, or a branch of philosophy. 'So this is part of political
    [philosophy].' [A]'s point is clearly that since statesmanship,
    politics, ultimately aims to achieve human flourishing for a
    whole state, the current question ('How *do* human beings flour-
    ish?') should be thought of as the first question of statesmanship
    (or of political philosophy). Both Plato and [A] assume that it
    is *politikē* that deals with questions of what is right and wrong
    and good and bad for human beings, and that is [A]'s point
    here too. 'These [ethical] questions are really a subdivision of
    politics.'

4. *made by craftsmen*: By a strict (and pedantic) reading of the
    syntax, [A] might be saying: 'We shouldn't always expect the

same precision in different subject areas, just as we don't [always expect the same precision] in [different] things made by craftsmen.' So the idea is that, e.g., a painting is more detailed (because it has colours) than a sculpture, or a lead sculpture is less detailed than one of ivory or bronze. Thus [E] and [Asp.]. But the commentators are mistaken. It seems much more likely that (with a slightly loose expression) [A] means this: we shouldn't demand absolute precision in ethics and politics, just as we don't demand it from craftsmen (i.e. any craftsmen). A round table doesn't have to be a perfect circle; two legs of a chair don't have to be equal in length to the nanometer. [A] makes the same point again at 1098a26, where he explains it more fully. See also 1104a. The basic claim here, that ethics is not an exact science, is of great importance to him, and one of his principal disagreements with Plato. It is discussed at length in VI.3–7.

5. *or by their bravery*: Some scholars think that this second point, about good things, is [A]'s own response to the suggestion that 'fluidity' in what's right and wrong is a reason to be a moral relativist. [A]'s response (on that reading) is: But even good things – money, health, strength, friendship – are 'variable' and 'fluid' (i.e. they're sometimes bad for us); yet nobody would be a relativist about those. Nobody would say health is only a good thing 'by convention', on the grounds that health sometimes hurts us.

I think, instead, that [A] is simply saying that variability is a feature of all value claims. In any case, ancient relativists (e.g. Protagoras) were, in fact, just as relativist about good and bad as about right and wrong. See Plato, *Protagoras* 334a–c, *Theaetetus* 166d–167c.

6. *grand and pretentious*: Or 'grand and above them'. Perhaps a reference to very demanding Platonic and Socratic views of what makes us flourish. See below, note I.15. Also perhaps a reference to Plato's theory of the Form of the Good in particular. [A] immediately makes a reference to that theory, which makes it seem a little like an illustration of what he has just said.

7. *some [of you] used to think*: [A] is referring to Plato's theory of the Form of the Good (see below, chapter 6). But he does not say 'some people [i.e. Platonists] think'; he says 'some people *used to* think'. The tense is puzzling. I think that it is best explained if he means: 'and I know that some *of you* [perhaps some *of us*] used to be Platonists, and used to think that . . .'. All of [A]'s

students, when he began as an independent lecturer, were former Platonists, like him.

8. *arguments . . . from our first principles*: I.e. deductive arguments. Once you have the axioms of a science in place (e.g. the axioms of geometry), you can use them to construct deductive arguments for further claims. 'Arguments that get us *to* first principles' are inductive arguments, which work by extrapolating from particular cases, or particular experiences, to general principles that explain them or best capture our intuitions about them.

Because this is the start of an investigation into ethics, most of what follows (and indeed most of the treatise) will take the form of inductive reasoning. [A] will try to arrive at some (rough) general principles by reviewing the details of our ethical and practical experiences, and giving some kind of order to them. Hence his earlier point that young people cannot study ethics: they don't yet have the experiences that the more general claims are based on.

9. *why X is the case*: [A] means that if the basic moral facts already seem obvious (e.g. that we should treat people fairly; not steal; not murder; be brave; be generous, etc.) then there's no need to argue about why those things are the case. [A] is not interested in meta-ethical disputes. He does not think that ethical starting points are objects of knowledge, strictly speaking, or can be argued for. (See e.g. VI.2, VI.6, VI.7, VI.13, and 1151a17, 1178a16.) He thinks they are fundamentally tied to desire; grounded in human character. By disavowing such debates [A] also avoids having to be explicit about his humanism. A humanist like [A] and a theist like Plato can fully agree that we should treat people fairly. Protagoras and Socrates can agree on that, too. So can Charles Darwin and Moses. They might disagree when they start to ask *why* people should act fairly. But that's the question that [A] says we needn't bother with at all, if we're all agreed on the fact.

10. *you're pretty much hopeless*: From Hesiod, *Works and Days* (293–7). 'Hopeless' translates *achrēios*, 'useless', but probably taken by [A] in the sense 'there's nothing that can be done with you'. [A] is saying that if you approach ethics without already having basically sound ideas about right and wrong, or at least a decent character that makes you receptive to good ideas – then don't bother with these lectures at all.

11. *where we were*: Literally, 'Let's speak from where we went off to the side.' This is one of many places where the text seems to

preserve [A]'s unscripted lecturer's banter. The brief 'tangent' started with the words, 'And let's not forget' at 1095a30.

12. *life of [well-fed] cows*: [A] means, as we know from the parallel passage in [EE], 1216a, that a life of physical pleasure and comfort is one that in principle even a cow *could* lead. He doesn't mean that ordinary cows typically live such a life. (Working cows live a life of boredom and servitude.) He says in [EE] that there is a cow in Egypt that is revered as the god Apis, living a pampered life in a temple, its every need attended to by priests. That cow, he says, lives as well as any monarch devoted to physical pleasure.

13. *like [King] Shardanapal*: I.e. throw themselves into physical comforts and pleasures. Shardanapal was (supposedly) an Assyrian king devoted to wild partying and luxurious living. The name, rendered in Greek as 'Sardanapalos', seems to be a corruption of Ashurbanipal, a mid-seventh-century Assyrian ruler, son of Essarhaddon.

Judging by the testimony of Cicero (*Tusculanae Disputationes* 5.35.101, *De Finibus* 2.32.106) it seems that [A] discussed 'Shardanapal' and his (alleged) tomb inscription in his published dialogue *Protrepticus* (the subject of which was approximately the same as that of our book I). The mention of 'public' writings a few paragraphs later almost certainly refers to that text. Diodorus (2.23.3) reports the tomb inscription as follows: 'Know that you are mortal, and enjoy yourself! Once you're dead you've nothing more to gain. Look at me. I was King of mighty Nineveh. Now I'm just ash. My enormous wealth I leave behind. All I take with me is my feasting and whoring!' On this, [A] remarked that this is an appropriate epitaph for a cow (see last note). The tomb inscription (which exists in various equally ridiculous versions) is Greek fiction. The real Ashurbanipal was a scholar-king, who built the world's first library.

But, in general, [A] means that rich and powerful men (kings, emperors, tyrants), i.e. people with the freedom to live however they choose, often devote themselves to lives of extreme physical luxury and self-indulgence. And, he says, that's a partial argument in favour of that kind of life.

14. *higher classes ... statesmanship*: [A] takes it for granted that politics is exclusively the domain of the wealthier, more educated class. In fact this was only roughly true, not invariably true.

15. *defending some [crazy] theory*: Literally, 'defending a *thesis*'. As all the commentators note, here [A] uses *thesis* in a technical

sense that is clear from the context. He explains elsewhere, at *Topics* 104b19: 'A "*thesis*" is a crazy notion associated with some well-known philosopher, e.g. Antisthenes' idea that contradiction is impossible, or Heraclitus' idea that everything is in flux'. Here, the relevant 'crazy' idea (I use the English term to mean highly counter-intuitive and contrary to common sense) is the Socratic *thesis*, that 'as long as you are a good person, then you prosper in life, no matter what'. But [A] does not actually name Socrates, apparently out of respect.

The most famous discussion of that Socratic view, and related ideas, is Plato's *Gorgias*; a version of it can be found fairly neatly stated at 470e8. It is also formulated as early as the *Apology*, 41d1: 'Nothing bad can happen to a good man.' The same idea was also favoured later by the Cynics and Stoics, and is at that point discussed as a Stoic 'paradox'. *Paradoxon* ('counter-intuitive') is the later term for what [A] here calls a *thesis*.

[A] rejects this view, preferring the more common-sense view that some things in life matter, quite a lot, besides how good a person you are. For further direct references to it see e.g. the end of I.8, V.11, and especially 1153b19.

16.   *drudgery, pretty much*: Literally, 'the money-making [life] is sort of a life of force' (or 'a forced life'). The language is a little odd, and commentators ancient and modern are unsure as to its meaning. Here are some suggestions. [E]: 'money-making is a life of violence' (you acquire money by violence); [S]: 'it is an unnatural life' ([A] believes that some forms of money-making are 'unnatural'). These two readings largely depend on taking 'money-maker' – wrongly – as if it meant 'usurer'. [R]: It 'is a life that is forced on you' (i.e. by material and economic necessity). I favour the last reading, with a slight tweak: 'a life of forced [labour]', 'drudgery'. This is consistent with [A]'s attitude to labour. It is also confirmed by the parallel passage at [EE] 1215a26, where it is clear that [A] is talking (in both places) about menial forms of employment. Like other aristocratic Greeks, [A] regards working for a living as socially demeaning (because slave-like). These attitudes play a major part in his discussion of 'generosity'. See especially from 1121b30.

Incidentally, this is why [A] never considers artistic or literary achievement as a possible form of human flourishing any more than money-making. He sees skilled artists (painters, sculptors, poets, playwrights) as tradesmen and labourers. Their life, in his mind, is not a candidate for being an ideal, 'blessed' form of living, however spectacularly successful they may be. (For confirmation that snobbery extended in that way even to the fine arts, see Plutarch, *Pericles* 2.1.)

17. *a sin*: Literally, 'it is pious – *hosion* – to respect truth more', in the sense, 'it is a religious duty', 'it would be impious not to'. This is the only place in [NE] where [A] himself invokes the concept of piety. (Strictly, he does not think that piety as traditionally conceived could be a virtue, since he denies that the God, or the gods, have any connection with ethics.) It is perhaps a subtle joke that rejecting the Platonic view of the cosmos (and by implication, Platonic theism) is the only duty of piety he can think of.

It's also a cute reference to a similar and infamous claim made by Plato in the *Republic*. Plato says that the works of Homer will have to be banned in an ideal society. 'We love Homer, but it's a sacred duty to love the truth more; so Homer will have to go.' (See 607a1, c8.) [A] responds: 'We love Plato, but it's a sacred duty to love truth more. So Plato will have to go.'

18. *Form for the [set of all] numbers*: I.e. a single Form ('number') for 1, 2, 3, 4, etc. That's to say, they never tried to define a single concept, 'number', that would be equally applicable to all numbers. The point seems to be that 1 is ontologically prior to 2 and 3, and so on. The number 1 is thus ontologically prior to all other numbers. But the Form of 'number' would also have to be ontologically prior to all numbers, including 1. And that doesn't make sense. See also [EE], 1218a1–7.

19. *good qualities (virtues)*: Or 'in what sort of thing [something is], the virtues'. [A] means that being brave, fair, honest, generous, or kind are good ways of being. So 'good qualities' is the more generic notion, of which 'virtues' are a particular example. As it happens, English likes to use the generic expression as a standard pointer for moral virtues. You are somewhat more likely to speak of someone's 'good qualities' than their 'virtues'.

20. *(habitable)*: [A] here says *diaita*, apparently implying that it can mean, in itself, 'a good place'. Its normal sense is 'mode of life' (hence 'diet'), but it can also mean 'dwelling place' or 'quarters', and I think [A] has in mind a biological use: an animal might have this or that place as its *diaita*, i.e. its habitat. So it's like saying 'a habitable zone', a 'Goldilocks zone' – the spatial equivalent of the last example, *kairos*, 'the right moment'. As a marine biologist, [A] is aware that many species live at particular depths, or in very particular tidal zones.

21. *Just in one of them*: [A] takes it for granted that if we are to give a general account of something – anything – it has to belong to only one of these categories of predication. (His term here, *katēgoria*, strictly means 'predication' rather than simply 'category'.) You can give a unified definition of 'bird' (applicable to all birds) or of 'green' (applicable to all things that are green) or of 'past' for all things that (only) existed in the past; but not of all things that are birds-or-green-or-in-the-past. Intelligible universals must belong to one 'category'.

22. *There'd be no difference in what makes them good*: [A] means something like this: 'Even if there were a single definition of "good" that applied to all good things (as there is a single definition of "human"), it wouldn't need to be a separate thing, this independently existing Form of the Good; it would be enough just to give a general account of what makes actual, particular good things good. So he has made two points in quick succession: (a) 'there is no universal definition of good'; and (b) 'we don't need Platonic Forms for universals anyway. Ordinary (purely conceptual) universals will do.'

23. *'Unity' in their column of good things*: I.e. they claimed that unity was a good, i.e. made the far more modest claim that unity is what makes (some) good things good, as opposed to claiming, like Plato, that 'the Good is a unity'. 'Even Speusippus', [A] then says, the current head of Plato's Academy, prefers that more modest claim. The Pythagoreans constructed two paired columns of good and bad things, to account for goods by way of a variety of different concepts. (See *Metaphysics* 983a23.)

24. *Speusippus*: Plato's nephew and head of the Academy after Plato's death. It was perhaps a sore point for [A] that he had been passed over for this role.

25. *pointless*: What's the point of grasping the nature of what is good, if it turns out there are no good things in human life anyway?

26. *random homonyms*: I.e. things that just happen to be called by the same term, like a 'fair' (a public festival) and 'fair' trade; or zero in tennis, 'love', and the emotion, 'love'.

27. *different area of philosophy*: I.e. metaphysics. An important subtext here, understood by [A]'s listeners, is that Plato's ideas about the Form of the Good are tied to cosmology and theology. In the *Phaedo* (97–9) Plato tells us that thinking about the wider cosmos in terms of 'the Good' means (a) rejecting the idea (favoured by Greek naturalists) that the cosmos achieves its organization through mindless, physical causes, and (b) accepting

that it is purpose-driven, shaped according to 'what is best'. Elsewhere Plato implies that we have to understand the principles that shape the whole cosmos, and only then try to understand human life and human morality. That is the claim made by the famous parable of the cave in the *Republic*, for example. [A] does not think that we gain any direct insight into human right and wrong by contemplating the nature of God. This disagreement is taken up (again) at greater length in VI.7 and X.8.

28. *one of you might have the idea*: Or 'someone might think'. My strong suspicion about this kind of formula is that it is the editor's way of recording an actual objection raised by a student. Perhaps one with Platonist sympathies, feeling a little riled by [A]'s dismissal of Plato's venerable theory, made this point from the floor. Then notice that [A]'s next remarks sound just like a response to a student (especially when, towards the end of the point, it begins to sound snippy). For another clear example of what appears to be an exchange with a student, see III.5, 1114a2, a31, b2.

29. *be a better doctor*: Consider an analogous version of this question that [A] may have in mind here: 'How is anyone going to be a better *person* by understanding "The Good" – the first principle of the cosmos?'

30. *don't ... investigate health that way*: I.e. don't try to define or understand 'health' universally. Doctors don't concern themselves with the health of horseshoe crabs, giant sequoia or fungus, or with a broad enough understanding of health to cover all of those.

31. *more than one, those*: A very brief allusion to X.7. See below, note I.45

32. *back where we started*: The reference is to the claim made at 1094a18 (near the very start of the lecture) which is indeed identical to what [A] has just said. Literally, 'the argument progressing – *ironic* – has arrived at the very same thing'. 'Has arrived at the same' means not just 'the same claim', but the place it started from. This seems to be a joke.

33. *wealth, bridles, any sort of tool*: All the manuscripts here read 'wealth, and *flutes* and tools/equipment (*organa*) in general'. I emend 'flutes' (which is abrupt and rather mysterious) to 'bridles'. See [TA].

34. *And if more than one ... most ultimate*: Another cryptic reference to X.7. See below, note I.45

35. *family ... citizens*: [A] does not mean that if you are flourishing you must be able to provide for all your family and friends and

all your fellow citizens. He means that if you are flourishing, then life has to be going well for those people too. You can't flourish if, e.g., your children are suffering horribly. And if you are, say, Venezuelan or Syrian, then you cannot flourish if things are going badly for Venezuelans or for Syrians. [A] thinks that being a citizen, and having ties to your fellow citizens, is a central and natural part of being human.

This is a distinctively Aristotelian view (at least, in comparison with other Greek philosophers). For Plato, 'meeting your own needs', being 'self-sufficient' meant being able to possess within yourself everything that has value in life. But [A] reparses 'self-sufficient' as '[it]self-sufficient', i.e. 'that which *itself* – i.e. without further addition – meets all your needs', and he is happy for *eudaimonia* to expand outwards to the people and events around us. This amounts to rejecting the Platonic, and more usual, concept of 'self-sufficiency'.

36. *count alongside other good things*: The point, tersely expressed in this paragraph, seems to be this: that you cannot treat flourishing (*eudaimonia*) as one good thing among the rest of the good things in your life. *Eudaimonia* is the whole set of good things that comprise your flourishing, blessed life, so to speak. For this interpretation – found in [Asp.] and [H] – compare *Topics* 117a16, on which Alexander of Aphrodisias comments (247.5): 'A flourishing life [*eudaimonia*] isn't more desirable if you add the moral virtues to it than *eudaimonia* is on its own; because the virtues are already included in *eudaimonia* . . . The things included within X can't then be counted alongside the X that includes them – as is stated in *Ethics* book I.' Saving everyone in the world doesn't get more heroic if you save everyone in the world *and your kids*.

37. *more desirable*: I.e. and that would not make sense, because flourishing is by definition the most desirable thing there is. So it cannot become more desirable.

This aspect of [A]'s conception seems unnecessary. Plenty of people are flourishing. It seems absurd (and whiny) to say otherwise. But do we need to claim that those lives could not possibly improve, in any respect? That seems equally absurd. Perhaps human flourishing, as a usable concept, must embrace the imperfection of all things human, rather than being, as [A] claims, perfect by definition. [A] would do better to have fuzzier boundaries for *eudaimonia*, like the ones he sensibly allows for moral virtues (see the end of II.5). (Arguably, he concedes this point in I.10, where he says that you can suffer various misfortunes – imperfections of a sort – and still be flourishing.)

38. *life of doing*: [A] has a rather enriched concept of 'doing', or 'action' (*praxis*). He takes it to imply, or involve, by definition, practical reason (aims, intentions, goals, deliberation, choice, etc.). Hence, only animals that possess reason are capable of doing things. [A] perhaps mostly has practical reasoning in mind here, and by definition that is a capacity tied to action. In the parallel section of [EE] we find a helpful statement of this connection (the topic is the question of what virtues are distinctively human, but the thought can be easily adapted): 'Distinctively human virtues must involve reasoning (which is in charge) and also action. And reasoning isn't just "in charge" of more reasoning; rather, it governs desire, and emotion; so those parts of us have to be involved too.' In other words, the presence of (practical) reason automatically implies the presence of desires, emotions, character.

[A] eventually discusses, in X.7–8, two different kinds of activity that constitute flourishing. One is the life of exercising of our moral virtues, the other a life of contemplating the cosmos (a life of science and higher philosophy). But in this first formulation of human flourishing, he calls it 'a life that is *praktikē*: a life of action'. And he tells us in VI.2 that pure thought (the sort exercised in contemplation) is by definition 'not *praktikē*: unconnected with action. So this first definition appears to exclude, or at the very least not to be paying much attention to, pure contemplation.

Most commentators, ancient and modern, assume that the contemplative life must somehow be included here, because otherwise there would be an inconsistency with X.7. So several translators offer 'active life of the part of us that has reason', implying that our reasoning part itself has to 'be active', (as in, 'she has an active mind'); as if *praxis* here were a synonym for *energeia* (activity), which is simply not feasible. 'Active life' means 'a life of actually doing things'. The qualifying phrase ('of the part that has reason') means 'that goes with reason', 'that is enabled by, or depends on, [practical] reason'.

39. *the part that's responsive to reason*: Emotions, feelings, likes and dislikes, physical desires, strivings in general: the material of character. For the crucial role that these play in our moral virtues see II.3–6, VI.2, VI.12–13.

40. *more natural sense of 'living'*: That is, 'living' is (by its more
     normal sense) the exercising of biological capacities, rather than
     just the possession of those capacities. A frozen acorn and a
     growing oak tree are both alive; but the growing tree is (in the
     normal sense) 'living the life of an oak'; the acorn is not. A wild
     lion and one confined to a tiny cage both have the same capaci-
     ties; but the wild lion, exercising those capacities, is 'living a
     lion's life' in the normal sense.

41. *soul's . . . [elements]*: For [A], the soul (*psuchē*) is (sometimes, in
     the context of biology) what makes something alive, and hence
     a collective term for all the biological capacities and functions of
     a living thing. He has just worked his way, swiftly, through our
     main biological capacities, from the most basic to the most com-
     plex: growth and reproduction; perception and sensation; desire,
     emotion, thought, reasoning. He is looking for the capacities
     that are special to us and characterize the human niche. So the
     biological sense of *psuchē* is prominent, and we might para-
     phrase this sentence like this: 'our function is the exercising of
     the rational or partly rational parts of our biological nature'.

     Of course, once you are talking about the soul's capacity to
     think and reason, and feel desires and emotions, you are talk-
     ing about the human mind – which is in many contexts also
     the standard sense of the term *psuchē*. And elsewhere in this
     treatise *psuchē* will typically refer to the human soul only, and
     hence the human mind: the seat of thought, reason, deliber-
     ation, desire, emotion and character.

     I shall retain the traditional term 'soul' rather than 'mind',
     because English speakers often fail to assume that 'mind' includes
     features of character. But it is important not to think that extra
     theoretical or metaphysical commitments are imported just by
     [A]'s use of the term 'soul'. If you believe that you are alive, and
     have thoughts, emotions, desires, ideas, and reasons, then you
     believe you have a 'soul' as the term is used by [A] and through-
     out Greek philosophy.

42. *same in general as the task of a good X*: It is hard to determine
     exactly how this premise fits into the argument, or exactly what
     [A] means. [A] may mean (a): that to fully describe the task of
     any X we have to describe the task of a good X. So, a reference
     to *aretē*, goodness, has to be added here, to make our account
     of the human task complete. That reading would make good
     sense in the context, and leave the argument relatively easy to
     follow. The problem is, it isn't what [A] actually says (although

I have been tempted to squeeze the Greek into that construal). Instead, he seems to say (b): 'and if we want to stipulate the task of a good X, as opposed to an ordinary X, it's broadly the same; we just need to add a corresponding qualification to the task'. That is, he seems to take it for granted that we want to describe the task of a good X. But he hasn't said why.

Comparison with the parallel argument in [EE] (1218b37–1219a39) suggests the second, more problematic, reading is correct. We find exactly the same claim there (1219a19–23): 'We say that the task of a [given] thing, and of its goodness, are the same, but with a qualification. E.g. the task {or product} of shoemaking, and of a shoemaker, is a shoe; and the task of shoemaking *aretē* (if I can say that) – i.e. of a good shoemaker – is a good shoe; and that holds across all cases.' But in the [EE] version, [A] has implied from the outset that understanding something's task and its *aretē* go hand in hand. (In fact, the whole argument starts as a discussion of *aretē*.) In our version this is less clear, so the reference to *aretē* arrives a little unexpectedly at this point.

It is as if there is a missing premise, just before premise (2). Something like this: 'Also, we're not just interested in the task of a human being, but more precisely of a good human being; because a better X implies a correspondingly better version of X's task, and obviously we want the best possible version of the human task. But that's easy enough, because . . .' (now proceed to premise 2). With that small but apparently missing premise, (b), the argument goes like this:

(1) Our task is the exercising of the soul's rational and part-rational (i.e. moral) capacities.

(2) But we need to specify the task of a good human being, of course.

(3) The task of any good X is broadly the same as the task of an X, but with the appropriate small qualification, corresponding to its goodness. E.g. the task of a guitar-player is 'to play the guitar'; and the task of a good guitar-player 'to play the guitar *well*'.

(4) So, the task of a good human being is to exercise rational {and moral} capacities well.

(5) That means exercising those capacities with the appropriate goodness {or virtues}.

So the human task is: exercising of the soul such as expresses our goodness {or our virtues}.

43. *in every sense*: Literally, 'well[a], and well[b]'. But the second well
     is *kalōs*, which also very often means 'honourably', 'ethically'
     (depending on context). So the text almost comes to mean:
     'well, and hence also honourably'. It seems better just to hint at
     the further sense, as the Greek does. I have done this as best I
     could in English by a paraphrase: 'in every sense', by implica-
     tion, includes the ethical sense of 'well' (as in 'he behaved well',
     'he acted well', 'she conducted herself well').

     [A] is shifting – without argument – from the generic notion
     of performing any task well to the more specific idea of per-
     forming human actions honourably and ethically. In the same
     way, the wider passage executes a shift from an (implied) non-
     ethical use of *aretē* ('being good at the guitar') to its standard
     sense, 'being a good person', 'goodness'.

     It is important not to assume a generic sense for *aretē* all the
     way through the argument. Some interpreters think that [A] is
     saying here that we flourish by 'cultivating excellence' in general;
     i.e. by being very good at something (e.g. basketball, curling,
     Scrabble). Others think [A] is saying that we need to cultivate
     'excellence of the soul', which for now must be understood gener-
     ically and rather vaguely (to be filled out in more detail later).
     Those are both misunderstandings. [A] takes it for granted that
     aretē has different senses in its different applications. So, the
     claim is that a guitar-player does well (as a guitar-player) by
     being (actively) a good guitar-player, and a human being does
     well (in life) by being (actively) a good person. And obviously a
     good person is good in the specific, familiar, moral sense imme-
     diately implied by that particular usage.

     The term *aretē* in its normal and unqualified sense – rather
     like 'being a good person' in English – always refers to character
     goodness anyway, and the term slots back into that sense, in all
     its detailed implications, in the conclusion. Absolutely no fur-
     ther, later explanation of what is meant by 'human goodness' or
     'human virtues' is required.

44. *(or the appropriate virtues)*: I offer the plural, virtues, as a
     secondary translation to show that [A] certainly means for the
     exercise of our particular virtues to be (loosely) covered by this
     expression. (It also assists with the qualification that follows.)

45. *more than one sort of goodness*: Almost certainly a reference
     to the claims made at X.7 (especially since the wording there
     very closely matches what we have here). So the 'other good-
     ness' is goodness of the mind: the intellectual virtues used in

contemplation. [Asp.] agrees. He thinks [A] is alluding here to 'contemplative virtue'. Notice that the remark is brief and cryptic. The other (probable) references to contemplative activity in book I are all very minimal. It is worth considering that they may have been added by an editor, to bring this book I discussion of *eudaimonia* into line with X.7. (On this view, an original version of this discussion only argued that we flourish in life by exercising our moral virtues.) Certainly, the remaining arguments of book I only seem to defend the ethical conception of *eudaimonia*. (And several of them actually exclude contemplation.)

None of this is to say that the X.7 passage is inauthentic, or that it is not extremely important. This is a purely editorial issue. [NE] is a poorly edited text with many similar problems.

46. *a summer*: Actually, the Greek version is 'One swallow doesn't make a spring.'

47. *Anyone can do that*: [A] means that he expects all other thoughtful people (perhaps especially his students, the people he is now addressing) to take his rough sketch further. A fundamentally new idea – a whole new *Bauplan* – is often quite hard to arrive at, but once it is in place it is easy to improve upon. Likewise, [A] is probably quite proud of his humanistic blueprint for human flourishing; and with the main idea in place, he thinks it should be quite easy to fill it out and improve it. He is conceding that it is bound to have imperfections.

48. *induction . . . perception . . . habituation*: The paragraph seems completely general to me, almost like a footnote on the concept of 'starting points', 'principles'. [A] is talking about the principles of all the sciences, as well as ethical principles. Induction (i.e. generalizing from experience) is the main source of principles in the empirical sciences. In mathematics, a starting point like 'this is a triangle, hence . . .' is simply a matter of perception. But in ethics, our normative principles (e.g. 'being brave is a good thing'; 'you should treat people fairly'; 'it's good to have friends') are arrived at by our being habituated into those attitudes, i.e. by our upbringing (in combination with the substantial promptings of human nature). See II.1.

49. *the start is more than half*: The word for 'start' here is the same as the one that serves as 'starting point' or 'principle'. So [A] can in effect pun with the saying: 'the start {starting point, principle} is more than half'.

50. *Something we've got right*: Strictly, the text says '*also* something we've got right is . . .'. But this looks like a close repetition

of the preceding point. (This seems proved by a complete lack of
consensus among commentators as to why the second point is
being made, and how it differs from the last.) I have speculated
that this is a deliberate, prompted repetition.

A question that arises here is: why are actions (straightforwardly) 'goods of the soul'? It is [A]'s own view that actions
require, and tie us to, external goods in multiple ways. (The
results of actions are external, for example, and an important
part of their value.) So [A] may have been saying here that by
thinking of actions as 'exercisings [of the soul]' (i.e. think of
a brave action as an exercising of your bravery), we can class
them as goods of the soul.

51. *higher philosophical knowledge*: I.e. *sophia*, which for [A]
means the most exalted areas of philosophy: metaphysics, theology, cosmology. See VI.7, VI.12, X.7.

52. *win the Olympic crowns*: Olympic victors were crowned with
laurel wreaths. [EE] 1219b9–11: 'It isn't people who could win,
but don't, who take the prize; it's the people who do win.' The
text given here, 'the strongest athletes on the practice ground',
is my proposed correction for the manuscript text, which curiously reads: 'It isn't the most beautiful and strongest who win
the prizes.' (I find support for the correction in a discussion of
this passage between Julian and Themistius. See Julian, *Letter
to Themistius* 9. See [TA] for the text.)

53. *fighting*: 'Resisting', we often say in English. A majority view
here is that [A] says that the things most people enjoy 'conflict'
(i.e. conflict with one another). [Asp.] agrees with my reading
('their pleasures are at war *with them* . . .'). Also, see IX.4,
1166b7.

54. *in themselves*: [A] uses 'naturally pleasurable' and 'pleasurable
in themselves' to mean, in effect, pleasurable for psychologically and morally normal people. For this convention see III.4;
also 1152b31, 1173b20–25, 1176b24–6.

55. *inscription . . . at Delos*: The parallel treatise, [EE], starts by
quoting this poem. But its position here is far more natural,
after [A] has argued for an account of human flourishing that
combines all these elements.

The poem cheekily argues that these three aims conflict with
one another. It is saying (by implication) that if you always do
what's right you won't stay healthy (e.g. because you will have
to fight for your country) and won't have much fun; and if you
stay healthy you'll have to shirk your duties and live a boring

life; or, if you just try to have fun (by indulging all your desires) you won't always be doing the right thing, and you'll probably harm yourself.

56. *but they've died*: People's children die in several famous Greek tragedies (*Medea, Hippolytus, Bacchae, Antigone*). And this was far more common in real life for Greeks than for modern developed societies. The example of King Priam, whom [A] mentions shortly, may be in his mind. 'I am utterly wretched. I fathered the finest sons in all of Troy. And not one of the good ones is left alive' (*Iliad* 24.255).

57. *some people think*: What people? [A] is almost certainly refer-ring to the view found in Greek tragedy, and in Homer, and hence in much of wider, popular Greek culture. The tragic view is that human life is fragile; that horrible things happen even to good people, and that how well your life goes is a matter of luck. Tragedians and Homer often express this through the idea that the gods decide (capriciously) whether your life goes well or badly. So there is an allusion to etymology here, too. To be *eu-daimon* is to be 'well treated by the gods' and hence fortunate.

58. *rather different from the view*: Literally, 'while others say'. [H], astutely, reads the broader point as being not 'So that's why some people say it's all about luck', but rather 'So that's why people disagree so strongly on this, with some saying it's all about luck, and others that it's all about goodness.' These two views, set alongside one another, are indeed strikingly different. [A] likes to adjudicate between big disagreements of this sort, and to find something to say for both sides if he can.

59. *different investigation*: I.e. 'that question really belongs to the-ology, not ethics'. Note that anyone who thought that the gods did play an important role in our lives would certainly want a discussion of that fact to be placed within ethics, or before it.

60. *still feels*: [A] is rejecting the common Greek view that the gods make good people prosper (and more generally, watch over human affairs). But he is offering that view some respect. This is his courteous humanism. 'Even if' we flourish by our own efforts (this is [A]'s own view, but notice the hypothetical), flourishing still 'seems' or 'feels' divine. This means, in effect, 'it still feels divine, even though it isn't'.

[A] means, I think, that his definition of flourishing retains a traditional, theistic feel because he has kept the core idea that you flourish by being a good person, i.e. as if rewarded for your goodness by the gods.

61. *congenitally incapable of being a good person*: Literally, 'deformed/handicapped with respect to goodness'. [A] is probably referring to severe intellectual disability (**Asp.** thinks so), which sometimes prevents the development of our moral virtues; he may also be thinking of sociopaths or psychopaths, who apparently have innate moral defects (e.g. an inability to feel any empathy). He discusses such cases at VII.5, under the category of 'bestial' states. [A] is perfectly happy to concede that it's only roughly true that people can flourish by their own efforts. It's certainly not always the case.

62. *(especially the very best one)*: The argument works like this: *eudaimonia*, the best and finest thing in human life, is surely not a product of chance. After all, look around the world and you'll see that, as a general rule, the best and finest and most beautiful things are never results of chance. Biological nature and human design and art (*technē*) produce the most beautiful things, and those are, for [A], two primary examples of processes that do not involve chance. (This is so obvious for him that he doesn't need to say it.)

What is this 'best [such cause]'? It probably refers to the first cause, which orders the wider cosmos (the stars and planets, etc.). [A] tells us elsewhere that the heavens are the most perfect example of an arrangement that does not involve chance (see e.g. *Physics* 196a24–b5) because the movements of the heavenly bodies are perfectly regular. He also assumes that the heavens are an example of astonishing beauty and perfection. I follow [**Asp.**] on this. He assumes [A] is referencing the 'necessary causes of the heavens'. And the cause of that order is, ultimately, God: the 'best cause'. Compare VI.7 for similar terminology.

Regarding the concluding remark: some Greeks would say that 'to make human flourishing depend on luck is *impious*'. (Plato says exactly this, for example, at length, at *Republic* 379c–80c). The theistic version of this claim is able to point to the unfairness of wicked people flourishing through dumb luck, while good people suffer through mere misfortune. [A] does not think that God has any sense of fairness (see X.8), and thus cannot present the case in those terms. But he seems to be trying to defend the same basic idea by other means. So he argues that *eudaimonia* is in some senses like a product of biology or design.

63. *behave honourably*: [A] claimed that statesmanship is the branch of knowledge that aims at the highest human good. Notice the rather doubtful premise here that laws aim at promoting virtues

themselves, rather than their results (or both). You could easily argue that the laws (or social norms) against (e.g.) murder, injury and theft, imply that statesmanship assumes that survival, health and money are among the highest human goods.

64. *other animals 'blessed'*: [A] implies that it is a standard Greek view that animals cannot be *eudaimones*, perhaps more in the sense of 'prosperous' than 'flourishing'. (In English it makes no sense to say that animals cannot 'flourish', since that term derives from the metaphor of growth, and hence we absolutely do speak of both animals, and plants, as 'flourishing'. But it is true that we would not call, e.g., squirrels 'prosperous'.)

   He makes the same claim at X.8. It does not seem to follow straightforwardly from [A]'s own principles (it is far from clear why animals cannot prosper or flourish in their own forms of life). And is it a common Greek view? It is rejected by some Greek philosophers. See my longer note on this, X.47.

65. *Solon*: Sixth-century Athenian lawmaker and 'sage', founder of Athens's main democratic institutions. He visited King Croesus of Lydia, a man of (still) legendary wealth, and was asked by him who, in his view, was the most prosperous man in the world (expecting to be told, of course, that he was). (The word Herodotus uses is *olbios*, 'wealthy', 'prosperous', not *eudaimon*; but [A] treats this as a synonym.) But he refused to congratulate Croesus, or to call him prosperous. His idea was that to be truly prosperous or blessed you have to maintain your enviable life all the way to death. He hadn't yet seen Croesus' life end. (He also did not think much of material wealth. His preference was for people who lived simple and morally upright lives, and died honourably.) There is a certain fatalism, or superstition, to Solon's view. It is as if he felt that a person's life might seem to be going extremely well, but if some disaster then struck, this showed that the gods had been plotting against them all along. So they were never 'blessed'.

66. *successes . . . of your children* [A] is, among other things, trying to account for the common-sense view that lots of things that will happen to others, and to the wider world, after you die, matter to you. Since he assumes that 'X matters to me' means 'X affects my life; affects my *eudaimonia*', he seems to conclude that, e.g., 'my child's future (after I die) matters to me' implies 'my child's future (after I die) must affect (will affect?) my *eudaimonia*'. (The problem is in the very first premise. 'X matters to me' does not imply 'X affects me'.)

67. *miserable wretch the next*: Does [A] just mean that changes in the fortunes your descendants might make people reconsider how your own life went; how successful it was, *in retrospect*? Or does he mean that dead people might actually become blessed, or wretched, after death? He surely means the former at least some of the time. But [A] is considering popular ideas here, so he is probably considering the idea of people being actually affected after death as well.

68. *not true to say that he is*: This certainly seems to be [A]'s meaning.

The interpretation of Solon's maxim is a little unfair. Solon (and various others) say that we 'should never call a man blessed while he's alive'. This obviously has an epistemic sense: you never know what might happen to them next. You can never be sure. [A] instead seems to treat it as a pure truth claim: 'It is never true, during a person's life, to say that they are blessed.' But these are different. It might now be true that it will rain fifty times in Boston next year; it might also be the case that nobody can make that claim with any confidence.

69. *more durable even than bits of knowledge*: Technically, the subject is the activities that [A] just referred to: the exercisings of our virtues. But it seems that, in effect, the subject is now the virtues themselves.

Our virtues – i.e. our virtues of character, our moral virtues – are very stable, and even more stable than scientific knowledge or technical expertise (probably included in the claim). You might easily forget the mathematics or the chemistry or physics you once knew (even if you went through all the proofs at the time). You can easily forget how to play the piano or bake a cake. You are far less likely, if you are a fair and generous person, to forget, one day, to treat people fairly and generously, or whether or not you should, or how to do so. This is a point that [A] makes elsewhere, e.g. at 1140b29, 1156b12 and 1159b4.

This claim, incidentally, makes it as good as impossible that [A] is here referring to, or including, the purely contemplative life that he discusses in X.7. That is a life of exercising certain kinds of higher philosophical knowledge. And he could not be saying that the exercising of knowledge is more durable than knowledge. So he appears to have only moral virtues in mind.

70. *the most precious*: In my view, probably a reference to *philia*: friendship and family relationships, and the moral virtues that we exercise, pretty much constantly, in the context of those.

(Many scholars instead assume a reference to X.7, and the exercising of pure contemplation. See next note.) Taking the text my way, consider (a) how continuously you exercise your love and friendship for the people closest to you, and (b) how unlikely you are to forget how you feel towards those people. The last phrase shows [A] adding the qualifier that you will at any rate have relationships of that kind only if your life is going well.

71. *and contemplating [in others]*: Seems most likely to refer to the claims made at 1170a about friendship. An important reason for having friends, says [A], is that you can more easily contemplate virtues, in action, in other people than in yourself.

The phrase may mean that good people will both do morally good things, and also think and reason about them.

It's also possible that the reference is to the contemplative activity of X.7: 'they'll do the things that express their [moral] virtues; and contemplate consistently with virtues [of intellect]'. That's a *very* awkward reading. But it is so taken by [Asp.], [H] and [S]; and [R], as it seems. (All those readers assume, perhaps wrongly, that the X.7 passage must already be in view here.)

A final possibility is that the words 'and contemplating' have been added by an editor; a minimalist addition to make the claim fit with X.7, resulting in a clumsy text.

72. *truly good; straight as a die, without a . . . flaw*: Literally, 'truly good, square, without flaw'. The square is used here by the poet Simonides as a metaphor for moral perfection. Simonides in the quoted line is saying that it is impossible for anyone to be flawless, and that everyone will, at some point, behave shabbily under the pressure of some awful situation. So Simonides thinks that even how good we are depends on luck. [A] proceeds to deny this, which he must, if he wants to defend his claim that *eudaimonia* does not (really) depend on luck. The poem is discussed by Plato in *Protagoras* (339–47).

73. *no effect on us whatsoever*: Literally, 'make no contribution at all [to our blessedness]'. There is an interesting interpretive crux here.

Reading (a): You might assume that [A] means here – though he does not say it – 'have no effect on us after we die'. That is how [Asp.] and [S] take it, assuming the qualification from the context.

Reading (b): You could take the words to mean simply, 'have no effect on us at all, in general, i.e. whether we are alive or dead', and think that [A] then makes the further distinction between our being alive or dead below, at 1101a31. That is how [E] and [H] both read it, and [R], as it seems. It is unusual for all the main authorities to be split in this way.

I prefer reading (b), because it seems truer to the text. To import the qualification 'when we are dead' from the context seems steep. Also the reference to 'friends and loved ones in general' seems to be precisely the moment of generalizing the question. And, crucially, when [A] says, below, that it would take a very long time to discuss all the ways that the lives of our loved ones affect us, he surely means in general. It seems absurd to think this means that we could make a long series of fine-grained distinctions about all the different ways we are affected after death. On the contrary, [A] is not sure that there is anything to say about that.

So, the 'unloving' view is that the fortunes of our loved ones do not affect us at all, ever. That is indeed unloving, and clearly does 'go against common sense'.

[Asp.] and [S], given their reading, are forced to assume that the 'unloving' claim is that we are not affected after death by what happens to our loved ones. (That's not absurd. It's certainly unloving to say that *you don't care* what happens to your family after you die.)

74. *acted out [before our eyes]*: Some scholars think [A] is referring to terrible incidents in the backstory, before the play starts. But he is surely referring to the common convention of Greek tragedy whereby the really ghastly and grisly bits of the plot always take place off-stage, and then, once they have taken place, are reported to the audience, typically by a dazed messenger. Thus, Medea kills her children off-stage; Clytemnestra axes Agamemnon off-stage, etc. [A] implies that it would be horrifying to have to actually watch those parts of the plot. The metaphor is clear. It makes a huge difference if you have to witness and watch the misery of your loved ones unfolding. King Priam in the *Iliad* (24.244–6): 'As for me, I just hope that I go down to Hades before I have to see, with my own eyes, my city being sacked and torched.'

75. *absolutely, or at least for them*: You could think that whether your children suffer or flourish after your death is very important, but also have the further thought that it won't matter *to you*. [A] seems to be making that distinction here. Without it, you might make the mistake that Epicureans later did, of insisting

that you have no reason to worry about anything that happens after you die. [A] hints that you can take future events to matter *absolutely*, even if they won't affect you. And that is a common-sense view.

76. *rob them of their blessedness*: It now seems extremely likely that here, and in the next paragraph, [A] means that the quality of a person's life cannot be changed retroactively, by what happens later to the people they loved. The upshot of this, in combination with certain other points, is that the afterlife should not form any part of our thinking about human flourishing.

77. *because of their actions*: The manuscripts read: 'We praise a good person, and their goodness, because of their actions ...'. I make a slight emendation. The revised text makes much more sense and is supported by [Asp.]. See [TA] for details.

78. *relation to some kind of good*: We praise a fair person for being a fair person; but also because we value the fair actions that they reliably perform. Likewise, we praise someone strong or fast for being strong or fast, but also because, e.g., they might be able to perform some physically demanding, useful task, or (perhaps [A] means this) win a wrestling match or a race.

79. *It makes the gods look ridiculous*: Here [A] treats the traditional Greek religious view as absurd. In his view, God is certainly (in some sense) the organizer of the whole cosmos; but He could not possibly have any special interest in, or direct relation to, human needs. [Asp.] explains: 'For example, some people praise Dionysus for giving us wine, and Demeter for giving us bread. But that's silly. What's special about the gods is not in their relation to us, but purely in their own nature. So, that's like praising a human being, not for [the central human qualities of] being moral, or rational, but for being good at feeding goats.' That seems right as a reading. [A] is not saying that it is absurd to compare the gods to us (though it is). He is saying that it is absurd to think of the gods as stooping to the service of human goals.

See [A]'s rather similar claims at 1178b8, where he says that it is absurd to think of the gods having any of our virtues, or engaging in any actions at all.

80. *mind (or character)*: Here this translates 'of soul'. See above, note I.41.

It is a little hard to see how this section slots into the wider context. It is often taken as somehow directly illustrating what has just been said. But I find the line of thought extremely hard

to make out that way. I follow [Asp.], who assumes this is a new
point: 'Next, he distinguishes praise from *encomia* (eulogies).'

I think the argument (as so often, very elliptical) goes back to
the main question (is *eudaimonia* something we praise, or just
something valuable, but not praiseworthy?) and works like this:
'No, [it's not something we praise], because we praise people
for being good (so, not for their *eudaimonia*); and we offer
encomia (a bit like praise) for exploits (so, again, not for their
eudaimonia) ... *Eudaimonia*, and our attitude to it, clearly
must be put in a different class.' Compare [EE] 1219b14–16.

81. *that part of the soul can be good ... not human goodness*: I
confess to a slight paraphrase here. More literally: 'The *aretē* of
that part of the soul [or of that capacity of the soul] is a sort of
common *aretē* [i.e. common to all living things], not human
aretē.' The *aretē* of the nutritive part of the soul means its goodness, but in the sense of its being good at its thing. So the claim
is that when that part of the human soul is good at its thing,
that doesn't count as human goodness. It's a fundamental, universal biological quality: being good at growth and reproduction.
So (clearly) not the same as being a good human being.

Passages like this lead some scholars to think that the term
aretē must, standardly, have some more neutral sense ('excellence' or suchlike). But in fact [A] is the only Greek writer of his
time (or later, outside his school) who uses *aretē* in this way
of our nutritive capacities. The usage is, objectively, extremely
rare, and presumably strange. 'The goodness of your stomach
and liver' (i.e. their being good at blood regulation and digestion) is probably no less strange in English than this expression
is in Greek.

Notice, too, that the wider point here is that human goodness
is something quite different from this mere biological *aretē*.
[A] means, in effect, that 'being a good human being', or 'being
a good person' – quite obviously – has nothing to do with merely
being good at digestion and growth. And for that claim [A]
falls back on the normal, unqualified sense of the term *aretē*,
'goodness', that he has employed throughout book I. Thus
even this passage shows that the standard sense of *aretē* is not
'excellence'.

82. *the dreams of decent people are better*: [A] means that good
people may have 'better' dreams not considered as dreams (more
vivid, more amusing). He means that good people's dreams might
in some sense be morally better. (Perhaps nasty people are even

nasty in their dreams.) Hence, good and bad people can be somewhat distinguished even in sleep.

83. *are 'virtues'*: This is true. [A] and other Greeks sometimes call good qualities of the intellect 'virtues'. But it is also misleading. In particular, it would be wrong to read [A] as saying that 'virtues' means, indifferently and equally, 'any praiseworthy qualities of intellect or character'. In reality, when the term is unqualified, *aretai* always automatically means 'moral virtues'; to have the other sense, it has to be so qualified. It also never means, when unqualified, 'virtues of either sort'. The intellectual sense is also much, much rarer. (Most writers in [A]'s time do not acknowledge it as acceptable Greek at all.) Also, it is possible for [A] to use the term *aretai* (unqualified) in the sense 'moral virtues' even in a context where the intellectual virtues are being discussed. There is evidently a huge weighting in favour of the moral sense of the term, which [A]'s comment here does not bring out.

Also, though we (and the Greeks) certainly praise both kinds of virtue, the other things closely associated with praising specifically people's moral virtues are not found in attitudes to the intellectual virtues. [A] explains that virtues of character are always connected with honourable and shameful actions (i.e. failing to exercise them is shameful); also, that we blame people for not having them; and that laws and norms of society enforce them (i.e. there are laws against not having them). By contrast, no Greek thinks of, e.g., not being good at epistemology as shameful; no Greek would ever blame anyone for not being good at geometry; and there are no laws, in any Greek city, enforcing purely intellectual attainments. There is a large, complex set of reactive attitudes and practices that apply specifically and only to moral virtues. The Greeks distinguished moral virtues exactly as sharply as we do.

BOOK II

1. *through teaching*: The manuscripts read 'are developed through teaching, and hence need time and experience'. Adopting a long-standing suggestion, I move the latter phrase to the next sentence, where it makes far more sense. See [TA] for details.

2. *character virtues*: Virtues 'of character', *ēthikai aretai*, are not simply all and any desirable or functionally useful qualities of character (I find this a common misconception about the term

aretē in this context). It would be easy to list dozens of desirable, highly functional character traits that no Greek would think to call *aretai*. [A] gives several examples himself in the treatise; see below, note II.45; and IV.7, 1127a14ff; and [EE] 1234a24, where he explains that good qualities of character aren't *aretai* if they don't involve (morally significant) choices.

In normal English (which I try to respect throughout the translation), 'moral virtues' typically means, precisely, 'qualities that make you a good person' – without further meta-ethical implication. As such, it is an accurate translation of *ēthikai aretai*, at least when [A] just means to pick out those qualities. At other times it is helpful to make his theoretical assumptions about the role of character more explicit. So, 'character virtues'.

3. *with technical skills*: [A] actually says 'the way it is with other technical skills'; but either he means 'other [dispositions, notably, our] technical skills', or the text is slightly corrupt.

4. *fair and honest*: Translates *díkaios*, which [A] later explains has both a broad sense (someone who generally does the morally right thing; so, 'moral', 'ethical', 'righteous') and a particular sense ('fair', but also 'honest'). In his detailed discussion of the particular virtue he omits the second of those particular senses, 'honest', but it is nevertheless an important implication of the Greek word and he shows, at times, that he is fully aware of it, e.g. at 1127a33, 1178b12. In fact, honesty is central to the idea of being *díkaios*. (Plato, for example, has one of his characters offer this as his first definition of being *díkaios*: 'telling the truth and giving back whatever you take from someone', which implies honesty on both counts: *Republic* 331d2.) So, where it is convenient, I add 'and honest', to bring us closer to what Greek speakers are hearing here.

Throughout the treatise I follow the rule that when *díkaios* is presented immediately alongside other particular virtue terms, as here, it very probably has its particular sense ('fair', 'honest'); but when used in proximity to other very general notions (e.g. 'being a good person') it probably has its general sense ('righteous', 'ethical', 'moral').

5. *system of government*: [A] thinks that government should aim, above all, to make us good people. This seems true, in a sense. Laws and institutions do indeed aim to make us treat each other decently. But it is also a distinctive view of a government's main aim, and similar to Plato's. [A] has mentioned this idea in I.9 (see 1099b29–32, 1102a7–10), and the theme will return in X.9.

6. *They'd all just be born already good or bad at it*: [H] para-
    phrases this point usefully: 'If you didn't acquire skills by
    exercising and practising them, if nature alone made you, say, a
    builder or guitar-player, why would there even be any teachers?'
    I.e. this point only defends the main claim, that you acquire
    skills through practice.

    The further point, that you also become a bad player by play-
    ing the guitar, is separate. And slightly odd. Isn't someone who
    can't build houses at all a very, very bad builder? But [A] means
    that 'a bad guitar-player' normally implies someone who regu-
    larly plays the guitar, and does so badly. (If I say 'my son is a
    very bad cook', I imply that my son cooks. I can't mean, e.g.,
    that my one-month-old son, if asked to cook lasagna, would do
    it extremely badly.) [A] makes this point because of the analogy
    with virtues: you become a bad person only by doing certain
    things regularly, and badly; infants clearly aren't bad people
    (or only in the sense that they are also bad cooks and bad sur-
    geons). There is a connection here with his definition of 'lack of
    skill' in VI.4.

7. *character traits*: Translates *hexeis*, as does 'dispositions'. Not
    every *hexis* is a character trait; just as not every 'disposition' is
    a disposition of character. Technically a *hexis* is just a 'state', a
    'way of being': e.g. being brave, being fair, but also being wise,
    being a good builder, being healthy. But when [A] uses the term
    of the virtues, 'character trait' is a useful translation. In [EE] he
    often uses *diathesis* as a close synonym for *hexis* and also in one
    section of [NE], II.7–8, which perhaps has a different editorial
    source. *Diathesis* means 'disposition'.

8. *correct reason*: Orthos logos. I follow the majority, and the
    traditional, view of the sense of this phrase. The ancient com-
    mentators, in particular, clearly assume that *logos* in the phrase
    refers to reason (the faculty) and particular bits of reasoning.
    The concept is elaborated in book VI.

    'Correct reason' is probably in fact a catch-all, covering (a) a
    conscious, articulate conception of your goals ('reason tells me
    that I should treat others fairly'); (b) deliberation and means-
    end reason*ing*; (c) awareness of pertinent facts, or what we call
    'common sense'; (d) an ability to weigh up competing moral
    demands. All those things help to direct and regulate the impulses
    of good character. But for now [A] wants to concentrate on the
    non-rational elements of the virtues: our pleasures and pains,
    emotions, feelings, etc.

He probably uses the term 'correct' because of the central connection with means-end reasoning, arguably the main sense of the phrase. An inference is correct or incorrect, not true or false. (In the same way he calls desires 'correct', because desires aren't true or false either.) He does also sometimes say that *logos* can be 'true', but probably in the sense of 'truthful', i.e. meaning that 'reason [the faculty] is saying something true', as in 'reason tells me I should X; and it is true that I should X.' See VI.2, and VI.12.

9. *across the board*: The modern consensus is that the term here (*koinon*) means 'everyone agrees' that this is the case. The older consensus (all three commentators) is that it means it is a 'general point', a 'universal point', i.e. a fact common to all virtues and actions. I prefer the older view. This is a completely characteristic use of *koinon* (see e.g. 1097b34, [EE] 1226a6).

10. *we said ... suit their subject matter*: See I.3, and I.7, 1198a25.

11. *can't be precise*: This seems to contradict [A]'s usual view that particulars are more reliable (see 1107a31), or that the right or wrong thing always depends on particular circumstances. Isn't the claim that 'person A, in situation X, should do Y' going to be both precise and true?

    [A] presumably means here – given the comment that immediately follows – that if we try to apply rules to particular situations, they become less likely to be true. We can offer general ethical rules that are roughly true or typically true: ('you should obey your parents'), but if we add detail, they become proportionately more prone to being wrong. (Should you obey your father when he asks you to lie?) General rules are increasingly useless for more detailed scenarios. (See IX.1–2 for a discussion of how particular situations tend to undermine general rules about how to treat family and friends.)

12. *set of rules*: General moral claims are only ever roughly true. So we cannot be good people by following a finite set of rules.

    Of course, laws are something like rules of behaviour. But [A] has the view that we cannot simply 'follow' laws, either. (We have to recognize their flaws; interpret them; apply them, case by case. See his discussion of being 'kind and decent', V.10.)

    This view also implies that we cannot be good people by following the instructions or commandments of enlightened superiors – at any rate not if 'following' them means simply obeying, without understanding. (The rules, or their commands, would have to be infinite to cover all the variability of human life.)

13. *subject*: I.e. *logos*. [A] has just used the term to refer to claims, arguments. But I think that here it naturally means 'discourse', '[area of] discussion'. Hence 'the present *logos*'.

14. *dour yokels*: Agroikoi. See below, IV.8 and note 11.46.

15. *feel-nothing person*: Anaisthētos. [A] in effect invents the word (and later claims to be inventing it). He means it in the (new) sense of 'not having any feeling'. But it did also already exist, in the sense of 'obtuse', 'clueless'. He uses it that way himself at 1114a10. I think [A] plays with that double sense. He has little respect for people who avoid all physical pleasure. Contrast [A]'s idea here with Socrates' claim in the *Phaedo* (83b–d) that we should strive 'to get away from the body' and from physical pleasure as much as we possibly can. See 1151b23–31, and the two discussions of pleasure (VII.11–14, X.1–5).

16. *same [sorts of behaviours]*: [A] means, e.g., that you become brave by the way you (repeatedly) face frightening situations; but you also become a coward by the way you (repeatedly) face frightening situations. Not that you will be acting in exactly the same way, of course.

17. *Plato says*: For Plato on the importance of this sort of early childhood education see *Laws* 653a–c, *Republic* 401d–402a.

18. *through opposites*: A medical theory at the time was that cures should (in some sense) aim to bring to bear on an illness something that is the opposite of its symptoms. E.g. treat a fever with something cold, and a chill with heat. (Reports of the theory are rather vague.) In the same way, if a child enjoys X, which is wrong, make X painful for them (by the punishment); if they shy away from Y (the right thing to do), because Y is painful, then make Y pleasurable for them (by the reward).

19. *reason may determine*: The conclusion is left unstated. 'Hence those dispositions must naturally relate to pleasures and pains.' I assume that 'reason' here refers to the *orthos logos* qualification (see note II.8).

20. *tranquillity states*: Apatheias, 'states of being free from emotions/free from feelings of pleasure and pain'. This is probably a reference to Speusippus (and hence to the Platonists of [A]'s day), who seems to have had a related theory about pleasure: that ideally you should pursue not pleasure, but freedom from both pain and pleasure. See VII.13, and X.2, 1173a5. 'Or whatever' translates tinas. [A] literally says 'some sort of *apatheiai*', a standard way, for him, of indicating uncertainty about a term. And in fact he gets the term wrong. Speusippus claimed

that good people should aim for *aochlēsia* – 'a state of being untroubled, undisturbed'.

21. *being a good person*: Is the sense of *aretē* here general ('goodness', 'being a good person') or particular ('a virtue', 'each of our virtues')? [A] has been switching back and forth from talk of 'virtues' to generally good and bad people. (At 1104b13 he seems to make an inference about general *aretē* on the basis of the very same claim about the particular *aretai*.) The claim that will shortly follow uses the more general subject ('a good person', 'a bad person'), so I prefer that here, for continuity.

But with a particular sense, we could translate: '[Every] virtue is a matter of [always] feeling pleasures and pains [in some particular domain] in such a way that you do what's best; and every vice, the opposite.'

The syntax is a little loose. But compare the nearly identical claim at [EE] 1220a29: 'So, goodness is the sort of disposition that . . . gives rise to the best actions of the soul.'

22. *as our standard*: I take this as a general claim about human motivation. We tend to do the things we enjoy, and to avoid the things that pain us or, simply, that we don't like doing. (The next sentence follows very nicely from the claim taken that way.) So I take it this is not a reference to hedonism. Hedonists use pleasure and pain as their standard in the different sense that they are *aiming for* pleasure. But [A]'s point, I think, includes people who are guided by their likes and dislikes (a kind of internal 'regulation') but aren't only pursuing pleasure per se. The claim that 'some of us [do this] more than others' refers to the fact that most people do the things they enjoy doing, but some people avoid things that they enjoy, and do things that they find painful (i.e. people who have to exercise a lot of self-control). [P] and [S] think the point here *is* about hedonism.

23. *task*: *Pragmateia*, 'whole business', 'whole concern', not 'whole enquiry'. [A] is talking about what we have to do to become good people, not what the main subject of the philosophical discussion is. For this other sense of *pragmateia*, cf. [EE] 1215a115, *Politics* 1274b37.

24. *of statesmanship*: Because the goal of statesmen is to make people good. But it is also possible to read this as a reference to the *topic*, 'moral and political philosophy'. And that decision depends on how you are reading *pragmateia*. (See previous note.) In defence of my reading, note that the *Politics* example discusses precisely the *pragmateia*, the task, of statesmen.

25. *So that's another reason . . . bad one*: This point seems slightly out of place, or displaced by extra material. It would follow nicely right after 1104b35. But if you place it there, start with 'That's why . . .'.

26. *know [what you're doing]*: This probably just means 'you can't be doing it by mistake'. For this term in that sense, see 111a23, 1135a24, a34, 1136a32. But in what follows there may be a sort of slide in the sense of 'knowing'. When [A] says that, for virtues, 'knowledge doesn't really matter much at all' he may now mean, e.g., knowing what you should do, or perhaps knowing what bravery is, or what fairness is. Clearly, the first sense of 'knowing' (not acting by mistake) is unimportant. It's easy to do X not by accident. But [A]'s view is also that the other kinds of knowledge are not as important as some people (e.g. Plato) think. He thinks you can know what you should do, but still not do it, if you lack self-control, or because you are still too young for that knowledge to be embedded in your character (see I.3 and VII.2–3, and V.9 from 1137a4). And he thinks that knowing what bravery is plays a very insignificant role in being brave. See [EE] 1216b3–25. There seems to be a glance here at Socrates, who argued that goodness just *is* (some kind of) knowledge. See VI.12–13 for more on that disagreement.

27. *most [young men like you]*: Literally, 'most'. The commentators think he means 'most people', i.e. *ordinary people*. But given what follows, that is absurd. It seems clear he means 'most people like you', i.e. he's saying 'most young men who do philosophy just theorize about ethics and politics, without actually ever doing anything'. This sounds like a reference either to Plato's Academy, or to the Socratic model of philosophy as lifelong but *inactive* moral self-examination. When [A] says that these people 'fancy themselves "philosophers"', the point is not that purely theoretical philosophy somehow isn't really philosophy (it is paradigm philosophy). He is criticizing people who feel morally superior because they spend all their time arguing about right and wrong, but who never actually do anything.

28. *joy*: Or 'happiness'. In standard, modern English 'happiness' is an excellent fit for *chara* (the word used here) and its verb, *chairein*, standard Greek for 'to be happy' or 'to feel happy'.

29. *involve making choices*: 'Choice' translates *prohairesis*. A virtue (arguably) 'is a choice' (a *prohairesis*) in the sense of a very broad, general choice, a life-choice ('your choices' in that sense, in Greek as in English, can mean something like 'your values',

'your commitments'). So a brave person chooses [in life] to act bravely (is committed to being brave); a fair person is someone who chooses to treat people fairly. And certainly virtues involve making (lots of particular) choices; a virtue by definition 'reliably causes you to make certain choices'. (See below, 1106b36.)

For the detailed discussions of *prohairesis* see III.2 (and note III.29) and VI.2.

30. *in general*: I.e. the broad kind or class; its *genus*. Not every disposition is a virtue, but every virtue is a disposition. Technical skills and intellectual virtues are also 'dispositions' (now rather more in the sense 'faculties'); and there are also physical and biological 'dispositions', i.e. one's 'physical condition' (see e.g. 1129a19, 1152b34).

31. *virtues*: I use the plural (though the Greek is singular) to make it clear that [A] is analysing particular virtues. I take the singular here to mean, from context, 'a virtue, in general'. But we could take the subject to be singular, 'goodness'; and indeed these kinds of claims (a very rare extension of the use of *aretē*) are typically singular: 'the goodness of the eye is (by definition) whatever makes it a good eye'. That sounds odd in English; but it is equally odd in Greek.

32. *then human virtues ... a human being*: Here is an alternative translation with (general, singular) goodness as the subject: 'then human goodness, similarly, is presumably a disposition [of character] that makes someone (a) a good human being, i.e. a good person, and (b) good at performing the task of a human being'. Note that the first claim is now hardly more than an analytical truth. Goodness makes you good. But with particular virtue(s) as the subject, the same is true. Virtues are by definition parts of (general) goodness; so by definition virtues make you a good person.

33. *already*: I.e. he has already set out the theory that virtues are middle states in II.2.

34. *the exact nature of a virtue*: The reference to 'nature' (*phusis*) signals that [A] is going to approach the question more theoretically, by way of a closer study of the psychology of our virtues, and his theory that virtues are 'middle states'. Compare with similar moments at VII.3, 1147a24, and IX.9, 1170a13.

35. *relative to us*: Probably in the sense 'relative to each of us individually'; 'relative to each person and their particular circumstances'. For other clear instances of this individualizing use of the 'us' pronoun see 1109b1–3, in II.9, and 1118b13, in III.11.

36. *ten pounds of food is a lot*: In Greek, ten *minae*. A *mina* is little more than a pound. I think we may understand the example like this: suppose that the most any athlete eats (per day) is ten pounds of food. Let's say that's a kind of athletic maximum. And suppose the least anyone eats is about two pounds. (A normal amount of food to eat in a day is about four pounds. So two pounds is approaching a minimum for a healthy, active adult.) It doesn't follow that every trainer will assign an athlete six pounds of food per day, on the grounds that that's the 'mid-point' between the maximum and the minimum. Rather, the mid-point has to be relative to the particular athlete.

   In the same way, there is such a thing as, say, the angriest that a human being can possibly be (incandescent with rage) and the least angry they can be (completely unmoved). It does not follow that in every situation you should aim to be set exactly between completely calm and incandescent. Rather, 'too angry' and 'not angry enough' and hence 'the middle amount of angry' (i.e. the right amount of angry) have to be relative to you and your exact situation.

37. *a Milo*: Milo of Croton, in southern Italy, a champion wrestler who lived about 200 years before Aristotle's time. He won multiple victories at the Olympics and other festivals.

38. *better, as nature is*: [A] means that nature – i.e., here, biology – produces works of wonderful beauty and complexity, far superior to human design. An eye is far more perfect and complex than any human artefact. Our virtues are grounded in our nature, and, when well developed, a 'perfection of' our nature (see II.1). So we should expect them to perform their functions with extreme perfection and precision.

39. *optimal . . . characteristic*: Optimal, or best possible states and best possible actions, characterize the virtues, and characterize good people, in [A]'s view – which seems reasonable. (Brave people are the best at facing things we fear; generous people make the best use of money.) See 1104b28, [EE] 1218b37ff.

40. *characteristic of good people*: 'Characteristic of *aretē*'; 'characteristic of goodness', or 'of virtue(s)'. But I take this to be a very quick supporting claim. [A] isn't just repeating himself. Getting it right and being praised are things we (already) naturally associate with good people. So that common view, he is saying, supports his claim.

41. *gloating*: Or 'malicious gloating'; 'gloating over people's misfortunes'. (But that's pretty much what 'gloating' means anyway.)

Epichairekakia: an emotion term that means 'delight at others' suffering'; *Schadenfreude*.

42. *from our chart*: The chart does not survive in the manuscripts. But there is an equivalent chart in [EE], at 1220b37. I give a Nicomachean version. But I place the virtues in the middle, where they surely belong.

43. *feel-nothings*: See above, note II.15.

44. *[the ways] they make money*: See IV.1, 1121b31. [A] means that some people stoop to disgraceful and degrading ways of making money, and in that (ethical) sense 'go too far' in making money; like pimps and pickpockets.

45. *to help us to see*: [A] makes a similar point at IV.7, 1127a14–17. Note, in passing, that [A] does not say that these particular middle states are virtues (*aretai*). That term has strong moral implications (see above, note II.2). His point is that even minor qualities help us to see the general claim that all attractive and useful dispositions of character (a much wider category than 'virtues') are middle states. This is also why he says the extremes, here, are merely 'not correct' (i.e. 'there's something not quite right about them') as opposed to 'shameful' or 'disgraceful'.

46. *humourless yokel*: *agroikos*, a country bumpkin, a provincial. [A] shares the urbanite Athenian prejudice that people from the countryside are humourless. Cf. English 'boorish', 'churlish', which can have similar implications ('churl' and 'boor' both once meant 'farmer'). Elsewhere he uses the same term to refer to people who lack interest in physical comforts and pleasures. The model for this stereotype is the gruff, sinewy old peasants of Greek comedy – like the chorus in Aristophanes' *Acharnians*, or the grumpy old man in Menander's *Dyskolos*. Obviously, the term is slightly abusive in tone. English supplies plenty of similar terms ('hick', 'rube', 'redneck', 'hillbilly', 'bumpkin', 'hayseed'), but I don't think any of them implies a lack of sense of humour. [A]'s thought is clearly that such people lack the ability to engage in sophisticated, witty repartee – a rather unfair standard for a sense of humour, which, in reality, is quite obviously a universal human quality.

47. *'gloater' ... delights in it*: The supplement here (in square brackets) appears to have actually dropped out of the text, rather than being something you could just understand from context. My suggestion comes from Rassow, in [S]. It appears that something to that effect must be right.

48. *elsewhere*: The set of virtues and other attractive dispositions are discussed from III.6 to the end of IV, in the same order as the 'chart'. There is never any further discussion of indignant and envious people, or gloaters. It's possible it dropped out. But the parallel 'full' discussion at [EE] 1233b16 is actually about the same length (nine lines) as here (seven lines, nine if you restore the missing clause). So I think this just is the discussion, and it's in the wrong place.

49. *in what sense they're middle states*: See V.1–5. It turns out that actually only one of these is a middle state, namely the virtue of being fair, and in a different sense from the other virtues (because its middle has to be described externally, in terms of its outcomes).

50. *and the equivalent with the other virtues*: Except perhaps for lecherous men, who are, by definition, quite happy to be the way they are (and perhaps that includes labelling themselves as lecherous). See VII.8–10.

51. *more natural opposites*: I.e. 'more naturally thought of as opposites', 'a better instance of opposites'; 'we more readily think of it as the opposite'. I do not mean 'natural' in any technical sense.

52. *Odysseus*: [A] gets this wrong, in two different ways. The lines are uttered by Odysseus himself (12.219) to his helmsman, and the original advice came from Circe, not Calypso (12.108–10). [A] always quotes Homer from memory.

53. *as they say*: I have cheated slightly. [A] quotes a proverb in the other part of the clause: 'by a "second sailing" (as they say).' 'Second sailing' means 'if you can't use the wind, use your oars'. So, the next best thing.

54. *Lady Pleasure*: My sense is that [A] in effect personifies pleasure at this point, treating her as a kind of goddess by poetic licence; hence the easy comparison with Helen.

55. *mantra*: This is what the old men say as they watch the fighting from the walls of Troy (*Iliad* 3.156ff.): 'Lovely as she is, she should sail back home, and not give us and our children so much grief.' The citation makes it clear that [A] has sexual pleasure in mind. The old men also say, as they leer at Helen: 'Who could blame the Greeks and Trojans for fighting over a woman like that? She's as lovely as an immortal goddess.'

BOOK III

1. *by the wind*: [A] means blown off-course in a ship. (*Pneuma* is a standard term for wind in sailing contexts. See e.g. Thucydides 2.84.2, 2.97.1.) E.g. Odysseus gets to within sight of Ithaca, but then goes away again – extremely unwillingly. His ship is blown back out to sea (*Odyssey* 10.54–5).

2. *if you refuse*: A helpful real-life example, suggested by [Asp.]: Socrates was ordered by the 'Thirty Tyrants' to arrest an innocent man, Leon of Salamis, and in effect collude in his murder (see Plato's *Apology* 32c–d). There was a clear threat of harm to Socrates, and to his family, if he did not comply. But he refused to take part in any crime. So then the question is, if Socrates had arrested Leon – and many other Athenians were pressured into similar crimes – would his action have been wilful?

3. *[at that moment]*: [A] makes the point just by emphatic use of the present tense. [H] is helpful here in confirming what this means: 'Actions take place at a particular moment; and at that moment you are doing it willingly.'

4. *broadly speaking*: I.e. *haplōs*, 'simply', 'absolutely', 'without any qualification'; also 'normally' or 'under normal circumstances'. Here [A] means, in effect, 'other than in special circumstances'.
    His way of putting it is, I think, slightly awkward. You would very naturally say here: 'I wouldn't normally do that; but I did it in that case, to save people's lives.' (And that is exactly how [A] then explicates it.) So the action is really something you 'wouldn't normally do willingly', rather than, as [A] describes it, something you 'normally do unwillingly'.

5. *extreme humiliation*: 'Extremely shameful', but in the sense 'extremely *shaming*'. [Asp.] rightly sees that we have to take the term here in that other, slightly weaker sense. [A] does not think you should ever do shameful things, in the sense of 'wrong', 'unethical'; see IV.9. [Asp.] suggests the example of a tyrant ordering a man to dress up in women's clothing and appear before his fellow citizens (and if he refuses his wife and children will be killed). This is humiliating, but you might well praise a man (for example, if you were his wife and children) for submitting to it. [Asp.] is probably thinking of the time that the Emperor Nero forced Roman aristocrats to perform as actors on stage (including in women's roles) – to their undying shame. Likewise, we would probably praise the people who played

along with Stalin's humiliating show trials, given that their self-debasement saved their families from torture, imprisonment or death.

6. *Alcmaeon ... ridiculous*: Alcmaeon (in the Euripides play) killed his mother, Eriphyle, because his father, Amphiaraus, upon departing to his death in battle, asked him to because he was angry with her, and threatened to 'put a curse on' him if he disobeyed. [A] no doubt finds the latter detail especially silly – like killing your mother because your father made you 'pinky-promise' that you would.

7. *X to avoid [outcome] Y*: Or 'X instead of Y' (as in 'I'll walk down the street naked rather than see my children be killed'); hence 'to avoid my children being killed'. The same pronoun can mean 'in exchange for' or 'instead of'; but it works either way. 'I'll walk down the street naked in exchange for my children's lives.'

8. *stick to your decision*: [Asp.] suggests, e.g., that having decided to submit to watching your children being killed rather than betray your country, you might break when they're actually before your eyes and about to die. Having decided not to betray a friend, even if it means being tortured, you might lose your resolve once you're being tortured.

9. *more like things ... willingly*: There are two interpretations of the overall idea here. One is that, e.g., throwing your cargo overboard is not normally a willing action, but fully willing under certain (rare) circumstances. So throwing your cargo overboard in a storm is fully willing. It's the abstract category – 'throwing your cargo overboard'– that's 'mixed'. Alternatively, 'mixed' actions are 'mixed' even when you do them, i.e. the particular action of throwing your cargo overboard is not fully willing or wilful, it's just *kind of* wilful, but arguably 'a bit more like' a fully willing action. I assume the second reading, followed by [Asp.] and [H], is the right one. It's those actions themselves that are 'a grey area', 'ambiguous', 'a bit of both'.

10. *so easily hooked*: 'Easily hunted', 'easy prey'; but the same verb is used for fishing, and I think that's the metaphor here. At this point [A] must have only pleasures in mind, especially sexual pleasures. He wouldn't speak of being 'hooked' by honourable actions. He's imagining someone who explains an illicit liaison. (For young Greek men, most liaisons were illicit.) 'It wasn't my fault; she was so beautiful. I was powerless to resist!'

11. *what's best*: Or 'what's in their interests'. But [A]'s view is that being a good person, and exercising all the virtues, is very much

in your interest. So a bad person is, in a sense, wrong about what is best for human beings. Note that there is a direct reference here to the Socratic paradox that 'nobody ever does wrong willingly'. Socrates means that people who do wrong, because they are mistaken about what's best for them, are not strictly doing what they themselves want or aim to do. (Everyone aims to do what's best for themselves.) They 'don't realize what they're doing'. [A]'s reply: that simply doesn't qualify as an example of 'not realizing'. Such people aren't only different in their knowledge; they also have a different character. And the whole point of saying that somebody did something 'by mistake' or 'without realizing' is to signal that their action does not indicate anything about their character. So the Socratic claim is clearly false, by the normal rules of conversational implicature.

12. *intended result*: Literally, 'the for-sake-of-what' or 'the purpose'. But what does [A] mean by not knowing, or being mistaken about, 'the purpose'? I take this to be a loose expression, but with a pretty clear sense. It refers to those cases where you say 'But that's not what I meant to do'; 'That wasn't my aim.' So you intended one outcome, but brought about something else. You didn't realize that your action was serving some quite different purpose, or, as we would more naturally say, having some harmful effect different from the one intended. In *Physics* II.8 [A] uses the same terminology to discuss things that 'serve a purpose' (i.e. objectively have some significant, useful effect) rather than in reference to being done *for* that purpose. (See *Physics* 196b15–30, also *Metaphysics* 1065a26–31.) Lucky events serve a purpose (have a useful effect in some sense) but are by definition not done *for* that purpose. And clearly the current case is also fundamentally about bad luck. 'I meant to do A, but unluckily caused B to happen.'

But you could take the phrase more directly: perhaps [A] means literally not knowing the purpose of something (an implement, say). 'I didn't know this powder was for killing rats; I thought it was for sweetening tea.' (But that, I think, just reduces to ignorance about 'what you're doing it with'. So the other interpretation seems more likely.)

13. *it just slipped out*: 'Sorry! Slip of the tongue!' Plutarch (*Pericles* 8.6) reports that 'Pericles was so cautious in his speech that every time he walked to the speaker's platform he used to make a little prayer, that not so much as a single word should slip from his lips against his will that did not suit the needs of the hour.'

(The example arises from the fact that in some circumstances there are things you must not say, but which you might say by a slip of the tongue. Certain swear words, for example, in many settings, or words of ill omen, or impiety. Or getting your bride's first name wrong in your wedding vows.)

14. *Meropē*: In the lost Euripides play *Cresphontes*, Meropē wrongly thinks her son has been murdered and then, much later, mistakes her son for the man she thinks murdered him. (She hasn't seen him for a while.) She is about to clobber him with an axe when she realizes – 'when the old man arrives in the nick of time' – who he is. Plutarch says that that scene of the play is particularly terrifying and suspenseful. (See *On Eating Meat* 998c; also [A]'s *Poetics* 1454a5.)

15. *fighting spirit, {anger}*: *Thumos*. The word means (a) 'spirit' (as in 'they showed a lot of spirit and put up a good fight'; or 'their resistance was very spirited'), i.e. something like 'fighting spirit'; but (b) increasingly in [A]'s time it means simply 'anger'. (This is not unlike the way 'temper' has evolved to mean 'anger' in English.) Unfortunately, [A] still very much uses both senses, and we will just have to keep track of that. This is also an older, quite different sense found in Homer; see below, note III.19.

16. *motivated in that way*: Here this translates *oregesthai*. This is [A]'s general term for all forms of push – or motive force – that come from physical desire or feeling and emotion, including when those are shaped by deliberation (wanting to X). In English (especially in philosophical contexts) we normally call this catch-all concept 'desire' (in a very broad sense), and that's my usual translation too. But here it needs to be able to (immediately) cover anger as well.

17. *things we should desire*: It's quite true that we should desire health and learning. But [A] here uses a verb that he usually confines quite strictly to physical desire (whereas the previous term 'motivated' covers both emotion and physical desire). So my suspicion is that these objects have been suggested by the editor ('He means, e.g., desire for health and learning'), whereas in fact [A] means that there are some physical pleasures that we should desire. For this claim see III.11, from 1119a5.

It would be bizarre to deflect responsibility in those cases. No Greek man, for example, would ever think to say that he 'shouldn't be blamed' for sleeping with his own wife. 'I just couldn't help it!' That would be absurd, [A] says. So why is it less absurd to say you 'couldn't help' sleeping with someone else's wife? Desire plays the same role in both.

18. *caused by [poor] reasoning*: [A]'s point is that we never accept poor reasoning as grounds for treating an action as unwilling. Suppose you invest in company X to make money; but your reasoning is poor, the investment is foolish, and you lose money. Does that mean you invested the money unwillingly? Of course not. Your reasoning led you astray. So when it happens to be your anger, or some other passion, that leads you astray, why think of the action as unwilling?

19. *[impulse] of spirit*: This is *thumos* again. See above, note III.15. But why on earth would anyone think that choice is 'fighting spirit' or 'anger'? That seems rather bizarre.

Perhaps [A] is using 'fighting spirit' as a stand-in for the emotional or passionate part of the soul as a whole (see, for example, *Politics* 1327b36–1328a4; *Topics* 113a33–113b3). So, on this interpretation, the position he's considering is that choice is an emotion- or passion-based impulse to do something.

More likely, this idea comes from the fact that the Homeric use of the term does indeed suggest a connection with choice. Homer frequently describes the moment of a character's choice, or their preference, by saying, 'it so pleased his *thumos*'; or 'his *thumos* is set on it'; or 'his *thumos* bids him': e.g. *Iliad* 1.24, 173, 378, 4.263, 6.444, 7.68, 9.703, 10.220, *Odyssey* 4.10, 5.89, 8.27 etc. So you can reasonably claim that for Homer at least *thumos* – in its older sense – is something like the seat of choice. For Homer the word usually means 'mind', 'heart' and 'spirit' in that older sense (as in, 'I do as my spirit bids me'; 'the spirit is willing but the flesh is weak').

So the claim [A] is reporting was probably something like this: 'Choice is *thumos* – and here are thirty well-known lines from Homer to prove it.' Homer was frequently appealed to as a kind of authority in this way, including by [A] himself.

But [A] dismisses this idea as if it is, fundamentally, about anger and passion. (It is characteristic of [A] to be rather insensitive to the older senses of Greek words.) His point is that when a passion-based impulse directs us towards things, then the stronger the impulse – imagine that we fly into a rage – the less we seem to be making a choice.

20. *can't desire the opposite of what you desire*: That is to say, you cannot long to eat a piece of chocolate because you crave chocolate, and be repulsed by the chocolate and have a strong desire

not to eat it. You can't love coffee and hate coffee. But you can love coffee and choose not to drink it; or hate it and choose to drink it.

21. *doesn't target pain or pleasure*: Choice, by definition, targets what's good. To make a choice is to judge that something is good, desirable, worth pursuing.

22. *even less*: [A] reverts to the ordinary sense of *thumos*, 'fighting spirit', 'anger'. See above, note III.19.

23. *actor or athlete to win*: Plays in Athens were performed as part of a competition. Plays competed against other plays, and the actors would 'win' by being in the winning play.

24. *say [we're blessed]*: Usually this is taken to mean 'and we say we do', i.e. 'and we say we want to be blessed'. Only one commentator of the three, [H], has a view on this, and that's his view. But this doesn't add anything. Better to take it as 'we [sometimes] *say that we are* blessed'. That's different from wanting it; but also still short of choosing it. I.10 discusses, at length, the circumstances under which we can call others and ourselves blessed. Also, to 'say someone is blessed' is the Greek idiom for a common speech act; it means 'to congratulate'.

25. *things that are in our power*: [A] does think that being blessed is mostly in our power (see I.9–10); but it is a more standard view that it is mostly out of our power. Most people assume that being blessed largely depends on the gifts of fortune (see 1179a15) and that fact shapes common intuitions about whether you can 'choose to be blessed'. It sounds a bit like saying, 'I choose to be lucky.'

26. *more usual way*: Especially a broad choice, a life-choice (see 1106a3, and note II.29). Choosing to treat people fairly, to be brave, to be honest, to be a good friend – those are good choices. Of course, we also often describe particular choices as good and bad as well. But the broader they are, the more readily we do so. (It would be odd to say 'I've made some really bad choices in my life. Like choosing ketchup over mustard the last time I had some fries.')

27. *kind of people we are*: I.e. good or bad people. Every vice and virtue involves choosing, valuing certain things and not others. That's why virtues and vices aren't just forms of expertise or know-how. In most cases this is perfectly obvious. But it even holds for minor qualities of character. [A] says, for example (see 1127b14), that a 'charlatan' isn't just someone who *can* fool people about how great he is, or who knows how to do that,

even if significant know-how is involved. You're a charlatan only if you also regularly *want* to act that way.

28. *because they're bad people*: Or maybe, 'through [a] vice'. Taken the second way, you might read this as (another) reference specifically to lack of self-control. People who lack self-control may have the right beliefs about what to do, but then they make poor choices.

But that doesn't quite make sense. [A] just defined lack of self-control as acting against your (correct) choice, because of physical desire; not as having the right beliefs and then choosing something else. He also does not think lack of self-control is really 'a vice'.

In general, our (moral) beliefs surely are rather detached from action, and quite capable of coming apart from our choices. We all have plenty of moral beliefs we never act on.

[A]'s thoughts here may be about philosophers and their belief systems. An Aristotelian might say: 'Hedonists have worse beliefs than we do about right and wrong, but Eudoxus was a good man and made much better choices in life than plenty of (rakish) Aristotelians I know.' (This thought is roughly implied by 1172b15–17.) Or, conversely, 'Critias spent time with Socrates and shared many of his excellent philosophical beliefs; but he still made bad choices and committed terrible crimes, because he was an evil man.' (Most people agree that religious belief systems do not reliably predict good or bad character either.)

29. *A over B*: Or perhaps A *before* B? The preposition *pro* can mean either. But the accompanying claim makes it very clear that [A] means the former. Choosing one thing rather than another in itself implies that you are thinking about your options. You are deliberating. Should I do this? Or that? That's deliberation, by definition.

But the ambiguity of the preposition is worth noting.

It seems clear that *prohairesis* sometimes means, for [A], something like 'aim' or 'intention' rather than 'choice'. And that is a standard usage in wider Greek, too. [A] uses it that way in his own natural idiom (rather than in self-conscious analysis) when he says, for example, that his discussion is 'achieving its *prohairesis*; its aim' (at 1102a13, and 1179a35). There the translation 'choice' is clearly unworkable. For another example see 1144a20–34, where he says that 'goodness makes your choice (your *prohairesis*) correct' and then immediately glosses that as 'your aim' (your *skopos*). Likewise at [EE] 1228a2–4.

[A] says that every *prohairesis*, every choice, involves choosing X for the sake of Y (see III.3 and [EE] 1227b34–1228a4); that may be why it's natural for [A] to use *prohairesis*, at times, to designate the 'purpose' or 'intention' of an action. But I don't think that's the reason.

The true explanation, I think, lies in the fact that the verb itself was used in two different ways. In effect, there are two verbs:

(a) Sometimes *prohaireisthai* means, as [A] claims here, 'to choose A over B'; hence to choose, or prefer. (To choose, in English, likewise always implies choosing something over something else.) In this sense, *prohaireisthai* is very similar to the plain *haireisthai*, also standardly translated as 'to choose'.

(b) Sometimes it means 'to fore-choose', 'to choose-beforehand', in the sense 'to intend', 'to have as your plan, or purpose'.

The noun may represent both senses of the verb, and hence can mean either (a) 'choice', or 'choosing'; or (b) 'intent', 'aim', 'purpose'.

[A] quite often uses the second sense of the noun (as noted). That gives rise to the oddness of his claiming, here in book III, that you choose 'the things that get you to your goal', so that *prohairesis*, in sense (a), means choosing the means to your goal, but also, e.g. in VI.12, that your *prohairesis*, now in sense (b), is 'your goal' (your *skopos*, 'your aim'), and that our means-end reasoning then figures out 'how to do things for the sake of that *prohairesis*'.

30. *nobody deliberates about their goal*: [A] doesn't mean that we can never, under any circumstances, deliberate about things that we take as goals. Clearly, we can deliberate about whether to heal someone (if it will be far too dangerous or costly, say) or whether to persuade an audience. Or consider [A]'s example from the opening paragraph of the treatise. The goal of bridle-making is to make bridles, but clearly we can ask whether we need any bridles; and the goal of generalship is victory, but we can also choose not to fight the war in the first place.

So the idea is rather that every act of deliberation, by definition, has to be relative to some goal. If we do deliberate about whether to heal the patient, or whether to go to war, we must be doing so in the light of some further, higher goal. And given what [A] says in book I, he presumably thinks that there is at least one goal that we cannot deliberate about (without being insane, perhaps): the goal of flourishing.

31. *the thing they want is unwantable*: The position that you can
     only want what's good is associated with Plato. Socrates argues
     in *Gorgias* 467a–468d that, since we want what's good, if we
     do something under the mistaken impression that it's good for
     us we're not actually doing what we want. See also *Meno* 75b–
     78b1. Thus, murderous tyrants are failing to do what they want.
     Is [A] being a little uncharitable in characterizing this position?
     Plato wouldn't say that people who are mistaken about what's
     good 'want things that are unwantable'; he'd say that they are
     mistaken about how to achieve what they want.

     But then again, the claim invites the paradox. Suppose you
     want to be rich (at all costs), and being rich (at all costs) is a bad
     thing, and on this theory you can't want something bad; then
     the claim really is, apparently (assuming normal language), that
     you can't want what you want.

32. *good person [can only want] what's really wantable*: The wider
     issue at stake here is this. If we tie good and bad to human desires
     and human strivings – as [A] is inclined to do – is there a danger
     of losing any possibility of their being objectively good and bad
     things, or at any rate good for all human beings, regardless of
     their particular desires and wishes? The people who argue that
     'wantable' just means whatever you happen to want are in effect
     also saying that 'good' just means 'something that somebody
     happens to want' and that could be anything at all. The people
     who say 'you can only (really truly) want what's good' are assum-
     ing an objective standard for what's good.

     [A] splits the difference, by arguing that good and bad are
     tied to human desires, and to what we human beings want; but
     in the sense of being anthropocentric – tied to the facts of
     human nature and human character and the facts of the human
     condition, and hence to human desires and needs – rather than
     to individual desires and whims. Good things are the things
     that good and wise people want. (Here, I assume he literally
     means that a good person can only want good things, just as
     good eyes can only see colours the right way, and good health
     can only make your body function well.)

33. *measure of them*: A clear reference to the Protagorean claim that
     'man is the measure of all things'. Whatever else he may have
     meant, Protagoras certainly means that 'human beings are the
     ultimate measure or standard of what is good and bad, right and
     wrong for human beings'. Plato's *Theaetetus* discusses this claim
     at length (152–71), but perhaps rather uncharitably. The passage

at 166–7 in particular seems very close to [A]'s thoughts here. [A]
substantially agrees with the Protagorean view, but with his
important qualification. That addition implies his willingness to
defend a universal (but still human) standard for right and wrong.

34. *so is doing it*: For centuries this phrase was misread as 'And
if saying no is up to us, then so is saying yes.' 'So is yes' is [A]'s
way, here, of saying 'so is doing it'.

35. The idea that no one is willingly a bad person is associated with
Socrates. See *Apology* 25d–26a; *Cleitophon* 407d–e. [P] tells us
that a very similar line appears in the works of Epicharmus, a
famous comic poet. The speaker is Heracles: 'I am doing all
these things only because I am forced to. Nobody is willingly
beset by troubles or by woe.' But then it seems to have been
recycled in the form quoted by [A]. He takes *ponēros* in the
moral sense of his own day, 'wicked', 'evil', but in Epicharmus
it means 'beset by toil', a 'toiler'. Even the version [A] uses probably meant 'No one is willingly beset by troubles [i.e. wretched],
or unwillingly blessed.' (In Greek many words that originally
meant 'labourer' came to mean 'bad person', a common phenomenon in slave-owning or otherwise caste-based societies.)

36. *cheating people*: I assume a particular sense of *ádikos* here
('unfair', 'dishonest'). For the corresponding narrower sense of
this verb *kakourgein*, here in the sense of 'cheating', 'tricking',
see 1165b12. (It's also the verb used when people accuse Socrates
of cheating, or being dishonest, in philosophical argument: e.g.
Republic 341a7, b1, b9; *Gorgias* 483a3, 489b4.)

37. *of character*: Literally, here, 'of the soul' – the term standardly
used for contrasting both mind and character with the body.

38. *for being born ugly*: This discussion closely matches Plato's *Protagoras* (323c–324a). But [A] seems to want to slightly improve
the argument.

39. *suppose someone said this*: It seems extremely likely, here, that
this is the editor's way of recording a further objection from the
student who started the exchange. (For the same formula used
in this way see I.6.)

[A]'s student Theophrastus argued in his own ethical works
that luck has a major role to play in how well our lives go, and
that it can even affect how good or bad we are (see Plutarch,
Pericles 38.2.1; Cicero, *De Finibus* 5.12.12). The objection considered here has just those implications. It implies that good
character might be a matter of luck; and hence that our *eudaimonia* is radically, not just superficially, dependent on luck. So

perhaps the student raising this objection is Theophrastus himself. (Plus, as I explained in the Introduction, [NE] perhaps derives from his records of [A]'s lectures.)

40. *every bit as involuntary*: [A] assumes this is a powerful rebuttal, since it is clearly absurd, he thinks, to argue that we should not be praised for being good people, any more than criticized for being evil people. But it seems very likely that the objector would simply reply, 'Yes, that's exactly my view.'

41. *innate, fixed goal*: Or 'goal set by nature'. Throughout this translation, the few times I use the term 'innate' (translating Greek *phusei*, 'by nature') I mean 'determined by your nature'. I do not mean that the relevant trait or feature is something you already have when you are born. This conforms with normal English usage. 'Innate tendencies' are tendencies we are 'born with'; but they might well manifest long after birth, at the appropriate age. 'Innate' is sometimes a better translation than 'natural'. Even habits and culturally instilled practices can be 'natural' if they conform with human nature. It is natural for human beings to form societies, and to have laws, for example. But laws are not innate.

42. *(whatever it might be)*: The manuscripts read 'fixed innately or however'. For the slight change to the text see [TA].

43. *(as we've claimed)*: [A] has made this claim in II.1–4, and again at 1114a4–31.

44. *violence being done to your wife and children*: It seems likely that [A] is responding here to a Platonic claim, found in the *Phaedo* (68d5–e1), that when 'ordinary people' (non-philosophers) are brave in the face of death, they are still acting out of fear: they think dying is a very bad thing, but they face it through fear of something worse. Hence they are (absurdly) 'being brave out of cowardice'. Hence, ordinary bravery is defective. Plato has in mind men who face death in battle to protect their families, i.e. because they 'fear' their wives and children will be abused by the enemy. [A] makes the point that being afraid of that is not cowardice. It is a perfectly legitimate motive for facing death bravely.

45. *[afraid that X might make you feel] envy; or anything like that*: The manuscripts read simply, 'or envy, or anything like that'. The point is cryptic, and highly abbreviated. The [EE] version of the same point goes like this (1229a37–9): 'You aren't a coward for fearing pains that are not directly associated with [the threat of death]; e.g. it isn't fear if you anticipate that [if X happens]

you are going to feel envy, or jealousy, or shame.' (The previous example may be part of the same idea. To fear the suffering
of your family is to anticipate, and imagine, feelings of anger
and grief – not at all the same as feeling fear in the standard
sense.)

46. *a whipping [from your master]*: The verb very strongly suggests
the whipping of slaves. [Asp.] confirms: 'Nor if you stay calm
under the lash, as many slaves do' (emphasis on do). But why
isn't that a form of bravery? I wonder if [A] tried it himself, to
get a good sense of whether it takes bravery not to flinch while
being savagely whipped. Underlying this rather mean point is
[A]'s prejudice that slaves cannot be brave. The problem with
slaves being brave, especially in war-mad cultures like ancient
Greece, is that if they can be brave men – which for many Greek
men means good men, period – then why are they slaves? (Cf.
the argument made by Howell Cobb, Confederate politician
and general: 'If slaves seem good soldiers, our whole theory of
slavery is wrong.') [A]'s views on slavery are, in fact, somewhat
mixed. See *Politics* 1.4–6. And 1161b, and my note there.

In a similar vein, [A] will shortly claim that animals can't be
brave either.

47. *the Celts*: Cf. [EE] (1229b28–9), where [A] says that the Celts
'take up their weapons and charge at the ocean waves'. According to Strabo (7.2.1.15–22), Ephorus, a Greek historian of [A]'s
time, reported that local Celts built their homes on the tidal
flats around (what is now) Mont Saint-Michel (where, as the
locals say, the tide rolls in across the bay 'at the speed of a gal-
loping horse'). They would then rebuild their houses in the same
spot, after they were destroyed by the surging tide. This story,
or a related one, seems to have made its way to [A] in some gar-
bled form. (Strabo adds that it is patently absurd. Why would
you build your house where you see the tide come in, twice a
day?) The claim about 'charging at the waves' may also derive
from the fact that travellers were, and are, sometimes caught by
the tides in that treacherous bay.

These kinds of wild beliefs about distant people (see VII.5 for
more) are not philosophically insignificant. See 1148b22, and
note V.37.

48. *Sicyonians*: The incident is described by Xenophon in *Hellenica*
4.4.10–11. Some Spartan infantry – by far the best heavy armed
fighters of the time – happened to go into battle with Sicyonian
shields (with large *sigmas* painted on them).

49. *actually more brave*: Compare what [A] says here with Socrates'
    claim in the *Apology* that we shouldn't fear death because it
    probably isn't a bad thing at all (40b–41c). According to [A],
    to be brave in the face of death you have to love life and be
    deeply attached to it, and recognize that death is a very great
    loss indeed. It is the loss of everything. In [A]'s view, Socrates at
    his trial was fearless (because of his beliefs about death), but not
    brave. Also, here [A] seems to concede that this kind of death is
    a sacrifice. The dying man accepts that he is giving up his won-
    derful life, his *eudaimonia*. He is putting the interests of others
    before his own. (And this is a common-sense, or at least com-
    mon, view of actions of that kind.) But in IX.8 [A] seems to
    backtrack, and deny it.

    [A] thus here seems to adopt, or toy with, a more tragic view.
    The brave man has powerful reasons to risk death; that doesn't
    change the fact that his death will be a disaster for him. This
    doesn't fit particularly easily with [A]'s tendency to claim that
    exercising our virtues very reliably makes us 'blessed'. The
    dying soldier in this passage loses everything – period. The dying
    soldier in the book IX passage loses his life, but [A] there seems
    keen to argue that, in some sense, his death still makes him
    blessed.

50. *So it's not true*: I.e. he has partially modified the claim made
    at I.8, 1099a7–31. He will modify it again at IX.11, and indeed
    every time he claims, in books VIII and IX, that we share the
    pain of the people we love.

51. The Greek for 'lecherous' or 'gluttonous' is the single term
    akolastos. This originally meant 'unruly' or 'undisciplined', 'out
    of control', used especially of unruly animals, slaves and 'mobs'.
    It came to refer to wild, self-indulgent living: the boozing, feasting
    and whoring of wild young men. The sexual sense ('lecherous',
    'lascivious', 'libidinous') is especially prominent throughout
    the treatise, and probably the main reason this is a vice. It is,
    above all, the vice that makes you sleep with other men's wives
    or unmarried daughters, or sexually abuse your subordinates,
    without compunction.

    [A] thinks the term went from 'unruly' to 'a man of unruly
    appetites', which is not quite right, but near enough. (It actually
    passed from a general sense to a more specific one.) He also else-
    where specifies that it covers people who drink too much (see
    [EE] 1231a19). The reader is invited to assume that being 'glut-
    tonous' covers that. But (a) sex and food seem to be the objects

he has in mind for most or all of this particular discussion, and (b) of those, the sexual sense is undoubtedly the dominant one in wider Greek.

52. *apples*: You can eat apples, of course, and even be gluttonous over them, arguably. So does [A] mean the blossom? Cf. [EE] 1231a10, where his example is 'flowers'. Theophrastus (fragment 4.5) notes that 'nuts, apples and pears' have an intrinsically pleasant smell, 'independently of being consumed'. (In fact, he says, they typically smell better if you don't eat them.) That seems to be the background thought here, too. You don't call someone a glutton for hanging an orange-scented air-freshener in their car; but you might if they had a bacon-scented air-freshener.

53. The next sentence reads: 'Taking pleasure in those kinds of smells is the mark of a gluttonous, lecherous man, because those things are the objects of his desire.' This seems to be a close alternative version of the sentence four lines before.

54. *pleasures of touch are*: It is extremely unlikely that the Greeks had their attitudes to this vice because the sense of touch is animal-like. [A] is trying to explain why these things are seen as vices – that's the fact he is starting from – and his analysis is philosophical speculation, not cultural anthropology. It is far more plausible that 'being lecherous' was viewed the way it was because of its close association with adultery, rape and sexual misconduct, as opposed to sexual desire in general. [A] himself often reveals this, by offering those as his core illustrations (see 1130a24ff., 1149b15ff.; *Politics* 1263b10 is very clear on this, too). It is the moral flavour of those wrongs (in VII.6 [A] calls sexual violations 'the things we're most right to be angered by') that underpins the attitude to 'being lecherous', not the role of touch, and not the role of physical pleasure per se. No Greek ever suggests that a man should be criticized in this way for sleeping too often, or too lecherously, with his own wife.

There are other difficulties with his analysis. Animals clearly enjoy the general pleasure of touch (i.e. beyond eating and sex) as much as 'a gentleman' enjoys a massage. Dogs and cats enjoy massages, too. Elephants enjoy baths. Some monkeys even enjoy hot baths. But that does not make those human pleasures 'animalistic' and disgraceful. Also, the appeal to the sense of touch cannot accommodate some paradigm forms of 'gluttony', e.g. alcoholism and drug-taking (see next note).

55. *entirely tactile*: As an account of people's excessive consumption of alcohol (or in a modern context, drugs) this can hardly

be right. True, the subtleties of the flavour are irrelevant. (Bill Maher: 'People don't drink bourbon to taste subtle hints of marzipan, pear and nutmeg. They drink it to forget that their life peaked in high school.') But the sense of touch is also irrelevant. I think this detail shows us clearly that [A] wasn't a drinker.

56. *famous foodie*: Philoxenus, the son of Eryxis, according to [EE] 1231a15–17. Note that Philoxenus is quite happy to boast about being a glutton. (Like Churchill on drinking: 'The water was not fit to drink. To make it palatable, we had to add whisky. By diligent effort, I learnt to like it.') This is a defining feature of all forms of *akolasia*, and what separates it from lack of self-control; it is unabashed. See VII.7, and notes VII.49–50.

57. *to 'bed' someone*: Literally, 'desires bed'. [A] is alluding to Homer's use of an older word for 'bed' (*eunē*) as a reference to sex. E.g. *Iliad* 24.129–31: 'My son, how long will you mourn and moan like this, with no thought for food or bed? Come on, it's good to sleep with and love a woman.' [A] seems to use the quote purely as a circumlocution, as if he were a little uncomfortable referring to sex directly. That may be why he calls sex, very oddly, 'sexual activity, so-called' at 1118a32.

58. *individual thing*: Literally, 'our thing'; in the sense, 'a matter of what each of us is like'; with implication of 'a matter of personal taste'. The 'us' pronoun is probably used in this sense in II.6, where [A] says that the mid-point, in each of the virtues, has to be 'relative to us', i.e. to each of us individually.

59. *{X-addicts}*: [A]'s claim would work for that English formulation: e.g. 'sex addict', 'coffee addict', 'chocolate addict', etc. The Greek formulation – '*philo*-X' – works in a similar way. [A] must have in mind terms like *philogune* ('womanizer'), *philomeirakios* ('mad about young boys'), *philoinos* ('wine addict'), etc.

60. *We use the same term*: The Greek term *akolastos*, in other contexts, can mean 'unruly' or 'undisciplined', and that seems to be its earlier sense.

BOOK IV

1. *not in warfare*: This sentence means that generosity has a domain that is distinct from the domains of bravery, moderation and fairness respectively.

2. *money*: Some translators, on the basis of this passage, and especially this remark, assume his term here, *chrēmata*, must mean

'wealth' or 'property'. In fact at this time the word simply meant 'money'. [A] means that he wants to use the term 'money' broadly, so that 'giving people money' includes giving people the things we spend money on. What he should have said – and does say, later – is that it is the notion of giving that he is using broadly ('giving money to others' will include spending money on them). As for 'making money' (literally 'taking/getting/getting hold of money'), that is the domain in which the other sense of *eleutherios* ('gentlemanly') comes into play. [A] will discuss ungentlemanly, low-class ways of making a living. We do not call those 'ungenerous' in English; hence the need for a double translation throughout most of the discussion. For [A], pimps and gamblers and petty thieves are *aneleutheroi* in the sense of 'ungentlemanly', not 'ungenerous'.

3. *no self-control and spend a lot*: That is, *asotia* sometimes means 'extravagant debauchery'. [A] reports that the word *asōtos* has two uses, and says that he only regards one of them as 'proper'. The one he doesn't accept (and does not discuss in what follows) persisted in Greek, with the sense 'wild living', 'debauchery', just as he reports. (It is the eponymous term in Luke's parable of the prodigal son.) It is virtually synonymous with *akolasia*.

4. *self-destructive*: [A] implies that *asōtos* literally means 'self-destroying'. How so? The standard derivation is from *sōzo* (to save, preserve), which seems morphologically somewhat plausible. But then *a-sōtos* would mean 'unsaveable', which (a) does not mean 'self-destroying' and (b), curiously, is not one of the word's recorded meanings, until centuries later. Aeschylus, a century earlier (*Agamemnon* l.1597) apparently uses it in the sense of 'destructive' – close to the etymology implied here by [A].

   I think that [A] is deriving it from *aaō*, 'to damage, harm' (aorist *asai*), along with the Ionian form, *ōutos* for *autos* ('self') – familiar to him from his native dialect – giving *as-ōutos* (ἀσ-ὠυτός), 'self-damaging'; analogous with, e.g., *philautos* (self-loving). The true origin of the term is obscure. [A] may be right.

5. *more about giving ... less about making money*: [A] here all but distinguishes the two senses of *eleutherios*. When it applies to giving, it means 'generous'; when it applies to how you make your money, it means 'gentlemanly'. And he is reporting, through this section, that the former sense ('generous') is the more important or dominant sense of the term. He made the same point in the opening lines: 'more about giving'.

It is striking that he never distinguishes the two senses of the term more explicitly. He shares the aristocratic attitude that blends the two together. The attitude is, approximately, that an interest in money is characteristic of the lower social classes; after all, they spend all their time making it and dealing with it directly. Genteel, 'decent' people, by contrast, never mention it or worry about it, so obviously they are less interested in it. This attitude is parochial, to say the least. In some societies, where more egalitarian attitudes prevail, the opposite idea often arises: that it is the wealthy classes who are greedy and obsessed with money. (And in some societies both attitudes exist side by side.) A culture's ethical vocabulary often reveals which of those attitudes is dominant.

6. *for not making money*: I.e. for not making money in a socially unacceptable way. All references to making money depend on the second sense of *eleutherios*, 'gentlemanly'. So [A]'s point here is that although it's ungentlemanly to make money by being, e.g., a pimp, you wouldn't thank someone for not being a pimp.

7. *easy-going*: Almost certainly this here has the colloquial sense of 'a softy in financial dealings'. [H] correctly paraphrases: 'naïve in financial dealings ... doesn't get upset when he's treated unfairly and makes a loss'.

8. *anti-Simonides*: Simonides was a shrewd and unabashed money-maker. He was once asked which is more desirable, being rich or being *sophos* (smart, an intellectual), and replied, 'I don't know. But I notice a lot of intellectuals knocking on rich men's doors.'

9. *going too far*: Consider the question, 'How far are you prepared to go to make a living?' [A] means that a pimp or pickpocket 'goes too far' in making money by their willingness to violate or ignore social norms and moral standards. He is talking about ungentlemanly ways of making a living. What he certainly doesn't mean here is that 'ungentlemanly' people make too much money, or 'go too far' in that sense. Hence the qualification 'albeit on a small scale'. Compare in English 'petty thief', 'small-time crook'. The qualification is repeated and explained later (1122a5–7) when [A] says that people who make money unethically on a vast scale tend just to be called 'criminals', not 'ungentlemanly' (because they are not typically associated with low social class).

10. *not making any money*: In this paragraph and the next, [A] has in mind wealthy young aristocrats who spend freely, but who by the social conventions of the time regard earning money as

degrading, and hence rapidly run out of it. Later, [A] gives examples of degrading ways of making a living: being a pimp, petty thief, loan shark or gambler. But his examples are inadequate as a portrait of the aristocratic attitudes he is relying upon through these passages. Upper-class Athenians considered it equally degrading to be a professional painter, guitar-player, sculptor, schoolteacher, etc. [A] discusses this fact in *Politics* 1337b. But here, all of [A]'s examples are disreputable by almost any standard. (I wonder if he finds it awkward to state, bluntly, that working for a living is a moral failing.)

11. *as we said*: He didn't quite say this. What he said was that it's rare for both aspects of extravagance to be found together. By implication, you usually find the first (large spending) without the second (gentlemanly horror of money-making); i.e. most big spenders are also ungentlemanly.

12. *ungentlemanly*: [A] is now discussing wealthy men who spend freely but make their money in 'ungentlemanly' ways. He gives no examples of how exactly these men make their money. (His later examples are far too small in scale. How many pimps or pickpockets would have 'hangers-on' and paid entertainers?) What he has in mind are wealthy businessmen, merchants, traders – men of self-made wealth. The nouveau riche. Such people – e.g. Cleon in the 420s, Anthemion and Anytus in the late 400s, Ismenias (the Theban) in the 390s – were much reviled by more genteel Athenians like Thucydides, Plato, Xenophon and [A].

13. *not honourable . . . right way*: Literally, 'Their givings are not honourable, or for that reason [i.e. they don't give because it is honourable to do so], or the right way.'

14. *cumin-splitters*: A Greek expression; people who will cut a cumin seed in half rather than let someone have half of it for free. Like English 'skinflints': people would even skin a flint to save money.

15. *gamblers, petty thieves, muggers*: This completes the examples: pimps, money-lenders, gamblers, petty thieves, bandits. [Asp.] adds 'and tax-collectors' (another much-detested profession, familiar from the New Testament).

16. *in a way that's fitting*: Probably not correct. The compound was formed with the original sense of 'befitting a great [man]', or possibly 'in a grand style'; but not 'grandly and fittingly'.

17. *I gave [food] to a drifter*: *Odyssey* 17.420: 'I too once lived in a wealthy house, and was a prosperous man, and many a time I gave [food] to a drifter.' I.e. feeding the homeless is generous, but never lavish or grand.

18. *qualities*: [A] uses the term *aretē* here in its (rare) generic sense.
     'The *aretē* of a public work is not the same as that of a posses-
     sion', literally, 'The goodness of a work isn't the same as that of
     a possession.' He means 'we don't judge a public work the way
     we judge a possession', but is working towards the claim, below,
     that *megaloprepeia* (lavishness, grandeur) is itself the *aretē* of a
     public work, i.e. is what makes such a work as good as it can be.
     [A] is the only writer who ever speaks of the *aretē* of a 'work'
     (*ergon*), so it must have sounded very odd, as in the first, literal
     version above. I wonder if he is not revealing here that *megalo-
     prepeia* was primarily a quality of things, not of human beings.

     My assumption, with the ancient commentators, is that the
     point here is to explain the difference between lavishness and
     generosity. They explain: 'A merely costly object (e.g. some-
     thing made of gold and precious jewels) might be a generous gift
     to one's city, but not grand or lavish.' For that matter, a cash gift
     can be generous, but lacks grandeur.

19. *background*: Some good scholars interpret these words to mean:
     'It suits people who already have the resources.' But it probably
     means: 'people who already have a tradition or history of such
     things'; i.e. people who come from lavish-spending households
     of long standing. The sense seems proved by [EE] 1233b11,
     where [A] says – using the same term – that Themistocles (though
     rich enough) was criticized for spending on a religious embassy
     to Olympia because of his humble background. Cf. Plutarch
     (*Themistocles* 5), who adds that Themistocles offended people
     by spending 'above his station' – [A]'s phrase from 1122b28.
     [A] means that the silver spoons are best provided by people
     born with them already in their mouths.

     In the next phrase, when [A] says 'either personally or . . .'
     (literally, 'either themselves, or') I assume he means 'either
     because they have already done such things in the past, them-
     selves, or their relatives have'. It is extremely unlikely that he
     intends a reference to self-made wealth. A clear implication of
     the entire discussion (and bluntly asserted in the [EE] passage)
     is that this kind of spending does not suit the newly wealthy.

20. *whole city is enthused*: What does [A] have in mind here? [Asp.]
     offers the example of 'the whole city being excited about arms,
     or horses', by which he probably means gladiator shows and
     chariot races. The first is a (Roman-period) anachronism; the
     second may be right. Funding a four-horse chariot at the Olym-
     pics, say, was a private matter, but at the same time aroused

enormous excitement in the whole city. (Cf. billionaires who buy a famous soccer team and fill it with expensive players, and generate great excitement in Manchester, or Barcelona.)

21. *modest*: Literally, 'ungentlemanly' (*aneleutheron*). The small cost is within reach even of the lower classes. Yet a lavish (aristocratic) man will spend even that relatively small amount with superior style and taste.

22. *in Megara*: Megarian comedy was famously crude, but also apparently involved very luxurious costumes. Athenians seem to have looked on the Megarian style in something like the way that we regard Liberace's pink sequin tuxedos; or late Elvis.

23. *sense of pride*: *Megalopsuchia*. Literally, 'greatness of soul (or spirit)', but strongly implying 'proud-spiritedness'. The traditional (Gringlish) translation is 'magnanimous' (this does not mean 'magnanimous'; it stands for the Latin word *magnanimus*). The word has been more or less correctly translated as 'pride' for over a century, first by [R]. It is sometimes translated etymologically, as 'great-souled'. But that literalism is not really even literal, since the *mega-* component of the word here directly implies pride for Greek speakers: *mega legein* and *megalēgorein* both mean 'to speak proudly' (sometimes 'to speak haughtily', 'to boast'), *mega phronein* means 'to be proud', 'to feel pride at'; *megalo-phron* means 'proud-minded' or simply 'proud'. Those sister idioms do not exist in English, and the connection with them is rendered invisible if we say 'great-souled'.

'Sense of pride' must be taken in a positive sense, as in the following characteristic uses in English: 'Socrates was too proud to beg for mercy'; 'Don't let him disrespect you like that; where's your sense of pride?' 'My sense of pride won't allow me to be part of your corrupt scheme.' That is why I have chosen 'sense of pride' over simply 'pride'. The former is always used positively; the latter less reliably so. It is also more literal. *Megalopsuchos* could reasonably be analysed as 'proud-minded'.

We associate a sense of pride with standing up to oppression, mistreatment, inequality or humiliation; also with integrity, and maintaining our moral standards. *Megalopsuchia* has a very similar pattern of usage. [A] is no egalitarian, and does not see the virtue as applying in (all) those ways. In fact he sees it as appropriate only to certain men in their dealings with certain other men. (I reflect this fact in my pronoun choices.) For him, the paradigm is a kind of philosophically revised version of aristocratic pride – which he also discusses – and the discussion is laced with implied criticisms of people of the lower classes who aspire to rise above their station. But, for all that, there is a recognizable virtue here, and he describes it well.

A sense of pride is a matter of knowing your worth, demanding respect, not accepting a position that is beneath you, not acting in a way that is beneath you (hence, not being petty or vindictive). In *Posterior Analytics* (97b16–26) [A] offers examples of people famous for being *megalopsuchoi*: Achilles, Ajax, Alcibiades, Socrates, Lysander. The Socrates example is helpful. Think of his defiance at his trial; his unshakeable self-belief; the way he questions his supposed 'betters' (living or dead) on equal terms; his equanimity in the face of death.

(Incidentally, the Gringlish term 'magnanimous', after centuries of slow semantic drift away from its Latin origin, now only picks out one of these several features in normal English, namely a lack of pettiness and a willingness to forgive, as a virtue of the powerful and victorious. As such it is now much closer to *epieikeia*, discussed by [A] in V.10, than to *megalopsuchia*.)

Pauline Christianity, with its idea that we are all sinners, does not always sit well with the idea that a strong sense of self-worth is an important virtue. That is irrelevant to the accuracy of the translation, obviously. But it may be the origin of a traditional anxiety about using 'pride' in connection with *megalopsuchia*.

24. *sees himself as being of little worth*: [A] is concerned to head off the possible misunderstanding that a sense of pride is just a matter of having an accurate sense of self-worth; the right amount for whatever one's worth happens to be. He so often claims that a given virtue is about having, or feeling, just the right amount of something or other, that it is easy to see why that mistake would arise here.

25. *sensible*: I.e. *sōphrōn*, elsewhere 'moderate'. [A]'s claim (see III.10) that *sōphrosunē* strictly applies to physical pleasures does not even match his own usage, let alone wider Greek. Here he uses the term in a different, older way: 'sensible', 'of sound mind'. For this see *Protagoras* 323b: 'Telling the truth about your abilities [e.g. not claiming to be an expert doctor when you aren't] is seen as *sōphrosunē* [sensible behaviour]'. The word also has social implications: people of lower rank who know their place and stick to it are 'sensible', 'well behaved'.

26. *greatest of all external goods*: Elsewhere (1169b10) [A] claims that friends and family are 'surely the greatest of external goods' – which on balance seems rather more plausible.

27. *nothing is all that important*: Since your sense of pride means
    you don't really care about money or poverty, why would you
    ever steal, or cheat anybody? And since it implies that you face
    death with equanimity, why would you ever panic on a battle-
    field? There is something undignified, degrading, about behaving
    that way in the face of those rather petty setbacks.

28. *case by case*: [A] means, 'If you think through each virtue in
    detail, imagining someone with a sense of pride doing the cor-
    responding wrong or shameful thing (i.e. failing to exercise that
    virtue) . . . it will be clear that' etc.

29. *every success or setback*: Compare Kipling, 'If you can meet
    with Triumph and Disaster / And treat those two imposters just
    the same / . . . you'll be a Man, my son!' Kipling's popular poem
    'If' has several other clear points of contact with [A]'s *megalo-
    psuchos*; perhaps by direct influence. [NE] was strongly in
    vogue in the 1890s, when the poem was written.

30. *the point is to be respected for them*: [A]'s prudishness gives
    him a blind spot here. For lots of men, the point of acquiring
    money, power and especially respect {prestige, status} is to
    make them more attractive to women. (And for others, even if
    that is not their goal, it remains part of the explanation for how
    those kinds of interests, in general, evolved.)

31. *for no good reason at all*: Or 'for any old reason' – i.e. snobs
    feel superior for empty reasons, like the fact that they drive a Mer-
    cedes, attended a prestigious university, or have a certain postcode.
    We might add here that physical beauty, a classic 'advantage of
    fortune', can make people scornful and disdainful too.

32. *take risks . . . seek out danger*: The manuscripts are divided as to
    whether [A] says, he does not 'constantly face danger' (*pukno-
    kindunos*) or does not 'bother with small risks' (*mikrokindunos*),
    which itself might mean 'he does not face risks over small mat-
    ters'. I prefer the former. He may also have said both. But the
    overall sense is clear. A sense of pride makes you brave, but not
    reckless, and not a serial risk-taker.

33. *not every form of life is worth living*: E.g. better to die than
    live a life of slavery, or of grovelling deference, or a life in which
    your country has been invaded, or (Socrates' case) a life in which
    you have had to renounce your principles, or (Achilles' case) a
    life in which you have failed to avenge your friend. [Asp.]: 'He
    prefers to do the honourable thing, and to die for what's hon-
    ourable.' This matches what I said in my note above: that we
    associate defiance with a sense of pride.

34. *doesn't like work*: Sounds strange as a compliment, especially as it could also be translated 'he's lazy'. On the aristocratic view, work is degrading. This sentence nicely catches the contradiction between the aristocratic love of idleness (i.e. a life of high-status leisure) and their admiration for certain kinds of high-prestige activity (war, politics, hunting). Expending effort is acceptable as long as it reflects high social position. So hunting is respectable; but not being a fisherman. Guitar-playing is all right, but not for money (see *Politics* 1337b).

35. *they ... talk about it ... those things*: Most translators (by punctuation) take this as: 'and they speak as if they'll be respected for them'. But the faux pas here is that they talk about those things, i.e. at all. From [A]'s gentlemanly point of view, you should not mention your wealth.

36. *back at the start*: A reference to II.7 (1107b25). The discussion there promises a longer explanation later, but is in fact almost as long as this one.

37. *leans a bit towards the shortfall*: I.e. 'good-natured' implies someone who does not quite get angry enough.

38. *touchy*: Or 'quick-tempered'. In Greek, *akrocholoi*. People with a short fuse. [A] may be suggesting that the word refers to their over-the-top fieriness (*akro-* can mean 'top', 'highest'). Or he may be emphasizing the fact that they get angry 'at anything'. The *akro-* more likely implies someone who reacts to the slightest touch (*akro-* also means 'tip').

39. *they 'know how to lead'*: The thought here reminds me of Xenophon's description of the Spartan general Clearchus (*Anabasis* 2.6.8): 'He was a natural leader. He knew how to look out for his army and make sure it had what it needed, and how to make his troops obey him. And he did it by being harsh. He was grim-faced and had a rough, rasping voice; and his punishments were firm, sometimes angry, such that even he regretted them – but there was a point to them.'

40. *As for humouring people*: [A] means 'as for those who always humour people'. But he then distinguishes between people who do so to everyone, and people who always humour one particular person, like those odd generals who follow Kim Jong Un around taking notes on his every word and laughing at his feeble jokes.

41. *these kinds of qualities*: almost certainly means 'these rather minor, morally less important qualities'. See next note.

42. *that's how it works for everything*: The 'everything' pronoun is neuter, not feminine. This shows that it cannot mean 'for all the

virtues'. If you look closely, you will see that [A] stopped using the term *aretē* ('a virtue') after the first line of his discussion of ambition. He does not refer to morally less important qualities as 'virtues'. (For that matter, he expressed ambivalence even about some of the 'vices' connected with generosity and sense of pride – he twice qualified himself by noting that they 'don't really make you a bad person', which means that they are not quite 'vices' in the full sense.) At a parallel point in [EE] (1234a24) he tells us explicitly that several of these same qualities are not *aretai*, because they do not involve (morally significant) choices. In the light of these facts, it seems clear that in the current passage [A] means that we'll be more confident that virtues – morally important qualities – are middle states if we also find that all good qualities of character of whatever sort – even the ones that are not *aretai* – are likewise middle states. (Having said that, even these minor qualities are still clearly of some moral importance, and that too explains their being discussed with the *aretai*.)

43. *straight-talker*: *Authekastos*, almost certainly meaning 'a person who [calls] each thing just what it is'. [Asp.] agrees. We might translate 'someone who calls a spade a spade', but for the fact that [A] would not like to think of any person he admires having any occasion to see a spade.

44. *we're not talking . . . morally right*: [A] means that the character trait – preference for truth-telling per se – shows itself most, and best, in the absence of the clearest moral reasons for not lying to people. So the purer cases justify the entire proposal of a distinct character trait.

But perhaps [A] is also ducking a problem. He means that he wishes to leave to one side the question of honesty in the context of contracts, oaths, treaties, vows, promises. For Greeks, those would paradigm cases of doing what is *díkaion* – paradigm moral obligations, as we might say. So the 'different virtue' [A] alludes to could only be some particular form of *dikaiosunē* – namely, the particular virtue we call being honest, (straight, trustworthy). The implication here is that [A] will indeed discuss this virtue elsewhere, presumably in his treatment of *dikaiosunē*, in book V. But he never does. [NE] curiously offers no discussion at all of promise-keeping, oaths, perjury, etc. The only particular virtue he discusses in connection with being *díkaios* is fairness. And fairness is not what makes us keep our promises, nor does [A] in any way imply that it is.

The explanation for this may be that promise-keeping and oath-taking, for Greeks, are so tightly bound up with piety (taking an oath, by definition, involves appealing to a god's oversight) that [A] cannot discuss it without being blunt about his views on piety. (Indeed, for many Greeks, the 'other virtue' that [A] alludes to here would actually be piety itself; or piety construed as one branch of *dikaiosunē*.)

45. *commendable*: We likewise, in English, associate truth-telling of the morally important kinds (e.g. 'being honest' by returning someone's wallet, not overcharging people, admitting to what you owe, not lying about an opponent, etc.) with pure truth-telling ('I'm just being honest' – now in the sense 'frank'). [A]'s idea here is that the one kind of 'honesty' overlaps with the other. Lying about yourself even in what seem harmless ways might shade into, or make you more inclined to, forms of deceit that do harm or secure unfair advantages.

46. *overstatements being kind of annoying*: A condensed thought. [A] means that it's classier to understate yourself slightly, so as to make sure you avoid ever overstating your abilities or accomplishments, which people will find annoying. This is an application of his general principle that one way to 'hit the middle' is to push deliberately too far away from the side you want to avoid (see 1109b5).

47. *or material gain*: [A] means that 'being a liar' is likewise not just an ability. You aren't a liar just if you know how to lie. You have to like lying, or have a tendency to lie, for money (or whatever). It has to be a feature of your character and your choices. Likewise being a charlatan or phoney.

48. *intellectual*: [A] almost certainly means sophists in particular. See 1164a31, where he describes sophists as making money from extravagant promises. His quip at 1095a25 may be a reference to intellectual charlatans, too.

49. *again*: I.e. phonies mostly lay claim to very noteworthy abilities ('I can cure cancer with crystals'; 'I can talk to your dead grandmother'; 'I can solve the paradoxes of human suffering') and self-deprecators typically disclaim the same ('I have no special wisdom'; 'I have no very amazing talent').

50. *upper-class tramps*: This is a guess, and could well be wrong. The word is *baukopanourgoi*. It seems to be Athenian slang. The commentators are unsure what it means. No other Greek writer ever uses it. [Asp.] records the tentative suggestion that it refers to people who pretend not to have money. You might

(just about) parse it as 'luxury scoundrels', 'pampered rogues'. If 'scoundrel' has a social-class sense, then perhaps it refers to wealthy Athenians who affected working-class dress and tastes. So they pretend not to have wealth and disguise their class. The next example (Athenians who wear Spartan clothes) then seems rather similar, if we take *baukopanourgoi* that way. (Compare English 'trustafarians', 'mockneys', 'bohemians'.)

51. *Spartan clothes*: Spartan clothes were famously plain. So wealthy Athenians who dressed in the Spartan manner were dressing down – pretentiously. Plato teases the same people at *Protagoras* 342c. (Obviously, it isn't the Spartans themselves that [A] is saying are 'phonies'.) Athenians in general tended to dress down (perhaps a feature of any democratic society), a fact noted by the grumpy aristocratic author of *Constitution of the Athenians* (see I.10), who bemoans the fact that in Athens most people dress just like their slaves, making it frustratingly hard to slap impertinent slaves in the street without striking a citizen by mistake.

52. *humourless yokels*: See note II.46.

53. *character in motion*: [A] cannot just mean that telling jokes is an exercise of character, and in that sense 'motion' of character. All virtues (and vices) involve the exercise of character. He means that telling jokes is the character equivalent of dancing, or juggling or acrobatics (as opposed to walking or running): i.e. pure display. [**Asp.**], rightly I think, sees dance imagery in the term *eutropoi*; he glosses, 'rhythmical'. *Eutropoi* can also mean 'of good character'. That's playing a role in [A]'s etymological claim, too.

54. *older comedies*: E.g. Aristophanes' plays, which are indeed often very obscene, even by late-twentieth-century standards. 'Recent comedies': [A] would have to mean what we now call 'Middle Comedy', none of which survives. But Aristophanes' last play, *Plutus*, shows some of the changing fashion. It has none of the obscenity of his earlier plays. New Comedy (which survives in the works of Menander and then indirectly in Roman and Shakespearean comedies) illustrates the same transformation. [A]'s claims here about what makes for good humour are rather debatable. Most people find Aristophanes funnier than Menander. Also, he does not mention that Aristophanes' plays were also far more political than Middle Comedy. He makes no note at all of the important civic role of satire.

55. *irrelevant to our moral virtues*: This seems inconsistent with [A]'s claim in book III (1110a20–33) that people are sometimes

put under pressure to do 'shaming' and degrading things, and
deserve praise for their reluctance and resistance. Obviously,
the relevant virtue there is a sense of shame. 'I would be deeply
ashamed to parade down the street naked'; 'I would be ashamed
to scrub the pavement in front of this crowd' becomes more
than a meaningless hypothetical if someone is trying to force
you to do it. Clearly, even if you are actually forced into it, you
still feel the shame and embarrassment. In general, it also seems
extremely unrealistic (almost inhumane) of [A] to assert that
good people simply never find themselves in positions that cause
them shame – as if good people never make mistakes, or as if
it is not completely human to feel shame and embarrassment,
sometimes, even if we do not also feel responsible.

BOOK V

1.   What follows is [A]'s discussion of *dikaiosunē*, the virtue of *being
díkaios, that is, of being someone who (reliably) does what's
right. In normal English we typically refer to this as the (very
broad) quality of being a moral or ethical person. In slightly older
English we called it righteousness, the broad quality of being a
righteous person. (For reasons of historical tone, and because of
the more direct and obvious connection with the underlying
adjective, 'right', I will mostly use the latter translation.)

   The opposite of *dikaiosunē* is *adikía*, the vice of *being ádikos*.
That is the (very broad) quality of being an immoral or unethical
or unrighteous person.

   These are the 'general', i.e. broader, senses of these terms, based
on the broader sense of the underlying, more basic concepts of
díkaion and *ádikon*: right and wrong.

   Those more basic terms also have a particular, narrower sense:
fair and unfair. (They can also mean 'honest' and 'dishonest',
but [A] does not discuss that sense of the terms.) Corresponding
to that narrower, particular sense of *díkaion*, the virtue term
dikaiosunē picks out the more particular virtue of being fair;
i.e. of being a fair person, and *adikía* refers to the more particular vice of being an unfair person.

   So, since the single term *díkaion* means both 'right' and 'fair',
the reader must understand that in the opening section of this
book [A] addresses a problem that does not arise in English. We
have, and use, two words here, not one. And in so far as it does

arise, it is easy to solve. If we want to explain in English that 'right' (in some context) means 'fair', we can say that it means 'fair'. If we want to describe someone as specifically a fair person, as opposed to a more generally ethical or moral person, we call them 'fair'. [A] can't do that because he doesn't have a separate word for 'fair'. That's the point.

So, to distinguish between *díkaion*-right and *díkaion*-fair, he initially sets up approximate pointers, to direct Greek speakers to the two senses (assuming, of course, that they are already fully familiar with them) before going on to analyse them in more depth. It's rather as we might say in English, 'Let's talk about what's funny, i.e. both funny-ha-ha and funny-strange' (assuming, of course, that the listener is perfectly familiar with both senses). [A] briefly explains *díkaion*-right as being equivalent to what is required of you by laws and social norms. So he labels it '*díkaion*-lawful'. And he picks out *díkaion*-fair as being tied to ideas of equality. He labels it '*díkaion*-equal'. Both seem reasonable ways of pointing his listeners towards the concepts of right, and fair, respectively. Then the analysis begins.

Since the opening discussion involves detailed claims about the Greek words themselves, I have left those words in the text, as the only feasible way of showing you what [A] is doing. At no point is the reader required to know the meaning of any Greek terms. All terms are explained as we go along. And wherever possible, I revert to translating *díkaion*-right as 'right' and *díkaion*-fair as 'fair' (including, for example, in the second sentence of the book, where we can be sure that the reference is to fairness only).

After the account of *díkaion*-fair comes to an obvious and signalled end, the original editors of the treatise added a miscellany of related discussions that have *díkaion* as their subject in some way or other. These subsequent passages quite clearly deal with right and wrong in the broad sense. I will discuss this again at the point where the added material begins.

2. *do the opposite of X*: [A]'s expression here is awkward, but this seems the right reading. Literally: 'But as for a disposition, one that is the opposite [of a certain kind of behaviour] can't also be of [i.e. produce] that opposite [behaviour].' So, although knowing how to play the guitar can also make you good at playing it badly (if you so choose), bravery, the opposite of cowardice, cannot cause you to behave in that opposite way, like a coward. Generosity cannot make you behave ungenerously. The key point here is that character traits are partly desiderative. [A] discusses

this further in chapter 9 (see 1137a4–30) and in book VI, chapters 2–5 (see especially 1140b22). The idea that righteousness,
dikaiosunē, paradoxically might enable opposite forms of behaviour was raised by Plato (see *Republic* 334a): 'If a righteous,
{honest} man is [by definition] someone who's good at looking
after other people's money, isn't he also bound to be good at
stealing it?' [A] here (and in book VI) offers his solution to that
problem, which is that an honest man isn't just someone who
knows how to do something: he is also someone who characteristically wants certain things. He is, in fact, extremely bad at
stealing people's money, because he strongly wants not to steal
anything. [A] returns to this point in the latter part of chapter 9.

3.   *unfair person*: From this point on, except in those places where
      [A] refers to the double sense of the relevant terms, I will trans-
      late *díkaios* as 'righteous [person]', or 'fair [person]', depending
      on which of the two senses is in play, and *díkaion* as 'right' or
      'fair'. Similarly for *ádikos* and *ádikon*.

4.   *normally good things*: E.g. money, status, health, beauty, chil-
      dren, victory etc. These are good under normal circumstances,
      but sometimes do you harm.
            Most people pray for these things. Instead they should pray
      that they will be able to make the best use of them. E.g. not
      'I hope I win the lottery', but 'If I find myself with a lot of money,
      I hope I'm able to do some good with it.' And they should
      primarily choose, or aim for, or value, a life of exercising good
      character. That raises the possibility that in [A]'s view people
      have no need to pray at all. Most Greeks take it for granted that
      you only pray for external goods.

5.   *laws and social norms*: I.e. *nomoi*. The Greek term very easily
      means both (it can also mean 'customs', 'conventions'), and
      in those places where I judge that [A] intends to cover both I
      translate the term with this doublet. Sometimes the term means
      'laws' to the exclusion of unofficial norms (as at 1162b22). But
      in this discussion it is perfectly clear that [A] means that right
      and wrong depend on society and its rules of all kinds, formal
      and informal. See 1180b1 for an explicit reference to those two
      senses of the term. (Also Thucydides 2.37.3.)

6.   *or the people in charge*: See next note.

7.   *good thing for someone else*: I.e., as the line originally implied,
      your being righteous (ethical, law-abiding) is a good thing
      for everyone else, not for you. [A] does not wholly accept this
      view – he certainly thinks being righteous is good for you as

well. But he does partly accept it. He agrees that being an ethical or righteous person fundamentally implies respecting and
serving the interests of others. He also probably even agrees
that it means serving others to your own detriment, if the laws
and moral norms under which you live are corrupt, and stacked
in favour of the powerful.

The saying is found at *Republic* 343c1–5, where it is placed
in the mouth of an amoralist character, Thrasymachus. But [A]
is probably not quoting Thrasymachus, or the *Republic*. The
humanist – not amoralist – thinker, the sophist Antiphon, a
contemporary of Socrates, is more likely the actual source of the
saying (and, at the same time, the model for Thrasymachus).
Plato vigorously attacked him by that fictional recasting. [A] is
partly agreeing with Antiphon, and defending his view. 'Antiphon is at least partly right in his claim that doing what's right
is typically good for someone else.'

Antiphon (in *On Truth*) proposed that codes of right and
wrong (even the ones sanctioned by our deepest notions of piety)
are created by and for human beings, and sustained by each
society's particular laws and cultural norms. Hence, he argues,
to be righteous is 'to follow the laws and norms of whatever city
you are a citizen of'. But moral norms are often corrupt or
defective or stupid, and do not always best serve the people who
abide by them; 'doing the right thing' often just means serving
others, and harming your real ('natural') interests.

It seems fairly likely that he used the example of slavery:
slaves do not benefit from 'doing the right thing', i.e. observing
the laws and rules that require them to obey their masters. By
being 'righteous' in that sense they only benefit their masters,
against their own natural interests. Another example he offers
is the common Greek view that children must always obey their
parents. When parents are cruel and abusive, says Antiphon,
that religious and moral norm harms the people who obey it.

[A] is not referencing all of these views here. But notice that
he explicates the motto in a distinctly Antiphonian way, by noting that 'doing the right thing' sometimes means 'serving the
interests of a ruler'. Similarly, back at 1129b15 he conceded that
'doing the right thing' (basically) means abiding by the laws and
social norms of your society, and therefore sometimes means
serving the interests of 'the people in charge', i.e. by clear implication, not your own. Antiphon's ideas are referred to again at
1134b24, where [A] says they are 'not correct . . . but they're

sort of correct'. And see *Politics* 1.3 and 1.5–6, where [A] outlines (what was probably) Antiphon's anti-slavery argument
and agrees with parts of it. He also raises Antiphon's question
of whether children must always obey their parents, in 9.2.

8.   The example seems strained. It's true that if a man seduced a
married woman just for money (e.g. to rob her, or trick her out
of her money) we might not call him lecherous. But would we call
him 'unfair'? And even if we would, is a lecherous adulterer any
less unfair? (Why not think that it's very unfair to treat your sexual pleasure as more important than someone else's marriage?)

[A] is right to say that Greeks would call a purely mercenary
adulterer *ádikos*, and not lecherous (*akolastos*). He is accurately
reporting Greek usage. But contrary to his own analysis, I suspect that that would be the general sense of *ádikos* ('wrongdoer',
'unethical'). Even a thieving adulterer is still a wrongdoer; but
he's not lecherous, like a lustful or romantic adulterer. In the
same way we might say that a professional assassin who coldly
commits a violent murder is certainly unrighteous and a criminal (*ádikos*), but not bad-tempered, like the man who commits
the same crime in a fit of anger.

Still, [A]'s idea here could be expressed with an emended
example. In the opening of Homer's *Iliad*, Agamemnon, although
he already has plenty of concubines, expropriates Achilles' only
consort, Briseis, out of wounded pride (not sexual desire) and to
assert his dominance. Achilles, who does most of the fighting,
flies into a rage. Agamemnon is being unfair, but not lecherous.
(The story of David and Bathsheba is similar. See 2 Samuel 12.)

9.   *besides adikía*: [A] means that Greek speakers only ever call this
adikía, as if there were no special term for it, because *adikía*
is (apparently) just the general word for 'wrongdoing' (or for
'being unrighteous'). He infers that in this context *adikía* must
in fact have a special, narrower sense (namely 'unfairness').

10.   *unequal [dealing]*: Here are these two claims as they would normally be expressed in English, with its larger vocabulary.
(1) 'Unfair' is not the same as 'wrong', it's a particular form of
'wrong'. (2) 'Every unfair action is wrong, but not every wrong
action is unfair.'

11.   *assault, imprisonment, manslaughter ... insult*: These 'unwilling dealings' are, of course, crimes and wrongs. But it is important
not to understand [A] as meaning that they are themselves his
examples of particular *adikía*. (With the traditional Gringlish
translation, 'injustices', that mistake is easier to make.) It is only

the subsequent compensation, or redress, awarded by a judge, that counts as the particular *díkaion* or *ádikon* here (a fair, or unfair, compensation), not the wrongs themselves, which are clearly general wrongs (although a few of them may also be, as it happens, acts of distributive unfairness).

It is unclear whether [A] also means for this analysis of 'making amends' to cover the question of punishments. He does not say so explicitly, or at any other point address the issue of punishment directly. See below, note V.14.

12. *Democrats say*: The implied context here is debates over who should rule, and the sharing of political power. [A] is reporting the debate over who should rule. (He discusses this with great insight in the *Politics*, especially book III, chapters 9–13.) This is such a central example of 'distributive fairness' that he can signal the domain with just the barest allusion (unless a more explicit reference to political power has dropped out of the text). But the preceding claim about desert obviously applies to all cases of distributive fairness, not just this one.

13. *with an overlap*: The Greek term is *sunechēs*, a 'continuous proportion'. Elsewhere that has a technical mathematical sense. But here, as explained by the commentators, [A] means a proportion with an overlapping term. A is to B as B is to C. The common term ties the two parts of the proportion together; makes it 'contiguous'.

14. *harm done to the victim*: Do these claims also cover the notion of fair punishment? In a criminal case, a punishment might, in a sense, be thought of as 'evening things out' between criminal and victim (or 'settling the score'); and we speak of a perpetrator 'paying the price' for a crime just in reference to punishment rather than literal payment. And [A] notes that Greek for 'penalty', *zēmia*, is also the term for 'loss'. The implication is that penalties (and punishments?) by definition impose a corrective loss on the perpetrator. 'The loss to the victim was such and such; therefore the following loss [i.e. penalty] now needs to be imposed on the perpetrator.'

[H] assumes that punishments are included here: 'The judge restores the difference by fining the wrongdoer ... or hurting him ... or killing him.'

But on the other hand, punishment, especially when carried out by the state, is often primarily a deterrent; and deterrence might have nothing whatsoever to do with compensation or score-settling.

The deterrent aspect of punishment is well known to [A]. It is discussed prominently in Plato's *Protagoras* (324b), one of his favourite texts. Plus, [A] himself alludes to the deterrent role of punishment at 1180a5–10. He compares legal punishments to whipping unruly animals into line. (And he certainly doesn't think that the point of whipping a donkey is to impose a loss on the animal that settles the score with the owner.)

So, this cannot be [A]'s full treatment of punishment. It is best to assume that the primary setting is what we now call 'civil' law, where the victim of a tort or a crime (the analysis covers both indifferently) petitions a court for redress, or a restoration of their loss. Some aspects and forms of punishment will be covered by this, but certainly not all.

In fact, under ancient Athenian law all trials were, in effect, civil suits. It was the victims of a crime (or the relatives of a murder victim), not state-appointed prosecutors, who pressed the charges and presented the case, in the form of a demand for redress (of which punishment might form one part).

15. *the whole line is divided exactly in two*: There is no doubt that [A] drew a diagram here to illustrate his divided line. The diagram would have been similar to the one I provide a few paragraphs below. (The second diagram makes the same point in a slightly more elaborate, three-line version. These appear to be duplicated sections, and duplicate diagrams, just like the duplicated diagrams in chapter 5.)

16. *three equal lines*: The diagram described in this paragraph very closely matches the one described in the previous paragraph (so much so that I can supply a single illustration for both). The concluding sentence is missing; something that would explain exactly how to restore the two lines back to parity (by taking C'D from CD and giving it to AA'). Presumably it was so similar to the equivalent point in the last paragraph that the editor felt it was mere repetition. But that leaves the paragraph oddly unfinished.

17. *no restrictions*: I.e. in such contexts, making a profit, even a huge profit, is not illegal. But in 'unwilling exchanges' – i.e. crimes or torts – any 'profit' is by definition illegal.

18. *Rhadamanthus*: Legendary judge of the underworld. The lines are from a lost poem of Hesiod. 'If a man sows evil, evil shall he reap; let him suffer exactly . . .' etc.

19. *He also needs to be punished*: [M]: 'If a slave hits a free man, he shouldn't be struck just once in return, but many times.' This example is in [A]'s mind here.

20. *Proportional reciprocity*: I.e. trade, where people exchange things of equivalent value. 'Exactly equal payback' seems to refer, here, to the idea just mentioned, of doing to others exactly and whatever they do to you.

21. *a temple of 'the Gratitudes'*: Or of 'the Graces'. The Greek term *Charis* (always translated 'Grace' when personified as a goddess) also means, depending on context, 'favour', 'gratitude' and 'thanks', and related verbs mean both 'to do someone a favour' and 'to thank'. This translates better into (e.g.) Latin, Italian or Spanish, where 'the Graces' (*Gratiae*, *Le Grazie*, *Las Gracias*) still means 'the Thanks'. (In older English, too, *charis* was translated *thonke*, not 'grace'.)

The received text here reads: 'That's also why they[?] treat[?] a temple of the Graces as in the way[?].' The text is hopelessly corrupt, but usually taken (unconvincingly) to mean: 'That's why they build temples to the Graces in prominent places.'

The Gratitudes, or Graces, were new gods in the Greek pantheon. Their cult was invented by King Eteocles of Orchomenos in early historical times. Several writers (Strabo, Pausanias, Theocritus, Hesiod) mention this curious fact – that he built the first temple 'of the Graces' and invented some goddesses out of thin air – and it is far more likely that [A], likewise, was referring to the creation of the cult, rather than commenting on the position of temples. That point makes good sense in context: 'Gratitude is so important they even made a goddess out of it.' (Compare [EE] 1233b26 for a similar claim about *Nemesis*.) See [TA] for the text.

22. *have to be equalized*: There is a sentence following this that I excise: 'This is also true of the other crafts. Because they would be annihilated if, when A did something to B, to a certain extent, and in a certain way, B did not have the same thing done to it, to the same extent, and in the same way.' The same sentence also appeared at 1132b9 in chapter 4, where, likewise, it seemed irrelevant, and there it is excised in Bywater's text (and hence not registered at all in my version). But Bywater includes it here. I agree with [S] that the sentence doesn't belong in either place.

It seems to be a general claim about objects acting on each other, e.g. a knife cutting a rope, a hammer striking a nail. If the knife cuts, the rope is cut; if the knife cuts slowly, the rope is cut slowly. We find similar claims, in the same terms, in Plato's *Gorgias* 476b–d. If this is relevant here it could only be as a claim about reciprocity. But it is a claim about one action (a cutting, a striking) viewed from two points of view (subject and object).

The thought may have wandered in from [A]'s physical theories, especially given the reference to 'annihilation'. This sounds a little like the claim that elemental contraries must act on one another reciprocally or they would be annihilated. E.g. if hot things heated cold things, without any hot thing being cooled, then everything would end up hot; cold 'would be annihilated'. For a closely related idea, see *Physics* 204b26. On this view, the subject of the sentence was *archai* ('elements'), not *technai* ('skills').

23. *what builder is to shoemaker*: I.e., as I read it, his equal. This brief phrase is otherwise very difficult to make sense of in this context.

It is clear that [A] is saying that a shoemaker and a builder need to trade goods, but cannot trade one house for one pair of shoes. They need to trade one house for an equivalent or proportional amount of shoes (or, in practice, a sum of money representing that equivalent amount). He twice expresses this 'proportion' like this: 'what builder is to shoemaker, x amount of shoes must be to one house'.

The second part of this seems easy enough: it means that x amount of shoes must equal or be the equivalent of one house in value. (He says nine times that the exchanged products have to be 'equalized'.) But what does the first part mean – 'what a builder is to a shoemaker'?

Commentators (ancient and modern) have made several contradictory suggestions here.

(a) Some think he means that 'as the labour of the builder, in making one house, is to the labour of the shoemaker in making the shoes'. But it seems impossible to read a silent reference to labour into the very thin expression.

(b) Some – including some ancient commentators – think that [A] means that in some sense a builder, the man, is worth more than a shoemaker, the man, and that their products should be traded at a rate that matches their worth (so 'what builder is to shoemaker' means, e.g., worth four times as much, as a man). But [A] surely doesn't mean that builders are worth more than shoemakers, whatever that would mean; plus that is a farcical way of working out the price of a house, or anything else.

(c) As I see it, [A] takes it for granted that 'what builder is to shoemaker' is *his equal*. There are several points in favour of this: (1) He repeatedly states that builder and shoemaker must be equals for the purposes of their civic partnership. (2) This would imply, simply and clearly, that 'x number of shoes' must equal one house in value, as required. (3) 'Builder to shoemaker', considered in itself, far from implying an unequal relation seems a natural example of social equals. (Contrast with master and slave, ruler and ruled, parent and child.) (4) Builder and shoemaker are offered as examples of citizens engaged in the 'civic partnership' that constitutes a *polis* (the examples match *Republic* 369b–370d, where they likewise stand for the theoretical first and equal members of a *polis*); and [A] states that citizens are, by definition, equals at 1134a27.

So the sense is: 'Builder and shoemaker can only be partners and cooperators (as required) if they can use proportionality to equalize the goods that they trade, in line with their (foundational) civic equality.'

24. *when they trade*: Most manuscripts here read: 'But they must not bring [their goods] into a form of proportion when they trade . . . but rather, when they have their own things.' That is sometimes taken to mean: 'They should not proportionalize their goods once they have completed the trade, but when they [still] have their goods.' This is deeply obscure by any standard; and '*once they have* traded' is not a feasible reading of the phrase 'when they trade'.

[A] is in fact making the same pretty simple claim that he made at the beginning of the duplicate passage, viz. that 'they need to get their goods into proportion when they trade'. See [TA] for details.

25. *advantage over the other, both ways*: This difficult phrase, literally, 'otherwise one of the top terms will have both excesses' – which has confused commentators, ancient and modern – is, on the duplication theory, a reference to the fact that if the traders don't use proportion (i.e. if they trade one item for one item), then one or other of them will get more from the trade – the 'excess' or 'the advantage' – since one product is worth more than the other. What's more, he'll get a double advantage: 'an advantage . . . both ways'. Suppose a pair of shoes is worth five obols, and a bushel of grain one obol. The advantage, or excess, that goes to the farmer, if they trade one bushel for one pair of shoes, is not the four obols difference in the value of the goods, because the farmer both pays less (one obol's worth) and receives more (five obols' worth). That's a both-ways advantage; his wealth increases by eight obols relative to the shoemaker's. [A] made

the same claim in simpler form in the duplicate passage, at 1133a12–13. The expression 'at the top' shows that [A] is using his diagram as he makes this point.

26. *promise*: Or 'guarantee'. [A] means that if you pay money to, say, a shoemaker, your coins represent a promise on your part to supply him with goods of equivalent value when he needs them. 'Whenever you present these back to me, I will hand over my goods.' In effect, [A] is suggesting that currency arose as a sort of IOU, or token of credit. (Once an IOU becomes fully transferable, from anyone to anyone, it is currency in the full sense.) This is in contrast to a standard view that currency arose from some intrinsically valuable commodity. (On the IOU theory, a currency doesn't need to be intrinsically valuable; it just needs to be a trustworthy token.)

27. *doesn't always have the same value*: This seems to be a reference to inflation. 'The very same thing happens to money' means that money, just like other goods, is sometimes less in demand, sometimes more.

28. *produces a middle*: Literally, 'is of a middle'. A virtue that is 'of a middle' here means a virtue that is productive of a middle, i.e. a virtue that targets, brings about or produces a middle through your actions, namely a distribution of goods that is right in the middle of you getting too much and you getting too little. The sentences that follow illustrate this.

What makes fairness different from the other virtues is that here the sliding scale is of outcomes only, rather than emotions or desires, and so has to be defined externally.

[A] does not have a specific emotion that he associates with unfairness or fairness. (*Pleonexia*, which he does closely associate with unfairness, means 'getting too much', 'taking too much', or 'taking advantage'. It names a state of affairs, or a kind of action, not an emotion or a desire.)

The claim that 'unfairness produces both extremes' refers to another difference between fairness and the other virtues. If someone gets too much, that's unfair, and if they get too little, that's also unfair. Hence 'both extremes' (of the range of possible distributions) result from (someone's) unfairness. That can't be said of any of the other virtues or vices.

29. The next several discussions return to general *díkaion and ádikon*: right and wrong. This is obvious for several reasons. (a) The examples require it. Adultery, theft, assault, murder, disobeying religious rules, inflicting bodily harm, battlefield

cowardice – these are all clear-cut instances of general 'wrongs', not of distributive or compensatory unfairness. Several of them appeared earlier as [A]'s own examples of general wrongdoing offered in contrast to unfair actions. (b) Early in chapter 6, [A] says he is discussing *díkaion* 'between citizens', as sustained (and, in a sense, created) by law. This very closely matches his earlier definition of general right and wrong, and should be read as another treatment of its origin and its basis. (c) Several of the particular discussions in chapters 8, 9, 10, 11 and 12 can only be understood at all as being about general right and wrong, and (at least) three times [A] indirectly asserts that that is his topic. (d) In chapter 11, [A] makes the distinction between particular and general *díkaion*, without the slightest indication that he has already done so. He uses the distinction to make a brief point about unfair actions (that you cannot be unfair to yourself) as part of his broader claim (that you cannot wrong yourself). That proves that the wider context there is a discussion of general *díkaion*.

So it is impossible that his topic in these chapters is particular *díkaion* (fairness) and *ádikan* (unfairness) only. But that does not mean that there is no further mention of fair and unfair actions. They enter the discussions at various points, as one type of the broader class of right and wrong actions, or at least as the examples that he probably has in mind.

It seems likely to me that here and there the editors try to tie these later materials too tightly to what preceded. In particular, they try to fulfil [A]'s claim at 1130b20 that general *díkaion* has now been 'put to one side'. They perhaps wrongly assumed – as many more recent readers do – that particular *díkaion* must be the topic from there on, and they seem to have made some clumsy additions to that effect. In reality, though general *díkaion* was indeed put to one side for a while, it now returns, probably because these other discussions had a different source.

30. *fully equal*: I.e. equals in the sense that they all get actually equal, 'numerically equal' shares of power, status, etc. They would be 'equals by proportion' under aristocracy or monarchy (where, e.g., 100 members of the working class equal the political clout of one aristocrat). See [EE] 1241b35–7. 'Proportionate equals' is an Orwellian phrase. It means, of course, 'people who are *not* equal'. I suspect the qualification does not belong here. I am very doubtful that the phrase can properly be used of persons at all.

31. *who can do one another wrong*: Literally, 'laws [arise] among people for whom there is wrongdoing (*adikía*)'.

[A] is sketching a social-contract theory of the origins of right and wrong. These claims are similar to (and in my view another version of) the idea already set out at 1129b11. The key idea is that right and wrong are functional; they enable cooperation, and society more generally, in the 'political animal' that we are. And here [A] emphasizes the fact that it is cooperation between non-kin, beyond the boundaries of the family, that is the real challenge. Hence it is the relation between citizens that is central to the origin, and basis, of right and wrong. (He made a closely related point at 1129b33.)

(But see VIII.9 for a different view. There [A] implies that right and wrong between family members is stronger than (and hence prior to?) right and wrong between citizens.)

It might seem circular, or incoherent, to say that right and wrong depend on law, but also that laws arise where there is [already] wrongdoing. But in fact we find exactly this feature in versions of the theory reported by Plato, and they show us what [A] means. E.g. *Republic* 358e: 'When people [forming the very first societies] found themselves wronging one another [and sometimes gaining, sometimes losing out] they made a general agreement not to do wrong to, or to be wronged by, one another; and that led them to institute laws; and what was commanded by the law they called right.' Notice that the account says that they 'wronged' one another before anything was even called 'right' or 'wrong'. (Likewise, *Protagoras* 322b–c: 'They kept doing one another wrong . . . So they needed to acquire a sense of right and wrong.') 'Wronging' appears to mean 'harming' in the first part of these formulations.

[A]'s view can make good sense of this, too, as follows: he believes we are civic animals, social by nature (1097b11, 1169b18, [EE] 1242a23, *Politics* 1253a3), hence harming a natural equal – a would-be fellow citizen – has a natural, proto-wrongness to it. Then, laws and social norms formalize that fact, and create right and wrong between citizens in the full and standard sense.

32. *being an unrighteous, {unethical} person*: The term *adikía*, in the previous point, and again in its continuation below, means 'wrongdoing'. But the same word can also refer to the character-state of being *ádikos*, being unrighteous. In this (miscellaneous) observation it has that sense. [A] has made a similar claim at the start of this chapter (being a thief means you steal stuff, but stealing something doesn't always make you a thief). He makes it again at 1135b22, and again, in similar terms, at 1138a34

('maybe not every wilful wrongdoing makes you a [fully] unrighteous person').

33. *tyrants*: This passage has a political subject. It appears to be part of an argument against monarchy, in favour of constitutional or republican government. The idea that the sovereignty of law (rather than of any individual human being) amounts to the rule of 'reason' appears again at 1180a21 (and see also *Politics* 1287a27). The notion that powerful rulers are prone to corruption (and should be restrained by law) features in [A]'s arguments against monarchy in *Politics* III.16. (And for the point that good rulers are rewarded only with prestige and respect, see 1163b5.)

The only reason for this fragment of argument to be here at all seems to be that it happens to mention the saying that 'being righteous' (i.e., here, being a law-abiding, fair and honest ruler) 'is a benefit to others, not to yourself'. See above, note V.7.

34. *master and slave*: This passage must be taken as continuing the argument begun before the three miscellaneous points. This seems obvious enough. It is also fully confirmed by the [MM] author, who paraphrases the argument here as if the three intervening points were not there at all. Here is that paraphrase (MM 1194b5–27):

> Some sort of right and wrong {and obligation} – we say – holds even between master and slave, and between father and son. But that seems like a metaphorical extension of the [central] kind, between citizens. The right and wrong that we're investigating here is the kind that holds between citizens, and that kind (in the paradigm case) depends on social equality. Citizens are partners, of a sort, and supposed to be naturally alike (even if they differ in personal character). By contrast, you might argue that right and wrong don't really apply at all between parent and child, or between master and servant. I have no obligations to my own foot or my own hand or any other part of my body; and surely that's just what a son is to his father. A son is like a part of his father until he takes his place as a man and becomes independent. Only then is he his father's equal (as fellow citizens are supposed to be). Likewise with master and slave. No right or wrong exists between them because the slave is an extension of the master. (The only obligations the master has to the slave are those of householder, [who has an obligation, of a sort, to preserve his property], and we aren't investigating those.) And as for husband and wife, well,

the kind of right and wrong that holds in their partnership is close
to the sort you get between citizens. Because although a wife is
the inferior of her husband, she is more closely tied to him and has
more equality with him, so their shared life is similar to the partnership of fellow citizens.

The extract seamlessly blends the sentences that come before, and
after, the three miscellaneous points. Clearly, those were not in
the text when this [MM] paraphrase was written, or its author
decided (as I do) to edit them out of the main argument. The
former seems more likely.

35.   *obligations*: I use this strictly as a noun corresponding to *díkaion*.
The Greek term can be used as a countable noun rather than
abstract noun. E.g. 'a father's [several] *díkaia* with respect to his
children', i.e. things-that-are-the-right-thing-to-do with respect
to them (but in the sense, things-he-must-do rather than things-
he-may-do); so, in English, his several obligations to them. That
sense of the term seems operative here; e.g. 'there is *díkaion*
with respect to your wife' means 'you have obligation(s) to your
wife'. See VIII.9 for further and clearer examples of this usage.
      No meta-ethical theory of any kind is implied here by the
term 'obligations', either in normal English or by me. Just think
of it as the noun form of the concept already in play as soon as
we speak of right and wrong at all. (An objection to the use of
'obligation' in translations of [A] is that it is specifically Kantian
in sense. The objection has no foundation in the facts of English
usage.)

36.   *as a husband*: [A] is saying (see last note) that 'your wife is
closer to being your equal, and hence your relationship with her
comes closer to your relationship with fellow citizens'.
      'Obligations as a husband' here translates *oikonomikon díkaion*.
Perhaps 'obligations of householder', or 'of head of the family'
(*oikia* standardly means 'family'). A later passage, at 1138b5,
suggests that [A] sometimes uses the term as a way of referring
to the relationship between husband and wife. (Note also that
English 'husband', at least historically, means 'householder'.)

37.   *could be some other way*: [A] means that some moral norms,
e.g. the notion that it is wrong for parents to eat their children,
or basic norms of fairness, or family obligations, obviously have
a basis in human nature, even though, in principle, and under
certain circumstances, a society might reject or significantly
reshape even those 'natural' forms of right and wrong. Note that

it is one of [A]'s beliefs that in some parts of the world people do actually eat their children (see VII.5). He is open to the idea that somewhere in the world there is some barbarian tribe doing literally anything you might think of, ethically speaking. His anthropological ignorance undermines his case. In reality, there is no human culture where people eat their children; or where people do not value fairness over unfairness, or generosity over stinginess. A quite detailed set of norms and virtues are to be found in recognizable form in all known human societies. It is simply not true that all social norms are variable in the same way. [A]'s argument here would have been stronger had he known that.

38. *Buyers use larger ones*: Where merchants buy their goods wholesale, they use large units (tons of wheat, amphorae of wine), but when they sell them on to customers, they use small units (bushels, cups, etc.). I suspect a misguided attempt by an editor to explain what [A] meant. It seems more plausible that [A] had in mind the fact that different countries use different units for the same things (kilos and pounds, miles and kilometres, etc.), something just as true in ancient times (e.g. Greeks used *stades*, Persians used *parasangs*, Romans used *miles*). That is a very good analogy for the phenomenon of arbitrary norms and customs that vary conspicuously between different cultures.

39. *We usually call . . . wrongdoing*: To me this reads like an editor's note. The editor seems to be sheepishly correcting the way [A] used the term *dikaiōma*. ('He should have said *dikaiopragēma*.')

40. *getting old or dying*: This brief explanatory sentence seems to make the point that some of the things we do are not in category (a) or (c) – they are natural, hence not forced on us, and we do them knowingly – but they are still not willing or voluntary. So the point justifies the existence of category (b). (The category is a little weird. Is getting old something we do?)

The manuscript text here reads: 'and none of those is willing, or unwilling'. There might be a way of making sense of it, but it undercuts the note's ability to explain category (b) or indeed any of these categories. I accept [S]'s view that 'or unwilling' should be deleted.

41. *mistake . . . mishap*: E.g. a child swerves out in front of your car on a bicycle. You aren't speeding. You have absolutely no time to react, and you injure the child. That's a mishap; an unfortunate accident. But if you hurt someone in a moment of careless driving (you didn't check your side mirror): a mistake.

42. *they can't remember*: There is disagreement here among both ancient and modern commentators about what [A] means. He obviously has in mind a case where, e.g., X sues Y over an unpaid debt. Y disputes the facts. I.e. he claims to have already paid the debt, or that he never owed X any money in the first place. In such cases, [A] says, it is obvious that someone, X or Y, is deliberately trying to cheat the other. So one of them must be a crook. 'Unless it's just because they can't remember.' That might mean either (a) 'unless they only committed the alleged wrong because they forgot' (e.g. Y forgot that he owed X the debt); or more plausibly, given the plural pronoun, (b) 'unless they're only disputing the facts because they've both forgotten [what happened]'.

43. *the other feels otherwise*: Again this is unclear. But I take it to describe how the two parties feel after the wrongdoing, not before it. So, suppose X punched Y out of anger, then [A] is saying that X admits to punching Y, and they only argue over whether the punch was justified, provoked, understandable, etc. 'Y feels that he's been wronged; X thinks not', i.e. Y feels the punch was a wrongdoing; X thinks that Y hasn't been wronged, i.e. that in being punched Y got what he deserved. (Note that I have repositioned one phrase here. The phrase Bywater puts in parenthesis makes much more sense if it comes at the end of the sentence.)

44. *an unrighteous person*: I excise one clause here: 'when they [i.e. your wrongdoings] violate proportion or equality'. This has the effect of tying this discussion of wrongdoings to the earlier definitions of particular *ádikon*, i.e. unfairness. It is easy to see that the qualification makes no sense. To say that 'deliberate unfair acts make you an unfair person when they violate proportion or equality' implies that some deliberate unfair acts do not violate proportion or equality. But if the actions did not violate proportion or equality, then they would not be unfair at all. (It is as if the editor simply wants to read the claim as: 'You are being unfair if you violate proportion or equality.' But [A]'s claim is about when your actions do or do not indicate your character; he is not defining either wrong or unfair actions.) The extra clause has the effect of spoiling [A]'s simple and important claim: that deliberate wrongdoing (as opposed to accidental wrongdoing, or wrongdoing after serious provocation) indicates that you are a fully unethical person.

45. *can you be wronged incidentally*: The Greek is more elliptical here: 'Or is it the same with being [wronged] as with

doing [wrong]?' The context and phrasing make it clear that the 'same' feature that [A] means is the possibility of incidental wrong.

46. *man who lacks self-control*: [A] seems slightly confused here. If I knowingly ask someone to harm me (e.g. inject me with a dangerous drug) through a lack of self-control ('I really don't want to do this; I know it's bad; but I can't resist'), then that person *would* then be acting 'contrary to what I want', as I myself am. Hence, I am being 'willingly wronged'. (What [A] would need to claim, for his conclusion, is that if in any sense you wilfully allow someone to harm you, you aren't being wronged.)

47. *gratitude . . . revenge*: I.e. when a judge makes an unfair or otherwise wrongful decision affecting others, he is himself 'taking advantage', he is 'gaining something' (*pleonektei*), in much the same way as people who act unfairly in their own favour. Obviously [A] does not mean that gratitude or revenge are in some sense being shared out, and the judge is taking an unfair share of them. This is best taken as an empirical claim about third-party unfairness. Corrupt adjudicators are almost always advancing their own interests in some sense (taking a bribe, pleasing a dictator, helping family or tribe, favouring their political party, etc.); so in some form they too are 'taking advantage'.

48. *not in our power*: [A] makes two points here. (a) Doing right or wrong implies a certain disposition of character and it is not in our power, at any moment, at will, to acquire, or lose, that disposition. Rather, it takes long habituation to acquire either disposition, and that habituation is not easy. (b) The actions considered in themselves are, in a sense, physically easy. It's also easy enough (usually) to know what action would be right or wrong. But for people with one disposition or the other, the opposite kind of actions are not easy. For an unethical person, doing the right thing is very, very hard. Physically easy, but not psychologically. [M]: 'For a righteous person, doing wrong isn't just hard, it's impossible.' For this point, compare 1114a12–21 and 1129a11–16.

49. *being a doctor*: This paragraph can be read as following on from the previous one without trouble. But you can also easily see that it says the fundamentally same thing in only slightly different terms; even to the point of using four identical examples. These two passages look like Nicomachean/Eudemian duplicates.

50. *kind and decent*: The term being analysed here is *epieikēs*. This has a range of senses:

(a) It's often used by [A], and many others, to designate higher social class: 'decent folk', 'the decent class of people'.

(b) It is used in a very broad sense, a virtual synonym for *agathos* or *spoudaios*: 'a good person'; rather like English 'a decent person', and from that also came to mean 'good' more generally – [A] mentions this in his discussion.

(c) It has a more precise and particular sense when used of a person – the one being analysed here: 'kind', 'forbearing', 'decent', 'lenient', 'nice', 'reasonable', 'merciful'. ([A] gives a very helpful list of examples of *epieikeia* in *Rhetoric* 1374b4–22.) The large vocabulary of English means that we tend to chop it up into different terms in subtly different contexts. A certain softness, an implication of empathy and forbearance, is fundamental – notice [A]'s helpful metaphor of bending – which is why 'kindness' overlaps with it very well (even if 'kindness' is broader, and has other uses beyond the one [A] discusses here). I also like 'forbearance' as a translation. But unfortunately that term lacks lexical range. (You can't say 'she did the forbearing thing'.)

If we turn to Latin, we find that *epieikeia* was translated or paraphrased (e.g. by Cicero) as *humanitas* ('humaneness', 'kindness') and *clementia* ('kindness', 'forbearance', 'leniency', 'mercy').

A common context for this concept, in the ancient world, especially given the prevalence of monarchs, was that of powerful rulers carrying out punishments. A willingness on the part of a ruler to be *epieikēs* in the exercise of power and force came to imply 'clemency' and 'mercy' in particular. (For this connection with forgiveness see VI.11.) This part of [NE] lies behind Portia's lines in *The Merchant of Venice*, when she appeals to Shylock not to insist on his pound of flesh: 'And earthly power doth then [seem most similar to] God's / When mercy seasons justice.'

51. *the more decent, the better*: In English, 'decent' is indeed used as a general term of approval ('that's a pretty decent beer', 'he's a decent player') like *epieikēs* in Greek. (In reality, it was really only the adverb form that took on this very general sense; as in 'he is fairly good at the guitar'.) Match-ups like this across languages are really just a matter of luck. Still, [A] may have a point. The fact that we take a word that means 'kind' and use it as an all-purpose word for 'good' perhaps reveals something important about current attitudes to that quality. And the same broad extension of use is found with the rather similar English term 'nice'.

52. *builders in Lesbos*: Apparently refers to building from irregular
stones – perhaps natural, rough-cut stones, as used in rustic
masonry, or perhaps the large, polygonal 'Cyclopean' blocks
used in city walls in the Mycenean period. The mason uses a
lead ruler to model exactly the shape of a stone, then can use the
ruler to search for a stone that will be a good fit. This is a piece
of local knowledge. [A] spent several years in Lesbos.

53. *this kind is … distinct from the other*: Obviously this repeats
the distinction between general and particular *adikía*, already
discussed at 1129a31–1130b29. But nothing in [A]'s wording
suggests that he has already discussed this, and overall it reads
as if a fresh point is being explained. If so, that would indicate
that this section of book V has a different source from chapters
1–6, which in any case already seems likely on other grounds.

54. *at the very same time*: This is a sophistic argument; i.e. basically
a joke argument. (See VII.2, 1146a21 for two other examples,
with a brief discussion by [A] on the nature of such arguments.
The next two arguments are also jocular.)

Imagine you have a large chocolate cake and you are dividing
it up, but only with yourself, and in doing so you try to 'treat
yourself unfairly', 'cheat yourself', by giving yourself less than
half. The trouble is, you get the other bit too. Foiled!

55. *the very same thing that's being done to you*: A joke argument.
The idea is that retaliation is widely regarded as justified, and
hence not wrong. But if we define retaliation as 'doing the same
thing as is done to you', then technically – but absurdly – it also
covers self-inflicted harm. When I kick myself, I am 'doing what
is being done to me'. Hence, it can't be wrong.

Self-punishment is clearly possible. But it has to involve two
actions. E.g. you 'kick yourself' for some foolish mistake. (Suicide, in some cases, is self-punishment for some unbearable
mistake.) Obviously, I can't kick myself as simultaneous instant
payback for this very act of now kicking myself.

56. *Having said that . . .*: [A] is the only Greek philosopher (that we
know of) who dared to reject Socrates' venerated maxim that
'doing wrong is always worse [for you] than being wronged' (see
Gorgias 469c). His disagreement is understated, and even presented as a qualified agreement. But it is a powerful critique.

[A] surely agrees that, e.g., being a lifelong violent thief is a
much worse state to be in than being a decent person who has
something stolen from them by that thief. Any reasonable person would rather be the victim than the thief.

But what if being wronged has very, very substantial consequences for you – e.g. your death? In that case being wronged
might easily be worse than the moral self-harm of being the
wrongdoer.

If someone causes the death of a young person through an
uncharacteristic moment of careless driving, it seems incompar-
ably worse to be the dead young person than the (somewhat)
reprehensible, careless driver. The Socratic view here seems ridiculous and inhumane. (Socrates does not think dying is a bad thing.
[A] thinks dying is obviously a bad thing. See 1115a26. [A]'s view
gives him the more credible attitude to cases of that kind.)

The text here is difficult, and I have slightly rearranged the
order of the phrasing. The Greek text reads: 'Of course this is
irrelevant to the art [of medicine] . . . it says a lung infection is
worse than a stubbing . . . and yet, the other [i.e. the stubbing]
could be worse, if . . .' etc.

57. *in those relations*: In *Politics* 1254b1–20 [A] explains that the
rational mind's control over the physical body is rather like a
master ordering around a slave (he sees slaves as animate tools
of their master), while the rational mind's relationship with
emotion and desire is still unequal, but a little more cooperative,
rather like (the Greek idea of) the relationship between husband
and wife. (He also discusses both these relationships in similar
terms in VIII.11.) The text here says that the different parts of
the soul, literally, 'stand apart in these *logoi*' – and, agreeing
with [M], I take *logoi* here to mean 'ratios', i.e. relations. 'Stand
apart' is a reference to the vertical gap between the parts: the
fact that one is set over the others. (The same verb occurs in this
sense at *Politics* 1254b16.)

BOOK VI

1. *calculating part*: Plato uses the same term, *logistikon*, to refer
to the entire rational part of the soul. Here [A] uses the term in
connection with practical reasoning (*logismos*). (He separates
practical reason from purely scientific thought, because of the
former's connection with emotion and desire.)

2. *Affirmation and denial*: In this context, [A] means affirmations
and denials about what we should do, or of what is good or bad.
'I should help my friend'; 'I should not break the law'; 'I should
pay my debt.' These have to correspond to, be underwritten by,

the right *orexeis*, 'desires' broadly conceived: features of character that push and pull you in the appropriate directions. (See next few notes.)

3. *making ... doing*: This distinction between making and doing seems to be one that [A] became interested in only between the two treatises. In [EE], he uses *poiētikē* ('concerned with making') synonymously with *praktikē* ('concerned with doing'). E.g. 1216b17, 1221b6, 1227b30. In ordinary Greek, *poiein*, like French *faire*, or Spanish *hacer*, can mean both 'make' and 'do'. Because of the blending of the common books, we find one Eudemian usage of *poiētikē* in [NE] as well, in book VII, at 1147a28.

4. *object of desire*: This probably means 'and that cannot be anything other than the object of desire', or 'and that's by definition the object of desire', i.e. it takes desires (*orexeis*, strivings of whatever sort) for us to have goals at all. Goals only come into the world – including all human practical and moral goals – with the strivings of living things.

5. *cognition-tied-to-desire, or desire-tied-to-thought*: Or perhaps: 'Choice is desire-y cognition, or thought-y desire.' Or, more expansively, 'Choice is what you get when cognition (awareness, sense) overlaps with desire; or if you like, it's what you get when desire overlaps with thought.'

    The key question to ask here – and about the whole passage – is what [A] means by 'desire' (i.e. *orexis*, desire very broadly construed). Does he mean desire that results from, or issues from, deliberation and choice, or desire that precedes and feeds into deliberation?

    I do not rule out the former reading; but I think it really helps to assume that he means the latter. When you choose to help a friend, say, your thought and deliberation might well produce a particular desire (to do this, or that, in her aid). But [A]'s point is that you also have to have background, standing desires, likes and dislikes, ingrained patterns of emotion, etc., to be able to undertake that deliberation correctly in the first place: you care about your friend, love your friend, want what's best for her, fear for her safety, would be upset by her death, etc. Those 'desires' combine with thought and deliberation to produce your choice (and, yes, generate some new, particular desire and action).

    You can see that this is the right reading from the fact that [A] twice uses 'character' interchangeably with 'desire'. 'Character' is obviously a reference here to our standing desires, our permanent likes and dislikes, etc. (For that, compare 1178a16ff.)

So earlier, when [A] said that 'reason has to be asserting something true, and desire has to be correct', he means, e.g., that (a) your reason has to be saying, 'I should help my friend' and (b) your character has to (already) have the desiderative features that underlie that thought and give it motive force: that's 'correct desire'. A thought of that sort expresses those desires, and further correct reasoning figures out how to act on them. (The claims here about 'correct desire', tied to character, closely match claims about 'correct starting points' and 'correct aims', likewise issuing from 'good character', at 1140b16ff., 1144a32ff. and 1144a20ff.)

6. *human way*: The point is to distinguish human beings from animals on the one hand and from God on the other. Animals are pure desire; they have strivings (many of them very similar to our own) but, on [A]'s view, they do not think about them, articulate them, reason about them or make choices. God is pure thought, without needs, desires or character. Thus, only human beings are this combination of desire and thought, and only they initiate action in that distinctive way, through practical reason and choice. This is (another) helpful delineation of [A]'s humanism. Clearly, on this view only human beings can be morally good or bad, not God; only they make good or bad choices; only they have thoughts about right and wrong. For similar statements see 1137a26, 1145a25, 1178a9ff, 1178b8ff.

7. *accidental*: Suppose you hypothesize that X is true, and it *is* true, but that's just a guess, or your reasons for thinking X are rather feeble. If you then deduce Y from X, and Y is true, you don't scientifically know that Y; that Y happens to be true is just a matter of luck.

8. *concerned . . . not with doing*: Hence (a key anti-Platonic point), moral wisdom is not a skill or craft or technical expertise (*technē*). Similarly, the previous point was that wisdom is not a form of scientific knowledge (*epistemē*).

9. *lack of skill the opposite*: You might think that lack of skill or lack of expertise is also the result of simply not having any ability to make something. [A] seems to be straining too hard for symmetry; or perhaps here he means *atechnia*, in the sense of 'being poorly skilled at X', e.g. being a poor guitar-player, a bad pilot. This seems to relate to his claim in II.1 that you can't be a bad guitar-player without being a guitar-player. (In natural language, you might think that someone who isn't a guitar-player at all is a very bad guitar-player.)

10.   *'wise' even in a particular field*: E.g. a wise general, a wise
      captain, a wise mother, a wise friend, a wise investor. We use
      the word of people who are good at figuring out how to achieve
      the goals of those particular domains. But a wise general isn't
      just an expert general.

11.   *doing well is itself the goal*: I have moved this sentence from
      three lines below. In the manuscripts it comes just after the con-
      clusion of the section (the definition of wisdom), where it seems
      out of place, rather than just after the claim that doing is differ-
      ent from making, where it seems perfectly apt.

      The claim that making has a separate goal means, for
      example, that while the goal of building is a house, the goal or
      purpose of the house itself must come from somewhere beyond
      the art of building.

12.   *preserves . . . our wisdom*: In the sense that it enables us to stick
      to, or abide by, what our wisdom is telling us to do. Strictly this
      makes moderation sound rather more like self-control. Self-
      control is matter of sticking to our better judgement against
      contrary desires, while moderation (in [A]'s understanding of it)
      is a matter of not having bad desires in the first place. But per-
      haps even the lack of such desires can be also thought of as
      'preserving our wisdom'.

      [A]'s etymological speculation is – as often – wrong. In reality
      the adjective *sōphrōn* (meaning, by [A]'s time, 'moderate') ori-
      ginally meant 'of sound mind', 'sensible'. (*Sō-*, 'safe', 'sound';
      -phron, 'minded').

13.   *wisdom must be*: This seems to be a duplicate of the definition
      of wisdom given fifteen lines earlier. What immediately follows
      is likewise rather disconnected from what preceded. It returns
      to the earlier (apparently completed) argument over whether or
      not wisdom is a form of technical expertise. I leave the text as is
      (except for the one minor transposition at 1140b6).

14.   *good at being wise*: [P] explains, correctly I think, that [A] means
      you can't be good (or bad) at being wise, because wisdom is
      always a matter of being good at something, namely, good at
      deliberating. If you're 'bad at being wise', you're simply not
      wise. In that respect it is more like being bad at being brave, or
      being bad at being generous, which just means you are not brave
      or not generous.

15.   *mistake on purpose*: If two guitar-players, A and B, are both
      playing horribly, but B is doing it on purpose (in a skilled imita-
      tion of a bad player), then clearly B is the better player. B is the

player you'd want to be. But if B does something ungenerous or
unfair on purpose, while A does the same only by accident, then
clearly B is the worse person. A is the person you'd want to be.
And wisdom is like the latter.

16. *abilities*: Strictly, *hexeis*, elsewhere 'dispositions', 'states [of character, mind]', 'character traits'; but in English we're more likely
to call them abilities, e.g. being good at arithmetic or trigonom-
etry or Latin. We easily lose such abilities, but we do not forget
the evaluative attitudes that make up our moral wisdom, and in
that respect wisdom is much more like, say, generosity or fairness. [A] made the same point at 1100b16.

17. *can't themselves . . . scientific knowledge*: I.e. for them to be
known scientifically you would have to be able to prove them,
i.e. deduce them, i.e. from something else; but then they would not
be your first principles after all. So starting points by definition
have to be unproven, and hence cannot themselves be part of
scientific knowledge as [A] defines it.

18. *directly intuit*: I.e. by induction; by extrapolation from experience.

19. *most exact of all the sciences*: [A] seems to mean this: when we
use the term *sophos* of craftsmen and artists, we use it of the
most precise and finely honed arts and technical abilities. But
sophia also refers to the kind of knowledge acquired through
higher philosophy. And in the light of its other use, [A] thinks it
should refer to the most exact kind of knowledge; it must be, as
we say, an exact science.

    This is a rather weak, etymological argument for his view
that *sophia* is an 'exact science' – and hence, the main point,
very different from moral wisdom. (Consider the times he has
noted that ethics is not an exact science: I.3, II.2, V.10.)

20. *direct cognition*: See chapter 6. [A] means that the first principles of the higher branches of philosophy, like metaphysics,
theology and physics, have to be grasped by direct cognition, through a process of induction, just like with all other
sciences.

21. *people even call*: [A]'s point seems to be that (a) any species that
could know and reflect on its own interests would naturally be
called 'wise', and obviously each species would have a very different version of 'wisdom', and (b) this fact is already recognized
in common speech: we call some animals 'wise' or 'smart', e.g.
foxes, cats, owls, elephants, bees, crows; but obviously their
wisdom has a very different content from ours.

22. *as 'philosophical'*: Remember to take this only in the sense of higher, non-practical philosophy. 'If our ideas about what's best for us derive from metaphysics, then every animal will have to have its own metaphysics.'

23. *multiple forms . . . [which is absurd]*: [A]'s target is Plato, who aimed to tie the highest realms of philosophy – our understanding of the cosmos, and its organizer, God – to ethics. The objection is, in basic structure, rather similar to the earlier criticisms of Plato's Form of the Good, except that there the point was about the many different forms of 'good' in human life; here the point is applied to the fact that 'good' means different things for different species.

   Imagine the specific case of multiple versions of theology. (Theology is one branch of *sophia*, and probably uppermost in [A]'s mind here.) If theology is to underwrite our notions of good and bad, right and wrong, then each species of animal will have to have its own theology; i.e. its own conception of God. If human beings get their notions of right and wrong from a god who is righteous, fair, generous, and, e.g., angered by fratricide, then great white sharks clearly can't get their values from that god. Their god will have to be ruthless, solitary and angered by overfishing.

   Something like this underlies [A]'s point here. He seems to be channelling the philosopher Xenophanes from two centuries earlier: 'If cows believed in gods,' said Xenophanes, 'their gods would be cows.' Xenophanes' point was that there is something very suspicious about our gods being so very human in bodily form and character – which they have to be, to be the source of our values. We see the problem more vividly, he suggested, if we imagine cows believing in a god who looks like and behaves like a cow, and reflect on just how absurd that seems to us. So he too used the idea of multiple theologies – one for cows, one for us – to make [A]'s point, that we should not be tying human concerns to theology, or to our wider conception of the cosmos.

   Notice [A]'s exact phrasing here: 'Philosophical knowledge [e.g. metaphysics, theology, physics] is not the same thing as statesmanship.' The term suggests a deliberate and clear repudiation of the philosopher-kings of Plato's *Republic*. On Plato's view, people who study the wider cosmos, in the right way, are thereby uniquely qualified to be statesmen.

24. *how you should manage your own affairs*: I suspect that this sentence belongs somewhere else, or should have come before

the preceding one: 'But what exactly do we mean by "managing your own affairs"? It's not obvious. Maybe "your own interests" include being a family man and a citizen?'

25. *grasps particular facts*: [A] is not saying that this is all that wisdom does. Rather, in this paragraph he is discussing the fact that this is one of the things that wisdom includes: our grasp of pertinent particular facts and general sense and awareness of the details of human life. That part of it is like perception, or at any rate global perception. In fact, the conclusion of the argument as I read it is that that kind of perception, and that aspect of wisdom – awareness of all the pertinent facts of your situation – are more or less the same thing.

26. *correctness in deliberation*: Following these words, I excise one sentence: 'So we first need to work out what deliberation is, and what it's about.' [A] does not, in any sense at all, stop here to explain deliberation in general. He carries straight on with the discussion of good decision-making only.

27. *done himself a lot of harm*: [A] usually says that someone who lacks self-control deliberates correctly, and has the right goals, but then fails to act on those goals. Here he's imagining someone working out how to achieve the wrong goal; something that (in fact) harms them. So – unless [A] is confused or there is something wrong with the text – we have to imagine a case where, e.g., someone who knows that they should not smoke nevertheless gives in to their craving and then figures out, brilliantly, how to get hold of some cigarettes. They might 'deliberate correctly' (in a sense), even though they're pursuing something that's bad for them. We don't really call that 'good decision-making', [A] says – which seems right. See also 1152a10ff.

28. *false middle premise*: I think [A] has in mind not – as the commentators suggest – cases where you achieve a good end by immoral means, but cases of deliberation where you get to the right conclusion for the wrong reason, through a false premise, and hence do what is in fact the right thing but for a silly or invalid reason. (E.g. you decide to stop smoking because you are convinced your cigarettes contain mind-controlling nanobots.)

29. *we'd all be 'insightful'*: [A] means, I think, that it's easy to have the right moral beliefs, or to know what's right. But that's not enough to make us morally insightful. See 1112a10 and 1137a9–14 for rather similar claims.

30. *offering judgement*: We can, of course, make judgements about what we ourselves should do; but in this context it seems clear

that the verb *krinein*, 'to judge', is used by [A] specifically to connote judging third-party problems, as opposed to our own. Rather like English 'to adjudicate', 'evaluate', 'give an opinion'.

31. *seeing your way into it*: There is a tricky etymological argument here which, naturally enough, does not work very well in English. Greek for 'insight' is *sunesis*, which literally means 'understanding'. The quality [A] is discussing here is all about taking in new information; solving fresh problems, i.e. other people's. To do that, obviously you have to learn things. (A judge has first to learn the facts of the case.) And to do it the way [A] is describing, you also need to use existing knowledge, so as to also understand them. The combination is 'insight'. (In English, we might say that 'insight' is when you can, with your own existing moral wisdom, as it were, see your way into someone's problem.)

32. *you can see this*: See the previous note. The verb [A] mentions, *manthÁno*, means either 'learn' or (in a common usage) 'understand'.

33. *sympathetic outlook*: There's another etymological point made here. 'Sympathy' (also 'forgiveness', 'pardon') in Greek is *sun-gnomÉ*, literally 'co-understanding', or 'seeing it their way'). [A] says that '*sun-gnomÉ* is the kind of *gnomÉ* (judgement, understanding) where . . .' etc.

34. *because of course kindness*: Literally, 'because kind things . . .'. I assume this means 'kind acts', i.e. doing what is kind is common to all good people. It seems extremely likely that the words I have obelized are a fragment that quite closely duplicates the passage where [A] defined *sunesis*, 'insight', about fifteen lines earlier. It also seems to interrupt a sentence.

35. *the whole set of virtues*: Translates *holÉ aretÉ*, 'the whole of goodness/virtue'. I have translated it twice to help the reader see the connection to the other uses of *aretÉ* that follow.

Here [A] uses this phrase (and the term *aretÉ*) in an unusual way by the standards of normal Greek, and even his own standards. He has said that *sophia*, 'higher philosophical knowledge', is 'the virtue of' the contemplative, scientific part of the soul (i.e. it arises when that part of your soul is in its best possible state, and doing its thing well). Hence it is part of 'the whole of *aretÉ*'. Here, this obviously means 'the whole set of possible virtues, of any sort, moral or intellectual, or whatever'.

Earlier in the treatise (1130a9, b7, b18) [A] used the same expression, *holÉ aretÉ*, to refer only to 'the whole of [moral] goodness', 'the whole of being a good person' – a much more natural usage, given the default tendency of *aretē* to have a moral sense. (Notice, too, that even in the lines that immediately follow here he reverts to using *aretē*, without any qualification, repeatedly, in its standard sense of '[moral] goodness'.) The discrepancy in the sense of the phrase may come from the double source of the common books.

[A] explains elsewhere that there are some virtues (in the broadest sense), namely physical and physiological 'virtues', that do not count as part of this 'whole of virtue' (see I.13, 1102b1–12, [EE] 1219b20). So 'the whole set', oddly, is not the whole set. He dismisses nutritive/reproductive 'virtue'. Here [A] expels it from the set on the grounds that it is not a moral virtue (it does not shape action); just as he did at 1102b11. That is true, but unsatisfactory, because exactly the same holds for *sophia*, higher philosophical knowledge (e.g. metaphysics). [A] doesn't think that has a bearing on action either.

So the 'the whole set' appears a bit gerrymandered. This seems like a problem for the argument. [A] is saying, in effect, 'To flourish you need to cultivate *all* the virtues simply because they are virtues – except some virtues, because even though they're virtues too, they aren't very important to flourishing.'

36. *no equivalent 'virtue'*: Going by [EE] 1219b, 'no equivalent "virtue"' seems to mean here 'no virtue that qualifies as having the same central importance to human flourishing'.

This part of the soul is 'the fourth part' as follows: first part, pure scientific reasoning and contemplation; second part, practical reasoning and moral wisdom, including emotions, desires, and character; third part, perception; fourth part, nutrition, reproduction, growth.

37. *your [basic] choice, {your aim}*: Translates *prohairesis*. For my discussion of how *prohairesis* means both (a) 'choice' and (b) 'aim' or 'intention', see 1112a17 (and note III.29). The second sense is prominent here. In fact [A] very shortly glosses *prohairesis* as 'your *skopos*' ('your aim'). He is able to run the two senses together by thinking of 'our choices' very broadly: our basic choices. For example: as a person of good character you choose to treat people fairly; but it takes wisdom to know exactly how to carry out that 'choice' (i.e. intention, aim, purpose) in a given situation.

38. *That explains . . . called 'wise'*: I.e. it is the overlap, and the general closeness, of the two concepts that explains their being run together.

This reading involves a slight alteration of the text. The manuscripts say: 'That explains why we also call wise people clever and cunning.' See [TA] for the change.

I take 'clever, cunning' to mean, in effect, 'clever, i.e. cunning', or 'clever in the sense of cunning'. The first term is fairly neutral, the second unmistakably negative: 'cunning', 'devious', 'sly', 'knavish', 'unscrupulous rogue'.

BOOK VII

1. *godly man*: [A] reports Spartan dialect. Apart from being known for using this word a lot, Spartans pronounced it differently, saying *seios* for *theios*. (As it happens, the *seios* spelling probably represents the way Greeks now pronounce *theios*, with a fricative, as in 'thanks'. In [A]'s time it was pronounced *teios* or *tios*, as preserved in Spanish *tio*.)

2. *bad person . . . good person*: If we took *aretē* here in its particular sense (which also seems feasible), then we translate like this: 'We shouldn't treat the one as simply a virtue, or the other as simply a vice; nor should we treat them as entirely distinct from those things.' Later [A] tells us that he understands this point in *both* senses. Lack of self-control is 'sort of a vice' *and* 'sort of makes you a bad person'. See 1148a3.

3. *feeling and emotion*: Pathos. In the standard case, the relevant feeling is physical, especially sexual desire, and desire for food; in another common case, anger.

4. *don't realize*: This is a broad scepticism about, and rejection of, the strong Socratic view that people who experience a loss of self-control cannot possibly *know* what they should be doing.

   But also, the particular expression [A] uses here, 'not realizing', is the one he uses to refer to doing something unknowingly, or by mistake (see 1110b18–1111a21; and 1136a7). So perhaps [A] is also implying that this is a very odd sense of doing something 'by mistake'. Drinking too much wine because you thought it was grape juice is a case of drinking too much wine 'by mistake', or 'without realizing'. Drinking too much wine, fully aware it is wine, and believing that you shouldn't drink it, is absolutely not a case of drinking too much 'by mistake'. Compare 1110b28, where [A] critiques the closely related Socratic view that people always do wrong 'unwillingly'.

5. *really awful things*: Imagine a sexual case in particular, e.g. adultery or sexual assault.

    A good question raised by [S]: how is [A]'s claim that wisdom is incompatible with a failure of self-control so different from the Socratic view that knowledge is incompatible with such failures? The answer is that for [A] wisdom involves features of character, including ingrained habits and patterns of feeling and desire. Having the right desires, the right 'character', is part of wisdom, and in some respects a prerequisite for wisdom. (See VI.2 and VI.13.) The Socratic view seems to be that something purely cognitive – some kind of knowledge or enlightenment – is strictly all you need.

6. *a particulars guy*: A wise person doesn't just have good general principles; they also, indeed especially, get things right in particular situations. See 1141b14ff.

7. *needs to use self-control*: Literally, 'a moderate person will not be a person with self-control ...' etc. But it is clear that [A] means here that having to use self-control is not compatible with being moderate.

8. *end up always doing good things*: The argument, though clearly expressed here as a joke, is not completely silly. It is similar to [A]'s own last point about good failures of self-control (the Neoptolemus case). Neoptolemus had rationally accepted a (morally) stupid idea which he then failed to act on. So he did the right thing. Often our best moral intuitions have to overpower bad ideas that we have accepted under social pressure. The sophists' argument could be slightly adapted to capture that case: 'Having terrible ideas (adopted from your culture, or peers) and *failing* to live up to them (because of powerful moral intuitions) is (at least part of) being a good person.'

9. *A is morally better than B*: E.g. a man whose conscious goal is to cheat on his wife as often as possible is morally better than one who's convinced he shouldn't cheat, but succumbs to a temptation. (The first man can be persuaded that cheating is wrong; the second already thinks cheating is wrong; so he's incurable.) This is another sophistic argument. The conclusion is clearly absurd. It misuses the notion of 'persuasion'. It makes it sound as if it were a relatively simple thing to persuade someone to change their character, which is in fact far more difficult than fixing a lack of self-control. [S]: 'The fallacy of the argument lies in [its] transformation of moral depravity into [mere] intellectual error.'

10. *even water makes you choke*: Water is the best thing to wash something else down with; but if you even choke on water, the best washer-downer, what can you do? If even knowledge, the best thing there is for making you do the right thing, still doesn't prevent your mistakes, what on earth will?

    There is a rival view as to the sense of the saying, found, e.g., in [P]: 'If you're drowning ['when the water chokes' can have that sense], what's the point of having another drink?' (Rather like our expression: 'When you're in a hole, stop digging.') That seems to work quite well here, too. The person with no self-control is already swimming in knowledge (and it isn't helping); what use is more of it?

11. *The starting point*: I obelize this section because it is something of a false start. I suspect poor editing (and the issue of the double source for the book). In what immediately follows, [A] does not address the two questions that he says here he will begin with. Instead, what comes after this section carries on seamlessly with the previous question: 'In what sense, if at all, do people know what they should be doing when they experience a loss of self-control?' The other questions return only in chapter 4.

12. *distinguished*: Most translators take this to mean 'distinguished from each other'. It is more likely to mean: 'Are people with and without self-control to be distinguished from everyone else . . .' etc. [A] is asking what characterizes the whole phenomenon of self-control: using or lacking it. He will go on to argue that people with and without self-control behave the same way as certain other kinds of people, but with a distinct psychology.

13. *the sorts of things they do*: Literally, 'by the what things they are about'. I interpret 'the what they're about' behaviourally: it refers to the kinds of things they do; the kinds of actions that self-control and lack of self-control involve. The contrast is between the domain of behaviour, externally described (e.g. 'eating too much') and psychological states.

14. *he does the same things*: Literally, 'he is about the same things'. See the previous note.

15. *using the universal one, not the particular*: Example: you know that 'drinking too much is bad for people' (universal premise); but you fail to have the conscious thought that 'this third glass of wine is too much' (particular premise). Hence, you don't act on your universal knowledge.

16. *but you don't know [the particular]*: [A] is saying that with the one kind of universal, you are bound to know the relevant

particular. But with the other kind, you might not. Here is [H], in full: 'When the universal is such as to embrace the person doing the reasoning, the particular is [automatically] known along with it. E.g. "Hellebore is harmful to all humans; I'm human; so hellebore is harmful to me." There the particular is known [automatically] with the universal. But when the universal [only] embraces a thing, then the particular isn't necessarily known along with the universal. E.g. "All hellebore is harmful; this is hellebore; so this is harmful." There you won't know the particular automatically with the universal. So that's the kind of particular that someone who lacks self-control might not know.'

17. *alter your physical state*: [E]: 'For example, when someone is in a rage, you see their eyes turn red; and when someone is in love, their face is pale.' (Other physical changes are caused by sexual desire; [A] may have those in mind.) The idea is that we should be open to thinking of failures of self-control as physiological.

18. *mature and grow*: Compare 1095a1–3, 1142a11–19. I read the content of what children are 'learning' to be implied by the context. (People who lose self-control can mouth true claims about what they should be doing; i.e. about right and wrong.) One commentator thinks that [A] means 'when children learn lines of Homer'. In that case, they can recite the lines, but cannot yet understand its adult psychology. That would amount to pretty much the same idea, but I think the terminology suggests arguments, not lines. Philo later offers the same phrasing, filled out like this: 'In philosophy class they string together arguments about how to be a good person, but what's the point if they pay no attention?' (*De congressu eruditionis gratia* 65.1).

19. *in other cases*: The text is extremely terse here. [A] means by 'in other cases' (or 'sometimes') that in non-practical cases of inference, when you put a universal belief (e.g. 'all whales are mammals') and a particular belief (e.g. 'Shamu is a whale') together and infer a conclusion ('Shamu is a mammal'), you inevitably believe it: your soul must affirm it. When that inference is the special case of a practical inference (of the form, 'So, I should do X'), the equivalent inevitable result is that you do it.

Note that in the practical case we might also 'assert' the conclusion (and are bound to do so if it is a conscious choice to do X), but we will not *always* assert it; we might just do it. The 'practical syllogism' is not always conscious, as I understand it. It is an attempt to describe the psychological mechanics of action, i.e. all action.

20. *this particular bit*: The qualification is added so that the premise is not taken as another universal 'Such and such a kind of food – e.g. chocolate – is sweet.'

21. *that's the one that's active*: You could take 'that's the one' to refer to the whole universal-with-particular combination. 'That's the one – i.e. that universal and its particular – that is the active syllogism occupying your thoughts.' Or, if the Greek is a little loose, 'that one' may refer only to the premise just quoted; so then [A] means that 'that's the operative particular premise' (the other particular premise being inactive).

   [A] does not give us the whole of the good syllogism, presented by reason. He only says, 'you have one universal belief telling you not to have a taste of something' opposing itself to the desire that drives you on. Perhaps the whole syllogism should have been in the text. Whether or not that is so, we can reconstruct what he has in mind as follows. Here, the syllogism on the left is 'telling you not to eat something' (I supply, 'because it is unhealthy, because it is very rich'). The syllogism on the right, given in full by [A], is the one that activates desire. [A]'s theory is that desire both silences (stupefies, extrudes, otherwise neutralizes) our grasp of P1, the particular fact that should be activating the first universal, U1, and fixates on P2, and pushes us into acting on it.

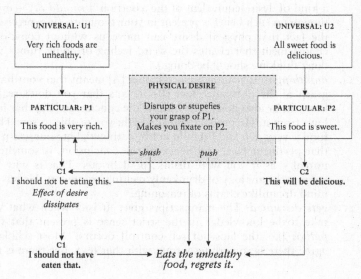

It is worth noting that the food-based example [A] uses would have a sexual equivalent, and perhaps, more than that, actually has a sexual subtext. Here is the simplest sexual equivalent for the two syllogisms, in a form [A] probably has in mind:

U1: 'I should not sleep with married women or respectable young girls.' P1: 'This woman is married [or otherwise off-limits].' C1: 'I should not sleep with this woman.'

U2: 'Sleeping with a beautiful woman is a great pleasure.' P2: 'This woman is very beautiful.' C2: 'Sleeping with this woman would be a great pleasure.'

So then sexual desire extrudes or stupefies your in-the-moment awareness of P1, 'this woman is married [or otherwise off-limits]', and fixates on P2, 'This woman is very beautiful.'

22. *set all your bodily parts in motion*: Compare 1110a15. Plenty of 'bodily parts' are involved here. Desire makes your legs move towards the fridge, makes your hand reach for the ice cream, etc.

23. *not the belief*: I.e. the belief, P2, 'This is sweet' (or the P2-C2 combination, 'This is sweet; this will be delicious') does not contradict either the belief expressed in U1, 'Rich food is unhealthy', or its particular, P1, 'I should not be eating this.' (The claims, 'This is delicious' and 'I should not eat this' can both be true. Likewise, 'I should not sleep with this married woman' and 'This woman is beautiful' can clearly both be true.) But desire supplies a kind of desire-equivalent of the assertion 'I *should* . . .' – even though no such belief is present in your thoughts. (It is precisely the fact that physical desire can move us without conscious endorsement that creates the weird feeling of doing things we don't think we should be doing.)

24. *mouthing it*: It is ambiguous whether [A] means that your hazy grasp of the particular fact [P1] means that you don't really know it, or also don't really know the conclusion [C1] that follows from it. He probably means both: you're able to say 'This food is very rich and I should not be eating it', but your grasp of that pertinent fact, and hence of the conclusion, is somehow unreal – as if you were drunk, or delirious. That is why he stresses the analogy of drunkenly reciting arguments. He has in mind dreamlike chains of reasoning.

25. *gets disrupted*: The manuscripts give: 'It isn't when what we take to be knowledge in the strict sense is present that the *pathos* [i.e. the lapse of self-control] occurs.' Most scholars agree there is something wrong with that text. But there is no

real controversy over what [A] is saying here. See [TA] for the details of my fix.

26. *just your perceptual knowledge*: The concession to Socrates would not satisfy him. The Socratic claim quoted by [A] from the *Protagoras* (352b5–c7) is that 'If someone knows what's good and bad, nothing can overpower them and force them into doing something other than what their knowledge is telling them to do.' [A] is only saying here that desire does not erase your universal knowledge from your mind. It's still in there, somewhere, though temporarily neutralized. Socrates thought that if real knowledge (of the universal) is 'in there', it is bound to lead to action in all relevant circumstances. It cannot be neutralized. So in fact [A] and Socrates disagree, and [A] has defended exactly the view that Socrates so disliked.

27. *can't control his temper*: [A] is saying that in Greek you use the same word of these people, *akrateis* ('lacking self-control'), but qualify it for their particular domains (*akrateis* of money, *akrateis* of fame, *akrateis* of anger). We might more naturally call the first two types 'obsessed with money' and 'obsessed with being famous'; or we say 'she has a weakness for X.'

Inability to control one's temper seems a bit more like the standard case, and later [A] will give it a separate treatment, admitting as much.

28. *Man, the Olympic champion*: A curious aside. The simplest way to read this is as an example of a small qualification that makes a major difference to the sense. I.e. 'Man, the Olympic champion' ('Man, the guy who won at the Olympics') is very different from just 'Man'. Similarly, 'I have no self-control when it comes to buying Pre-Raphaelite art' is very different from plain 'I have no self-control.'

This interpretation is confirmed by the equivalent example in Version B, at 1148b7, where the point is made that 'He is a bad doctor' is very different from 'He's simply bad [i.e. a bad person].'

Here's a parallel. If we say 'John is intolerant' or 'Mary is an extremely intolerant person', that unqualified term carries a quite precise and morally important sense. When qualified – 'John is gluten-intolerant', 'Mary is extremely lactose-intolerant' – it takes on a clearly different and morally unimportant sense. [A] is saying that *akratēs*, to the Greek ear, works very much like that.

The commentators had long reported there was an Olympic champion whose actual name was Anthropos, i.e. 'Man' (or 'Human'). That seemed bizarre, and impossible to accept as the explanation for [A]'s text, until a papyrus (*P. Oxyrhynchus* 222) confirmed that there really was a boxer called Anthropos (probably a slave or ex-slave) who won at the Olympics in 456 BC.

I assume that *logos* here means not definition but 'expression'. 'Man-the-Olympic-champion' is itself a *logos*, i.e. an expression that picks out this person. (See *Posterior Analytics* 93b31, where [A] refers to 'names, or name-like expressions'.) Then, a little loosely, [A] uses *logos* to refer to the general term 'man' as well. This works just as well in English as in Greek: 'the general expression, "man", as opposed to the expression that specifically picks out Man the boxer'.

(Note that unqualified or 'standard-sense' *akrasia*, lack of self-control, is not the same as a 'universal' or 'general' *akrasia*. 'Standard' *akrasia* has a very specific, not a general, sense.)

29.   *or is (sort of) a vice*: Most translators take this as: 'not just as a mistake, but as a vice – whether it is standard [lack of self-control], or a particular kind'. That is an impossible construal. The final two phrases certainly qualify *kakia* ('badness', 'vice').

What [A] says here, more literally, is: 'We think of it as a sort of badness (*kakia*), either absolute [i.e. it sort of makes you a bad person] or particular [i.e. it's sort of a vice].' The 'sort of' qualifies both options. ('Being a bad person, in general' is the 'absolute' sense of *kakia*; a 'particular' *kakia* is 'a vice'.) This closely matches what he says at 1145b1 (lacking of self-control is somewhat like being a bad person) and at 1149b20; and 1152a17 (a person who lacks self-control is 'semi-wicked'). Conversely, the very end of book IV describes self-control as 'kind of' a virtue.

30.   *excessive pleasures † . . . †*: At this point the sentence contains a parallel reference to avoiding pain: 'and avoids [excesses] of painful things (hunger, thirst, heat, cold, all the pains to do with touch and taste)'. The reference to pains seems to me to have been inserted rather clumsily. It asserts, strictly, that avoiding *excesses* of pain is a lack of self-control. That seems wrong on two counts. [A] only ever says that shirking *ordinary* levels of physical pain is a failing; and he calls it being 'soft', not a lack of self-control. (He makes a reference to being soft in the next sentence. That fact may have caused the awkward insertion. In fact, it is not required. You can be soft with respect to pleasures too.)

31. *do the same things*: Literally, 'they are certainly about/involved with the same things'. In this case, a reference to outward behaviour. See above, note VII.13.

32. *obsessively*: Literally, 'who are overpowered beyond reason'. 'Is overpowered by' is a Greek way of saying, e.g., 'she can't resist X', 'is addicted to X', 'is obsessed with X'.

33. *Niobe ... Satyros*: Once again [A] takes his examples from Greek drama rather than real life. Niobe had fourteen children and boasted that she had out-mothered Leda, who had only two, Apollo and Artemis. So Apollo and Artemis killed all her children. We have almost no evidence as to what [A] is talking about with the second reference, but [E] reports the following: 'Satyros fell in love with a young girl, and then found that his father Sostratos was colluding in his love affair with her, and from then on loved his father so much that when his father died he threw himself off a cliff.' (The girl in question was probably Sostratos' own second or third wife.)

34. *Phalaris*: Phalaris, King of Akragas in the sixth century BC, reportedly burned people alive in a bronze bull, so constructed that their agonized screams would resonate through its mouth and make it bellow like a real bull. He became a byword for savagery, unsurprisingly.

The report about 'tribes' supplying their own children 'for banquets' is absurd. Something was lost in translation. My guess is that the original claim was that local chieftains would send their sons or daughters to one another 'for [*marriage*] banquets', i.e. not *to be eaten* but to be married, to form alliances.

35. *eating charcoal, or clay*: Likely a reference to pregnancy cravings, or pica more generally. Both of these particular cravings are known in pregnant women. [A] (probably) refers to these again at VII.12 (1153a5); and more explicitly at *History of Animals*, 584a20.

36. *female sexuality in males*: The manuscript text here contains an ungrammatical fragment, usually loosely rendered as 'sex with men'. It can only mean that in pig-Greek. See [TA] for details.

Greek attitudes to homosexuality were complex. Many cities, including Athens, tolerated relationships between an older 'lover' (the *erastes*) and younger, late-adolescent 'boyfriend' (the *paidika* or *erōmenos*). [A] discusses those relationships as if they were commonplace and normal (see e.g. VIII.4 and IX.1). But the relationships had rules: the younger men were not expected to stay in them into manhood. Also, the younger man – who played the quasi-feminine role – was supposed to be the sexually passive partner. Older men who were passive sexual partners (in that sense) throughout their lives were considered unusual, and teased with accusations of 'effeminacy' and 'softness'. (There are various graphic terms of abuse for men known for having those tastes, preserved by Aristophanes.)

Given these cultural facts, and the physiologically explicit remark about women that follows, and [A]'s attitudes elsewhere, we can be certain that he was not referring here to homosexuality in general or to the cultural practice of the *erastes/erōmenos* relationship in general ('pederasty', as [R] wrongly translates), but to sexual passivity (i.e. a preference for being penetrated) in (older) men.

Victorian scholars, because of their own attitudes, took [A]'s phrase 'outside the bounds of being a bad person' (which means 'something it makes no sense to regard as morally bad') to mean 'beyond depraved', i.e. unspeakably evil – pretty much the exact opposite of its actual sense. Note that [A] says that God is outside the bounds of badness, too, at 1145a26.

[A]'s treatment in fact has elements of defence. Some men have female sexual tastes, he says, and it makes no more sense to criticize them for those, or accuse them of 'not controlling themselves', than it does to criticize women for the same. And notice that he appears to place such tastes on a moral par with biting your fingernails and pregnancy cravings.

A key Peripatetic text to compare here is *Problems* 879a36. There the question is raised, 'Why do some men enjoy the passive sexual role?' There is no hint of condemnation. But [A] – or whoever the author is – does say, as here, that the natural version of the condition is a 'physical impairment' that 'distorts' reproductive functioning. The terms are biological, not moral.

37. *human levels of lechery and gluttony*: [A] means this: to do X 'through a lack of self-control' (in ordinary language) requires that X falls within normal human levels of lechery or gluttony if and when it is done by choice.

38. *self-control*: Rather, of *akrasia*, lack of self-control. [A] uses *akrasia* as the catch-all for the topic. In English we use 'self-control'.

39. *follows reason*: Oddly, [A] made a very similar-sounding claim about lack of self-control caused by desire, too, at 1147b1.

40. *non-necessary*: The idea is that (standard) lack of self-control always involves those. [A] is willing to treat sexual desire, in

general, as 'necessary' (see chapter 4), but not, say, the desire to sleep with someone else's wife.

41. *But lust certainly schemes*: [P]: 'If a man wants to sleep with a [respectable, unmarried] girl he can't just seduce her openly, or immediately; he has to plan his seduction, and make sure nobody notices it, and that's why Homer calls Aphrodite a weaver of wiles (Aphrodite stands here for sexual desire).' This interpretation is exactly right. For a vivid contemporary example of adulterers' schemes, see Lysias 1, *In Defence of Killing Eratosthenes*.

42. *abuse*: I.e. *hubris*. An act of *hubris* is by definition unprovoked. The term can imply 'an assault', 'violation'; but also cruelty, an outrageous wrong, a deliberate humiliation. [A]'s point here is that if you react violently out of anger, that is by definition not an act of *hubris*: i.e. it is not an act of abuse or cruelty, etc. By contrast, lust certainly motivates acts of *hubris* (i.e. sexual transgressions, sexual assault, sexual abuse). See next note.

43. *nothing abusive*: There is no *hubris* in having an angry reaction (to mistreatment). *Hubris* (abuse, violation) often has a sexual sense, obviously in play here. The observation here is that sexually based offences are considered especially heinous. And the common perception is that they are caused by lust. The things we do out of anger, when we lose our temper, seem more understandable – at least by comparison.

44. *violently randy*: E.g. goats, rabbits (at least in common perception). Literally, 'in abuse and randiness'. The first term, *hubris*, (as we just noted) implies *sexual abuse*. The second term is *sinamōria*, an extremely rare word and apparently Athenian slang. The commentators all seem puzzled by it, and one wrongly reports that it means 'destructiveness'. (It can, in some dialects.) But context strongly suggests a sexual sense, and this is confirmed by, e.g., Aristophanes' *Clouds*, line 1070, and by its use in Callimachus (fr. 366) of a 'randy' satyr; and by later lexicographers' reports that *sinamōros* (sometimes) meant 'whorish' and 'lewd'.

45. *crazy and impulsive*: The verb can have this meaning; and the claim makes good sense. But the manuscript text, as preserved, seems instead to say 'animals deviate from their nature'. See [TA] for the emendation.

46. *lion*: The text here reads, 'So [comparing these things] is like if you compared, say, unrighteousness with an unrighteous human being.' This makes no sense, and I will spare the reader the convoluted attempts that have been made to explain it.

I read 'a lioness' (or 'a she-lion') for 'unrighteousness', which makes good sense for a fairly easy change to the text. [A] uses 'lioness' as an example of a ferocious beast. See [TA] for details. [MM] at this point paraphrases: 'Which can do more harm, a lion or [an evil man like] Phalaris?' (2.6.33).

The run of thought seems to be this. Being bestial isn't as bad – as destructive – as being evil. [A] has in mind, for the first, people suffering from extreme forms of mental and psychological and social impairment. People like that may be ferocious and violent, but they lack the intellect that, in evil people, can be a source, through strategy and cunning and deliberation, of vastly larger amounts of harm.

In making this point, [A] makes two comparisons.

(a) A 'bestial' state, compared to an evil human intelligence, is almost like inanimate evils, i.e. the mindless harm of a landslide or an earthquake. Those are terrifying in their way, but not capable of devising harm.

(b) Comparing bestial states to normal evil is very like comparing an actual beast – a lion, say – to an evil human being. The lion is worse in certain respects (more savage, worse table manners). But a lion can't become a tyrant or initiate genocide.

I read the two comparisons as running in parallel. The first should not be made to explain the second. Earthquakes, and lions, both lack reason; the two comparisons both follow on from the claim that 'bestial' people lack powers of reason.

47. *various ways you can be*: I have reorganized [A]'s sentence structure here, for conversion into English. The actual sentence structure is as follows: 'You can be in a state (a) such that you can't resist {or handle} the ones most people can; or (b) such that you can resist {control/handle} the ones most people can't; and of those, when that's about pleasures, [that means] you lack, or have, self-control [respectively]; when that's about pains, [that means] you're soft, or resilient [respectively].'

48. *lean . . . to the inferior states*: I.e. most of us tend towards over-indulging in pleasure, and pull away from physical hardship. So we're constantly tending towards a lack of self-control and softness, even if we succeed in resisting the pull. [A] makes closely related claims at 1109a13–17, 1119a5–11.

49. *incurable*: There is an etymological claim here. [A] is implying that *akolastos* directly implies 'incurable' by its literal or historical sense, 'unstoppable'.

50. *worse person*: By far the best way to understand this (often
     repeated) claim is to concentrate on the sexual sense of *akolas-
     tos*: lecherous. Think of someone who pursues excessive sexual
     gratification by choice: a womanizer and serial adulterer; a
     tyrant who sexually exploits his subjects; a slave-owner who
     assaults his slaves; a man who drugs women for non-consensual
     sex. What they have in common is that they all act by deliberate
     choice and without regret. [A] is saying that (a) this is very dif-
     ferent from sleeping with the wrong person through a lapse of
     self-control and regretting it; and (b) it makes you a worse per-
     son. An equivalent point can be made for gluttony, but that is
     far less prominent in [A]'s thoughts.

51. *Philoctetes ... Xenophantus*: [Asp.] says that Philoctetes, in
     this version, was bitten by a snake while hiding from the Greeks.
     He endured the pain as long as he could, then gave in and started
     screaming – thereby revealing himself. Cercyon's unmarried
     daughter Alopē was raped (or perhaps seduced); he demanded
     the name of the offender, promising that he wouldn't punish
     her; but then flew into a rage (and possibly killed himself, or,
     more likely, her). Nobody knows what the Xenophantus refer-
     ence is about. Evidently he was known personally to [A] and his
     students. Perhaps he was an actor who cracked up on stage.

52. *kings of Scythia*: We are not sure what this hereditary 'softness'
     was. It seems to be referred to by Herodotus (1.105): a heredi-
     tary Scythian illness he calls the 'female disease'. Notice that
     [A] moves into the example after a mention of illness.

     I suspect this is a reference to hemophilia. Note that (a) hemo-
     philia conspicuously runs in families, and (b) is largely confined
     to men, and (c) its most obvious effect is to make men dramat-
     ically less able to endure physical hardship (especially those in-
     volving any violence) and (d) it historically often causes men to be
     labelled as 'soft' and 'effeminate'. The same condition ('woman-
     liness among wealthy Scythian nobles') is also mentioned by
     Hippocrates (*De aere, aquis et locis* 22.1). He describes men
     who shelter themselves from outside life, thereby living 'women's
     lives', when they notice pain and swellings (*kedmata*) in their
     hips and ankles resulting from their horse-riding. Also, that
     they test themselves for the condition by making a small incision
     behind the ear and observing the bleeding. This surely supports
     identification with hemophilia. Hippocrates seems unaware that
     the illness is hereditary; but [A] is reporting that fact. (If this is

correct, this pushes back the first recorded medical reference to
this illness by about 500 years.)

[A]'s point, then, is that hemophiliacs are not 'soft' in the character sense that he is discussing; neither are women, just because
they are (in certain respects) physically less hardy than men.

53. *still do wrong*: The switch to the language of wrongdoing rests
on the examples of desire-based lack of self-control that [A]
mostly has in mind: adultery, seduction of unmarried women
and sexual abuse. In a modern context, we might add people
who steal, e.g. from their own family, because of an addiction.
They feel really bad about stealing; but they steal.

54. *it isn't reason's job*: This is the key point. Since starting points
of this kind (e.g. basic principles of action that constitute people's goals in particular contexts: 'I should not sleep with other
men's wives'; 'I should respect unmarried girls') come from
character, not from reason or reasoned justifications, it follows
that no form of reasoned argument can persuade someone who
has the wrong ones to adopt different ones (e.g. someone whose
starting point is 'I should sleep with as many married women as
possible'). You'd actually have to alter their entire character – a
much, much harder process, and one not based on reason (or
certainly not only on reason). The person who lacks self-control,
by contrast, also needs to alter their psychological make-up –
not a matter of argument either – but less drastically, since they
already have 'the right starting points'.

55. *makes us have*: Most translators supply 'teaches us about' from
the previous clause. I think the syntax is looser, and we should
understand a general notion of 'being responsible for'; 'being
in charge of'. See VI.12, from 1144a11, for [A]'s more detailed
discussion of this.

56. *incidentally, yes*: Example. Suppose you firmly believe that
smoking is good for your health (as some people once did). So
you choose to smoke. And though you really hate it, you make
an enormous effort and stick to your decision to smoke ten
times a day, for your health. Is that self-control? Absolutely. Is
it also a case of sticking to a false belief? Not really. [A] is saying
that it counts as self-control because you are sticking to your
commitment to health. Your per se target is health, and your
per se belief is 'that you should do things that are healthy'. You
are only incidentally choosing to do something unhealthy
because you happen to be misinformed. So this is self-control,
because you have the right per se goal. It is also, in a sense, a

case of sticking to a false belief – but only incidentally. The same applies, *mutatis mutandis*, to a lack of self-control.

If you were sticking to a, per se, false belief ('I believe I should harm my lungs as rapidly as possible'), then [A] thinks that would not be a case of self-control. The whole concept of self-control presupposes a familiar set of pressures and temptations, and a standard set of reasonable, morally normal aims that people then stick to, or fail to stick to. (A psychopath who one morning lazily fails to stick to his earlier resolution to kill and eat someone that day is not experiencing a loss of self-control.)

57. *X in order to get Y*: Using my example, this means: 'If you choose smoking, X, to become healthy, Y, then your per se (and real) object of choice is Y, health, and you are only incidentally choosing to smoke.' What's more, the normal sense of 'choosing' is the per se sense. So it is overall misleading to say you are 'choosing to smoke' (just as it is clearly misleading to say that a mother who chooses to give her son a vaccine is 'choosing to stab her son with a needle').

58. *lack self-control*: [A] means that since fanatics are motivated by pleasure and pain, they resemble people who lack self-control. I use the term 'fanatic' here of someone who is obstinately devoted to the superiority of their own views whatever they happen to be. ('Bigots' would also be a decent translation, in its older sense; but it is now more often associated specifically with racial and religious animosity.) The analogy with self-control goes further. A fanatic, to be rational at all, must have the belief, 'I should, and will, change my views if someone presents me with a compelling reason to do so' – but the pain of admitting to being wrong is so completely overpowering that they never act on that principle. (This is the powerful intellectual vice that Karl Popper calls the 'unfalsifiability' of pseudo-rational dogmas.) So they act against their own principle. (On the other hand, unlike people who lack self-control, fanatics never acknowledge that failure, and never feel any regret – until their fanaticism fully breaks.)

59. *the honourable thing for him to do*: The thought is compressed and elliptical (to the point where some editors suggest adding to the text). But it is clear enough that [A] means: 'Telling the truth, which is the thing he took pleasure in doing, was also the honourable thing to do, and he was persuaded, rationally, that he should lie, which is shameful.' So in this case, backing away from his rational decision, and going with his feelings, was the

honourable thing. An interesting question that [A] does not
raise is how often this is the case, and why this kind of 'lack
of self-control' shouldn't be a fairly common feature of good
people's character. (Instead of denying that it is a real case of
akrasia, why not just allow the possibility of good *akrasia*?)

60. *between*: [A] is trying to cast self-control as a middle. He likes
the idea that all character traits fit that model (see IV.7,
1127a13). So one obvious idea would be to imagine people who
have too much self-control. But [A] does not go for that idea.
Nor is it clear what it would mean. Instead he proposes someone who does not have enough physical desire. He has already
discussed such people in connection with moderation, but here
the idea is that there might be people who initially decide to
enjoy certain physical pleasures – 'I really should have two
glasses of wine tonight' – but then fail to stick to their decision
because they just don't get enough pleasure from drinking wine.
That character trait is then the lower extreme on the scale of
self-control; a lack of desire that undermines your plans and
commitments.

61. *being lecherous*: That is, people typically discount or ignore the
vice of not enjoying physical pleasures enough, which [A] elsewhere calls being a 'feel-nothing'. Likewise, we hardly ever
notice the vice of not sticking to a commitment to physical pleasure because of a lack of desire. Does it even exist? Consider the
question, 'What is the opposite of being sexually faithful to
your spouse?' We would all say 'Being unfaithful; having an
affair.' But there is another opposite: never sleeping with your
spouse at all. Being sexually faithful requires that there is at
least some sex going on. Two rocks aren't sexually faithful to
one another just because they don't sleep around. [A]'s wider
point here is that since these vices are so rare, some philosophers do not recognize them at all. Plato, for one, sometimes
seems to imply that less physical desire is always better. The
Stoics sometimes seem to have a similar view. But the more
common-sense view is that a complete lack of physical desire,
when it occurs, is clearly a bad thing, a form of mental illness.
Hence [A]'s passing comment, 'just as people assume they are'.

62. *choice {and intent}*: The reference here is to the discussion at
VI.12, 1144a23. A 'clever' person might just be good at working out how to achieve bad goals. A wise person, by definition,
has morally decent goals, because wisdom by definition includes
grasping and valuing what's good and right. The term *prohairesis*

is here used in the sense of 'aim' or 'goal', i.e. 'life-choice' or 'overall choice' (e.g. 'I choose/prefer to treat people fairly', 'I choose/prefer to pay my debts'). It is so used in the earlier passage too, at 1144a20.

But how can a clever person lack self-control, if 'clever' here means someone who is skilfully pursuing the wrong goals? Doesn't lack of self-control by definition imply having the right goals, and then failing to act on them? [A] seems to allude to this same case earlier, at 1142b18 (see note VI.27). Someone who lacks self-control has the right goals in a sense, somewhere inside them; but they might temporarily entertain bad ones, and pursue them cleverly.

63. *use as our criteria*: The point seems to be that the study of human life, and *eudaimonia*, gives us the right criteria for judging the value of all goods, including pleasure and pain, by way of the question, 'How does pleasure contribute to *eudaimonia*?' Or [A] may mean that we are studying the overall goal of life, and a well-known candidate for being, itself, the highest good in life is pleasure (i.e. according to hedonists). So this is the right place to look at that view carefully. (In effect, this is just the very broad claim that a discussion of hedonism belongs within ethics.) I suspect [A] is mostly implying the second. The [MM] author also takes it that way (1204a21). He paraphrases: 'After all, we are discussing *eudaimonia* here, and everyone thinks that *eudaimonia* (flourishing) either is pleasure, or the same as living a pleasant life, or at least involves pleasure.'

64. *made the claim*: See 1104b26, 1105a5, a11.

65. khairein: Or *chairein*: Normal Greek for 'to enjoy' or 'to rejoice' or 'to be happy [at, with]'. [A] is saying (as elsewhere) that *eudaimonia* must include pleasure (i.e., as we would say in normal English, a perfect life includes being happy). He is not asserting that *eudaimonein* is synonymous with *khairein*.

The etymological claim probably derives from some hedonist philosopher; perhaps Eudoxus. It is – as usual – wrong. *Makarios* does not have anything to do with *khairein*. The word *makar* perhaps originally meant simply 'great' (related to *mega*, big, *makron*, large, long, *makos*, length, size, *makistos*, largest). *Makares* is frequently used as an epithet of gods in Homer (perhaps originally 'the great/big/mighty gods') and hence came to be reconstrued as 'the blessed gods'.

66. *process ... endpoint*: So, as the house is a greater good than the process of building, so the state of calm satisfaction, untroubled

by pleasure or pain, must be a greater good than the pleasure that leads to it.

67. *simply {or normally speaking}*: This translates *haplōs*; sometimes translated 'without qualification' or 'unconditionally'. In connection with pleasures, it is [A]'s way of referring to things that are pleasurable for most people; for people in a normal condition, with the right set of feelings and attitudes. That is not the same as pleasurable always, or for everyone (for some people, these things are not pleasurable); nor does it mean 'unconditionally pleasurable'. We do not call hot soup 'unconditionally hot'. We say that hot soup 'normally feels hot; but may not feel hot to some people'.

68. *corresponding distinction*: [A] begins with a very general point that if the critics of pleasure observed all of these distinctions, then all or most of their claims would turn out to have much less force. But he is not completely clear about how each distinction, exactly, would make a difference to the argument.

Some examples of the sort of things [A] has in mind: surgery, and powerful drugs, are not good things normally speaking, but they can be very good things for people who are sick. Eating and drinking (which restore a certain natural physical state) may not be good things strictly speaking, or absolutely, but they are good things for some people, namely people who are thirsty and hungry. Or at any rate they are good for those people for a while.

Also, people who claim pleasure is bad in general wrongly assume that pleasure is always the restoration of our natural state (like the pleasures of eating and drinking). They fixate on a subset of physical pleasures. Then they argue that since restoration is by definition a kind of repair, it cannot be a good thing. [A] will argue that some pleasures involve no repair or restoration. He also seems to say that even restorative pleasures are good, not *qua* repair, but *qua* the normal functioning of certain healthy parts of the soul.

In a nutshell: 'They say pleasure is bad, but it turns out they really just mean physical pleasures; so they're just saying that some kinds of pleasures, for some people, under some conditions are bad: a far weaker claim.'

69. *aren't . . . pleasures at all*: [A] makes the same or a very similar point, more clearly, in the parallel treatment in book X: 'if the things a good person finds distasteful seem pleasurable to someone else, what's so surprising about that? . . . Those things

aren't [really] pleasurable. They're just pleasurable . . . to people in that condition.' There are two related claims here: things that physically ill people find pleasurable are not really, or naturally, pleasurable; and things that morally depraved people find pleasurable are also not really pleasurable. [A] treats physical health as analogous with moral health as a determinant of what is 'naturally' (or 'normally speaking') pleasurable. See also III.4, 1113a29–33 and I.8, 1099a7–20 for general statements of this point. The claim that these are 'not really pleasures at all' serves as part of [A]'s defence of pleasure, because it is often precisely those kinds of pleasures that anti-hedonists focus on.

70. *the remaining, [intact] physiological disposition*: The sense here is difficult, because it is very dense, and there are some doubts about the text, specifically the term translated as 'remaining'. But [Asp.] and [MM] both confirm the text, and both say that [A] means this: when you are extremely thirsty, say, then you are dehydrated and your 'natural [physiological] state' needs to be restored. The pleasure of drinking accompanies that restoration. But it is not restoration per se that causes pleasure, says [A]. Rather, pleasure (in general) arises from the normal exercising, or activity, of your various physical (and mental and moral) dispositions. Even in the case of drinking, you still have physiological states and mechanisms that are functioning normally and need no 'restoration' or repair. In one sense, yes, your 'nature' is experiencing a lack (you are dehydrated), but in another your physiology is intact and just doing its thing. To see this, consider a different case where a person is extremely dehydrated, and also fails to feel any thirst. That would mean that some other part of their physiology was malfunctioning and not properly active. So clearly, in normal thirsty people, that 'natural disposition' (here *hexis* in effect means 'physiological mechanism') is active in the normal way. (Here [Asp.] says that it's the nutritive part of the soul that is active when you are thirsty; and [MM] says more vaguely, 'some part of the soul' is active.) In spite of your extreme thirst, that mechanism 'remains intact'; and that activity, says [A], is what results in pleasure. It's a 'merely incidental' fact that its operation accompanies the restoration of the body's required level of hydration. Pleasure does not, per se, require or depend on restoration.

The point of this is to defeat the claim that pleasure in general depends on restoration, which would mean, in effect, that you only experience it at all when some part of you is defective or damaged, which in turn implies that ideally you never want to experience it at all. (It would have the implication, for example, that God never experiences pleasure, since He never experiences any lack or deficiency. And for most Greek philosophers, even Epicurus, that is a powerful argument against hedonism.)

71. *You can see this*: I.e., probably, that it is only an incidental fact that pleasures accompany restoration. Once you remove those particular and temporary conditions, people resume their normal, non-restorative pleasures.

72. *sharp or bitter, for example*: Commentators assume that 'sharp' here refers to a kind of taste. Vinegar, for example, is 'sharp' (i.e. acidic). Indeed 'sharp', *oxos*, was a term for cheap, low-quality wine. So [P] explains: 'When you are not thirsty you prefer fine wines (e.g. Chian), but when desperate with thirst even sharp, [low-quality] wine gives you pleasure.' [A] may have that in mind. Or he may mean that when people are in a non-standard physical condition, their actual tastes alter. E.g. pregnant women crave pickles (sharp), lemons (bitter), black coffee (bitter), etc. (Their 'cravings' would make that a case of 'restoration'. [A] is aware of this phenomenon. He mentions it at *History of Animals* 584a20, and probably at 1148b28.)

73. *some people say*: The argument originates with Plato, as an attack on pleasure. I offer, e.g., *Philebus* 54c (I will use the same translation of *genesis*, even though Plato's Greek is in reality rather more elegant): 'I say that every becoming, {every A-to-B process}, occurs for the sake of something that then is; and becoming, taken as a whole, occurs for the sake of being, taken as a whole. So pleasure, since it is an A-to-B process, necessarily occurs for the sake of something that [then] is. And when something always occurs for the sake of something else, then the thing that it's for the sake of belongs in the class of what's good, while the thing that occurs for the sake of it has to be placed in a different class. So doesn't that mean, since pleasure is an A-to-B process, that we'd be correct in classifying it as other than good?'

74. *changing from A to B*: Again translates the Greek term *genesis*, which means 'becoming' but in this context has to have a predicative sense: 'becoming X (from not being X)'. (Hence 'changing from A to B'.) E.g. changing from thirsty to hydrated, from hungry to full, from exhausted to rested, from cold to warm, etc.

75. *exercising of our natural dispositions*: Whether physiological, mental or moral. The last would be the exercising of our virtues,

which [A] has discussed in connection with its accompanying pleasures at I.8. But here he has mostly been discussing bodily pleasures, which he construes as the unimpeded exercise of physiological dispositions, i.e. of our normal biological functions. See above, note VII.70.

76. *paradigm good*: Or 'a strictly good thing'. The term is often used of something that is the clearest, best paradigm case of X. (E.g. earlier, 'knowledge in the strict sense' at 1147b15.)

77. *activity is an A-to-B process*: [A] means that some people see pleasure as a process (and for that reason, an inferior thing) because it is activity, and they confuse activity with process; which means, absurdly, that they think it is bad on account of the very thing (its being an activity) that in fact makes it a paradigm good. Thus [Asp.], correctly, as it seems.

78. *bigger is the opposite of smaller*: Speusippus agrees that pain is bad, and the opposite of pleasure, but thinks pleasure is bad too. Only the neutral state (no pleasure, no pain) is good. So pleasure has two opposites (pain and neutrality) just as bigger has two opposites (smaller and equal).

79. *by definition, a bad thing*: Speusippus defines good as a kind of tranquillity (*aochlēsia*), the absence of both pleasure and pain. So he is asserting that pleasure is, definitionally, a bad thing. [A] replies that this is just obviously silly. The commentators all assume that '[he] would not say' means 'a person would not say', i.e. 'nobody would say', and I think they are right. But you might also take Speusippus himself to be the subject. 'Even he wouldn't say that.'

80. *flourishing is . . . perfect*: The conclusion: hence, flourishing, or being blessed, must be an unimpeded activity; and that is how we just defined pleasure. This is a near-repeat of the last argument. (But a natural repetition, as it seems, not editorial.)

81. *and nobody thinks they do*: [A] is apparently now talking about human beings only, because he uses the masculine pronoun. [A] sometimes makes sweeping claims of this kind even when he knows that some people disagree. He is asserting that different human beings have different natures and different best-possible qualities (of mind and character) that they can attain. This maps onto his views about differences between men and women, adults and children, and perhaps his views on 'natural slaves'.

82. *there's nothing wrong with you if*: [A] says simply, '*He* doesn't avoid excess [of pain].' That means (with subject supplied from three lines earlier): '*A bad person* doesn't avoid excessive pain',

which in turn means 'A bad person here isn't someone who avoids excessive pain.' Here and in the last sentence 'bad person' (*phaulos*) seems to be used to mean 'person with the relevant fault or failing in this context'.

BOOK VIII

1. *philia*: *Philein* means 'to love'. A corresponding noun, *philos*, can mean a 'loved one' or 'a friend' (and is often used of family members). The translation here respects the full scope of *philia*. It is usually quite easy to tell, from context, how the term is being used. Here, and through the opening two chapters, *philia* is being used broadly. This is perfectly normal. In ordinary Greek *philoi* often translates accurately as 'family and friends' or 'friends and loved ones'. Hence [A]'s inclusion of family relationships in his examples here.

    Soon, though, friendship in particular will become the main topic, until chapter 7. Friendship is a cooperative relationship of some sort between non-kin. That is the underlying natural fact about it that makes it recognizably the same phenomenon across all human cultures. Relationships with non-kin are always reciprocal, in some form. Relationships with family are not, or do not have to be. So *philia* in its other sense (love between family) is importantly different, as much for [A] as for us.

2. *a sort*: [A] says that *philia* is *aretē tis*. The *tis* qualifier very often means 'a sort of', or 'sort of a', and it almost certainly has that sense here. [A] mostly means that being a friend is sort of a virtue. But he may well also mean that love for family – e.g. being a loving son, a loving mother, a loving husband, a loving sister – is likewise 'a sort of virtue'. He does not ultimately think *philia* is a separate particular virtue like the others he has discussed. Rather, it implies, uses and depends on several of them. (His second suggestion clarifies his actual view.)

3. *better when two men go together*: Iliad 10.224–5: 'When two walk together: one may notice, before the other, where an advantage lies.' [A] leaves out the rest of the well-known lines. But he quotes their next verb in his next clause. But he recasts 'notice' (Homeric sense) as 'thinking' (its sense in his time).

4. *travelling*: I take this to be about the actual travelling (not just the being in other countries). Ancient travel was unlike (most) modern travel. It was dangerous and arduous. To get anywhere

any great distance away you (or you and a few companions) would be spending time on empty country roads, in wildernesses etc., passing through dangerous places. In those circumstances, you are delighted to encounter anyone at all who is willing to be helpful. So you learn that any fellow human being is a potential friend. Thus [Asp.]: 'When you are travelling, people tell you the way; they offer shelter; they protect you.' Likewise [H]. And the word for travels here is *planais*, 'wanderings', assisting this interpretation. Think of the parable of the good Samaritan (Luke 10: 25–37) for a similar sentiment: out on the road, any kind and decent person, of whatever nationality, may prove to be your 'neighbour'.

5. *when people are friends*: I take this to be separate from the previous point about laws and citizens, but related to it. It furthers the claim that, in a sense, friendship is better than, and subsumes, righteousness. (Being friends is better than merely doing what is right by one another, and includes the latter, as a given.) But the point is made by considering (as I read it) just two individuals. [A] literally says: 'if people are friends, they have no need for righteousness'; and this clearly means: they have all the righteousness (with respect to one another) that they need – i.e. they are already bound to treat each other rightly, just *qua* friends. In the same way, 'we don't need any food' can easily mean 'we have all the food we need'. [A] makes exactly this point at 1157a23: 'Friends [of the best kind] would never do one another wrong.' And at the equivalent point in the opening remarks of the [EE] version, at 1234b28: 'If you want to guarantee that someone will not do you wrong, make them your friend'; and 1234b24: 'It's impossible for people to do one another wrong and be friends.'

6. *clearest case … friends and family*: 'Clearest case' translates *malista*, 'of the [forms of] right and wrong, the most [i.e. most paradigmatically, strongest, most obvious] right and wrong is between friends and family'.

    See [TA] for a very slight emendation I make here to the text (I restore a definite article). There are other ways of taking these words. Perhaps 'and of the different forms of right and wrong [between citizens], the best kind is friendly; friend-ish'. [A] does say things to that effect elsewhere too, e.g. at [EE] 1243a33. But I do not think that he is talking here about citizens. And while the claim as I take it might seem to contradict V.6 (where right and wrong is said to hold, 'standardly' and paradigmatically between citizens), it matches and, I think, looks ahead to VIII.9, where [A] seems to offer a rather different view: that the closer the friendship or family tie, the stronger the form of right and wrong. Decisively, there is a closely parallel claim at the equivalent point in [EE], at 1234b26: 'Right and wrong apply most [*malista*] between family and friends.'

7. *people disagree about*: Several of the questions about friendship that [A] raises here (and elsewhere) are raised by Plato in the *Lysis*. See, for example, 213e5–214b2 for the idea that friends are similar to one another; 214b7–214d7 for the idea that only good people can be friends; 215a6–c2 for why good people need friends. [A]'s discussion is a continuation of, and a response to, Plato's earlier treatment.

8. *proverbial*: A Greek proverb (from Hesiod, *Works and Days* l. 25): 'Potter loathes potter; carpenter loathes carpenter.' (Fortunately, translators feel nothing but goodwill and affection for all other translators.)

9. *talked . . . before*: Not in the text as we have it.

10. *xenia*: Your *xenos* is a friend who lives in a different city, with whom you have an arrangement that every time you, or any of your family, visit that city, you will stay in his home and be hosted by him; and vice versa. So the word means both 'guest' and 'host'. *Xenia* is a long-term, long-distance inter-family support network.

11. *something about them*: There seems to be an equivocation here. [A] appears to claim that loving someone because of the way they are intrinsically, or 'for who they are', thereby implies loving them, and wanting the best for them, *for their sake*. But those are not the same. Clearly there are people we care about and help for their sake without also admiring (or knowing) their character or thinking that they are good people (e.g. when we help earthquake victims, or strive to eradicate treatable diseases, or alleviate extreme poverty).

On the other hand it is probably true, if we confine the claim specifically to friends (not distant strangers, and not family), that the friends we consistently help purely for their sake – i.e. our closest, dearest friends – are also people that we've found to be trustworthy, honest, kind, generous, etc. over a long period of time. So the correlation between having altruistic attachments to those people and believing in their good character seems correct – even if the argument here is too quick. (In reality [A] has a number of other motives for this central thesis about close friendship.)

In fact, I would go further and say that [A]'s main idea is deeply insightful. Our moral virtues (very plausibly) are intimately and essentially connected to these relationships, both in their present function and in their evolutionary history. They make us attractive to potential friends and partners, and they obviously sustain those relationships once formed.

12. *resemble this one* † . . . †: There appears to be a hole in the text here. Perhaps the argument went something like this: 'The other two kinds resemble this one [in so far as they supply some sort of good or pleasure (incidentally). But in friendship based on goodness, the friends are good things in themselves, and absolutely]; and what's good absolutely is also pleasurable absolutely.' The apparently missing section is similar to what [A] says at 1157a32.

13. *in it for something useful*: The plural here seems to refer (confusingly) to people who enter into those relationships for material benefit with partners who are in it for the pleasure, i.e. not to cases where both parties are only after material gain. Because there is no such thing. (At least one lover in a sexual relationship is in it for the pleasure. People never pay *each other* for sex.)

[**Asp.**] thinks this is a reference to (male) prostitution. 'He means people who go with someone for money.' [A] probably means something less crude, but perhaps along those lines.

14. *something in common*: Usually taken as 'in so far as these friendships [have] something good, or [have] something in common [with the primary type of friendship]'. But as I read the grammar here, [A] says: '[good people are friends] in so far as they *are* good people; and the other types *are* friends, in so far as they *are* a good thing of some sort and *are* in some sense a similar thing'. These other kinds of friends are similar to one another in some respect. They both like drinking, say. (Translators are put off by the neuter gender: 'in so far as they are a good *thing*, etc.'. But we find the same idiom at 1159a8 and 1157b34.)

15. *(prosperous)*: *Makarioi*, i.e. one of [A]'s two words for 'blessed', synonymous with *eudaimones*. But here he falls back into its sense by common usage, 'wealthy'. On the other hand, when he then says that you'd never expect such people to be solitary, he seems to use its other sense again. (People whose lives are going well will spend their time with family and friends – obviously.)

16. *involves choice*: I.e. choosing to spend time with your friend (or loved one), to help your friend, choosing what's best for your

friend, etc. Thus a friendship or close family attachment, very
like a moral virtue, is 'a disposition to make certain [regular,
predictable] choices' – it is a firm, standing intent to help your
friend. (You can't say that you love someone, or are their friend,
but choose to harm them, or choose never to speak to them. In
that case you just aren't their friend. Friendship implicates
choice.)

Or [A] may mean that a friendship requires choosing to be
friends with a given person in the first place – a little closer to
saying, in English, that friendship implies not just an emotion but
also a conscious decision and commitment. But that less clearly
implies an ongoing disposition of character. The next two
sentences make the first reading much more probable. Plus, [A]
certainly means this as a claim about love between family members as well as friends; but we do not choose our family.

17. *the Form of the Good itself*: This is probably intended as a joke.
Plato is being teased again. I suspect it is a fragment of an argument between Plato and his hedonist opponents (with whom [A]
often sympathizes, given his own views on pleasure).

Plato argued that what's good for human beings must have an
absolute basis. His (rather cryptic) doctrine was that all good in
the whole universe derives from, or depends on, the Form of the
Good. Hedonists argued that what's good for human beings
should simply be identified with whatever gives us the most
pleasure or happiness. ('Happiness' works well as a synonym
for 'pleasure', conceived broadly, rather than as a translation of
eudaimonia.) So one could imagine a hedonist argument going
like this: suppose Plato's mysterious Form of the Good exists,
and suppose you were communing with it directly, like the
philosopher-kings in the *Republic*; even so, if it were painful to
be in its presence, then you wouldn't be able to stand it. So it
wouldn't be good after all. It would be bad. So, even the goodness of the Form of the Good itself is subject to *our* principle,
that what's good is pleasure!

18. *[rulers] to be like that*: I.e. it is unusual for rulers to be supremely
good men, better than 'a good man' to a degree that matches
their much higher social status.

Friendship between social inferiors and superiors by definition is not between equals, and so, says [A], has to be based on
some form of 'proportional equality'. To be friends with someone much more powerful than you, you have to balance out that
gap by offering proportionately greater deference and service.

His idea here seems to be that this would require the ruler having a moral superiority that made such deference acceptable, rather than demeaning.

Suppose you consider yourself a decent person. Why would you live at the beck and call of some tyrant who you think is a horrible man? Certainly not for the perks. You're no man's flunky or hanger-on (see 1124b31). It would be humiliating; and you don't care about perks. But good people are interested in spending time with other good people. So you might willingly attach yourself to a monarch, even as a subordinate, if you were convinced he was a really fine ruler, a wonderfully good man. That superiority of his in goodness would compensate for and justify your deference and subordination. As long as you are surpassed by him proportionately in both domains, the relationship might be workable.

But very few [rulers] are like that, says [A]. I.e. hardly any rulers are so exceedingly good as to surpass even 'a good man' in goodness to the same degree that they surpass him in power. That's clearly true.

[Asp.] thinks that the text here means that a good man can only be a friend to a tyrant if 'he [i.e. the tyrant] is also morally inferior [to him, the good man]' so that the good man's inferiority in one domain is balanced by superiority in the other. The idea is that wicked autocrats might befriend good men for moral self-improvement. This is not an absurd reading, but it involves a harsh change of subject. It also makes less sense of the last claim. (Most kings and dictators, rather than 'hardly any', are 'surpassed in goodness' by good people.) Also, it is very hard to see why a good man would ever enter into that relationship, on [A]'s view.

I suspect that [A] is answering a student question here. (I italicize what I take to be the objection from the floor.) [A] does not answer it particularly well (just as you might expect in an off-the-cuff response). What he should have said is that although good people are indeed both useful and a pleasure to their friends at the same time, they are certainly not useful, or a pleasure, in the ways valued by powerful rulers (which is what [A] was talking about). People never combine the two features of being court jesters and ruthless henchmen.

19. *probably not all*: I read this as a half-joke and half-truth. Do you want your best friend to win that Oscar for best actor? Of course! Unless you've been nominated for the same

Oscar in the same year. But IX.8 suggests [A] is not fully serious about this.

20. *unequal to be friends*: Suppose a poor man is to be friends with
a very rich man, or an ordinary citizen with a king. Their social
inequality can be 'equalized' – i.e. compensated for – if the
poor man 'loves' the rich man more than the rich man loves
him back, or if the subject 'loves' the king more than the king
loves the subject. This sounds strange in a modern, more egalitarian context, but it is a perfectly accurate description of
relationships between different social classes in highly strati-
fied societies. A loyal citizen loves his monarch, and would do
anything for him – even die for him. But the monarch needn't
lift a finger just for that citizen. A slave is expected to be 'devoted'
to his master; the master owes no similar 'devotion' to the slave.
Under these conditions, the relationships are acceptable to the
social superiors.

[A]'s terminology is uncritical. Social inferiors have to offer
greater 'love', he says, to compensate for an inferiority which he
takes for granted. It would be more accurate to say that requir-
ing social inferiors to offer this 'greater love' is the same thing
as maintaining the (fictive) inferior position in the first place.
'Love' in these contexts is a euphemism for deference.

But in [A]'s defence, we might also note that when an ordinary
person interacts with someone of truly extraordinary ability or
achievement – someone of a deserved higher status – then 'greater
love' is perfectly appropriate. It's all right for Albert Einstein or
Tenzing Norgay to expect a little deference in a social setting.

21. *obligation*: Translates *díkaion* when used as a countable noun.
See note V.35.

22. *partnership*: *Koinōnia*. I usually translate *koinōnia* as 'partnership'. It also means 'sharing' (in the sense 'holding in common',
not in the sense 'dividing up'); 'association'; 'cooperation'. In
the special case of the partnership of citizens, [A]'s terminology
here is the origin of the word 'community' (*communitas*, 'sharing', literally translates *koinōnia* into Latin) and also 'society'
(original meaning, 'partnership'). So 'the partnership of citizens' is also society; the community. In the Greek context, at
least in [A]'s time, that means the *polis*, the city state.

23. *friends are partners*: The saying *koina ta philōn* perhaps more
precisely means '*philoi* [friends and loved ones] share everything'; i.e. whatever they have and do they have and do together.

The saying more easily refers to family (something like: 'there's no "mine" and "yours" for family').

I think [A] uses it more as a reference to joint action (i.e. cooperation) than to property. At any rate, most of his examples of *koinōnia* are clearly examples of cooperation and common purpose, rather than common property.

24. *anything that serves the common interest*: See book V, 1129b14.

25. *government 'by property-holders'*: an arrangement whereby all men who possess some minimum amount of property have a say in the government, are entitled to vote, or are eligible for public office. In Greek this is called *timokratia* (a *timēma* is the term for a census, or property assessment). But since 'timocracy' has no currency in English I will stick to the phrase 'rule by {or open to} all property-holders'.

Of the three mentioned so far, this is the form that spreads power most widely, because the property qualification in practice tended to be quite small. (Similar qualifications existed for voters in various countries in the eighteenth and nineteenth centuries, and in that context too such qualifications always had the effect of spreading power far more widely than under the earlier feudal or aristocratic governments.) 'Democracy' (*démokratia*) in [A]'s terminology, differed from *timokratia* by opening up political participation to all free men, regardless of property (but not to women or slaves).

26. *republican*: In Greek this form of government is called *politeia*. This is also the general term for 'constitution' or 'form of government' – so used by [A] in the opening words of the chapter, for example – and his point here is that Greeks also happen to use this general term to refer to what we would call (approximately) a 'republic'. (Incidentally, this double use of the term, and an early error, explain why the title of Plato's famous dialogue is *The Republic*, even though the government it describes is extremely unrepublican. Its title, correctly translated, is *The Constitution*, or [*Outline of an Ideal*] *Form of Government*.)

27. *Democracy is the least bad*: It seems very hard not to read this section as a kind of stealth argument for democracy. You just need to read the subtext. 'Monarchy is the best, as long as we find a superhuman, morally perfect king [*which we never will*]. Aristocracy is the second best, as long as the ruling class is morally enlightened, fair, public-spirited and unselfish [*which won't happen*]. [So those two will, in practice, lead to tyranny and

oligarchy.] Democracy is the least bad of the bad forms [i.e. *it is the best that we can realistically attain*].'

There is a famous and similar line attributed to Churchill: 'Democracy is the worst form of government there is, except for all the others that have been tried from time to time.' What Churchill actually said (in Parliament in 1947) is that 'It has been said that democracy . . .' etc. People are unsure who he was referring to. He is, almost certainly, referring to [A], by way of someone's report of these arguments.

28. *[members of the] 'decent' [class]*: Literally, 'decent people' (*epieikeis*). The term often designates social rank ('decent folk', i.e. the higher classes). Having just discussed the idea of superior and inferior classes in aristocracy in the previous paragraph, [A] is clearly saying that in rule by all property-holders there supposedly is no inferior class. People are supposed to be equals. But the phrasing of the second part is a little odd. See [TA] for my slight emendation.

29. *love*: I.e. *philia*, meaning, as usual, reciprocated, dispositional love (as between friends or family). Here this might also be translated 'friendship': 'So there can be no friendship with a slave, considered as a slave. Considered as a human being – maybe that's different . . .' etc. But I feel that 'love' is better here. [A] began with the claim that a king loves his subjects in the same way that a father loves his sons, while a tyrant does not. The tyrant is then compared to a master who does not love his slaves because slaves are mere tools. The father's love for his sons sets the sense of *philia* for the paragraph.

The point of the claim that a slave is an 'animate tool' is not that the slave cannot love you back – in fact, slaves clearly can love their masters – but that a slave has no interests that a master is bound to respect. [A] means that a master cannot want the best for his slaves for their sake, as a carpenter cannot want the best for his hammer for the hammer's sake.

30. *capable of being a partner*: For the idea that right and wrong fundamentally depend on law, and similar remarks about slaves, see book V, 1129b11ff. and 1134a35ff. Yet there is something different here. The claim that right and wrong apply to anyone 'capable of being a party to law' hints at a criticism of slavery. 'This person here might be, through their bad luck, your slave; but purely in terms of their capacities they could have been your fellow citizen, had things turned out differently for them (e.g. had they not been born into slavery).' So there seems to be an

allusion here to the idea discussed in the *Politics* 1.6, that perhaps slaves are slaves by law only (and by bad luck), not by
natural inferiority – i.e. that all slaves could be, in principle,
subject to the same laws as free people, and could be citizens.
There, [A] partially accepts that view (he agrees that it is true
of many slaves, but not all). Here, too, he seems to flirt with it.
Notice that he does not say, here, that some slaves are capable
of being partners under law and some aren't. (There is no hint
of the idea of 'natural slaves' here.) Rather, the simplest way to
take the sentence is as implying that all human beings, as such,
have the capacity to be citizens; it's just that some of them are
slaves.

31. *because they're equals*: It's clear from the preceding discussion
that [A] means that (a) tyrants have limited love for their
subjects, and recognize only limited obligations to them (i.e.
citizens have very few rights), and (b) that in a democracy the
government has a much more friendly relationship with its citizens and recognizes much greater obligations to them (citizens
have far more rights); but also (c) that citizens in a democracy
are more likely to be friends with one another, because they are
equals. Of course (b) and (c) are really the same idea, since in a
functioning democracy the citizens are the government.

32. *mothers love their children more*: I.e. than fathers. This claim
should almost certainly be taken with the point made before the
parenthesis. (The parenthesis is probably an in-text note.) 'Parents love their children more because they know them more
easily – which is also why mothers love their children more than
fathers.' [A] means that mothers more easily know that the children are theirs than fathers do. The interpretation is confirmed
by 1168a25–6.

33. *both desire the [same] good*: I take this to mean that if two
friends are 'competing' at helping one another – e.g. both insisting on paying for lunch – and one of them outdoes the other, i.e.
pays much more, and hence succeeds at what she was trying to
do, then it would be bizarre if she turned around and com-
plained about paying more. Plus, in that case 'they both want
the same good': e.g. friend A wants to pay for B's lunch; friend
B, even if he also wanted to pay, is happy to be treated to lunch;
so in two different senses they both want B to get a free lunch.
So they 'both desire the good [in question]'.

34. *a matter of character*: [A] means that even when you are not
formally or legally obliged to pay for goods or a service, you

may be under moral pressure to pay, or to return the favour. 'That's what a decent person would do.'

35. *settle accounts*: [Asp]: 'Suppose A gives B fifty coins, as a loan to a friend, with no mention of interest, and by an informal deal – with no written contract – and then later demands interest on the loan. In that case he made the deal one way but wants to settle accounts in another.'

36. *take your chances*: Or 'accept however things may turn out'. [A] means that because contracts with delayed payments imply an arrangement between friends, some cities treat them as a private matter and don't allow one party to sue the other. (For confirmation that *stergein* has this sense here, see [EE] 1243b9).

37. *on the same [friendly] terms*: Virtually all translators take this to mean: 'and he will complain if he doesn't come out of the exchange as well as he went into it', i.e. if he doesn't recoup the money he put in. But that is a different matter. Of course people complain when they get the worst of an exchange, but here [A] is discussing the complaints that arise when there is ambiguity about the form, or terms, of the friendship. What he means here is that when a friend changes his tune halfway through the exchange, from being friendly and informal to acting as if you are legally obliged to repay him, he will complain about the fact that you have not repaid him. A true friend doesn't ask for repayment. To start grumbling about repayment is to switch to those less friendly terms. (Also, for grammatical reasons it is impossible that the Greek here means '*if* he ends the exchange . . .' etc.)

The whole argument here is very compressed. [A] appears to be describing how the 'informal' kind of exchange typically works; but in fact he is only describing the situation where people switch from the one form of friendship to the other. Informal exchanges will involve no complaints if the two parties stay informal throughout.

38. *you shouldn't force him*: I.e. by not paying him back, which in effect forces him into the position of friend, since if he were a friend he would not expect repayment. Clearly this is both absurd ('I've decided not to pay you back; thanks for the generous gift, friend'), and a bad idea (you should not want such a person as your friend). I suspect [A] means both; but what follows expands on the latter.

39. *choice (or intent)*: I.e. *prohairesis*, frequently [A]'s term for referring to the intent or motive (that in turn implies traits of character) behind an action. See note III.29.

Suppose you're starving, and a friend offers you a crust of bread. If his kitchen is conspicuously bursting with delicious food and drink, you would probably be offended. If he's desperately poor, and you're both starving, and that's his last piece of bread, you'd feel grateful. The objective benefit to you – a piece of bread – is the same in each case, but your debt is measured by the friend's intent or choice (e.g. 'he chose to share his last piece of bread with me'). By contrast, in a shop – where the customer has a 'mutually useful friendship' with the owner – such considerations are irrelevant. You pay less money, you get less food: end of story.

40. *a good man*: I.e. a man of high social rank. It is clear that through the passage [A] is using 'good' and 'worse' in their (fairly frequent) social-class sense (like English 'your betters'). See 1132a1–4 for another important instance of this. He sometimes seems to merge the two usages (as if higher social class automatically makes you a better person). But 1124a21–1124b5 proves that he is also able to distinguish them very sharply.

41. *you just get the money*: This passage seems to be a response to an argument in *The Republic* (343d6–e7) where Thrasymachus claims that dishonest, immoral men gain far more than honest men from public office. The honest men, he says, lose out financially (because they neglect their own affairs and of course refuse to take any bribes) and lose the respect of their families and friends (who are angry at not profiting, illegally, from a friend in office). To this [A] replies that, actually, honest men would not tolerate public office if it meant losing out in every way. In reality honest politicians are respected, and dishonest ones may make more money, but there's a trade-off: they are not respected. So in fact each is compensated in his own way. This paragraph does not seem to connect particularly well with what precedes or follows – except that it serves as a case of people exchanging material goods for respect.

42. *made a better person*: 'Helped towards goodness'. [A] probably has in mind relationships between teachers and students, especially philosophers and their students. These are very often seen as cases of people morally improving their friends.

BOOK IX

1. *asymmetrical friendships*: Anomoioeidesi, literally 'of the unlike type', apparently meaning friendships where the friends

want and get different things from the friendship, in whatever sense. In practice that applies to most utility friendships, some pleasure-friendships, and combinations of the two. The wording of the first six lines of the chapter closely matches a discussion not in the preceding friendship book, but at V.5. A relevant line from there: 'cooperative partnerships like this aren't between a doctor and another doctor. They're between, say, a doctor and a farmer, and in general between people who are different . . .' So the point is that citizens get different things out of the civic partnership. Note that [A] insists that civic friendship is between social equals. So 'asymmetrical' friendship does not refer (or does not only refer) to friendship between superiors and subordinates. He also stated that civic friendship is utility friendship for all parties. So 'asymmetrical' friendship does not refer (or only refer) to one in which, e.g., one friend gets pleasure and the other material benefit. (If one person gets money and the other bread, that's asymmetrical, but a two-way utility friendship.)

2.   *And now you're not doing anything*: [M] interprets the chronology here sexually: 'before sex he promises he'll do whatever the other wants; and he isn't following through [i.e. afterwards]'. This seems likely to be right about the implication of [A]'s phrasing.

3.   *neither do those kinds of relationships*: It is of some importance that both here, and at the parallel passage at VIII.4, [A] does not give even the slightest indication that a homosexual relationship of this kind is, per se, shameful. His only criticism, in both passages, is that the *erōmenos/erastes* relationships are sometimes (but not always) a bit shallow. This has a bearing on how to make sense of 1148b30 (see note VII.36).

4.   *love of people's characters*: Most naturally understood in the light of a similar point made in the parallel discussion at 1157a11: lovers will stay together 'if . . . they become fond of each other's characters'. Both sentences have the same plural 'characters', as an object of love. [A] never elsewhere refers to full friendship ('the friendship of good people' or 'friendship based on goodness') in this way, as 'friendship/love of characters'. So the phrase here is probably equivalent to: 'But if they love each other's characters . . .'.

5.   *[the king] promised to pay the guitar-singer*: One Byzantine commentator, [M], remarks: 'I don't know who this is about and I can't be bothered finding out.' (I sympathize.) As it happens, the original story was about Dionysius, King of Syracuse. As Plutarch tells it (*De Alexandri Magni fortuna aut virtute*

333 F), he promised a well-known singer a talent of silver for a night's work (rather like offering about half a million dollars, or ten years' wages). The next day, when asked for the promised fee, Dionysius said: 'I really enjoyed your singing last night. And you really enjoyed thinking you were going to get all that money. So we're even.'

6. *what you focus on*: This means 'those are the things you focus on when you come to assess the value of this kind of friendship, or this sort of deal; nothing else matters'. Compare [EE] 1243a31: 'Citizens [in trading] look to the thing [i.e. the material object that they want from the trade: are they getting it?]'

7. *You'll give X so as to get Y*: Literally, '[Someone] will give these things only in order to get that thing.' The phrase is most easily read as generic: *this* for *that*, X for Y. [A] is discussing all (non-kin) relationships that are not full friendships. All of them work by some form of tit for tat, and you stay in them only as long as you are getting what you need.

8. *[even with friends]*: [A] only quotes three words of the saying *misthos d' andri*, 'fee for a man' (or 'payment for a man'). The full line (immediately implied for any Greek listener) is: 'There should be a stated, sufficient fee, [even] for a man who is friend {or family}.' The poem continues: 'even if he's your own brother, don't hesitate to make a contract before a judge'.

9. *because of who they are*: I.e. because of who the friends are; because of what the friends are like, and for their sake. I have deliberately allowed the ambiguity because the original (depending on how you accent a key word) is ambiguous enough that several commentators took the text the other way: 'because of themselves'; 'spontaneously, because of their own goodness'.

10. *choice {and intent}*: See note VIII.39 on the parallel passage at VIII.13.

11. *philosophical mentors*: The key phrase is not completely clear. More literally, he says: 'people who have shared in philosophy'. So, philosophical colleagues? This might mean (a) 'people who have done philosophy together', but with the clear implication of students and their teachers, rather than colleagues. Or it may instead mean (b) 'people who have shared, i.e. imparted, their philosophical knowledge'; or (c) 'people who have studied philosophy under [someone]'. On any of those readings, [A] is talking about mentorship (and of course, indirectly, about his teacher, Plato). The grammar is highly elliptical: 'and that way it seems also for' probably means 'and that's surely how [we

should repay]' (assumed from the previous clause), or 'it also seems that way [i.e. there's no fixed agreement] for' (assumed from the sentence before that).

12. *the gods*: For the thought, see VIII.14, 1163b15.

13. *it's against the law*: See VIII.13, 1162b29. But why is this point being made here? Presumably because it illustrates, in an extreme form, the idea that the person who receives the goods should get to decide the payment – even to the extent of deciding not to pay at all or paying much less than expected. The laws in question, which [A] seems to somewhat admire, treat broken contracts as purely private matters, like spats between friends. And presumably in these societies it makes no difference whether the agreement has or has not been written down. Strabo (15.1.34) reports on such customs in India: 'There are no lawsuits except in cases of murder and assault; ... in contracts, everything is left to individuals to sort out. If someone breaks a promise, you just have to accept it (but also take notice of who you should trust) and not fill the city with lawsuits.'

14. *people think he is*: This is the natural way to take the plural ('they think he is'). It is important that people generally think he's a crook. If it was just your (personal and ignorant) opinion, then it would be wrong of you to refuse the request.

15. *wouldn't be so wrong of you [to refuse]*: 'You surely wouldn't be doing *atopa* [if you refused].' In classical Greek *atopa* means 'absurd', 'strange', and it may mean that here: 'you wouldn't be doing anything odd [i.e. strange, absurd]'. But in later (Koine) Greek *atopon* came to mean simply 'wrong', with no implication of strangeness. (For clear examples of this see Diogenes Laertius 2.93.3; or Luke 23:41.) The same usage seems to occur at 1165b3 and b21. In at least one of those, the sense 'wrong' (or 'untoward') seems required. Even in [A]'s time, this was probably a colloquial usage. (Book IX in my view has a number of distinctive purely linguistic features that raise the possibility of a different editor.)

16. *many times before*: See 1094b11–25; 1103b34–1104a11; 1172a34.

17. *only offer sacrifices to Zeus*: Literally, 'people do not sacrifice all things to Zeus'. This is open to being taken – wrongly, I think – to mean 'there are some things we don't sacrifice to Zeus'. (The idea would then be that there are some things you should not do for your father.)

18. *better*: Literally, 'it's more honourable'. The comparative does not quite make sense. [A] means that 'the only honourable

choice is to keep your parents alive rather than yourself'. But another good possibility, I think, is that *kallion* here has its later, Koine sense: 'better'.

19. *offering them a seat*: The setting seems to be a dinner. When an older guest arrives younger people should rise; and an elder should be offered the higher seat. At Greek dinners, people ate reclining on individual couches, and their position marked the relative importance of the guests. The gesture meant by 'offering a seat' is referred to in one of Luke's parables (14:10): 'When you are invited [to a wedding], take the lowest place, and maybe when your host comes, he'll say to you, Friend, move up to a better place, and you'll gain respect before all the other guests.'

20. *speak frankly*: One implication is that with parents and elders, it's not appropriate to speak freely. ('Children should be silent in the presence of their betters.') The claim here also has an obvious connection with the virtue discussed at IV.6, and that would give more sense to the idea that you owe it to your siblings to speak freely (i.e. especially to tell them when they're in the wrong, or making a terrible mistake). [A] also notes (1124b29–31) that someone with a sense of pride speaks freely, because they refuse to treat anyone as being above them. Hence, speaking freely is a mark of equals.

21. *at the start*: Not clear what this refers to. [A] makes a related point at VIII.13, 1162b23–34; and again at IX.1, 1164a13–22. If [A] means the latter, then 'at the start' means at the start of book IX (so, perhaps, 'at the start of today's lecture').

22. *wrong of you*: Atopon. Possibly 'odd'. See above, note IX.15. In this case, it seems that *atopon* must mean 'wrong'. All the surrounding questions are about what sort of behaviour would be justified. The claim that it wouldn't be 'strange' to drop the bad friend seems much too weak.

23. *to each other*: This might mean, (a) that they will not even like each other any more; or, more likely, (b) that they won't even share each other's pleasures and pains. When one gets upset, or is pleased, by something, the other won't sympathize. Children don't notice or understand adults' worries; adults often don't take childish concerns very seriously.

24. *mothers ... a falling-out*: [A] means that mothers want their children to be alive even if they are not with them (he gives the same example with more detail at VIII.8, 1159a28); and that friends and family who have fallen out can continue to want the best for each other even if they are no longer in each other's lives.

25. *the measure*: See III.4, 1113a29 for the earlier version of this
     claim. Both times [A] means this with an important (and obvi-
     ous) qualification. He means good people are 'the measure' in
     human matters. Good people's characters and attitudes do not
     determine, say, how many moons there are around Jupiter, or
     the atomic weight of potassium. Here, he means that what self-
     love is like for good people is what self-love is really like. That
     should be regarded as the normal case. And for good people, it
     closely resembles love of others.

26. *as what you are*: The manuscript text here is very obscure, and
     probably corrupt. Bywater brackets one whole phrase that I
     leave in the text ('that other thing that's now come into exist-
     ence') – perhaps wisely. The reference to God, too, seems to
     come out of the blue, and perhaps should not be there at all. I
     have done my best to retain the manuscript text as far as pos-
     sible, with one slight emendation. (See [TA] for the details.)

     The claim about not wanting to turn into a god seems to have
     no bearing on [A]'s thesis here, that self-love is similar, in detail,
     to love of others.

     The solution may be that the equivalent part of the descrip-
     tion of love of others, to which this point would correspond, is
     missing here. It is striking that [A] did make exactly the required
     corresponding claim in VIII.7. If we place that claim alongside
     this one, the argument works fairly well:

     We want what's good for our friends {and loved ones}; but
     of course, that means as what they are. We don't want them
     [to become something else]: gods, for example. Because then
     they couldn't be good things for us. They have to stay human
     (1159a6–11).

     Likewise, you want what's good for yourself. But of course
     that means as what you are. You'd never choose even to have all
     possible good things if it meant first becoming something else;
     a god, for example. You have to stay what you are, human.

     The final, extra claim, that 'what you are' is the part of you
     that thinks, seems closely related to similar claims made in
     IX.8 and X.7, to the effect that the thinking part of you is you.
     On the other hand, unlike the twin claims about human iden-
     tity reconstructed here, the extra point has little to do with the
     similarities between self-love and love of others, and in fact
     works against it. [A] never says that love of others mostly
     means love of their thinking part. (Love of others is love of
     character.)

27. *God already has the highest good*: Seems a rather odd point. Perhaps it can be unpacked like this: 'You wouldn't want to become a god to have every good thing in the universe, because that wouldn't be you; so you wouldn't have them. It's really just the same as wanting some god to have them, instead of you (which is doubly absurd because God already has all good things anyway).' Alternatively, perhaps the text should say, more pertinently, 'because then that god would have the benefit of them, not you'.

28. *conflicted*: Observe that here [A] starts to show, point by point, that bad people's relationship with themselves is the exact opposite of that of good people. His first point is that they do not want, or do, what is best for themselves.

Elsewhere [A] says that people who lack self-control suffer an internal conflict, whereas 'lecherous' or 'gluttonous' men are quite happy about their immoderate desires. Does that mean that only people who lack self-control are ever conflicted?

No. He means bad people in general, exactly as he claims. In the special case of desire for food, drink and sex, people can have immoderate desires that they are morally comfortable with. But that is not the case with the other vices. [A] never suggests that people can be quite happy to regard themselves as murderers, liars, cowards, bad friends, etc. We should assume that in his view such people are prone to an uneasy view of themselves. And that is what he is discussing.

But that also raises an objection. It might be more accurate to say that bad people can love themselves (and be free of remorse) in so far as they can believe, including by self-deception, that they are good. And that seems to be exactly what many bad people do. Remorse is a common emotion in good, but imperfect, people. (It's one of the things that keeps them good.)

[A]'s view of remorse is related to his view of shame (see IV.9) and self-control. He thinks, implausibly, that good people do not need any of them. In reality, good people need all three, even if not all the time.

29. *hate being alive*: Most manuscripts say 'and are hated for being so horrible'. See [TA].

30. *nothing to love*: The point seems out of place here, and exactly matches what [A] says in summary a few lines later. But perhaps he means this as an extra point about why such people don't like being on their own. (You only hang out with people you like.)

31. *attractive*: The manuscripts say 'when someone strikes you as *kalos*'. In classical Greek, used of a person, that strictly means

beautiful. And we do feel goodwill towards attractive people. But would [A] be saying that? In Koine Greek *kalos* (used of a person) became standard for 'good' (as in modern Greek). It is possible that the word has that later sense here. Another fair possibility is that *kalos* is a corruption of *díkaios*, 'fair {and honest}', which [A] so often elsewhere pairs with 'brave' as his go-to examples of moral virtues.

32. *sun, moon and stars*: Literally, 'things in the heavens'. Elsewhere [A] states that the study of the wider cosmos – physics, cosmology, theology – has no connection with moral and political wisdom (see VI.7). Hence, agreement on the nature of the cosmos should have no bearing on political or moral harmony.

But this view is unrealistic. Views about the wider cosmos include views about God. And while [A] himself holds that theology has no bearing on ethics and politics, almost nobody agrees with him about that. Others (both among the Greeks and throughout history, including [A]'s teacher, Plato) have thought that the right views about the gods, or God, are central to morality, politics and law. And because of that, disagreements about 'things in the heavens' have often been a source of murderous civil strife and wars between nations. Conversely, people often align themselves with others who have the same metaphysical and theological – i.e. religious – views. [A]'s idea here is more of a naïve hope than a statement of fact. See 1095b6 for a related claim (and note I.9).

33. *same values*: Our notion of 'values' comes close to [A]'s concept of what we choose in the broad sense that he so often employs: what we choose in life. In this context it seems worth noting that the idea of a society with 'shared values' is exactly what [A] has in mind here.

34. *Pittacus*: Pittacus was elected dictator of Mytilene by popular demand, and was willing, for a while. After ten years he decided he didn't want the job any more because it was corrupting him.

35. *scoundrel's view*: Epicharmus was a writer of comedies, and [A] obviously here quotes a well-known phrase from one of his plays. Literally, '[you're only saying that] by looking at things from [the point of view of] an evil man', or 'spoken from the point of view of a scoundrel!', meaning, of course, from a point of view that attributes only the worst character, and worst motives, to others. In English we call this a 'cynical' view.

36. *another thing that might apply*: I.e. if you've helped someone, you know whom you've helped. If you've been helped, you don't

always know who helped you. In support of [A], notice also that when you help others without knowing whom you've helped, e.g. by taxation or donations to very large organizations, you tend to feel less attachment to the people you've helped.

37. *sayings*: [A] means that all of these are true of your relationship with yourself, in most cases literally. You *and you* are one soul; you share everything *with you*; you are *your* exact equal; you are closest of all *to you*. The last saying, 'knee's closer than shin', seems to have been used to mean 'I have to look after people who are closer to me first.' So it is a little like 'blood is thicker than water'. It is only actually used in one place in surviving Greek: Theocritus (16.18), living as a travelling poet on people's charity, reports it as an excuse he hears from people for not offering him any money. I.e. 'Sorry, I have a family to feed.'

38. *'fought-over' goods*: Money, power, status, land, etc. See 1168b19, [EE] 1248b27, *Politics* 1271b8 (the last implying 'goods that people go to war over'). The idea is that they are bound to be fought over since most people want them, and they are limited. (There is also the fact that some of them, especially certain kinds of high status and prestige, only exist at all in the way they do if most other people do not have them.)

39. *your mind is you*: For this point to work in English, you have to analyse 'self-control' as meaning 'control, by the self, of your emotions and desires'. In Greek, the term for 'lack of self-control' does not contain the word 'self'; it literally means simply 'lack of control', and [A] assumes that implies 'instance of you failing to control [your emotions]'. Hence the concept implies you are your mind, controlling those somewhat less you-ish elements.

The claim here does not square with what [A] says at 1111a33–b3, that emotions and desires are 'very much of the person', i.e. very much part of the self. Also, in English, 'self-control' implies 'control of the self', not 'control by the self'. Thus it implies that desires are part of the self. The same is true of Greek. *Akrasia* cannot ever refer, e.g., to a failure, by you, to control a rowdy toddler; it necessarily implies a failure, by you, to control *you*. So it precisely implies that your desires and feelings are you.

40. *give up actions*: So, for example, you let your friend take the chance to do something brave, or fair, or generous, in a case where there is one particular thing to be done and only one of you can do it – rather like passing to a team-mate to let them score the goal, even when you could probably have scored yourself.

Oddly, this gives rise to a sense in which *to kalon* – honourable action – can be a 'fought-over' good as well if, e.g., people fight over who gets to be generous to the other (see e.g. the Youtube video of Larry David and Rosie O'Donnell fighting over who gets to pay the bill).

41. *gifts of god*: The line is Euripides, *Orestes* 667. In context: 'It's in times of trouble that friends and family have to help one another. But when the gifts of god are good [i.e. when fortune smiles on you and things are going well], what need of friends and family?' The 'family' sense of *philoi* is prominent in the passage: Orestes is asking for help from his uncle. [A] seems to slightly misread the line as 'if the gods, and fortune, give you good things [in life], why do you need friends [at all]?'.

42. *A good person*: The point does not seem to belong here. (Attempts to explain the train of thought seem far too convoluted, and I will not bother with them here.) But it clearly fits the general context. It would make sense if preceded by something like, 'And you'll also take pleasure in your friends' actions, if your friend is good. Because a good person . . .' etc. Alternatively, it would fit nicely right after the fifth premise of the argument given just above.

43. *very close friends*: The type of friendship is that of *hetairoi*, 'best friends', 'mates' or 'best mates'. The famous fictional pairs that [A] probably has in mind: Orestes and Pylades, Achilles and Patroclus, Ajax and Teucer, etc. This seems to remain true: Don Quixote and Sancho Panza; Holmes and Watson; Chewbacca and Han Solo.

44. *may even outdo his friends*: This phrase has caused commentators (ancient and modern) a lot of trouble, and given rise to several different readings. [A] says: 'even if he doesn't surpass in not being upset, he doesn't tolerate . . .' etc. For the basic idiom and logical structure here, compare English: 'he is, if not the best, the second best', which means 'he may be the best, and, if not, he's at any rate the second best'. Likewise here: 'he may surpass his friends in not being upset' [i.e. he may be even less upset about his own misfortunes than they are], and, if not, then at any rate he doesn't let them get upset too'.

The example that springs to mind is Socrates, who, as described in the *Apology*, *Crito* and *Phaedo*, was less upset at his own death than his friends were. Thus he 'outdid them in *alupia*', in not being troubled or upset by his (supposed) misfortune. And he got annoyed with them for being as upset as they were. He told them to stop being so silly. That is the meaning here of 'not tolerating' your friends' distress (it means not allowing it, rather than not being able to bear it). This is proved by the following clause.

BOOK X

1. *account of pleasure*: [NE] has already done this, of course, at the end of book VII. The two accounts of pleasure obviously do not both belong in the same treatise, and represent two different phases of [A]'s lectures on ethics. Little or no attempt is made by the editors to harmonize them. No doubt one account (probably the book VII one) originally belonged with the [EE] set of lectures, while the other belonged with the [NE] set.

2. *how life really works*: In Greek, *ta erga*. [M] takes this to mean that what we *say* (on practical and moral questions) is less credible to others than how we *act*. That interpretation goes fairly well with what follows. And certainly, *erga* can refer to 'actions' or 'behaviour' (it also means 'products', 'works', 'tasks', 'results'). But here I think it refers to 'the facts' or 'the realities' of human life more generally. [A]'s remark sounds very similar to the claim (at 1145b28) that Socrates' theories about self-control clash with 'what clearly seems to be the case'; and see also 1098b11.

    [A] makes this same claim again at 1179a21. For this distinctive sense of *erga*, compare its use at 1168a35 ('the facts') or 1131b18 ('actual cases'); see also *Politics* 1264a6 ('in the real world'), 1333b15, 1268b39, 1270a31, 1308a2, 1326a26 etc.

3. *in any form*: [A] means that when ordinary people see a philosopher pursuing any kind of pleasure, they infer that his actual view is that every kind of pleasure is a good thing, and desirable. (They won't distinguish between the kinds he pursues and the kinds he doesn't.) This hints at the 'truth' that [A] thinks gets thrown out along with the false claim that all pleasure is bad: the truth that some pleasures are bad.

4. *Eudoxus*: Eudoxus of Cnidus (*c.*390–337 BC); mathematician, astronomer, doctor and (alleged) translator, who like [A] came to Athens and studied with Plato. So [A] must have known him personally. The fact that he favoured hedonism in ethics reveals that he was humanistic in basic outlook, like [A]. But the details of his hedonism are only known from [A]'s report. A version of the premise discussed here, that 'what all things strive for' must be

good, is approvingly cited by [A] in the very first sentence of book I.

5.   *more desirable*: [A] employs this same principle in book I, at 1097b17, in his discussion of *eudaimonia*.

6.   *what we're looking for here*: [A] means that the highest good is 'what we are looking for here'. This seems false, since the current subject of investigation is pleasure. This remark makes it seem that this discussion originally came from a wider discussion of 'the good', the key good in life (like the book I and book X discussions), rather than of pleasure per se. Notice that the opening sentence of chapter 2 can easily be read in the same way, as having 'the key good' as its topic, not pleasure; and the final paragraphs of chapter 3 raise the same suspicions (see below, note X.15).

7.   *natural [force]*: The text here reads 'some natural good'. But that seems very likely to be wrong. [A] is agreeing with Eudoxus' claim that all animals, we should assume, instinctively gravitate towards their own good. I.e. even if they lack conscious intelligence, we should assume they have a natural, biological wisdom, or capacity to track their own good. This is 'stronger than they are' or perhaps simply 'superior to them' in this sense: a spider is not a very intelligent animal, but its nature directs it wisely, to make its highly complex web, etc. Its nature is smarter than it is. (For that matter, the same is often true of human beings.)

      The 'good' of 'natural good' may have been added here by a confused editor; or it may conceal some other missing noun (e.g. 'a natural ruling part' or suchlike). Bywater suggests deleting the whole phrase, leaving just 'there is something superior to them'. Or it may be that the text is correct, and 'they have a natural good' here means 'they have an instinctive better part'. But that's very awkward.

8.   *isn't A or B*: The argument is attributed to Speusippus, Plato's nephew and successor at the Academy. His idea is that pleasure and pain are both bad, and both are opposites of tranquillity, the absence of both pain and pleasure. So 'neither' or 'neutral' in Speusippus' argument seems to have meant 'neither pleasure nor pain', and that is how my version renders it. (This seems proved by the parallel claim at VII.13.) But it might, in itself, be taken to mean 'neither good nor bad'.

      [M] offers, as an illustration, the fact that recklessness is the opposite of cowardice, but those are both bad, and both opposites of bravery, which is not recklessness or cowardice. [A] would agree with that example, and hence, as he says, he agrees with the general point. [M]'s example, if correct, suggests that 'neutral' means 'neither pleasure nor pain', not 'neither good nor bad': bravery, the 'neutral' middle, is good. [M] also tells us that Speusippus in effect used the term 'neutral' to mean 'good' (at least in this argument).

9. *or both equally*: The standard reading of this phrase is this: 'whereas [if they belonged to] the neutral class [i.e. the class of things that are neither good nor bad], then neither of them [should be undesirable] or both equally'. This is just about possible, but notice the large amount of the syntax and detail that has to be restored. And the larger problem is that it has [A] using 'neutral' in the wrong sense, 'neither good nor bad', as opposed to Speusippus' sense: 'neither pleasure nor pain'.

In Speusippus' argument 'neutral' becomes a kind of synonym for good. (The idea is that when in pain we desire to be free of it, and when distracted by physical desire, and pleasure, we also desire to be free of that, through satisfaction. The neutral state, the state of freedom from both pleasure and pain, is good.) Given that terminology, the sentence goes like this: 'If they're both bad, as he claims, they should both be undesirable, and neither should be of the desirable class [the 'neutral' class, he calls it], or both equally – but that's clearly not the case.'

10. *our [moral] goodness*: The moral virtues themselves are qualities, of course. But the exercising of them is not a quality. And [A] takes it for granted that the activities that express them are good things. He may be referring here to the exercise of intellectual as well as moral virtues; but I follow the normal rule, that when the noun *aretē* is unqualified, as here, it refers only to the latter. Also, by [A]'s usage, intellectual virtues are not 'qualities' in the relevant, technical sense: they do not make you 'a certain sort of person'. For this see [EE] 1220a12, 1227b9, 1228a3; *Politics* 1323b25. More generally, I believe we have other reasons for thinking that the other kind of *aretē* – of the intellect – only enters the conversation at the start of chapter 7.

11. *pleasures [as such]*: The previous suggestion was that Speusippus thinks pleasures are 'indeterminate' because we feel pleasures in degrees. Or maybe he thinks all pleasures, just as such, are indeterminate. That idea probably rests on the notion that all pleasures are changes of state – which [A] discusses shortly in more detail. And he will argue that only some are changes of state, namely the 'mixed' ones, but not the 'pure' ones.

12. *the cosmos*: To say of something that it is fast or slow, typically means fast or slow for what it is (a fast runner is faster than a fast glacier, but slower than a fast car); or faster or slower than it usually is. Each thing in that sense has its own way of being slow or fast. But there is only one cosmos – [A] means the rotating sphere of the fixed stars – and it turns at perfectly uniform speed, so it makes little sense to speak of it going fast or slow.

13. *when you're being cut*: [A] seems to be saying, in abbreviated form: 'It's like the way that you feel pain at being cut, but nobody would say the cutting *is* the pain.' The 'just as' has to be added to make this work. Some editors think 'being cut' is corrupt and there may have been something more general here: 'and you feel pain when you're being emptied'; or 'and when it doesn't happen, you feel pain'.

   'Being cut' is a standard Greek way of referring to surgery, by the way; going 'under the knife'. There were no anaesthetics, so this was a favourite philosopher's example of excruciating pain.

14. *just anything*: [A] means that though health is a good thing, you certainly wouldn't eat something monstrous, like human flesh, say, to stay healthy.

15. *not the highest good*: [A] here appears to switch into arguing (i.e. himself) against hedonism, i.e. against the claim that pleasure is the highest good. He had been defending Eudoxus against his Platonist critiques in the previous paragraphs, so this seems a little unexpected. But it is confirmed at the end of the chapter. So there is perhaps some poor editing here.

   The phrase 'or . . . that there are different kinds' is not grammatical (in the Greek), and may have been added to make a better connection with what came before.

   Flunkies and hangers-on are 'friends' that exist for your pleasure; they amuse, entertain and flatter you. True friendship aims at what's good: it makes you a better person, and true friends join with you in doing morally important things. Those two aims are different; hence pleasure is not the same as good. Or at any rate, the distinction is a good reason to think that pleasure is not our only goal in life. The argument, like the next three, clearly shows that pleasure cannot be *identified* with good. It certainly does not show that pleasure could not be a good thing at all. See [TA].

   The next arguments are clear, direct arguments against hedonism, with no rejoinder to them by [A]; thus they appear to be his arguments, or at least arguments he approves. The topic again appears to be the highest good, rather than pleasure per se. (Pleasure is being considered as one candidate.)

These are the only explicit and direct arguments against hedonism in [NE], and as such are rather important, though quietly tucked into the end of this section.

[M] thinks that with all four arguments [A] continues his report of the Platonist anti-hedonist case, and doesn't endorse these claims. But they all rest on standard Aristotelian views: his own analysis of friendship, his own view that the virtues would be intrinsically valuable even if nothing else (including, by implication, pleasure) ever resulted from them (see I.7, 1097b2). So I suggest that this is a snippet of anti-hedonist Aristotelian thinking that happens to have been slotted in here.

16. *never going to experience any pain*: All ancient hedonists tended to argue that hedonism was fully compatible with (more or less) normal moral standards. Our reason for not doing wrong, they said, is that it will inevitably lead, at some point, to greater pain (for ourselves). (Epicurus later argued, for example, that your reason for not doing wrong, even if you aren't caught or punished for it, is that you will always worry, painfully, about being caught. See *Principal Doctrines* 35.) Here [A] points out, plausibly, that even if there was absolutely no prospect of any pain whatsoever arising from a pleasurable but wrong action, you still have ample reason not to do it. That is, you have strong reasons unconnected with your pleasure. And that disproves hedonism. (The 'nobody' in the sentence is a little loose. It means 'no decent person'.)

17. *freeze*: Literally, 'grab'. [A] is imagining grabbing hold of and stopping the pleasure, as one might stop or freeze something in motion. This is pure thought experiment, of course.

18. *over the whole time*: I.e. if building a house takes three weeks, you can think of it as a 'complete three-week house-building'; or as complete at the end of the three weeks; but not as complete at any earlier point during the three weeks.

19. *safe to say*: Most translators think that [A] says here: 'I've given a detailed discussion of *kinēsis* elsewhere, and from that it seems that . . .' etc. But the opening clause implies something more like this: 'We don't have time for a really detailed discussion of this here (I've done that elsewhere), but it seems . . .', i.e. 'but at any rate it seems safe to say that . . .'.

20. *most processes are incomplete*: [A] may just mean that most processes are incomplete in the sense that making foundations, or

triglyphs, is incomplete because they are only part of the temple. Or he may mean that most are incomplete at every moment (with the latter qualifier carried over naturally enough from the first part of the sentence). That also makes decent sense. Only very few cases of *kinēsis* are complete at every moment (the movement of the sphere of fixed stars, for example). The second claim, that they differ in kind at each moment, then seems to be illustrated by the example that each particular section of an object's movement through space counts as a different kind of movement.

21. *object of a process*: A tricky section of text to interpret, and apparently corrupt. I have agreed with the several editors who think [A] must have said here that there is also 'no *kinēsis* of pleasure' and 'no bringing about of pleasure' rather than (yet again) that pleasure is not a bringing-about (of something else). But the first part would then be asserting that there is no process of change or movement that is the changing or moving of pleasure. That seems reasonably well explained by what follows.

22. *brings about seeing*: Compare building a house with seeing a house. This can illustrate several of [A]'s recent points. Building a house breaks down into different stages, takes a long time and is not complete until its final moment. Seeing a house has no detectable parts or stages and is instantaneous. There is no moment of it small enough that you could say that it does not yet count as complete seeing. Every instant of seeing is complete seeing. (It is 'complete in its form' at every instant.) Also, between opening your eyes and seeing, there's no 'process' or 'movement-towards' that brings about your seeing. Of course, [A] might have a different view of seeing (and of pleasure) if he could slow down the relevant physiology.

23. *working well*: [A] inserts, as a qualification here, 'when they are good', applied to both object and faculty, i.e. 'when they are good versions of what they are'. This is shorthand for double the condition just stated: the object needs to be a good object and the faculty in good working order. So this is a double translation. But I didn't want to write '{(when working well)}'.

24. *health and a doctor*: Pleasure does not 'perfect' the activity in the sense of bringing it about (or being its 'efficient cause'). Rather, the idea is that without its corresponding pleasure that kind of activity would not be perfect. The pleasure is the 'formal perfection' of the activity. Similarly, the doctor is the efficient cause of your being healthy, while health is the 'formal' cause. So the analogy is between pleasure and health in these

respective roles. But it is not a strictly exact analogy, and [A] qualifies it in what follows.

25. *disposition ... already being in place*: The physical disposition(s) of the eye, say, give it the power of sight, and in that sense that disposition, which exists, ready, in the eye at all times, 'brings about' sight (or accomplishes it). 'Accomplish' is one of the senses of the verb also translated here as 'complete' and 'perfect'. (A doctor brings about, accomplishes your health.) And for any faculty of perception or thought there is a corresponding *hexis*, disposition, that plays that causal role. Pleasure, by contrast, arises once every other aspect of the activity is already there; it is an emergent property of the activity.

26. *specific to them*: The conclusion is left unstated: 'Hence, the pleasures corresponding to activities that are different in kind must themselves be pleasures different in kind.'

27. *don't vary*: I.e. all donkeys enjoy the same things; all chimps enjoy the same things, etc. This seems false, and typical of [A]'s anthropochauvinism. If animals can show personality (as countless species can), then their pleasures must vary within the species.

28. *which sort, or which of them*: [A] may (in effect mean) which kind, intellectual or sensual, and of those, which one in particular? (There are also the important pleasures that go with exercising our virtues, which are a sort of mixture of the two because they involve feelings and emotions and reasoning.) The question anticipates chapter 7, as does the reference, in the answer, to activities 'of the second rank'.

29. *of a human being*: That is, it is our human nature that ultimately determines which are the best pleasures, and best activities, available to us.

30. *second rank*: Or 'in a secondary sense', as opposed to human pleasure 'in the strict (or proper) sense'. Then 'or in the third or fourth sense' (which does not quite work in English). Literally, 'or in-the-more-than-two-sense' (which works even less well).

Moral and political activity, [A] will say, makes us flourish 'in a secondary sense', or in a second-rank sort of way. (And a life of purely physical comfort and self-indulgence is probably what he means by activity of the 'third or fourth rank'.) But while these terms undoubtedly hint at the later discussion, there is a difference. Here [A] implies that the best pleasure available to us is also 'the distinctive human pleasure'. Later, he says the humanity of our practical life is exactly what makes it 'second-rank', compared to the divine activity of pure thought. So the later discussion seems at odds at least with the terminology used here.

31. *spoudaia*: The Greek word for 'serious matters' (if it is in the neuter gender, and plural) is also, in a different usage, one of [A]'s standard ways of saying 'good'; especially 'a good person' (*spoudaios*). His point here rests on an etymological connection, not on the actual meaning of the personal adjective.

Spoudaios derives from the noun *spoudē*, which can mean 'earnestness', 'care', 'attentiveness', 'concern'. Hence *spoudaia*, a few generations earlier, typically meant 'things that require attention', 'serious matters'. But *spoudaios*, used of a person, meant 'attentive', 'considerate'; in particular, considerate *towards others*, or attentive *to one's obligations* – and from that it acquired (before [A]'s own time) a new sense: 'a good person'. The term then also became an all-purpose word for 'good', i.e. used even of things. (The etymology and history of the English term 'nice' is rather similar.) So *spoudaios* never meant 'a serious man' in any period of the language.

Here [A] is noting the two existing senses of the word. *Spoudaia*, he says, which means 'good things', can also mean 'serious things'. He is implying that the etymological link shows that 'good' implies 'serious'. This is pretty implausible. Good things do (often) demand our attention. But Greeks would also have said (in an earlier period of the language) that earthquakes, wars and famines are paradigm *spoudaia* – very serious matters.

32. *even living*: Literally, 'unless also of life', i.e. 'unless [they] also [allow that the slave has some share] of life'. The meaning is: nobody would say a slave 'is flourishing'. To do so, they would first have to think that a slave is living at all – which they shouldn't. In [A]'s view, a slave is deprived of so many basic human activities (choice, deliberation, reasoning, being a citizen etc.) as not to be living a human life at all. But his highly abbreviated expression matches English fairly well here. 'That's not living.'

It is unclear whether [A]'s view here is that slaves are *wrongly* deprived of a human life, or as a result of their own defective, slavish nature. In the *Politics* 1.4–6 he argues for the idea of an inferior slave version of human nature. But see note VIII.30.

Notice that it is supposed to be obvious that slaves are not flourishing. And surely it is obvious. Taking it for granted that a slave's life is utterly awful is a sane and humane view. It is the necessary first step towards the idea that slavery is wrong; an idea that [A] is willing to consider (see *Politics* 1.4–6).

33. *(and the rest)*: Extremely dense, but probably means 'and the other categories of good person' (brave, generous, moderate, etc.); taken up again in what follows. (For that reading, compare 1099a18–20.) But it may mean 'or for that matter anyone else'.

34. *all the rest*: This means all the other categories of good person: generous, wise, fair etc. [A] seems to compare two people, as if separate individuals, each with only that feature (so, an amoral cosmic-contemplator and a non-philosophizing morally decent person). But what he actually means is that contemplating and, e.g., being fair both demand the bare necessities; but to be fair (or brave etc.) you also need lots of extra stuff, e.g. other people. He is not talking about two people, but two activities of any one of us.

35. *other than [the search itself]*: Or, more strictly, 'other than [political activity itself]'; or 'a different one from [the activity itself]'. [A]'s point here is that political activity, statesmanship, consists in the quest for the flourishing of a community of citizens. He made the same claim in the opening remarks of book I (1094b6–7). [A]'s point, that political activity has goals beyond itself, seems obviously right. But it involves a slight shift of subject: the statesman flourishes by exercising his virtues; the flourishing he pursues, a goal beyond that activity, is the flourishing of others.

36. *is exceptionally leisurely*: Here I adopt a slightly different text: 'exceptional for its leisure (*scholē*)' rather than 'exceptional for its seriousness/concern (*spoudē*)'. See [TA].

37. *[. . . the required features]*: [A] now lists three key features abstractly, in the neuter. He's saying, 'So it ticks all the boxes.' I take the three features to be the ones just mentioned. Contemplation meets its own needs because it does not aim at anything beyond itself; and we don't get tired of it because it brings its own pleasure. And leisure (with the corrected text) has also been referred to.

38. *think human*: [A] may be thinking of what Socrates says, in rather similar terms, in Xenophon, *Memorabilia* I.1.12. Socrates is ridiculing the study of physics and astronomy and cosmology and suchlike. [A] is defending natural science against that kind of defeatism, and against the idea that lay behind it: that such matters should be left to the gods.

39. *other type of virtue*: Note that this 'other type' (bravery, fairness, moderation etc.) is also the standard sense of *aretē* in [A]'s

Greek. In connection with that, notice that two lines later [A] uses *aretai*, 'the virtues', in that standard (moral) sense, without needing to say which kind he means (its default sense simply reasserts itself).

40. *All the ways we exercise that are human*: I have given this claim its own paragraph, as a kind of heading, because it is itself an important thesis that is advanced in what follows. [A] begins to argue that moral virtues are human, i.e. not divine; i.e. that morality has no connection with God or the gods. Technically the claim is offered only to support the wider, surrounding thesis that contemplation is in some sense a superior form of activity. But the supporting claim was of greater interest to other Greek philosophers, and much more controversial.

Notice, also, that much of what follows appears only to make the case that moral virtues are human, not divine, without referring back to the wider thesis, or at any rate without the connection being very clear. (The connection is this: since our moral virtues are strictly human, not divine, it follows that the exercise of them must be a kind of second-grade activity. But [A] never actually says that. In particular, he fails to say it at the start of the argument, where it seems required. Nor is it at all obvious, given that elsewhere in the treatise he claims that an activity's being distinctly human is a strong point in its favour.)

41. *to one another ... in [meeting each other's] needs*: The point in saying that we only do these things to one another is that it is only for social animals, interacting with one another, that these virtues have any purpose at all. God is not a social animal.

Earlier [A] argued (see 1133a27, b6) that human needs, in particular, give rise to exchange and cooperation, and hence, in a sense, to the very existence of human societies. The relevant virtue here is fairness. The reference to needs emphasizes, again, the humanness of that virtue and related virtues. God has no needs. So God has no occasion for fairness, or any of the experiences required to develop that virtue.

42. *the body*: Notice, again, that this argument does not support the wider thesis particularly well or at all clearly. (Why does the involvement of the body make an activity second-rate? Does that make surfing inferior to counting imaginary sheep?) But it directly supports the narrower thesis, that moral virtues are unconnected to God. Our moral virtues are intimately tied to the body and its emotions. God does not have a body, or emotions. Therefore God cannot have our moral virtues.

43. *power*: Perhaps [A] means physical strength (thinking of an individual on the battlefield; the bravery of a soldier); perhaps 'military power; forces' (thinking of a general or a leader; the bravery of a Churchill). I cannot decide. But the reference to power (i.e. political and military power) at 1099b2 perhaps supports the latter.

44. *opportunity*: I.e. the opportunity or freedom to overindulge, which most often will come from wealth. You can't be moderate if you don't have a fridge full of beer; or inappropriate sexual partners lavishing you with offers. You could almost translate *exousia* here as 'temptation'.

45. *doesn't need any of those kinds of things*: It's perhaps worth pointing out here that to be a contemplator, as [A] surely understands it – a philosopher, or mathematician, or scientist, embedded in the intellectual community of a *polis* – you actually need other people and resources far more than you do for exercising moral virtues. You need other people to sustain a city for you, feed you and generate leisure for you by doing all the drudge work, keep your city law-abiding, allow and protect your intellectual freedom, build and maintain schools and libraries, and fight wars for you so that invaders don't sack the libraries, burn your books and murder your students. A philosophical life floats on an ocean of other people's sweat.

46. *much less making things*: [A] means that since the gods do not do anything, it hardly even needs saying that they also don't make or create anything, because making anything is part of, and dependent on, action. Notice that in this aside, a mere five words, [A] dismisses the idea of God as creator.

   I think there is a very Aristotelian social attitude behind the aside, as well. [A] is in part suggesting that it is demeaning to think of God making things, in the manner of an 'ungentlemanly' craftsman (a grubby blacksmith, cobbler, tailor, etc.). His social prejudice is being put in service of his deism. 'God doesn't *do* anything, much less – ugh! – *make* anything, like some cosmic bricklayer.' (The 'Watchmaker' God of later theology would displease [A] in part just because watchmakers are manual labourers.)

47. *other animals*: Unless the argument is circular, [A] must be relying on a prior, uncontroversial view that nobody (in his time) would attribute any share of *eudaimonia* to an animal. I think this is correct (as a report of Greek attitudes and language use) and relies on the standard, wider sense of the term 'prosperous',

'fortunate'. Even in English, you'd never say 'Look, what a prosperous goat!' Or perhaps his claim rests on the idea that no sane person would envy, or aspire to, the life of a mouse, or a cow.

But it may also be that attitudes on this have changed. We may be more willing now to think of animals as flourishing, or being fortunate, lucky, blessed, at least in their form of life. Indeed, there is no clear reason why [A] should be against this. Why shouldn't a lion flourish by exercising all the distinctive capacities and virtues of a lion, over a whole life? In fact, animal rights advocates often use Aristotelian thinking about flourishing. For a killer whale to flourish, live a good life, it has to be able to exercise all the distinctive capacities and virtues (social, emotional, navigational, venatorial) of killer whales. That's why no killer whale can possibly be other than wretched if confined to a tank.

The Stoic Chrysippus later argued that animals do flourish. They flourish by living according to their nature (and hence in harmony with the nature of the wider cosmos) exactly as human beings flourish. Oddly, that actually seems a natural Aristotelian view.

48. *for contemplating*: These words seem fairly likely to have been added, to tie this section to the discussion of contemplation just concluded. In the text that immediately follows (i.e. up to 1179a22) [A] implies, seven times in all (1179a3, a4, a5, a7, a11, a12, a13), that he has claimed that we flourish by action; by exercising our moral virtues. He makes no further mention of contemplation within this argument about resources. There is a similar editorial oddity before the discussion of contemplation. [A] treated *eudaimonia* as a matter of exercising moral virtues in I.6 as well, four times (see 1176b7, b8, b25, b27). It appears that we do not quite have a continuous discourse. One discussion of *eudaimonia* (X.7 and most of X.8) seems to be intruding into another.

49. *Solon*: See note I.65. Solon thought the most fortunate, enviable man he knew was Tellos, an obscure Athenian citizen who had several fine sons and saw them all have children of their own, all of whom survived infancy. Then he died gloriously in battle. When asked who he thought was the second most enviable man, Solon named Cleobis and Biton, two young Argive farmers of modest but adequate means and fine athletes, who one day hauled their mother on a cart for six miles on an urgent pilgrimage to a religious festival (oxen weren't available for some reason), and

after being applauded for their act of filial and religious piety promptly dropped dead. Solon had particular admiration for going out in style.

50. *as he saw it*: [A] would probably think that dropping dead after hauling a cart for six miles purely out of religious piety is not so much 'glorious' as a rather silly thing to do. (Recall his comment about ' "father-loving" Satyros', at 1148a34.) Hence the 'as he saw it'. I put 'glorious deeds' in quotes because *kallista* here echoes Solon's own words. *Kallista* has a common tie (as here) to glorious death. (See e.g. III.6, 1115a28.)

51. *And who act correctly and honourably*: This is not something [A] believes. See X.8 especially. You could take the phrase like this: 'and who, as a result, act correctly and honourably'. But then [A] has strangely turned into Plato. Alternatively, perhaps it is supposed to say: 'Surely it makes sense that the gods would love people who exercise their intellect, *rather than* people who act correctly and honourably.' His earlier argument that the gods do not share any of our moral virtues would support that neatly and directly (rather than flatly contradicting it, as with the current text).

    You could then take that argument either to be another part of his rather complex and difficult views about contemplation, or as yet another indirect argument for separating the gods from ethics.

52. *as we said*: [A] is referring to his claim at the start of II.2. Literally, 'as is said'. [R] took that to mean 'as the saying goes'. But there is no such 'saying'. [A] uses this expression of his own earlier claims ('as we've been saying').

53. *lives by their emotions*: [A] means that the young person, 'someone who, [like all young people], lives by their emotions', would not listen to any mere philosophical argument unless their feelings were already in alignment with that argument.

54. *'wilfully or otherwise'*: 'Wilfully, or unwillingly'. It's a stock phrase, in its basic sense rather like: 'You must never, whether you mean to or not, do X.' But also a little like 'under any circumstances'. It was a legalistic stock phrase, used, for example, in laws against killing: 'No citizen shall kill any other, wilfully or otherwise'; 'under any circumstances'.

55. *public education*: Literally, 'public forms of care', 'public provisions'. In this context, this unambiguously means 'public care over education' or 'public care over making young people good' and is thus functionally synonymous with 'public education'.

56. *opponents*: Literally, 'doesn't apply the same style of fighting to all'. By normal standards of Greek this straightforwardly refers to boxers fighting different people in different ways (rope-a-dope for some; all-out attack for others). And that is how it is taken by [P]. But most translators think it refers to boxing trainers 'assigning' different styles of fighting to their students (a far harder sense of the verb, and the phrase). It is taken that way by [H]. The more convoluted reading seems unnecessary. After all, the doctor, in the other example, is curing people, not teaching them medicine. Why can't the boxer just be punching people? [A] does have education in view, but by metaphor. Raising and educating children is like a simultaneous boxing match against several very different opponents.

57. *exactly what happens, every time, with each thing*: I take this as a reference to the various things you might do, and have done many times in the past, in e.g. looking after your patient. You know that if you give them wine, it reduces their fever; if you make them drink lemon tea and go for a run, it cures their indigestion, etc. That sense is suggested by [A]'s own example of medical treatments five lines earlier. But the phrase might refer more broadly to all observed causes and effects in your patient or student (not limited to the effects of your efforts).

Index